MW00906483

THE
FRANCHISING
HANDBOOK

THE

ANDREW J. SHERMAN — editor

FRANCHISING

 Endorsed by the International Franchise Association

HANDBOOK

amacom
American Management Association
New York • Atlanta • Boston • Chicago • Kansas City • San Francisco • Washington, D.C.
Brussels • Toronto • Mexico City

Library of Congress Cataloging-in-Publication Data

The franchising handbook / Andrew J. Sherman, editor.
        p. cm.
        ''Endorsed by the International Franchise Association.''

    Includes bibliographical references and index.
    ISBN 0-8144-0118-X
    1. Franchises (Retail trade)   I. Sherman, Andrew J.
II. International Franchise Association.
HF5429.23.F72   1993
658.8'708—dc20   *92-30868*
                                                CIP

Printing number

10 9 8 7 6 5 4 3 2 1

This book is dedicated with love
to my second franchisee,
Jennifer Rachel Sherman,
and to my wife,
Judy Joffe Sherman.

Contents

PART VII
Current Trends and Topics in Franchising   441

Preface: The Management of Franchising in the Twenty-First Century

As franchising as a method of business growth approaches the new century, there are several issues and new challenges that must be addressed. After over twenty-five years of rapid growth, franchisors must take a hard look at their management and financial structures to ensure that they are properly positioned for another twenty-five years of unbridled success.

After twenty-five years of being the darlings of the business media and the propellant of small-business creation and jobs, franchisors must reexamine their franchise relations strategies and legal practices to ensure that these positive trends continue.

After twenty-five years of pioneering global markets and dominating the domestic retail economy, the franchising community must double-check its training programs, operations manuals, and computer systems to ensure that it is properly positioned for even greater U.S. and international market share.

The Franchising Handbook has been written *by* professionals and executives in the franchising community *for* use by professionals and executives in the franchising community. Each chapter is designed to stimulate new ideas, share different approaches, present various tools for analysis, and leverage on each author's experiences—with a view toward the concerted purpose of making your franchising program even stronger and your management team even wiser.

The Handbook is *not* a how-to book on franchising, though prospective and start-up franchisors should carefully review its contents. *The Handbook* is *not* text that solely discusses legal and financial issues, though lawyers and accountants who serve the franchising community shouldn't be without it. *The Handbook* is *not* a guide for prospective franchisees on how to select a franchise, though any current or prospective franchisee looking for insight into the dynamics of the franchising relationship may want to read it.

The Handbook is a working tool for the community of franchisors, written by many of the most recognized executives and advisers in their respective fields. Their collective experiences and advice bring together one of the first resources of this kind at a time when it is most needed.

Franchising as a Strategy for Growth

Many companies prematurely select franchising as a growth alternative and then haphazardly assemble and launch the franchising program. Other companies are

urged to franchise by unqualified consultants or advisers who may be more interested in professional fees than in the long-term success of the franchising program. This has caused financial distress and failure at both the franchisor and
franchisee level, usually resulting in litigation. Current and future members of the
franchising community must be urged to take a responsible view toward the creation and development of their franchising programs.

A commitment to quality, fairness, and effective communication among
franchisors and franchisees should go a long way in reducing disputes among
franchisors and franchisees. Current and prospective franchisors must be committed to supporting and servicing the franchises they sell. Franchisors who develop strategic plans that focus on the *quantity* of franchisees and expansion,
rather than on the *quality* of franchisees and training, are surely headed for disaster. These franchising management philosophies will be emphasized throughout
the course of this *Handbook*.

Franchising in the Year 2000

In preparing for the year 2000, new, emerging, and mature franchisors must be
deeply committed to the success of their franchisees and the strengthening of their
franchising program. They must act responsibly in the review and selection of
franchisees; in the hiring of training, operations, and support staff; and in the
management of their marketing staff. Responsible franchising is the *only* way that
franchisors and franchisees will be able to harmoniously coexist in the twenty-
first century. Responsible franchising means that there must be a secure foundation from which the franchising program is launched. The key components of this
foundation are as follows:

1. *A proven prototype location* (or chain of stores) that will serve as a basis
for the franchising program. The store or stores must have been tested, refined,
and operated successfully and be consistently profitable. The success of the prototype should not be too dependent on the physical presence or specific expertise
of the founders of the system.

2. *A strong management team* made up of internal officers and directors (as
well as qualified consultants) who understand the particular industry in which the
company operates as well as the legal and business aspects of franchising as a
method of expansion.

3. *Sufficient capitalization* to launch and sustain the franchising program to
ensure that capital is available to the franchisor to provide both initial and ongoing
support and assistance to franchisees (a lack of a well-prepared business plan and
adequate capital structure is often the principal cause of demise of many franchisors).

4. *A distinctive and protected trade identity* that includes federal and state

registered trademarks as well as a uniform trade appearance, signage, slogans, trade dress, and overall image.

5. *Proprietary and proven methods of operation and management* that can be reduced to writing in a comprehensive operations manual, not be too easily duplicated by competitors, be able to maintain their value to the franchisees over an extended period of time, and be enforced through clearly drafted and objective quality-control standards.

6. *Comprehensive training* program for franchisees, both at the company's headquarters and on-site at the franchisee's proposed location at the outset of the relationship and on an ongoing basis.

7. *Field support staff* who are skilled trainers and communicators who must be available to visit and periodically assist franchisees as well as monitor quality control standards.

8. *A set of comprehensive legal documents* that reflect the company's business strategies and operating policies. Offering documents must be prepared in accordance with applicable federal and state disclosure laws, and franchise agreements should strike a delicate balance between the rights and obligations of franchisor and franchisee.

9. *A demonstrated market demand* for the products and services developed by the franchisor that will be distributed through the franchisees. The franchisor's products and services should meet certain minimum quality standards, not be subject to rapid shifts in consumer preferences (e.g., fads), and be proprietary in nature. Market research and analysis should be sensitive to trends in the economy and specific industry, the plans of direct and indirect competitors, and shifts in consumer preferences.

10. *A set of carefully developed site selection criteria and architectural standards*, based on market studies and demographic reports, that require sites be readily and affordably secured in today's competitive real estate market.

11. *A genuine understanding of the competition* (both direct and indirect) that the franchisor will face in marketing and selling franchises to prospective franchisees as well as obstacles that the franchisee will face when marketing products and services.

12. *Relationships* with suppliers, lenders, real estate developers, and related key resources that will benefit the franchisees overall through group buying programs and discounts, financing and site preferences, and contributions toward national advertising.

13. *A franchisee profile and screening system* in order to identify the minimum financial qualifications, business acumen, and understanding of the industry that will be required to be a successful franchisee.

14. *An effective system of reporting and record keeping* to maintain the performance of the franchisees and ensure that royalties are reported accurately and paid promptly.

15. *Research and development* capabilities for the introduction of new products and services on an ongoing basis to consumers through the franchised network.

16. *A communication system* that facilitates a continuing and open dialogue with the franchisees, including franchise associations, national and regional meetings, random calls and visits, and a commitment to being supportive of franchise ideas.

17. National, regional, and local *advertising, marketing and public relations programs* designed to recruit prospective franchisees as well as consumers to the sites operated by franchisees.

Understanding the Franchisee of the Year 2000

One way to avoid failure is to truly understand the profile of the franchisee of the future. A wide variety of marketing, planning, operational, and strategic decisions can be made by the growing franchisor once certain basic premises are understood. As a general rule, franchisees in today's competitive markets are getting smarter, not dumber. The better educated, better capitalized franchisee is here to stay. As franchising has matured, prospective franchisees are provided more resources (such as seminars, media articles, trade shows, and International Franchise Association programs) than ever before for information and due diligence. These new, sophisticated franchisees are much different from their mom-and-pop predecessors. This new prospect is better trained to ask all the right questions and hire the right advisers when investigating and negotiating the franchise agreement. These new franchisees are also better heeled, and more likely to organize themselves into associations and take action if they are not receiving the required support and assistance. As we discuss in Part V of this *Handbook*, franchisors who fail to mold their sales and support systems around the characteristics of these new franchisees, and continue to do business the old-fashioned way, are headed for disaster and litigation.

Curbing the Failure Rate of Early-Stage Franchisors

One of the underlying premises of this *Handbook* is that successful franchising takes proper planning, capital, and management. The various components of a successful franchising program, as well as the legal and strategic issues in developing a franchise program, are discussed by the various franchising veterans in the chapters that follow. Our mission is to avoid the mistakes made by hundreds of franchisors that have failed over the past few years. That's right, hundreds. Each year since 1986, between seventy-five to a hundred franchisors *went out of business*. This figure represents between 3 and 5 percent of all franchisors operating during those years. Some of the more common reasons why franchisors fail include:

- ▲ Difficulty in attracting qualified franchisees
- ▲ Lack of proper disclosure documents and/or compliance system
- ▲ Failure to provide adequate support
- ▲ Lack of an effective franchise communications system
- ▲ Complex and inadequate operations manual
- ▲ Inadequate site selection criteria
- ▲ Lack of a proper screening system for prospective franchisees
- ▲ Unworkable economic relationship with franchisees
- ▲ Lack of effective financial controls

This *Handbook* has chapters on all of these topics, written by veteran franchising executives and consultants who have handled these problems from the trenches. Their experiences and insights are in the pages that follow.

Andrew J. Sherman
Washington, D.C.

Acknowledgments

I am very grateful to the individuals who worked time into their busy schedules to write a chapter for this *Handbook*. I am especially grateful to those individuals, such as the team at Management 2000, who somehow found the time to write multiple chapters.

The support for this project by Bill Cherkasky and John Reynolds at the International Franchise Association and, once again, Andrea Pedolsky and Barbara Horowitz at AMACOM Books, really made the publishing of this *Handbook* possible.

I would like to give special thanks to my loyal and ever-growing base of clients, especially the wide variety of domestic and international franchisors whom I have had the pleasure of serving over the years. This *Handbook* is truly dedicated to the achievement of their goals and objectives.

My secretary, Michele Lewis, was once again instrumental in orchestrating this project, not only with her assistance in the preparation of my own chapters but also in coordinating the submissions of nearly twenty-five contributors.

Finally, I would like to acknowledge the expression on my wife's face when I told her that I'd be working on a third book as well as the sigh of relief when Judy found out that I wouldn't have to actually write all the chapters. My family has, and always will be, my greatest source of strength and support.

Introduction to Franchising and the International Franchise Association

William B. Cherkasky, International Franchise Association

While franchising as a method of doing business in the United States can be traced back to the 1850s, when the Singer Sewing Machine Company established a network of salesmen and dealers to distribute its sewing machines, the modern concept of business-format franchising can chart its origins from the early 1960s. It is no accident that the International Franchise Association (IFA) can trace its beginnings from the same period.

After World War II, as Americans became more mobile and as large segments of the population began to shift to the suburbs, local and regional chains of drive-in, quick-serve restaurants began to develop. Franchise chains such as A&W Restaurants and Tastee Freez were quickly joined by McDonald's, Burger King, Dunkin' Donuts, Kentucky Fried Chicken, and many others. But franchising was also expanding beyond the granting of a license to distribute or sell a product to many different types of businesses, such as hotels and motels, automotive repair shops, and tax preparation services. These franchisors, such as Holiday Inns, Midas Mufflers, and H&R Block, granted the rights to adopt an entire business concept and method of operation.

It was during this evolutionary period in the early 1960s that the IFA came into existence. The IFA was founded in 1960 by a small group of franchise-company CEOs who, in the words of IFA founder Irl H. Marshall, "banded together to protect the good name of franchising." Marshall, who was founder and president of Duraclean International, later recalled that, "We knew franchising had something great to offer, but the public perception was quite negative." Marshall was later involved in drafting the association's first *Code of Ethics*.

In his study of nonprofit organizations, consultant James Dunlop writes that trade associations pass through fairly predictable stages in their development, which mirror the growth and changes taking place in their respective industries. These stages advance from embryonic to growth to maturity to aging.[1] It is certainly true that the International Franchise Association, which was founded during the embryonic stage of franchising in the early 1960s, has grown and matured during one of the most dynamic periods of franchising. In turn, IFA has helped to mold the environment in which franchising has flourished.

The IFA was the brainchild of William Rosenberg, who was founder and chairman of Dunkin' Donuts. Rosenberg and others were brought together at a

"Start Your Own Business" show in Chicago in 1959. Rosenberg recalls, "We started IFA as a mechanism to police ourselves. At the time this was a necessary effort. Franchising was growing and attracting the fast-buck con artist. People were getting hurt by unscrupulous businessmen."

Other entrepreneurs at what became IFA's first organizational meeting were A. L. (Al) Tunick, founder of Chicken Delight, who became IFA's first chairman in 1960 and 1961, Grant Mauk and Irl H. Marshall of Duraclean, Robert Grover of Snap-On Tools, Matthew Lifflander of Hertz Corp., Donn Lynn of International French Cafes, Burr McCloskey of the Biddle Company, Edward Morgan of ServiceMaster Industries, John Osterman of A&W Root Beer Company, Don Slater of Mister Donut of America, Frank Thomas of Burger Chef Systems, Charles Wilson of Western Auto Supply Company, Elmer Winter of Manpower, Dansby A. Council of the Council Manufacturing Corporation, Donald Hamacher and John Connolloy of Roll-A-Grill Corporation of America, David Barnow of Beltone Electronics, and Monte Pendleton.

Elmer Winter, founder of Manpower, Inc., described the IFA's mission at the first meeting. "We wanted to go to the American public and say that franchising was a responsible method of doing business. It was an idea that many entrepreneurs ought to examine because of its many advantages. As franchisors we operated successful businesses that had proven methods and patents. We were willing to share our methods with others under a fair and equitable franchise arrangement."

Then and now, IFA members share this common purpose, which has not changed since the founding of the organization: to promote franchising as a responsible method of doing business. Through service on IFA committees; participation in workshops, seminars, and franchise shows; and a wide array of other programs, IFA members work to educate the public, lawmakers, the business community, and the media about franchising. As a condition of membership, all IFA members must subscribe to and uphold the IFA *Code of Ethics* (see Figure I-1). In the truest sense, IFA's mission is a living one, as relevant to the present and future as it was to the past: to serve as an instrument to bring franchisors together and to uphold franchising as a responsible method of doing business.

IFA and the Continuing Growth of Franchising

IFA counts among its members the world's largest franchise chains—McDonald's, Kentucky Fried Chicken, H&R Block, Radio Shack, Century 21 Real Estate, International Dairy Queen, Burger King, Subway Sandwiches and Sales, Pizza Hut, Domino's Pizza, ServiceMaster, Taco Bell—companies whose products and services, advertising campaigns, and signs along the highways have made them household words. It can be truly said that franchising has come a long way from the early 1960s. Most recently, as the walls of communism came tum-

Figure I-1.   Code of Ethics of the International Franchise Association.

IFA CODE OF ETHICS

I.

In the advertisement and grant of franchises or dealerships a member shall comply with all applicable laws and regulations and the member's offering circulars shall be complete, accurate and not misleading with respect to the franchisee's or dealer's investment, the obligations of the member and the franchisee or dealer under the franchise or dealership and all material facts relating to the franchise or dealership.

II.

All matters material to the member's franchise or dealership shall be contained in one or more written agreements, which shall clearly set forth the terms of the relationship and the respective rights and obligations of the parties.

III.

A member shall select and accept only those franchisees or dealers who, upon reasonable investigation, appear to possess the basic skills, education, experience, and personal characteristics and financial resources requisite to conduct the franchised business or dealership and meet the obligations of the franchisee or dealer under the franchise and other agreements. There shall be no discrimination in the granting of franchises based solely on race, color, religion, national origin or sex. However, this in no way prohibits a franchisor from granting franchises to prospective franchisees as part of a program to make franchises available to persons lacking the capital, training, business experience, or other qualifications ordinarily required of franchisees or any other affirmative action program adopted by the franchisor.

IV.

A member shall provide reasonable guidance to its franchisees or dealers in a manner consistent with its franchise agreement.

V.

Fairness shall characterize all dealings between a member and its franchisees or dealers. A member shall make every good faith effort to resolve complaints by and disputes with its franchisees or dealers through direct communication and negotiation. To the extent reasonably appropriate in the circumstances, a member shall give its franchisee or dealer notice of, and a reasonable opportunity to cure, a breach of their contractual relationship.

VI.

No member shall engage in the pyramid scheme of distribution. A pyramid is a system wherein a buyer's future compensation is expected to be based primarily upon recruitment of new participants, rather than upon the sale of products or services.

bling down in the Soviet Union and Eastern Europe, the lines were longer outside the McDonald's restaurant in Moscow than to get in to see Lenin's tomb.

As John Naisbitt, futurist and author of *Megatrends* and *Megatrends 2000*, reported in a special 1986 study on the future of franchising, commissioned by the IFA, "Franchising is entering an era dominated by changing consumer attitudes. . . . The franchise explosion has penetrated all areas of business and retailing and has helped reshape consumer habits and expectations worldwide."

Since the 1960s, the IFA has played a significant role as both scribe and trumpeter of what Naisbitt has described as the franchise explosion. With this explosion has come a rapid growth in the number of franchise companies, the number of franchisees, and the diversification of franchising itself. Today, franchising accounts for more than 35 percent of all retail sales in the United States— more than \$758 billion. More than 542,000 franchised businesses employ more than 7.2 million people spanning sixty different industries.

Many people may still think of fast-food chains such as McDonald's when they hear the word *franchise*, but houses are bought and sold; painted, cleaned, decorated; and carpeted through franchises. Cars are purchased or rented, tuned, and washed through franchises. We can have our hair cut, clothes cleaned, pets cared for—all in franchised businesses. IFA's membership now represents this great diversity in franchising, including more than 650 franchise companies, 173 supplier members organized as the Council of Franchise Suppliers, 21 sister associations organized in foreign countries around the globe, and 15 educational members (institutions of higher learning).

To keep pace with the rapid changes taking place in franchising, the IFA provides its members with lobbying and government relations, seeking to safeguard the very practice of franchising at state, national, and international levels; it offers hundreds of educational programs and seminars throughout the year and extensive marketing and public relations campaigns, franchise shows, and publications to educate the public about franchising as well as international trade missions and special programs to encourage minority participation in franchising.

IFA members benefit from the collective strength, expertise, and experience of other IFA members, the staff, committees, and board of directors. IFA members frequently rank networking as the number-one benefit of membership in the association, and rate the staff and programs of the association as excellent and above average.

One of the early goals of the IFA's founders was to dispel the negative image of franchising. IFA's marketing and public relations efforts have focused on protecting and promoting the good name of franchising by providing reliable and accurate information to the public about franchising. Among these information sources are publications such as the IFA's *Franchise Opportunities Guide*, which provides a comprehensive listing of the leading franchise companies grouped by product and service, and the IFA's bimonthly magazine, *Franchising World*. (A complete catalog of IFA Publications is available by writing to: IFA Publications, P.O. Box 1060, Evans City, PA 16033.)

IFA committees include the following:

- Awards
- Council of Franchise Suppliers
- Education
- Educational Foundation
- Finance, Audit, and Budget
- Franchisee Relations
- International Affairs
- Legal and Legislative
- Long-Range Planning
- Marketing and Public Relations
- Membership Development
- Minorities and Women in Franchising
- Nominating
- Past Chairmen's Council
- Board of Directors
- Executive Committee

IFA is the oldest and largest association representing franchisors in the world. It serves as a resource center for both current and prospective franchisors and franchisees as well as for government and the media. In addition, the IFA has been instrumental in developing legislation that regulates and safeguards franchising from abuse by fraudulent operators. The association has testified at the state, national, and international level on behalf of programs that encourage women and minorities to become more involved in business through franchising.

Living up to the mission of its founders, IFA's many committees, task forces, individual members, and staff have contributed countless hours of time and effort to—to coin a phrase—make the world a better place for franchising.

IFA and the Future of Franchising

The franchise boom, which began in the early 1960s and exploded in the 1970s and 1980s, shows absolutely no sign of slowing down in the 1990s. In fact, experts predict that franchising will account for half of all retail sales by the end of the 1990s. As an economic and social force, franchises with their familiar trademarks, systematic business formats, and global marketing power help make the world an even smaller place.

Six major factors will influence the growth and expansion of franchising to what some experts have called the globalization of franchising. These trends are:

1. *A leveling off of sales growth among franchise outlets in the traditional fields such as fast-food, convenience stores, hotels and motels, and rental car*

agencies. By the year 2000, these businesses will share top billing with a handful of new service-oriented businesses.

2. *The continuing rapid growth and expansion of service-type businesses.* Such businesses as home repair, decorating and remodeling, business aids and services, maid services, lawn care, child care, and educational services will become dominant in the marketplace. Naisbitt reported in his study for the IFA that "franchising will continue to embrace specialization as new companies enter the field."

3. *Continuing mergers and acquisitions of small chains by large chains.* Corporate America will become increasingly interested in ownership and control of franchise chains as a way to reach consumer markets.

4. *Conversions of independent businesses to franchises.* Aggressive franchise companies will increasingly look to broaden their market coverage, while independent owners assess the competitive advantage of joining the franchise system.

5. *Globalization of franchising.* Franchise companies in the United States will continue to expand overseas and foreign companies, on a smaller scale, will develop subsidiaries and master franchises in the United States.

6. *An increasingly mature and diversified franchise company ownership and management.* Many of the best-known franchise chains are less than thirty years old, and the majority have been founded since 1975. As many franchise companies grow, corporate management styles will replace entrepreneurial styles of operation. With changing management styles, companies will develop new and different approaches to marketing, franchise development, and financial management.

All of these future forces will shape the direction of the International Franchise Association as its leadership, its members, and its staff seek answers to the questions of the future. The association's programs in the international area will increase in both number and depth. The association will expand its programs to encourage minority participation in franchising. As franchisors embrace management specialization, IFA's educational programs will become more tailored to individual needs, both in content and in the method and mode of instruction.

With a new franchise opening in the United States every sixteen minutes (it is currently growing at a rate six times faster than the economy as a whole), with the rapid expansion of franchising abroad, and with the diversification of franchising in the United States, the International Franchise Association will live up to its mission to unite franchisors around the globe.

NOTE

1. James Dunlop, *Leading the Association* (Washington, D.C.: American Society of Association Executives Foundation, 1989).

PART I

DEVELOPING A MANAGEMENT STRUCTURE FOR EFFECTIVE FRANCHISING

The growth and development of a franchised business must be carefully managed. The strategic process of franchising raises a host of management challenges that in many cases are not faced by nonfranchised businesses, such as the need for flawless training and impeccable field support systems.

The chapters in Part I of *The Handbook* focus on the core management issues that must be addressed in building a successful franchised business. Emphasis is placed by the various authors on training, field support, administrative systems, and the management of quality control.

1

Strengthening and Supporting the Franchising System

Jan Kirkham and Timothy McGowan, Management 2000

Most franchisors at some point become frustrated when franchisees are reluctant to do what needs to be done for the franchise to be successful. The reluctance is manifested by not following prescribed systems, devoting insufficient resources to marketing, not cooperating with other franchisees, remitting royalties late, or declining to support expansion of the system in the area. In turn, the franchisor's frustration is marked by name calling, nasty letters, and forced compliance with the terms of the franchise agreement.

We believe most parties enter the franchise relationship with the sincere intention of making it work for mutual benefit. People normally do not wake up in the morning, thinking "How can I wreck this relationship?" So what happens to make the relationship turn sour? Why does the franchise relationship evolve to an adversarial state? And what can be done to remedy this unpleasant situation or prevent it from occurring in the first place?

This chapter provides a context for these questions. We explore these concerns by focusing on four issues:

1. The nature of the franchise relationship
2. The relationship between field support personnel and the franchisee
3. The consulting skills needed by field support personnel to strengthen the franchise relationship
4. The situations commonly encountered by field consultants when dealing with franchisees

After examining hundreds of franchise companies in all stages of development, Management 2000 has concluded that most problems between the franchisor and franchisee are a result of no shared understanding or shared meaning about the relationship. Normally, neither party has a clear grasp of what is expected of each party's role—and why this expectation is important: the intent. Consequently, the ability to develop a relationship based on solid communication is difficult at best. Understanding the role and intent of each party in the relationship is key to building a successful relationship.

There is a sequence of events that normally molds the franchisor-franchisee relationship. First, the franchisee recruitment and selection process establishes communications—or lack thereof. In fact, franchisors create most their problems by what they say and do during this critical process. For instance, the franchise prospect is told that he is "sold" a franchise and that he has an "independently owned and operated" business. As a result, franchisees come to believe they can change the operating system at will. Based on the franchisee's "independent" actions, the franchisor then concludes that the franchisee is not operating the business the way it should be operated. The "independent owner" is not in compliance with the franchise agreement.

Second, this franchisor focus on compliance defines the role of the field support staff, who become compliance inspectors with the intent of getting the franchisee "back into compliance." The compliance inspector works within this "we-they" relationship. Once on the scene, the field support personnel feel they should dictate to the franchisee how he should be running the business—a business the franchisee believes he owns! Understandably, the franchisee becomes resentful. He says, "How can this inspector, who has been on the job three weeks, possibly know how I should run my business? She isn't here every day. She hasn't a clue."

Third, once an adversarial relationship develops, it is increasingly difficult for field personnel to develop a feeling of trust and rapport with the franchisee. Without trust and rapport, the intent of both the franchisee and the field personnel (and the franchisor they represent) are suspect.

As a franchisor, assess your relationship with your franchisees. Determine their perception of franchising and critically evaluate both your role and intent and those of the franchisees. Assess your consulting skills of facilitating, questioning, and listening. Review your choice of words to uncover negative descriptions of franchisees. Determine whether you really have established trust and rapport with your franchisees.

The Franchisor-Franchisee Relationship

What Is Franchising?

The first step in understanding the franchisor-franchisee relationship is to understand franchising. Franchising is a business strategy for getting and keeping customers. It is a marketing system for creating an image in the minds of current and future customers about how the company's products and services can help them. In short, it is a method of distributing products and services that satisfy customer needs.

The power of franchising is realized when the franchisor and franchisee work as a team, with a mutual commitment to market share. This mutual commitment enables the franchise system to get and keep more customers, who consume more products and services more often, so that the system grows faster than the market demand for the product or service and faster than the competition. When these conditions exist, franchising as a business strategy, as a marketing system, and as a method of distribution works best.

Franchising is a business relationship based on a legal structure. The franchisor grants to the franchisee a license to use the franchisor's brand name, operating system, and support system to accomplish the business purpose of the relationship, which is to get and keep customers. When this business purpose is accomplished, the franchisor and franchisees are better able to satisfy individual motivations and achieve individual goals, dreams, and objectives.

The franchise relationship begins when the franchisee is recruited. During this process, the franchisor's and franchisee's expectations of each other are established, based on what each wants from the relationship. Contrary to popular belief, a franchisor can not "sell" a franchise to a candidate. The use of the word *sell* to characterize the relationship can set the basis for misunderstanding that will dominate the relationship. The franchisor does, however, *grant a license* to the franchisee. This concept should not be dismissed as mere semantics; indeed, the franchisor must understand the impact of language on this long-term relationship.

The premise that a franchise license is *not sold* and the franchisee *does not own* the franchise license is supported by the following facts:

- A franchisee cannot incorporate using the franchisor's name because the franchisee does not own the name.
- Should the franchisee want to exit the business, the franchise license is not sold; rather, the franchise license is transferred upon approval of the franchisor. The franchisee enters into a separate transaction to sell her assets.
- The franchise agreement has a stated term and must be renewed if the franchisee is to continue in business under the franchisor's brand name. If a franchisee owned the license, it would not need to be renewed.

The market, the brand name, operating system, and support system are owned by the franchisor. The franchisee is delegated the right to use the brand name in a defined market, for a designated period of time, to develop a market share for the franchise system.

From a franchisee's perspective, franchising is one of several strategies available to build a career. Figure 1-1 provides an overview of these strategies.

A person can be employed by others, and in this relationship the employee is dependent on the employer. A person can be self-employed, and there are two options: as an independent businessperson or as a franchisee. The option of independent businessperson affixes total responsibility for the direction and development of the business on the owner. The franchisee option affixes mutual responsibility for the direction and development of the business. The latter is therefore an interdependent relationship.

Figure 1-1. Your career strategies.

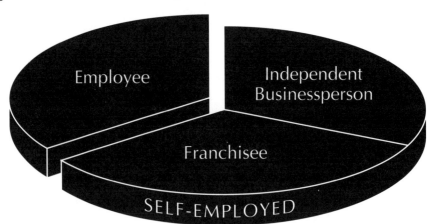

What is the advantage of franchising? A franchisee invests in a company's brand name, operating system, and ongoing support system in the hope of obtaining a return on the investment. This investment is returned to the franchisee in two ways:

1. From current revenue, as a result of using the brand name, which creates customers, and from using the operating system, which gets those customers to come back
2. From the increase in value of the franchisee's assets owing to the association with the franchisor's brand name, which enhances the franchisee's ability to produce future revenue; this enhanced value is the goodwill of the franchise system

The Relationship Between Vocabulary and Behavior

The use of the words *sell*, *buy*, and *owner* sends a message that is contrary to the real purpose of the franchise relationship. These words focus on the legal structure of the relationship rather than on the business purpose.

Let's explore the logic of *selling* and evaluate the impact of this word on future franchisee behavior. First, the logic:

- ▲ If I sell you something, you have bought it.
- ▲ If you have bought it, you own it.
- ▲ If you own it, you can do what you want with it.

This owner mentality leads to unilateral changes in the operating system. This, in turn, leads to inconsistent application of the operating system, with variations from franchisee to franchisee and from unit to unit. This inconsistency confuses customers by invalidating their expectations of the brand name created by marketing. The owner mentality also leads to a perception that franchisees are competitors of each other rather than teammates responsible for enhancing the value of the brand name.

Likewise, an owner mentality makes franchisees believe the operating system is the way the franchisor controls them, rather than seeing the system as how customers are retained and the value of the brand name is built. In addition, an owner mentality prevents the franchisee from understanding why it is important to implement legitimate changes to the operating system as the system grows. The franchisee does not understand the need for these changes because franchising was never adequately explained—*that the operating system is for the customer, not the franchisee*. Changes in the operating system, when adequately tested and consistently applied, are made for marketing reasons—to fulfill the business purpose of the relationship, which is to get and keep customers.

There is rarely a context provided to franchisees for understanding the real purpose of the initial franchise fee and the ongoing royalty fees. Franchisees mistakenly believe that the initial fee is for the brand name, operating system, and training. They also believe that the ongoing royalty fees are only for the support the franchisor provides, which they take as a promise to make them successful. This thinking creates a dependency among franchisees and causes them to constantly ask, "What has the franchisor done for me today?"

These are only a few examples of how the words *sell* and *owner* adversely affect the franchisor-franchisee relationship, potentially dilute the franchisee's investment, and prevent the system from realizing the power of franchising to get and keep customers.

New Words and Behavior

Almost every problem franchisors face regarding franchisees originates in how the franchisees think about the relationship when they are first recruited and selected. The problems can be greatly diminished by establishing a proper context for understanding the franchisor-franchisee relationship early on.

The franchisor should constantly communicate the following to franchisees:

▲ *Unit-to-unit consistency is imperative to the success of franchising.* If franchisees do not follow the operating system as prescribed, differences among units will create a negative impact on the customer's perception of the product and service. As a result, lack of consistency dilutes the investment made by all franchisees in the system. Candidates need to understand that the operating system institutionalizes the customer's buying experience. The operating system reinforces the image created by marketing and builds customer expectations. The brand image is enhanced if the operating system consistently delivers what the customer expects.

▴ *Franchisees are not competitors, even if located in the same market.* All franchisee-managed and company-managed locations share the task of establishing the brand name as dominant in the market. This focuses on the business purpose of the relationship, which is to get and keep customers. When brand-name awareness increases, there are more customers to use more of the products and services. Everyone in the franchise system, especially franchisees located in the same market, has a responsibility to work as a team to grow the system and increase its market share.

▴ *The franchisor and franchisee have an interdependent relationship.* The franchisor and franchisee each must accept responsibility and accountability for the success of the system. It is not the responsibility of the franchisor to make franchisees successful. Franchisees must market the brand, work the operating system, and use the support system to get and keep customers. Likewise, the franchisor must provide the best operating system and assist the franchisee to become more effective, efficient, and profitable by providing support services. The franchisor and all franchisees must work as a team for mutual benefit.

▴ *The franchisee must understand the purpose of the initial franchise fee and the ongoing royalty fees.* The initial franchise fee goes toward the following, which protect the franchisee: (1) franchisor's expenses in connection with selecting quality franchisees; (2) training and support provided by the franchisor prior to opening; (3) costs of developing and organizing the franchise and related systems; (4) trademark and trade name registration and protection; and (5) compliance with various laws.

The royalty fees are paid for revenue generated in the prior reporting period because: (1) using the franchisor's brand name created a customer; (2) the operating system got the customer to come back; and (3) the support services provided by the franchisor helped the franchisees acquire and develop their ability to use the brand name and operating system to get and keep customers.

Franchise Recruitment and Selection Process

The franchise recruitment and selection process offers the first opportunity to shape the franchise's thinking about the relationship. Recruitment and selection creates the future of the company by granting franchises to people who understand the realities of self-employment, have the financial resources to make it happen, understand franchising, and find this form of business compatible with their personality.

The recruitment and selection process should also help the franchisee candidate to articulate her motivations and goals (both short- and long-term) and allow her to discover how franchising can be a career strategy. These motivations and goals will provide a context for the relationship between the field support personnel and the franchisee.

The Relationship Between the Field Support Personnel and the Franchisee

If the field support personnel are not compliance inspectors, what is their role? How do field support people build communication, trust, and rapport with the franchisees? What skills are needed to be a successful field support person?

The Role of Field Support Personnel

The field support person should help franchisees acquire and develop their ability to become successful and profitable by using the franchisor's brand name, operating system, and ongoing support system. To do this, a field person must acknowledge the franchisee's motivations.

First, the franchisee has made the decision to be self-employed. The field support person must now understand why the franchisee has decided to do this. What are the franchisee's goals? Does the franchisee understand self-employment or has the candidate just bought a job? These answers are vital to understanding the franchisee's motivations, and they will define the franchisee's intent. They will focus a franchisee on where he wants to go and facilitate his business-planning process.

Second, the franchisee has selected franchising as her career strategy. The field support person needs to determine whether the franchisee understands this strategy and how to use it to achieve her goal. Does the franchisee understand that the purpose of the franchise relationship is to get and keep customers? Does the franchisee understand why a royalty fee is paid? Does the franchisee understand the importance of a consistent operating system to the success of a franchise system? The answers will enable the field support person to help the franchisee understand how to get where she wants to go. The discussion will also establish a teamwork environment among all franchisees in the local market, so together everyone can achieve more.

Third, the franchisee has decided on a particular industry. Does he understand how to make money in this industry? Does he understand what marketing is? Does he know the difference between a condition of business and a problem in business? These answers will help focus the franchisee on the purpose of the business—to get customers, keep the customers, and grow. The franchisee will come to understand that *conditions* of business are recurring situations that must be planned for and addressed in the daily operation of the business, while *problems* are usually not recurring or, if recurring, are conditions not adequately planned for. This distinction will be important during the business-planning process discussed later in this chapter.

Discussions between the franchisees and the field support person will also enable the franchisee to take a broader view of marketing. *Marketing* is everything that creates a real or perceived image in the minds of current or future customers about what the business is, what the products and services are, and what the customer can expect. When integrated into the concept of franchising, this definition will help distinguish between marketing as advertising and marketing as everything else, from rent to payroll. The franchisee will come to appreciate that most marketing occurs within the walls of a business.

Building Strong Communications

PERCEPTIONS ARE REALITY

If the role of field support is to help the franchisee think about these issues, how is that done? The first step is to assess the perceptions of the franchisee. Perceptions affect our thoughts, feelings, and actions. If perceptions about a franchisee relationship are negative, the field staff cannot work as well with the franchisees. Negative labels create a ''we-they'' attitude and soon become reality.

When a field support person labels a franchisee with negative words, such as *stubborn*, *jerk*, *uncooperative*, or *uncaring*, these are behaviors the field support person comes to expect. The perceptions then cause the franchisee to truly become a negative force rather than a partner in the business. Remember, language is the most significant shaper of our behavior, thus the first step in building strong communications is to eliminate negative labels. We suggest that franchisors do the following:

- Bring the relationship beyond one based on compliance to one based on business planning.
- Include the franchisees on the company's organization chart.
- Make a conscious effort to eliminate negative labels throughout the company (see Figure 1-2).
- Involve the franchisees in major decisions affecting the company, including strategic and operational planning, and solicit ongoing feedback.

Figure 1-2. Positive perceptions of franchisees.

- As partners in profit
- As people we respect
- As part of our franchise system
- As if we want them to succeed
- As our internal customers
- As investors in our brand name, operating system, and support systems
- As our method of distribution
- As people with good ideas
- As developers of market share
- As the critical element in our growth strategy

THE BUSINESS PLANNING PROCESS

To build strong communications, get franchisees to use business planning. The business-planning process is the foundation of the relationship between field support people and the franchisees. By encouraging planning, field support people can be consultants rather than compliance inspectors.

The primary question asked by field support personnel is how to get franchisees to prepare and follow a business plan and, furthermore, if business planning is so great why don't franchisees do it? These are excellent questions, best answered by first distinguishing between the business planning process and the business plan.

The business planning process is the rational ("what") and emotional ("why") assessment of where a franchisee is, where he wants to be, how he wants to get there, and how he will measure his results. The business plan is the documentation of this thinking process. The objective of planning is not the development of a business plan but rather the establishment of an ongoing business planning process. Many times people focus on the plan rather than the planning process. Ultimately, the plan may not be as important as the learning that goes on during the planning process.

There are many reasons why franchisees do not plan. Some say it takes too long, they don't have enough time, they can't predict the future. Others feel things are going to change anyway, so why bother. The field support person must go beyond these traditional responses to what underlies them.

First, people do not plan because they don't know how. They do not plan for the future; they only plan for what they want to happen, or what they have decided will happen, or for what is inevitable. Most people are not driven by long-term goals, dreams, or objectives. Rather, they are guided by short-term needs, wants, or desires. Indeed, it is difficult to focus on the long term when you can't get your "to do" list done on a daily basis. Many franchisees have a hard time thinking past Monday morning, therefore planning is uncomfortable and seems a waste of time. To be successful at helping franchisees plan, field support personnel must discuss planning on a human plane, showing how everyone does it and that it works.

Second, people begin plans from the wrong vantage point. Most people plan from the present and look to the future—the future to them is a point in time that has not occurred yet. This method of planning causes procrastination because, "If my goals do not get done today, they can always be done tomorrow (the future)." Instead, a person should project a date into the future that she is comfortable thinking about, and then define, as specifically as possible, what her life will look like on this date. The day becomes the "present," and the period of time between this "present" and "today" is called the "extended present." What is done within this extended present becomes the "goal." The action plans are steps that get her there—the strategies, the means to use. Successful businesspeople live in the extended present. They define their future and make this future happen, rather than wait for it to happen. They have no doubts that their goals will be accomplished, and they take actions every day to move closer to meeting these goals.

Third, people really do not have goals. They have a wish list. When things go wrong, most people adjust their goals rather than adjust their strategies to get to those goals. They conclude, "That goal was not realistic anyway." But this is where the distinction between *conditions* of business and *problems* in business is important. Recession and employee turnover are conditions of the food-service business; they must be anticipated with contingency plans made during the planning process. Such conditions become problems only when the business has not adequately planned how to handle them.

Fourth, most people do not know how to plan. Planning starts with four basic questions:

1. Where are you today? (analysis)
2. Where do you want to be at some predetermined point in time? (goal setting)
3. How will you get there? (strategy)
4. How will you measure your success or results? (control)

Field support personnel can ask franchisees these questions and use their responses as the basis for a business plan. Then field support personnel can facilitate the business planning process to arrive at the business plan.

Monitoring the Business Planning Process

Once franchisees go through the planning process, the action plans that result become the basis for field support's follow-up feedback and monitoring. The follow-up focuses on how successful the action plans were, where the franchisee wanted to be, and where he ended up. These gaps are then the basis for ongoing support the franchisee receives from the field staff.

The field staff and the franchisee should meet periodically to discuss items of concern to both parties. Keep these meetings focused by building a common agenda prior to each meeting, identifying items to be discussed, with priority ranking for these items.

Building a common agenda focuses energy on what is really important, clears everyone's mind for listening, truly involves the franchisee in the meeting, and helps gain commitment. The process helps the franchisee understand that the field staff's role is not to run the business but to stimulate the franchisee's thinking. The franchisee then looks at the meetings as worthwhile rather than as another activity taking up its time. The franchisee thinks about the business and takes responsibility for the results.

While conducting the meeting, the field staff uses the agenda to stay on track. If additional issues come up, these issues are added to the agenda, with priority assigned. At the end of the meeting, the field staff person summarizes what was accomplished, notes any issues or problems resolved, and lists action items to follow up. The franchisee has a chance to react, question, or make additional comments. The meeting results are documented on a consultation report.

The key to getting franchisees to follow through on commitments is involvement. Franchisees are not usually mentally involved in meetings or consultations because they have no ownership of the meeting. Thus, the agenda must focus on the *franchisee's* plans and goals. The field support person must encourage the franchisee to take responsibility for results by facilitating the thinking process, using questioning and listening skills to gain commitment to specific action plans.

Building Trust and Rapport

Building trust and rapport is key to developing the relationship between the franchisee and the field support staff. Field support personnel will know they have established trust and rapport when the franchisee opens up and shares his thinking. But to do so, a franchisee must feel that the field support person is trustworthy. Until franchisees get to know and trust their field support person, very little can be accomplished. Consultations end up being "visits," without results.

The following questions and actions help field support personnel develop trust and rapport.

Trust and Rapport Questions

▲ What do you know about the franchisees and their operations? Learn about each franchisee. Review past performance. Understand the market area in which the franchisee operates. Determine what's happening that is significant—both troubling and exhilarating. How long has each been in business? Why did he get into business? Is it a family operation? Are the offspring working in the business?

▲ Have you gained an insight into who the franchisees really are and what motivates them? Determine what motivates each franchisee, in both business and personal lives, both short and long term. Why are franchisees doing what they are doing?

▲ Do the franchisees know you? Share your background. Indicate your knowledge about the industry. Be sincere but confident.

▲ Do you respect the franchisees as individuals? Do they project the image the franchisor desires? If not, why not? Focus on the issue and not the person.

▲ Do you appreciate each franchisee's fears, uncertainties, and doubts? What is troubling them? Why is it troubling? What threats to their business is each franchisee facing? What is each's impression about franchising?

Actions to Develop Trust and Rapport

▲ *Clarify the role of consultant.* Explain to the franchisee that your responsibility is to help him acquire and develop the ability to become successful and profitable in using and appreciating the franchisor's brand name, operating system, and support systems. Your intent is to be a resource in the business planning process. The franchisee must see that your motives are honest and that your purpose is to help him build the business and solve problems to everyone's benefit.

If your role and intent are not clear, a franchisee may assume you are there to inspect his business and make sure he is complying with the franchise agreement. Instead, establish that your responsibility includes helping franchisees analyze where they are relative to where they wanted to be; understand how using the operating systems can help them be more successful; learn how to problem solve; develop their abilities to grow their businesses; understand and appreciate the value of belonging to a franchise system; and focus on improving service to the customer.

▴ *Demonstrate empathy for franchisees.* Empathy is the ability to identify with another person's feelings. Since each franchisee's situation is slightly different, the field support person must be able to put himself in the shoes of the franchisee and understand her feelings and concerns, thus communicating empathy. While empathy does not mean *agreeing* with franchisees, it does require a willingness to look at situations from the other person's point of view. A field support person must first understand, then be understood.

One way to demonstrate empathy is to discuss the franchisee's concerns. Discussing these matters up front is a way to reduce tension, which then earns the franchisee's respect because she has been treated as a person rather than as a potential problem.

▴ *Establish credibility.* The field support person has credibility when she knows how to help franchisees think about what needs to be done or changed so as to become more profitable. Credibility is obtained by association and by working for it. Being associated with the franchisor company lends a certain amount of credibility automatically. But credibility must also be earned, through the franchisee's perception that the field support person has the skills, expertise, desire, and ability to help him build his business. Consulting skills of facilitating, questioning, and listening help.

▴ *Identify common ground with the franchisee.* What family or personal common ground do you share with the franchisee? Same schools? Children of the same age? Association memberships? Similar attitudes about events? Similar opinions?

▴ *Focus on the strengths of franchisees and the business.* Every franchisee has skills, knowledge, abilities, and experience; recognize these strengths and build on them. Has the franchisee been in the system a long time? Has she made any special contribution? Make a list of the franchisee's strengths, and make notes as new strengths develop. Give the franchisee feedback as the new strengths develop. Get her to identify what strengths need to be developed to achieve her plans. When citing strengths, choose those that are specifically meaningful to the franchisee.

▲ *Establish integrity.* Integrity is a value, not a skill. It means doing what you say you are going to do. It means keeping your commitments to franchisees. It means not promising something you know you cannot deliver.

The Consulting Skills Needed by Field Support Personnel

Helping the franchisee acquire and develop the ability to think is a noble goal for any field support person. But how do you get people to think for themselves? When does a person learn? How do you get people to commit to and actually change their behavior? The answers to these questions rest on the ability of field support people to create an environment for learning. This new environment will enable an exchange of information to take place for mutual benefit. To create this environment, field support people use the communication skills of facilitation, questioning, and listening. These skills, coupled with both parties' motivations, will enable everyone to focus on results.

Facilitation, questioning, and listening are skills grounded in the principles of psychology, psychotherapy, and adult learning. They are not activities but rather a process leading someone to learn and change behavior. These skills are used by many professions and form the basis of all productive human relationships.

Questioning

The questioning process gets people to think and discover solutions for themselves. Questioning allows the field support person to gain insight into what the franchisee is thinking and why. The process enables the field support manager to better understand what the franchisee wants and why he wants it.

Questioning also opens up the communication process by encouraging people to talk. This keeps the defenses down, expands the thinking process, and allows everyone to learn how to think about things.

Finally, the questioning process allows a person to "own" her solutions. Through questioning, the field support person allows franchisees to discover solutions for themselves rather than telling them what the solution is. Solutions then have more meaning and generate greater commitment.

There are two types of questions: fact finding and feeling finding. Fact-finding questions uncover objective data or factual information. They deal with the "what" of the message and use words like *what*, *how*, or *when*.

Feeling-finding questions obtain subjective information. They are targeted to emotions, feelings, opinions, or desires, and deal with the "why" of the message using words *like*, *why*, *think*, or *feel*.

Facilitation

Facilitation allows a person to think for himself and make decisions. The field support person helps franchisees identify their personal and business motivations, develop goals that support these motivations, focus on specific areas to achieve the desired results, and monitor the results to ensure the target is reached.

Through this facilitation process the franchisees gain confidence in their ability to respond, build on strengths, and enhance their relationship with field support people. The challenge for the field support person in this process is to avoid jumping in and "doing it" for the franchisee. Field support people must allow franchisees to make mistakes as a natural part of learning. Telling, without a context in which to learn, only satisfies a desire to tell.

Facilitation is a stepping stone between questioning and listening skills, and helps build trust and rapport with a franchise candidate. Facilitation, questioning, and listening skills are most effective when they complement each other.

Listening

Listening is the ability to open your mind to the thinking of others. Correctly used, it is more persuasive than talking. When you think about it, it's easy to understand the psychological power of listening. When a field support person is listening and suggesting, the franchisee feels more in control and, therefore, more comfortable.

Listening is the field support person's biggest challenge. It requires patience, discipline, and focus. Effective listening uses these four principles:

1. *Your mind is blank.* Assume your mind is a computer terminal with information zipping across the screen. Blank the screen so that all attention can be focused on the person doing the talking.
2. *You are able to repeat the actual words spoken, and not use the excuse "I have no memory."* An effective listener can clarify what was said or keep a discussion on track.
3. *The listener implies that what someone has to say really matters.* Have you ever had a conversation in which the listener does all sorts of things while you are talking, such as opening mail, taking telephone calls, or having conversations with others? Does this person really care what you are saying?
4. *The listener listens long enough so that the speaker knows she's been understood.* Have you ever listened to someone and after five seconds got what was being said? Have you ever put up your hands and said, "I understand." At the same time, the speaker is thinking, "No way this guy understood me. I haven't said five words!" Ask what he meant and let him talk.

Common Situations Between Field Support Personnel and Franchisees

Up to this point we have discussed the need for understanding and for developing trust and rapport. Now let's apply these to typical situations: problem solving, confronting and resolving issues, and managing change and resistance.

Problem Solving

A problem can be defined as anything that is off target or a deviation between what should be happening. The deviation between the expected and the actual is usually caused by a change of one kind or another. Field support people can help franchisees think through their problems, not help solve them.

The following process will help the franchisee problem solve:

1. *Collect information and describe the problem.* By describing the problem, you gather enough information to identify what change occurred that prevented the expected from happening or resulted in the unexpected happening. Ask who, what, where, when, and why to identify the problem.

2. *Consider the possible causes and decide on the most probable cause.* Brain-storm every possible cause and write them down. Do not discount any as foolish or illogical.

3. *Develop possible solutions and decide on the best solution.* Once the cause of the problem has been identified, you can develop solutions. The solutions should focus on the future. In considering possible solutions, reexamine the cause of the problem and identify the resources for solving it. Draw on the franchisee's prior experience and the experience of others in the system. Do not stop at the first possible solution; brain-storm for all possible solutions.

4. *Develop a plan for implementing the solution.* The plan should include a clear statement of the goal and how it will be achieved, plus a schedule for reaching it.

5. *Follow up.* Inspect what you expect to happen. Specify what follow-up will occur and when.

Confronting and Resolving Issues

COMPLIANCE PROGRAM

Consistency and standardization are important to a franchise system. Consistency reinforces the expectations of the consumer, and that results in brand loyalty. Compliance protects the investment that all franchisees have made in the system. What happens if a franchisee refuses to comply with the terms of the agreement? How should this situation be handled?

In dealing with compliance issues, field support people should identify the deviation to the franchisee, reeducate him as to acceptable standards, demonstrate how the deviation hurts the whole business, and document any further deviations. An important point here is that the field support person is not a compliance officer. The compliance officer has the power to terminate a franchise agreement. In contrast, the field support person's role is to communicate, educate, and document. He also needs to be sure the compliance procedure is consistently applied. The procedure should be explained to the noncomplying franchisee so there are no surprises. At all times, field support personnel should handle compliance in an adult-to-adult manner and help the franchisee make an informed decision about appropriate behavior.

When dealing with compliance issues, the field support person should handle the deviation from a marketing perspective, highlighting how the deviation impacts on the franchisee's ability to get and keep customers or achieve his goals.

CONFRONTING THE ISSUES

Working through issues with franchisees is a skill that can have a positive impact on franchisees. Tactfully handling potential and existing problems involves the following steps:

1. Identify the issue.
2. Clarify the franchisee's understanding of the issue.
3. Ask questions to determine the franchisee's intent or goal.
4. Listen. Demonstrate empathy when appropriate, and reinforce positive intent.
5. Help the franchisee understand why the issue is important and how it will impact on his business.
6. Discuss alternative strategies for achieving that intent or goal.
7. Ask for agreement or a commitment to a different strategy.
8. Document the conversation and decisions made.
9. Follow up on actions to be taken.
10. Reinforce compliance.

Dealing With Change and Resistance

Change is and will continue to be a constant in today's business environment. The effective field support person deals with change by getting franchisees involved and leading them through the change.

Change is threatening to most people. One of the reasons why franchisees feel threatened by change is that normally they do not initiate changes, yet they are most affected by them. This is where trust and rapport is important, and the field staff person's skills of facilitation, questioning, and listening help the franchisees cope. The key question is, "How will the franchisee benefit from the change?" Remember, the franchisee pays a franchise fee to ensure change.

It is natural for field support personnel to feel that if ideas are presented clearly and logically, and if they are in the best interest of the franchisees, then the franchisees will accept those ideas. But as most field staff have probably already discovered, franchisees still resist change.

Franchisees may be viewed as stubborn and irrational. Field support people may become adamant. But resistance is more understandable if it is seen as:

- An emotional reaction by the franchisee
- Not a reflection of logical, rational conversation
- A predictable, natural reaction to a difficult situation
- A necessary part of the learning process

People use the phrase "overcoming resistance" as though resistance or defensiveness were an adversary to be wrestled and subdued. Overcoming resistance uses data and logical arguments to win a point. But there is no way to talk franchisees out of resistance, because resistance is an emotional reaction.

Behind the resistance are certain feelings, and the field support person needs to help the franchisee get past those feelings to get on with solving the problem. The basic strategy is to encourage the franchisee to surface the resistance, not fight it head-on. Feelings pass when they are expressed. To bring this about:

- Identify when resistance is taking place.
- Prepare people ahead of time for change.
- Get the franchisee's input. Ask questions and listen. Let the franchisee be part of the change process.
- View resistance as a natural process and a sign that you are on target.
- Support the franchisee in expressing the resistance directly. Avoid arguing or showing hostility. (Don't make the other person wrong.)
- Do not take resistance personally.
- Resistance is not the same thing as NO!

Summary

At some point, most franchisors experience frustration over a franchisee's reluctance to do what the franchisor knows should be done for the business to be successful. The key to strengthening and supporting the franchisee relationship is communication. The franchisor has an obligation to communicate what franchising is as business strategy, a marketing system, and a method of distribution. This should be done during the recruitment and selection process, defining the franchisor-franchisee relationship in terms of getting and keeping the customer.

The role of the field support person needs to evolve from that of compliance inspector to that of consultant. The basis of this relationship is the business plan, and facilitation of the business planning process becomes the primary vehicle for helping the franchisee become successful and profitable, using and appreciating the franchisor's brand name, operating system, and support systems.

The relationship between the franchisor and franchisee will be improved if everyone becomes aware of perceptions that create reality. Negative labels need to be eliminated and franchisees must be brought into the decision-making process. These changes will create an environment that develops trust and rapport. Field support personnel use the skills of facilitating, questioning, and listening to enhance communications. These skills encourage the franchisee to think, learn, and change.

By encouraging an understanding of franchising, developing strong communications links, and using basic consulting skills, the field consultant can strengthen and support the franchise system.

2

Developing Effective
Training Programs

Sid Henkin, Prism·CLS

Training is the lifeblood of a franchise organization. It is the vehicle that ensures the continuity and replicability of all the systems that make a franchise unique. When customers walk through the door of a franchise, they expect the same level of service and/or product as received at each of the franchisor's other stores. What happens in one franchise store reflects on every other store in the system. Good experiences create repeat customers for the franchisee; poor experiences drive customers to the competition. Training provides the foundation for the good experiences that will allow a franchisee to prosper.

When a person purchases a franchise, there is both an explicit and implicit understanding that the franchisor will provide the training necessary to lead the franchisee to success. The explicit understanding is stated in the offering circular and is generally detailed during the franchise sales cycle. The information provided is more than an understanding; it is a contractual obligation. The implicit understanding is based on the assurances, usually made during the sales process, that the franchisor will provide ongoing training to help the franchisee. These assurances are rarely detailed and create high levels of expectation on the part of the franchisee.

The Four Levels of Franchise Training

Besides the training of franchisees, there are three other audiences that require specific training within the franchise organization. These are the franchisor itself, the internal franchisor staff, and the staff of the franchisee. The training of these people is as critical to franchise success as the training of the franchisee, although rarely is there as much training attention paid to these people as there is to the franchisee. Training at all levels is the responsibility of the franchisor.

The franchisor must continually be aware of new ways of managing a franchise organization. It must stay abreast of changing needs within the franchise market to keep the organization alert and alive. The franchisees have invested their money and their trust in the franchisor's ability to provide direction and support. It is the franchisor's responsibility to stay current with the market and new management practices to meet the expectations of the franchisees.

The franchisor's staff must continually upgrade their skills to maintain a meaningful and positive relationship with their customers, the franchisees. Every person who comes in contact with a franchisee, whether it be by phone, correspondence, or face-to-face, must understand the needs and expectations of the customer and have the skills necessary to meet them. We often focus on training the development and field (operations) staffs, but neglect other staffers who also interact with the franchisees. These include the receptionist, accounting staff, advertising and marketing personnel, and legal staff as well as other departments.

The franchisee must be trained in how to operate her new business in the prescribed professional manner that you have mandated. The training must cover every area of the business, from daily operation to compliance reporting. One rule of thumb: If a topic is important enough to be in the operations or policy manual, then it is important enough to be in the training schedule. Franchisees come into the system with a variety of backgrounds and experiences that may contribute to their long-term success, but no one comes to the business with the specific knowledge to operate your franchise. The thoroughness of franchisee training is your assurance that the franchisee will understand and remain in compliance.

The franchisee's line people, who actually deliver the goods and services to the consumer, require detailed and continual training. These people *are* the franchise in the eyes of the customer; they are the ambassadors who add value to the name of the franchise and who determine whether a customer comes back. If these people are not well trained and cannot perform their jobs well, it does not matter how well anyone else in the organization is trained. If there are no satisfied customers, there is no business!

Franchise training must be developed as a long-term commitment. It must be developed as a curriculum, not as a single event. Many franchisors have been very successful with a training schedule that spans several years. This indicates that the needs of participants have been given planning and consideration. In the eyes of franchisees, it shows that there's a lot to learn and that their business has room for growth. Another benefit to long-term training is that it answers the ever-present franchisee question, "What have you done for me lately?"

Basic Questions for a Training Program

Several basic questions must be answered whenever you are considering a training program. The answers to these questions provide the guidelines for developing and implementing a training program. In the following section we address each of these questions:

- ▲ What is the issue or problem that you want to resolve?
- ▲ What do you want people to do differently as a result of the training?

▲ What are the specific measurable objectives of the training program?
▲ Who is the audience that must be trained to do the job?
▲ How should the training be delivered?
▲ Who should deliver the training?
▲ When is the best time to deliver this training?
▲ Where should the training be conducted?
▲ What skills and knowledge do the participants need as a prerequisite for the training?
▲ What are the possible sources for this training?
▲ What measurements will you use to determine if the training was effective?

What Is the Issue or Problem?

Successful training programs focus on specific skills to enhance the performance of a particular task. The better we define the task, the better defined are the skills necessary to accomplish that task.

If a customer survey indicates that the satisfaction level is lower than you hoped or has dropped from the last time you conducted the survey, you obviously want to correct the problem. One immediate response might be to ignore the situation or blame it on the season or the way the study was conducted, and hope the problem goes away. Another solution might be to reinforce among the franchisees the importance of customer satisfaction; you might send a powerful memo or make an impassioned speech at an owners' meeting. You might also consider charging up your field consultants and directing them to meet with store owners to reinforce the importance of customer satisfaction. These solutions can raise awareness, but they do little to address the specific problem. Furthermore, they do not provide any solutions or specific activities to change the situation.

The franchisor must break down the generalized problem into specific issues. Customer dissatisfaction may be due to factors such as:

"I had to wait a long time before I was served."
"The staff didn't seem to care whether I was there or not."
"The store was dirty."
"The product or service I received didn't meet my expectations. It was [late/cost more than I expected/didn't look like the pictures]."

These issues are clear, concise, and manageable. At this point you can begin to decide the best plan of action for correcting these matters. If the complaints are important they deserve the time and attention to resolve them properly. Too often we compress too much into too little time, and important issues blend into a morass of other matters. Sometimes the truly important issues are tacked on to the tail end of other issues, treated as afterthoughts rather than serious points.

It is always worth taking the time to analyze what the real issues are before moving ahead with plans for correction or improvement.

What Do You Want People to Do Differently as a Result of the Training?

Now that you've isolated the specific issues causing lower customer satisfaction, you must examine what you want people to do differently to eliminate those problems.

In this instance most of the behavior changes are apparent. For example, as a result of the training, you might like to see the following:

- The counter people greeting the customer quickly and politely
- The counter person being attentive to customer needs
- The store staff maintaining the cleanliness and appearance of the store
- The counter person determining the customer's satisfaction at the time of delivery

What Are the Specific Measurable Objectives of the Training Program?

The objectives of the training program must be stated in action terms that are measurable. Adults, especially, must know what is expected of them and have a means for determining when they are meeting those objectives.

For instance, as a result of the training, the participant will:

- Greet the customer within one minute after he or she enters the store.
- Greet the customer using the standard ABC Franchise greeting.
- Determine the customer's needs by asking the ABC Franchise Six Magic Questions.
- Ask all customers to comment on their level of satisfaction using the ABC Franchise Customer Satisfaction Guide.

All these issues fall into the same category: face-to-face customer skills. The issue of store cleanliness and appearance does not fit this context, so it may be better handled at another time. But if you were to deal with it now, the objective might read: LEARN THE ABC FRANCHISE STANDARDS OF CLEANLINESS AND THE SKILLS NECESSARY TO MAINTAIN THESE STANDARDS.

Who Is the Audience That Must Be Trained to Do the Job?

Determining the proper audience is generally simple once the objectives are stated. In the example we are using, it is clear that the counter people are the ones who must be trained. When the satisfaction issue arose, the immediate reaction was to go to the franchisee to correct the problem. Now you can see why training the franchisee in this case would have been ineffective.

How Should the Training Be Delivered?

There are several methods to deliver training. The most common forms are:

- Group training using a trainer or facilitator
- Self-paced instruction using a workbook and/or audio- or videocassettes
- One-on-one training using an experienced staff member

Group training using a trainer or facilitator provides the following:

Benefits

- High levels of interaction
- Participants having the opportunity to share ideas with one another
- High levels of buy-in and commitment
- Easily modified as needs change
- Well suited for "one time, one of a kind" training such as launching a new product or promotion

Limitations

- Groups of employees off the job at the same time
- A trained facilitator or trainer required
- Variations in the consistency of the training according to the temperament of the trainer and the group
- A committed time block with limited flexibility required
- Someone missing the session having to wait for the next go-round
- Travel to a central training location often required

Self-paced instruction using a workbook and/or audio- or videocassettes provides the following:

Benefits

- Training completed at the convenience of participants
- Absolute consistency and replicability every time
- Consistency in delivery
- Repeat training at any time
- Well suited for skills that must be taught repeatedly

Limitations

- No guaranteed buy-in or commitment on the part of the learner
- Time consuming and expensive to produce
- Possibility of material becoming dated in both content and image—five-year-old cars or outdated clothing in the pictures

▴ Difficult to modify and update
▴ A capital purchase of equipment such as a VCR often required

One-on-one training using an experienced staff member is the simplest and quickest form of training, but it offers the highest risk: There is no guarantee that the experienced staff member is teaching the right skills. The staff member may well have been taught by her predecessor, who was taught by his predecessor and so forth. There is a tendency in one-on-one training to fall into a "let me tell you the way it's really done around here" syndrome. The trainee may learn shortcuts before he ever learns the right way to do things.

One-on-one training using an experienced staff member offers the following:

Benefits

▴ Inexpensive
▴ Readily available
▴ Little or no preparation required
▴ Well suited for on-the-job coaching and skill improvement

Limitations

▴ No consistency or replicability
▴ Wrong information often conveyed
▴ Shortcuts encouraged, rather than full-process training

In our customer service example, self-paced instruction provides the longest benefit, since every current and future counter employee needs these skills to be effective. Since the skills are specific, they must be replicated exactly, every time the training is offered. The initial cost may be high, but when amortized over the number of stores and the number of employees going through the program, the cost becomes relatively low.

In this particular instance, where there is a short-term goal to bring up customer satisfaction in a hurry, group training using prepared materials may be worthwhile. The buy-in of the current staff is important, as is the need for a forum for employees to discuss the importance of customer satisfaction. Group training provides this.

Who Should Deliver the Training?

The best possible training personnel are professional trainers. Most franchise organizations have limited training resources and must rely on personnel from within the organization. The field consultants are generally a reliable resource for training outside of the office. They are the most knowledgeable liaisons with the franchisees. Initial franchisee training at the home office should be shared by every department on the staff. At the home office, you have the opportunity to have the experts in each area interact with the new owners. The training forum allows staff members to get to know the new owners as well as address their specific concerns. For major events such as national meetings, or for specific events such as legal updates, consider using outside resources such as training companies or nationally recognized experts.

The customer service program could be introduced to the franchisees by the field consultants. Training and support in the stores could be provided by the franchisees themselves. The self-study program requires no trainer but should be introduced to the trainee by the franchisee or store manager.

When Is the Best Time to Deliver the Training?

Training is most effective when new skills can immediately be applied to a real-life situation. To determine the best time to deliver training, see how quickly it can be applied; teaching month-end accounting to a new franchisee before his store has even opened has limited value. But teaching it on-site during the first month of operation is very meaningful.

In our customer service example, the best time to teach these skills is on-site during operating hours, so employees can immediately put the skills to work.

Where Should the Training Be Conducted?

Skills training should be conducted as close to the actual work site as possible. If a person is learning to operate a printing press, he must be in a properly equipped pressroom. If the real pressroom has not been built, then the training must be conducted in a facility that has the same equipment and same environment as he will be working in later.

Awareness training can be conducted off-site as long as the facility is conducive to learning. If the training is a major event, the site must reflect the importance of the event. But regardless of the location, the training facility must have good lighting, good ventilation, and comfortable seating. No one can learn in an environment that bombards with distractions or is uncomfortable.

What Skills and Knowledge Do the Participants Need as a Prerequisite to the Training?

Rarely can you teach a new skill without assuming some basic knowledge. If you were training individuals to be income tax preparers, you would assume that they had some basic mathematics skill. If you were training a person in sales skills, you would assume that they had some basic communications skills. Unfortunately, these assumptions often lead to disappointment or disillusionment. There are people who cannot add and others who cannot talk to strangers.

When designing a training program, you must challenge all your assumptions and create a checklist of basic, intermediate, and advanced skills that trainees should have. Once you have determined these, state them prior to the training. This avoids a great deal of frustration, embarrassment, and wasted time, while you strive to help one individual catch up to the rest of the group.

What Are the Possible Sources for This Training?

As a franchisor it is your responsibility to provide the training, not to create it. Many of the dollars expended on developing training programs could be saved if you look to programs that already exist. Many times you can find existing resources for training at a fraction of the cost of developing new ones.

If the skills you are training are generic to the industry, trade sources can often provide training. Trade associations usually have numerous offerings. For example, management training is available through the American Management Association; franchise-specific training is available through the International Franchise Association; food-service training is available through the National Restaurant Association. Suppliers often provide training on their equipment or systems.

The development of effective training programs is a discipline unto itself. When you have to supply your own training programs, be certain that the people developing them have a successful track record. The growth and success of your franchise depends on how well your franchisees deliver the goods and services. Their ability to deliver depends on how well you have trained them. Training is an investment, not an expense.

What Measurements Will I Use to Determine Whether the Training Was Successful?

Every successful training program has measurable objectives. At the end of the training there should be some type of measurement system to ensure that the objectives have been met. Usually participants are asked to evaluate the training at the completion of a program. This type of evaluation—the smile sheet—tells you how much the participant enjoyed the training and provides some insight into how the participant feels the training will help her in the future, but it does not show if the training has indeed changed real performance.

The true measurement of success is the training program's impact on the issues the program was designed to address. In the customer satisfaction example, the results of the next survey will tell you if the training succeeded. Continual measurement and feedback often highlight areas that need greater attention.

Ultimately, every training activity should be measured as a return on investment. If you do not measure the long-term effectiveness of your training programs, you may be throwing away time and dollars.

The Development of a Basic Franchisee Training Curriculum

Many franchisors have felt the frustration of watching new franchisees coming into the system and stumble during their first few months of operation. A great deal of this is due to ineffective training. We try to compress too much into too short a time, and expect new owners to absorb it all. Unfortunately, adults don't learn that way. Adults learn by relating new knowledge to past experience and then applying that new knowledge to a new environment. Too much of new-owner training is based on the ability of an individual to warehouse knowledge until it is needed.

The other aggravating aspect of new-franchisee training is that franchisors often expect franchisees to use their wits to figure things out, but they don't. People don't buy franchises to figure things out. They buy franchises to have someone show them how to do it. That's what new-franchisee training is all about.

The new franchisee is excited about her new opportunity and is ready to learn. There is probably no better training audience than the new store owner. It's your job to deliver the training in understandable and meaningful terms.

The following training matrix provides a format that has proved successful for many franchisors. The matrix is based on the premise that if a topic is important enough to be in the operations or policy manual, it is important enough to be in the training curriculum.

To develop a training matrix, list every topic found in your operations and policy manual. For each item listed, ask the following questions:

- Is this item really important for the operation of the franchise?
- Who is responsible for the implementation of this item? The franchisee? The manager? The front-line person?
- When does this person have to first implement this item?
- When is the best time for the person to be trained in the skills necessary to implement the topic?
- Who is the best person in the organization to deliver this training?
- How will the person know he is implementing this topic satisfactorily?
- What are the measurable standards?

The responses to these questions are then plotted on the training matrix shown in Figure 2-1. The completed matrix defines who should be trained when and in what. The process of developing the matrix highlights redundant items in the operations manual as well as redundancies in the training process. From the matrix you will then be able to determine the areas that require revision or new training programs.

Once you have instituted this matrix you can reference the available training resource on each page of the operations and policy manuals.

Figure 2-1.   Sample training matrix.

SAMPLE TRAINING MATRIX

X = Common to both Franchisee and Company

O = Specific to Franchisee or Company

Training Course (Content Blocks)	Current Source	Preferred Source	Franchise (Owner)	Store Manager	Assistant Store Manager	Cashier	Parts Clerks	Gas Attendant	Service Center Manager	Service Writer	Mechanic Technician	Basic Service Technician	Operations Manual Interface
I. Management Orientation	TM/AMT	TM/AMT	O	O					O				Philosophy in Action
II. Store Management Training	TM	TM											
A. Introduction	Pres.	Pres.	O	O	O				O				Philosophy in Action
B. Sales and Marketing	S&M	S&M	X	X	X				X				Marketing and Merchandising
C. Security	SEC.	SEC.	O	O	O				O				Store Security
D. Inventory Control	TM	TM	X	X	X				X				Supply Operations
E. Scheduling and Payroll	RM	RM	O	O	O				O				Store Organizations
F. Gas Operations	TM	GC	X	X	X				X				Gas Operations Manual
G. Business Reports	CFO	CFO	O	O	O				O				Financial Reports
H. Customer Relations	RM	RM	X	X	X				X				Philosophy in Action
I. Safety and MIOSHA	RM	RM	X	X	X				X				Store Security
J. Employee Handbook	PD	PD	O	O	O				O				Appendix
K. Management Techniques	TM/AMT	TM/AMT	X	X	X				X				Employee Relations
L. Service Operations	TM	SD	X	X	X								Service Operations Manaul
III. Store Manager and Assistant Manager	CT	CT											Transactions
A. Cash Register Training	CT	CT	X	X	X				X				
B. System 36	CT	CT	X	X	X				X				
C. End of Day Processing	CT	CT	X	X	X				X				
D. Setting Security	CT	CT	X	X	X				X				
E. Cashier File	CT	CT	X	X	X				X				
F. Ordering Supplies	CT	CT	X	X	X				X				
G. Problem Determination	CT	CT	X	X	X				X				
H. Response Line	CT	CT	X	X	X				X				
I. Gasoline Procedures	CT	CT	X	X	X				X				
IV. Employment/Personnel Administration Seminar	TM/AMT	TM/AMT	O	O					O				Employee Relations

© CLS

Summary

The quality and thoroughness of your training programs directly reflect the quality and thoroughness of your franchise operation. The first true exposure a new franchisee has to how your organization does business is the training process. When the training process is presented in a professional manner, with professionally prepared materials presented by professional people, the franchisee feels good. If the training, materials, and presenters are poorly prepared and ineffective, the franchisee begins to resist and questions his choice of business partner. In short, during the development process the franchisee was told how good everything was going to be. The training process is his first fulfillment of this promise.

When your franchisee hires her staff, the training she provides will have the same impact and importance as yours did for the franchisee. When the staff is confident and well trained, then customers will keep coming back for more.

3

Establishing an Effective Administrative System for the Franchise Network

Mark E. Czekaj, Safeguard Business Systems, Inc.

A great deal of time and effort goes into developing the individual franchise system. Every precaution is taken to ensure that each operating phase of the business is carefully evaluated and proved. Procedures are defined in great detail. Required operating compliance is documented and followed to the letter.

During the formal training period, new owners or operators are rigorously schooled and tested in their ability to run the business in accordance with the strict business format prescribed by the franchisor. Considerable attention is given to the proper execution of the recommended business plan. There is passionate emphasis on the importance of product or service standardization throughout the training program. Every question or concern is addressed with great zeal, confidence, and *enthusiasm*. The system *does* work if new owners follow the guidelines established by the franchisor.

Unfortunately, many franchise training programs fall short of delivering a true turnkey package to their new franchisees. While a great deal of emphasis is placed on the actual operation of the business, little is done to prepare the new owners for actually managing their businesses. Record keeping, accounting, and tax-related issues are often perceived as the responsibility of the individual owner, not the corporate franchisor. A limited amount of time, if any, is spent discussing this critical aspect of running a successful small business. Except for instructing new franchise owners to secure the services of a "good" accountant, many franchise programs leave this important area of the business to chance. But in this economic climate, can a franchisor afford to take the risk?

Record Keeping Compliance at the Franchise Level

Today, corporate franchise organizations are rethinking their position in this area, and with good reason. The benefits of introducing consistent, standardized record keeping systems and procedures go far beyond the needs of the individual franchisee. Franchisors stand to gain as well. Although expansion of the franchise network through new unit sales remains a major thrust of every organization, facts indicate that long-term success ultimately rests on the franchisor's ability to track and collect royalty revenues. Uniform, well-planned record keeping and reporting systems play a critical role in maintaining the integrity of that process. Developing a structured approach to effectively monitor franchise business activity has great merit in today's business environment. By establishing defined reporting procedures and general record keeping systems, franchisors can proactively maintain financial compliance standards capable of minimizing abuse at the franchise level.

Clearly, it is the franchisor's responsibility to develop, implement, and maintain such financial compliance systems. The corporate organization's future success is dependent on its willingness to deal directly with this issue early on in the franchise-development process. Properly devised systems and controls can dramatically improve the franchisor's ability to maintain quality, isolate format inconsistencies, and detect negative trends long before they become business disasters. And with the franchise business environment becoming more complex every day, a second look is well advised for well-established franchise organizations as well.

Benefits Derived at the Headquarters Level

With a franchisor's business success highly contingent on the generation of royalty revenues, franchisors have a great deal at stake in ensuring the accuracy of weekly, monthly, or daily sales revenue reports. While some retail establishments enjoy the benefits of using computerized cash register systems, noncomputerized franchised businesses rely solely on the personal integrity of individuals completing the sales recap reports designed to capture periodic revenue data.

Unfortunately, new franchisors often assume that all reporting at the franchise level is truly accurate. Why not? They selected those people themselves. But according to industry statistics, over 30 percent of all franchise owners underreport their earnings for royalty compilation. Let's face it—they are human beings too! Unless the franchisor creates a disciplined method or system to track sales revenues, abuses at the network level will grow over time.

Many small corporate franchisors do not have the ability to periodically audit the franchise reports. Surveys indicate that less than 30 percent of all franchisors do so on a consistent basis, since it costs time and money. Therefore, in the absence of direct field monitoring, a franchisor can supply a formal record keeping procedure that says the company is in fact committed to financial integrity in the field. In the event an audit is conducted, the standardized reporting systems will enhance and streamline the process. Revenue reports can easily be compared with disbursements or cost expenditures to determine trends and variances. If franchisees experience cash-flow problems or other financial weaknesses that affect their performance, corporate headquarters can help identify the operating problems. Owing to record keeping standardization, the information is accessible and relatively easy to define. Most important, the problems can be resolved in relatively short time.

Through standardized record keeping systems, franchisors can help the franchisees while helping themselves. Indeed, with so much on the line, many franchise organizations are making such an effort to upgrade this aspect of their business.

Benefits for the New Franchise Candidate

During the 1980s, a small-business revolution occurred in the United States. Franchising as an industry took great strides in developing its position as the leading source of new small-business opportunities. Simultaneously, major adjustments within the corporate industrial sector began to produce an abundance of displaced employees yearning for a piece of the American Dream: business ownership. In addition, more and more women entered the workplace and soon began to dominate small-business startups through the decade.

Of most significance to today's franchisor is the fact that over 50 percent of all candidates interviewed and selected by franchisors have *no* prior small-business ownership experience. As a result, more emphasis is needed on helping them understand the basic fundamentals of small-business management.

Unfortunately, there is no foolproof plan to guarantee success. According to statistics, the risks of small-business ownership are quite high. Small Business Administration studies indicate that 75 percent of all new business owners fail within five years. Furthermore, 60 percent of those going out of business do so as a direct result of poor record keeping practices. The lack of basic management skills is the leading cause of these small-business failures.

For many reasons, record keeping has never received the proper attention it deserves in the small-business community. Even today, record keeping is perceived as a tedious exercise, full of boredom and futility. But it is far more than just numbers on paper. It is a working part of a system of business controls that capture important information. This information is necessary for making timely, intelligent business decisions. Record keeping's primary purpose is to format pertinent business information in a simple and easy-to-use manner. With decisions to be made every day, the businessperson needs accurate information at a moment's notice.

Record keeping should not be confused with "accounting"; rather, good record keeping is an important component of the accounting process. Actually, intelligent record keeping systems *complement* the accounting needs and objectives of a business.

More important, detailed and consistent record keeping systems can assist both accountants and franchisors to solve business problems at the individual franchise level. Disciplined, well-defined record keeping management can significantly improve communication and facilitate the ability to consistently monitor current business performance. Consequently, critical issues and trends can be addressed long before they become major business problems.

Disciplined Record Keeping—A Shared Responsibility

While no one would argue the positive value a good record keeping system represents to the individual franchise, a more important question concerns the level of responsibility assumed by the corporate franchisor at the training level. Whose responsibility is it to initiate the defined systems and procedures—the individual franchisee, the accountant, or the corporate franchisor?

Today, after considerable debate, more and more franchisors see that active participation in the development of network financial controls is indeed warranted and cost-justified. They realize considerable benefits when they are committed to establishing and maintaining record keeping compliance throughout their networks. Depending on the degree of small-business experience among the franchisee candidates, the franchisor's perceived corporate responsibility varies from organization to organization. Nevertheless, most franchisors include some aspect of business management in their formal training process.

As the key influence in the business development process, the franchisor has both the ability and responsibility to develop good working habits at the grassroots level. Long before a formal relationship with an accountant begins, corporate franchise personnel are often looked upon as the primary source of business advice and experience. Eager to achieve success, the new owner or operator seldom rejects logical recommendations given by the franchisor during the training. In fact, the new owners come to expect that advice as a benefit of investing in the particular business.

Contrary to once-popular opinion, there is little if any liability in establishing record keeping procedures at the headquarters level. The risk of destroying the ''arm's length'' relationship between the franchisor and the franchisee is far too often misunderstood as it pertains to this critical area of business management. Unlike giving tax-reporting advice, recommending general IRS-approved record keeping systems and procedures poses no threat to the corporate organization. Of greater concern is the liability that results from knowing your franchisees need help and offering no clear direction for securing assistance. In today's litigious business environment, it may be wise to provide specific directions, limiting corporate exposure in the event franchisees fail or file bankruptcy.

A variety of approaches have been taken by leading franchise organizations to initiate good business practices at the individual franchise level. More and more franchisors are recommending and/or mandating the use of professionally designed record keeping or data-retrieval systems. In many cases, specified record keeping systems are included as part of the initial franchise fee. In that way, both the franchisee and franchisor benefit.

Leadership best describes the role franchisors play in developing a strong network of successful entrepreneurs. To fulfill their responsibilities, franchisors must take an active role in determining how franchisees conduct their business on a daily basis. The opportunity to help entrepreneurs become good managers is one of the primary goals of the training program. It is never too late to introduce solid record keeping methods to promote good business practices. Some of the world's largest franchise organizations, including the McDonald's Corporation, have initiated proactive programs to improve network record keeping efficiency. Even the best organizations find new and innovative ways to become better.

Indeed, the responsibility for having good record keeping systems and habits extends far beyond the individual franchise owner and his accountant. Today's leading franchise organizations are realizing the positive benefits of active participation in this important area.

The Accountant's Role

The vague advice "go find a good accountant" is insufficient direction for corporate franchisors to give their new owners and operators. If the new franchisee lacks small-business management experience, he will not appreciate the full value a professional accountant represents. It's no surprise that a majority of established small-business owners today underutilize their accountants. Instead, the accountant must be seen as a source of financial advice and management counseling. The new franchise owner must be told that the accountant does more than keep books and prepare taxes. Through no fault of their own, new franchise owners know little about the business problems they will encounter, or the value an accountant represents in solving those problems. Considering the high cost of business failure, for both the franchisor and franchisee, both parties need to revise their view of the accountant.

Communication, or the ability to communicate, is the highest hurdle facing new franchise owners in developing a working relationship with a local accountant. Finding it difficult to express his exact needs in detail, the franchise owner often receives a fraction of the help and professional guidance available from his accountant. Yet the ability to develop a meaningful dialogue with the accountant is critical, particularly during the initial meeting. The accountant is eager to be of assistance; it is up to the client to articulate the level of assistance required.

In dealing with an accountant, franchise owners need to be comfortable explaining the financial reporting needs of their business, including those requirements set forth by the franchisor. Even though the accountant may have a solid understanding of small business, she may in fact have little knowledge concerning the specific franchised business. With proper training, franchisees can better develop meaningful, productive relationships with their chosen advisers.

In addition, new franchisees should be given direction in developing an accountant relationship. A discussion of the evaluation process is often helpful; in that manner, franchisors can assist new owners to make a better, more intelligent choice of adviser to serve their best interests.

In many cases, franchisors incorrectly assume that the accountant will discuss in great detail the need for a defined record keeping system. More often than not, accounting professionals aggressively promote good habits in this area, but others maintain a neutral position or recommend potential solutions only upon a specific request from their client. This ambiguous situation creates the further need for specialized record keeping training.

Like other professionals, accountants differ in the way they interpret the regulations and procedures of business. Of great concern to today's franchisor is an accountant's willingness to conform to the system and guidelines established by the corporate headquarters. To attain reporting uniformity, the franchisor must establish specific record keeping requirements, and then the individual account- ants will better understand their role in bridging the franchisor-franchisee rela- tionship.

Leaders at the corporate franchise level must promote a strong, advisory franchisee-accountant relationship. Through corporate-sponsored workshops, seminars, and targeted classroom development, franchisors can communicate fun- damental management needs. In that manner, franchisees can enjoy a more mean- ingful relationship with the outside adviser so vital to their long-term success.

Program Development—The Assessment Process

In determining how much of a part a franchise record keeping system should play in the overall training package, the franchisor needs to analyze the company's objectives, franchise information requirements, staff capabilities, and internal fi- nancial resources. During the needs-analysis process, it should be understood that a variety of tools and outside resources are available for developing a solid pro- gram. Today's franchisor is not required to be a record keeping expert in order to promote good franchisee business habits. It is more important that the organiza- tion accurately assess the information needs of both the corporation and the fran- chisee, as well as identify appropriate outside vendors capable of designing inte- grated solutions consistent with those objectives. By no means a complicated process, incorporating a professional record keeping module into an overall train- ing program is simple and cost-effective.

With today's sophisticated management information systems, determining the appropriate management system can be tedious and time-consuming. There- fore, more and more franchisors are actively researching and evaluating record keeping alternatives, and then recommending those that best suit franchise- reporting needs. From manual record keeping systems to computers, franchisors are finding that these systems can greatly enhance their management effective- ness.

A major part of the assessment process is determining the capability of the headquarters staff and the franchisees. Oftentimes, the preferred solution is the easiest to initiate, support, and use in the field. Remember, the objective should be to make franchisees good business owners, not accounting professionals. The franchisor recruited the new owners to sell its product or service. A proper record keeping system should help maximize their time doing business with customers while minimizing their time and effort keeping track of it.

Basic Franchise Record Keeping Goals

Although franchise formats differ from organization to organization, all owners share one thing in common: each must capture and document day-to-day financial events to properly manage the business. The IRS demands it. Government regulations dictate it. Small business survival depends on it.

To begin analyzing the record keeping options, focus on needs at the headquarters level; a majority of the financial controls are mirrored at the field level. Although the aggregate numbers may be higher, the franchisees will measure their performance using the same general guidelines the franchisor has established at the corporate level. Thus all good financial records answer three basic questions vital to management:

1. Where am I?
2. Where am I going?
3. Where will I be in five years if I continue this trend?

At the franchise level, owners must be keenly aware of the overall cash-flow process. They cannot sit back and wait for their accountant to compile summary reports on a quarterly basis. Business conditions change daily. These changes demand flexibility for making appropriate, timely corrections. Therefore, record keeping is not a passive exercise of data collection. Rather, it is a daily barometer measuring the core of the business. A living, breathing component of the business itself, record keeping as a business function has grown immensely.

Applicable Franchise Record Keeping

Three basic business functions occur on a daily basis:

1. Revenue generation
2. Cost control and operation management
3. Management, planning, and strategic development

Within the revenue-generation process, small-business owners document the receipt of cash, credit card, or credit purchases made by customers. Depending on the nature of the business, accounting may be on a cash or accrual basis—a decision usually made by the corporate controller or CPA. Record keeping is a cash receipt and accounts receivable system that tracks the cash received or due the business, providing a clear audit trail for reporting taxes and royalties. In retail situations, computerized cash registers often facilitate this process. Again, the approach may vary, owing to the individual nature of the business. In the event that customers are invoiced for future payment, it is critical to establish sufficient paper controls to ensure that proper accounts are debited for future payment.

Accounts receivable represents the largest single asset carried on the balance sheet of many small business entities. When applying for a business loan at a local bank, the major focus is not only on the quality of the receivables but also on the time those obligations have been carried on the books. The longer a receivable goes unpaid, the less chance the obligation will be collected. According to the accounting firm of Alexander Grant and Company, $1 in accounts receivable represents only 80 cents when collected over a 120-day period. Without a mechanism to properly record, track, and follow up on accounts of this type, cash-flow problems are inevitable.

Cost control and *operations management* have come under great scrutiny since the late 1980s. With margins shrinking, there is greater emphasis on this area of the business. Efficient inventory management, business expense analysis, and payroll and benefit management now receive greater attention from businesses both big and small. As the cost of doing business rises, the need for disciplined controls increases proportionately.

Payroll processing can be a big problem for today's small-business owner, particularly those with ten or more employees. Tedious and time consuming, payroll tax procedures continue to grow more complex.

Proper *accounts payable* management can also save substantial revenue annually. In addition to taking advantage of available discounts, a good record keeping system helps avoid paying invoices twice or more. Proper procedures and documentation can have a positive impact on the bottom line.

Cash disbursements, or check writing, is best associated with, but not limited to, cash accounting procedures. Since there is a need to pay vendors each day, a proper system similar to the accounts payable function can simultaneously record both the check and the account as credited. It is unwise to write a check without understanding its impact on the business's cash balance the same day. Indeed, owners need to be fully aware of every business transaction, including individual contributions to the business at hand. Likewise, proper bank reconciliation should be performed monthly. Good management involves ongoing intelligent decisions, rather than a few major decisions scattered along the way.

Petty cash and gift certificates are highly suspect by the Internal Revenue Service. All too often during an audit situation these accounts appear to lack controls. Simple procedures can be implemented to track these activities, providing an excellent audit trail for both internal and external reviews.

Businesses that require maintaining substantial inventories must be on guard against mismanagement. For instance, without proper *inventory control*, cash flow can be negatively affected. Again, depending on the type of business, there are a variety of solutions that help minimize problems.

Today's competitive environment has forced all small-business owners to become better managers and planners. However, not every person who buys a franchise will have the necessary experience to achieve that goal. Therefore, franchisors must provide more direction and prepare these new owners for the challenge. Good record keeping systems can help owners and operators make better decisions, as well as assist them in planning the future of their businesses. Making available to them solid business information will give them more time to better evaluate their results and, more important, recognize the series of events that led to those results. Their business planning will then be even more meaningful. Most important, franchisees will know when it's time to ask for help. Their relationship with the franchisor will indeed be one of mutual effort, respect, and trust.

Tools of the Trade—Solution Analysis

A variety of new business tools and solutions emerged during the 1980s to help franchise owners run their businesses. The computer age had revolutionized the way big business managed its affairs; with the advent of the PC, high technology was now available to anyone else interested in streamlining at the small-business level. No more paper. No more problems. Right? Unfortunately, this has not proved to be the case. Along with the benefits derived from technology have emerged many new problems. The computer was not the total answer. Computerization has come to represent an important part of the solution, but along with it must be a comprehensive record keeping system.

Business information or record keeping systems can be categorized as follows:

1. Manual
2. Semiautomated
3. Automated or computerized

Typically, the new small-business owner begins manually. Owing to limited financial resources, this is often the most practical method of recording business activity. In many start-up situations, the owner often handles the record keeping duties as well. At this point it is important that the franchise owner fully understand the nuts and bolts of record keeping. Manual systems are easy to incorporate and simple to use, and can easily be applied to every aspect of the business. Day-to-day control over operations is achieved, and the system provides an excellent foundation for future automation.

Semiautomated management systems use computer-related technology without the large hardware investment. Simple to incorporate, semiautomated solutions are relatively inexpensive and easy to use. These semiautomated solutions are discussed later in more detail.

The term *automated* can be misleading. Although its obvious implication is the day-to-day use of a computer, most small-business owners find it difficult to manage all areas of the business using a single computer system. Also, only the most proficient computer advocates utilize the computer to its full potential. Computer hardware is expensive while the software requires special training and demands constant updates and technical support. Hard data are still required for input and backup purposes.

It is no surprise to find that most efficient businesses combine elements of all three systems. The systems are carefully integrated to complement each other. Even independent systems become interdependent upon each other, though each is capable of standing on its own. Thus total system failure becomes a remote possibility. As the business expands, the emphasis shifts to meet different processing demands; nevertheless, the foundation systems remain in place, thus there is maximum benefit per investment dollar. The best integrated solutions are the ones that meet today's needs and are flexible enough to anticipate tomorrow's requirements as well.

Manual Solutions – One-Write Accounting Systems

Accountants have the phrase ''the shoe box syndrome'' to describe the clutter of financial information so often dumped on them by disorganized small-business clients. Most accountants prefer not to spend their time playing financial archaeologist, sifting through unlabeled receipts, illegible invoices, and undated journal pages. Ultimately, franchise owners pay the price for the resulting clerical work.

Today's most popular alternative to the shoebox syndrome is the manual *One-Write Accounting System*. Often referred to as a ''pegboard'' system, this tool is highly recommended by CPAs. Far from being old-fashioned, one-write systems have up-to-date features and a contemporary look. Many leading franchise organizations recommend or include such systems in the franchise package. Pegboard accounting is fast, accurate, and easy to use. The systems can effectively reduce by 75 percent the time required to record business activity. Unnecessary repetition is eliminated. Account balances are always up to date. The systems are literally error free and provide timely, organized information.

More than 200 different types of one-write systems are available. In addition to basic payroll, accounts receivable, accounts payable, and general disbursement systems, there are many industry-specific systems available. Cash receipting systems are very popular, because receipts can be numbered to assure full report of cash transactions. But all one-write compliance systems are easily adapted to meet other franchise-related record keeping situations. Should the organization upgrade to a computer technology, one-write systems provide the necessary backup and data-input capability. There's also computer software for one-write accounting, which includes a tutorial to learn the operation.

Semiautomation – Low Investment and High Technology

Semiautomated record keeping has expanded over the past decade. Many applications have emerged to fill the void between manual systems and computer systems. The reality is that even when there is a need for accelerated processing, both the financial and staff resources may not be available. Semiautomated solutions present a significant opportunity for both large and small franchise organizations by supplementing their operations with outside services.

Automated payroll processing services are now available from a number of companies in North America. These processing services help franchisees and franchisors deal with the payroll function of the business. In particular, franchisees with more than ten employees benefit greatly. They are cost-effective and can save a tremendous amount of time. Payroll processing companies offer features such as direct deposit, quarterly reporting, and government documentation, including W-2s and 1099s. What once required hours can now be accomplished by simply picking up the telephone.

Service bureaus are another tool gaining interest in the franchise marketplace. Also referred to as batch processing or outsourcing services, this record keeping alternative combines the benefits of high technology with minimal capital investment. Many franchisors make the service available to their franchisees, in efforts to guarantee that record keeping is given proper attention. Monthly reporting documents are forwarded to a centralized computer location capable of preparing the detailed financial reports. Customer billing can also be automatically processed, if required. Typically, the information is processed by a third-party corporation; however some franchisors provide the service themselves. (Owing to trust issues associated with the franchisee-franchisor relationship, third-party participation is most often the better choice.) Some accounting firms offer this service as well.

The demand for *collection letter services* has risen dramatically. Past-due accounts and bad checks continue to plague both franchisee and franchisor. The collection process is time-consuming and people-intensive. Companies offering collection letter services provide a professional approach to reducing receivables, improving cash flow, and minimizing unnecessary write-offs. Not to be confused with collection agencies, which actually will pursue a collection matter, collection letter services help streamline the process of informing problem customers. Cost-effective and easy to initiate, this third-party service produces results!

Automation—Integrating Computer Technology

Computer technology continues to romance franchisors and franchisees at all levels. Seen as the solution to all management problems, computer operations have been tried by franchise organizations, with mixed success. On the surface, the solutions appear simple. Beneath the surface, however, are a variety of complex factors that hamper headquarters efforts to automate the reporting process.

During the 1980s, a number of franchise organizations attempted to design software programs. In an attempt to justify the thousands of dollars in time and money, many franchisors truly believed that the unique nature of their business required a custom software solution. Existing small-business record keeping packages with proven records were ignored. In some cases, ego was the dominating force.

Today, a new awareness helps guide franchisors down the road to greater technology. Good office-management software is available at affordable prices. Indeed, many software manufacturers customize their product to meet franchise requirements. "Data-link," or system interface programs, facilitate the merger of data generated by two independent systems. Depending on the needs of the franchise organization, it may no longer be necessary to start automation from the ground up.

Applicable low-cost small-business software has measurably reduced the investment necessary by both the franchisee and franchisor. Attaining systemwide uniformity is now both realistic and achievable. Therefore, the main focus of today's franchisor must be on selecting the right software. More specifically, the software must address needs at both the field and headquarters level. In any event, consistency in the system used will enhance the value of the individual franchise as well as assist the franchisor in managing transitions owing to terminations or buy-sells.

A systemwide software program brings many great benefits, including the fact that computer-related reporting documents—invoices, receipts, statements, mailers, and checks—are standardized and can more effectively be monitored and controlled. Achieving uniformity throughout the network, franchisors gain valuable insights from studying the business activity generated at individual locations. Likewise, variances in the reorder process can prompt an in-depth investigation. And franchisees benefit as well. The fear and mystery of computerization can be significantly reduced when the franchisor helps individual owners make a good business decision in this area.

Some franchisors consider it a top priority to have a computer system that integrates the best interests of both franchisee and headquarters. But only when headquarters' objectives are clear should the franchisor begin the evaluation process. The success of computerized cash registers or a P.O.S. (point-of-sale) system comes in part because the franchisee perceives a great benefit in using the tool. Inventories are more easily tracked; daily sales summaries are provided with a touch of a key. Therefore, the benefits should be clear to *all* parties.

The biggest challenge facing franchisors attempting to automate is the privacy issue. Let's face it, individuals buy a franchise to be independent, not to run a company store. Regardless of the system you recommend or mandate, changes could be perceived as a threat to independence. Therefore, some organizations try to involve franchisees in the decision to automate. In that manner, a spirit of mutual interest is maintained. For best results, these systems are introduced during the initial stages of franchise development; greater resistance results when changes are forced upon a mature organization.

Regardless of the franchisor's posture, franchisees may at some time request assistance in choosing appropriate accounting software. The franchisor should consult the corporate accounting team for its advice.

Software manufacturers are glad to send demonstration disks to show their program's capabilities. The final decision should rest on the simplicity of use, not the availability of complex features. Remember, franchisees are not computer specialists.

Expanding Your Team Through Meaningful Vendor Relationships

Building a first-class record keeping compliance program does not have to be expensive or complicated. Smart franchisors, large and small, seek the experience and expertise of worldwide suppliers. Insist on personal training and support at all levels. No matter how good the product or how inexpensive the price, follow-up service ultimately determines how successful the system will be. Insist that suppliers be part of the team, not the payroll. Especially if the franchise organization lacks internal support personnel, select suppliers can greatly compensate if they are committed to helping build a first-class organization. Quarterly consultative reviews should be part of any vendor-client agreement, since changing conditions require periodic adjustments. Finally, vendors offering multiple services under one umbrella greatly maximize efforts and minimize overlap and confusion.

*   *   *

More than ever before, the need for accurate record keeping and financial reporting at the franchise level demands a proactive franchisor role. Great benefits await the organization dedicated to developing, implementing, and maintaining standardized record keeping systems and procedures. Though the degree of sophistication at the individual franchise level may not seem to demand it, the franchisor must transcend basic operational issues and cover business and financial management.

Establishing proper record keeping programs at the headquarters level can also promote consistency, uniformity, quality, discipline, and control system-wide. Royalty income is indeed the lifeblood of any franchise organization. Failure to accurately monitor the flow of revenue through the organization will inevitably impact the bottom line.

Furthermore, the absence of proper record keeping at the franchise level can and will result in business failures owing to poor financial management. The high cost of franchise development and training necessitates a proactive role for the franchisor in recommending proven record keeping systems.

Today's franchisors must take dramatic steps to control their financial destiny. They must be true leaders in the franchise business community. With proven solutions available now, tomorrow's industry leaders can indeed capitalize on the opportunity at hand.

4

Managing Quality Control in a Franchising Operation

JoAnn T. Hackos, Comtech Services, Inc.

Quality is actually quite simple to define—it's just difficult to achieve. William Thurston, in his article "Quality Is Between the Customer's Ears," defines *quality* as "what the customer perceives when he feels the product [or service] meets his needs and lives up to his expectations."[1] Quality, then, centers on the perceptions of the customer. Quality is not about high cost and luxurious treatment. Not all customers need, want, or can afford the most expensive and luxurious products and services. Customers do, however, want the product to equal or exceed their expectations. They want to be treated, in all instances, with courtesy, integrity, and respect.

AVCO Financial Services of Canada, a company that has led in the development of a quality planning system, defines "quality in perception" in the following way:

> Quality in Perception, which is how our customer perceives our people, products, and services, is achieved by:
>
> ▲ Delivering the right product
> ▲ Satisfying our customer's needs
> ▲ Meeting the customer's expectations
> ▲ Treating every customer with integrity, courtesy, and respect.[2]

To achieve quality in our operations, we must understand our customers and respond to their needs and expectations. Quality in perception is, of course, quite subjective and difficult to measure. The customer's perceptions and expectations may be best known to those on the front line, those who directly interact with customers every day. However, those who are further removed or less perceptive in their observations are just as important to meeting customer needs. Our job in establishing and managing operations is to ensure that all people engaged in the activities of the business are aware of the customer and the customer's perception of quality.

In a franchise operation, we attempt to translate the understanding of customer needs that was developed by the original business creator into a set of requirements and guidelines that permit the franchisee to achieve that same level of business success. As a result, we move from quality in perception to the other side of the quality coin—quality in fact. In franchising, quality in fact is best represented by the information provided to franchisees through the operations manual, training and orientation programs, and regular visits to the franchisee locations by field support services.

In his seminal book *Quality Is Free*, Phil Crosby provides us with another simple definition of quality: "Quality is conformance to requirements".[3] This definition, which focuses on measurement of success or failure in meeting requirements, is a more traditional definition that leads us directly to the significant franchising issue of quality control. To achieve quality in fact, we must provide franchisees with comprehensive rules and regulations, thorough training, and consistent enforcement. The obligation of the franchisor is to figure out what will satisfy customer needs and perceptions and figure out how to meet these customer needs by developing systems to be followed by its network of franchisees.

AVCO Financial Services also describes quality in fact in its company literature:

> Quality in Fact . . . is achieved through first-time performance in the execution of our duties and responsibilities. It is defined as:
>
> ▴ Doing the right thing
> ▴ Doing it the right way
> ▴ Doing it right the first time
> ▴ Doing it on time

A simple example will serve to clarify the distinction between quality in fact and quality in perception. A franchised restaurant operation purchases a new accounting program designed, it hopes, to provide accurate financial reports and a detailed picture of its daily operations. The salesperson from the accounting software firm assures them that the program complies with government reporting requirements and adheres to generally accepted accounting principles. The restaurant manager also learns that the computer program has been thoroughly tested and has no bugs; that is, the program is guaranteed to make no mistakes. In terms of both accounting and programming requirements, the accounting people believed that they have achieved quality in fact.

Unfortunately for the restaurant franchise, the new accounting package is extremely difficult to learn and use. The on-screen menus and forms are so complicated that the restaurant employees make frequent mistakes entering basic data. No one at the restaurant franchise can make head or tail of the manuals and, as a result, they have no idea what the many reports that spew out of the system are trying to tell them. The customer service people at the accounting company can explain how the computer program works, but they can't or won't give the franchisor any insight into how to use the program to operate the business. The accounting product, in terms of meeting customer needs and expectations, fails to exhibit quality in perception.

Quality in Perception

Quality in fact has no meaning in the absence of quality in perception. We may be very successful in designing a product that looks good to us, but unless it appears good to our customers, we're unlikely to sell it.

Quality in perception should be the central concept that drives quality in fact. To achieve quality in perception, we must do four things:

1. Understand the customer's needs.
2. Understand the customer's expectations.
3. Deliver the right product.
4. Treat the customer with integrity, courtesy, and respect.

It is the job of the franchisor management to identify and understand the customer's needs and expectations, define the right product or service, and communicate this understanding to the franchisee.

There is nothing simple about the process of achieving quality in perception, as anyone knows who has ever tried to establish and operate a successful business. Keeping abreast of changing customer needs and expectations is perhaps the most difficult aspect of the process. Fortunately or unfortunately, success in identifying the customer needs and expectations accurately and comprehensively is easy to measure. If we succeed, we make money; if we fail, we don't. Admittedly, this equation is something of an oversimplification in a time of shrinking capital and a complex global economy. Nonetheless, in franchising we are perhaps closest to the basics of business success. Because many franchises are service businesses, we remain nearer to the customer than do many who engage in fundamental research and development or in manufacturing. In fact, much of the success of franchising comes from our ability to remain close to our customers and meet their needs effectively.

It is beyond the scope of this discussion to explain the complex process of developing a sound business concept and creating the mechanisms to deliver products and services to customers. Let us assume that, as a successful business developer and operator, you have identified your customers and developed the right products and services to meet their needs. Your problem is to translate what you know into something that can be transferred to the franchisee—or to translate the business's original quality in perception to quality in fact.

Quality in Fact

One of the greatest fears of prospective franchisors is that they will lose control of the quality once the business is in the hands of the franchisee. The franchisees are equally concerned that without adequate instruction in how to achieve quality in the business, they will not succeed in developing a profitable operation.

A number of effective mechanisms already exist for achieving quality in fact. These mechanisms center on defining and enforcing standards, or constructing and ensuring, in Crosby's terms, "conformance to requirements." The primary mechanism for quality control is the franchise operations manual. The operations manual describes the policies, procedures, and specifications that must be followed by the franchisees. If the operations manual is carelessly written and the instructions ambiguous, a carefully planned franchise organization can deteriorate into chaos.

Creating the Franchise Operations Manual

Ensuring that the franchise operations manual is an accurate yet reasonable document begins with adherence to some basic guidelines:

- ▲ Get involved from the start and stay involved.
- ▲ Recruit an expert to develop the operations manual.
- ▲ Ensure that the operations manual is carefully reviewed by everyone involved in the development of the franchise system.
- ▲ Bring in outside experts to review the information as needed.
- ▲ Field-test the procedures once they're written.
- ▲ Update the manual as new concepts and systems are created and implemented.

Participate Fully in Developing the Manual

The franchise operations manual is the critical underpinning of quality control and must be carefully developed and reviewed. Nothing should be omitted that is expected of the franchisee. It is especially important to avoid the trap of buying a generic operations manual that does not specify explicitly the components of your unique business operation.

Use Experts in Manual Design

Select someone to develop the manual who understands how to create clear, easily understood, and unambiguous policies and procedures. It is difficult to write a comprehensive policy statement or detailed procedures and specifications that will be completely understood by newcomers to the business. The task of creating the operations manual must not be delegated to amateurs.

Review the Manual Carefully

As the key element in the definition of quality, the operations manual must be taken seriously. A thorough review of every word will save a great many problems later. Bring in outside experts to review the information. Franchise attorneys and other key advisers will help ensure that the operations manual will not create legal difficulties in the future.

Conduct Field Tests

Not even the most experienced professional who analyzes and writes policies and procedures can ensure that a new franchisee will be able to understand and follow instructions. Give sections of your operating procedures to new franchisees and ask them to explain what they understand and don't understand. Ask them to perform the procedures indicated. Watch what they do and listen to their comments and questions. Only through on-site testing can you anticipate problems and correct information that is incomplete, inaccurate, difficult to understand, and easy to misinterpret.

Creating a comprehensive, clearly written, and accurate franchise operations manual is a critical element in the success of franchise quality control. However, it is only the starting point. The operations manual identifies the customer and the product or service, and details the steps required to achieve customer satisfaction. But having the rules and regulations in writing does not guarantee that they will be followed effectively. Effective adherence to requirements requires training and consistent followup and enforcement.

To understand the importance of effective training and enforcement requires an understanding of the concept—the cost of quality—and the process of total quality management.

What Is the Cost of Quality?

The cost of quality is the cumulative cost of building a good product or service balanced with the cost of making mistakes. Every time we have to throw away a product because it isn't made correctly, every time we have customers who don't come back because they were treated rudely, every time we have to redo work that was done wrong the first time, we increase the cost of quality. If we are able to solve problems quickly or keep them from occurring in the first place, we can avoid substantial costs and ensure more satisfied customers.

In looking at two remarkable examples, we can see first what can happen if problems go undetected. Then we can see what can be saved with an approach that leads us to discover potential problems before they become catastrophes.

Hiroshi Hamada, the CEO of Ricoh Corporation, reports that it cost Ricoh $590,000 to recall from customers a fax machine that had a manufacturing defect. If it had detected and corrected the defect before it shipped the machine from the plant, Ricoh calculated that its total cost would have decreased to $17,000. If they had found and detected the defect during the production of the machine, the cost to repair the problem would have been $368. If they had caught the defect while they were procuring the subassemblies, it would have cost $177 to fix the mistake. And if they had identified the defect in the design stage, a mere $35 would have corrected the problem (see Figure 4-1). Ricoh spent $590,000 fixing the defect in customer machines; the cost of lost sales and poor customer opinion has not been calculated.

As a result of this experience, Ricoh was determined never to allow such a situation to occur again. Many companies have instituted quality programs under similar circumstances. They want to ensure that problems are detected and solved as quickly as possible. Following an analysis of a manufacturing process at ITT, Phil Crosby tells us that ITT was able to save an amount "equivalent to 5 percent of sales" by eliminating manufacturing defects.[4] In one year alone, that savings added up to $530 million.

Three major cost areas are associated with the cost of quality:

1. The cost of conformance
2. The cost of nonconformance
3. The cost of lost opportunity

The first of these costs is positive and necessary to the success of the franchise operation. The other two are the costs of doing it wrong and need to be minimized or eliminated.

Figure 4-1.   The cost of nonconformance.

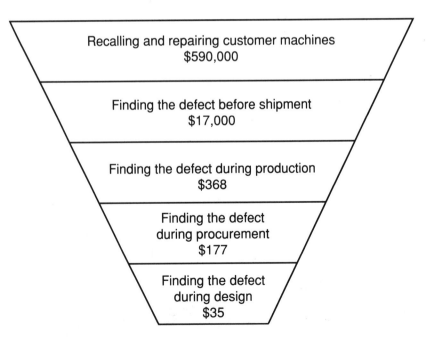

Recalling and repairing customer machines
$590,000

Finding the defect before shipment
$17,000

Finding the defect during production
$368

Finding the defect
during procurement
$177

Finding the defect
during design
$35

Cost of Conformance

The cost of conformance includes the cost of three significant parts of a successful franchise operation:

1. Prevention
2. Inspection
3. Appraisal

The cost of prevention is the cost of doing things right the first time and represents some of the best money spent in developing a sound franchise operation. It includes, first and foremost, the development of a comprehensive, accurate, and unambiguous franchise operations manual, as described above.

Once a good franchise operations manual is in place, the next requirement is training. People do not learn how to run an effective operation simply by reading about it in a manual. They need practice and feedback to ensure they understand what needs to be done. We need to provide training for the franchisee and for members of the staff who will run the daily operation, from managers to administrative staff to core skill workers, as defined by the business. This training, while it may be administered by the franchisee, should be defined and developed by the franchisor. If the goal is consistent, high-quality operations, then training at all levels is essential.

In some organizations, learning to use a Total Quality Process (TQP) has become an integral part of the training provided every employee (see Figure 4-2). The focus of TQP is the customer. The customer, both internal and external, is the core of the business. All employees must be aware that their primary function is to serve the needs of the customer. They must understand that while the key customer is the external one who pays for a service, customers also include all the people around them.

Establishing a TQP system and engaging each employee in continuous quality improvement has some cost. We have labeled it the cost of prevention. Remember, however, that you must include in the cost of prevention the monies you will save by preventing the problem from occurring in the first place.

Closely linked to the cost of prevention through manuals and training is the cost of inspection and appraisal. Franchisors must establish a regular and comprehensive system of inspection to ensure that individual locations are being operated in accordance with the franchise agreement and according to the best practices defined in the franchise operations manual.

Regular inspections help ensure that the franchisee is operating the business in a manner that will lead to profitability. If procedures and policies were initiated because they resulted in a profitable operation, then adherence to the procedures is in everyone's interest.

Field support services move beyond inspection, however, into continuing

(Text continues on page 60.)

Figure 4-2.   TQP in franchising.

Incorporating TQP in a Franchise Organization

Many people confuse Total Quality with producing high-priced products or services. Not all products and services should be high priced; not all customers want to buy the most expensive product or service on the market. TQP is not about end products; it is about planning. Basically, if you improve how you do the job, the quality of that job will necessarily increase. We call this process improvement.

For many years, organizations have tried to set standards, thinking that standards alone would result in quality. We have only to look at the history of government regulation to see the fallacy of this assumption. The government produces all sorts of standards; those standards have rarely resulted in quality products or services. Some years ago, my company was involved in producing manuals for a government project. We were handed stacks of standards that outlined what size paper to use, the size of the type, the length of each column of text, the presentation of graphics, even the exact organization and the correct wording for the headings. Missing from these standards was any concern for the user of the manuals. We could follow all the regulations, comply with all the standards, and easily produce manuals that were useless for the people doing the job. In our organization, we have long insisted that it is the process, not the standard, that leads to quality.

The danger in relying upon the franchise operations manual to enforce quality standards is that without a quality process in place and the full participation of all franchise employees, quality will remain elusive.

By *process,* we mean every discrete activity in our businesses that has a goal. For example, a process might be taking a customer order. That process has some *input.* In the case of the customer order, the input might be a personal statement by a customer who enters our place of business, a telephone call, or a completed form sent by mail or fax. Once the input is received, we *transform* it into something that we can use. An order clerk might enter the information from the customer on a form, onto a computer screen, or into a point-of-sale terminal. The transformation leads to an *output* that has new value in our organization. The order form may be transferred from the clerk to the cook in a fast-food operation. The cook then begins a new process to prepare the food. To improve a process we must look carefully at each piece in this sequence, from input through transformation to output.

A Typical Process Model

Many people in an organization will be interested in improving the order process to make it more efficient and more accurate. They may note flaws in parts of the process that cause orders to go wrong, resulting in wasted food, service delays, and unhappy customers. If your franchise employees are trained in TQP, they will know automatically how to attack a process problem.

Step 1. Planning. Once employees or managers or both have identified a process that needs improvement, they should carefully define what they want to improve. For example, they might write that they "want to decrease the number of incorrect orders to the cooks."

They then organize themselves into a small team to look at the process. Everyone who is interested or involved in the process should be part of the team. The team looks at each step in the process and who will be involved in implementing a decision to change how the step is performed.

The team members may want to study the process to discover the frequency of incorrect orders. If they learn how to measure the problem, they will be able to gauge improvements. Then, they investigate the possible causes of the problem. They should rank the causes so that they concentrate their efforts on the most significant causes first. Each cause should lead the team to the development of a solution.

Step 2. Doing. Once the team has decided on a solution, it should set up a trial run. You don't want to implement a new process on a wide scale before you've tried it on a small scale.

Step 3. Checking. The team should find out, using its measuring system, if the new process actually improves the results of the process. Are their fewer incorrect orders and are customers served quickly and accurately? Customer satisfaction is one of the key results to measure. But employees must remember that the end customer or external customer is not the only customer they must address. Some of the most important customers are those who have to perform the next process down the line.

Step 4. Acting. Once the results of the experiment look positive, particularly after appropriate tweaking, implement the improved process organizationwide. That means changing the operations manual and the training program. In addition, continue the checking program to ensure that the gains remain high and no one reverts to the old, inefficient process.

This TQP system may seem like simple common sense; it's not. It's a more analytical approach than many of us ever take in solving a problem. We tend to assume that we know the customer and the process, and we can fix problems without ever examining their root causes. We tend to settle for downstream solutions—solutions that fix the problem at the end—rather than upstream solutions that address the process from the beginning.

education. If field support is perceived by franchisees as strictly a police action, they will resent such visits and engage in practices that are orchestrated more to deceive the inspectors than to maintain good business practice. Instead of acting as police, field support personnel must themselves be trained in quality. Their role is service and their customer for that service is the franchisee. With a strong service orientation, field support will engage in educating franchisee personnel so that they recognize the underlying intent of standard policies and procedures. If they understand why something must happen or be done in a particular way, they will become as interested in enforcing standards practices as the franchisors. When people feel they must do something simply because it is a rule, they make mistakes, experience a decrease in productivity, and feel resentment toward the enforcer. When they understand that the standard practices will result in business success and increased profitability, and when they see the connection between a practice and the bottom line, they become their own inspection agent.

Cost of Nonconformance

Thus far, we have been reviewing the issues surrounding the cost of conformance to quality standards. The costs of prevention, inspection, and appraisal all become part of the credit side of the account in measuring the cost of quality. The costs of nonconformance and of lost opportunity are firmly lodged on the debit side of the account (see Figure 4-3).

   The cost of nonconformance is the cost to the organization of doing the job wrong—of failing to deliver quality to the customers, both internal and external. For example, if the order-taking process that we used as an example in Figure 4-2 does not function correctly, it is likely to result in incorrect orders. The cost of discarding unwanted materials or goods plus the cost of producing the wrong thing all contribute to the cost of nonconformance. Whenever an organization must scrap a product, pay to have work redone, or pay for the wrong work in the first place, the organization is losing money and drastically affecting profit. The costs outlined by Hiroshi Hamada in the Ricoh example are all contributors to the cost of nonconformance. Ricoh lost more than half a million dollars because it had to recall and repair faulty equipment.

   If we take a typical franchise organization example, we can see the costs of nonconformance emerge when management skips the critical steps of planning,

Figure 4-3.   The cost of quality.

Credit	Debit
Cost of Conformance	Cost of Nonconformance
	Cost of Lost Opportunity

training, documentation, inspection, and appraisal. One of our clients, a major fast-food franchisor, discovered that its food-preparation operations were not running efficiently. Workers seemed confused about how to prepare the menu items correctly. A great deal of raw material (food items) had to be discarded because they were not prepared properly. In our review of their food-preparation manuals, we discovered that the workers could not understand the instructions provided in the manuals. The instructions were badly organized and poorly written. The information workers needed most was buried in information that they really did not need at all. The goal in redesigning and revising the manuals was to ensure better performance and simplify the training process. The ultimate goal was to develop a more efficient, standardized operation that would result in a substantial cost savings for the franchise. We were able to save the franchise a minimum of $1 million in the first year as a result of only a single, small change in the information design. The more substantial savings came over a longer period through improved performance. It had clearly been costing this company well over a million dollars a year in nonconformance to customer requirements.

Experts in quality process report that the average American company loses 15 percent of its revenue to the cost of nonconformance. By using systems such as the Total Quality Process described earlier, an organization has the opportunity to recoup a substantial proportion of that loss.

Another kind of nonconformance is the cost of exceeding requirements. You have almost certainly received reports you did not need or detailed information when all you wanted was a quick estimate. Recently, we discovered that one of our clients spent a great deal of time and effort developing an installation manual that its customers—internal system engineers—simply threw away. They already knew and did not need the information in the manual. It cost this company many thousands of dollars a year to produce information that the internal customer did not need. At the same time, it had failed to produce the critical information that its customers were clamoring for.

Nonconformance to the needs of both internal and external customers usually means that an organization must spend time and money fixing the problems that occur as a result. If we can do things right the first time, by putting more resources into planning, training, and standards, we can reduce nonconformance costs and increase profitability. If we can do things right the first time, we also increase productivity and make better use of our assets. We need fewer people, equipment, materials, and buildings to do a job right than to do it wrong and then have to repair the mistakes.

Lost Opportunity

The cost of nonconformance is not the only cost on the debit side of the quality equation; a substantial cost of failing to meet requirements and satisfy customer needs is much more difficult to track but perhaps more significant. The cost of lost opportunity is the business that does not return. We all know that it is easier and substantially less expensive to sell additional or new series to an old customer than to find and convince a new customer to buy. We do not want to lose old customers; we want them coming back.

However, if we have processes in place that fall short of achieving customer satisfaction, those customers will not come back and the goods and services we might have sold then go unsold. Furthermore, one displeased customer can have a negative influence on other potential customers. Organizations are often amazed at the speed at which problems move through the customer and competitor grapevine. One disgruntled customer influences many others.

In the Ricoh example, we noted the cost of nonconformance, or the cost of doing something wrong. The accounting, however, did not consider the cost of lost opportunity. That cost, including lost future sales and unhappy customers, is more difficult to measure but extremely significant. We can get an idea of what has been lost by monitoring canceled orders and declines in new business orders. If we can reduce our lost opportunities, we have the potential of increasing revenue and profitability. It means producing more revenue with the same staff and assets.

Opportunity Gained

Another way of looking at the cost of lost opportunity is to examine what happens when opportunity is not lost—when customers are satisfied. My company presents workshops and seminars on quality planning and development processes worldwide. In the course of operating these seminars, we deal with many hotel sales and catering departments. Often these hotels are franchise operations.

Most of the time, the hotels give us poor service—so poor in fact that we frequently change hotels in an effort to find one or two that will treat us with courtesy, integrity, and respect. We're even willing to spend a lot of money to buy service from high-priced, luxury hotels, but how much we pay appears to make very little difference. At one point a year or two ago, we became discouraged enough with paying high prices for poor service that we decided to arrange our workshops with lower-priced hotels. We contracted with a Holiday Inn in Walnut Creek, California, for a workshop. Holiday Inn is not a five-star hotel. However, when I arrived to set up the workshop, two young men worked closely with me to prepare the room, searched for the right equipment, and delivered it quickly, continually asking if I needed anything else, and in general made themselves available and showed genuine concern about my satisfaction.

I was so impressed and so pleased with the unusual quality of the service that I mentioned the fact to the manager on duty when I checked out. I also wrote a letter to the management when I returned to my office. I've told others about the high-quality service offered in that establishment and have used it and other Holiday Inns again. I don't know what's going on at Holiday Inn, but it seems to have service quality under control. Perhaps Holiday Inn hasn't reaped a great deal of profit from my small operation, but they've certainly enjoyed a lot of goodwill. It certainly must have some influence on the bottom line.

How Can the Cost of Quality Be Controlled?

In their outstanding book, *Service America*, Karl Albrecht and Ron Zemke summarize the basic business proposition of a service organization: "IF the target customer comes in contact with the organization, and IF the organization performs the promised service to specified standards, and IF the service meets the customer's expectations, THEN the organization has achieved its mission and will return a profit (or something else of value) to us."[5]

Our entire examination of the quality process is based, at heart, on a business proposition such as this one. If we concentrate on understanding our customers' requirements, and if we establish standards and processes that ensure that we will meet our customers' requirements, we will more likely operate a successful organization. All of us, from senior management to the newest person on the loading dock or in the mail room, need to think of our jobs in terms of service to our customers. We must involve everyone in an effort to provide better and better service, and we must involve them continuously. It is essential that we set up sound systems of policies and procedures through documents like the franchise operations manual, and that we create comprehensive and ongoing training programs. But setting standards is never enough; we cannot legislate the responsibility to treat customers with courtesy, integrity, and respect. By implementing a quality plan, we have some hope that we will learn to operate our organizations in the most effective way possible in the marketplace.

NOTES

1. Thurston, William R., "Quality Is Between the Customer's Ears," *Across the Board* (January 1985), pp. 29–32.
2. As quoted in Townsend, Patrick L., *Commit to Quality* (New York: John Wiley & Sons, Inc., 1986).
3. Crosby, Philip B., *Quality Is Free: The Art of Making Quality Certain* (New York: New American Library, 1979).
4. Crosby, p. 11.
5. Albrecht, Karl, and Ron Zemke, *Service America: Doing Business in the New Economy* (Homewood, Ill.: Dow-Jones-Irwin, 1985), p. 140.

PART II

OPERATIONAL ISSUES IN FRANCHISING

Operations—we all talk about it. We all readily acknowledge its overall importance in the growth and success of the franchising program. Yet when we search for resources, guidelines, and experience in this critical area of franchising, there is often a lack of information.

Part II focuses on key operational issues, the preparation and maintenance of the operations manual, and the use of computer systems and technology to improve the operations of the franchisor.

Certain special topics that have a direct impact on operational issues, such as real estate and territorial issues, management of the renewal and transfer process, and demographic and marketing analysis in site selection are also addressed in this part.

5

Key Issues in the Operation and Management of a Franchise System

R. M. Gordon, The Original Great American Chocolate Chip Cookie Company

A franchisor is in two businesses: the underlying business (such as hamburgers or auto repairs), and the business of franchising. Successful franchisors are successful in both businesses. Franchisors who are good at the underlying business but not good at the business of franchising often fail.

Because of the dual nature of franchising, some of the key issues of operating and managing a franchise business are the same as for operating any other kind of business, while other issues are peculiar to franchising. It is the key management and operation issues that pertain to franchising that this chapter discusses.

Allocation of Responsibility

The franchising method is powerful because it distributes responsibility between the franchisor and franchisee. The logic of franchising is that certain jobs are best performed by someone (the franchisee) close to the final customer and with a financial investment and interest in the success of that performance. Other jobs are best carried out by someone (the franchisor) who is large enough to take advantage of economies of scale and make those advantages available to the customer-level person (the franchisee).

Some of the responsibilities that must be allocated to either the franchisor or the franchisee include financing unit-level construction or development, training, product and service development, development of marketing and promotional materials, media placement, sources of supply, and ancillary services such as bookkeeping and insurance.

How does a franchisor determine how to allocate responsibilities? If you are operating and managing an existing franchise company, the first sources you turn to are the franchise agreements in effect. You should already be familiar with their terms, which theoretically allocate certain responsibilities. While most franchise agreements put such terms in writing, a greater number of responsibilities are determined by habit and custom—what the franchisor and franchisee have been doing over the years. Therefore, you should also be familiar with what the company currently does for its franchisees, as well as what it expects its franchisees to do themselves.

If responsibilities are to be reallocated or assigned for the first time, there are several approaches to determine an advantageous arrangement.

1. *Skills analysis.* What skills does the franchisor have? What skills do the typical franchisees have, or do you expect them to have? What skills can you easily develop? What skills can typical franchisees easily develop?

For example, if you have been in your franchise business for some time and have developed substantial site-selection skills, it makes sense for you to control site selection. In fact, this will be one of the assets you bring to the table in return for your franchise fee. If you have developed and perfected a method of delivering a service and intend to recruit franchisees who have heavy sales experience, it makes sense to allocate the responsibility for seeking new end-user accounts to your franchisees.

2. *Economic considerations.* If you can create economies of scale with respect to a responsibility, it may make sense for you to assume that responsibility.

For example, once ad slicks are produced, it is relatively inexpensive to send copies to all your franchisees. It makes sense for the franchisor to produce the slicks, not each franchisee. The cost of the creative work is paid only one time and can be spread over all the outlets. The franchisor can deliver something that has a greater value to the franchisee than the cost of producing it for that franchisee. That is part of the joy of franchising.

The economics of allocating responsibilities should be considered in the aggregate, not just on a case-by-case basis. If a franchisor assumes too many responsibilities in relation to its franchise fees, it will go broke. If a franchisor allocates too many responsibilities to the franchisees in relation to the franchise fees, the franchisees might go broke. Experienced franchisors sometimes get the impression that franchisees expect them to do everything at no additional cost. A franchisor can unwittingly end up with financial problems if each year it assumes yet another responsibility that does not cost much itself but which when combined with other tasks becomes burdensome.

3. *Legal matters.* There are general laws, such as antitrust, that affect franchising, as well as laws that specifically regulate the franchise relationship. You don't have to become a lawyer, but you do have to have enough acquaintance with these laws to be able to spot the traps.

For example, the antitrust laws affect how you can package goods or services (called *tying* by antitrust lawyers). A classic case involves packaging. If you decide that it would be efficient to go into the packaging business and require all your franchisees to buy their packaging from you, you may find that even though you may be selling them high-quality, low-cost packaging, you may possibly be sued by suppliers who would like to provide that packaging instead.

Staffing

How you staff your franchise organization reflects how you have allocated responsibilities. For example, if you've assumed responsibility for the franchisees' bookkeeping, you will need a substantial bookkeeping staff. At minimum, most franchisors need staff for training, unit-level consulting, unit-level monitoring, and marketing.

Most franchisors have to train their franchisees in the underlying business. One of the assets of franchising is that it successfully puts people in a business they previously knew nothing about. If you are a conversion franchisor (for example, a real estate franchisor who recruits existing independent brokers for your chain), training is less of a factor, but you still will want to retrain your franchisees to do things the way your system does them.

Most franchisors provide franchisees with some sort of unit-level consulting, even after training. Even a genius franchisee needs help in keeping up with an evolving business. Franchisees also experience personnel turnover and need help in training new employees.

Franchisors need unit-level monitors to provide feedback to determine areas in which owners need help and whether franchisees are operating in compliance with the system. Imagine a McDonald's with the crew wearing tank tops, selling hot dogs and beer, and renting videocassettes. Franchisees occasionally are overly creative, willing to do bizarre things in hopes of making an extra dollar. Franchisors need to make sure they remain consistent with the franchise concept.

Most franchise businesses are market-oriented. Because of this, and because of the economies of scale often available in marketing, franchisors generally need to be well staffed with marketing people.

In addition, the franchisor staff should be nonauthoritarian. Franchisees do not like to be bossed around. They feel an internal tension between being independent businesspeople and being dependent on the franchisor. When they want help, they lean toward dependence; when you tell them what to do, they lean toward independence. Authoritarian dictates from a franchisor remind the franchisees of their dependence and push them to assert their independence.

At the same time, franchisor personnel must not be easily intimidated. Franchisors must insist that individual owners comply with certain requirements. As many franchisees have personal relationships with someone higher up in the franchiser organization, and as franchisees often become richer than the franchisor staffer, it is not hard for intimidation to succeed.

Franchisor staffers must have mature judgment capabilities. Yet, ironically, franchisors often place their most immature people in positions that involve most contact with franchisees.

Training Franchisees and Their People

Training generally is one of the most important responsibilities assumed by the franchisor. There is both the initial training and the subsequent training of franchisees. A number of factors influence the scope of initial training. First, the nature of the underlying business determines the scope of training. After all, some businesses are simpler than others or easier to teach. Another factor is the level of experience among franchisees, in either the direct business or a related one.

Training is not an either-or matter; rather, it is a spectrum. For example, if you franchise jewelry stores, you may not convert independent jewelry stores to your franchise, but you may accept as franchisees only those people with some retail experience. These people require more training than a conversion franchisee, but less training than someone with no retail experience at all.

How you allocate responsibility influences the scope of the training you need to offer. The more responsibilities you allocate to the franchisees, the more training you must offer so that they are capable of handling those responsibilities.

The initial training helps set the tone for a relationship that extends years into the future. This is important, because a franchise relationship is similar to a marriage: Both parties are together for a long time, sharing joys and sorrows. More to the point, divorce is expensive.

Franchisees are most impressed and impressionable at initial training. They know nothing or little about the business, and they look to the franchisor for guidance. Later, they may believe they are more expert and become less amenable to franchisor influence.

The initial training is the time to explain what is important and to sell the idea of why it is important to them. It is the time to set high standards if you later want high standards to be followed. It is also the time to show that you know what you are doing, that you are capable of transferring that to them so that they can be successful, and that you are capable and willing to make a substantial, professional effort to lead them toward success.

Later in the relationship the franchisees will need additional training. When you make additions and improvements to your system, you will need to train the franchisees to implement those improvements and additions. And when franchisees experience turnover in their personnel, they will want help training their new people. All of this is expensive. Inexperienced franchisors often underestimate the cost of initial ongoing training. Yet it is not a matter to scrimp on.

Monitoring

Franchisors must monitor the operations of their units for at least two reasons.

First, the franchisor is in a position to help its franchisees succeed. It has greater depth and breadth of experience in the business (provided it moves up the experience curve by learning from the experiences of its units). The franchisor is also better positioned to spot areas in which franchisees can improve operations. But in order to spot these opportunities, a franchisor must monitor the franchise operations.

In addition, monitoring ensures that units are complying with the system rules. There are two reasons why such compliance is important. First, franchisees who effectively executive the system have a better chance of succeeding than franchisees who don't. (If this is not true, what is the benefit of the system?) Second, the trademarks, service marks, and goodwill of the system is valuable in proportion to the consumer's perception of a uniform, expected quality of services and/or products. The value of McDonald's marks and goodwill does not stem from food that is superior to all other food in town. It arises from the food and service being of uniform quality, so that the customer knows what to expect at any McDonald's, in any town. There are legal reasons for uniformity as well, but that is beyond the scope of this chapter.

Consider a franchise system that does not monitor the operations of its units. Some franchisees wander from the proven methods, and of those that wander, a few may do better, but the greater proportion are likely to fail.

The wandering franchisees damage not only themselves but also the franchisees who comply with the system. The varying quality confuses customers and makes them less likely to stop at any unit, because they cannot tell in advance whether it will have the standard service or product.

Franchisors have some options as to how to monitor the units. Many use the same staff people who counsel franchisees. This is economical, and the two functions are highly related. But other franchisees use separate monitoring staffs, and this has advantages also. For instance, the monitors do not "pull their punches." The consultant-monitors generally wish to maintain good relationships with the franchisees, and fear that if they grade a franchisee too severely, they will not get the smiling reception that everyone likes to receive.

In many industries, outside services can monitor certain aspects of franchisee operations. For example, retailers may use "mystery shoppers" from independent market research companies. The mystery shoppers visit a store and report on certain aspects of the experience.

Staying in Control

As is clear from the preceding discussion, control is an important aspect of managing franchise operations. We have discussed how control over quality and uniformity is crucial from the viewpoint of the ultimate consumers. We also have mentioned why control over quality and uniformity is important to other franchisees. And there are other consequences of losing control of the franchise system.

Franchisors who lose control may be unable to get anything done. For example, if control over marketing plans or the introduction of new products passes from the franchisor to the franchisees, the franchisor may find it impossible to introduce new marketing plans. Marketing is highly subjective, and getting any large group to agree on a particular marketing plan (or even on a particular advertising scheme) can bring your marketing to a screeching halt. The same is true when it comes to deciding what new products to introduce. This is not to say that franchisees should have no input in these areas, or that their input is not valuable. Their input often is valuable. But in the end, some one person or unit has to be able to make the decision.

Losing control of the franchise system can also result in responsibility passing to certain dominant franchisees, that may not act in the best interests of the system. For example, dominant franchisee units may well block improvements to the system that require spending money, such as for remodeling or adding equipment for new products or services. They may not see any need for these new assets because their costs are fully amortized, and they can make more money in the short term by milking old assets.

Maintaining control can be difficult. As a franchise system gets older, the franchisor is likely to be stuck with deals made long in the past, when the franchisor was not sophisticated. Its early agreements did not provide the ability and flexibility to update the system later on. There are franchise systems that were leaders in the 1960s, but whose time has passed. Sometimes this is because the franchisor was asleep at the wheel; other times the franchisor knew what was needed but had not retained enough control to push its franchisees to make changes.

Franchisors have problems with control also because it is a sensitive issue. As already discussed, franchisees do not want to feel compelled to do anything, although they may like the benefits of having other franchisees do things that help their business (such as remodeling their stores or participating in a city-wide promotion).

Even if a franchisor has a legal basis for requiring units to upgrade, add new products, or remodel, the franchisor must be skilled in exercising that control.

In addition, franchisors must consider the legitimate economic circumstances its franchisees face. Not every franchisee can afford to implement new programs. In some cases, this is because the franchisee has milked the business, putting nothing aside for reinvestment. In other cases it is weak through no fault of its own. The franchisor may wish to consider creative and flexible approaches with franchisees that wish to comply but that have legitimate problems.

One other circumstance that makes control difficult is the ''special deal'' syndrome. Franchisors occasionally make special deals, often when the franchise is young and often to influential units or personal friends. The special deals may seem smart at the time, but later can haunt the franchisor, including when a special provision prevents the franchisor from exercising reasonable and necessary control.

Providing Continuing Value

Franchise companies must provide continuing value to their franchisees. Franchisees who pay franchise fees every month expect services every month. The franchisor may have intended to charge service fees either as a way of allowing franchisees to finance the initial purchase of the franchise or as a simple royalty for the use of the system mark. But no matter how carefully you explain this, franchisees are unlikely to see it that way. Franchisees who don't think they're getting value are likely to leave the system or stop paying royalties, no matter what the franchise agreement says.

There are endless ways to provide ongoing value, depending on the business and the franchisor's own creativity. One valuable ongoing service is research and development of new products or services. These can either be primary additions, such as new menu items in fast-food restaurants, or support items, such as new types of training aids. They can even be ancillary items such as group insurance for employees.

Marketing support is another area where franchisors often can provide continuing value. As mentioned earlier, economies of scale often allow the franchisor to provide materials with a higher value to the franchisees than it costs to produce them.

If your name or mark is an important aspect of your franchise's value, as is often the case, there is continuing value in franchise support and enhanced customer recognition of that mark. Training is ongoing support, although its importance depends on the nature of the business and whether or not the units are conversion franchisees.

The franchisor can provide ongoing psychological support. For example, a franchisor can give the franchisee a feeling of support by a strong, capable, caring franchisor. The value of this should not be underestimated, because many franchisees are "half entrepreneurs"; that is, they will take some business risks, but not on their own. They often are willing to pay for support, not just to get technical support but also for psychological comfort. Indeed, franchises often are rightfully sold by telling the prospective owner that she will be in business for herself but not by herself. Many people, including franchisees, like belonging to a group. For some small-business people, belonging to a franchise group is an important social part of their lives.

Whatever the ongoing support provided, that support should be visible and appreciated. A franchisor can do a lot behind the scenes, but if there isn't tangible evidence of that support, franchisees are unlikely to appreciate it. Franchisors should provide value and should get credit for having provided it.

In addition, the value must be value to the franchisees, not simply something that the franchisor wants to do. Franchisors have spent a lot of money generating publicity about themselves and buying franchisees dinners and gifts. But franchisors place more value on these than do franchisees.

Staying Competitive

Times change. Consumer tastes change. Competitive conditions change. Franchisors must make changes to stay competitive. Developing and implementing changes is an important value that franchisors provide franchisees.

The franchisor's ability to make changes is related to its areas of control. If the franchisor has insufficient control in an aspect of the business, it can be stuck with a system doomed to extinction. If it is sad to see a franchisor who has not initiated changes to stay competitive, it is even sadder to see one that wants to implement changes but has franchisees who care little about long-term prospects.

Making a Profit

Businesspeople do not need to be exhorted to make a profit. The peculiarity of a franchise system is that the franchisor wants to help the franchisees make enough profit to have a reasonable return on investment, after having paid franchise fees that are high enough to provide the necessary services and make its own profit.

Franchisor profits are a sensitive issue. Some systems are like the old communist regimes: Profits are perceived as a sign that the franchisees are being exploited. The franchisor should educate its units to understand that if the franchisor is making a healthy profit, it can reinvest that profit in the system and help protect their investments. Franchisees should be reminded that the opposite situation—a franchisor who is broke because it charged its franchisees too little or spent too much on them—does not provide a happy situation.

*   *   *

This chapter has highlighted some of the attributes of managing and operating a franchise company. I don't need to emphasize the importance of franchisor experience in the business. On the other hand, it is also important to have special sensitivities to people and franchise situations. A good franchise manager combines the skills of entrepreneur, management consultant, group therapist, and psychologist.

6

The Operations Manual

Margaret Dower and Robert Gappa, Management 2000

Franchise development is recruiting, but how can a franchisor know whom to recruit when its recruiters don't understand the operating system?

The people training new franchisees are doing it off the top of their head. There is nothing written, so they create their own version of the system, and that's what they teach.

In the field, franchisee Dave Smith is operating a Mexican-food restaurant that he has decided to turn into a fern bar and that's outside the operating system, so what happens?

Then, there's the fact that no self-respecting prospect is willing to invest $100,000 when there are no written operating procedures.

The conclusion? The franchisor needs an operations manuals. In this chapter, we discuss what you need to do and what your writer needs to do to get a manual out the door.

Issues to Resolve

You probably think the biggest issue is, *Who will write it?* But there are issues you must resolve before appointing someone to write, or you'll find yourself wanting to shoot the messenger (the writer) for bringing you a bad-news message (that you have a lot of holes in your system). Before beginning such a project the franchisor must answer these questions:

1. What business am I in?
2. What is my operating system?
3. What resources will I make available to document my operating system?

What Business Are You in?

Are you in the heating and air-conditioning business? Or are you the leader of a franchise company whose franchisees are in the heating and air-conditioning business? Or are you a franchised service business whose service is heating and air-conditioning?

If you are the leader of a franchise company, you know that franchising is a completely different enterprise from the one in which you found your initial success. What is that enterprise? Do you view it as a legal arrangement that allows others to go into your business so you can capitalize your "real" business? Or is it a business relationship with a legal structure? If it is a business relationship, what is the nature of that relationship?

Once you have determined your vision of franchising, you must then ask what your vision is for the future as a franchise. What is the mission of your franchise company? What values do you and your franchisees live by? By defining your vision, mission, and values, you define your vision of franchising, which in turn affects the type of people you seek as franchisees, how you view your relationship with them, and the way you conduct business together. Of course, you will want these vision, mission, and value statements in your operations manual; you'll want your trainers to teach them; and you'll want your entire organization to be guided by them.

There are other subjects that pertain to the relationship you have with your franchisees. These are spelled out, primarily, in the license agreement—though spelling them out in plain English won't hurt either, particularly when franchise development is recruiting new prospects. These subjects include:

- The meaning of franchising
- The franchisee's responsibility to enhance the brand, use the operating system, and take advantage of the ongoing support
- Protecting the franchise brand, name, and logo
- The franchisee's responsibility to penetrate, retain, and dominate the market
- Territorial rights and responsibilities
- Payment of fees
- Submitting required reports
- Licenses, permits, and other requirements
- National, regional, or cooperative advertising
- Structure and purpose of an advisory council
- Requirements or standards for purchasing equipment and supplies
- Computer systems
- Audits and inspections
- Compliance with the franchise agreement
- References to specific sections of the franchisee agreement
- Insurance

Once you've decided what business you are in, the next step is to document the way the business operates.

What Is Your Operating System?

The purpose of an operations manual is to document (not create) your operating system. One of the first discoveries you will probably make when someone attempts to document your system is that you don't really have an operating *system*—or if you do, you might be the only one who knows for sure what it is. This becomes evident when you attempt to describe your operation in detail. You may find, for example, what you believe is quite different from what franchise development believes, so the people being recruited as franchisees aren't the kind of people your business needs.

You might find that what you believe is central to the success of your operating system is not being taught in training, so once franchisees are on their own they flounder and everyone wonders why. Our franchisor clients frequently make observations related to this point. One franchisor said in the *Wall Street Journal* (October 9, 1991) that he was surprised at how much franchisees needed to know. They were often unaware of how to purchase an ad in the Yellow Pages or how to set up a checking account for a business.

At a seminar, another franchisor related how amazed he was to find that people didn't know how to open bank accounts and make deposits. Another said how popular her concept was with franchisees because they loved the environment of her designer furniture store, but she was shocked to find they knew nothing about inventory control.

But let's think about it a minute. Qualified prospects have money to invest; they may bring the necessary technical skills to produce the product or service being sold. But that doesn't mean they know how to run a business, not to mention how to *build* that business. If they did, they would be running their own. And you can be sure that for their franchise fee, they expect you to teach them these things. Whether you do or not is up to you, but if you don't, you can be fairly sure your franchisees will falter. If you don't plan to do so, perhaps you should ask if franchising is right for you.

ADMINISTRATION

Two very broad areas must be included in your operations manual. These can be included in one book; usually they are in two, although it can be more, depending on how extensive your system is. These two areas are operations (what product or service you sell and how you sell it) and internal, administrative control. If you have anything that is written, it usually concerns the operations side of the business.

It is the administrative side that is most often overlooked. The administration manual is addressed to the franchisee or unit manager. It concerns questions of control, such as: *How do I make money in this business?* It includes a business plan: *How much money do I want or need to make and how will I go about doing it?* From that comes marketing: *What will I do to generate business?* And cost control: *How do I plan and project future sales so I can control labor and inventory costs, yet still achieve my major objective, which is serving the customer?*

You will find, as did the franchisors discussed earlier, that you must spell everything out in clear, complete detail, from what franchisees do when they open the door in the morning to closing at night. Administrative controls include:

▲ Controlling costs and managing cash flow
▲ Preparing budgets and budget reports
▲ Writing and implementing a business plan
▲ Accounting and record keeping systems: monitoring and controlling financial performance and profitability
▲ Financial reports: balance sheets, profit and loss statements, financial statements, cash-flow analysis, cost analysis
▲ Evaluation of financial performance: standards, norms, key ratios
▲ Taxes and tax planning
▲ Payroll and payroll taxes
▲ Financial reports to the franchisor

OPERATIONS

The operations manual is addressed to everyone within the organization. The franchisee and anyone who works for the franchisee should be able to pick it up and read how to do what needs to be done on a daily, operational basis. (Usually this includes some administrative duties, such as making and recording the day's deposit and other record keeping activity; but if this is an activity anyone can be appointed to, it belongs in an operations manual.)

The most obvious benefit to documenting your system is that it allows you or your training staff to teach your system the same way each time. It provides a resource to your franchisees, once they leave training, that lets them continue doing things according to the operating system.

Why is this important? Because franchising institutionalizes the buying experience, removing the element of surprise. The buying experience is institutionalized through an operating system that is followed every time by everyone. The operating system is designed to keep customers coming back once they try the franchise. Operations emphasizes matters of quality, convenience, cleanliness, consistency, friendliness, unparalleled customer service, and price value. Specifically, operations includes:

▲ Using the franchisor's unique system day to day (techniques, procedures, packaging, recipes, ingredients, services, delivery)
▲ Indicators of efficiency and effectiveness
▲ Franchise unit hours of operation, scheduling, supplies, equipment, forms, reports
▲ Physical layout of the unit, if this is not included in a Grand Operning manual
▲ Equipment use and maintenance
▲ Inventory controls; preventing losses
▲ Cash control; preventing losses
▲ Quality control
▲ Customer service and courtesy

▴ Purchasing procedures
▴ Government regulations
▴ Required records and their retention

What Resources Are Available?

Writing a manual isn't simply a matter of going into the field and writing down what you see. Experience has taught us that no matter how creatively we write about what we see, what we see is not always what is correct. (On more than one occasion clients have said, *Where did you get that?*—"that" being the first time they'd ever heard of a procedure.)

To document your operating system, there are resources you must make available—people, time, and materials. As we proceed, you will see that whether you assign a writer or hire an outsider, the people, time, and materials required are pretty much the same in both cases.

THE PROJECT MANAGER

The first people resource is a project manager. The project manager can't possibly be the writer; the task is too big. But you will also see that the project manager has to be someone with a thorough understanding of the operating system, an ability to communicate it, and the authority to delegate additional resources to document it.

The project manager defines the scope of the project. That includes deciding on or approving an outline for each manual. It includes defining:

▴ *Who the audience is*
▴ *What the purpose of the document is*
▴ *What areas will be covered—operations, marketing, administration, personnel, franchise relations, training*

The project manager is responsible for supplying any existing resource information. It is when the writer begins working with this information that "holes" first appear—outdated procedures, nonexistent procedures, obsolete forms, and so on. The project manager is then responsible for providing the information that doesn't exist, which can be time-consuming if it's done right.

The project manager must either serve as the subject-matter expert for the writer or have the authority to delegate responsibility for subject matter to others. This is not without its perils. It is not at all uncommon for the project manager to direct others in the organization to write procedures—what they do and how they do it—only to get in return essays photocopied from popular business magazines. Such filler wastes everyone's time and money, and it certainly does not provide useful operating instructions to the franchisees. A good writer can judge the usefulness of the writing, but both the project manager and the writer must be sure that what is received from within the organization is actually what the organization is doing, or wants done, in the field. Subject-matter experts in the organization are rarely writers. They bring all the bad habits to the written page that everyone else brings. So you can bet that additional time will need to be spent conducting in-person interviews to get information.

The project manager must see the project to the end. This means, principally, reading through as many drafts as necessary (because there is *always* more than one draft) and approving it: *Yes, this it is. You've got it right. This is our operating system.* This process—reading and correcting drafts—takes time.

A client, like any consumer, doesn't like surprises. So ideally you want the writer to stay as close to the form and content as was originally agreed to. But this is not always possible. When the writer finds holes in the operating system, both the writer and the project manager may have to go back to the beginning: information gathering, writing, reading, correcting, redrafting, and so on. A good example of this occurs when a client wants a writer to edit existing material but the existing material doesn't really reflect the operating system; it may be a collection of exhortations to do good and avoid evil, or ''shouldy'' writing—writing that tells the reader what *should* be done as opposed to what to *do*.

In light of this—the time, authority, and ability required of a project manager—you may conclude, *There's no way I can afford to take one of my top people and assign them to this job!* So what can you do?

The Writer

Part of the solution is to relieve the project manager of some responsibility by assigning it to the writer. To do this, you must have someone on your staff who can devote the time it takes to gather, organize, and write the information. If you have such a person, can you afford to take him away from the work he is already doing? It won't do simply to say to Susan, *Take care of this as soon as you can get to it, okay?* First, Susan may not have the ability to write it. Second, if she is a full-time staff member, she doesn't have the time; she's already got a full-time job.

You could remove her from her full-time job and give her the writing assignment, but most people consider this a threat worse than death. They aren't writers; that's why they don't have writing jobs. But if you have someone on your staff who *can* do the writing, who *will* do the writing, and who will be given the people, resources, and materials to get the job done, this is one way to lessen the operational responsibilities of the project manager. If not, hire an outside writer.

An advantage of having an outsider write your manual is that the writer *is* an outsider. Directions and procedures that, to you, are so obvious, are often seen by an outsider as anything but obvious. For example, suppose your franchisees are to mail a weekly report to you. Your directions might say, ''Mail the weekly report for the previous week to Company XYZ at such-and-such address.'' But *how* is that form filled out? What is the information used to complete it? Is it taken from some other document—register tapes perhaps? Exactly what do you do to transfer the information from one source to another? In this respect, an outside writer is like a new franchisee: The person really must start from zero if they are to understand how to make your system go.

Let's suppose you have decided to use an outside writer. What should you look for? What follows are some general guidelines:

Finding a Writer

1. Don't put an ad in the newspaper for a "writer." Everyone who is looking for a job can honestly call themselves a writer. You will be inundated with applicants, and on what basis would you screen them, in any case?

2. Recognize that there are different types of writers. There are ones you don't want, even if they are fine writers, because their area of expertise is not what you need. You don't want feature writers (people who write human-interest pieces in newspapers and magazines); copywriters (the ones who write advertising copy, marketing brochures, and so on); technical writers (people who write for their peers, such as those in the oil and gas fields); or documentation specialists (the people who document computer programs). You want a how-to writer—someone who can tell a reader how to operate a robot coupe; how to make a bank deposit; how to take inventory; how to do guerilla marketing. Cookbooks are great how-to books. They tell you how to do what you need to do, what you need to do it, why you are doing it, and what to do when you're done. That's the kind of writing you need.

3. Contact your community college to find writers because they usually have courses on business writing. Call the community college and ask to speak to the head of the business department. Tell the department head you have a writing project and you are looking for someone to write your operations manual. Ask if any of the business faculty does such writing on a contract basis. A student might also do, but students generally lack experience. Hiring experience lessens the burden on the project manager because an experienced business writer should already understand, generally, what your manual needs to include.

4. Ask your fellow franchisors if they have operations manuals and who wrote them. It might also be relevant to ask how long ago they were written. Anything over ten years old probably was not written on a computer. (More about this later.)

5. Check with consulting companies. Be sure to get a clear understanding of what service they will provide. Like legal writing, a lot of operations writing—personnel, marketing, for example—can be boiler-plated. That isn't necessarily bad. There's a lot of good information on these subjects. But you want to be sure that the operations and administrative procedures will be your own.

6. Ask for references and check them out. This doesn't really tell you anything about someone's writing ability, but it will tell you if the reference had a

good working relationship with the writer. Ask how well the reference felt the writer worked with the material that was provided. Ask if the writer's material was used in training or in developing training programs. Ask what the feedback was from within the organization about the manuals. Did they use them? Were they helpful? Do they feel it was worth the time and expense?

7. Ask to see a sample of an operations document the writer has written. This will give you a good idea of the writer's style, and how clearly he or she writes. Ask for a sample table of contents and index. They don't have to be from the same manual, but you do want to confirm that the capability of producing both is there.

Presentation of the Document

Desktop publishing is everywhere—a popular, fast-growing field. But do you want or need it? It depends in part on the purpose of your manual and in part on the skill level and equipment within your own organization. You can physically put together the materials to be printed using desktop publishing techniques or more standard publishing materials. More about this later.

Binding

If you are going to use the document as a marketing document—that is, to select and impress qualified prospective franchisees—appearance is more important than content. You can have an easy-to-use document inside but create "curbside appeal" with a padded, silk-screened three-ring binder and colored, preprinted tab dividers.

Don't overlook the scotch-whiskey effect. Remember the blind-tasting story? If the panel members knew only the price of the scotch and nothing else, they invariably chose the more expensive as their favorites—not based on taste but presumably on the assumption that, If it's more expensive, it must be better. High-end document bindings have the same effect. Notice it the next time you attend a franchise exposition. Look at the manuals displayed. See if those that are attractively bound aren't more effective than the others.

Formatting

The more complex your document, the more difficult it will be for your production staff to replicate it. Lots of graphics, fancy fonts, different typefaces—nowadays you can create a manual that looks like *USA Today*. But what you want is an uncluttered book, clearly written, in easy-to-understand sentences, with a table of contents, a line on each page that identifies the document, and a date. A small header with your logo also makes a nice appearance and is usually not difficult to duplicate. Figure 6-1 shows an example of what a table of contents and a page from a manual might look like that is not difficult to do. See pages 84–85.

Regardless of the use, most companies want a manual that can be used immediately and modified or updated quickly and easily. In the best of all possible worlds, the writer and the franchisor will be using the same software package for ease of transferring data back and forth. That is rarely the case, however, even within organizations. But recognize that these are issues that must be discussed before the project begins. You don't want a high-end technical document if no one on your staff can use it.

What the Writer Needs to Do

In the material that follows, let's assume that you have hired someone outside your organization to do the writing. There still are things that must be done before a word can be written.

Gather Information

A writer cannot clearly and concisely write a policy or procedure if the policy or procedure the writer is supposed to convey is not clear. The first task is to determine what message you want the writer to convey and provide the resources that can convey it.

A good how-to writer will know what questions to ask as well as how to put the information in writing. Getting someone within the organization to relate what it is they do on a day-to-day basis, in conversational English (in their own words), is a good way to gather information, although the project manager is the ultimate authority as to the correctness of a procedure. That's why—although this is not the favorite task of any project manager—reading each draft is so important; you must be sure that what is written is, in fact, correct.

Trainers are good resources. They know the system and they have to explain it to others. Attending franchisee training sessions is an excellent way for a writer to gather information. Under these circumstances, the writer is like the new franchisee, with the trainer explaining the operating system so it can be understood. The only difference between the franchisee and the writer is that the franchisee doesn't have to put it in writing. (Writers in no way participate during franchise training; they only observe. Questions, comments, and observations must be reserved for a later time.)

Define Your Purpose, Know Your Audience

Who your reader is determines what the writer writes about.

Franchise Development

Franchise development can use the operations manuals in several ways. The manuals create a visual statement by themselves. If they look good, the franchise

(*Text continues on page 86.*)

Figure 6-1. Sample table of contents and text page.

Our Company _____

TABLE OF CONTENTS

What About an Operations Manual?

Operations Manual   1   October 15, 1992

Our Company _____

What You Need to Do

If you come fully prepared to a manual-writing project, you probably think the biggest issue is, *Who will write it?* But these are issues you must resolve before appointing someone to write, or you'll find yourself wanting to shoot the messenger (the writer) for bringing you a bad-news message (that you have a lot of holes in your system). The issues are:

1. What business am I in?
2. What is my operating system?
3. What resources will I make available to document my operating system?

What Business Are You in?

Are you in the heating and air conditioning business? Or are you the leader of a franchise company whose franchisees are in the heating and air conditioning business? Or are you a franchised service business whose service is heating and air conditioning?

If yours is a heating and air conditioning business, for example, your manual will be oriented to the technical side of the heating and air conditioning business. If, on the other hand, you're in the service business, your emphasis will be on getting and keeping customers to serve—in which case your manual will focus on customer service.

What Is Your Operating System?

The purpose of an operations manual is to document (not create) your operating system. One of the first discoveries you will probably make when someone attempts to document your system is that you don't really have an operating system, or if you do, you might be the only one who knows for . . .

Operations Manual   1   October 15, 1992 looks good. They can also be used as a demonstration tool, as if to say, "Here you have tangible evidence that we are committed to franchise support. These manuals are a good example of how we do that. How many other opportunities have you explored that can offer you something like this?"

The manuals can also be used as teaching tools. Ordinarily, presentation books are used in recruiting prospects, but these can be supplemented with the operations manuals to strengthen the presentation and stress a benefit of critical interest to a prospect: the franchisor's ongoing support.

TRAINING

Can you imagine a movie director saying to the cast, "Just get up there and say whatever comes to mind"? That, in effect, is what is expected of trainers who have no training book. Not only does this guarantee that different systems will be taught but also that every time there's a new group of franchisees, the anxiety level escalates within the organization as people have to contend with, *What shall we do with them this time?*

FRANCHISEES

If the document(s) is positioned correctly from the outset—that is, if it is used during training and if it continues to be used by the field or phone support staff—franchisees will become accustomed to using the operations manual. They will see it repeatedly used within the organization and conclude that it must be useful. This is a benefit to both of you: to them because they can use a resource they have on hand, rather than calling your support staff; and to you because you can be confident that the system they are following is the correct one.

While it is a big task, solicit the opinions of franchisees during the course of the manual project. Their suggestions and ideas are important and may be useful. But even more important is the *process* of seeking those suggestions and ideas. The process confirms in their minds that their ideas and opinions count and that they are worthwhile. Their contributions make the manual *theirs,* which will encourage them to use it. This, again, makes it worth the investment: to you because they don't have to be so dependent on your staff; and to them because they have a resource they can use.

EMPLOYEES

People don't like surprises. That's one of the reasons why franchising is so popular with the public. They know that when they go from one unit to another they will find basically the same product, served in the same way, under the same circumstances. An operations manual strengthens this likelihood because the franchisees use it to train their employees, just as you used it to train the franchisees. When procedures are written, the manual becomes an objective standard for judging whether or not someone is in compliance with the operating system. It helps diffuse personal conflict because the standard is in a book, rather than coming "from above." This is true both for you and your franchisees and your franchisees and their employees. It's a lot more effective to say, "Let's see what it says on page 24," than to say, "I don't care how you did it yesterday, my point is. . . ."

How Will the Document Be Managed?

This question is becoming more pressing with every new personal computer that is sold. It used to be that manuals were typed and updated every five or six years. It was an expensive undertaking and updating was so awkward it wasn't often attempted. Faxes and computers have changed all that, and companies must assess the implications for their organizations.

1. How will the manual be updated? Will someone be put in charge of the updating?
2. When changes are made, how will changes get into the field? (This question has to be decided before writing begins because it will affect how the document is formatted.)
3. Will changes be printed on hard copy and mailed? Will they be faxed? How will you know that changes have been made to existing manuals? Will manual inspection be a part of a quality-control audit? Will an acknowledgment of receipt be faxed to you from the field confirming that changes were received and entered into the unit's manuals?

How the Writing Is Done

It is rare for clients to take much interest in the writing procss. Their knowledge of computers is limited, at best. Most have never worked with them, so they have little understanding or appreciation of the complexities involved in producing documents. But for those of you with an interest in what a writer actually does, the pages that follow talk about the process.

In a nutshell, here is how you write a manual:

How to Write a Manual

1. Keep track of your time. Begin a log, or, if your computer lets you, do it there. Write down when you start writing; what you're writing about; client requests for additions, changes, deletions, and so on; and when you stop. This adds to your experience in gauging how long a project will take and it is a useful record, particularly when questions of cost and deadline overruns arise.

2. Get hold of all the information you can; the more recent, the better. Make file folders for everything you collect. Particularly, make a separate file folder for all the forms you will collect. (It makes it easier to find during the project; and they don't get lost.)

3. Make photocopies of everything. Restore the originals to exactly the way they were when you got them. Put them away where they will be undisturbed and work from the photocopies.

4. Separate the work into categories (Operations, Administration, Personnel, Marketing, or whatever categories seem to make sense at that point; these can change later.)

5. Further separate the material within each category. Personnel is an easy one to use as an example. Make one file folder "Recruiting," another "Interviewing," another "Orientation and Training," and so on. It doesn't matter how you categorize the information. Doing it chronologically works best in operations manuals. In a manual entitled *Equipment, Safety, and Security*, where events don't necessarily occur in chronological sequence, arranging things alphabetically is effective.

6. Create an outline based on the way you've sorted the material. Get the project manager's agreement.

7. Talk to people.

8. Start writing.

Here are some tips. They are addressed primarily to writers, but a project manager will find them helpful, too:

1. *Photocopies.* Working from photocopies is preferable. When you begin the project, usually the first step is reorganizing the client's material. (Effective reorganization is probably the biggest contribution a writer can make to a client.) Reorganizing means pulling things out of notebooks, folders, binders—wherever you find information—and assigning them to new places. But you'll find the client is still accustomed to referring to the previous organization. Or you'll find that once upon a time, the organization of that data meant something to someone, and you may have to know what that is. Also, as you work, you will mark or write on documents. (The most common example of this is in filling out forms.) Unexpectedly, you may get directions over the phone and you won't want to write on the originals.

2. *Forms.* There are a number of observations to make about forms, or the records the client keeps to control business. Record keeping and record keeping forms are at the administrative heart of the franchisor's business, and documenting their use is a major contribution a writer makes to create a manual that is practical and useful. Notice that when clients explain their operating system, it almost always revolves around some record keeping procedure. But it is rare to find written directions explaining their use—perhaps because companies are so

close to them, or because they've been using them for so long—but in any case, clients assume people know how to fill out those forms properly.

A writer must specifically ask for forms as well as for directions for filling them out. Here are some tips to make that easier:

- Get copies of all records, both filled in and blank. Records include everything, even register tapes. You want the blank ones so you can include them in the new manual. You'll want examples that are filled in so that you have them to refer to when you write directions for them.
- Almost inevitably, questions, suggestions, criticisms, or reconsiderations of the forms or record keeping procedures stall the writing project. This is understandable. Different discoveries are made: the forms are too long, or no one is filling them out completely, or the form is outdated, or the information is no longer needed, or the directions for filling out the forms (if there are any) don't match what's on the form. An experienced writer knows this will happen, but the client doesn't. Client education on this point is an equally important aspect of a writing project.
- Keep the forms in a separate folder marked "forms." Most of the records businesses use function for more than one procedure, so you'll be referring to them over and over again. It makes it easier to find them if they are all in one place.
- Different writers treat forms in different ways. Some insert the directions for their use in the body of the text with a standard-size copy of the form alongside them. Others create a separate section in the manual devoted solely to forms. They are filed alphabetically for quick reference, the idea being that the reader can remove them and photocopy them as needed. Sometimes, if the forms are lengthy or complicated, the directions for their use can be included with the forms in the stand-alone section. (Not all clients will want their forms photocopied. Some have preprinted forms for which users are billed. Be sure to ask how it's done.) Discuss the options with the client beforehand because moving forms around at the eleventh hour creates changes in the entire document, including the table of contents and the index. Proofreading can be a nightmare.

3. *Project Time Line*. Forced deadlines can sabotage a writing project, usually because in the haste to finish, attention isn't paid to details (spelling, accuracy of page cross-references, or consistency of copy). Project managers find these lapses highly irritating, though they are bound to happen if deadline pressures are too great. There isn't a ready solution to this difficulty, but be alert to it because these relatively minor problems are the first thing the client sees. The quality of the work can be dismissed out of hand if the reader is drawn to matters merely cosmetic. Spellcheck and proofread the document every time you change copy. Page through it to be sure the pages are in order, to be sure there aren't duplications, to be sure the document looks the way you *think* it looks, before you send

it. It can be discouraging, after putting in ten 12-hour days making an inventory procedure understandable, only to have a client say, ''There's another page two in here.''

There is another matter that demands attention—this, much more important yet not much discussed, perhaps because it was only ten years ago we traded our yellow legal pads for computer keyboards: Save hard copies of every change the client directs. People make mistakes; computers crash; things happen. It is very comforting, on that final copy, to be able to sit down with those original drafts and confirm you have made the changes you were directed to make.

4. *Organization.* Certainly the most dreaded word a writer can hear is *confusing.* Anything that can be done to avoid confusion should be done. This involves materials handling as well as writing. Some things that work well:

- ▴ Don't change the writing too much after the first draft.
- ▴ Print your work on three-hold punched paper. Put it in a three-ring binder. (There are colored cardboard binders that are not too expensive.) Use numbered tabs to divide your work. This organizes the work for the client rather than obliging the project manager to decide what to do with sixty pages of unmarked, loose-leaf paper.
- ▴ When sending subsequent drafts, print them on three-hole punched paper, but don't bind them in notebooks. Have the client remove the previous draft and insert the new draft in the notebook. But be sure to tell the client to save the previous draft in case it has to be cross-referenced at a later date. You will be surprised how frequently this can occur. Alerting clients beforehand can save both of you hard feelings later on.

Your franchise license agreement no doubt has a statement to the effect that franchisees are expected to return their operations manuals at the end of the contract. This implies that there are operations manuals to return. If you keep your end of the bargain, your franchisees will thank you, your trainers will thank you, and you can feel confident that you have made a good-faith effort at ongoing support by providing useful, readable documents that help everyone standardize the operating system.

7

The Role of Computers and Automated Systems

Robin Ballard Simeonsson, University of Maryland,
and Neal Anstadt, Parcom Technologies, Inc.

Technology plays a large role in business today, and this is especially true for franchised businesses. Many franchisors have realized that upgrading their computer and communications systems provide a competitive edge. In doing so, franchised businesses gain an added advantage of increased buying power when deciding which systems to purchase. The franchisees can benefit from corporate discounts owing to high-volume sales. Also, integrated computer systems allow quicker response to market demand and corporate needs. Smart registers, or point-of-sale terminals (POS), provide tighter inventory control and better tracking of sales data. POS terminals are able to save sales data that then can be used to improve inventory decisions and better identify target markets. Many POS terminals run sophisticated software that can manage everything from the payroll to the sales mix in individual units. In almost every case, improved technology increases the efficiency and profitability of a franchise business.

It has become increasingly important to provide customers with fast, accurate, and efficient service, whether the franchise business is new or well established, and whether the franchisee operates from a home or office or storefront. This translates into a need for complete business control without excessive working hours or a large staff. The right computer system, along with software designed to meet the specific requirements of the franchise business, can accomplish this goal. As a result, the franchisor and franchisee work together better to ensure the growth and longevity of the franchise.

Computers, ranging from notebook-size portables to mainframes, now play a significant role in every businessperson's life. Use of computers has increased vastly during the last ten years for the following reasons:

1. PC systems and software are cost-effective.
2. The consumer expects services and products in a fraction of the time once considered acceptable. This requires speedy retrieval of sales, inventory, shipping, and cash-flow information—only accomplishable with computerization.

3. Computerization requires fewer employees to accomplish more tasks, more efficiently.

The integration of computer systems between franchisors and franchisees has been slow to gain acceptance, however. Price previously was the major hindrance. Though prices of technology have fallen, franchisees are still slow to accept technology for two reasons: loss of privacy and loss of control of information. Offering a system that meets the needs of both franchisor and franchisee will encourage acceptance of an integrated system.

Developing an Integrated System for Franchisor and Franchisee

Each franchise corporation has specific needs for its business or market, and these needs must be addressed in the system design. For example, there are certain areas of management and control that each franchisor requires. Likewise, the franchisee has the responsibility of performing the sales and services of the franchisor's business, while also acting as bookkeeper, personnel administrator, customer service specialist, and more.

Franchisor Information

- *Franchisee database*. A file that includes the name, location, financial arrangement, and purchase price of each franchise unit. It may also include store build-out features and costs, initial inventory, and percent of royalty to be paid.
- *Demographic information*. Data on population density and businesses that use the franchise services in a given geographic area. This information helps the franchisor determine where to split regions or areas and what values to assign to each.
- *Inventory and product movement*. Data for franchisors that intend to supply forms, products, and other materials to their network of franchises.
- *Accounting system*. General ledger, accounts receivable, accounts payable, and payroll data needed to reconcile accounts with franchisees.
- *Franchise sales tracking*. Valuable analytical data to help the franchisor determine how to better support and market the services of the franchise operation. In addition, the franchisor can assess seasonal sales trends overall, by location, and by product line. This feature helps in product forecasting if the franchisor is stocking and shipping inventory for sales to the franchisees.
- *Royalty control*. Data to permit the franchisor and franchisee to determine the royalty payments due the franchisor, with accurate sales revenue re-

ports from the franchisee. As more sites are placed, this revenue stream becomes increasingly important and increasingly difficult to monitor.

Franchisee Information Needs

▲ Automatic sales and service recording, including capture of credit card information
▲ Cash register entry and reporting functions
▲ Unique operations related to the franchisee's business
▲ Accounting system functions like inventory tracking, purchase order creation, check printing and bill payment, payroll or time card processing, and accounts receivable tracking as well as statements and credit limits

Interesting and innovative technology is in use in franchised businesses in many different industries. Most businesses have sought a customized system that gains them a competitive edge. This chapter surveys the technology used by the service, food and beverage, and retail industries. It analyzes the impact of computers and technology on these specific businesses.

Technology in the Service Industry

Within the service industry, the focus of competition is on improving the speed and quality of service. Technology has had a positive effect on both of these goals.

The Hilton hotel chain has developed a powerful computerized sales and marketing system that links all its units, allowing faster and more efficient transmission of information. Called Answer Net, the system was written in COBOL and runs on an IBM 3090 380J mainframe. IBM personal computers are connected to the corporate mainframe via phone lines and satellite transmission channels. The database in the mainframe holds client files, including booking activity of large clients over the past five years, and is accessible from any Hilton in the country. Each client file contains a minimum of four pages of stored notes per client, including business or personal information such as birthdays, spouse names, or wine preferences. This allows the Hilton sales staff to tailor presentations to specific clients among its larger sales accounts. The database groups client files by event, making it user-friendly for the sales staff. The ease of access allows local sales staff to conduct quick availability checks for large customers who are deciding among several locations for large conferences. For example, the system allows an employee in Atlanta to meet with a client, discuss a potential booking in Hawaii, send electronic-mail messages to a Hilton in Hawaii, and allow that local salesperson to pursue the sales lead (i.e., book the conference). The system is flexible in that it allows salespeople, to dial in using their IBM P/S2 from home, on the road, or in the office. The system provides up-to-the-minute information regarding which guest rooms or conference rooms are in use. Messages can also be left for clients via the system when the client is staying at any Hilton location. The system was fully functional in all sixty-three corporate hotels by June 1991, and was being offered to the 235 U.S. franchises. Hilton proclaims that the major benefits include both the ability to tailor sales to specific client needs and the speed and accuracy of information transfer between Hilton personnel. For the future, Hilton is trying to integrate a software package into the system that will track demand. Hilton will use this information to accurately determine peak periods and adjust pricing to obtain maximum occupancy levels.

In the video rental business, two keys to success are quality of selection and speed of service. The technology pioneer in the video rental business was David Cook of Blockbuster Video. Cook used technology in several ways to increase video selection and speed of service to his customers. First, he invested in a powerful computerized inventory system, utilizing point-of-sale terminals, so that he could manage a large inventory and selection of tapes. His first Blockbuster store had 8,000 tapes and 6,500 different titles. Cook was among the first to move tapes from behind the counter out into the store, so that customers could browse and pick their own tapes. To do this, he used magnetic stripes on each tape to prevent theft. He originated the use of bar codes on each tape. Each customer had a membership card with a unique bar code. As the customer's video selections were scanned at the POS terminal, a receipt was printed at the register and the customer's account was updated to reflect the rental. The entire customer transaction took merely seconds. Interestingly, the Blockbuster system is so sophisticated that the individual membership cards can be programmed to provide information about the customer to the clerk. For example, parents can request a special code for their children's rental card so that the children cannot rent R-rated movies. The sales tracking allows Blockbuster to maintain the optimal inventory (both in quantities and titles). Thus, Blockbuster's innovative use of technology brought a higher quality standard for service and selection in the industry.

Maryland's Erol Onaran of Erol's Video recognized the role of computers in providing quick service when he opened his first store in 1980. As he expanded, Erol continued to upgrade his system. By 1988, each store had ten POS terminals with bar-code readers, ten matching printers, and one microprocessor. The POS terminal recorded each customer transaction as it occurred. At the end of the day, all transactions were analyzed by the in-store microprocessor to verify membership and update inventory counts. Nightly, the microprocessors from each store downloaded the transaction data over leased lines to a mainframe at the corporate headquarters in Springfield, Virginia. Daily sales reports were printed and both membership and inventory databases were updated. Erol's system sped up customer transactions, sales-report generation, and inventory management.

The recent development in high-tech systems has fueled rapid growth in some franchise industries. One of the most obvious is that of copying and quick printing. Sales in this industry were close to $8 million in 1969 and grew to $1.9 billion by 1991. Two of the most important technological developments to affect this industry are color copying and desktop publishing. With the advent of desktop publishing software packages and reasonably priced laser printers, the quick-printing shops took on the role that commercial printers had in the past. One of the most technologically well-positioned franchises in the industry is Alpha-Graphics Printshops of the Future. AlphaGraphics has a network in place, called AlphaLink, that includes sufficient bandwidth over satellite transmission links to transmit camera-ready text and graphics among any of its 325 units in twelve countries. In fact, AlphaGraphics markets its services in a manner where the customer doesn't even need to come in to the print shop at all. The client can create her own camera-ready material and transmit it directly to AlphaGraphics for printing. Computer development and sophisticated communications networks give AlphaGraphics a major competitive edge.

The Albert Andrews, Ltd., franchisor, with locations in Washington and Boston, has made extremely innovative use of technology in the tailoring industry. Andrews makes custom-tailored suits, with pricetags ranging from $400 for low-end models to $3,000 for top-of-the-line silk suits. The innovative part involves the method of measuring and cutting the suits. Andrews franchisees can operate with a minimum of capital investment: a laptop computer, a measuring device, and a modem to send measurements to the Cleveland factory. The salesperson or franchisee carries the electronic measuring device to the client's location, takes about forty electronic measurements with the measuring device, and stores these measurements on a floppy disk. The franchisee also records the client's choice of style and material. The visit can actually be very brief. Then the franchisee returns to his office (which can be in his home) and transmits the client's information to the factory over his phone line via modem and laptop. Another computer at the factory receives the data and manipulates it to produce a unique pattern for the client. Then a computer-aided machine, using laser technology, cuts the material to the exact measurements of the unique pattern. The suit is in the factory and shipped directly to the client within four to six weeks. From the time of measurement forward, the client can order additional suits that will fit exactly the same, merely contacting the franchisee over the phone. This is possible since the client's measurements are stored on disk and the cutting technology produces the exact same suit each time. Using this technology, the franchise targets upscale clients who dislike or have no time for shopping in the traditional way. In 1989, after its second year in business, Albert Andrews, Ltd., produced more than 1,500 made-to-order suits.

Technology in the Food and Beverage Industry

In the food and beverage industry in particular, a labor shortage was expected to occur in the late 1980s. As a result, many franchisors geared up with increased computing power. The labor shortages did not materialize to the extent expected, however the technology implemented in this industry is fascinating. Many of the large fast-food chains implemented intelligent systems to ease the paperwork load on managers and further automated the food delivery process. Even franchised restaurants that are not considered fast-food establishments have found systems beneficial to their daily operations.

In 1988, the Burger King management decided to try a Consumer Response Line (1-800-YES-1800) at 200 company-owned stores. At first, only one PC was needed to handle the database. But the customer response (both criticisms and compliments) was so great that management decided to go nationwide with the response line. Now, customers from over 5,600 Burger King units call in, with an average 4,000 calls per day. The system utilizes an IBM AS/400 mid-range system and twenty-six operators taking calls twenty-four hours a day. When customers call in, the operator simply requests the name of the caller's city. When the first letter of the city is entered into the computer, all Burger King cities beginning with that letter appear on the screen. The operator selects the correct city and then the exact Burger King location can be identified. With this extensive database, compliments and criticisms can be channeled directly to the individual restaurant and reacted to more quickly. For Burger King, technology is allowing the company to keep in constant touch with customer sentiment and make appropriate changes quickly.

Burger King is a good example of the interesting problem mature franchisors face when franchisees resist integrated technology. The Burger King corporate management decided to standardize on a PC-based POS (point-of-sale) system in 1989. The system would link the microcomputers at the counter to video screens in the kitchens for displaying orders and to the manager's PC in the back office for tracking sales and inventory. There was no doubt that the system would increase efficiency and manage inventory more effectively. The problem was how to convince the franchisees to invest in this new system. The franchisor did not want to strain relations with the franchisees by forcing them to purchase the new system. So Burger King attacked the problem in two ways. First, it gave the franchisees a choice between two different vendors. As an example, Burger King converted the corporate stores using different vendors, hoping that franchisees would focus on the benefits of an upgraded system rather than the resentment of having one system forced on them. It converted half the corporate stores to an IBM system and half to NCR. Second, to encourage the franchisees to buy, Burger King offered the new systems to its franchisees at the same corporate discount rate it negotiated from each of the vendors. Burger King hoped that by offering selection and discounted prices, the franchisees would buy in to the new technology. They did not focus on the issue of information transfer, but rather stressed the benefits that upgrading could provide for the franchisees. The standardization problem can be avoided with new franchisees by incorporating the purchase of the new system into the franchise agreement.

The increased sales volume that results from combining corporate and franchised units gives franchisors an interesting advantage when shopping for computer systems. The large volume of the purchase puts franchised businesses in a position to negotiate lucrative discounts from systems vendors. For example, Taco Bell, Kentucky Fried Chicken, and Pizza Hut, the three largest franchises under the Pepsico umbrella, combined their corporate buying power and received a good price when they decided to upgrade to PC-based POS terminals and Mlink software. The software package allowed corporate headquarters to download price and menu changes to the PC-based POS terminals in each unit and upload sales and transaction data nightly. The three chains also collaborated on a transmission link that allowed transmission of software, video, and Muzak.

How the system operates at Pizza Hut is of interest. Pizza Hut[1] successfully implemented an integrated POS system that tracks sales, sales mix, inventory, payroll, labor scheduling, promotions, and training. Each unit's PC-like POS terminal is capable of performing calculations independently and also of interfacing with a host computer at Pizza Hut headquarters. This relieves the managers of many calculations previously performed by hand, allowing them to spend more time out front, providing better service to customers. First, the host computer downloads product codes and pricing (both regular and promotional) for each item on the menu. This preprogrammed pricing ensures that customers are charged accurately, since the employee at the register simply identifies the item purchased. It also allows the system to track promotional pricing. Pizza Hut claims that thousands of dollars are saved simply because the system accurately applies promotional pricing. It allows individual restaurants to monitor how well promotional items are selling. The POS terminal also calculates and adds the sales tax. As orders are inputted into the POS terminal at the order counter, a printer in the kitchen outputs the recipe for the order to ensure that the pizza is made correctly. This improves customer satisfaction, since fewer mistakes are made in delivering the pizza as ordered. As sales are made, the POS terminal tracks dollar volume sales, but more important, it tracks the quantities and combinations of items sold. Accurate tracking of quantities allows accurate cost-of-sales figures, better budgeting for individual stores, and better monitoring of inventory variances. Restaurants can accurately forecast future sales and order correct quantities of daily inventory required to match actual sales. This is extremely important in the restaurant business, since the "inventory" is perishable. Sales data are transmitted to the host computer nightly and posted automatically to the general ledger on a weekly basis.

With regard to labor management, the Pizza Hut POS system contributes at both the corporate and local level. At the corporate level, Pizza Hut has claimed cost savings of one staff position immediately, since information was transmitted from individual units directly into the host computer and no longer needed to be inputted manually at the corporate level. At the local level, the POS can use sales forecasts for the unit to more accurately forecast hourly labor requirements. Also at the local level, the system provides on-line training for employees. Employees are more adequately trained since installation of the system because corporate management is able to monitor the amount of time the employees have spent with the computer training program and can identify inadequacies. The payroll improvements have provided benefits at all levels. When employees arrive at work, they "clock in" at the POS terminal and enter job-function codes according to which job they will perform (cook, waitress, hostess). Information regarding hours worked per employee, hours worked per job code, employee expenses, and tips is transmitted to corporate. Checks are cut and accounting ledgers are updated automatically. The system also allows for two-way transmission of electronic-mail messages between corporate headquarters and restaurants and transmissions between restaurants. This means quicker information transfer.

Many times, computers can be used by a franchisor to produce better economies of scale. A good example is the way Strings[2] pasta houses in California utilize computers. Each unit produces its own pasta, however all sauces, dressings, and soups are made in a centralized kitchen. That's where the economies of scale come into play. Strings utilizes an electronic accounting system that transmits sales data from individual units to a central host computer. This method of tracking sales and inventory by unit allows the kitchen to produce and deliver precise quantities of each food item for the individual units. Strings boasts that its production loss is always less than 2 percent. The franchisor had twelve units that produced $11 million in sales in 1990 and was scheduled to open twelve more units in 1991. Strings attributes its success to a streamlined menu and the economies of scale afforded by its centralized ordering system.

In some cases, the franchisor is more familiar with computer technology than with the business of the franchise. Donald Boensel, an electrical engineer and computer consultant, bought into the original The Soup Exchange restaurant in 1983, with the express purpose of computerizing the business and franchising it out. The California-based franchisor expects to have 250 units by 1993. Each unit is equipped with a POS system that tracks sales and the cost of labor and food as a percentage of sales. The data are transmitted daily via modem to a mid-size computer at corporate headquarters. Corporate headquarters produces a weekly status report of sorts, and distributes it to all franchisees, specifically to breed competition among the units. Investment in computer-aided design technology contributed to The Soup Exchange's rapid growth. It allows corporate management to develop and tailor complex floor plans to individual sites, accomplished within forty-eight hours. Thus, when a potential franchisee considers The Soup Exchange for a site, she can request and receive floor plans very quickly. The Soup Exchange also attributes its success to investment in the appropriate council to develop its operations manual, offering circular, and franchise agreement. Finally, Boensel expanded by selling multi-unit territories only to experienced and well-capitalized businesspeople. This sophisticated franchisor uses the power of technology as one of several important strategies in expanding the business.

Technology in the Retail Industry

Competition in the retail industry is fierce. Franchises, as with most other businesses, try to find the most profit while still pricing their goods and services competitively. To help, computer technology can track costs more efficiently than manual methods. Some franchises try to foster customer loyalty by improving service with computer technology. While there are many uses for technology in this industry, the most common are to "reduce inventory" and "increase profits."

The computer retailing industry has moved from a period of large profit margins to one of slim margins, as large discount warehouses and mail-order businesses came on the scene. In order to squeeze the most profit from their small margins, computer retailers have had to become more innovative in their inventory and delivery systems. For example, ComputerLand has used a new ordering and delivery system to decrease inventory, decrease floor space, and decrease its labor force. When a customer walks in to one of the new ComputerLand units, the only stock on site is demo units. The new target customer is the medium to large buyer who wishes to order in volume. The order is placed via computer and transmitted to one of three national warehouses. At the warehouse, a small centralized staff assembles the personalized order. The computer system also feeds into the offices of a contracted trucking business responsible for transporting the product from the warehouse to the customer. ComputerLand claims to deliver within two days. By allowing the trucking business quick access to the order system, the latter can plan efficient routes and ensure quick delivery. The new computerized process allows ComputerLand to decrease its operating costs and get the most profit.

A different computer franchise has used desktop publishing technology to improve service by providing a monthly informational newsletter. MicroAge Computer Stores stopped its mass-mailing marketing approach and narrowed its focus to targeted businesses and existing accounts. MicroAge tries to build relationships with existing accounts by providing the makings for a monthly newsletter. Corporate headquarters, located in Arizona, creates a newsletter on disk. The disk, called "NewsDisk," is mailed to each of MicroAge's 200 franchisees. (This is admittedly not the most high-tech mode of transmission, but the makings for a customized newsletter is innovative.) Each franchisee has standardized with headquarters by purchasing the same software and hardware: Ventura desktop publishing software and PCs. When the franchisee receives the "NewsDisk," he can pop it into his PC, add or delete articles of interest, insert sales reminders, or include anything else he needs to personalize the newsletter for his customers and geographic area. Then the disk is delivered to a printer for reproduction. MicroAge customers receive a professionally designed newsletter containing valuable information.

Athlete's Foot[3] uses its POS terminals to control and allocate inventory, control ticketing errors, and reduce paperwork. Each unit has DataServ software running on POS terminals. At night, the software dials into the corporate mainframe via a modem to exchange sales information. The software manages an average of 50,000 different products in each of the 203 company-owned stores and 190 franchises. The POS software tracks each product's sales so that management can most effectively distribute its stock among the stores. For example, some stores demand more basketball products while others demand more hockey products. The sales data allow management to determine customer demographics down to the unit level. Tracking of this information also allows management to maintain smaller inventories, since the sales history can be used to predict future demand for each item. The system is a more efficient and effective method of tracking inventory than doing it manually. Product codes and prices are captured by the register at the time of sale. This means fewer errors and better tracking of markdowns and promotions; previously, employees tracked markdowns and promotions manually. Finally, the POS system runs the credit checks on credit cards automatically and records the authorization information on the system's detailed transaction log. This reduces the amount of time required in tracking problems.

Remington Products[4], while not a franchise, has used a POS system to track in several innovative ways that could be applied to a franchise business. The system is unique in that it must track labor and thousands of tiny parts on the service side of the operation, as well as record retailing and wholesaling sides. The Remington stores service Remington, Braun, and Norelco products. Remington also tracks sales based on the placement of items in the displays. This way, Remington can rearrange the displays to determine the combination that results in the highest turnover. The POS software is able to provide perpetual inventory data on each of the many small products in the store. This allows Remington to monitor inventory turns and operate with the smallest inventory needed to meet demand. Remington also uses the system for electronic mail and claims to have cut mailing and phone costs between headquarters and the stores by 60 percent. The POS terminals in each store are polled from corporate headquarters each night. Sales data are compiled into a report and transmitted back to the stores before morning. These sales reports keep individual stores up-to-date on performance and also inform individual sales clerks of their personal sales numbers. These reports are used to motivate the sales clerks, who work on an incentive basis. Interestingly, corporate headquarters does not have an expensive mainframe. The polling and report generation are conducted by three PCs.

A popular concept in franchising is operating a business out of a pushcart-type stand, thus the name "standchising." These stands are usually located in heavy-traffic areas, like malls. This type of franchise has emerged because it demands an extremely low outlay of capital and avoids long-term leases required by most franchisees. But expanding through standchising brings unique problems of management and control. A standchised business can use technology to maintain control. For a capital outlay of under $25,000, a franchisee like the Historical Research Center obtains a computer and the supplies to produce family-name histories printed on colorful placards. The computer contains an extensive name database, but the technology also comes into play when tracking sales. The franchisee pays a set fee and receives a "counter key" good for 250 outputs. The software key is loaded into the computer and the computer will print 250 name histories. The software program running on the computer operates only as long as the counter key is valid. After 250 prints, the computer locks until another key is installed. The franchisor can thus be assured that the franchisee is accurately reporting its sales.

New Technology for the 1990s

Many fast-food restaurants feel that their ability to compete in the future lies in providing fast service. Many realize that the increased efficiency from technology is one of the final frontiers of speedy service. With the goal of speed in mind, Wendy's[5] restaurants is testing an interesting POS system that involves a hand-held, wireless order-entry device that uses radio waves to transmit orders to the POS register. This speeds the ordering process, since it allows employees to greet the customers virtually at the door.

Symbol Technologies has developed a portable, wireless point-of-sale device to further automate retailing. The unit weighs two pounds and measures 8 by 9 by 2 inches. It is PC-compatible, has a full (small) keyboard and a magnetic stripe credit-card reader, and can print customer receipts. It can attach to a hand-held PC capable of scanning inventory tags for inventory audits, price markdowns, and orders. Using this technology, retailers can roam the store during busy times and "check people out."

How the Computer System Simplifies Business Operations

Although computer technology provides benefits to franchised businesses, in the past the expense of most sophisticated systems has prevented many from realizing these benefits. However, as the price of technology has fallen, an increasing number of franchises are taking advantage of the latest technology to gain a competitive edge. For instance, businesses in the quick-printing and custom-tailoring industries have used these systems to separate themselves from their competition, in both speed and quality of service. And many franchises are standardizing their business with intelligent point-of-sale terminals and high-power mainframes so that personnel, pricing, inventory, and back-order information is available to download to the franchisee system; this is the case, for example, in food and retailing businesses. Computers are able to take over many of the manual computing tasks that previously tied up management, putting businesspeople in a position to handle labor shortages and promote customer service. Integrated systems result in the minimum effort to transfer sales, inventory, and general ledger data from the franchisee's system to the host system in the franchisor's headquarters. Powerful new systems increase the accuracy and speed of this information transfer and better support nationally integrated sales and marketing programs.

From an integrated-systems base, the franchisor and franchisee have important data from which to determine the success of the franchise operation, make changes or improvements that need to be made, and determine how well they are responding to market needs.

NOTES

1. "Accounting for Remote Locations," *Management Accounting*, 73 (5) (November 1991), pp. 58–60.
2. "Success With Strings Attached," *Restaurant Hospitality*, 75 (1) (January 1991), pp. 112, 114.
3. "Point of Sale: Athlete's Foot Steps Up Inventory Control," *Chain Store Age Executive*, 66 (11) (November 1990), pp. 128, 130.
4. "POS Flexibility Keeps Remington Sharp," *Chain Store Age Executive*, 66 (7) (July 1990), pp. 49–50.
5. "Business Strategies: Food Fight," *Computerworld* (Section 2), (40) October 2, 1989, pp. 22–25.

8

Site Selection and Territorial Issues

Kenneth J. McGuire, Performance Group, Ltd.

Throughout my franchising career I've repeatedly encountered the weather-beaten rule of the three prerequisites for success in a small retail business. This is typically referred to as the Three L principle, or Location, Location, Location. From my perspective, the rule is at best a gross overstatement if not factually misleading. There are numerous elements that contribute to success in providing a product or service for the public. However, the most essential elements are a trio of factors I call "LOC," or Location, Operator, Commodity. There is no question that proper site selection is critical in most ventures providing a consumer service or product, but must be combined with the other two major ingredients. Moreover, location doesn't always warrant primary significance and is often superseded in importance by either the operator or the commodity. As a former fast-food franchisor, I placed tremendous emphasis on choosing excellent locations. Our company already had a high-quality product and strong trademark identification. Nevertheless, an inept franchisee or operator could not achieve optimum success, and in some cases avoid failure, through location and product acceptance alone. Likewise, the double drive-through hamburger operations—that is, Rally's and Central Park U.S.A.—go to extremes to secure prime locations in their targeted markets. This is because of the nature of their customer's eating needs and habits, but also because they would also suffer without the good commodity and management. At the other end of the spectrum, however, are franchises such as employment agencies, where operating management and the service or commodity offered takes precedence over location. Location, of course, cannot be totally ignored; it has to be accessible and inviting. Therefore, how important site selection is depends on the type of business. The extent to which the commodity for sale is predominantly an impulse or planned purchase is highly influential.

The importance of location, operator, and commodity must not only be acknowledged but also assigned sequential emphasis. This evaluative process is absolutely essential. Failure to acknowledge the interlocking relationship here could seriously impair a franchise system's growth and vitality. Ask yourself the question "If I had to choose only one of the three primary success elements, which two would I do without?'' If you are able to embrace one and discard the two others, you either have a problem with analysis or a nontypical business.

A Site-Acquisition Philosophy

One of the franchisor's early considerations in network building is formulating a policy regarding location. This policy can range from the very narrow to a quite diversified one. There are many variations and combination philosophies, including:

▲ Purchasing and developing vacant property, which requires extensive capital or borrowing capability, but certainly builds a strong real-estate asset base. Conversely, it could develop considerable potential liability, particularly if the company is overleveraged or the locations demand changes in the franchise system.

▲ Long-term leasing of property and erecting special buildings, which has the same potential advantages and disadvantages as purchasing and developing vacant property.

▲ Purchasing property by a sale-and-leaseback arrangement with a third-party investor. This approach allows a franchisor to acquire prime sites without a substantial investment in land and buildings, which in turn frees up capital for other growth objectives.

▲ Buying existing buildings and remodeling them to comply with standard program features, e.g., trade style, adaptability to equipment and fixture layout, and operational efficiency.

▲ Traditional leasing of existing premises from a third party. This is probably the most common technique, particularly in retailing. It requires the smallest initial capital outlay combined with the least down time between acquisition and commencing operations.

Determining which individual or combination of methods to employ for site acquisition involves both long- and short-term financial and marketing goals for the franchisor, as well as criteria for the franchise system, such as (1) desirability of maximizing the asset base for obtaining future debt or equity capital; (2) a preference toward real estate ownership for long-term asset appreciation; (3) the availability of desirable sites; and (4) the amount of control the franchisor desires over possession of the locations, as determined by the effect relocating might have on consumer patronage.

Selection Criteria

There are several criteria applicable to competent site selection, depending on the location's ability to capitalize on the franchise trademark and its commodity magnetism; that is, its influence in creating impulse versus planned consumer purchases.

Demographics

There is available vast information on demographics to use in site evaluation. Several companies specialize in providing that information—for example, Urban Decision Systems and CACI Marketing Systems.* Such information includes:

- ▲ Population density by ethnic, sex, marital status, age, and income categories
- ▲ Households by per capita and family income
- ▲ Owner and rental occupied units
- ▲ Property values
- ▲ Education
- ▲ Occupation
- ▲ Vehicle registrations
- ▲ Retail sales broken down by several product categories

This helpful information can be obtained for almost any community in the United States, and limited to specific mileage radii from a proposed targeted location.

Accessibility

Locations that require a high degree of vehicular traffic for maximum patronage have to be researched carefully with regard to accessibility. In such instances, the speed and flow of traffic are critical. Islands or other physical obstructions separating directional lanes must also be evaluated, as must be the positioning of traffic signals. Actual entry into and exit from the proposed location are also important. The density and regularity of traffic as to days of the week and time of the day must be ascertained. Even when vehicular and/or walking traffic is not significant, as in the case of home-delivery food franchises, some of the above are crucial with respect to delivery vehicles.

Market Range

Businesses vary with respect to the distance from which they can readily attract customers, ranging from several miles to eye visibility. Consequently, the fran-

---

*The addresses of these companies are as follows: Urban Decision Systems, 2040 Armacost Avenue, P.O. Box 25953, Los Angeles, CA 90025 and CACI Marketing Systems, 9302 Lee Highway, Fairfax, VA 22031.

chisor must know how well the location's position will attract maximum patronage from the primary and secondary market.

Residential vs. Commercial Mix

It is imperative that a franchise system's customer profile be clearly defined, and if that profile indicates a customer who comes from either the residential or commercial sector, or both, this information must enter the site-selection process.

Visibility

Franchisors with strong product recognition should continue to maximize efforts to display their recognizable mark. Consumer awareness grows in large part through repetition. Likewise, franchises with a strong impulse-purchase orientation should consider locations that permit product recognition.

Signage

This element is of major importance to most franchisors, particularly those in retailing and even more so when impulse purchasing is a major factor. Too often franchisors fail to check for either municipal or landlord signage regulations before the location is acquired. After acquisition, the battle for desirable or essential signage is either futile or at best one-sided. Matters such as size, materials, and construction of signage as well as permissibility of illumination and flexibility of placement *must* be determined before acquisition.

Longevity

All too often franchisors apply most of the criteria for location analysis but fail to objectively appraise the length of time they can economically remain there. Short-term desirabilities tend to camouflage the negative consequences of short-term possession. This is a major concern of franchisors that hold prime leases with parallel subleases to franchisees, who may have been granted franchise agreements that extend past the negotiated lease agreements. This often develops into a serious conflict when the lease expires and a comparable site is unobtainable.

Direct and Indirect Competition

Many franchisors attempt to locate as far from their direct competition as possible, whereas others seek locations in close proximity—for example, McDonald's, Burger King, and Wendy's. Whichever path a franchisor takes, it should be aware of all competitors considered helpful or distracting.

Tenant Combinations

Sometimes called piggyback franchising, the sharing of a location by two or more franchises is a recent trend. Certain franchisors, particularly those in fast-food retailing, not only want to locate in close proximity to an indirect competitor but choose to be either adjacent to or within the same location. The strategy is synergism, whereby differences in each competitor either offsets or augments their similarities. The piggybacking permits both businesses to deal with the same customer base during different time frames or satisfy compatible needs simultaneously. This theory, combined with the ability to share facilities, equipment, and personnel, enhances the economic picture. Although a relatively new marketing technique, it appears to have merit, and more examples of this strategy will emerge in the coming years.

Types of Locations

There are a wide variety of types of sites where a franchised business can be located. The franchiser should include in one development of its site selection criteria a profile of the ideal location, which may be in an enclosed mall or a shopping center, or may be a free-standing unit.

Enclosed Malls

The enclosed mall comes in a variety of sizes ranging from 200,000 square feet all the way up to 1 to 2 million square feet. Recently there have been efforts to build superregionals that exceed 3 million square feet and attract customers from hundreds of miles away. There are several advantages to enclosed malls, the major one being temperature uniformity. Climatization in combination with high tenant density and variety generally mean enormous traffic flows that would be otherwise unattainable. Another feature is the ability to promote the enclosed mall via advertising assessments and mandated expense requirements by each tenant. The resulting market penetration would certainly not be possible if individual tenants promoted their own businesses individually. However, these favorable factors are often outweighed by the extremely high occupancy cost, which often places operational expense far beyond the range for many franchise operations. Nevertheless, one cannot overlook the fact that locating in a major regional mall in a new market, where a franchisor's trademark or presence is either unknown or minimal, can gain rapid recognition and acceptance in a wide geographic area in a relatively short period of time.

Strip (Unclimatized) Shopping Centers

Outdoor shopping centers are the bastions of retail sales and service. Generally they are affordable and targeted to a relatively local consumer base. They are also usually much less strict with regard to regulatory uniformity and compliance, are more easily identified with a particular segment of the population, and are easier to negotiate terms in accordance with tenant needs and objectives. The strip center is probably a more desirable site for franchisors governed by planned purchasing, as opposed to impulse buying, and those less reliant on traffic flow.

In-Line (Storefront) Facility

Often these are desirable locations for tenants with unique, high-impulse, or strong repeat-oriented products or services. In-line positions often appeal to tenants offering either high-ticket unit prices requiring minimal traffic or low per capita sales offset by an unusually high traffic flow. Usually this type of location is most desirable by franchisors geared to walking patronage. Needless to say, these sites often suffer from relatively poor parking availability. On the other hand, they often provide good billboard sites by virtue of their signage visibility to fast-moving, high-density vehicular traffic.

Downtown Business Districts

In a highly active business district, this type of location can generate substantial traffic if the product or service is targeted to the office worker, city dweller, or in-town shopper. Prime downtown locations are not easily obtained, are extremely expensive, and usually entail relatively short-term leases. Moreover, businesses that benefit most from that type of location must be able to generate most of their revenue during work days, since traffic comes to a virtual halt in the evenings, on weekends, and on holidays.

Specialized Shopping Complexes

Depending upon customer profile, product or service characteristics, and price structure, there are locations available within environments that attract high-volume, specialized traffic. These include discount or factory outlet centers that have one or more well-known major tenants offering substantial price advantages often combined with name-brand merchandise. There are also "power" centers that combine several small retailers with one or more high-profile, effective merchandisers with substantial consumer appeal.

Public Facilities

More and more franchisors are seeking high-rent locations in periodic high-traffic facilities designed for noncommercial functions. Included in this category are sports stadiums, airports, universities, military bases, and hospital complexes. Although these sites produce considerable pedestrian traffic during specific times and events, they are governed by irregular traffic patterns.

There may be other, less popular location categories that have been over-looked here. And undoubtedly new location categories will emerge as commerce changes and entrepreneurial imagination expands. Nevertheless, these examples cover the vast majority of possible franchise locations.

The Economics of Location

No matter how potentially viable or alluring a prospective location might be, acquisition should never be undertaken without a careful analysis of both the cost of acquisition, if any, and also the expense involved in getting the location oper-ational, as well as ongoing total occupancy costs. There are endless examples of locations that were analyzed and met all demographic criteria, but proved unprof-itable because of overbearing acquisition and occupancy costs. Certainly, occu-pancy costs—since they are ongoing—are critical and deserve greater scrutiny. Nonetheless, the cost of obtaining and readying a site must also receive proper attention.

Land and/or Building Costs

The maximum amount allocable to land or building costs depends on whether or not the franchisor intends to retain these assets for appreciation and/or resale. The alternative is to acquire the land and/or building as part of an eventual franchise purchase; in that event the acquisition portion of the total investment significantlys affects the projected return on investment, as well as the potential for recruiting prospective franchisees.

Site Preparation

Purchasing land with the intention of building demands intensive study of certain factors:

- Condition and composition of soil, excavation difficulty, drainage, and EPA regulations
- Proximity of water, sewer, and power
- Restrictive easements
- Accessibility to vehicular thoroughfares

Renovations Costs

In general, leasing of existing premises is most common for franchisers. Unfor-tunately, in too many instances, there is insufficient time and effort spent deter-mining the conditions of those premises and existing problems in need of correc-tion. Typical problems include the ease and efficiency of operation as well as municipal ordinances, which can vary considerably from community to county to state. Moreover, these ordinances often require corrective action ranging from minor to major expenses. Yet remedying these deficiencies could be too expensive. Some problems fall into different departmental jurisdictions, requiring negotiations with several different authorities in addition to the landlord. These can include plumbing, electrical system, structural problems, sanitation, fire protection, and provisions for handicapped customers.

Depending upon the viability of the location, and the relative willingness of the lessor and lessee to make a deal, responsibility for correcting these deficiencies can be negotiated.

Control of Premises

There are divergent views regarding who should have ultimate legal possession of the premises—the franchisor or franchise operator. The largest factor is the importance of location continuity for operational success. In those systems where location is critical, the franchisor needs to be able to repossess the premises. When location is of importance, the franchisor usually requires that the franchise holder purchase or lease his own location. In so doing, the franchisor may aid the franchisee to negotiate the lease, but is usually not obligated to fulfill its obligations. Occasionally, to enable the franchisee to secure a desirable location, particularly one with competitive bidders, the franchisor might guarantee the franchisee's performance to either a limited or full degree. When the franchisor finds it either desirable or essential to have ultimate control, there are two major methods to accomplish this.

PRIME AND SUBLEASES

Franchisors who demand eminent control over selected locations usually negotiate and execute the prime lease with the landlord, even though they then assume liability for nonperformance and are not the actual occupant. To offset that disadvantage, the franchisor subleases the premises to the franchise holder under the same terms and conditions, with a rental often higher by a certain amount. The franchisor then has contractual recourse to his franchisee or sublessee for uncured infractions. In the event of termination of the sublease or threatened termination of the prime lease, the franchisor can, through appropriate legal action, continue occupancy of the premises. One essential aspect in this approach is the understanding in the sublease that loss of the franchise can be considered a default on the lease, resulting in its termination.

COLLATERAL LEASE ASSIGNMENT

An alternative to the prime-sublease arrangement is to have the franchisee enter into a direct lease with the landlord and simultaneously execute what is called a Collateral Assignment of Lease. This document, signed by the prime landlord, the franchisor, and the franchisee, provides that, under specific uncured default conditions caused by the franchisee (lessee), and at the sole option of the franchisor, the lease would inure back to the franchisor. This is probably the most realistic approach, in that it gives the franchisor ultimate control over the location, at its election, in lieu of involuntary assumption of considerable liability as prime tenant.

DIRECT LEASE

The most common method employed by franchisors, surprisingly, is a direct lease between the owner of the premises and the franchisee, with no contingent rights accruing to the franchisor, under the premise that there is no ongoing or contingent liability. That might be a sound practice when the relationship with a landlord is for a single location. However, when there are multiple locations, with major national developers or landlords, the franchisor is perceived to be the principal responsible party and is looked upon to fulfill the conditions of the lease, even though not legally required to do so. Therefore, although the franchisor may not be bound to perform, failure to do so usually impairs, if not ends, any future relationship with such a multiple-location landlord.

In summation, what is the best leasing option depends on the economic liabilities of controlling and retaining a location, as opposed to a possible forced relocation to a site of lesser viability, with the accompanying potential of diminished consumer patronage and identification.

Occupancy Cost

There is still a big "if to acquire" consideration: the initial economic burden, whether assumed by the franchisor or ultimately taken over by the franchise owner. Unfortunately, many prospective lessees confine their evaluation to the base rent obligation without due regard for the numerous additional rental charges. It is a grave mistake and a common error to overrationalize the maximum contractual rental ratio to reasonable projected sales. If the total rental charges or occupancy costs exceed that maximum ratio, the location is unlikely to be viable. It is an even greater and more common error to fail to include the often hard-to-calculate miscellaneous charges with the base rental when evaluating that maximum ratio. Depending upon the type of location, these additional charges include:

- Common area maintenance costs
- Real estate taxes
- Insurance
- Merchant association assessments
- Heat and air-conditioning
- Excess percentage rent based on sales

It is not unusual for miscellaneous charges to exceed the base rental on a per square-foot basis. Obviously, they can't be overlooked.

Liability

Finally, no lease, regardless of the location's perceived viability or acceptable economics, is properly balanced unless it contains a mutual, although differing, limit on the lessor and lessee exposure. A landlord should expect a certain minimum dollar productivity from each tenant to maximize the total value and appeal of his complex. Likewise, the tenant should be subject to limited penalty for an inability to maintain the operation in business despite full compliance with the lease and all reasonable efforts to perform profitably. These exposure limits should be negotiated and incorporated in the lease agreement for ultimate implementation without the necessity of costly litigation.

Types of Territorial Protection

One of the most complex and adversarial issues in franchising is territorial sovereignty, or what I call the ''noncompetition fallacy.'' It's a common but mistaken belief among franchisees that territorial exclusivity is directly related to economic results, or the less competition, the broader the potential market. Nothing could be further from reality. On the contrary, well-planned and encouraged competition nurtures consumer activity and contributes to faster and greater success. It is not always easy to convey such a free-enterprise philosophy to prospective or existing franchisees. There are, however, several different ways to contractually address the matter of competition. Some of these restraints are external, while others are internal.

External Competition Restraints

Almost all retail leases have so-called retail restriction covenants that prohibit a tenant from locating another unit offering the same or similar products or services within a prescribed distance from the leased location. Usually the distance is arbitrary and varies depending on tenant category. Obviously, the landlord's intent is to prohibit duplicate tenancy in a competitive center; the radius restriction typically is much broader than justifiable for the retailer. Unquestionably, this type of competitive restriction—dictated by an external party—should be vigorously opposed and every effort be made to remove it from the lease. If removal is impossible, then the restrictive clause should agree with the distance normally granted to a franchisee in the system, if that is the practice.

On the other hand, most landlords will not agree to tenant exclusivity, and normally refuse any prohibition against tenant duplication. Although many landlords try to establish and maintain a balanced tenant mix, some abuse their reserved right and subject tenants to damaging competition. In such circumstances a franchisor cannot control the competitive situation nor protect its franchisee from severe competition. The franchisor is powerless to prevent restrictions or control competition that materialize outside the franchise system.

Internal Restrictions and Competitions

The most common form of territorial protection relates to a single-location franchise, whereby the franchisee must operate his business from a specific, pre-approved location. With this type of franchise it is customary to provide exclusivity ranging from minimal to extensive. From the franchisor's perspective, the protective radius should not be one bit greater than required to give the franchisee a reasonable opportunity to capture and retain an acceptable market share. There should be a formula uniformly applied throughout the system, based on factors such as population density, proximity of nonsystem competition, projected growth for the area, and prior system experience. The formula should also be flexible enough to compensate for changing demographics or extraordinary circumstances. It is most important that the franchisor clarify the extent to which the protective covenant applies. Except in rare cases, the protection should only prohibit the franchisor from establishing another corporate or franchise unit within the restricted area; it should normally not prohibit the franchisee from marketing her product or service outside of the area nor should it prohibit another franchised unit from locating outside the protected territory. This is a free-enterprise matter that should be resolved solely by the parties to the competition.

There's no avoiding the sensitive and intense nature of exclusivity. The most practical solution is for the franchisor to develop criteria that are consistently applied to all corporate-owned and -operated facilities.

Territory Licenses

Another, broader form of noncompetitive protection is afforded to an area or territorial licensee wherein the franchisee is granted geographical sovereignty for an entire community, county, or even larger jurisdiction in return for establishing a mutually agreeable number of additional franchised units within the territory. Regardless of the range of competitive protection offered by a franchisor, there are at least two quasi-protective devices that are frequently employed.

▲ *Limited Exclusivity.* The franchisor reserves the right to establish other franchised locations within the same primary market or trading area in which the franchisee is located, but stipulates a maximum allowable number subject to changes in demographics. It also provides a minimum radius from the franchisee's location within which none of the permitted additional units will be placed.

▲ *Conditional Exclusivity.* As an alternative to limited exclusivity, a franchisor may grant competitive protection to a franchisee for a single-location franchise or a geographic territory, provided the franchisee achieves minimal annual sales per operating unit. Should the franchisee fail to meet those goals, the exclusivity ceases and the franchisor may establish additional units within the territory.

Notwithstanding these options, some franchisors steadfastly refuse to grant any type of competitive protection because of the complexities of establishing an equitable formula. Franchisors prefer to rely on their own experience and fairness to expand their system and position locations in the best interests of the system as well as its individual units. This approach can work well when the franchisees and franchisors have confidence in and respect for each other.

Regardless of which territorial-protection technique is employed, generally no restrictions should be placed on how far-reaching a franchisee's marketing efforts can extend. As stated earlier, within certain parameters, franchise holders should be able to sell their wares to customers anywhere from their franchised location or territory.

Methods for Determining Exclusive Territories

There are two separate but related aspects to the concept of exclusivity. One involves determining the extensiveness of an exclusive area surrounding a franchised location so that it is sufficient to enable the franchise owner to achieve maximum productivity but not so broad as to prevent or impede the franchisor's need to obtain optimum market share. The other relates to establishing the geographic boundaries within which the exclusive franchisee has the obligation to franchise and/or own and operate a minimum number of units.

In either instance, the objectives of franchisor and franchisee are in opposition to each other. The franchisee would like to secure as much restricted territory and as minimal a unit quota as possible, whereas the franchisor's goal is to minimize the geographic exclusivity and optimize the replication of units in order to achieve maximum market coverage. It should be the franchisor's self-imposed, disciplined mandate to manage this conflict with consistency and firmness tempored by prudent foresight. This can only be accomplished by steadfastly embracing two principles: (1) don't grant excessive territory that might hinder optimum growth by virtue of the exclusive franchisee's inactivity; and (2) only award exclusivities that retain flexibility for modification owing to changing market conditions or improved marketing knowledge.

Of course, the ultimate best solution is for the franchisor to develop irrefutable historical evidence of (1) the maximum effective radius of a unit with various population densities, (2) the minimum population serviceable without competition from another unit within the system, and (3) the expected effect on revenue stream of one unit by addition of another unit within the shortest practical distance. Once that information is documented, it becomes much easier for a franchisor to deal with the controversial issue of territorial exclusivity.

Determining the grantable geographic exclusivity to a single franchise is uncomplicated once the franchisor establishes the maximum customer base unaffected by additional competition. Resolving the issue of territorial exclusivity with respect to an area-development franchise requires settling the single-unit exclusivity issue plus dealing with the additional and more complex issue of the number of units to appropriately serve the markets within the territory, both currently as well as in the future.

Likewise, defining geographic boundaries in an area-development franchise is relatively simple as long as the methodology is consistent. Most commonly, it is based on multiples of contiguous communities, cities, counties, states, or population clusters established as metropolitan statistical areas (MSAs), or areas of dominant influence (ADIs), which are often used by franchisors whose products or services are heavily marketed via television. Some franchise systems—such as those marketing automotive products or office supplies or those marketing their product or service via direct mail—might use automotive registrations, business licenses applications, or zip codes to determine the size and boundaries of an exclusive territory.

Whichever methodology is employed, it should be intelligent, rational, mutually agreeable, and clearly defined in an exhibit attached to and part of the franchise agreement, including conditions under which the exclusivity could be either withdrawn or modified.

Conclusion

Site evaluation and selection is far from pure science. It's an art, the intricacies of which vary from one franchise system to another. As a franchise system matures, however, the techniques for proper site selection should improve. There's no question that time-tested methods and disciplined evaluation criteria are essential. Although gut feeling often influences a decision, emotions should be minimized and nonstatistical rationalization discounted. When an evaluation process proceeds from past experience and is reliable, it should be implemented and followed. On the other hand, since business and economic conditions are constantly changing, no selection process should be etched in stone. It should be reviewed regularly and modified as required. Despite various evaluation techniques, it is naïve to not recognize that site selection is often determined by intuitive judgment. It is equally foolhardy to forget that straying from objectivity can be fraught with risk.

Most experienced franchisors make few mistakes in location evaluation when they use appropriate criteria. Rather, the facts and other information on which they base their decision change after acquisition. Because of that possibility, and because location "inadequacy" is often one of the major complaints in litigation between franchisors and franchisees, franchisors should anticipate change and incorporate a disclaimer in the franchise offering circular that rejects liability for location selection, based on the inability to predict changes in demographics, competitive factors, or other obstacles over which the franchisor has no control.

Above all else, the franchisor should never "fall in love" with a proposed location if the economics don't measure up. Rationalizing high occupancy costs puts the landlord in the driver's seat and usually leads to disaster. Always have at least one substitute location if the numbers aren't right. An alternative site selection that more favorably meets overall criteria will invariably prove superior to one that appears preferable to the eye but can't pass muster in the "head."

9

Demographic and Marketing Analysis in Site Selection

Gary Blake, The Blake Group, Inc.

Since the infant days of the franchise industry and the signing of the first franchise agreement, every franchisor (and franchisee) has been on the hunt for the ultimate franchise location—that singular property which will generate the highest possible revenue in its market. Of course, back in the 1950s, there wasn't the volume and quality of information that is available today. However, since that first franchise agreement, and the first store opened, franchisors have followed one basic rule: *location, location, location.* As Ghosh and McLafferty (1987) tell us:

> In the extremely competitive retail environment, even slight differences in location can have a significant impact on the market share and profitability. Most importantly, since store location is a long-term fixed investment, the disadvantages of a poor location are difficult to overcome.[1]

Even with the enormous changes in franchising in the last forty years, and with the ever-increasing diversity of the American population, the basic rules haven't changed much. What has changed is the information available to locate a new franchise and how to analyze that information. Not too long ago demographic and market analysis for franchise site location consisted, at best, of looking at a series of basic census data reports. If a company were somewhat sophisticated, the potential locations would be mapped out, complete with red dots and three-mile radii (drawn with the appropriate size coffee cup) on a Rand-McNally map. Then the director of real estate would hop on a plane for a trip to the target market and tour the available real estate with a local broker, getting a firsthand look at locations and local site issues.

In the 1990s and beyond, the key to continued growth of franchise systems is the franchisor's ability to adapt to an increasingly diverse landscape. As the industry grows and matures, and as competition continues to intensify, competition for prime sites also intensifies. Franchisors are forced to find better and more innovative methods of designing territory strategies, locating and evaluating sites, and delivering marketing support at the local level. The ultimate test of strength for any franchise system is how each *individual* unit performs, and the ultimate measure of success is the return on investment (ROI) generated by each franchisee. Therefore, a key challenge facing every franchisor today is how to quickly identify the factors that determine a successful franchise location. Beyond that is the need to minimize risk for both franchisor and franchisee through better information, including better demographic and market analysis. The result is better and more informed business decisions.

However, be forewarned. More information does not guarantee more informed business decisions. Better decisions come from a rigorously defined process that lifts out necessary information from the deluge of data now available. And in the end, no matter how much information is gathered and analyzed, there is always risk attached to the site-location process. As opening day approaches for each location, the team will always wonder, "Will they come?"

To attain a better perspective on demographic and market analysis in site location, let's take a brief look back in time.

Location, Location, Location—1950s

The 1950s. We all have an image of that decade when life was simple and uncluttered. The United States had just emerged victorious from World War II, and even a bad Korean experience couldn't put a damper on the enthusiasm felt from coast to coast. As Frank Flack, one of the founders of the International Franchise Association (IFA), tells it:

> Eisenhower initiated the country's first mass transportation system and the Interstate Highway system (which gave Holiday Inn and McDonald's their prime exit locations). Shopping malls and strip centers were just beginning to be an influence on American shopping habits. There were no FTC regulations, no state regulations, and there was no such thing as a Uniform Franchise Offering Circular (UFOC).

The country was ready to fulfill its destiny, and the infant known as "franchising" was ready to play an important part. With a wide-open market and pent-up demand for consumer goods and services, all signs pointed toward a rosy business future: "In the 1940 census . . . the population of the country was put at 131,669,275. Three years later, the Bureau announced confidently that, with birth rates declining and immigration unlikely to be of any great future consequence, the nation's head count would reach its ultimate peak in 1980, at 153,000,000. That figure was passed in 1951."[2]

Ralph Weiger, one of the early Midas executives, in recalling what it was like during the heady days of their growth, said that the company simply "looked for a site with 100,000 population and 50,000 cars. It had to be a visible location, didn't have to be on a corner, had to be findable, and had to have the proper zoning.'' He then went on to say that the site needed to be ''a good site for twenty years. If we had chosen a downtown Cleveland location, it might have been bombed out twice by now. On the other hand, a location on the edge of Chicago would now be in the center of the market.''

There was a lot of art and little science in site location in those days, primarily because there was very little census data or other market information available to franchisors. But in the last few decades, the census—which has been the basis for much of the information used by franchisors in site-location work—has evolved from what was basically a head count, used primarily for congressional redistricting and allocation of federal funds, to ''a collective portrait of the American population's race, income, employment, education, housing and commuting habits. The census provides the underpinnings for most marketing plans. As computer modeling has expanded, the data have become crucial to consumer profiles, test-market selections and new-product development.''[3]

Location, Location, Location—Forty Years Later

According to Tom Krieck, director of marketing analysis at Avis Rent A Car System, ''The selection of a potential site for a future facility is accomplished through the interactions of various data sources. It is a combination of our internal proprietary data with demographic and syndicated data. . . . The internal data is composed of two years' worth of current customers with the appropriate geo-code variables.''

Even the way we talk about site selection in the 1990s might sound like a foreign language to most people. Franchise companies *are* becoming more sophisticated in their approach to site selection and demography. That's because as we move toward the next century, a strong site-location program will continue to be a significant factor contributing to continued profitable growth of franchise systems. Franchisors will find it imperative to have better and more innovative ways to design territory-development stategies. It is quite likely that new and better demographic and life-style information, as well as new distribution channels, will lead to new location possibilities and strategies, just as the development of shopping malls and strip centers led to new and better locations in the 1960s and 1970s.

Improved methods of site location and evaluation, and delivery of better marketing support to franchisees at the local market level, will be prerequisites to a successful franchise program. In fact, savvy franchisees will put pressure on the franchisor to better understand and deal with local market information and issues in order to ensure better site locations and a reasonable return on investment. In turn, as the franchisor becomes more adept at dealing with the local markets, there may develop a stronger franchisor-franchisee relationship.

Site Location and the Information Age

Rapid advances in technology and technologically driven strategic planning systems, coupled with more and better data, offer a viable solution to the problems franchisors now face in real estate development, site location, and strategic planning. The foundation for these information systems is the 1990 census, whose TIGER database (Topographically Integrated Geographic Encoding and Referencing) links detailed geographic and visual information with customer and market data. Now, franchisors can create proprietary definitions of customer profiles to drive an integrated site-location and marketing process.

The 1990 Census

There was a plethora of population and marketing studies during the 1980s, and many of them were able to give site location and marketing departments the information they needed to make informed decisions. However, the 1990 census provides information that gives every company the unprecedented ability to look into the future. Some of the key factors the census shows are:

- Twenty-three million Americans will be added to the 1980 national head count, for a total of 250 million, an increase of 10%.
- Immigration was the biggest reason for that uptick. The Asian population has grown by 65%, doubling its population share to 3% since 1980.
- The number of Hispanics has increased by 44% and now accounts for 8% of all Americans, up from 6%.
- Blacks maintain their 12% share of the population base.
- The population continues to shift toward the South and the West.
- While cities continue to lose residents, the metropolitan areas surrounding them continue to grow.
- Sixty percent of the growth of the labor force can be attributed to women.

An obvious question is: Just how good are the census and the census data? In 1940, the census missed 7.9 million persons, or 5.6 percent. It is estimated that the 1990 census missed 4.7 million persons, or 1.9 percent. The census bureau provided several programs to validate the data it collected. A local review program provided preliminary reports to 39,000 local governments, giving them an opportunity to review the numbers for their area and challenge them. Any changes in the numbers had to be backed up with solid evidence (tax records, building permits, etc.). Only one in six local governments gave any type of response. Coverage and undercount are being handled by statistical adjustment. As an additional checkpoint, the bureau conducted a post-enumeration survey of

150,000 households to determine whether or not each of these households participated or were counted in the census. The census bureau has determined that sample size is reliable. Three-fourths of the census data come from a sampling of one out of six households, or 17 million. Finally, expanded geographic coverage by the census bureau means expanded small-area coverage. There are three times as many census blocks in 1990, and as a result there is now more geographic detail along with a new geographic hierarchy.

The site-location implications of this detailed information are staggering. For instance, cross-referencing client files with TIGER files and large databases allows real estate divisions to locate and rank markets with large numbers of non-customers sharing similar attributes of the company's current customer profile.

Information Technology and Micromarketing

In the early 1900s pedestrian counts were used to locate tobacco shops. Today's needs are more sophisticated. The availability of information at the household level, and the recognition that we need information portrayed graphically to understand it more easily, has given birth to a new discipline—micromarketing. The original micromarket was a one-on-one relationship between a buyer and seller who knew each other in a village setting. But this relationship changed as America moved from an agricultural to an industrial society. Now, paradoxically, as we become an information-based society, we are moving back to a one-on-one relationship with customers. However, this time around the relationship will be much more impersonal, since it will be driven by large databases.

There is a wealth of information available on U.S. households. Want to know the net worth of households in the trade area of a proposed location? Is the presence of children important to your business? You can easily access the information. In fact, up to 350 variables are given for household data. Soon it will be possible to look inside the household at characteristics of individuals residing there. As an example, in the 1990 census, it was discovered that 24 percent of all single adults between ages twenty-five and thirty-four reside at home with their parents. Information like this could have considerable impact in choice of location.

Today's micromarketing is built on the premise that understanding the dynamics of the household and business worlds is prerequisite to a site-location strategy. In the United States alone, over 90 million households and over 9 million business locations have been geo-coded—that is, they have been assigned a precise latitude and longitude—in a database. Other important databases have been linked to these household and business databases, including demographic, lifestyle, automobile, and market-potential databases. Additionally, there are syndicated databases such as MediaMark Research (MRI) and Simmons and Stanford Research's (SRI) VALS and VALS II.

There can be no doubt that we are in the midst of an information revolution. The keys to this revolution are (1) the realization that *geography* is the common denominator to all site location and marketing decisions; (2) phenomenal growth in the capability of microcomputers, coupled with a dramatic drop in computer prices; (3) the rapidly increasing amount and quality of data available; and (4) integration of data elements with mapping software. As a result, a franchisor can usually understand critical data immediately, instead of having to wade through streams of confusing, disjointed facts.

Some of the key data available to link up with proprietary company data are:

- ▲ Demographic characteristics (age, sex, income)
- ▲ Geographic characteristics (MSAs, ADIs, Interstates, streets, highways, neighborhoods)
- ▲ Life-style characteristics (product purchasing behavior, psychographics)
- ▲ Business locations (malls, strip centers, competitors)
- ▲ Automobile information (make, model, year)
- ▲ Media consumption patterns (TV, radio, print, direct)

This information, when linked with sales data on existing stores, allows the development of a predictive sales model. In addition, the data on households gives real estate and marketing people the insight into factors that make a good location good and a distressed location bad.

However, even though technology has extraordinary potential, the rules that have always applied to franchise growth strategies, including territory and site location, remain: (1) a company must have a thorough understanding of all aspects of a problem to find a viable solution; and (2) no computer system or information base can replace common sense and creative thinking. Franchisors still need a good intuitive sense. And some very basic questions must be answered:

- ▲ Where are you now?
- ▲ Where are you going?
- ▲ How do you get there?

The "New" Geography

Asking and answering the basic business questions is best done in the new context of today's trade areas. This means learning the "new" geography.

Utilizing data as previously described has led to a new way of looking at markets. It is particularly important to understand the implications of two critical factors in site location. In gaining this understanding, the franchisor creates a new way of looking at present and future markets, on the basis of valid information.

1. *Trade-area dynamics vs. market-area dynamics.* Typically, a franchise license is granted for a particular "geography," such as a three-mile radius from the store location, or a population of 100,000 in a radius from the store location.

While this may provide a good legal definition, frequently more than 25 percent to 40 percent of a retail location's business comes from outside that specified trade area. This influences the franchisor's development strategy, site-location process, and marketing support programs. It is crucial that the franchisor be aware of the difference between a defined trade area and the *actual* market area.

2. *Demographic profile vs. actual target customer profile.* Franchisors frequently create a demographic profile in the absence of valid criteria. But a target customer profile should *always* start with actual customer names, addresses, and sales data. With this information, a precise target definition can be created. This definition can then be used to better support existing locations and be the basis for developing the site-location process.

Building a Site-Location Process

Sound planning reduces risk. Good information reduces the risk of unsound planning. We all know there is nothing more expensive than opening a franchise in a poor location. So make a resolution now that future location decisions will not be made without the *right* information.

In fact, the best franchise systems recognize the value of information gathering and sharing. A few astute franchisors have linked their corporate planning, operations, and marketing functions with their real estate division. Thus, site location is part of their integrated corporate strategy.

There are some key questions that all departments need to answer.

A process that answers these questions enables the franchisor to determine where, and in what order, new units should be opened. Fortunately, the answers are readily available.

1. *Who are the customers?* If the past, finding this information meant undertaking expensive primary research. Now the answer is affordable; all that is required is a valid number of customer addresses. With this list, up to 350 demographic and life-style variables can be appended at the household level, leading to a rich information base that goes beyond demographics to include media habits, product purchase habits, and sports habits. Of all the information, the most important is an understanding of which key customer types drive the majority of the business. This is typically achieved through "clustering," a system of looking at "like" individuals displaying similar geographic, demographic, and life-style characteristics.

The Appendix to this chapter contains examples of clustering data put together by different companies.

2. *Where are the customers?* Once a franchisor knows precisely where the customers live relative to its store locations, because all information is now in the context of geography, there is, in effect, a digital pin map of individual trade areas and the *actual* trade-area dynamics.

3. *How can we find more of the "right" customers?* Once the target customer is clearly defined, the next task is to find markets and subsequently trade areas that have a high concentration of target customers. Using micromarket technology automates what once was a tedious process. Using a cluster definition and key demographic and/or geographic variables, a microcomputer system "scans" the entire country using a set definition and criteria for the target customer. The country is then mapped and prioritized to allow development matching the company's opportunities and resources. But don't get fooled by the beauty of the maps. Franchisors still need to interpret the information. It's not uncommon for a state like Montana or Utah to show great target customer potential for a franchise system. The only problem is, not too many people live in those wide-open spaces.

4. *Where are the competitors located?* Often the success or failure of a location depends partly on the existence or absence of competition. For most retail locations, it is frequently critical to know precisely where the competitor is located relative to an existing or proposed location. Several business databases have been geo-coded, including Dun & Bradstreet's *BusinessLine* and NDS/Equifax's Business-Facts. Thus, you can map out competitive locations inside a given trade area and make the appropriate decision about the site. Competition may or may not be a factor for a service concept; however, if you are in a service business, do not neglect to consider the ramifications of competition.

5. *What is the market potential for the product or service?* Having found a high concentration of target customers and a prospective site, and having located the competition, it is imperative that the franchisor complete a market-potential study. Market-potential information is readily available in report form from models based on the U.S. Census of Retail Trade. These reports are available from Claritas, DMIS, NDS/Equifax, and other sources, including syndicated sources such as MRI or Simmons. No decision should be made about a site without studying both current and forecast market-potential information. Then the franchisor creates user pie charts. (See Figure 9-1.) These charts show market share for each of the competitors or for each of the users by market segment.

To help better understand the process, see Figure 9-2, which outlines the primary steps that must be taken in the site-location process.

In the Field

Having the best information and a sound strategy is just the beginning point. Remember, decisions about where to locate a site cannot be made in a vacuum. It is equally important to understand the dynamics of each community in which you will be doing business. That requires field work before a final site decision is made and time to consider the *ABC*s of site location:

Figure 9-1. Pie charts for market potential.

User Frequency

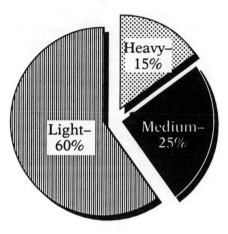

Competitive Market Share

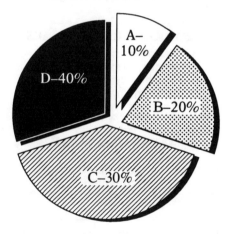

Figure 9-2. The franchise development process.

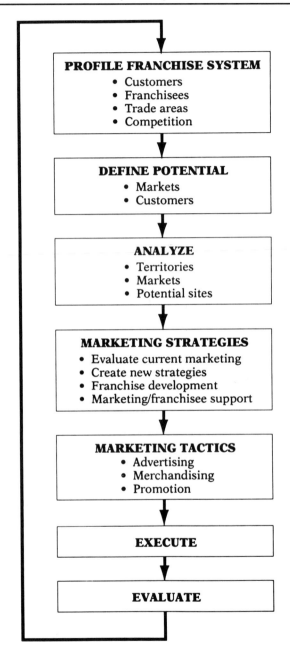

▲ *A* is for area: Feel the area, see the area, get in touch with property owners. Don't forget to talk to the property owners about the area as well as to the people at the courthouse. If you are not sure which department in city hall or the courthouse has the information you need, stop into any of the offices and tell them what you need; they should be happy to give you that information. . . .

▲ *B* is for best site. Keep the time crunch and your franchisee's *needs* on your mind. . . . How would I feel or what would I want if I were the franchisee? Location, location, location is important in real estate, but Better, Better, Better is critical!

▲ *C* is for competition. Your basic steps are to: Analyze the competition; check your user pie; and choose a site that is best. Love your ''other.'' Learn from your competition. Sharpen your skills and expertise against his experience and go for it. Take the *leading edge*.[4]

The Real Estate Broker

The right real estate broker is an essential element in any site search. Find a broker who is a Certified Commercial Investment Member (CCIM) of the Realtors National Marketing Institute. They know the market and their business. Screen at least three brokers and pick the one who can best serve your company's needs. The right broker can speed up the site-location process because he or she knows the idiosyncrasies of the local market. The broker also can point you to the right people at the courthouse or city hall.

The Courthouse and City Hall

The county courthouse can give you a good indication of the county's posture toward real estate and development. In the last few years, land-use planning has taken on ever-increasing importance. The county's comprehensive land-use plan may have a significant impact on your growth plans in the local market. Review it carefully, and if your planned location is within the city limits, be sure you also visit city hall. Study the zoning laws. They can affect factors other than just proposed usage, including parking, setbacks, and landscaping. Then study the four zoning ''what's'':

1. What's in?
2. What's under construction?
3. What's been announced to start?
4. What's in the throes of getting approval?

Other Departments

While you're in the courthouse or city hall, don't just quit when you've reviewed land-use and zoning issues. Visit the city manager, if possible. Schedule meetings with the county and city economic development departments. Educate them about franchising and the positive impact it can have on a community. Find out if there are small-business programs available for your franchisee. Be an ambassador for your company and for franchising.

And don't stop there. Visit all the other departments, too. The building department can provide you with the information and timing required for a building permit. The engineering department can assist you regarding pertinent ordinances and state and regional issues, if any. The utility department will provide information on critical utilities and fees for water, sewer, gas, electric, and telephone services. Study transportation issues, review tax issues. Don't hesitate to ask questions. Remember, these people work for you—the taxpayer or potential taxpayer.

To make your visit easier, prepare a checklist prior to viewing a market. Take copious notes, and come away from your visit with a feel for the local people and politics.

Will They Come?

You've done all the homework. You've found the best franchisee, the best market information and the best location, with the right number of target customers in your new trade area. You're ready for the grand opening of another franchise location. If you're like everyone else, you're a little nervous as opening day approaches. You're asking yourself: Will they come? Fortunately, because you *have* done all your homework, you can also identify every prospect within the defined trade area.

A fundamental element of every grand opening is the opening promotion. In some cases, there are already enough locations in the local market to support broadcast, print, and direct mail advertising. In many cases, there aren't enough units to justify the costs of broadcast advertising. What then?

Don't overlook the old standby, the local newspaper. And don't forget that one medium on its own is not as powerful as multiple media. Look at direct mail possibilities; the same micromarket technology that helps you develop a precise customer profile also allows you to find every household that matches your profile on an location-by-location basis. In fact, you can now order a mailing list complete with a telemarketing list, and have it delivered to your office on a magnetic tape or labels within days. You can create the proper media mix as well, because of information at the neighborhood level on micromarket media habits. Television viewership, radio listening habits, magazine and newspaper readership, direct mail responsiveness, coupon response, and promotion responsiveness are all measured, and the information allows you to create a more intelligent, workable, and measurable strategy.

In summary, institute a well-defined site-location process. Gather the right information. Visit the market. Pay attention to detail. Balance it all with common sense. Then there is no reason you should lose any sleep wondering, "Will they come?"

NOTES

1. J. J. Ghosh and S. L. McLafferty, "Locating Stores in Uncertain Environments: A Scenario Planning Approach," *Journal of Retailing* (1982).
2. E. J. Khan, Jr., *The American People* (New York: Weybright and Talley, 1973).
3. Nancy Youman, "Re-mapping the American People, Block by Block," *Adweek's Marketing Week* (April 9, 1990), pp. 2–3.
4. Kay Whitehouse, "Site Selection: Finding and Developing Your Best Location" (Pa.: Liberty, House, 1990).

Appendix to Chapter 9

Examples of Clustering Data From Several Companies

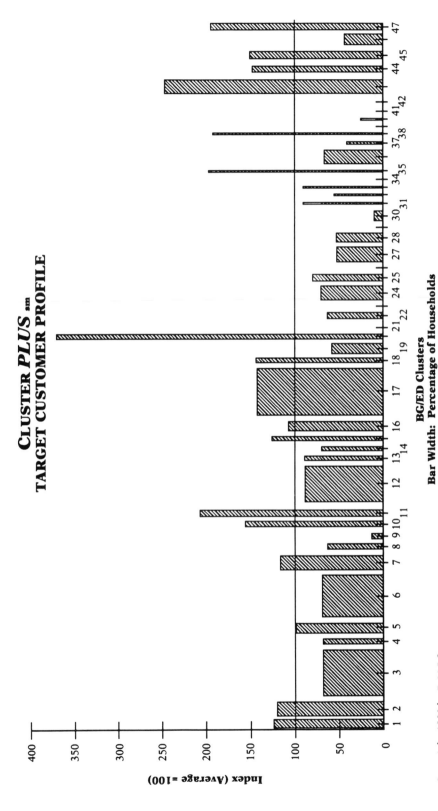

Cluster *PLUS* sm
TARGET CUSTOMER PROFILE

Index (Average = 100)

BG/ED Clusters
Bar Width: Percentage of Households

Copyright 1990 by D.M.I.S.

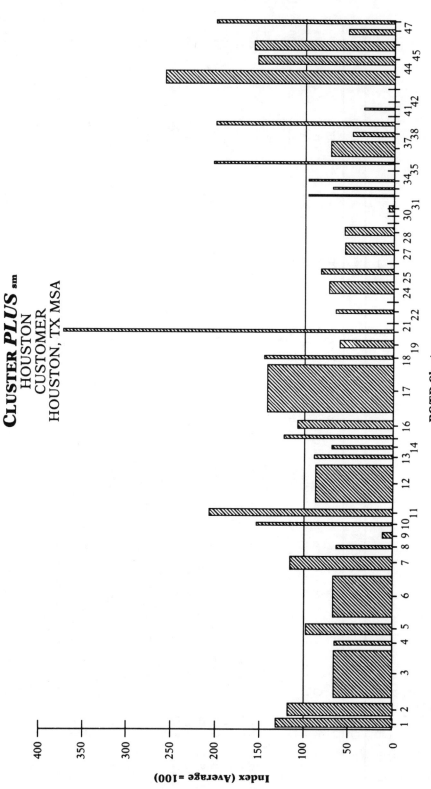

CLUSTER PLUS sm
HOUSTON
CUSTOMER
HOUSTON, TX MSA

Index (Average = 100)

BG/ED Clusters
Bar Width: Percentage of Households

Copyright 1990 by D.M.I.S.

CLUSTERPLUS CUSTOMER LIST ANALYSIS REPORT

Company : HOUSTON
Base : HOUSTON, TX MSA
Customers: CUSTOMER
Grouping : BG/ED Clusters
Ranking : Index

Rank	Code	Description	Base	% Base	Customers	% Cust.	% Pen.	Index
		Totals	1,220,849	100.000	13748	100.000	1.126	100
1	S 20	Group quarters: college dorms, hospitals, institutions	5,460	0.447	230	1.673	4.212	374
2	S 43	Unskilled southern Blacks, families with children	47,160	3.863	1,367	9.943	2.899	257
3	S 11	Average educated homeowners, teenagers, homes built in 1960s	20,836	1.707	488	3.550	2.342	208
4	S 35	Young, mobile, avg. educated, old homes & apartments	4,916	0.403	113	0.822	2.299	204
5	S 47	Unemployed, urban areas, Black women with children	2,001	0.164	46	0.335	2.299	204
6	S 38	Old, low income, retirees, urban apartment areas	3,428	0.281	78	0.567	2.275	202
7	S 45	Unskilled urban Blacks, old housing	24,459	2.003	441	3.208	1.803	160
8	S 10	Well-educated, young singles, apartments, professionals	6,156	0.504	108	0.786	1.754	156
9	S 44	Urban Blacks, singles, large metro areas	17,747	1.454	311	2.262	1.752	156
10	S 18	Working couples, children, larger families, homeowners	9,377	0.768	155	1.127	1.653	147
11	S 17	Well-educated, young, mobile, singles, apartment dwellers	158,918	13.017	2572	18.708	1.618	144
12	S 15	Older, nonmobile, urban, white-collar, old housing	7,715	0.632	112	0.815	1.452	129
13	S 01	Top income, highly educated, professionals, prestige homes	22,280	1.825	311	2.262	1.396	124
14	S 02	Well-educated, mobile professionals, new homes & condos	40,897	3.350	546	3.971	1.335	119
15	S 07	Apartments & condos, high rent, professionals, singles	44,575	3.651	588	4.277	1.319	117
16	S 16	Nonmobile working couples, older homes, urban areas	29,574	2.422	366	2.662	1.238	110
17	S 05	Nonmobile professionals, established communities	32,217	2.639	356	2.589	1.105	98
18	S 31	Older, nonmobile, low income, retirees, old housing	1,374	0.113	15	0.109	1.092	97
19	S 33	Nonmobile blue-collar workers, low home values, older homes	2,660	0.218	29	0.211	1.090	97
20	S 13	Older nonmobile homeowners, fewer children, older homes	6,800	0.557	70	0.509	1.029	91

21	S 12	Young mobile working couples, young children, new homes	124,080	10.163	1,236	8.990	0.996	88
22	S 25	Young, below average income, apartment dwellers	14,723	1.206	138	1.004	0.937	83
23	S 24	Young mobile singles, urban, ethnic, low income, apartments	40,420	3.311	342	2.488	0.846	75
24	S 36	Avg. income, Hispanic families with children	42,776	3.504	358	2.604	0.837	74
25	S 32	Old, low income, singles, retirees, few children	247	0.020	2	0.015	0.810	72
26	S 14	Retirees, apartments & condos, high home values & rents	3,966	0.325	32	0.233	0.807	72
27	S 06	Younger mobile large families, children, new homes	141,621	11.600	1106	8.045	0.781	69
28	S 04	Mature professionals, larger families, teenagers	12,051	0.987	92	0.669	0.763	68
29	S 22	Older, fewer children, single family homes	11,701	0.958	89	0.647	0.761	68
30	S 03	Younger mobile professionals, homeowners, children	153,712	12.591	1,159	8.430	0.754	67
31	S 08	Older, fewer children, white-collar workers	6,847	0.561	49	0.356	0.716	64
32	S 19	Younger, married homeowners, larger families, children	24,047	1.970	167	1.215	0.694	62
33	S 28	Younger mobile families, children, mobile homes	23,972	1.964	157	1.142	0.655	58
34	S 27	Lower valued single family homes built in 1950s and 1960s	40,549	3.321	254	1.848	0.626	56
35	S 46	Unskilled, Hispanic families with children, apartments	31,638	2.591	194	1.411	0.613	54
36	S 37	Average income, blue-collar, primarily north central region	4,369	0.358	24	0.175	0.549	49
37	S 40	Older, singles, retirees, old homes & apartments	760	0.062	3	0.022	0.395	35
38	S 09	Average education, two incomes, homes built in 1960s and 1970s	18,005	1.475	27	0.196	0.150	13
39	S 26	Below avg. income, retirees, mobile homes, fewer children	1,289	0.106	1	0.007	0.078	7
40	S 30	Poorly educated, low income, farm families, rural areas	23,231	1.903	15	0.109	0.065	6
41	S 42	Poorly educated, nonmobile, blue-collar, rural South	6,532	0.535	1	0.007	0.015	1
42	S 21	Blue-collar workers, children, homeowners, rural areas	4,497	0.368	0	0.000	0.000	0
43	S 23	Nonmobile married couples, old homes, farm areas	591	0.048	0	0.000	0.000	0
44	S 29	Older, nonmobile, avg. income, northeast urban ethnic areas	0	0.000	0	0.000	0.000	0
45	S 34	Older, avg. educated, rural nonmobile blue-collar workers	437	0.036	0	0.000	0.000	0
46	S 39	Older, nonmobile, blue collar, very old housing	7	0.001	0	0.000	0.000	0
47	S 41	Blue-collar workers, rural, manufacturing areas	231	0.019	0	0.000	0.000	0

AVIS POTENTIAL SITE

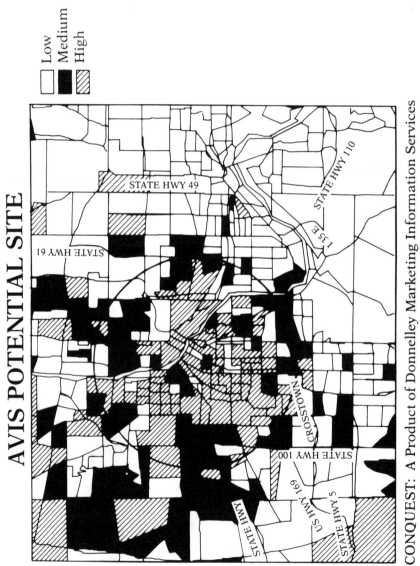

Low
Medium
High

CONQUEST: A Product of Donnelley Marketing Information Services

AREA SITE ANALYSIS

Total Score

0
1
2
3

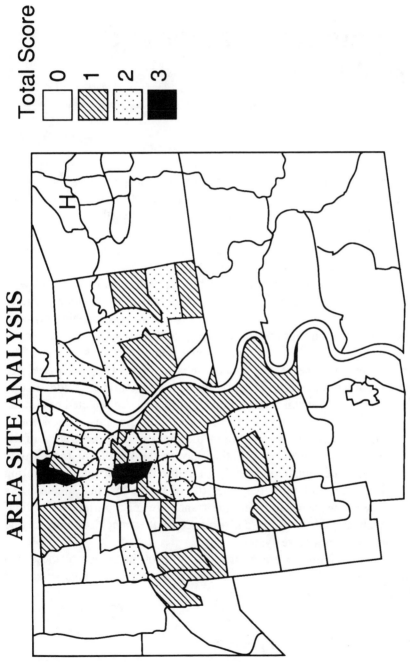

CONQUEST: A Product of Donnelley Marketing Information Services

10

Managing the Transfer and Renewal Process

Andrew J. Sherman, Silver, Freedman & Taff

One critical but often overlooked area of franchising management is the administration of transfer and renewal. Although the transfer of a franchise is a very different and usually more complex transaction than renewal, both situations highlight an important aspect of the relationship between franchisor and franchisee: *Franchises are awarded and not sold.* As a result, the franchisor has every right to impose certain conditions of approval for either event.

Renewal of the franchise agreement is similar to when a husband and wife renew their marriage vows, each restating his or her desire to continue the relationship. Renewal is the ideal time for the franchisor to impose certain new conditions on the agreement and for the franchisee to commit to another five, ten, or twenty years of meeting obligations and following the operations manual. The transfer process, on the other hand, is akin to a divorce. The franchisee, for reasons such as retirement, relocation, burnout, or frustration, has decided to end the relationship with the franchisor, and a third party has been selected to assume operation and management of the business. To protect itself against the unknown, the franchisor must impose certain conditions for approval or authorization of the transfer or sale. The franchisor should also stay in the middle of the transfer process to ensure that the transferee is viable, qualified, and capable of operating the business. The franchisor must play the role of facilitator, investigator, and traffic cop in order to protect itself, lest the franchisee misrepresent the obligations of the franchisor, the financial performance of the franchised unit, or the overall character of the franchise system.

This chapter highlights the key issues that arise in the course of these two critical transactions, with emphasis on the conditions that the franchisor should impose on the proposed renewal or transfer.

Managing the Renewal Process

Rights are awarded to franchisees for a specified initial term and are subject to meeting certain obligations and following certain standardized systems. The franchise agreement should also specify the obligations of the franchisee that must be met as a condition to renewal when the initial term is up. Certain key issues such as royalty rates, performance standards, territorial allocations, and advertising fund contributions may need to be revised. For obvious reasons, franchisees will resent any significant changes in the relationship, especially if these changes were not disclosed in the initial offering circular. Franchisees often complain that the renewal fee structure forces them to essentially ''repurchase'' their franchise at the commencement of each new term. Although the term *repurchase* shows an obvious misunderstanding of the nature of the franchise relationship, it reveals a legitimate concern of the franchisee—namely, that she does not want to be unduly penalized for building up local goodwill and capturing local market share. If the renewal fee structure is not viewed as fair and reasonable, or if key terms in the franchise agreement significantly change upon renewal, then the renewal process is likely to be a source of conflict.

A well-drafted franchise agreement should impose, at a minimum, the following conditions to a renewal of the term:

1. At least six (6) months prior to the expiration of the initial term of this Agreement, Franchisor shall inspect the Franchised Business and give notice of all required modifications to the nature and quality of the products and services offered at the Franchised Business, the Software, advertising, marketing and promotional programs, necessary to comply with the Franchisor's then-current standards; and, if Franchisee elects to renew this Agreement, shall complete to Franchisor's satisfaction all such required modifications, as well as adopt and implement any new methods, programs, Software updates, and modifications and techniques required by Franchisor's notice no later than three (3) months prior to expiration of the initial term of this Agreement.

2. Franchisee shall give Franchisor written notice of such election to renew not less than three (3) months prior to the end of the initial term of this Agreement.

3. Franchisee shall not be in default of any provision of this Agreement, any amendment hereof or successor hereto, or any other agreement between Franchisee and Franchisor, or its subsidiaries, affiliates, and suppliers and shall have substantially compiled with all the terms and conditions of such agreements during the terms thereof.

4. Franchisee shall have satisfied all monetary obligations owed by Franchisee to Franchisor and its subsidiaries, affiliates, and suppliers and shall have timely met those obligations throughout the term of this Agreement.

5. Franchisee shall execute upon renewal Franchisor's then-current form of Franchise Agreement, which agreement shall supersede in all respects this Agreement, and the terms of which may differ from the terms of this Agreement, including, without limitation, by requiring a higher percentage royalty fee and/or National Advertising Fund contribution, increase in the Minimum Local Advertising Expenditure and the implementation of additional fees; provided, however, that in lieu of the then-current initial franchise fee or its equiv-

alent, for such renewal period, Franchisee shall be required to pay a renewal fee of _____percent (_____ %) of the then-current initial franchise fee paid by new franchisees of the Franchisor but in no event shall said renewal fee exceed _____ dollars ($ _____).

6. Franchisee shall comply with Franchisor's then-current qualification and training requirements.

7. Franchisee and its shareholders, directors, and officers shall execute a general release, in a form prescribed by Franchisor, of any and all claims against Franchisor and its subsidiaries and affiliates, and their respective officers, directors, agents, and employees provided, however, that Franchisee shall not be required to release Franchisor for violations of federal or state franchise registration and disclosure laws.

8. Franchisee shall present evidence satisfactory to Franchisor that it has the right to remain in possession of the premises where the Franchised Business is located for the duration of the renewal term.

9. In the event that any of the above conditions to renewal have not been met, no later than three (3) months prior to the expiration of the initial term of this Agreement, Franchisor shall have no obligation to renew this Agreement and shall provide to Franchisee at least sixty (60) days prior written notice of its intent not to renew this Agreement, which notice shall set forth the reasons for such refusal to renew.

A sample Renewal Release Agreement is shown in Figure 10-1.

Managing the Transfer Process

There is a wide variety of issues and obligations triggered when a current franchisee (transferor) proposes to sell or transfer his rights under the franchise agreement to a third party (transferee), who must always be subject to approval by the franchisor. Some of the key issues in the administration and management of the transfer process include:

▲ *Franchisor's right of first refusal*. Many modern-day franchise agreements provide the franchisor with a right of first refusal to essentially match the terms offered by a bona fide third party in the event of a sale or transfer by a franchisee. All of the proper notification, approval, exercise, or waiver procedures set forth in the agreement must be followed.

▲ *Data gathering*. Assuming that the franchisor will *not* be exercising its right of first refusal, the franchisor must begin its due diligence on the proposed transferee. The franchisee and the proposed transferee must be diligent and timely in meeting all information requests of the franchisor in the areas of business experience, financial capability, employment, and educational history. The franchisor should *always* meet with the prospective transferee for a face-to-face interview.

Figure 10–1. Renewal and Release Agreement.

THIS AGREEMENT is made and entered into this _____day of_____,
19___, by and between _____, a _____ corporation whose
principal place of business is _____
("Franchisor") and _____ whose principal
place of business is _____ ("Franchisee").

WITNESSETH:

WHEREAS, on _____, 19___, Franchisor and Franchisee entered into
a written Franchise Agreement by the terms of which Franchisee was
granted a license to operate a _____ business in connection
with the Franchisor's System and Proprietary Marks (the "Franchise") at
the following location: _____; and

WHEREAS, pursuant to Section _____ of that Franchise Agreement,
Franchisee desires to renew the Franchise for an additional ten (10) year
period and Franchisor desires to allow said renewal.

NOW, THEREFORE, in consideration of the mutual promises, covenants and
conditions contained herein and for other good and valuable consideration, the receipt of which is hereby acknowledged, the parties agree as
follows:

1. Renewal of Franchise Agreement. Pursuant to Section _____of the
Franchise Agreement, Franchisee hereby renews the Franchise for an
additional period of ten (10) years.

2. Execution of Current Franchise Agreement. Concurrently with the
execution hereof, Franchisee shall execute Franchisor's current form of
Franchise Agreement which agreement supersedes in all respects that
Franchise Agreement executed by and between Franchisor and Franchisee
on _____and any other prior agreements, representations,
negotiations or understandings between the parties.

3. Renewal Fee. Concurrently with the execution hereof, Franchisee shall
pay to Franchisor the sum of $ _____ representing the renewal fee
as provided in Section _____ of the Franchise Agreement.

4. Release of Franchisor. Franchisee, individually and on behalf of Franchisee's heirs, legal representatives, successors and assigns, hereby
forever releases and discharges Franchisor, its subsidiaries and affiliates,
their respective officers, directors, agents and employees from any and all
claims, demands, controversies, actions, causes of action, obligations,
liabilities, costs, expenses, attorney's fees and damages of whatsoever

(continues)

Figure 10-1. (cont'd.)

character, nature and kind, in law or in equity, claimed or alleged and which may be based upon or connected with the Franchise, the Franchise Agreement or any other agreement between the parties and executed prior to the date hereof, including but not limited to any and all claims whether presently known or unknown, suspected or unsuspected, arising under the franchise, securities or antitrust laws of Canada, the United States, or any state, or municipality, to the extent permitted by law.

5. <u>Acknowledgement of Performance.</u> Except as provided herein, the parties hereto acknowledge and agree that all conditions to renewal provided in Section _____ of the Franchise Agreement have been satisfactorily complied with or performed.

6. <u>Execution of Documents.</u> The parties agree to execute any and all documents or agreements and to take all action as may be necessary or desirable to effect the terms, covenants and conditions of this Agreement.

IN WITNESS WHEREOF, the parties hereto have hereunder caused this Renewal and Release Agreement to be executed the day and year first above written.

ATTEST: FRANCHISOR

_____   By:_____
                                               _____, President

WITNESS: FRANCHISEE

_____   _____

▲ *Document control.* The franchisor should be provided with copies of all correspondence, listings, sales contracts, bulk sales, transfer notices, broker agreements, and any other paperwork related to the transaction to ensure against misrepresentations, inaccurate earnings claims, or false statements about the franchisor. The franchisor should play the role of document reviewer, not document validator. It is tempting for the transferee to contact the franchisor directly to get its opinions on the fairness of the sales terms, the accuracy of the store's financial performance, or the credibility of the transferee's proposed business plan or pro forma financial statements. Franchisors should help facilitate the process, but resist the temptation to go beyond the review and approval level, *unless* serving as a direct remarketer of the franchise.

▲ *Franchise remarketing.* Some franchisors have been remarketing their franchises, essentially serving as a broker on behalf of current franchisees who want to sell their businesses. The secondary market for franchised business flourishes now that franchising has matured. Many of the franchises awarded in the 1970s and early 1980s are now operated by individuals nearing retirement age and franchisees are ready to transfer ownership. Franchisors must decide what role they plan to play in this process and what their compensation will be for locating qualified transferees.

▲ *Transfer fees.* The franchisor must devote time and resources to reviewing and approving a proposed transfer. Often the franchisor's attorneys must review the terms of the transfer. The transferee, once approved, must be trained and supported. All these costs must be borne by someone, and it is typically *not* the franchisor. Therefore, the franchise agreement should provide for a transfer fee that at least covers all the franchisor's training and administrative costs in connection with the transfer.

▲ *Debt assumption.* A typical condition of approval of the transfer is that the franchisee pay all of his outstanding financial obligations to the franchisor. In the case of a troubled franchisee, the transferee may buy the business in exchange for a promissory note, leaving little or no cash for the transferor to pay his debts to the franchisor. If the franchisor is also taking a promisory note from the transferor (for its outstanding obligations or transfer fees), then the terms of repayment, the security agreements, financing statements, and personal guaranties of both transferor and transferee must be prepared. Any other defaults by the transferor which must be cured for approval of the transfer should be explained to the transferee, especially if any will be cured *after* consummation of the transfer.

▲ *Disclosure of the transferee.* Regardless of specific legal requirements, good franchising practice dictates that the franchisor provide the proposed transferee with a copy of its current disclosure documents and explain any new developments, obligations, or problems that may affect the decision to buy the business. Transferees do not want to hear about major changes to the system, class-action lawsuits against the franchisor, or impending bankruptcy of the franchisor just after they have invested their life savings.

▲ *Inspection and audit.* The franchisor should always have its field support staff visit the site of a proposed transfer in order to conduct an inspection and audit. This uncovers any fees still owed as well as helps determine whether refurbishment should be a condition for transfer. This is also an opportune time for the franchisor to collect from the transferor all copies of the operations manual and any other confidential information.

▲ *Execution of documents.* There are many legal documents to be prepared by the franchisor for execution by the transferor and transferee as a condition for approving the transfer. These documents may include mutual releases, guaranty agreements, representation and acknowledgment letters (for execution by the transferee, which represent his capabilities and acknowledge his undertaking certain responsibilities), lease agreements, or a consent-to-sale agreement. A sample transfer agreement is shown in Figure 10-2. There may also be certain ''standard'' documents that must be executed by the transferee, such as for local co-operative-advertising participation, sign leasing, equipment leasing, or inventory purchasing.

In addition to these key issues, a well-drafted franchise agreement should include, at minimum, the following specific contractual conditions, which must be met prior to approval of the transfer:

1. All of Franchisee's accrued monetary obligations and all other outstanding obligations to Franchisor and its subsidiaries, affiliates, and suppliers shall be up-to-date, fully paid, and satisfied.

2. Franchisee shall not be in default of any provision of this Agreement, any amendment hereof or successor hereto, any other franchise agreement or other agreement between Franchisee and Franchisor, or its subsidiaries, affiliates, or suppliers.

3. The Franchisee and each of its shareholders, officers, and directors shall have executed a General Release under seal, in a form satisfactory to Franchisor, of any and all claims against Franchisor and its officers, directors, shareholders, and employees in their corporate and individual capacities, including, without limitation, claims arising under federal, state, and local laws, rules, and ordinances, provided, however, that Franchisee shall not be required to release Franchisor for violations of federal and state franchise registration and disclosure laws.

4. The Transferee shall enter into a written assignment, under seal and in a form satisfactory to Franchisor, assuming and agreeing to discharge all of Franchisee's obligations under this Agreement; and, if the obligations of Franchisee were guaranteed by the Transferor, the Transferee shall guarantee the performance of all such obligations in writing in a form satisfactory to Franchisor.

5. The Transferee shall demonstrate to Franchisor's satisfaction that the Transferee meets Franchisor's educational, managerial, and business standards; possesses a good moral character, business reputation, and credit rating; has the aptitude and ability to operate the Franchised Business herein (as may be evidenced by prior related experience or otherwise); has at least the same managerial and financial criteria required of new franchisees and shall have sufficient equity capital to operate the Franchised Business.

6. At Franchisor's option, the transferee shall execute (and/or, upon Franchisor's request, shall cause all interested parties to execute) for a term ending on the Expiration Date of this Agreement and with such renewal term as may

(Text continues on page 148.)

Figure 10-2. Franchise Transfer Agreement.

THIS AGREEMENT is made and entered into this ＿＿＿day of ＿＿＿＿＿＿,
by and between ＿＿＿＿＿＿＿＿＿, a ＿＿＿＿＿＿ corporation, whose
principal place of business is ＿＿＿＿＿＿＿＿＿＿ (hereinafter the
"Franchisor"); and ＿＿＿＿＿＿＿＿＿＿, whose principal place of
business is ＿＿＿＿＿＿＿＿＿ (hereinafter the "Transferor"); and
＿＿＿＿＿＿＿＿＿＿, whose principal place of business is
＿＿＿＿＿＿＿＿＿＿ (hereinafter the "Transferee").

WITNESSETH:

WHEREAS, on ＿＿＿＿＿＿＿＿, Franchisor and Transferor entered
into a written Franchise Agreement by the terms of which Transferor was
granted a license to operate a Center in connection with the Franchisor's
System and Proprietary Marks (hereinafter the "the Franchise") at the
following location: ＿＿＿＿＿＿＿＿＿＿＿＿＿＿＿＿;

WHEREAS, Transferor desires to sell, assign, transfer, and convey all of its
right, title and interest in and to the Franchise to Transferee and Franchisor is willing to consent to said transfer, upon the terms and conditions in
the said written Franchise Agreement and upon the terms and conditions
herein; and

WHEREAS, Franchisor has elected not to exercise its right and option to
purchase the Transferor's interest on the same terms and conditions
offered to the Transferee, as provided by Section ＿＿＿＿ of the Franchise
Agreement entered into between the Franchisor and the Transferor.

NOW, THEREFORE, in consideration of the mutual promises, covenants and
conditions contained herein and for other good and valuable consideration, the receipt of which is hereby acknowledged, the parties agree as
follows:

1. Transfer. Subject to the provisions contained herein, Transferor hereby
sells, assigns, transfers and conveys all of its right, title and interest in
and to the Franchise to Transferee and Franchisor consents to said transfer, upon the terms and conditions in the said written Franchise Agreement and upon the terms and conditions herein.

2. Release of Franchisor. Transferor hereby releases and discharges
Franchisor and its officers, directors, shareholders and employees in their
corporate and individual capacities from any and all claims, actions,
causes of action, or demands of whatsoever kind or nature.

3. Transferee's Agreement. In lieu of an initial franchise fee customarily
paid under the terms of the Franchise Agreement and upon payment of a

(continues)

Figure 10-2 (cont'd.)

transfer franchise fee to Franchisor by Transferee in the sum of _____ ($ _____), which sum is equivalent to _____ percent (____%) of the initial franchise fee currently being charged by Franchisor to new franchisees, and concurrently with the execution hereof, Franchisor shall offer Transferee the standard form of Franchise Agreement now being offered by Franchisor to new franchisees and such other ancillary agreements as Franchisor may require for the Franchise. The term of said Franchise Agreement offered by Franchisor to Transferee shall end on the expiration date of the Franchise Agreement entered into by and between Franchisor and Transferor and with such renewal term(s) as may be provided by the Franchise Agreement entered into by and between Franchisor and Transferor. Except as provided herein, the Franchise Agreement offered by Franchisor to Transferee, if executed by Transferee, shall supersede the Franchise Agreement entered into by and between Franchisor and Transferor in all respects and the terms of the Transferee's Agreement may differ from the terms of the Transferor's Agreement, including, without limitation, a higher percentage royalty fee and advertising contribution.

4. Transfer Fee. Concurrently with the execution hereof, Transferor shall pay to Franchisor a Transfer Fee of _____ Dollars ($____) to cover Franchisor's administrative expenses in connection with this transfer.

5. Training. At the Transferee's expense the Transferee and the Transferee's manager shall attend and successfully complete any training programs currently in effect for current franchisees.

6. Upgrades. At the Transferee's expense the Transferee shall upgrade the premises referred to herein to conform to the design concepts now being used in other franchised locations and shall complete the upgrading and any other reasonable requirements specified by Franchisor and which relate to said upgrading on or before _____.

7. Receipt of Documents. On or before _____ Transferee shall sign an Acknowledgement of Receipt acknowledging Transferee's receipt of all required legal documents including Franchisor's Franchise Offering Circular, Franchisor's current Franchise Agreement, related agreements and documentation.

8. Transferee's Obligations. Transferee hereby assumes and agrees to faithfully discharge all of the Transferor's obligations under the Franchise Agreement entered into by and between Franchisor and Transferor.

9. Guaranty by Transferee. Transferee understands and acknowledges that the obligations of the Transferor under the Franchise Agreement entered

into by and between Franchisor and Transferor were guaranteed by Transferor and Transferee hereby agrees to guaranty the full and complete performance of all such obligations and agrees to execute a written guaranty in form satisfactory to Franchisor.

10. Transferor's Liability. Transferor understands, acknowledges and agrees it shall remain liable for all obligations to Franchisor in connection with the Franchise prior to the effective date of the transfer and shall execute any and all instruments reasonably requested by Franchisor to evidence such liability.

11. Transferor's Warranties. Transferor warrants and represents that it is not granting any security interest in the Franchise or in any of its assets.

12. Survivability. Transferor acknowledges, understands and agrees that those provisions of Section _____ and Section _____ of the Franchise Agreement entered into by and between Transferor and Franchisor, to the extent applicable, shall survive this Agreement.

13. Transferor's Obligations. Transferor acknowledges and agrees that each of its obligations regarding transfer must be met by the Transferor and are reasonable and necessary.

14. Transferor's Monetary Obligations. Transferor understands, acknowledges and agrees that all of its accrued monetary obligations and any other outstanding obligations due and owing to Franchisor shall be fully paid and satisfied prior to any transfer referred to herein.

15. Waiver. The failure of any party to enforce at any time any of the provisions hereof shall not be construed to be a waiver of such provisions or of the right of any party thereafter to enforce any such provisions.

16. Modifications. No renewal hereof, or modification or waiver of any of the provisions herein contained, or any future representation, promise or condition in connection with the subject matter hereof, shall be effective unless agreed upon by the parties hereto in writing.

17. Execution of Documents. The parties agree to execute any and all documents or agreements and to take all action as may be necessary or desirable to effectuate the terms, covenants and conditions of this Agreement.

18. Binding Effect. This Agreement shall be binding upon the parties hereto, their heirs, executors, successors, assigns and legal representatives.

(continues)

Figure 10-2   (cont'd.)

19. Attorney Fees. Transferor shall pay to Franchisor all damages, costs and expenses, including reasonable attorney fees, incurred by Franchisor in enforcing the provisions of this Agreement.

20. Severability. If any provision of this Agreement or any part thereof is declared invalid by any court of competent jurisdiction, such act shall not affect the validity of this Agreement and the remainder of this Agreement shall remain in full force and effect according to the terms of the remaining provisions or part of provisions hereof.

21. Construction. This Agreement shall be governed by and construed in accordance with the laws of the State of _____.

IN WITNESS WHEREOF, the parties hereto have hereunder caused this Franchise Transfer Agreement to be executed the day and year first above written.

ATTEST   Franchisor

_____   By:_____
                                            _____, President

WITNESS

_____
                                    _____

                                    Transferor

_____
                                    _____

                                    Transferee

be provided by this Agreement, the standard form of Franchise Agreement then being offered to new franchisees and such other ancillary agreements as Franchisor may require for the Franchised Business, which agreements shall supersede this Agreement in all respects and the terms of which agreements may differ from the terms of this Agreement, including, without limitation, a higher percentage royalty fee, National Advertising Fund contribution, increase of the Minimum Local Advertising Expenditure and the implementation of additional fees;

7. The Transferee shall upgrade, at the Transferee's expense, the Fran-

chised Business to conform to the current specifications then being used in new Franchised Businesses, and shall complete the upgrading and other requirements within the time specified by Franchisor.

8. Franchisee shall remain liable for all direct and indirect obligations to Franchisor in connection with the Franchised Business prior to the effective date of the transfer and shall continue to remain responsible for its obligations of nondisclosure, noncompetitive, and indemnification as provided elsewhere in this Agreement and shall execute any and all instruments reasonably requested by Franchisor to further evidence such liability.

9. At the Transferee's expense, the Transferee and its manager and employees shall complete any training programs then in effect for current franchisees upon such terms and conditions as Franchisor may reasonably require.

10. The transferee shall have signed an Acknowledgement of Receipt of all required legal documents, such as the Franchise Offering Circular and the then-current Franchise Agreement and ancillary agreement.

11. Transferor shall pay to Franchisor a Transfer Fee equal to _____ percent (____%) of the then-current initial franchise fee paid by new franchisees of Franchisor but in no event shall said Transfer Fee exceed _____ dollars ($_____) to cover Franchisor's administrative expenses in connection with the proposed transfer.

PART III

THE DYNAMICS OF THE FRANCHISOR-FRANCHISEE RELATIONSHIP

Understanding the dynamics of the franchisor-franchisee relationship and the importance of effective communications with franchisees is critical to the long-term success of the franchising program.

In these next three critical chapters, the contributors deal with important philosophical and practical issues in understanding the root of the franchisor-franchisee relationship, as well as certain steps that can be implemented to more effectively manage this relationship, such as the creation of rigid and objective selection criteria and the establishment of franchisee advisory committees.

11

The Dynamics of the Franchising Relationship and Recruitment Strategies

Timothy McGowan and Margaret Dower, Management 2000

Since 1972, the number of business-format franchisors in the United States has increased by over 1,600, or 175 percent. This growth in franchisors has increased the competition to find and sign qualified franchisee candidates. As franchising continues to evolve as a significant strategy for companies of all sizes to market and distribute products and services, the demand for qualified franchisees will increase accordingly. We believe the ability of a franchise system to maintain a competitive edge rests largely on the success of the franchisee recruitment and selection process.

After working with hundreds of franchise systems both large and small, we see that many of the problems experienced by franchise systems originate in the way franchisees are recruited, selected, and brought into the system. During this critical process, the focus traditionally has been on "closing the deal," rather than determining whether a candidate is right for the system and the system is right for the candidate. As a result, many franchise systems are shackled with poor franchisor-franchisee relationships. These relationships create an adversarial environment that eventually prevents the franchise system from realizing its potential.

The purpose of a franchisee recruitment and selection process is to create the future of the company. Doing this implies a new understanding of franchising, of the objectives of marketing, and of the role of marketing representatives. First, the franchisor must understand the nature of franchising and agree that franchises are granted, not sold. Once this is clear, there will be significant changes in the expectations the franchisor has of its licensing personnel; this will, in turn, influence the selection and recruitment of franchise licensing representatives.

Second, traditional marketing objectives must change. Rather than concern for the number of inquiries, the focus must be on the candidates and the value each will bring to the franchise organization over the life of the relationship. Granting franchises goes beyond a numbers game to a consultation process that produces more qualified applicants in less time, and results in better franchisees.

Finally, licensing representatives must change the way they see themselves. Rather than convincing prospects that they should ''buy'' a franchise, they must act as consultants, helping candidates make informed business decisions. Rather than focusing on what the franchise can do for the candidate, they must concentrate on the candidate and what she needs to do to make an informed business decision about joining the system. Listening and questioning skills must be developed and refined—not easy for traditional salespeople, used to finding hot buttons, overcoming the objection, and closing sales.

The results will be mutual compatibility, better franchisees, and effective use of resources in finding and signing on qualified candidates.

A focused franchisee recruitment and selection process comprises the following three interrelated parts:

1. *Market development strategy and plan.* A market development strategy and plan provides the direction for building the system to achieve the vision of the company. It documents the company's marketing and operational decisions related to market analysis, market selection and penetration goals, competitive analysis, and franchise structure and form.

2. *Structured franchise licensing system.* A *structured* franchise licensing system achieves the results of the market development strategy and plan. The system contains processes for identifying candidates, qualifying and interviewing them, following up, granting a license, and opening a unit.

3. *Skilled franchise licensing personnel.* Skilled franchise licensing representatives know how to use the structured licensing system to achieve the results of the market development strategy and plan. The representatives help franchisee candidates make an informed business decision as to whether the franchise system is the best opportunity to achieve their goals, dreams, and objectives.

This chapter provides a context for thinking about the franchise recruitment and selection process. It focuses primarily on the following questions:

▴ What does it mean to grant a franchise and why can't franchises be sold?
▴ How is the market development strategy and plan used to effectively build a franchise system?
▴ What are the components of a structured system and why does a structured system work?
▴ What skills are needed for the franchise licensing representative to effectively recruit, select, and grant franchise licenses to qualified franchisees?

As franchising increases in popularity, both from the franchisor's and franchisee's perspective, the competition for qualified candidates will intensify. As you read this chapter, evaluate your company's franchisee recruitment and selection process. After studying this material you will have a greater understanding of how and why your company's methods can be improved, how your relationship with franchisees can start on a firm foundation, and how your franchise system can reach its potential into the next century.

What Does Granting a Franchise Mean?

Most franchisors are under the misconception that franchises are sold. To effectively build a strong foundation for growth and to use the true power of franchising, franchisors must understand why franchises can't be sold, and how *granting* franchises establishes a proper context for a strong relationship with and between franchisees.

Why Can't Franchises Be Sold?

The premise that a franchise license is not sold and the franchisee does not own the franchise license is supported by the following facts:

- A franchisee cannot incorporate using the franchisor's name because the franchisee does not own the name.
- Should the franchisee want to exit the business, the franchise license is not sold; rather, the franchise license is transferred upon approval by the franchisor. The franchisee enters into a separate transaction to sell his or her assets.
- The franchise agreement has a stated term and must be renewed if the franchisee is to continue in business under the franchisor's brand name. If a franchisee owned the license, it would not need to be renewed.

The market, the brand name, the operating system, and the ongoing support system are "owned" by the franchisor. The franchisee is delegated the right to use the brand name in a defined market, for a designated period of time, to develop market share for the franchise system.

A franchise cannot be sold or bought. However, a franchisee does own the assets of the business. A franchisee has invested in a company's brand name, operating system, and ongoing support system in the hope of obtaining a return on this investment. This investment is returned to the franchisee in two ways:

1. From current revenue, as a result of using the brand name, which creates customers, and using the operating system, which gets those customers to come back.
2. From the increase in value of the franchisee's assets owing to association with the franchisor's brand name, which enhances the franchisee's ability to produce future revenue.

The Effect of "Selling" Language

The use of the words *sell*, *buy*, and *owner*, when referring to the franchisee, sends a message that is contrary to the real purpose of the franchise relationship. Such words focus on the legal structure of the relationship rather than on the business purpose.

Let's explore the logic of selling franchises and evaluate the impact of this language on future franchisee behavior. First, the logic:

- If I sell you something, you therefore have bought it.
- If you have bought it, you therefore own it.
- If you own it, you therefore can do what you want with it.

This message creates what we call an owner mentality. The impact of an owner mentality is as follows:

- There is a crippling impact on the growth of the franchise system. An owner mentality leads franchisees to believe they can change the operating system at will. These changes make the operating system inconsistent from franchisee to franchisee, and the inconsistency adversely affects customers' experience and expectations and invalidates the perception of a brand name created through collective marketing efforts.

- There is a perception that franchisees within the system are competitors of each other rather than teammates responsible for enhancing the value of the brand name. This perception originates when the franchisees are told they are "independent owners."

We have often seen franchisors reinforce this thinking by requiring franchisees to display a sign of the place of business which says, "This franchise is independently owned and operated." This again focuses on the legal relationship rather than the business purpose, which is to get and keep customers. It prevents franchisees, the franchisor, and the franchise system from realizing the power of franchising. Since the assets are owned by the franchisee, we suggest using the words: "This [Unit/store/office] is independently owned by [*name of proprietor*] and operated under a license from [*name of franchisor*]."

- Franchisees believe the operating system is the way the franchisor controls them, rather than seeing the system as the way customers are retained and value is built in the brand name.

- Franchisees don't understand why it is important to implement legitimate changes in the operating system as the system grows. The franchisee does not understand because franchising was never adequately explained—namely, that the operating system is for the customer, not the franchisee. Changes in the operating system, when adequately tested and consistently applied, are made for marketing reasons—to fulfill the business purpose of the relationship, which is to get and keep customers.

⬩ There is usually no context for franchisees to understand the real purpose of the initial franchise fee and the ongoing royalty fee. Franchisees mistakenly believe that the initial franchise fee was for the brand name, operating system, and training. They also believe that the ongoing royalty fee is only for support the franchisor provides that makes the franchisee successful. This thinking makes the franchisee dependent and causes him to ask, "What has the franchisor done for me today?"

These are only a few examples of how the words *sell* and *owner* adversely affect the franchisor-franchisee relationship, potentially dilute the franchisee's investment, and prevent the system from capitalizing on the power of franchising to get and keep customers. Almost every problem franchisors face with franchisees originates in the way franchisees think about the relationship based on how they were recruited and selected. The problems experienced by many franchise systems can, in many cases, be eliminated by encouraging an understanding of the franchisor-franchisee relationship during the recruitment and selection process.

Figure 11-1 outlines the differences between selling and granting franchises, and offers suggestions for new language and behavior.

Figure 11-1.   The difference between selling and granting franchises.

	"Selling" Franchises	*"Granting" Franchises*
1. The function	Franchise sales	Franchise licensing
2. The person	Franchise salesperson	Franchise licensing representative
3. The recruit	Prospects	Candidates
4. The role	Sell a franchise	Help candidates make an informed decision; create the future of the company
5. The process	Assume, convince, manipulate, pressure	Involve, facilitate, guide, stimulate thinking
6. The approach/ skills	Telling, presenting, and closing	Questioning, listening, facilitating, and confirming decisions
7. The language	Hot buttons, sense of urgency, objections, and close the deal	Motivation, candidates' decisions, basic issues, granting the license
8. Franchisees	Owners	Member/associate/affiliate

New Language and Behavior

To help the candidate better understand franchising and the franchisor-franchisee relationship, the franchise licensing representative should communicate the following to the candidate during the recruitment and selection process:

1. Unit-to-unit consistency is imperative to the success of franchising. If franchisees do not follow the operating system as prescribed, they adversely affect the customer's perception of the product and service being marketed. Lack of consistency dilutes the investment made by all franchisees in the system. Candidates need to understand that the operating system institutionalizes the customer's buying experience. The operating system reinforces the image created by marketing and builds customer expectations. The operating system is for the customer, not the franchisee. The brand image is enhanced if the operating system consistently delivers what the customer expects.

2. Franchisees are not competitors, even if located in the same market. All franchisee- and company-managed locations share the task of establishing the brand name as dominant in all markets entered. This focuses on the business purpose of the relationship, which is to get and keep customers. By increasing brand-name awareness, the units create more and more customers, who use more and more of the products and services. Everyone in the franchise system, especially franchisees located in the same market, share a responsibility to work as a team to grow the system and increase the system's market share.

3. The franchisor and franchisee have an interdependent relationship. The franchisor and franchisee each must accept responsibility and accountability for the success of the system. It is not the responsibility of the franchisor to make franchisees successful. Franchisees must market the brand, work the operating system, and use the ongoing support system to get and keep customers. Likewise, the franchisor must grow the system, provide the best operating system, and assist the franchisee to become more effective, efficient, and profitable by providing support services. The franchisor and all franchisees must work as a team for mutual benefit.

4. The purpose of the initial franchise fee and the ongoing royalty fee should be communicated. The initial franchise fee goes toward the following: franchisor's expenses in connection with franchisee selection; training and support provided by the franchisor prior to opening; costs to develop and organize the franchise and related systems; trademark and tradename registration and protection; and compliance with various laws.

The royalty fees are paid for the revenue that was generated in the prior reporting period because the brand name created a customer; the operating system used by the franchisee got the customer to come back; and the support services provided by the franchisor helped the franchisee acquire and use the brand name and operating system to accomplish the business purpose of the relationship, which is to get and keep customers.

The Market Development Strategy and Plan

Once franchisors and marketing representatives have a firm understanding of the purpose of franchising, a market development strategy and plan must be developed. This strategy and plan provides the direction for creating the future of a company. It is the first step in implementing a focused recruitment and selection process. A market development strategy and plan should do the following:

- Focus on the purpose of business, which is to get and keep customers.
- Evaluate various options and conditions that influence the development of markets.
- Document marketing and operational decisions that will chart the course of the development effort.
- Focus on key *result* areas—areas of activity that achieve the market development goals and vision.

Strategic Thinking

The market development strategy and plan are a result of an ongoing planning process that determines how the company will be developed. This process should focus on three strategic areas:

1. The goals and abilities of the company
2. The current and future customers for the company's products and services
3. The competition for getting and keeping customers

The strategic analysis should focus on some of the following strategic questions:

The Company

- What are the company's mission, values, and vision?
- What are the company's strengths and weaknesses?
- Will the company be international, national, or regional in scope?
- How fast does the company wish to grow?
- What resources (people, money, material, time, and space) are available to develop the company?
- What strategies besides franchising will the company use?

The Customer

- Who is the customer for the company's products and services?
- What are the market segments for the company's products and services?
- What is the market potential for the products and services today and in the future?

- ▴ What is the growth potential of the industry?
- ▴ How is market share measured?
- ▴ How will the products and services be marketed and promoted?

The Competition

- ▴ Who are the company's major competitors?
- ▴ What are the competitors' strengths and weaknesses?
- ▴ In what markets do these competitors have a strategic advantage?
- ▴ How do the competitors' products and services differ from yours?
- ▴ How will the company create a competitive advantage?
- ▴ How will competitive barriers be created or handled?

Impact of Strategic Analysis

Strategic analysis provides a basis for decisions regarding the direction of development efforts. It offers answers to the following questions:

- ▴ What business strategy (franchise or company managed) will be used to penetrate each identified market segment?
- ▴ What are the criteria for ideal geographic markets to be penetrated?
- ▴ What are the primary, secondary, and tertiary geographic markets to be pursued?
- ▴ What structure and form will the franchise take—single unit, multiple units, development agreements, subfranchisor, or area manager?
- ▴ What is the profile of the franchisee candidate?
- ▴ What will the franchisee performance standards be?
- ▴ How much market penetration (number of units and volumes per unit) will be required to support the initial marketing effort?
- ▴ What growth is required (number of units and volumes per unit) to maintain a competitive position in the market?
- ▴ What initial support will franchisees need to open and develop the market?
- ▴ What infrastructure will be needed to support the units in each market entered?
- ▴ What should the initial franchise fee, ongoing royalty, and marketing fees be?

To remain competitive, a business needs to increase its market share by growing faster than the growth in the market demand and faster than the competition. Marketing conditions are ever-changing and business is never static. New products, new market segments, and new niches are created almost daily. As market conditions change, it is a strategic necessity that the franchisor maintain flexibility and control over every market entered; otherwise, the system is vulnerable to competitive attack.

Lacking a market development strategy and plan, many franchisors abdicate their right to the market. In many cases, they select markets by reacting to candidate inquiries rather than having a focused strategy for market penetration. This situation is aggravated when the franchisor gives the franchisee an exclusive territory with no performance standards. The franchisee then thinks she "owns" the territory (market) and sees other franchisees as competitors. Consequently, when market conditions change or competition increases, neither the franchisor nor the franchisee is strategically positioned to respond, and the franchise system suffers as a result.

In summary, a market development strategy and plan consists of the following eight components:

1. The company's mission, values, and vision.
2. A definition of who the customer is.
3. Designation of the various market segments.
4. The market selection criteria.
5. An analysis of potential markets to be developed. This analysis may include:
   - Number of potential customers
   - Competitor analysis
   - Desired number of franchisees in each market
   - Number of units needed to penetrate and develop market share
6. A strategy to build and maintain brand name awareness.
7. A plan to coordinate the various departments in the company to accomplish the market development goal.
8. A summary of the target markets. This summary may include:
   - A description of the market
   - Units in the market
   - Timeline for development
   - Number of franchisees and units per franchisee
   - Marketing dollars to be generated to maintain a competitive position

Structuring a Franchise Licensing System

For many franchisors, a licensing system has consisted of putting an advertisement in one or more national magazines or newspapers, sending a brochure to those who have responded and, hoping the candidate calls back, conducting a prospect presentation that tells how great the concept is, and signing up whoever has the money. But this is a formula for franchise mediocrity. Recent growth in the number of franchisors has increased the competition to find and sign qualified franchisee candidates. To attract qualified candidates, a franchise licensing system must: (1) select candidates who are right for the system and a system that is right for the candidate; and (2) educate and prepare candidates to think the way they must to satisfy the business purpose of the franchise relationship, which is to get and keep customers.

The franchise recruitment and selection process creates the future of the company. The franchise licensing system should support this purpose by structuring a process that will accomplish the following goals:

- Help candidates make an informed business decision about whether the business opportunity will enable them to achieve their personal goals, dreams, and objectives.
- Grant franchise licenses to qualified candidates who will enhance the franchisor's brand name, consistently use the operating systems, and take advantage of the support services.
- Find and sign qualified candidates in the most cost-effective and timely manner.

The Process

Recruiting and selecting qualified franchisees is similar to recruiting and selecting employees. The franchise licensing representative is similar to an executive recruiter, in that she must determine whether the candidate is right for the system and if the system is right for the candidate. As in the employment process, there are several steps that lead to a decision to join an organization. Figure 11-2 compares the steps in the employment process with those used to recruit and select qualified franchisees.

The franchise licensing system should be designed to find, qualify, interview, and grant licenses to candidates who can proactively support the market development strategy and plan. The system should be a structured approach to promoting, qualifying, interviewing, following up, granting, and opening a franchise. These components are further described here:

1. Promotion process. The promotion process identifies candidates who meet the qualifications to become franchisees. The process focuses on who the franchisee candidates will be, how they will be contacted, what the budget will be, and what the anticipated results are. The franchisor should develop a candidate profile and qualification criteria. These criteria should be used to determine and evaluate promotion strategies that can best attract qualified candidates. The promotion strategies will then better support the market development strategy and plan.

2. Qualification process. The qualification process determines if the franchisor and a candidate have mutual interest in continuing the discussions. There is mutual interest when candidates:

- Have made the decision to be self-employed.
- Have necessary financial resources.

Figure 11-2. A comparison of the employment and franchise recruitment processes.

Step	Employment Process	Franchise Process
1. Define qualifications for the position	Job description and qualification description	Qualification profile and criteria
2. Promote the position	Search for candidate	Search for candidate
3. Initially qualify candidate	Receive response from applicant	Initial contact with candidate
4. Receive credentials	Résumé	Request for consideration
5. Meet to discuss the position	Interview	Interview
6. Conduct follow-up research by company and candidate	Additional interviews; reference checks	Candidate and franchisor validations
7. Decide to extend offer	Application and offer of employment	Application, approval, granting of franchise license
8. Accept offer	Employment agreement	Franchise fees paid and franchisee agreement signed
9. Develop skills	Employee training	Franchisee training
10. Start candidate	Employee is on the job	Franchisee's initial unit opens

▲ Have a time frame compatible with the franchisor's time frame for penetrating the market.
▲ Want to learn more about the industry, how the franchise operates, and how a franchisee makes money in the business.
▲ Have the special requirements or skills necessary for the business (certifications, for example).

Most franchisors are reluctant to disqualify candidates at initial contact. An effective qualification process enables them to focus on candidates who are in a position to proceed and results in quicker identification of better candidates.

3. *Interview and follow-up and process.* The interview process helps candidates understand the franchise opportunity and helps the licensing representative assess whether the candidate is a suitable franchisee.

The interview process and support materials should facilitate a discussion of the candidate's motivations, his qualifications, the franchisor-franchisee relationship, and the operation of the business. The franchise licensing representative uses questioning, listening, and facilitating skills to create an environment of mutual trust and effective exchange of information.

The relationship between a candidate and the franchise licensing representative, when properly positioned, enables both parties to make an informed business decision. The result is mutual compatibility, which forms the basis for continuing discussions.

To facilitate an effective exchange of information, the licensing representative must:

- Articulate a clear definition of the purpose and desired result of the meeting.
- Direct candidates to prepare for the meeting by listing questions about the franchise and by thinking about their personal motivations.
- Ensure all decision-makers are present.
- Use the skills of questioning, facilitating, and listening to lead the discussion.
- Use materials that support the purpose, agenda, and results of the meeting.
- Discuss the UFOC (Uniform Franchise Offering Circular) and franchise agreement from a marketing perspective and obtain the UFOC Acknowledgement of Receipt.
- Summarize results and make a list of outstanding questions.
- Gain commitment from the candidate for specific follow-up actions.

The follow-up process should enable the candidate to confirm his understanding of the franchise opportunity and help answer the question, "What else do I need to know or do to make an informed decision about this franchise opportunity?" The expected result of the follow-up process is the candidate's submission of the application package for the franchise.

Candidate follow-up includes discussions with existing franchisees and additional research, which helps validate the candidate's understanding of the franchise opportunity. The follow-up process should be systematic and completed within an agreed-upon time frame. The franchisor validates the candidate's qualifications through reference and financial checks.

4. *Granting process.* The granting process makes a final assessment of the candidate's qualifications. If this assessment is positive, the candidate is granted a franchise license. The process involves assessing the candidate's application by the operations, training, financial, and legal personnel within the organization so that the following questions can be affirmatively answered:

▲ Does the candidate possess the necessary qualifications to join the franchise organization?

▲ Will the candidate work within the system to achieve the business purpose of the relationship, which is to get and keep more and more customers?

Owing to the litigious nature of business today, more and more franchisors videotape their interviews to validate compliance with disclosure requirements and confirm the candidate's understanding of the opportunity.

The final step in the granting process is the acceptance interview. At this interview, the candidate affirms his understanding of the opportunity and the relationship. The franchise agreements are signed, initial fees are paid, and the opening process begins.

5. *The opening process.* After the franchise is granted, new franchisees become the responsibility of the operations, training, design and construction, leasing, and other departments. This process should be systematic and planned. As with other steps, the value of the franchise should always increase with every contact the candidate has with the organization. The result of the opening process is a new franchisee, ready to begin business.

Why a Structured System Works

Franchisee recruitment and selection is a process, not an event. Often, when people come to our seminar, "How to Recruit and Select More Qualified Franchisees," they are looking for the magic technique or set of words that will convince good candidates to become franchisees and sign the check. But granting franchises is a process that must focus on the candidate's motivations or reasons for interest. It is a process that can be organized and structured in a systematic way to accomplish this goal. Here's why:

▲ *An evaluation system is provided.* Candidates usually do not have a systematic methodology for evaluating the opportunity they are being offered, so the franchisor must provide that systematic method. A structured system also helps the franchisor evaluate the candidate's willingness to follow a system. If candidates fail to follow the system during the recruiting and selection process, they probably will not follow the operating system once they are franchisees.

▲ *Clear expectations are established.* A structured system gives candidates a clear expectation of what should happen next. It affixes responsibility on both candidates and the licensing representative to move the process forward. It requires candidates to take some action and to take that action by a specific date to move the process along. This action (or inaction) allows the licensing representative to decide about proceeding with the licensing process, a decision based not on the ambition to sell a franchise but on the genuine interests of the candidate himself.

▴ *Focus is on the candidate.* A structured system clarifies and focuses the candidate's motivations. Most candidates do not have clearly defined goals, objectives, and dreams. The franchise licensing representative facilitates a candidate's decision-making process by providing a structure for thinking. The licensing representative helps a candidate define her goals, consider whether self-employment is an appropriate personal strategy, and see how franchising can be used to accomplish her defined goals.

During a candidate's evaluation of the franchise, she will be exposed to events, experiences, and information that create perceptions about the franchise. The franchise licensing system structures these experiences so that there is an ever-increasing perception of value about the franchise. We call this the Franchise Value Curve, demonstrated in Figure 11-3.

The solid line represents the candidate's increasing sense of the value of the franchise. Conversely, the dotted line represents value fluctuations that occur with certain events, experiences, or information. With every value fluctuation, such as those that occur with standard sales procedures, it is that much harder for the licensing representative to bring the candidate back to her previous level of enthusiasm (sense of value) for the franchise. The franchise licensing system must be designed to prevent occasions of value decline and instead constantly increase perceived value and move the qualified candidate forward.

Value fluctuations occur because of inadequate preparation or follow-up, lack of candidate focus or commitment to moving the process ahead, and failure to use the various materials and documents to create value during the licensing process. A structured system, consistently followed, is one way to prevent these missteps.

▴ *Limited resources—people, time, money, space—are channeled.* Every

Figure 11-3. The franchise value curve.

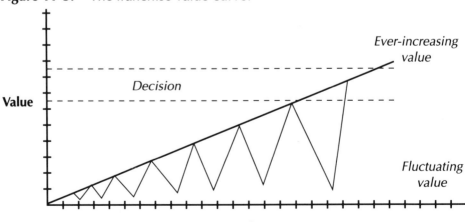

organization has limited resources of people, time, money, materials, and space. Many times a franchisor's resources are allocated without clearly defined goals, a strategy to develop markets, or a focused promotion effort to attract qualified candidates. A structured licensing system spells out every step, allocates a time sequence, and specifies the results expected. Figure 11-4 demonstrates a structured franchise licensing system.

The Skilled Franchise Licensing Representative

Helping a candidate make a decision about joining the franchise requires a fluid communication process that includes a mutual exchange of information as well as a candidate's commitment to specific actions. During the recruiting and selection process, the franchise licensing representative must know exactly where he or she is, exactly where the candidate is, and exactly what needs to be done to move the

Figure 11-4.   A licensing system structure.

Activity	Days	Expected Results
1. Implement promotional strategies	1–14	Generation of leads
2. Initial phone interview	5–25	Information package sent; candidate commits to return Request for Consideration
3. Request for Consideration returned	15–30	Franchise licensing manager follows up; schedules interview with qualified candidate
4. Interview	20–50	Candidate obtains understanding of franchise; franchisor gains insight into qualifications and motivations
5. Interview follow-up	25–60	Candidate commitments completed; demonstrates understanding of franchising
6. Candidate application received	40–75	Preliminary decision by franchisee selection committee to grant franchise
7. Acceptance interview	55–80	Agreement signed, fees paid
8. Pre-opening activities	60–240	Site selected, lease signed, store built out, franchisee trained, merchandise ordered, staff selected and trained
9. Store opens	120–270	Franchisee productive

process along. This can be achieved only through skillful use of facilitation, questioning, and listening. These skills, grounded in principles of psychology, psychotherapy, and adult learning, are used in every profession. They form the basis of all productive human relationships. Using them effectively during the franchise recruitment and selection process starts with understanding motivation.

Motivation

People do things for their own reasons, not for someone else's. The most important step in helping a candidate make an informed decision is to surface the candidate's personal motivations. Traditionally, franchise sales people spend very little time understanding why a candidate wants to pursue an opportunity. The tendency is to focus on the merits of the franchise. But telling about the franchise opportunity prior to understanding the candidate's reasons for acting only satisfies the desire to tell. The licensing representative must seek first to understand, then be understood.

To be motivated means to be aided by motives. Motives are reasons for acting—that is, *why* people do what they do. Motives change constantly and the licensing representative must be always alert to this. To learn what motivates a candidate, the licensing representative will use questioning and listening to explore these important areas:

- Needs, wants, and desires
- Goals, objectives, and dreams
- Fears, uncertainties, and doubts

Needs, Wants, and Desires

Needs, wants, and desires are the initial drivers that motivate a candidate's interest in self-employment and franchising. Either a person wants a change or he's tired of working for someone else, or she wants to be in control of her own affairs. Questioning and listening leads the licensing representative to probe these needs, wants, and desires, helping candidates define and close the first gap—that is, the gap between where they are today and where they hoped they would be.

Goals, Objectives, and Dreams

Once this gap is bridged and the candidate believes that it *is* possible to achieve change, he will have a reason and context for evaluating how the franchise opportunity will help close the second gap between where he is today and where he wants to be *at a defined future date*. Once the candidate defines his goals and personal vision, he will be more receptive to information about the franchise and better understand how to use the franchise to achieve these goals and personal vision.

The discovery process is one of constant flux. Questioning and listening skills are the franchise licensing representative's barometer for how the candidate is feeling and thinking at any one time. They enable the licensing representative to confirm information, uncover new information, assess feelings, and determine commitment to the franchise opportunity. Probing questions and active listening let the representative learn about the candidate as well as assess his compatibility with the franchisor.

Fears, Doubts, and Uncertainties

During the course of recruitment and selection, the candidate is asked to commit to specific actions to be accomplished within a specific period of time. It is usually at these points that candidates resist making those commitments. The logical question is, "Why the reluctance?"

The traditional sales approach would be to find out, "What's separating you from doing this deal?" And the candidate would respond with what are traditionally considered objections. The traditional salesperson would then try to overcome these objections by providing additional information that convinces the candidate the objections are no longer valid. A skillful franchise licensing representative goes beyond these objections and focuses on the source of the objections—the candidate's expression of a *basic issue*. A basic issue is a fear, uncertainty, or doubt about the franchise opportunity being in her best interest. It is the source of *why* the candidate feels the way she does.

Basic issues must be surfaced and resolved, because no matter how promising the match appears to be, it means nothing unless the candidate's fears, uncertainties, or doubts are resolved and that proceeding with the franchise seems in that candidate's best interest. The basic issue could be that, in fact, the candidate hasn't made the decision to be self-employed; or she has the money but is fearful of the financial investment; or he wants to be his own boss but lacks the confidence in his skills, knowledge, and ability to make it work.

Probing questions and active listening allow the licensing representative empathetically to surface these fears, uncertainties, and doubts and provide a forum for open discussion of them. Understanding continues to help candidates discover the gaps between where they are today and where they wanted to be today, or where they want to be in the future.

Getting Information

The licensing process should support the franchise licensing representative's need to get information. This is accomplished at various stages throughout the process by: structuring every contact the licensing representative has with the candidate, building a common agenda at the start of each contact, encouraging the candidate's involvement in moving the process ahead, and using the skills of facilitating, questioning, and listening.

Giving Information

Giving information involves supporting the candidate's need to know about the business opportunity. At every stage in the licensing process, the candidate is given information about the franchise opportunity. This information and related experiences are used by the licensing representative to build the value of the franchise as well as address the candidate's need to know, so she can obtain and confirm an understanding of the franchise opportunity. This information and related experience includes the following:

- Advertisements and other promotional materials
- Contacts with franchisor personnel throughout the process
- Interview materials
- The UFOC and franchise agreements
- Validations with existing franchisees and other testimonials
- Visits to an operating unit
- Statistics
- Business planning

Getting Commitment

Getting commitment involves responsibility on the part of both the candidate and the franchise licensing representative to move the process ahead. This is accomplished by affixing responsibility on both parties, As previously stated, commitment means that the candidate will take some action within a specific time frame to move the process along. These actions result in incremental decision making and discovery throughout the process:

- Candidates decide to be self-employed.
- Candidates decide to pursue franchising as a strategy.
- Candidates have the necessary financial resources.
- The franchisor decides that a candidate meets minimum qualification criteria.
- Candidates obtain and confirm their understanding of the franchise opportunity.
- Candidates decide that franchising is right for them.
- Candidates complete the application process.
- The franchisor grants the franchise.

Summary

The franchisee recruitment and selection process creates the future of a franchise system. To remain competitive into the next century and to reach the full potential of franchising, a franchisor must have a strong franchisee recruitment and selection process. This process includes a market development strategy and plan, a structured franchise licensing system, and skilled licensing personnel.

The market development strategy and plan provides the direction for building the system to achieve the vision of the company. A structured franchise licensing system achieves the results of the strategy and plan, and structures the candidate's evaluation process. Skilled franchise licensing personnel use the structured system to achieve the results of the market development strategy and plan.

Skilled licensing personnel help candidates make informed business decisions about whether the franchise is the best way to achieve their goals, dreams, and objectives. The franchise licensing process allows candidates and the licensing representatives to exchange information and make commitments that determine if the arrangement is right for each other—what Miller and Heiman in their book *Conceptual Selling* call a win-win situation.[1] This outcome means the ultimate decision is good for the candidate and good for the franchise. Leading a candidate through the decision-making process requires communication skills of facilitating, questioning, and listening.

Competing today requires franchisors to shift their thinking about the nature of franchising, understand the thinking of prospective franchisees, and transform the role of licensing personnel. First, the franchise organization must understand the nature of franchising and agree that franchises are granted, not sold. Once this understanding is reached, it significantly changes the expectations the franchisor has of its licensing personnel, which in turn influence the selection and recruitment process of franchise licensing representatives.

Second, traditional marketing objectives must give way to a new focus on the candidates and the value each brings to the organization. Granting franchises goes beyond a numbers game to a consultation process that produces more qualified applicants in less time, and results in better franchisees.

Finally, licensing representatives must change the way they see themselves. Rather than convince prospects that they should buy a franchise, they must act as consultants, helping candidates make informed business decisions. Rather than focusing on what the franchise can do for the candidate, the licensing representatives must focus on what the candidate needs to make an informed decision. Listening and questioning skills must be developed and refined—not easy for traditional salespeople used to finding hot buttons, overcoming the objection, and closing deals.

The result of these mental shifts is the determination of compatibility, better franchisees, and effective use of resources.

NOTE

1. Robert B. Miller and Stephen E. Heiman, *Conceptual Selling* (New York: Holt, 1978).

12

Key Aspects of Managing the Franchisor-Franchisee Relationship Over the Long Term

Robert F. Turner, independent consultant formerly with both General Business Services, Inc. and Decorating Den Systems, Inc.

By their very nature, franchise organizations tend to be geographically widespread, and franchisees are more inclined to independent thought and action than employees of conventional business organizations. These factors impose on the franchisor a greater need to communicate and manage the relationship effectively over the long term. They also mean the franchisor needs an organization that is self-motivating to the greatest extent possible. Variations on standard leadership techniques are necessary to accommodate the broad structure that characterizes franchise organizations. The wise manager in a franchise organization recognizes how these differences affect human relationships and adapts his methods to meet those needs.

Leadership in the Franchise Business

Leadership in a franchise organization is, in most ways, the same as leadership in any other organization. Yet there are some differences. The fact that franchisees have made an investment in their franchise—which they sometimes interpret as an investment in the total organization—causes them to look at the organization differently. Indeed, some franchisees feel they have a proprietary interest in the total organization, not just their franchise.

Some franchisees will have made a larger investment in their franchise than the chief executive has made in the franchisor. This large investment colors their outlook, and their reaction to changes, their attitude toward management, their views on marketing, and perhaps most important, their expectations of management are all affected by their stake in the business.

It is no wonder, then, that franchisees want to be consulted on key decisions affecting them. Whereas an employee might take the attitude that he can simply quit and move on to another job if he does not like management or the direction it is taking, a franchisee is locked into the organization. Significant changes in management, operations, philosophy, or company style are magnified if the company is a franchisor. Thus, franchise managements contemplating significant changes to their operations make such changes at the risk of alienating their franchisees if they do not confer with them first, advise them of the impending changes, and allow them to participate in the planning and implementation of the changes.

A representative body of franchisees can be a good vehicle to introduce change. A franchisee advisory committee, new-product committee, advertising committee, or similar group in which franchisees have a real voice, not just nominal participation, can be effective. But nominal participation will not meet the need; real participation is the key to good franchisee relations.

The franchisor must not yield control or abdicate responsibility when working with franchisee committees, however. Franchisees must always understand that there can be only one final decision maker in the organization. Decisions in a successful, well-managed company are usually not democratic actions, although frequently they are arrived at by consensus. The chief executive must give serious consideration to the recommendations of his franchisee working groups, but he alone is responsible for making the final decisions. Franchisees must understand that the chief executive has other constituencies to consider in addition to the concerns of franchisees.

How does someone lead an organization that is geographically diverse, and where the franchisees place their own profit goals ahead of the goals of the franchisor? How can a CEO give direction to a franchise organization? First, franchisees must understand the mission and goals of the franchise organization before becoming franchisees. When recruiting a new franchisee, the franchise marketing department must instill in the candidate a sense of the organization's goals, its mission, and the route the organization is taking to achieve its goals. The new recruit has the opportunity to opt out before signing on. But if the new recruit does sign on, then presumably he does so with an understanding of the mission, goals, and vision of the organization. He has bought into the mission, goals, and vision of the organization.

The next step is the training program. The training department has the responsibility to inculcate in the new franchisee an ever deeper understanding of the corporate mission and its goals. The franchisee must understand how she fits into the overall effort to achieve corporate goals. She needs to become a believer in the corporate religion and become a missionary for the company.

The new franchisee becomes the company's centurion in her community. It is her responsibility to carry the company flag. To do this she must have the corporate mission, the vision of what the company hopes to become, so clearly fixed in her mind that she doesn't have to think. She has been converted to the corporate religion. This is such an important issue that the training department should give it importance equal to the operational aspects of the business.

When the franchisee understands the corporate mission and its objectives, and buys into the vision of the company, then implementation of new programs at the franchisee level becomes easier. Implementation is a matter of showing the new franchisee how the new program helps the organization move toward achieving its mission and objectives. Assuming that the franchisee has bought into the mission in the first place, implementation should be a smooth process.

Franchise executives who have attempted to implement new programs before selling franchisees their vision of the company and instilling a corporate mission can attest to the difficulty of the implementation. Thus, top priority goes to selling the franchisees on the corporate mission, objectives, and vision, above all else. Business writer Peter Drucker once wrote that "Without understanding the mission, the objectives, and the strategy of the enterprise, managers [franchisees] cannot be managed, organizations cannot be designed. . . . The mission must be a clearly articulated call to action. Management must invoke the dream."[1]

Steady progress toward achieving the goals of the organization is critical to maintaining morale. When progress ceases or reverses, morale goes into reverse. Momentum begins to slow. If the situation is not quickly remedied, momentum will begin to accelerate in the wrong direction, but this will not happen without considerable warning. When top management senses that momentum is on the decline, action is required to restate the mission, repaint the picture of the corporate vision, and restate the corporate objectives. It is this restatement of mission, objectives, and vision that will reenergize franchisees if the restatement is backed by action. It will lead then in positive directions. They will be self-motivated, self-directed, and self-actuated.

Shared Goals

It is desirable to design the organization and structure the relationship in such a way that the goals of the franchisor and the franchisee coincide. To achieve this the franchisee must see how the accomplishment of corporate goals will help him achieve his personal goals. Similarly, top management must design the organization so that achievement of the franchisee's personal goals will help achieve the corporation's goals. While this is easily stated, successful execution requires very skillful management.

The Franchise Relationship

Franchising is based on a unique set of relationships not found in other business organizations. It is a business relationship *and* a human relationship, so success in franchising is dependent upon developing these relationships successfully. Franchisees look to the franchisor for leadership, support, vision, assistance, and profitable solutions to their problems. They do not look for employer-oriented attitudes. Direct orders given to a franchisee do not obtain the same results as one would expect from direct orders to an employee. Indeed, direct orders given to a franchisee frequently result in a negative response and negative reactions.

The best results are usually obtained when the franchisee knows the absolute parameters of what constitutes proper operation of her business. These parameters must be clear, easily understood, and inviolate. For example, in a restaurant franchise, absolute standards apply for cleanliness, food quality, and health matters. Failure to meet these standards is cause for corrective action.

Absolute standards differ based on the type of business. In the tax preparation business, accuracy rates are critical, and the IRS is the final quality control. A high error rate by the franchisee plus penalties imposed by the IRS can destroy the franchisor and tarnish the image of all franchisees in the organization. A company that has established a money-back guarantee if the customer is dissatisfied for any reason, and has promoted the policy in its consumer advertising, cannot allow a franchisee to back out on this responsibility. An interior decorating franchisor faced with an incident of this type was forced to step in and service the consumer at company expense. The franchisee was eventually terminated when a resolution with the franchisee proved to be impossible.

Too many rules and too close supervision will kill the franchisee's motivation. The best ideas come from motivated franchisees. The franchisee who has been active in the day-to-day operation of his franchise can be expected to generate suggestions worthy of consideration.

Human beings will behave as they are rewarded. Positive reinforcement for positive accomplishments encourages the franchisee to continue heading in a positive direction. The franchisee who understands the mission of the company and the corporate objectives, and is rewarded for positive accomplishments, will be a valuable, self-motivated franchisee. The franchisee who does not receive rewards for positive accomplishments will gain her recognition (notoriety) from negative actions dysfunctional to the company.

Franchisees as Long-Term Customers

Every business has more than one customer. The manufacturer must consider the wholesaler and the retailer as well as the consumer; the franchisor must consider the franchisee as well as the consumer. In fact, the franchisee is the most important customer the franchisor has, both in the short term and on a long-term basis. Customers are usually rational, and their behavior over long periods of time is rational. But remember that they behave rationally in terms of their own circumstances. Likewise, franchisees, being customers, can be expected to behave in a rational and predictable way, as they perceive their situation.

If fees are too high for what they receive (or perceive they are receiving), the franchisor can expect a negative reaction. The franchisor must be sure the services it provides to its franchisees (customers) have value as they perceive it. In some cases this will require explanatory selling, but no amount of selling will convince franchisees they are getting good value if they, in reality, are not. Fairness and competitive pricing must characterize all sales to franchisees.

Overcharging franchisees for products or services results ultimately in the same response one would expect from overcharging any other customer: The franchisee will acquire his products and services elsewhere. And the reaction is compounded by the fact that he thinks he is being taken advantage of because he is in a captive situation. Whereas nonfranchise companies never hear from the customer again, the franchisor can be sure the franchisee will most definitely be heard from again—much to the chagrin of the franchisor.

Dealing With the Outspoken Franchisee

So how does a franchisor deal with a franchisee who is outspoken? We all cringe at bringing the outspoken, disruptive franchisee into a position where she might have influence over others, but when done carefully, she can be changed from a disruptive force into a positive agent of change. Far better to have the disruptive franchisee where you can keep an eye on her, influence her positively, and know what she is doing than to have her out causing all sorts of problems you don't know about—but soon will.

If the troublemaker is given responsibility for leading a discussion group, moderating a subcommittee, or chairing a task force, either he will seriously try to do a positive job or his peers will quickly size him up for what he is and he will discredit himself. Those that can be turned into a positive force will soon be identified; those that are true troublemakers will be frozen out by the franchisees.

Franchisees cannot be fired like employees. Termination is so fraught with potential problems that only the reckless try to terminate an outspoken franchisee without first having taken every opportunity to discover the cause of her unhappiness. Try the positive approach first.

The Franchisee-Franchisor "Partnership"

Frequently one hears a franchisor-CEO describe franchisees as her *partners*. This term reflects a thought process that can bring a variety of problems. Obviously, franchisees are not partners in the legal sense. They are, at best, partners in some philosophical sense. Use of the term *partner* leads franchisees to the view that they, by right, have a say in the operation of the system. Some franchisors have unwittingly restricted their freedom to manage by blurring the boundary between the rights of the franchisor and the rights of franchisees. Each has separate and distinct rights and responsibilities, and those rights and responsibilities must remain clear. When a franchisee has been told that he is a valued *partner* in the organization, only to be rebuffed when he later tries to exercise his *partner* prerogatives, trouble brews. The relationship will suffer.

The term *partner* is used because it denotes a warm, shared relationship both parties want. Eventually our society will become more knowledgeable about the franchisee-franchisor relationship and the rights and responsibilities of each, but for now try not to use the word *partner* to describe franchisees.

Usually franchisees like to be called something other than *franchisees*. Companies have used terms such as *associate, licensee, area director, area manager,* and *owner* as the in-house appellation. But whatever they are called, they are the customers that make the business successful, and the staff in the national headquarters must recognize that the franchisee is the most important person in their daily business lives.

Negotiating With Franchisees

Occasionally disputes with franchisees will arise. The franchisor wants to negotiate a settlement quickly and get on with business. However, negotiating unique relationships, special deals, or one-of-a-kind contracts almost always results in problems. Franchise contracts issued during any given period of time should be identical for identical groups of franchisees. Whenever a ''special deal'' has been granted to one franchisee, it must be extended to all franchisees in the same class. Failure to do so will erode the franchisor's integrity and cause unhappiness among the franchisees who did not get the ''special deal.''

Experience has shown that it is almost always a mistake to negotiate contracts when the initial sale of the franchise is made. Some leeway can be extended in those few cases where an individual franchise is distinctly different for some explainable reason, or if very few franchises will ever be granted, but individual negotiation of franchise contracts leads to administrative problems and possible legal problems if a significant number of franchise contracts are unique. Negotiating a franchise contract with a franchisee only leads her to believe that everything is negotiable, and then the integrity of the system suffers. Soon franchisees want to negotiate everything from prices to royalties, from menus to operational details. Negotiating can and will get out of hand.

Selection of Franchisees

Successful franchising depends on the entrepreneurial spirit and motivation of the franchisees. But franchisees are sometimes referred to as ''leaners'' because they lean on the social relationships and support provided by the franchisor.

Individuals who are so strongly entrepreneurial that they see a franchise system as a series of constraints will not remain long within a franchise system. They can never be happy within a system and should be avoided as franchisees. Identifying the too strongly entrepreneurial before bringing them into the system is as desirable as identifying the incompetent.

Most franchisors have introduced testing systems into the selection process in an attempt to avoid both nonperformers and loose cannons. Very few screening systems have proved particularly effective, but they are worth trying to develop. Recruiting mistakes are costly—more so in franchising than in the usual business recruiting situation. Those who fail hurt the entire system, and those who are unable to live within the constrictions of a franchise system eventually leave, but only after having created more than their fair share of havoc.

Franchisee Supervision

Supervision of franchisees is not the same as supervision of employees. Franchise supervision should focus on quality control, maintaining standards, compliance with policies and approved procedures, and ongoing training. Assistance with goal setting, but not actually setting goals for the franchisees, is also an important function of franchisee supervision.

Whenever possible, supervision should be performed by individuals with franchise operations experience, although locating and hiring supervisors with successful franchise experience is difficult because the successful ones can earn more operating their own franchises than the franchisor can afford to pay as a salary. It is also beneficial if top managers have franchise experience. But "old" experience can be dangerous. A franchisee knows more about how to make, sell, and deliver a pizza than someone (the CEO for example) who has been away from the pizza oven for a few years.

Communications

All the good intentions, all the wonderful plans, and all the brilliant ideas are worth little if they are not communicated clearly in such a way that they guide, educate, and direct the organization. The mission and objectives of the organization must be continually before the franchisees in all that they do and read about the company. This is so important that the national headquarters must have a communications department tasked with the responsibility of inculcating the vision, philosophy, and objectives of the company.

The company's franchise manuals should be reviewed to determine if they are adequate in this area. They should be updated on a regular basis. Most franchisors have two publications they distribute to their franchisees in addition to their manuals. One carries only "must know" information. The other carries "nice to know" information.

The "must know" publication includes everything franchisees need to know to operate their franchises. It includes information bearing on their franchise contract, royalties, advertising fees, menu changes, operational changes and the like. The "nice to know" publication carries information about what other franchisees are doing, plenty of photographs and recognition of franchisees, both in the operation of their businesses and in their extracurricular activities. A little recognition can go a long way to building morale and togetherness. In fact, recognition of franchisees is so important it should dominate this publication.

Advertising Fees

Probably no issue is as controversial as the advertising fee. All franchise systems that sell to the public should require some form of advertising contribution by the franchisees. At stake is the long-term viability of the system.

More than one franchisor has tried to be a "nice guy" and keep the advertising fee small or nonexistent. Eventually the franchisees saw that their businesses were not prospering, and they blamed the franchisor for "not doing anything," rather than see their failure to pay an adequate advertising fee. On the other hand, an advertising fee set too high can result in a severe financial burden to the franchisees. Too much advertising, or poorly spent advertising, can result in failure of the business just as surely as too little advertising. The franchise contract should allow the franchisor some flexibility to adjust the advertising fee to meet changing needs of the business. Conditions change, products and services change, and the market will change.

The spending of the funds collected from the advertising fee creates its own set of issues. Experience has shown that the best procedure for budgeting and spending advertising funds results when the franchisor holds the ultimate authority, but consults with the franchisees and obtains their assistance in developing the advertising plan. It may be better to waste a few dollars on questionable advertising than get into a lot of wrangling with franchisees over the program.

Some franchisors establish an advertising council composed largely of franchisees, but allow the franchisor to appoint or otherwise select a few members of the council who have expertise in advertising and marketing. The council supervises the activities of the advertising agency retained by the company to do the creative work and implement the ad campaigns.

To eliminate as many issues as possible, the advertising fund should be set up as an independent trust with a trustee. Financial statements for the trust should be published to the franchisees periodically by the trustee along with highlights and many details of the advertising plan. Franchisees want to know how their advertising dollars are being spent.

The Self-Motivating Organization

The ultimate goal of good management could easily be described as building an organization that is self-motivating. Thanks to its unique structure, franchising already contains some of the basic ingredients of self-motivation, especially the profit motive. Franchisees have a profit motive that an employee can only dream about.

But more than the profit motive is necessary to motivate an entire organization. Ego satisfaction, positive feedback from peers, a sense of satisfaction, a feeling that one controls one's own destiny, and a positive contribution to society are also important motivators. Franchising can contain many of these motivators because the freedom of action granted to franchisees allows them to develop their own motivating interests.

Unexpectedly, the profit motive does not always work. Some franchisees don't grow beyond the comfort level they reach at only a modest level of profitability. The profit incentive loses much of its motivating force after the franchisee reaches this personal comfort level. Forcing them out of their comfort level by challenging them to achieve higher goals requires the same type of motivational leadership nonfranchise organizations require. Just like employees, franchisees respond to different goals and different incentives. It is a responsibility of management to create the motivational systems that motivate the greatest number of people.

Some can be motivated by a system of rewards, some by pats on the back, and some by pats lower down. Some can be motivated by recognition. Some can by competition with other franchisees in the system. Some can be motivated by the opportunity to grow within the system. The wise franchise executive creates a system of rewards for performance, recognition for positive reinforcement, educational opportunities, growth opportunities, expansion opportunities, as well as the pat on the rear, peer pressure, and as a last resort, the threat of termination. To motivate an entire organization requires a multiple approach. The company that relies on only one approach will motivate only a portion its franchisees.

Problem Solving

The franchise organization lends itself beautifully to the type of problem solving whereby the individuals (franchisees) in the organization are the resource that creates the solutions. Not only do the franchisees appreciate the opportunity to be of service but they recognize the need to contribute to the well-being of the organization.

Most franchisors have established franchisee advisory councils. The councils should always be set up as an advisory group and never given executive authority. Nevertheless, the council can have a very broad charter taking on any assignment where the chief executive desires advice or counsel.

The advisory council is best organized as an elected body representing the community of franchisees. Staggered terms, rotating chairmanship, and geographic representation typically characterize the advisory councils that are most effective. The council will have a charter and by-laws, and in some cases has a budget to cover certain designated expenses, such as the expenses to operate the council and reimburse the members for their legitimate expenses incurred in the execution of their council assignments.

The council consists primarily of franchisees. The greater the representation of the franchisees on the council, the greater the legitimacy of their recommendations. Nevertheless, some franchisors like to have one or two members of management sit on the advisory council with voting rights.

The council usually acts through a series of working committees such as an advertising committee, convention committee, new-product committee, supplier committee, and a grievance committee. Thus, problem solving where franchisees are involved can frequently be referred to the appropriate committee of the franchisees' peers for resolution. The committees will usually try to resolve the problems themselves, but will make recommendations to management for action where necessary. Indeed, one of the most useful functions of an advisory council is its problem-solving activity. Managements who use it skillfully will reap many rewards.

Quality Control

Among the many benefits of franchising for the consuming public is the high standard of quality associated with the system's name and trademark. It follows that establishment of the appropriate quality standards is a top priority of franchise management. The franchisor must have an effective quality enforcement program. Enforcement requires that the standards be easily understood and applied, and that there be a clear understanding of the interpretation and application of the standards.

Education of the franchisee beginning at the initial training is the single best way to infuse high-quality standards in the organization, explain the need for high standards, and discuss the company's interpretation of the standards.

We have just seen how an advisory council can be helpful in resolving or ameliorating a wide range of issues. The council can also be helpful in enforcing quality standards. Although management should never yield its responsibility to maintain quality standards, peer pressure exerted through the advisory council can exert enormous influence over the quality standards of the organization for the benefit of all franchisees.

Peer pressure from franchisees directed through the advisory council may be able to gain compliance more effectively than an inspector from headquarters. But putting teeth into the enforcement of quality standards is necessary from time to time not only to protect the company image but also to convince the franchisees that the company is serious.

Many franchisors have instituted inspection programs, with hired or contracted personnel making unannounced inspection trips or purchases to grade the franchisee on his performance. This can be very effective, but should be explained well in advance of the implementation of such a program. Regardless of the type of inspection, the inspector's report should be given to the franchisee and a representative of management should discuss it with the franchisee. Only in this way can improvement be effected on a long-term basis.

Conclusion

Successful management of a franchisor depends on recognizing both the similarities and differences between franchise organizations and traditional organizations. The wise manager of a franchise will capitalize on the strengths inherent in franchising, and at the same time adapt her leadership style to accommodate issues unique to franchising. Some of those issues are economic, some are control oriented, while others are motivational in nature. All of them involve human relations and require the manager to modify her leadership style from traditional methods if the business is to be everything that it can be.

NOTE

1. Peter F. Drucker, *Management: Tasks, Responsibilities, Practices* (New York: Harper & Row, 1974), p. 48.

13

Franchisee Advisory Councils

Robert L. Perry, The Hunter Group

Franchise executives maintain that their most important problem is building positive, productive, mutually beneficial relationships with their franchisees. The long-term success and continued growth of both franchisor and franchisee depend on this relationship. During the past few years, successful franchisors have built successful relationships by effectively communicating with their franchisees and ensuring they feel empowered.

Empowerment was one of the business buzzwords of the 1980s and it is still applicable in the 1990s. It may imply many things, but in franchising it means not only allowing but encouraging franchisees to suggest improvements in the system and—more often—to participate in decisions that affect the system. Successful franchisors state that the most effective structure to encourage franchisee participation is the franchise advisory council (FAC). A franchise advisory council is a group of established, successful franchisees who meet regularly to discuss essential business issues with company executives.

FACs differ from other types of franchisor-franchisee groups. First, many franchisors that collect advertising fees have set aside special advertising funds and have an advertising council to manage that money. These councils, whose members may include both company executives and franchisees or only franchisees, discuss advertising and marketing issues; work with advertising and public relations agencies; and determine future advertising, public relations, and promotional programs. Some franchise advisory councils, such as that for The Maids International, evolved from an advertising council and continue to manage advertising funds. But they consider other franchise business issues as well.

Second, some franchise companies, such as Precision Tune, have technical advisory groups that include franchisees, trainers, and technical experts. They develop new equipment, set up new training programs, and provide technical support programs. However, a franchise advisory council includes, but goes far beyond, technical issues. Its main purpose is to advise franchise executives about all the issues that directly affect franchisee business, such as field support, new product or service development, insurance costs, price structures, operations and distribution, and market trends.

Franchise advisory councils develop in many ways: to bring about specific

changes, correct situations, or solve problems; to reestablish positive communications; to encourage franchisees to participate more in the company's development; or to facilitate better communication.

Servicemaster's twenty-year-old Idea Review Council evolved from the company's need to cope with rapid growth and communicate effectively with its thousands of franchisees. The Maids International's council evolved from its advertising fund management group. Merry Maids' council, according to President Don
Parkhurst, evolved from a group of annual award winners, called the President's
Advisory Council, to a more representative council based on geographic location
and franchisee size. And Blimpie's president and cofounder, Anthony Conza,
explained that its new advisory council developed when "we created a new vision
for the company" and adapted two existing regional advertising cooperatives to
form a national franchisee association.

David H. Senseman, franchisee and chairman of The Maids International's
advisory council, explains that his group is concerned with five essential cost
areas: automobile and liability insurance, workers compensation, supplies and
equipment, advertising, and automobile expenses. His group urges The Maids
executives to establish nationwide group buying plans so its 180 franchises can
save money. On the other hand, advisory councils rarely have the power to make
decisions or set corporate policy. Their primary role is as adviser. Equally important, the councils act most effectively when they identify both problems and
opportunities, and when they urge the franchisor to work together to solve the
problems and take advantage of cost-cutting or profit-making changes.

Effective Advisory Councils

How effective an advisory council is depends directly on how franchise executives
respond to the council's advice. Successful franchisors use the council to solicit
ideas, encourage franchisee recommendations, and listen to criticism because, as
Tom Peters has insisted for the past decade, the people doing the work—the franchisees—know how to do their jobs best. Busy franchisor executives—concen-
trating on growth, financing, promotion, and similar issues—may lose sight of
what is happening at the franchise level. And corporate staff and field support
representatives—who may never have owned their own businesses—may find it
difficult to understand the perils that an independent franchisee faces.

For example, Don Anderson, president of the 5,800-franchisee Servicemaster ResCom Division, noted that its council "is an effective communication tool
so we don't get 'ivory tower-itis.' Our Idea Review Council gives us structured
feedback not only so we get our franchisees' ideas and perspective, but also so
they can review our plans and changes we believe will help."

To make an advisory council effective, franchise executives must set a positive tone, and franchisees must avoid the temptation to use council meetings as
sessions to complain about but not solve problems. Most important, franchise

executives must follow through on their promises to the council. States Dan Bishop, president of The Maids International:

> Our council works best when we are very open with them—when we create an honest, true partnership with them, not force our decisions on top of them. Our franchisees have seen us take action by the next council meeting on items we jointly decided at the last meeting. We do not just talk about changes; we are results-oriented. Even if we can't make the change, we report back to the council what we have done or not done and why. They know we respond.

Franchisee council members and franchise executives agree that if company executives do not respond or follow through, the franchisees learn quickly that the advisory council is a paper tiger. The franchisees then ignore the council, refuse to join, do not submit ideas, and feel even more frustrated.

Furthermore, for the council to be effective, franchisors must be patient. It may take three to five years for franchisees to understand and appreciate the council's purpose and actions, and then to begin to contribute ideas and participate. Franchisees tend to be busy and skeptical; they have a "show me" attitude that takes time to change. Before establishing an advisory council, franchise executives must understand what will make it successful.

Advisory Council Structures

How the council has evolved will influence its structure and its members' responsibilities, and yet its structure is essential to its success. Organizational development experts have found that structure both influences how well a group works and also is influenced by the corporate culture—that is, the prevailing attitudes, practices, and behaviors of top executives. For example, a top-down, authoritative structure will not support a participative, democratic culture; neither will it support a responsive, effective franchise advisory council. Any franchise planning to establish an advisory council should consider its basic structure and culture because, by its very nature, a council requires and encourages open attitudes, active participation, and a democratic culture.

An advisory council's structure usually consist of its membership, membership requirements, selection (election or appointment), length of terms, council officers, formal bylaws, council committees, meetings, meeting process and agenda, council duties, and franchisor's participation and roles.

Selection Procedure

Advisory council members are selected in myriad ways. The prevalent method is to combine nomination by other franchisees and appointment by company exec-

utives or current council members. The second most common method is direct
election by the franchisees. The third most common is direct appointment by
franchise executives, often after they consult with current council members.

However, the nomination process may take many forms as well. For example, Precision Tune solicits nominees from each region via a special FAC mailing
to all franchisees and then sends out ballots; franchisees within each region vote
for their region's representative. On the other hand, Servicemaster executives
discuss potential nominees with current council members and seek the nominees'
cooperation to serve. And The Maids International solicits nominees formally
from its council members and informally from all its franchisees.

The chosen nomination method reflects franchise attitudes toward the council. Some want it as open as possible so that even franchisees likely to disagree
with executives may be elected, while others want as council members only those
franchisees who have been successful and strongly support the franchise system.
Franchisees do not want "rubber stamps"; they want members who will bring a
positive attitude and concentrate on improving the system.

If franchise executives or former council members appoint the new council
members, then they appoint them if they are willing. For example, to obtain its
council's sixteen members, Servicemaster appoints two members—one franchisee and one distributor—from each of eight regions (seven in the United States
and one in Canada).

Election methods also vary. Usually, new members are elected in three ways:
(1) by region, (2) in a nationwide election, or (3) by a secret ballot among the
present council members. The council's method tends to follow the franchisor's
structure. For example, Precision Tune's council consists of twelve members: six
franchisees and six subfranchisors, one from each of six regions. But The Maids'
nine-member council comes via secret ballot from any location, and Blimpie's
elects the council members at the company's annual meeting.

Membership and Qualifications

The number of council members usually reflects the company's structure. Councils may have from five to twenty-one or more members, though the average is
from eleven to fifteen. Councils may include as members regional or state master
franchisors, area developers, regional distributors and/or subfranchisors as well
as regular franchisees. For example, Merry Maids' council consists of twenty-one
owners who act as regional coordinators.

Although some companies place strict qualifications on council membership,
almost all have at least minimum requirements. Members usually must have been
franchisees for at least one or two years, be in good standing with the company
(i.e., pay their royalties, fees, and bills on time), operate a successful local franchise, and in a more amorphous sense, be dedicated to the franchise system and
its success. A common informal qualification tends to limit membership to those

who are large enough and successful enough to afford the time away from their own business to carry out the council work.

For example, states Servicemaster's Anderson, "We are looking for creative, interested franchisees who are willing to take the time and whose business allow them to do this. They should have influence within their regions and be accessible to others because they must communicate with the other franchisees in their regions and represent their interests before the council."

Membership Terms

Furthermore, most franchisors stagger the terms of membership so new blood can come onto the council regularly. But members usually serve long enough to accomplish their personal goals or bring projects to fruition. The most common term is three years, so that one-third of the council members are replaced each year. In a common example, The Maids' council's nine members serve three-year terms, with three new members elected each year.

Most franchisors also limit how many terms a member can serve—most often just one three-year term, although sometimes two three-year terms or, occasionally, one one-year term, are allowed. Former council members also must wait from one to three years before they can be reelected or reappointed. The term limitation gives more franchisees the chance to participate.

Personal Benefits of Membership

Although at first franchisees may be reluctant to serve, as the council proves its effectiveness, franchisees begin to covet the positions. Members also receive direct benefits. Bonnie Jacobson, chairperson of Precision Tune's council, cites four key advantages: (1) networking with the most successful franchisees to find out how they run their businesses; (2) continuous direct contact with franchise executives and operations managers; (3) power to influence the franchise's future directions; and (4) immediate influence on daily operational problems. The Maids' council chairman Senseman adds a fifth advantage: a twelve- to eighteen-month head start on new technology that the company plans to introduce.

Council Bylaws

The length of terms, membership qualifications, and group's purpose, duties, and operations are usually written in bylaws. The International Franchise Association strongly recommends that formal bylaws be prepared and approved by the council members. This prevents arbitrary changes and assures the franchisees of the company's strong commitment to council independence.

Council bylaws range from a simple three-page overview, such as The Maids' version, to a lengthy legal document drafted by franchise attorneys that discusses every detail of a council's activities. In general priority order, a representative set of bylaws includes the following:

I. *Statement of Purpose and Objectives.* This presents a brief purpose or mission statement and then lists the council's five to ten key objectives. For example:

> The Franchise Advisory Council encourages open communication among the company's franchisees, its master franchisees, and company executives to discuss common problems and recommend mutually beneficial solutions. The Council acts as an advisory body and may recommend policy decisions, but it will not act as a policy-making board to make decisions which properly belong to company executives.

II. *Membership.* This section usually describes the qualifications or eligibility for membership, the council's composition or representation, members' term of office, and selection or election procedures. Sometimes, these issues are presented in separate sections. It should also address the nomination process and application procedures.

III. *Officers and Their Duties.* This section discusses the council's officers, how they are elected, and their specific duties which all members share. This chapter later discusses these duties.

IV. *FAC Duties and Powers.* This section lists or describes in detail the FAC's overall duties and limits its powers and roles to advising, recommending, or suggesting. It may also discuss how each member votes: as an individual; as a regional representative with one vote; or as a region rep with a weighted number of votes based on that region's number of franchises.

However, those councils that also manage an advertising fund may directly control and approve marketing and promotional programs, authorize spending, and hire and fire ad agencies and PR firms. This control gives the council significant power over one of the issues franchisees consider more important than all others.

V. *Committees.* This section describes the committees the council officers may appoint and their composition and duties. Most often, the committees cover these areas: advertising and marketing, operations, finance, new franchise sales, product and service development, and support services. Sometimes, they combine support services and operations.

VI. *Meetings.* This section outlines how often the council meets and its location and discusses who sets the agenda and how that agenda is determined before each meeting. It may also discuss procedures for regional council or franchisee meetings that precede a national council meeting.

VII. *Expenses*. This key section specifies whether or how much the franchisor will pay to cover the council members' costs of attending the meetings. This chapter later discusses this critical issue in detail.

VIII. *Amendments*. This section discusses the procedure by which the council and/or the franchise executives may change the bylaws. Usually, a bylaw change requires a simple majority vote (the most common method) or as much as a three-quarters majority (75%) to change the bylaws. Many bylaws also require 30 days' notice in writing to all council members before a vote on an amendment.

This outline does not include many of the details that bylaws can involve, such as voting proxies, membership termination, and area and regional councils. But some of these issues—including council officers, meetings, committees, expenses, and of course, a council's and its members' most important duties and tasks—require special attention.

Council Officers

Most councils elect their own chairperson, vice-chairperson, and secretary. The chairperson presides over the meeting, consults with franchise executives to determine each meeting's agenda, and gives a summary report to the full council. A chairperson is usually elected from the council's members and serves a one-year term. She may have to wait a year before she can be re-elected as chairperson.

Of course, the vice-chairperson serves in the absence of the chairperson and serves the unexpired term if some event prevents the chairperson from completing hers. In some cases, to give the council continuity, the vice-chairperson automatically becomes the chairperson the next year.

The secretary, usually with active support from the franchisor's administrative staff, takes minutes, reports those minutes to both the council and other franchisees, and sends any others letters or key information to the franchisees.

Council Committees

Each council committee considers the major issues and problems in its areas and works closely with its executive or operational counterpart—that is, the company's marketing vice-president works with the Marketing and Advertising Committee. The committee structure allows large councils to divide the work equitably and allows franchisees who do well in one area to share their expertise and experience. Some large councils appoint executive committees to meet with the franchisor's top executives between full council meetings.

Other councils use ad hoc committees appointed by the chairperson to consider special problems or issues as they develop. It seems that the older, more representative, more involved councils work through committees; they consider so many issues that studying each one would overburden the members and require them to take too much time away from their businesses.

Meeting Structures and Procedures

How the meetings are held shows the strong differences in attitude among franchisors regarding advisory councils. Councils usually meet two to four times a year; some large franchisors with large councils arrange two full council meetings and two council executive committee meetings per year. Others with small to moderate-size councils have two or three full council meetings; often one of these takes place at an annual convention. However, many franchisors believe too much activity happens at an annual convention to allow for an effective council meeting. Sometimes, the executive committee or a full council will meet briefly with franchise executives to review its presentations to these conventions.

The meeting location is very important. Some councils hold meetings at company headquarters so the council sticks to business and does not consider the meeting a vacation. Others use a resort or remote conference center for its relaxed, creative, and cooperative atmosphere.

Most council meetings last at least two, often three days. They require that much time to cover the four or five major concerns, listen to executive presentations, meet with advertising agencies, and so forth.

How the meeting takes place is essential. For example, many franchisors prefer to preside over and dominate the meeting with executive and operations presentations. They give council members information on new ideas, new programs, changes to existing programs, and progress on old issues. Although they may allow time for questions and feedback, they may not include time specifically for the franchisees to raise or explore issues they consider important. Franchisors rarely allow council members to meet without company executives.

On the other hand, more and more councils are asserting their need to caucus before they meet with franchise executives. Some councils allow the first full morning for this separate franchisee session; they discuss and decide the priorities to present to executives and the key questions they want to ask.

Who actually presides over the meeting can vary. In all cases, the figurehead chair is the franchisee chairperson, but in some cases the company CEO or president presides with the franchisee and leads the meeting. In other cases, the company CEO is the council chairperson. But usually the franchisee presides in fact as well as in title, and conducts the meeting.

The Agenda

The most important influence on how the meeting occurs is from whomever controls the agenda. Usually, franchise executives, with some advice from the council chairperson or members, draw up the agenda and send it to the members. The meeting follows that agenda strictly, often heavily oriented to what the franchisors want to discuss.

On the other hand, many councils control their own agendas and make sure thei committee reports receive ample time. They also set aside several hours or a full morning to discuss franchisee issues. But some franchise executives feel threatened by this situation, and the meeting structure itself may cause conflict between franchisors and franchisees.

The agenda raises fundamental issues about policy- and decision-making power. Some executives fear that agenda setting gives franchisees a wedge to determine policy, while others encourage council members to make sure the issues they consider most important receive adequate discussion.

Sample Agenda Format

Here is a sample agenda modified from a three-day council meeting that a major franchisor held in September 1991.

First morning:	Four-hour pre-meeting session for franchisees to discuss their issues that differ from company issues
First afternoon:	• Present financial update on company status
	• Discuss new franchise sales and new database for handling sales leads
	• Discuss performance of central toll-free telephone service
	• Consider fourth-quarter 1991 strategies
Second morning:	• Do general marketing review, including national ad fund status, toll-free number status, new advertising programs, new point-of-sale materials, and new tie-ins with corporate partners
Second afternoon:	• Review health and casualty and liability insurance programs
	• Discuss new products and equipment
	• List new and proposed programs and review with program development staff for council feedback
	• Discuss and update status of training programs, policies and procedures manuals, distributor development programs
Third morning:	Discuss important franchisee issues not covered by other sessions

With the exception of the franchisee issues, each item corresponds to a presentation by a company manager and a question-and-answer discussion with the members. Clearly, by the meeting's end the council knows exactly what the company has been doing, its members have had their say on every issue, and company executives have been made aware of every pertinent issue on the members' minds.

Of course, during the meals before, during, and after the formal meetings everyone discusses the issues, forms relationships, and shares ideas on how to improve the company or make individual franchises more successful.

Members and executives agree that to be effective, everyone at the meeting must maintain a positive attitude. Of course, tempers flare occasionally, but the underlying attitude must be of cooperation. As one council member put it, "We all want to work together toward the same end: making the franchise as strong and as successful as possible. Without successful franchisees, the franchisor cannot prosper; without a successful franchisor, the franchisees cannot profit."

Members' Duties During and After Meetings

The council bylaws discuss the formal duties and actions franchisees must take while they serve. These include the obvious, such as attending council meetings, attending annual conventions, participating in committee work, and formally reporting to franchisees each meeting's actions. If the members come from specific regions, they may have to attend regional council meetings or regional general meetings to communicate with franchisees and answer their questions.

However useful these formal actions are, the members' informal actions are probably far more important. On the most effective councils, members act as lightning rods for the other franchisees. They not only share what they learn at council meetings but also listen to the issues, ideas, problems, and complaints of other franchisees. They have a strong intuitive feel for franchisor actions that upset franchisees, and they have the confidence to bring these ill feelings to the council and company executives.

Of course, most problems become known through phone calls, private conversations at regional meetings, or open arguments between a franchisor's field support representatives and franchisees. In many cases, franchisors have a formal problem-reporting structure, but council members may work informally to solve a problem as well. For example, the company tells its franchisees to report problems first to their field reps, and if the field rep doesn't or can't solve the problem, to then report it to corporate headquarters. If the problem persists, franchisees then should report it to their regional council member or closest council member. Franchisors prefer that the council avoid individual problems between a franchisee and the company, and concentrate on issues that affect most or all franchisees.

Of course, this policy doesn't always carry through in practice, and council members often hear about individual problems before company executives do. Then, the council member often will make an informal survey via phone calls to see if this same problem affects other franchisees. And he may also report the problem to the proper operations manager or senior executive and urge its resolution.

On the other hand, some councils regularly and formally survey their franchisees. For example, James B. Ervin, Precision Tune's vice-president of business development, explained that the council solicits information before the meetings. The council chairman mails questionnaires weeks before to help identify problems and key issues. The company also frequently surveys its franchisees on specific interests, such as business-building techniques. In one seemingly unimportant but crucial difference, Precision Tune's FAC has its own letterhead—a small item that demonstrates its relative independence of company executives.

The Franchisor's Responsibilities

While council members can make recommendations for change, the buck stops at the franchisor. For the council to succeed, franchise executives must take several critical steps:

1. Give the council reasonable independence, especially setting its own agenda and conducting its own meetings.

2. Truly listen to what the council members say, including the implications of their comments, attitudes, and actions.

3. Devote staff and administrative time and money to the council. A significant part of at least one middle manager's duties should include working with the council. And that manager and the council's executive committee should have direct administrative support to manage mailing lists, correspondence, newsletters, or surveys and to coordinate council meetings, executive committee meetings, and regional council meetings. Without this direct support, the council members cannot trust that busy staff members, with other, more pressing duties, will address their activities quickly and completely.

4. Respond to every issue a council raises. From the start, franchisees are hesitant to speak out. If they do risk raising an issue and the company ignores it or brushes it aside, they may never again raise an issue, ask a question, report a problem, or suggest a new—and perhaps better and more profitable—idea or technique. Furthermore, franchisees may become reluctant to serve on the council; they may see it—accurately—as meaningless.

It is absolutely imperative for franchise managers and executives to act quickly on council issues and report their activities promptly to both the council and all other franchisees. For example, most council meetings set aside many hours for individual presentations from key managers: marketing, operations, franchise sales, product development, field service, and product distribution. Council members question these managers during their talks or raise pertinent similar issues when they can discuss their own issues.

During these franchisee sessions, executives should call in the manager responsible for that area or make sure that manager receives a full report on the issue immediately after. Then, the manager should discuss the issue either on the spot or by phone with council members and agree to report to the council by a certain date. Even if the manager can't solve the problem by that date, she should report what she has been doing about the issue and what she plans to do to resolve it.

Major issues, of course, may take months to resolve—for example, new products may take a year or more to be introduced. But the principle remains the same: managers and executives must regularly tell council members and other franchisees what they are doing. Otherwise, council members may become frustrated, feel ignored, or tire of raising issues the company refuses to consider.

Who Pays the Bill?

The last critical element to establishing an effective advisory council answers a simple, yet important question: Who pays the franchisees' expenses for participating in council meetings? The answer ranges from paying for everything to paying for nothing.

Some franchisors, such as The Maids and Servicemaster, pay all franchisee expenses, including travel, food, and room. They argue these two points:

1. Traveling to two to four meetings a year, often in distant locations, is expensive and may discourage or prevent smaller franchisees from serving as council members. Thus, they could lose the small or newer owners' valuable perspectives.
2. Paying expenses allows franchisees to spend time away from their business to do the council's work. They don't have to worry about hurting their own profit margins or reducing their salaries.

On the other hand, some companies refuse to pay any franchisee expenses; they argue that the council is serious business, and they want only serious franchisees willing to incur the costs serving on the council requires. They also tend to hold meetings at company headquarters to reduce costs.

But many franchises pay only part of the franchisee costs, ranging from $100 to $500 per member. They argue that sharing the costs impresses on the members the high value of the time they spend and sacrifices they make to serve on the council. However, to ease this problem, many franchisors—especially those whose councils administer advertising funds—pay franchisee expenses from these funds. They argue that all the franchisees should share the council's costs. They suggest that the ad fund is an appropriate vehicle because the council's main goals are to promote the franchisees and make them more successful and profitable. They also assert that using the ad fund is less troublesome than creating a new fund or charging a special fee to pay the council's costs.

Summary

Franchise advisory councils serve as an essential method through which, as franchisors grow, they stay close to their franchisees. It allows franchisors to communicate openly and share a positive attitude with their franchisees. Franchisors receive the best ideas from those who know best how to manage the franchises and make them profitable. And franchisees feel empowered and confident that their voice can not only be heard but can make their own businesses better by contributing to the franchise's overall success.

As Precision Tune's Jacobson concludes, "When I was a new franchisee, I realized that by working with the council, I might not be able to move mountains, but I could move some pebbles. When I become a FAC member, I realized I could move hills."

PART IV

MARKETING, ADVERTISING, AND PUBLIC RELATIONS

No experienced franchising executive would debate that marketing, advertising, and public relations play a key role in the development and growth of a franchising program. These three tools allow the franchisor to position its franchising program to reach the targeted franchisee.

The marketing strategies selected must be focused and aggressive, the advertising materials and placements must be targeted and exciting, and the public relations program must be professional and efficient. Bringing this all together is no easy task. The effort must be integrated to send a message about the mission and values of the franchisor.

In this Part IV, some of the best in the business walk you through this mine field safely. John Campbell's excellent chapter on developing the marketing and sales plan helps set the stage for specific articles on advertising, public relations, and trade show marketing that follow.

14

Developing the Marketing and Sales Plan

John A. Campbell, Franchise Masters, Inc.

I am certain you have heard about the man who woke up one morning and decided to drive from his small city in Louisiana to the big city of Minneapolis. He had always heard about it, knew what it looked like, but had never been there. He headed north in the approximate direction of Minneapolis, but did not have a road map. He had driven hundreds and even thousands of miles and, suddenly, there it was. He excitedly drove his car into the city he had always wanted to visit—Indianapolis.

"If you don't know where you are going, you'll probably end up somewhere else." Franchising had been an industry for many decades and new franchisors arrive on the scene every week. But the lack of sophistication in the marketing of franchises of many of these new as well as seasoned franchisors can be a sad epitaph for companies that do not plan. When a company seeks money, the first thing it must do is develop a business plan to present to banks, venture capital companies, and other investors. So why do those same companies move blindly along without the marketing plan (and a parallel sales plan) they so desperately need?

In 1980, a new franchisor that had recently entered the marketplace received a $2.5 million infusion of capital through the development of a very carefully worded and planned business plan. It set up its prototype and began marketing its franchise. After it had spent nearly the entire $2.5 million, it had only four franchises in the system. The business plan was excellent, but the company skipped the marketing plan completely. It felt the country was ripe for the type of franchise it was offering. But it forgot at least one major ingredient: the country didn't understand what it was it was trying to accomplish. The business and the franchise filled a niche, but the public didn't know what it meant to them.

A valuable lesson was learned from that problem. While it was marketing for franchises, the company needed to educate the public in what they had to offer. Once that educational process was in place and a small additional infusion of capital obtained, a marketing plan was carefully prepared. Now Sylvan Learning Centers is known by virtually everyone in the country and Sylvan is considered one of the foremost franchisors in the nation—all because the company developed a marketing plan that understood and met its target. Now it had a road map. (*If You Don't Know Where You're Going, You'll Probably End Up Somewhere Else* was a book written years ago by David Campbell.)

It is always interesting to listen to companies discuss marketing plans. They usually understand the terminology, but seldom understand the ingredients. They also do not understand the difference between a marketing plan and a sales plan. In the following pages I hope to generate the type of understanding and processes necessary to build a strong strategic marketing plan.

Marketing Plan Ingredients

A marketing plan looks at your present company activities and the competitive environment. That view forces the strategic and tactical changes required to move or stay ahead of the competition. It views how you will market your franchise and who you will market to, not how it will be sold at the grass-roots level. The sales plan is different. It is designed, once you have determined who you are selling to and where, to provide the *how* and *when* you will sell the franchise. In the sales plan, the questions of who will sell, where they will sell, and what the sales environment is will also be answered.

Following are some of the specific ingredients that should be considered and included in your marketing plan.

Environmental Analysis

Before beginning your journey, you must know your environment. The five environmental categories are: economic, societal, industry, markets, and franchising. Understand each thoroughly before embarking.

1. The *economic* evaluation includes the current economic condition of the country and the mood of the general public, the consumer. Timing of your franchise offering under certain economic conditions can be crucial. If recession is imminent, your offering must be geared to recessionary issues and well directed. The number of leads generated may be less, but the quality will be higher if the marketing is "well directed." A recession can be a good time to introduce a franchise opportunity that meets the proper requirements. For example, when people have lost or are about to lose their jobs and are looking for alternatives, a recession-proof franchise becomes one of those alternatives. Understanding interest-rate issues is also critical. Is borrowing expensive? Does your franchise require a large amount of borrowing? Does your franchise have tangible assets that can be used as partial collateral? Is your franchise riskier than others? (Fast-food or sit-down restaurant operations are examples of franchises that are considered riskier to lending institutions.) Direct marketing to people experienced in restaurant operations or management will reduce the risk factor to the lending institu-

tion. Even if a recession appears to be over, the mood of the population is also important. Small business generally reacts much later than large business to upswings following recessions. This could extend an apprehensive attitude within the investing public toward your franchise.

2. The *societal,* cultural, and governmental environment and the restrictions placed upon any of these noncontrollable entities will also affect your franchise significantly. Not understanding the tastes or governmental restrictions of a particular community can be fatal. In the 1980s, Popeye's entered the Detroit and other northern markets with a "hot" fried chicken product. The Detroit population was not interested. In a relatively short period of time, all the Popeye's stores in Detroit were forced to close. Popeye's did not understand that northern tastes were not accustomed to "hot" chicken products. These environmental issues may be different from community to community, and continual analysis must be made.

Also, what national, state, and local governmental restrictions have been, or may be, placed on your franchise business? What environmental issues face your franchisees? What are the problems on the horizon that could affect your franchise program in the future?

3. Understanding your own *industry* is also crucial. Where do you fit with your competitors? Do you have a specific niche you are attempting to fill, or do you look like all the rest? Picking a particular niche can be crucial to your marketing effort, but understanding your competition is most important before choosing that niche. This is more fully discussed in the next section.

4. Understanding each *market* is critical as well. While your franchise program may work well in Tampa, it may not be understood in Boise. Carefully planning how your franchise will be expanded market to market is critical to the success of your entire program. You will spend more time on one failing store than you will on twenty successful ones. Your marketing plan should include special attention to remote markets where you do not have a complete understanding of the consumer or the franchise buyer. Positioning your franchise expansion must be carefully evaluated, and should include testing of markets that are foreign to your knowledge. Is your goal to enter a market and then concentrate on saturating that market? Is "shotgunning" (opening wherever a franchise can be sold) the goal? Are there specific target markets?

5. The last analysis must be toward *franchising* itself. While you feel that your competitors are in the same field as you (fast food, house-cleaning services), your real competitors are every company that is a franchisor. Your marketing plan is geared toward finding and keeping franchisees for your system. Those franchise prospects could be looking at as many as 3,000 franchisors in their evaluation before making a decision. What the franchising industry looks like, who is doing what, where and when are critical. What marketing tools and degree of professionalism are they using? How does it compare to you? Joining the International Franchise Association, reading *Entrepreneur* magazine, randomly attempting to

buy franchises in competing and noncompeting franchise industries—all will become critical to your planning process. Be certain that you understand the precise profile of your franchise prospects: How to talk to them, who they are, and where to find them are all critical. It is important to pick your niche and understand the psyche of your potential franchise prospect. You can only do that when you understand what your competition is doing to approach that same prospect.

Competition Analysis

Before you begin the process of marketing your franchise to the general public, it is important for you to analyze companies in your own field as well as others in franchising. Choosing the top five franchisors in your specific industry is your first goal. Second, pick several new up-and-coming franchise companies in your industry. Third, determine other nonfranchised companies in your industry and evaluate those, obviously not for marketing franchises but, rather, for marketing their product or service to the consumer. Fourth, pick five companies who are not in your industry but are franchising, and evaluate how they are making their franchise and consumer offers to the general public. The first three processes are to determine the structure of your direct competitors; the fourth is for your indirect competitors. Both are important because they will affect the decisions of both you and your prospects.

Since you are evaluating how to market to the general public or your specifically profiled franchise buyer, you should review the business offering first and the marketing approach second. If possible, visit a store or business in each of these categories and attempt to buy a franchise from each of those competitors. Review their marketing materials, their sales approach, and their business plan. Question where they have their present stores and where they are planning to develop new stores. Understand the features their franchise has to offer. If possible, understand the performance of their business. Determine the decor, the sales, the profitability, the consumer approach, and the overall image. Then evaluate their strengths and weaknesses in the marketplace.

Once you have developed a matrix of all of these businesses, and complete the current franchise program assessment described in the next section, you will have a better understanding of where your company fits into the marketing equation.

Current Franchise Program Assessment

It's hard to know where to go if you don't know where you are. Another key element of the marketing plan is to understand your current positioning and what is successful or not successful about your present system. Part of the analysis must ask the following questions of your franchise system:

1. What are the key ingredients to making a new franchisee successful *rapidly*?

2. What are the major problems a new franchisee must face?
3. How can you solve those problems through your franchise system?
4. How can you keep your existing franchisees happy throughout the entire term and any renewal of their franchise agreement?

Often the key executives of a franchise company may not fully understand these issues. It can be enlightening to utilize focus-group studies with your franchise organization. Third parties should lead the group in order to obtain the quality information.

The analysis can be divided into the following components:

1. *Current franchise sales analysis.* A complete analysis of every franchisee's first-year sales by month, second year, and beyond sales to determine trends and growth patterns.
2. *Market coverage and penetration.* How successful has the franchisor been in developing its markets and successfully penetrating market share?
3. *Area strengths and weaknesses.* What areas are strong or weak and what increased penetration must be made in order to properly develop each area or market? Gaps between markets, where no penetration has taken place, should also be noted.
4. *Income and expense analysis.* What are the specific expenses of each franchisee (if known), as well as the net income (if known) of each franchisee in each month of year 1, year 2, and so on? The minimum level of your knowledge must be cost of goods, labor costs, and other controllable costs where support can be provided by the franchisor. Most other costs are of "franchisee's choice."
5. *Franchisees' return on investment.* What was the investment of each franchisee against the return received? A fast-food restaurant company based in the Midwest grew rather substantially. It was very successful in growing its franchise company, but after one year it found the franchisees were quite unhappy. None of them were getting a return on their investment because *their* business didn't grow. Customers were not returning because they weren't satisfied with the food. If they looked only at the growth of the franchise system they would have a false view of their success. Using the sales from item 1 above, the specific expenses from item 4 above, and applying a "miscellaneous" expense factor, the net profit can be reasonably assumed.
6. *Franchisee evaluation.* What are the strengths and weaknesses of each franchisee and unit?
7. *Franchisee profiles.* Who are the franchisees, what is their background, what are their financial capabilities? A matrix should be developed to determine the profiles of the most successful versus the least successful franchisees.

8. *Prospect evaluation.* What are the profiles of the prospects and where did each learn of your franchise opportunity? In this way you can determine how to best reach the best prospects with the least cost.

9. *Operational support.* Determine the strength of the management team and the support team. It is also important to test all support materials and their implementation along with the success ratios of franchisees. It may be necessary to survey the franchise system to determine their views.

10. *Contract review.* At least yearly review the franchise agreement and its components to determine if changes need to be made for the future franchise system based upon the system review.

11. *Administrative.* What administrative problems do you have in collecting royalties and communicating with franchisees?

12. *Recruiting methods.* What methods have been used to recruit employees for the various functions and how successful have they been?

13. *Communications activities and incentives.* What newsletters, public relations activities, and bonus or incentive programs are available to your franchise system and how successful have they been?

14. *Advertising techniques.* What advertising media have been most successful for the dollars expended?

15. *Location evaluation.* Determine the most to the least successful locations in the franchise system and attempt to decipher why each location performs as it does.

All of the above components must be weighed to determine the strengths and weaknesses of your current franchise program. In the following sections, this will help you better define your system as it relates to those strengths and weaknesses.

Overall Goals

OFFICERS' PERSONAL GOALS

The personal goals of the officers of the company and its majority shareholders must be considered in the development of your marketing plan. If a particular owner or officer is looking to maximize earnings or take the company public, you may seek to expand as rapidly as possible to build the profitability quickly. However, that creates substantial risk since the franchise system may suffer for lack of complete and proper support. Under these circumstances, the growth plan must be even more carefully planned. However, if the officers' personal goals are not taken into account, the plan could be in conflict and challenged. Each owner and officer must accept the final plan if it is to be successful.

CORPORATE GOALS

The number of franchises to be sold must be determined by the top executives as well as the line executives of the company. This must also include where they should be sold and under what circumstances. While these goals are only a standard to be met, they should be constantly changing based upon the program assessment in the next section.

It is not enough to state "We will sell 100 franchises next year." Where these franchises should be sold, the budgets that should be established for those franchise sales, the expected numbers of leads to be generated, the marketing tools that should be created, the timing of those sales, and how these sales will be serviced internally are all extremely important. The total will be only as good as the component parts in the preparation of these plans.

"What if" planning becomes important in this section. What if one segment of the plan does not work? How will it effect the other segments? Or, what if we would increase our advertising budget by 50 percent? These and many other questions should be addressed during the development of this plan. Once everyone understands the components of the plan, the final preparation of numbers can begin. Everyone who has any involvement in the sales of these franchises must be involved in the development of those numbers and be willing to accept those goals. Compromise may be required, and while it is important not to be too conservative it is equally as important not to be too aggressive. Reachable goals should show bottom and top limits.

Franchise Program Compared to Competition

You have undertaken a comprehensive study of your existing franchise system. The strengths and weaknesses of each of the components and franchises should have been clearly defined with your evaluation. If you thoroughly understand each of these components, you should be able to evaluate your competition based on these same components. Obviously there are some areas of competition that you will not be able to evaluate thoroughly. Understanding the competitive strengths and weaknesses will help to determine your positioning.

Let's evaluate some of the same components:

▲ *Current franchise sales analysis.* By obtaining competitive UFOCs and other financial data, you should be able to determine their average sales per unit and possibly even sales in various market areas. By evaluating the kinds of products you are selling versus the products they sell, you can also determine the strength of your sales program compared to theirs. If you would attempt to buy a franchise from a competitor through a third party and contact some of its franchisees in the process, you would be able to determine a franchisee's first-year sales, second-year sales, and beyond. Compare its growth patterns to your growth patterns. What is the effectiveness of startup advertising? What is the effectiveness of training and the field support system? Most of these areas will become evident as you make these evaluations.

▲ *Market coverage and penetration.* Look at your key as well as your up-and-coming competitors to determine where they are developing stores, in which markets, and what kind of market share they are achieving. This will help you determine in which markets you should concentrate. How did they develop new markets? Where are their successes and failures and why?

▲ *Area weaknesses and strengths.* You may begin to see a pattern of growth in your competitors. You can then determine whether you want to compete against their growth pattern or develop alternative markets. You might find they are developing major markets only and you might have strengths in the more minor markets. Again, this will help to focus your positioning.

▲ *Income and expense analysis.* It is very difficult to gather income and expense data about your competitors. However, if you evaluate their franchise system by attempting to purchase a franchise, you may be able to talk to their franchisees about income and expense data, such as cost of goods and labor factors. If your sales are lower and your costs are higher, you may need to change your product line or reposition your services in order to improve your franchise system. Keep in mind that if your system is built on image and the cost of goods is a part of that image, you should not destroy what has built your company despite the fact that the sales may be too low. Under those circumstances the concentration should then be on sales rather than on product costs.

▲ *Franchisee's return on investment.* It is hoped you will be able to evaluate the revenue and expense from the first and fourth items above. You will be able to determine the investment that was made on their franchise by evaluating the UFOC. You should also ask each franchisee their investment in order to accurately determine the range. While this is difficult and time consuming, it can be a valuable tool in preparing your plan and planning your growth. Hiring third parties to help in making this evaluation might become important in protecting your image with your competitors.

▲ *Franchisee evaluation.* This is also tough to evaluate because you do not have access to all of their franchisees. (The same will be true of franchisee profiles and prospect evaluation.)

▲ *Operational support.* You should be able to obtain information regarding the support that other franchisors give to their franchise systems. This can be done through your franchisee evaluation technique as well as observations of the market. Does your competitor have a store-opening specialist team? Does it have troubled-store or field support teams? Does it provide special incentive programs for its franchisees? Does it provide newsletters? Is its operations manual better than yours? Does it have corporate stores interspersed with its franchise stores? How many stores does each field support team member service? All of these should be compared to your franchise system.

▲ *Contract review.* It is easy to look at the contracts of your competitors because they are registered and available through various state agencies. A close review of your contract at each yearly renewal date can be very valuable, and comparing it to other contracts can prove enlightening.

     ▲ *Administrative.* A competitive analysis may be difficult to obtain in this instance.

     ▲ *Recruiting methods.* How good are your competitors in recruiting new employees and keeping existing employees? How does their franchise system feel about their support staff?

     ▲ *Communications activities and incentives.* Compare your competitor's newsletters and public relations activities. Your entire public relations activities should be compared, reviewed, and analyzed constantly. A concentrated program must be developed to improve the company's and franchisee's relationships with the public.

     ▲ *Advertising techniques.* The utilization of clipping services for your competitor's advertising across the country, as well as public relations stories, can prove invaluable. Understanding what your competition is doing and being able to position yourself against that competition is vital.

There will be 3,000 to 4,000 franchisors competing for your prospective franchises in the 1990s. If you don't know what the competition is doing in your own industry, plus other franchising industries, it will be difficult for you to keep up and stay ahead. Continual evaluation and development of marketing plans within this competitive atmosphere will be required.

Specific Franchise Program Tactics

After you analyze your own company and its activities, and compare them to the competition, you must develop the program tactics to use in your future marketing. This becomes the most critical portion of the marketing plan. These tactics are divided into segments, each of which should be evaluated separately and costs assigned for the changes required. These areas are:

     1. *Support programs.* Based on your weaknesses and strengths you must to know the kinds of support programs needed to build your franchise into a stronger system. Do you need store-opening specialists? Do you need troubled-store support teams? Do you need additional communications support efforts? Do you need better training techniques? And if so, at what cost?

     2. *Market direction.* What changes will be required in your franchise system to achieve the goals you have determined? What new markets will you enter? What markets must you penetrate more inclusively? Where and how will you need to increase the market share? How will you achieve this change in the market direction? It may require advertising. Incentives may be used with existing store owners to increase franchise sales in a given market. Increasing the number of

corporate stores to penetrate the market more successfully may be the solution. All opportunities and potential solutions must be evaluated and a cost associated with each change must be applied.

3. *Organization required.* Who are the people who can help you achieve your goals? Should you restructure your present organization or should you add to it? Where will you obtain the kinds of people you'll need? If possible, you should utilize internal restructuring rather than outside hiring. However, your people may lack some of the strengths required to carry your company forward to the new position and, therefore, outside staff people may be required.

4. *Image.* When you fully understand the current image, you may then define the image you wish now to achieve. What changes are required to achieve that image and what cost? This issue transcends to advertising, promotions, public relations, added resources, product line, and other issues.

5. *Accounting, control, or reporting systems required.* Do you need better controls internally? Do you need more information from your franchisees to help them control their business better? What reporting system changes will be required?

6. *Advertising and promotions.* Do you need to change the advertising and promotional fees involved? If a change is required, it is easy to upgrade and update the franchise agreement, but it is not easy to go the franchise system to ask for increased fees. If that is required as a revamping of the system, a careful plan of how that is to be accomplished must be prepared. With this plan there must also be included the type and intensity of advertising to be accomplished. If promotions are a part of the equation, these must be tested and rolled out accordingly. If public relations is required, careful consideration as to how it will be controlled must be made. Costs on all of these issues must be carefully planned and put into the budget accordingly.

7. *Training support requirements.* Do the training programs need to be changed significantly in order to accomplish the goals to be established? On many occasions the system does not grow adequately because the initial training was not correct or was inadequate. A company based in Texas was once reviewed because the franchise system was not growing and was, in fact, shrinking. Many existing franchisees were being lost within the first three years of their franchise experience. However, many franchisees who had been in business for five years or longer were thriving and successful. The problem was that the initial franchisees were not being trained in the entire franchise system and would only operate a portion of the system in the early years of their franchise experience. This would cause them to become disenchanted with low sales, hard work, and very little profitability. If they survived beyond the three to five years, their businesses would thrive substantially and profitability would increase. The problem was that the company felt that the profit centers should be trained gradually into each franchisee's business rather than all upfront. The franchisee became disgruntled with the amount of work required for, virtually, no reward. The company changed

this positioning by providing better first-year support to all franchisees and initially training them longer and more intensively in all of the profit centers of the business. It also changed the franchise profile. The result was that its franchisee retention rate increased substantially.

8. *First-year support programs needed.* From the previous item, you can determine what additional support programs might be required to enhance the initial training and improve first-year's sales of your franchise system. If you could develop an advertising or marketing program to provide substantial increases in sales, it would mean that future years' sales will be substantially higher as well. Over the long term, this means more profits to you and the franchisee. Careful evaluation must be made of your training and first-year support programs in order to maximize the sales and profitability level of your franchise system. Should a special team be assigned to all new stores? Should special promotional programs be developed for new stores? Should an advertising deposit be made to the company as part of the investment by the franchisee initially? What is required to get the franchisee off the ground more successfully and faster? Careful attention to the tactics of this issue might be the most important solution to your franchise marketing programs and provide a stronger selling point for marketing your franchises.

9. *Sales plan.* This is discussed in more detail in the next section.

10. *Financial planning.* What will be the cost of all of the added items from above? What will be the added revenue as well? Here is where "what if" planning can be very valuable to your company.

11. *Financial assistance needed.* With this financial planning, what financial assistance and borrowing will be required to achieve the goals? Will you need new lines of credit, asset-based borrowing, or other financial support structures to provide for the required changes in the system?

12. *Fees, royalties, advertising contributions needed.* What changes are required in the franchise agreement to increase the fees needed to cover the programs that will now be developed for franchisees? Careful evaluation must be made of the competition. Don't price yourself out of the marketplace. However, consider reducing franchise fees and increasing royalties in order to substantiate some of the programs that you intend to develop for your franchise system. Franchisees may not mind paying from their profits if you are providing the programs to make profits for them.

13. *Franchise agreement provision.* What changes are required in your franchise agreement in order to accommodate the new programs being developed?

14. *Registration states needed.* Does the marketing plan require penetration of new states which may require registration, and how soon will they be required? Understanding the time constraints of registering certain states will be important in order to make your marketing plan work. Contact your attorney to determine if this lead time is invaluable.

15. *New franchisee profile*. After evaluating your existing franchises and their success or failure, you should be able to determine the profile of the successful franchisee for your system. Has it changed from your original profile? Do you need to review who you are seeking as franchisees and what marketing techniques will be required to reach them? This can completely change your franchise marketing equation and could substantially reduce or increase the marketing costs. Pinpointing the franchisee often reduces the cost of marketing franchises. In addition, the sales plan (defined later in this chapter) will identify how to reach and follow up with each franchise prospect for a larger close ratio, which could reduce your marketing costs as well. If you profile properly this can help your overall plan substantially and target your markets much more easily.

16. *Franchise structure for the future*. After determining these issues, you can now determine what the franchise structure should be for the future and be able to monitor and evaluate the success of your marketing plan.

Overall Strategic Planning

The finalized strategic marketing plan narrative is now ready to be prepared. You have reviewed your own environment and your competitive environment, and analyzed the differences. You have determined the changes in tactics required in order to reach the goals you seek to achieve. Assumptions, changes in program tactics, and the costs associated with such changes will be part of the narrative. The expected benefit of each change should also be identified.

At this point, overall assumptions must be made to project the additional cost and benefits. Very specific objectives must be established. Assumptions for each of those objectives must be portrayed. This includes the number of franchises to be sold, the numbers of leads to be generated to sell that expected number of franchises, the costs associated with generating those leads, and the revenue amounts to be achieved as a result of those goals. Very specific measuring devices must be included in these assumptions. The first-year assumption should include the specific media and cost associated as well as all other costs to build the program to the level expected by the strategic and tactical positioning from above. The second year of this projection should be a ''what if'' planning year. This will also be a monthly plan with the same parameters as year 1. Assume that the goals projected from year 1 will be reached and, if so, year 2 will project the following results. The narrative for the second year might include fail-safe planning. If certain elements of the first-year projection do not produce the results expected, new decisions need be made based upon assumptions to be placed in this marketing plan. Specifically, year 2 may show two projections:

▴ Results as expected
▴ Forecast if results are not as expected

Years 3 through 5 should be yearly projections only, rather than monthly, and will make the assumption that year 1 projections and the tactical strategic plans produce the expected results.

Once the marketing plan is produced, every person responsible for any element of success of that marketing plan must make final approval of the plan. If any one person or department does not buy into the plan, the plan could be doomed to failure. The result will be only as good as the component parts, and each manager and department must commit to the plan as if it were his or her own.

From this marketing plan a task chart should be created, showing the responsibility of each person and department for execution of the tactical and strategic plans and results. A beginning and completion date for all of the tactical program issues must be prepared and a constant evaluation of these component parts must be made. Initially, weekly meetings may be required. Ultimately, tactical and strategic evaluation meetings must take place at least monthly. An overall coordinator for the execution of this marketing plan must be appointed and the responsibility for execution and follow-up should be in their hands.

If your company is large, obviously this will become a major undertaking. If your company is small, there are likely to be only one, two, or three executives involved in the plan. The danger with small companies is that objectivity in the preparation of the plan, as well as in its execution, is difficult. Determining who will control the plan is also more difficult in a small company. There is a tendency to procrastinate in the execution of certain component parts, which could cause the entire plan to fall behind.

There should be no question with any company as to the importance of having a marketing plan. Rather, the intensity by which a marketing plan should be devised is at issue. No marketing plan is complete without the entire objectivity of all of the components listed previously. It is not enough merely to forecast numbers; there must be reasons behind each number and understanding of how those numbers were reached and why.

Once the marketing plan had been completed, a sales plan must be developed for your company.

The Sales Plan

Most companies develop only one sales plan, but you really need many sales plans—one for each of the selling modes you wish to accomplish:

- ▴ Sales of individual units to new franchisees
- ▴ Sales of territories or multiple units to new franchisees
- ▴ Expansion through existing franchisees
- ▴ Affiliate or conversion franchisee expansion
- ▴ Other forms of expansion including master franchising, limited partnerships, joint ventures, and subfranchising

Each plan should include the various people who will be involved in the franchise sale. The salesperson is usually considered, but we often forget about the sales director and the "qualifiers." The qualifiers are people such as receptionists or secretaries who handle the phone calls and initial contacts of franchise prospects. The sale can often be lost by these people before it even gets to the salesperson. Including them in the equation is critical, and planning must be done in order to accomplish your goals.

Following are specific ingredients that should be considered and included in your sales plans.

Goals for Sales

The marketing plan previously discussed identifies the competitive and economic situations facing the franchisor as well as other input critical for growth. This section relates strictly to the sale of the franchise and the environment and technique of the sale, which, if properly handled, is considered an award of a franchise, not a sale. Being realistic will assure success toward development of the sales plan. Setting your goals too high may cause the salespeople to not accept them as their own, and create excuses for not reaching them. Setting them too low will not provide adequate incentive.

These goals must be established by month rather than by year. It is too easy to say "I've got ten months left." When sales don't occur during a given period, the salesperson could assume (or argue) that all sales would be made at the end of the term and the result would be that these goals will not be met.

Each franchisor must understand the cycle of franchise selling:

January 1–10:	There is not much activity in franchise sales and marketing.
January 10–April 10:	High activity in franchise sales and marketing.
April 10–April 30:	Most people are working on or paying taxes and are not interested in making investments at this time.
May 1–June 15:	Medium activity in franchise sales and marketing.
June 15–August 15:	Low activity in franchise sales and marketing.
August 15–September 10:	Medium activity in franchise sales and marketing.
September 10–November 15	High activity in franchise sales and marketing.
November 15 (Thanksgiving)–New Year's:	No, to very low, sales and marketing activity.

Each person responsible for any portion of the franchise sale should have separate responsibilities for action. These actions and responsibilities should be identified in the sales plan along with a timetable for their completion.

Once you have determined the goals for sales per month, you will be able to determine the corresponding revenue. In addition, you should know the budget for making these sales, including the advertising expense and all other expenditures. Also included in this sales plan should be a contingency plan. What if actual sales do not achieve the levels of the sales goals? What will happen to the expenditure budget? It is important to know how many leads are to be generated from each advertisement placed. Knowing how many leads should be generated, you can determine that one to four franchise sales will take place for every 100 leads generated. However, if you have direct marketing activities to a specific profile, your lead generation may be lower but your sales results may be higher. Evaluating past activity is the only way to understand this equation. Have you adequately tracked your leads to be able to build this section? Do you really know your level of activity and success rate?

Determining Franchisee Profiles

I previously discussed how to develop franchise profiles and recognize their importance. Knowing specifically who to market your franchise to will obviously result in lower marketing dollar needs. Target marketing becomes more critical in this age of competition. Understanding who had been successful with your existing franchise system and who can best service your franchise will build a more successful system and a less expensive, and more directed, marketing program.

Advertising, Media Analysis, and Media Selection

Once you have determined your franchise profile, choosing a medium to reach that profile may be easier and far less costly. If you have targeted *where* your market is, it becomes less expensive to market your franchise. The advertising media you select should directly reach the people to whom you wish to sell your franchise. If you were to utilize the *Wall Street Journal* as an advertising medium, and are attempting to sell your franchise to a blue-collar worker, you have obviously chosen the wrong medium. However, if your goal is to reach middle and top-line executives of medium to large companies across the United States, newspapers which reach these executives, such as the *Wall Street Journal,* or magazines like *Forbes* (and other such periodicals), would be the ideal medium.

During 1990 and early 1991, Union Carbide's Marble Life franchise used a shotgun approach to franchise selection. The company was seeking franchise prospects from all walks of life and spent substantial money in marketing franchises to those prospects. It was largely unsuccessful because the market did not understand the product and its use. The company also did not have a base of franchisees with financial knowledge of how good or profitable its business would be.

Union Carbide restructured its franchise selling process, and began to target-market to existing marble-care small companies across the country. Once it selected these markets and their target audiences, a direct marketing campaign worked and the franchise base increased.

Another company, the Kip McGrath Education Centers, was seeking only teachers and administrators who were dissatisfied with the U.S. educational system as its franchisees and master franchisees. Rather than advertising, it selected the specific markets it wished to approach and used a direct mail campaign. Lists were available for the specific target market, as they are available for almost any targeted market. In this instance, the target-marketing worked and the franchise program is rapidly developing throughout the United States.

Sometimes it's not easy to define specifically who your market will be. Under those circumstances, it is important to test the market and evaluate your results. Unfortunately, many franchisors plod forward, advertise wildly, and don't understand the significance of the results they obtain. If you have determined your market niche and your positioning is solid, franchise advertising should fall into place. You may not always be right the first time, but in constantly evaluating your advertising programs and quickly changing your positioning, you should achieve the levels you require.

Another example of media positioning and market strategy is Movie Warehouse Franchising, in Kentucky. It had developed fifty franchises as a regional and successful video chain. Attempts were made to market the franchise outside the local area, with limited success; the company attempted to market on a shotgun approach throughout the United States. But once it determined its niche and the franchise prospect was reasonably identified, it completely repositioned its marketing program. The company realized that the market niche was small-town middle America, and that it could beat out the competition and the local video stores in the marketplace. It targeted cities of 10,000 to 100,000 residents, in markets just outside existing store territories and did direct marketing to local banks, CPAs, attorneys, and video stores, plus business-opportunity advertising in those same local newspapers. The company could blitz these smaller markets inexpensively. A telephone campaign followed and new franchisees were the result.

Appeal to Your Potential Buyer

Though you have determined who your franchise prospect will be and which medium will reach that prospect, your work is not completed. It is important to understand the emotional psyche of that franchise prospect. What words will entice him to consider your franchise? What are that franchise prospect's goals? Creating a theme as a headline that causes the profiled franchisee to respond, to create an image of ''they are talking to me,'' is required. Saying too much can have an opposite effect. Better to say too little, and leave white space. Approaching the prospect's emotional psyche through words is critical.

Using focus groups to test your headlines and verbiage might also be valuable. When the advertising program and direct mail concept was conceived for the Kip McGrath Education Centers, tentative advertising copy that would reach administrators and teachers was given to several school districts, in a focus study meeting, to test reactions. When they looked at the master franchise program and the individual franchise program combined, the description made it look like a multilevel promotional scheme rather than a professional education system. The perception, although incorrect, was real. But changing a few words in the materials eliminated that problem and created a successful mail campaign. Remember, one seemingly minor error in advertising copy can be fatal. Understand the emotions of the *recipient* of any advertising before you place or send that material. A very successful campaign can turn into an ill-fated campaign if one word turns off the reader.

Creation of Response Material

Once you have prepared your ad for your initial franchise offering, people will contact you for more information. It is important that a response piece be prepared that, once again, is indicative of the franchise program you are offering and meets the concerns and questions a franchise prospect may have. The advertising piece should be of high quality. *High quality* does not always mean four-color, since one- and two-color advertising programs work as well if the right words and pictures portray the result the franchise prospect is looking for. The franchise response material should not overemphasize the franchise as much as tell the franchise prospect what she needs to know to make the proper decision. Once again, it is important to understand how that franchise prospect makes decisions before preparing the advertising materials.

Steamatic has been a strong franchise system for many years. However, in the mid-1980s it recognized a depletion of its franchise system: A substantial number of new franchisees abandoned the program within the first three years. The company didn't understand why this was happening, but focus groups consisting of their franchisees (one group of less-than-five-year owners and a second group of over-five-year owners) helped: The company was seeking the wrong type of prospect to begin the program and was not providing a comprehensive training program to get new franchisees off the ground. Steamatic changed its positioning and the type of franchisee it was seeking to a marketing-oriented rather than a blue-collar franchisee; it also improved its training program by teaching all profit centers the operations immediately and began to establish new, achievable goals. They now have attained that goal by reaching the right type of franchisee with the right type of advertising, saying the words that make a difference and providing the proper base for success more quickly.

The initial response material may not only be brochures. It could also include video presentations, audio presentations, and other materials that get the message across.

Franchisee Response Handling

If one were to ask a franchisor, Who is the person who receives the call from a franchise prospect? the answer is generally the franchise salesperson. In most instances, that is incorrect. The receptionist is the first person to receive that call and rarely is he or she trained to receive a franchise response. This can cause a franchise prospect to immediately discount your franchise if the response is incorrect or unprofessional. Substantial training must be provided so the receptionist can handle franchise prospect responses. The receptionist must know something about the franchise to be offered and be given the proper words to respond. Handling the calls in the absence of a salesperson can be fatal without training, while role playing should be attempted and there should be constant testing of technique.

Each prospect should be asked where she heard of your franchise and what caused her to call you. When prospect forms are prepared, the ad verbiage that caused the franchisee to respond should be included to determine the success of each theme. What caused her to call? What were her hot buttons? What was her attitude toward your franchise that heightened her excitement? All data obtained from the franchise prospect during the course of the selling process should be documented on the prospect form. The form and its use should be included in the sales plan. The time and date of each franchise call should be noted, and the time and date of the next franchise prospect contact should also be shown for the tickler file ("set the clock"). You should always let the prospect know what the next contact will be, whether by phone or letter or personal meeting.

The franchise prospect should also be given tasks to accomplish between phone calls and contacts—tasks such as "Please read the franchise brochure and list your questions for our next call," or "I would like to have you visit one of the stores in your area before we talk again for your views and observations," or "I would like to have you call ten franchisees in our system and give me your thoughts at our next phone conversation," or "Now call some of our competition to find out how they feel about their business before our next call." If you constantly guide the franchise prospect through the franchise selling process, you will not have to sell the franchise; you can award the franchise to her because she has made her own decision. The sales plan should incorporate all of these issues so the documentation can be presented and given to any new salesperson during the sales plan term.

Additional Materials and Responses

The franchise prospect wants to feel as if he is part of a team. Constant contact, yet not *over*contact, is important. A three-month plan of selling must be devised, to include the materials such as timing schedules and letters to be sent. It may be wise to forward newsletters as they are developed to franchise prospects. Use follow-up letters and testimonials periodically in the selling process. It may be wise to announce new store openings and sales of franchises. Additional sales literature that explains important points of the franchise program, which may not be outlined in detail in the initial response brochure, might be appropriate. This is the medium by which the franchise prospect is kept apprised of your franchise activity while he seeks the correct franchise for himself. While this may be more costly, if used for hot prospects, it is a very successful technique.

If you are shotgun advertising, you may receive responses from prospects located in states where your franchise is not registered. Your attorney will tell you that you cannot respond with any material to that franchise prospect. However, you can provide advertising materials on your *business* not relating to the franchise. You could also forward a personal profile form to be returned to the company, stating that if the person returns the form, when your franchise becomes available in his state he will be the first considered. Should you receive enough inquiries and subsequent responses from these potential franchisees, you should consider registering in that state. You can build an interest in the business, and an expectation for the franchise, with this response technique.

Public Relations

Many franchisors overlook the public relations aspect of franchise marketing. A special section in your sales plan should be devoted to public relations efforts. It is strongly recommended that franchisors utilize a public relations company, agent, or in-house person, especially if you have a story to tell. Careful consideration must be given to how to use public relations, however.

A press kit is required, giving the history of the business and an introduction to the company and its key people. These should be forwarded to all appropriate media initially, as well as each time an article is written or a promotion prepared for your business or your franchise opportunity.

Making your franchisees aware of public relations and promotion development techniques can be very valuable. Reading your local newspaper daily can develop creative public relations ideas. Several years ago in Minneapolis, a paraplegic had saved for years to buy a specially designed vehicle for transportation. He wanted to be productive in society and felt he needed to have proper transportation to work. He was proud of the van he had purchased. One day after the van was purchased, it was stolen and destroyed. The story made the headlines the next day. That same day, a local service station and convenience-store chain agreed to purchase a new van. Within twenty-four hours, every local radio and television station picked up the story. Local talk shows interviewed the paraplegic and national stories emerged as well. This publicity was all for the price of a new van. Publicity is oftentimes inexpensive, but priceless, advertising.

This kind of creativity in your public relations efforts can provide substantial mileage to your company. Articles should be prepared about what your franchisees are doing for their community. Franchisee activities with school boards, national associations, political organizations, and other special events should be noted and published. Your sales plan should structure how these stories are to be prepared, how franchisees should provide data to the company for such public relations, and how creativity can be enhanced in the field by use of these public relations techniques. Even though the sales plan is prepared for the company, these ideas should be promoted to franchisees to help them become a stronger part of the system.

Sales Promotion and On-Site Business Builders

There are many different techniques for creating promotions to sell franchises. The normal selling sources are media such as newspapers, magazines, and occasionally radio and television. There are other areas that can provide far less expensive franchise marketing, but special plans must be devised for selling franchises under these circumstances. Some of these are:

FRANCHISE LOCATION PROMOTIONS

In-store signage such as FRANCHISES AVAILABLE. CALL 1-800-555-3726. Or carefully planned brochures contained in plastic holders identifying that franchises are available and the benefits of being a franchisee in a system also promote franchise sales. These are especially effective where customers must wait for a product to be prepared or service to be performed.

For instance, an ice cream store in Georgia had a unique product. All ice cream was manufactured in the store in old-style churns, and customers would become intrigued by the method of preparation. While they watched the process, they became interested in the concept. A brochure was created and made available to customers while they waited. No franchise marketing was done for this company besides the in-store promotions, yet within two years eighteen franchises were sold. Very effective, very inexpensive, and the "touch and feel" aspect of franchise marketing was established.

FRANCHISEE REFERRALS

It is important to have your existing franchisees involved in your expansion program. They should understand that expansion is growth and that growth is positive. That positive growth attitude should be instilled in the franchisee at the sale of the franchise and reinforced throughout training. New franchises not only enhance an existing store's operation but also improves overall advertising clout, since more stores provide more in advertising dollars.

A referral system with real dollar rebates to franchisees who provide leads that turn into franchise awards could be established, but is not always necessary.

The objective is to have the franchise salesperson and all corporate officers enhance the need of each franchisee to be part of a growing system and assist in future expansion.

BUSINESS CONTACTS AND NETWORKING

Belonging to chambers of commerce, Kiwanis, American Legion, and various other community organizations should be a requirement for the franchisee and the franchise salesperson. Becoming active, talking about the business, giving speeches, and networking can be valuable tools in your marketing efforts.

SEMINARS

A franchise salesperson should understand how to prepare and give seminars. The sales plan should also include how to produce these seminars. The advertising structure, proposed ads, hotel or other meeting locations, response materials, presentation materials, and other data should be provided in the sales plan for a franchise salesperson to do a proper job. Seminars can be excellent tools for bringing people together in one place to listen to your franchise opportunity.

All of these sales promotion concepts and others should be considered while developing your sales plan. Don't leave any of these items to chance. They must be thought out and documented for the franchise sales department to operate effectively.

Salesperson's Presentation

How a salesperson presents himself in front of franchisees is another critical area of importance to the franchise sale. One company learned that asking women franchise prospects to meet at a hotel was not producing results. The reason, they learned, was a fear for personal safety. While the franchise and the salesperson were of high quality, the location was a hotel, in one-on-one meetings, so they would not respond. The company changed its policy to utilize a seminar format, and the problems went away.

The atmosphere where the franchise salesperson gives the initial and follow-up presentation is important. The image she provides, the appearance she projects, the clothing she wears—all are important. These items should be addressed in the sales plan along with information on how to handle questions about sales and earnings of the franchise, how to present success stories, and how to present other financial information about the company or its franchise stores, whether or not an earnings claim is part of the franchise document.

Franchisee's Perceptions

While you as a company or a franchise salesperson may view your franchise and its opportunity in one manner, the franchisee may not see it the same way. The Caswell Shooting Clubs brought many independent shooting-club owners together to do a focus group on perceptions, and included proposed materials that would be used to market these shooting clubs across the United States. The program was to be marketed first to existing shooting clubs. Since these were the marketing prospects, the company wanted to learn how they would view the franchise. The results were interesting: The clubs perceived the opportunity as an infringement on their business, whereas it was really a nationwide club business opportunity. The marketing materials were changed, and the perception changed accordingly.

Before you sell franchises, it is important that the company employees, franchise store operators, and general public have an opportunity to view the franchise from their own perspective. Role playing might be important. Focus groups can be important. But most important, place yourselves on the prospect's side of the table. Understand how he feels about issues, investments, time spent on the job, and other aspects of the business. Then learn as much as you can about what your franchise prospect has as a goal for himself. It is *always* important to award the franchise to a person who sees the opportunity to achieve his objectives, rather than to sell your franchise to a person you have convinced. Guiding the prospect in the process and letting him make the decision based on your input is the technique most profitable to the company. In this way, the franchisee doesn't doubt his decision or lose respect for the company. Understand the prospect's objections, his goals, and the kind of responses that he would expect. That way you award the franchise to the right prospect. Too often, companies do not understand perceptions and how they affect the franchise selling effort.

Interviewing and Qualifying

We've discussed the location of the franchise sale, the franchisee's perceptions, and other parameters integral to the franchise-selling process. Your approach will immediately impact a franchise prospect, and you only get one chance. The technique of your sale will do the same. If you downgrade or make a person feel insignificant, it will kill the sale. If she feels you are talking down to her, it will have an adverse effect.

Your technique of interviewing obviously is critical. Look for certain criteria in a prospect that include some or all of the following:

- ▲ Skills of being a successful franchisee
- ▲ Motivation for being a success
- ▲ Financial capabilities
- ▲ Cooperativeness

- Personal stability
- Openmindedness
- Ability to be sociable and personable with customers
- Integrity and honesty
- Tolerance for stress
- Aggressiveness, verbally and otherwise

Visual presentations are most often correctly remembered, whereas conversations are not. Having presentations, presentation books, and various other methods of showing *visually* what your business is can be effective. Consider a professionally prepared selling book, and test it on others before using it in front of a franchise prospect. Make it brief, make it understandable, make it promote questions; you want the prospect to converse with you to help you evaluate and understand his goals and potentials.

Analysis of Leads

A simplified but complete form must be developed for use by all your franchise salespeople. That form should consist of the franchise prospect's name, address, telephone number at home, telephone number at work, company she presently works for, her goals and objectives in buying a franchise, other franchises she has looked at, investment capabilities, and documentation of each call, mailing, or contact made. Periodically (but no less than once per month), an analysis of these leads must be made:

- How many leads have been generated during this period?
- How many leads have been generated year to date?
- How many hot prospects are in process (and their names and cities)?
- What happened to the hot prospects listed in the last update that are no longer listed?
- How many franchises were sold during this period?

This information should be segmented by medium, by dates of placement of those media, by the theme used in each medium, and various other information that will help track the success of your sales program.

Franchisee Selection Techniques

There are generally three ways of making decisions on selecting and awarding your franchises:

1. Always use a background checking system to determine any problems the franchise prospect may have in his past. This includes a financial analysis, criminal record check, and various other background-checking procedures you deem

necessary. Some years ago BioCare of California (a W. R. Grace Company) was in the final selection process of a franchise prospect. After the entire staff had approved the franchise prospect, the company did a background check and found that he was a sex offender in three states. Had that person become a franchisee, it would have proved disastrous to the franchisor.

2. Psychological testing has become a significant technique in the franchise selection process. There are many testing systems on the market today. Check with the International Franchise Association for tests they recommend.

3. The most important decision-making tool for your franchise selection is gut feeling. Each person who meets the franchise prospect should be part of the final selection process. There should be a meeting of people who have met the prospect to discuss the pros and cons of awarding the franchise to that person. If any one person blackballs the prospect, that person should not be chosen. While the guidance process of awarding a franchise is a good one and makes the franchisee "buy into the system," it is also important that the company and its personnel "buy into the franchisee." If any one person does not agree with the others, the "I told you so" syndrome can also create a problem.

Waiting Process for the Franchisee

The sales plan should include another important ingredient that is easily forgotten: the waiting process between the sale and the opening. How to maintain the franchisee's interest while waiting to open her unit or business may be the most critical time in the process. A detailed plan of involvement should be prepared and included in your sales plan. Prospects should be given a responsibility every week, such as:

- Finding a site
- Opening a checking account
- Contacting the Kiwanis Club
- Joining the Chamber of Commerce
- Contacting the city regarding water hookup
- Contacting the power company about electricity
- Contacting contractors
- Visiting similar businesses in town

A list of weekly involvement procedures should be included, and weekly contact made with the franchisee to be certain she is following the "to do" list. In that way the franchisee remains involved and keeps the pace exciting while waiting for the franchise to open. More franchises have been lost between the time of signing and the time of opening than at any other, especially if contact and involvement are not consistent and constant. New franchisees are vulnerable at this time. Doubt may creep into their thinking and they may wonder if they've done the right thing. Keep them active and involved from the very moment they sign the franchise agreement.

Review of Results

While it is extremely important to develop a sales plan, it is just as important to review that sales plan continually and update for results. What's working? What's not working? The salesperson's effectiveness, the media effectiveness, your image effectiveness—every aspect of your sales plan should be challenged once each year and changed accordingly. Reports should be prepared by each responsible party and reviewed by a group consisting of all those involved in the franchise award activity and the executive staff. Brainstorming should follow and changes made to the sales plan accordingly.

Expectations

Identify what you expect from each of your franchise salespeople, qualifiers, and screening staff.

Your franchise award staff may consist of a vice-president, director of franchising, one or more franchise salespeople, and several qualifier/screening people. It will be important to identify the responsibilities of each and establish goals for them. The sales plan should include a structure for each *position* as well as each *person* holding it. The salesperson on the East Coast may have a totally different sales plan and goals from the salesperson on the West Coast. Be certain to identify all functions and people separately.

1. Goals should be identified specifically and be established as minimums and expected, by month. Keep in mind the marketing and sales cycles identified earlier.
2. Budgets should be established for each person, department, or area with explicit costs and expected revenues.
3. The creativity allowed for each salesperson, qualifier, and/or screener should be specified. Are they allowed to develop their own advertising techniques and materials? May they create ads? Can they create their own sales books? What input are they allowed? What group evaluation techniques should be implemented?
4. The latitude allowed should be explained. What are negotiable items in the franchise agreement and what areas cannot be changed? What can they say about sales and earnings?
5. Required abilities of the salesperson and their tools should be given. These may differ from region to region and between screeners and qualifiers, who may have specific areas of responsibility.
6. The required reports and their deadlines should be listed.

7. The reporting relationships between each of the individuals and executive staff need to be outlined.

8. The sales techniques to be used must be listed.

9. You need to specify the continuing knowledge required and how salespeople should update their training, both in the company and outside the company.

10. Continuing contact should be required with the franchisees after signing the franchise agreement.

11. The territory availability for franchise sales, how market share is to be determined, and how these markets should be developed—shotgun vs. rifle marketing—should be explained.

12. The presentation modes to be used, such as shows, seminars, hotel meeting rooms, shared franchise presentation meetings, home office visitations, or field visitations, should be considered.

13. The franchise approval structure for each franchise salesperson, and who will visit the franchise prospect prior to awarding the franchise, needs to be described.

14. Role playing should be an important element of franchise marketing. Always use role play for each person involved in the sales process prior to contact with prospects.

You now have a marketing plan and sales plan for your franchise organization. Never underestimate the importance of these plans and their development, or the reaction you will obtain from your staff as a result. Use the plans as tools to develop and create a better franchise. Your company's success will depend on it.

15

Managing the Franchise Marketing Process

Jerry R. Darnell, Sterling Vision Inc.

Take a look inside the executive offices of several successful franchises in the 1990s and you'll always find one common trait: a systematic approach to the marketing of franchises. A systematic approach means that the marketing process is predetermined and documented in writing and, most important, respected by the users of the system—namely, the marketing staff.

If the system to locate new prospects system is overly rigid, it will have chilling results. If the system is too loose, it will create a multitude of legal problems. The system must be pragmatic, striking the right balance between the need to grow the system and the need to respect the laws of franchising. Management of marketing must provide leadership so the staff puts equal emphasis on both important objectives.

This chapter highlights some key aspects of a marketing system that can be respected by your marketing staff, and gives some guidelines for managing franchise-development personnel.

A Structured Marketing System

The first step in building an effective marketing system is to identify the objectives of the system. What is the marketing process trying to accomplish? Is it our goal to sell or to facilitate? Is our purpose to pressure a candidate or to educate the prospect? Should we be proactive or reactive? Talk a lot or listen a lot? Quite obviously, the correct answer is to build a system that facilitates the decision-making process of prospective franchisees and assists them in reaching an informed business decision—one way or the other. In the long run, your franchising system (and the prospect) will be far better off reaching a decision that this offering *isn't* really right, rather than forcing a wrong situation and living with the consequences.

Why is a structured system so important? People invest in dreams, in a factual and attainable way. Prospects need a clear notion of what should happen next, and since they generally do not have a systematic methodology for evaluating your opportunity, you must provide them with one. Prospects invest their dollars in a strategy to succeed—a strategy that will give them psychological and financial success. They expect your company to provide them with the steps that lead them to completion of their goal.

Your franchise development staff will not close sales. The staff will assist prospects in making decisions that open up possibilities in people's lives. Prospects buy for their own reasons, not for yours. Therefore, your system and presentation procedures must motivate and educate the prospect. That structured system focuses on results. It also provides an operational efficiency that can increase productivity. Licensing results are measured and evaluated against your own standards and goals. The effective communication this method establishes will, in turn, provide a higher quality prospect in the end.

From a budget standpoint, a structured marketing system mandates a higher lead-to-close ratio, reduces the time between initial contact and the close, enhances the value of your franchise in the mind of the prospect, and promotes future franchisees who "think" in a system-wide manner for success.

A Prospecting Strategy

Many franchisors spend thousands and thousands of dollars annually (and usually wastefully) to acquire prospect leads. Depending on the type of franchise being offered, leads can come from targeted marketing, trade shows, franchise trade shows, newspapers (both local and national), and magazine ads. Most new and some older franchisors don't know how to use those leads, or even measure their cost ratios in the media they use. For example, I recently had the opportunity to telephone an older franchisor. He expressed how disappointed he was because he had attended three franchise trade shows and acquired 2,500 leads. We later determined that he had asked everyone attending these shows to complete an information request card, without employing a preliminary qualification process. Furthermore, it is likely that each of these individuals did the same at each booth. Thus, he spent thousands of dollars and yet had no operating system to qualify or manage those leads.

Here is how you might start to track your lead inventory, in which you may have invested a large sum of money. Prior to computerizing our ratios, we use the three forms shown in Figure 15-1. They should assist you in visualizing the ratio tracking process.

In developing strategies for locating prospects, ask the marketing staff the following questions:

- ▲ Who are our ideal prospects?
- ▲ Where are they located?
- ▲ How are they to be contacted?

Figure 15-1. Licensing tracking system forms.

Franchise Licensing Manager

Source	Leads	RFC	%L	Presentation	%R	%L	Corporate Interview	%P	%R	%L	Awarded	%CI	%P	%R	%L
1.															
2.															
3.															
4.															
5.															
6.															
7.															
8.															
9.															
10.															

Franchise Licensing
Ratio Tracking System
Source of Leads

Source	Leads	RFC	%L	Presentation	%R	%L	Corporate Interview	%P	%R	%L	Awarded	%CI	%P	%R	%L
1.															
2.															
3.															
4.															
5.															
6.															
7.															
8.															
9.															
10.															

Franchise Licensing
Ratio Tracking System
Summary of Leads per Year

Source	Leads	RFC	%L	Presentation	%R	%L	Corporate Interview	%P	%R	%L	Awarded	%CI	%P	%R	%L
1.															
2.															
3.															
4.															
5.															
6.															
7.															
8.															
9.															
10.															

▲ What is our prospecting budget?
▲ What are the desirable results?

Once these questions have been addressed, the strategy becomes clear, but only if you monitor the results and hold the staff accountable. In short, everyone must be held accountable for maintaining high lead-to-close ratios, respecting the system, and following the qualification standards.

Qualification standards for new prospects should include the following factors:

▲ Does the prospect have or can he obtain the financial resources to become a franchisee?
▲ Does the prospect have the ability to make a decision within a given time frame?
▲ Does franchising fit the prospect's personality?
▲ Does the prospect understand marketing?
▲ Is there enthusiasm about your industry?
▲ Does the prospect enjoy working with people?
▲ Can the prospect follow the system you designed and mold his personality to fit the system?
▲ Does the prospect have high self-esteem and self-confidence?
▲ Does the prospect present the image that must be portrayed by your franchisees?
▲ Does the prospect possess business acumen, or understand profit-and-loss statements, balance sheets, and other financial matters?
▲ Are the prospect's values comparable to your standards?
▲ Has the prospect demonstrated the ability to make things happen?

Specific Steps in the Marketing System

In building the step-by-step process that ultimately makes up the overall marketing system, incorporate the following general procedures:

1. Each marketing representative must follow a written agenda for meetings with prospects, avoid oral statements inconsistent with the offering documents, and maintain compliance files on each prospect in accordance with guidelines established by legal counsel.
2. Each marketing representative should establish a strict timetable for each qualified prospect for initial meeting, data gathering, and follow-up calls and meetings.
3. Each marketing representative must be armed with literature developed and approved by the company to truly create value and help the prospect make an informed business decision.
4. Each marketing representative should include other executives in the mar-

keting process as well as existing franchisees (by providing testimonial mailers or addresses and phone numbers the prospect can call).

5. Each marketing representative must be trained to assist the prospect in investigating third-party contracts (landlords, commercial banks, etc.).

6. Each marketing representative must follow company procedures for execution and delivery of contracts.

Developing the Presentation Format

The presentation is critical. Equally important is the preparation, both mental and physical, for the first face-to-face franchisee meeting. The following steps should be followed in developing a presentation:

1. Determine the presentation format (one-on-one, face-to-face, or group).
2. Confirm the meeting time, date, and place with the prospect.
3. Confirm that all necessary arrangements have been made at the presentation site.
4. Review the prospect's paperwork to familiarize yourself with her background, possible goals, dreams, objectives, and doubts.
5. Be knowledgeable about the franchise concept.
6. Know the local market, the franchise, and the competition.
7. Know the content of your UFOC and agreements, and anticipate questions on areas of possible concern.
8. Make sure presentation and hand-out materials are complete.
9. Be skilled at using the presentation materials.
10. Maintain a high level of confidence and enthusiasm.
11. Remember that your role is to facilitate the decision-making process; you are helping prospects make an informed business decision about whether your franchise concept is the best investment opportunity for them.

Likewise, the presentation training of your franchise development staff is critical. What characteristics does a well-trained, effective presenter possess? The following are presentation-skill end results. Your development staff should rehearse to develop these results:

- Clearly understands and communicates the purpose of the meeting.
- Understands the prospect's needs, motivations, goals, dreams, objectives, fears, uncertainties, and doubts.
- Is professional (organized and prepared).
- Is credible (dress, demeanor, language, and temperament).
- Is impressive rather than tries to impress.
- Talks with prospects rather than to them.
- Builds value and trust.

▲ Is service minded.
▲ Shows perseverance and follows up.
▲ Understands how the franchise opportunity will help the prospect address basic issues.
▲ Leads the prospect to the decision that is best for both parties.

The follow-up is as salient as a good presentation. Each party must leave the meeting with specific assignments and target completion dates. We use a Decision-Making Checklist for a first talk or visit.

During the meeting, both parties must confirm understanding of several things. The prospect needs to understand the concept of franchising, how a franchise operates, how he can make money, and how your franchise is right for him. The franchisor must determine if the prospect is able to meet commitments, must know what actions are necessary to keep the process moving forward if it is in the best interest of both parties, and must provide additional information to assist the prospect in validating his decision.

The checklist (see Figure 15-2) illustrates how to develop an agenda for a meeting, future processes, and target dates. The agenda evolves from the questions (see Figure 15-3). This allows the representative to control the discussion, pace the meeting, keep the talk focused, and assist a prospect in making an informed business decision.

Closing

If the franchise licensing system has been followed, the results should be a closing process that began from the first contact and continued to the end. The most

(Text continues on page 233.)

Figure 15-2. What do we want to discuss at this meeting?

1. The candidate's motivation for becoming a Sterling Optical Centers franchisee
2. The details of the completed request for consideration
3. The basic principles of business format franchising
4. The Sterling Optical Centers Operating System
5. The Sterling Optical Centers Marketing System
6. The Sterling Optical Centers Support Center
7. The qualifications of the candidate
8. The candidate's goals, objectives, dreams, fears, uncertainties, and doubts
9. The basics of the Disclosure Document and License Agreement
10. The location(s) and funding being considered by the candidate
11. The mission, values, vision, strategy, and systems of Sterling Optical
12. The timetable for opening a center

Figure 15-3. Agenda for face-to-face meeting.

**What Do You Want to Discuss
at This Meeting?**

(List 5 things)

_____

_____

_____

_____

_____

**What Is Motivating You to Pursue
This Business Opportunity?
(Personal Goals and Objectives)**

(List 5 things)

_____

_____

_____

_____

_____

Figure 15-4.   Sterling Optical Centers franchise licensing process summary.

Description of Steps	Sequence of Calendar Day	Expected Results
1. Initial prospecting effort	1–15	Telephone call from prospect or return of in-store inquiry for more information.
2. Initial telephone qualification interview with prospect	5–25	Preliminary qualification; agreement to return Request for Consideration and Financial Verification Request; Send brochure, Request for Consideration, Decision-Making Checklist, and Financial Verification Request only if qualified.
3. Follow-up telephone conversation to prospect	15–30	Review Request for Consideration, Financial Verification Request, Decision-Making Checklist, and brochure; Schedule visit to meet with all decision makers.
4. Second direct-mail letter to people not responding to initial mailing.	25–30	Telephone call from prospect for more information. Go to step 2
5. Meeting with prospects	35–50	Prospect obtains understanding of franchise; UFOC, application or essay and completed franchise agreement given to prospect.
6. Follow-up telephone conversations	40–60	Answer remaining questions on Decision-Making Checklist.
7. Third-direct mail letter to people not responding to first and second mailings.	55–60	Telephone call from prospect for more information.
8. Prospect application or essay received	50–80	Application or essay reviewed and processed by Franchise Selection Committee. Decision is made to approve or reject the franchise award.
9. Prospect visits the Franchise Support Center	60–90	Franchise awarded and agreements signed by franchisee only and fees paid.

10. Site-selection process begins; local Sterling Optical Centers real estate rep works with new franchisee	90–120	Site confirmed.
11. Lease negotiated	100–130	Lease approved and build-out begins.
12. Training	100–160	Franchisee prepares for operation.
13. Build-out of lease-hold improve-ments	100–170	Site ready for opening.
14. Grand opening and other pre-opening activities	150–180	New franchisee guided in opening of center.
15. Center opens	150–180	New franchise in operation and agreement signed by Sterling Optical Center on opening day.

important skill in closing is the ability to listen . . . listen . . . listen. Representatives must have the ability to discard peripheral thoughts and listen to the prospect. They must be able to repeat the prospect's words for confirmation, give the perception that what the prospect has to say matters, and listen long enough so the prospect knows he has been understood. Representatives should never jump to conclusions without hearing the prospect's words, and should respond only after they are certain they have the prospect's complete point of view.

Summary

Only the basics have been discussed here; obviously, there is more to designing and managing a marketing process than making an outline and adhering to it. Our system at Sterling Optical (see Figure 15-4) has been the training tool for all of our development representatives, providing the documentation that demands results. Like all businesses, however, our planning perspectives are so close to home they sometimes become myopic and we are in danger of losing the bigger picture. In over fifteen years in the franchising business, I have adjusted the process many times.

The franchise marketing process is kept intact through steady leadership. The senior staff must lead by example and respect the system. This yields accountability, fewer legal problems, and, most important, results!

16

Working With an Advertising Agency

Ron Guberman, Media Reactions, Inc.

Multidimensional Advertising

Franchise advertising consists of two major and distinct segments. The first addresses the generation of franchise customers. This includes advertising in the traditional franchise or "business opportunity" magazines and newspapers.

In addition to traditional paid media, franchise prospect generation also involves public relations efforts and participation in International Franchise Association (IFA) expositions and selected business trade shows. The development of support tools such as brochures, slide shows, video presentations, convention displays, and promotional materials also fits in the prospecting segment.

The second major segment of a franchisor's advertising program is directed at generating retail customers for the franchisee. Possible advertising tools include everything from radio and television spots to newspaper ads, store signage, point of purchase displays, and local promotions. Although this advertising segment is primarily directed at the retail customer, it often has a dramatic effect on franchise sales.

When someone buys a franchise, he is looking to improve his odds for success by investing in a business that has a high likelihood of success. To the franchise prospect, success generally translates to "I'll get a lot of customers." After he reviews all your disclosure documents, listens to your presentations, and observes all the "due diligence" material, the prospect's main question often becomes "How do I know people will buy from me?" Since the answers to this question are as unique as your fingerprints, we discuss it here primarily as it relates to franchise selling.

The answer to the question usually comes from the franchise company's retail or consumer advertising. If a franchise prospect likes your advertising, sees it all the time, believes it creates a dominance in the market, and feels that it adequately sells the essence of the business, he will feel much more comfortable about buying your franchise.

The same "comfort factor" holds true for consumers. They patronize franchise operations because the advertising gives them the impression that each outlet is part of a sizable, dependable, national operation. The consumer is buying familiarity and consistency.

In each vendor's search for the elusive customer, competition is a major factor. This is especially true in most traditional franchise businesses. The decision to invest in a particular business or to investigate a particular franchise is frequently based on an emotional response, often generated more by consumer or retail advertising than by corporate or franchise advertising. In an increasing number of cases, the advertising itself provides a major competitive edge and plays a significant role in establishing the unique character of a franchise. To a good number of successful operations, advertising is a big part of what a franchise is all about.

Understanding Exactly What You Are Selling

When you get right down to it, the positive attitude you have about one business compared to another is usually nothing more than a feeling. It is an impression you have formed as a result of what you have been told or what you have been shown. As a franchisor, your retail advertising copy should convey both the spirit and the product of your business. What you have to sell is success—the look and feel of success. It must be communicated in every piece of promotional material you produce.

As a franchisor, keep in mind that while your retail advertising is directed toward generating direct sales from your retail customers, that same advertising is being seen and judged by the prospective franchise customer on a completely different level. Franchise prospects evaluate your advertising to determine how well it might generate customers for *them,* should they buy your franchise. They look at your company's advertising while thinking that it might be their advertising some day. In reality, many of the same rules that apply in personal contact also apply in advertising. First impressions are important and lasting. What kind of impression does your advertising convey?

Retail customers look at advertising from the standpoint of content. They want to know if your ad offers something they are in the market for. The franchise customer looks at your ad from the standpoint of quality and effectiveness. Her concern is not necessarily *what* the ad sells, but rather *how well* it sells. Does the ad look professional? Does it look expensive or cheap? Does it create excitement? Is it the kind of advertising that franchisees will want to run?

Advertising is a major part of the product you have to sell. Often, it can be your competitive edge in the marketplace. There is one common denominator that should underscore all of your consumer and franchise advertising: *What you have to sell is success.*

How to Attract Franchise Prospects

Although the following paradigm may seem oversimplified, prospect generation can actually be summed up quite easily. Find out who your prospect is. Find out what she wants to hear. Find out where she can be reached. Speak to her needs, and tell her exactly what she wants to hear. And don't forget to provide an immediate reason for her to contact you.

Unfortunately, as you attempt to generate franchise prospects, you may find that the first few are the easiest to get. Developing large numbers of prospects on a consistent basis is much more difficult. Breaking past that significant, growth-inhibiting volume barrier is the cause of frustration for many franchisors. Here are a few pointers that should help you increase your lead flow.

When you remember that you are selling *success* first and your particular business second, attracting franchise prospects becomes much more productive. Design the headline of your ads to stress the benefits of owning your own business instead of just listing the details of what your offering provides. Use words that convey benefits such as *potential, success, rewarding, satisfaction, profit, freedom, independence*.

Response: Your Primary Objective

Always keep your ad's objective in mind. As you develop your franchise ads, your only goal is to generate a franchise prospect. Your mission is to get your phone to ring. Nothing more.

If you develop your ad with the intent of telling your whole story, you'll lose on two counts. First, you will most likely run out of space. Second, if you do succeed in telling most of your story, you may have provided too much information, thereby failing to give the prospect a reason for calling you to "find out more." Ads are designed to entice a response, not to sell the offering. Sales presentations, owner testimonials, and site visits sell the franchise.

To help encourage a response, offer something of relevant value to your prospect as an incentive to respond immediately. A free booklet on the unique benefits of your franchise may work well. Again, use a benefit-related headline on the cover, such as: *Independence, Freedom,* or *Satisfaction.* Using nonrelated premiums or incentives in your ad may also help generate more leads, but these leads may be of poorer quality since the prospect may be calling just to get the premium. You shouldn't have to bribe someone to become a prospect.

Scoping Out the Competition

Face the reality. Regardless of your business area, competition for customers is always a factor. There is always business out there for the taking. Franchise sales are made every day. Someone gets them. The real question is, Is it you? You must establish a clear understanding of how competition will affect your particular endeavor and then determine precisely what you should do to compensate.

The story is told about two guys who just happen to be in the franchise business. One is in fast food, the other in some type of service industry. They are both campers who happen upon a bear while hiking through the woods. (I'm told this happens in franchising all the time.) As they both run from the bear, one franchisor stops just long enough to change from his hiking boots into his running shoes. When the first franchisor asks his companion if he thinks running shoes will really help him outrun the bear, his reply is, "No, but they will help me outrun you."

Although I use this story to put dealing with competition in its proper perspective, the story helps illustrate the value of having clear objectives in all your advertising endeavors. Get a good handle on exactly what you need to accomplish with each project. Who is your competition, and what kind of tools does *it* have? Don't limit your scope just to your industry. Keep in mind that your competition is often franchises that sell products or services other than yours. If your objective is to garner a bigger share of an existing market, whom will you have to beat?

Develop a clear understanding of what type of prospect you are looking for and what types of businesses other than yours might appeal to him. You can then better understand who your competition is and what you have to do to outflank it. For example, if your franchise is in the male-dominated automotive aftermarket field, you needn't worry about trying to develop ads designed to beat franchisors in the fast-food arena. If your franchise is in the decorating industry, don't worry about ads from the automotive franchises.

Once you have a clear understanding of who your competitors are, take a close look at the size, style, and placement of their advertising. If you have no direct competition, evaluate what size ad will be required to put you either on an equal footing or just ahead of other franchise offerings in the publication. Then, design your ads so that they do not get lost in all the advertising clutter. One of my favorite devices for gaining page dominance with small space ads is to use nonlinear or nonsymmetrical designs. This is advertising jargon for "Do something different." When everybody else is using straight lines, use crooked ones. When others design their ads to be horizontal, make yours run uphill.

Media Choices and Strategies

There are many media options available to the franchisor in search of increased prospect responses. In addition to the traditional national publications with regularly scheduled franchise or "business opportunity" sections such as *The Wall Street Journal, USA Today, Inc., Entrepreneur*, and *Franchising Opportunities*, most local newspapers have a business section that features a weekly business opportunity page. There may also be specialty publications directed at your particular industry. For example, a photography magazine presents a good opportunity to promote a franchisor such as One-Hour Photo Lab. An automotive magazine is a logical choice for an automotive service or aftermarket franchise ad.

You have to decide if you want to advertise where everyone else in the franchise business is advertising or if you want to place your ads in specialty publications where your offering presents a logical tie-in with the reader's personal interests. Although their audience may be somewhat limited, specialty publications offer a franchisor the opportunity to target prospects with a predetermined interest in their type of business. As an added bonus, competitive ads from nonrelated franchises are usually not a factor in specialty publications. If you do find ads from the competition, chances are the ads will be smaller in size. You can usually outflank the competition without having to spend the kind of money required to compete with a major fast-food company.

Prospect Qualifications and Prequalifications

The cost of your franchise and the financial strength requirements of your prospect will be factors in all of your media selection. You should check the average readership income level before placing ads in specialty publications. Be sure that your ad style and copy reflect the quality standards associated with the prospects you seek.

Prospect quality can be measured by both financial strength and ease of conversion. Financial strength is a measure of qualification; the ease of selling or closing a prospect is a measure of convertibility. Everyone in sales prefers working prospects who can afford to purchase even the largest item out of petty cash. Every salesperson would like her prospects to be so presold that closing the deal involves only a casual meeting over lunch to review the terms and sign contracts. This type of prospect does exist. Unfortunately, there are only twelve of them in the universe—and several thousand franchise companies hoping to get their hands on them.

As a franchisor, you can control the quality, convertibility, and quantity of responses from your advertising. But some words of advice: Use caution. If you make your ad's qualification factors too tight, the prospect will end up qualifying you before you have a chance to qualify him. For example, if you have an expensive franchise package with large cash requirements, publishing those requirements in your ads will scare off some individuals. In your efforts to keep from working prospects who cannot qualify, you may be eliminating some who could afford your offering but need to be convinced of its value first.

Here's a good rule to follow when considering prospect qualification in your advertising: First create value, then discuss price. *You* should be the one who determines if the prospect is to your liking. If prospects are disqualifying *you* as a result of your ads, you may be missing out on some of the advertising value you paid for.

There are additional prospect factors that vary, depending on the nature of the publication. The person responding to a classified ad in the Franchise Opportunities section of a major publication can be classified as a Shopper—someone who is actively looking to buy, or who is considering buying, a business. The person who responds to an Own Your Own Business ad in a specialty magazine is looking for a way out. Although she may not be as predisposed to buying a business as the Shopper, neither is she being bombarded with as many competitive choices. The Franchise Opportunity prospect may have responded to dozens of other ads. Keep these differences in mind when planning your ad strategy and placement options.

You can control both the quality and quantity of your respondents. Just remember, quality and quantity are opposing factors. By raising one, you lower the other. Adjust these values as you go along on the basis of measured and documented record keeping of your results. Be sure you factor in the abilities of your selling organization and the quality of the follow-up tools you provide. Remember, often the only difference between a good lead and a bad lead is the ability of the salesperson who gets it, the tools he has to work it, and the amount of effort he must put forth to close it.

Advertising Tools

In working with new clients, I find it helpful to have a shopping list of projects or campaign components developed early on in the relationship. Here is a list of some of the tools you might need to promote your franchise. See how many of these tools you presently have, and how many you need. Armed with that answer, you can then address the real question: Who is going to create the needed materials and ensure their effectiveness?

Prospect Generation

- Classified print advertising—creative and placement
- Display magazine advertising—creative and placement
- Direct mail program—design, production, fulfillment
- Ongoing public relations programs
- Convention/trade show booth
- Owner referral cards

Prospect Sales Support Materials

- Inquiry response mailer
- Main franchise sales brochure
- Presentation portfolio
- Owner testimonials
- Press clippings/stories
- A/V (slide or videotape) sales presentations
- Three-ring notebooks/sales presentation
- Advertising/public relations kits

Franchise Operations Tools

▲ Operations manual/notebook
▲ Corporate ID package with logos and stationery

Retail Advertising Materials and Co-op Program Details

▲ Logos and signage
▲ Coordinated radio/TV/print ads

Advertising Agencies Versus Do-It-Yourself

Ever since our industry and the media painted the advertising business as glamorous, exciting, and fun-filled, clients have wanted to become a part of the glamour. Temptation is what the advertising business is all about. In fact, the roots of the advertising business can be traced to biblical times. Some believe that Eve was actually the first advertising person. She was assigned the Garden of Eden Applegrowers account. Of course, media decisions in those days were much simpler. There were only two demographics, and Eve was one of them. Unfortunately, even though she delivered the desired target market, she ultimately lost the account.

Today, the advertising business is more complex and more exciting. Having lunch with a studio executive, scouting backgrounds for a commercial, or attending a dinner party thrown by the local media can be more exciting than an internal staff meeting to evaluate the merits of redesigning and repackaging the Wompedoodle line. Sure, some agency executives may try to convince you that the advertising business is not always upbeat and exciting—but you know it is.

A trip into the world of advertising can add new excitement, adventure, and rewards to a client's daily business routine. In fact, at my agency, we often insist on a high level of client participation in our efforts. My best advice is: Don't venture into this area alone. Take an experienced professional with you to be your guide. Together, you can accomplish a great deal more, sometimes for less money.

As you review the roles of client and agency, the real reasons for using a professional should become quite clear to you. As the franchisor, your job relates to the nuts-and-bolts operation of creating and offering a turnkey business. That includes making significant contributions to the development of the advertising and marketing strategy that helps build your business. It does not require you to write all the copy, design the ads, or develop the brochures. These are functions best relegated to an advertising agency.

Ad agencies can lend two distinct strengths to your ad campaign. These areas of strength are creativity and media selection know-how.

CREATIVITY

Your agency's job is to communicate a positive feeling and to motivate people to respond to your advertising. If your background and experience are in an area other than mass communications and motivational psychology, you need an agency. Even if you are completely clear on *what* you have to say, chances are an agency can show you *how* to say it better, more effectively, more memorably.

In the highly competitive franchise sales arena, a professional agency can bring talents to the table that will help your advertising and sales support materials cut through the clutter and competition and place you on top. The ability to work with copy, style, layout, design, touch, feel, and emotion simultaneously adds up to giving your organization an edge. This is especially important if your budget is small. Anybody can look big and successful given all the money in the world. It takes skill and professional help to look big when you're not.

MEDIA SELECTION

Another area where an agency can be very beneficial is in media selection. Today, media has become a very broad term that includes some of the newest forms of communications. In addition to the traditional forms, such as print advertising, brochures, and slide shows, the media now include many new and exciting high-tech options for sales tools. Examples are multimedia computer demonstrations, video presentations, audiotext, and interactive communications. The newest selling tool, called virtual reality (V/R), combines many of these functions into a beyond-space-age presentation where the prospect wears a special screen-equipped helmet that lets her tour, sense, feel, experience, and even smell a multidimensional computer representation or even take a mock demonstration ride in a new automobile. V/R users can simulate actually walking around, getting inside, and seeing what is there. Every year new and exciting additions to the list of media choices become available to you. One of those nontraditional choices may be exactly what you need to generate the audience and sales you desire. Remember, they laughed at television when it first came out.

Competition for audience awareness is very tough. In the game of exposure and viewer awareness, franchise companies are up against some of the biggest and most powerful advertisers in the business. Your advertising is judged against that of clients spending hundreds of millions of dollars annually. Even though you may have developed a vastly superior business concept, neither your retail nor your franchise customer will know of your superiority unless it is successfully communicated through some form of advertising.

Media choices are becoming increasingly complex, and the options are increasingly expensive. Knowing where to place your advertising resources is as important as knowing what to say when you do advertise. Many prestigious national magazines and newspapers offer regional or local editions to allow advertisers to concentrate expenditures in areas where they need business without having to purchase coverage in areas where there is less need. The media departments of most agencies have access to a wealth of research material that can help you identify your best media opportunities. Together, you and your agency can analyze costs and potential return for each relevant option and then make an intelligent and informed media purchase.

It is difficult for some clients to delegate advertising responsibilities, either because of what they see as the unique nature of their business or because of the importance of what needs to be said. It is vital to your success that you remain detached enough to be objective about what the agency submits for your approval. Fight the temptation to do it all yourself. Bring in agency professionals who can communicate the magic that you created.

Check Your Footing

I am often amazed at what some prospective clients try to pass off as a sales brochure. Obviously, they must have never heard the old expression "Put your best foot forward." After spending thousands of dollars in prospecting costs to generate a valid franchise lead, some companies try to get a potential investor to spend tens or hundreds of thousands of dollars to buy a franchise on the basis of a black and white brochure. The brochure in question wouldn't pass the trash test, in which the reader looks at what you sent him and then promptly tosses your treasured offering into the trash. When a prospect buys a franchise, he is usually making one of the biggest single purchases of his life. He must never lose sight of the value he is getting. He must never doubt that what he is buying, along with success, is quality. Ask yourself how well your brochure and sales material stack up.

When I am presented with a low-quality brochure, one of my favorite tactics is to pull out a very fancy brochure that our agency developed for a client in the mortgage industry. I place our brochure next to the client's. I ask, Which company gives you a warmer feeling in your tummy? Which seems bigger, more reputable, more established? The client flips through the large, full-color pages, ends up on the last page where there is a shot of *my* client's office building, and says, "Well, I guess yours is." I then let the client on the secret. I point to one corner of the office building pictured and state that our client rented just a small corner of this building. In reality, the client with the fancy brochure is much smaller in annual revenue and has far fewer employees than the client I am with. The point is made.

Through the advertising craft, we created a picture bigger than life. By not using this tool to its fullest, your franchise will be disadvantaged because your strengths and benefits to the consumer will be inadequately communicated.

There are thousands of business opportunities and franchise offerings on the market today. Your competition can outfox you by spending a couple of dollars more on creating a better impression with a simple but more professional-looking brochure. It doesn't matter that your offering may have significantly more going for it. Conversely, a really good brochure can give you a major edge over much larger and more established competition. A professionally produced video can easily outclass some of the toughest competitors, often for the same development costs as a color brochure.

The same rules hold true when it comes to packaging. Take your disclosure document, for example. Here are hundreds of pages detailing your history and distilling all your dirty laundry, some of your secrets, and untold years of your sweat equity. Answer these questions:

- ▲ How does this document look?
- ▲ Is it typeset?
- ▲ Is it easy to read?
- ▲ Does it say what you would *like* to say or what you *have* to say?
- ▲ Was it professionally prepared by an artist or was it drawn up by a lawyer's secretary?
- ▲ If you had a choice, would you send it?
- ▲ More importantly, if you had a choice, would you read it?

We live in the age of the executive summary. If your disclosure document came with an impressive sixteen-page color brochure or a ten-minute video, which would you look at first?

A good advertising agency can help you improve your disclosure document and provide you with a package that can provide a whole lot more sizzle. Agency professionals are experienced artists and writers who can take your strengths and embellish them to produce the desired results. By using simple yet very affordable devices such as color, textured paper, or a particular style and mood of photography, a good advertising agency can produce a brochure that creates an image that is bigger than life. More important, an agency can help you focus on the realities of what your customer is looking for. Often, this is different from what you, the client, feel is important.

Agency and Client: Some Philosophical Differences

A number of factors will influence your selection of an ad agency. Where you come down on each factor will determine your decision.

Cost Versus Effectiveness

Understandably, clients are often concerned about costs. What they should be more concerned about are results. I often pose a challenge to new clients, asking them how they would go about getting twice as many responses from their advertising. Would it be wiser to double their expenditures and buy twice as much advertising or to spend their existing budget more wisely, making it twice as effective? In reality, it is usually much less expensive to double your effectiveness. With ad layouts that jump off the page or with highly targeted media selections, most good agencies can help you increase your effectiveness without significantly increasing your costs.

In-House — or Not

Some clients feel it is less expensive simply to hire a graphics firm or an artist to convert their own ideas into ads and brochures. Others feel they can produce their advertising in-house, keep the agency commissions for themselves, and convert those saved dollars into extra advertising. In considering the wisdom of an in-house operation, the question that you have to answer is: *Are you really saving the 15 percent commission — or are you possibly compromising the remaining 85 percent?*

Although I must admit to a certain bias on this subject, there is a parallel that can be drawn. Let's suppose that a member of your family needs surgery. Would you run an ad in Help Wanted section of the local college newspaper for a graduating medical student to save on the cost of a delicate operation? An exaggeration on my part? Maybe just a little. But ask yourself: Are the direction, skill, and execution of your advertising efforts any less important?

This is not to say that a franchise company can't find and hire competent professionals to staff and run an in-house advertising agency. The real questions are these: Are the people you need available in your market? In your price range? Would working for your company offer these professionals both the creative and financial rewards they would get by working for a recognized advertising agency? Will your in-house agency's ideas be fresh each year, or will they reflect too much internal company influence? Remember, you are in competition with the agency marketplace for top talent.

Big Agency Versus Little Agency

Once you have decided that an agency can help you get more results for your advertising dollars, selecting the right agency for your needs becomes your next task. Agency size is often one of the tougher issues that needs to be resolved. The assumption that the biggest agency can do the most good for you is not always true. Granted, outstanding talent, a full range of services, and experience can usually be found at a large agency. The real questions are: Will your account get that service? Do you need all that service? And, can you afford all that service?

In recent years, some smaller yet very talented shops have successfully unseated some of the larger Goliaths of the advertising industry. We often comment that our shop has won accounts away from agencies that have more people in their men's room at any given time than we have in our entire building. This is not to say that smaller agencies are better than bigger agencies. Every agency has its own strengths and weaknesses.

Many clients have commented that when they interviewed at a big agency, they felt *they* were the ones being interviewed. Often, this is a reality. An agency is as concerned about what the client has to offer the agency as the client is about the agency. Smaller accounts and, especially, start-up companies require a great deal of extra service that may be disproportionate to the media billing or project revenues. A small account in a large agency does not usually draw the best agency staff members. Often, many small accounts find they get better service from a small or medium-size advertising agency where they can be assigned the "A" team.

My best advice is, shop around. Evaluate the talent and relevant experience of the people you will be working with, rather than the overall size of the agency. When you find the right agency, you'll know it. You'll sense the enthusiasm and the chemistry, often at the first meeting. If your advertising expenditures will be measured in millions, you will usually find you can get the service and attention you deserve in a bigger shop. If your budget is smaller, chances are that a medium-size or small agency will work a lot harder for your business.

Beauty and The Beast, or Art Versus the Budget

Major philosophical differences exist between agency and client. The agency is interested in seeing just *how good* it can make your company, ad, or brochure look. The client, on the other hand, is more often interested in *how inexpensively* the agency can get the job done. Obviously, this difference in viewpoint can become the foundation for a major conflict between client and agency.

In the agency business, *your* advertising is *our* product. You pay us to produce something that we can later show off as ours. It ensures that we take pride in your work, not just in your billing. In reality, it's good that it happens this way because it ensures that one of us will always be concerned about how good you look.

As the client, you inherit by default the job of budget watchdog. Unfortunately, in the battle of art versus budget, if the client wins by too much, he also loses. It's risky to regard cost as an expense rather than as an investment in achieving a desired outcome. Budget projects realistically so that the agency can produce a product you will both be proud of.

Here is a rule of thumb to use when faced with a creative budgeting dilemma. Art is no substitute for substance, even though in advertising it is often used that way. As long as the art and the associated costs are being used make a point in a professional manner, let it stand. If the art is used just for the sake of art, let your budget be your guide. On the other hand, if you find you cannot generate any substance, get the best art you can find.

Armed with a clear understanding of what needs to be done and not just what needs to be said, you and your agency can proceed to develop a persuasive package of tools.

Financial Considerations

Advertising and the Uh-Ohs

Many clients rank advertising purchases and budgeting with other needs that we affectionately call "uh-ohs." An uh-oh purchase is usually an unfortunate or an obligatory purchase that you make unexpectedly, generally not out of any real desire. This type of purchase got its name from the expression that usually precedes the purchase, such as:

"Uh-oh, I need new tires."
"Uh-oh, there goes the furnace [or the roof]."
"Uh-oh, Junior just got his driver's license."

Usually franchisees and franchisors look at budgeting advertising with the same enthusiasm they'd have for purchasing life insurance or visiting the dentist. They regard advertising as a necessary evil and expense. Here again, we're dealing with the need to put things in the proper perspective.

When was the last time you woke up and said, "I think I'll get dressed, go down to the local newspaper office, and buy that full page ad I've been thinking about?" Never?

The reality of the situation is that nobody really wants to buy advertising. What clients want to buy are results. Unfortunately, what they usually buy are ads. What they focus on is image. This creates a dilemma.

The advertiser is buying something that he really doesn't want (usually space in a publication). To make things worse, in return for his investment, he is getting something he often can't define and usually can't immediately see (usually, nebulous results). If clients were to focus on the level of results they could expect from running an ad, their attitude toward advertising budgets would quickly change from "uh-oh" to "good investment." Things start to get exciting when you stop viewing advertising as a liability and see instead an *opportunity* for growth.

Buying Customers, Not Ads

One of my favorite approaches when I am trying to unhook a client from another agency or from a traditional media campaign is to ask what she thinks about her existing advertising. Clients almost always say, "It's great!" When I then ask why they aren't buying more of it, they usually fumble for an answer. In reality, most advertisers do not know exactly what their advertising is doing for them. One in a hundred knows what her advertising *cost per sale* is. The reason advertisers are reluctant to spend more is that they find it difficult to invest heavily in something where the outcome is that unknown.

Knowing what it costs to buy a customer is not an unreasonable request. It is an essential request! As a businessperson, you know exactly what your products cost. You know what labor costs. You know how much to budget for rent, utilities, and taxes. Why not know what customers cost? That's just as valid a line item as all the other costs of doing business. How can you factor or plan growth without it?

If there is one thing that you and your agency should set as a goal in your relationship, it should be to learn precisely what it costs to buy more sales, more customers. Even if that cost is high you can factor it into your business equations as a cost of manufacturing or cost of goods sold and let the customer pay for it. Knowing your advertising cost of sale may force you to raise your price. But then, so would an increase in the cost of materials or labor.

Advertisers usually resist buying more advertising because they simply don't know what it will do for them. Your franchisees may fight promoting their business (and yours) because they have not been convinced of the real value of advertising. Your regional managers or advertising co-op groups may be having a difficult time getting participation because you are asking for a decision based on faith and not facts. Businesspeople are very smart. Talk to them about results, and then show them a good return on investment. They'll listen.

Advertising Accountability

The reason most advertisers can't tell you exactly what results they are getting from each of their ads is because they fail to ask. Often, the only tracking they do is known as *bottom-lining*. This is the act of judging ad results based on overall sales or bottom-line numbers. Nice, but not enough.

Recently, there has been a shifting of values and dollars to a segment of the advertising business known as *direct response*. Although it found its roots in direct mail, direct response has grown to become a major segment of the broadcast and magazine business.

Direct response (D/R) differs from traditional or institutional advertising in one significant way—direct response advertising solicits an immediate response or order. D/R can be identified by a phone number at the end of a television spot, a coupon at the bottom of an ad, or a reply card inside a mailer. What is amazing to many first-time direct response advertisers is that people actually do respond immediately, often in numbers much higher than anticipated.

Accountability has always been the watchword in direct response advertising. Response agencies talk results. Traditional agencies, on the other hand, tend to focus more on creativity and campaign execution rather than bottom-line responses. They speak in terms of long-range plans and use words such as *reach*, *image*, and *frequency*. These are valid considerations, especially when the client does not know, or has not yet started to focus on exactly what a new customer should cost them to buy; there is genuine value in repetitive, cumulative exposure. But in your dealings with advertising agencies, use caution when the emphasis is on lengthy exposure periods to generate specific results. Just about any advertising will generate some results if you run it long enough. We have a favorite expression at Media Reactions: *"Time is the salvation of bad advertising; good advertising works overnight."*

In direct response, you can't hide behind a less-than-effective ad, regardless of how good it may seem or how creative it looks. If the ad is good and if the copy requests a response, someone will respond right away. You can actually measure that instantaneous response more easily than you can measure the results of long-range exposure.

As you evaluate the myriad advertising choices to which you will be exposed, keep in mind that some traditional agencies and media sources shy away from speaking about instant results or from putting their reputations on the line on an ad-by-ad basis. If a medium has a record of working in your business, its representatives will be the first to tell you. The same holds true for agencies. What is interesting is what ultimately happens when clients do switch to response-oriented advertising. They usually don't go back to more traditional modalities.

Some agencies do make a significant investment in providing for results tracking. Without sounding too commercial, our agency has spent over ten years and untold thousands of dollars developing sophisticated computer software to allow our clients to know exactly what results each media purchase is achieving. The program is such a powerful decision-making tool that it is being used to direct the broadcast media purchases of two Fortune 100 companies whose advertising is handled by separate national agencies, which license the program from us.

Tracking results is not easy, nor is it free. An investment from both the client and agency is required to produce the numbers. Why spend the extra effort and extra cost to obtain the data? The answer is simple. Armed with dependable numbers that project future growth, you can make advertising decisions and purchases more easily, and results become much easier to forecast as well as to achieve.

The Bottom Line

Presenting Your Advertising as a Tangible Benefit

Advertising directed at motivating retail customers is both a business-generating tool and a major part of the product you have to sell. With that point in mind, knowing the cost of buying that customer is not only a plus, often it's the ball game. Consider these points.

Your franchise prospect came to you to buy a business she feels has a high likelihood of succeeding because of your research, testing, and experience. The biggest question often is "How do I know I'll get customers to buy from me at my location?" Imagine the value of your having a system that can project a range of anticipated costs for generating customers in markets where the prospect is considering purchasing a franchise.

In a highly competitive marketplace, wouldn't you have a competitive edge if you were the only franchise of its type that could reliably demonstrate and factor customer acquisition costs? Wouldn't knowing the cost of generating a predetermined customer level be worth a great deal to you in your own operations?

And what about your retail co-op advertising? How would it affect franchisee advertising participation if you could factor demonstrated results into the equation?

OPM and Who's Co-Oping Whom?

Most franchises offer some sort of cooperative advertising program to promote mutual growth and business generation at the area or even at the individual franchise level. There is a tremendous opportunity for both franchisee and franchisor to gain from co-op programs. The added value comes in the benefit you both achieve from spending **O**ther **P**eople's **M**oney.

Franchisors often allocate a percentage of local gross revenues to an advertising fund and then match those dollars with national dollars when advertising is done according to published guidelines. From the corporate standpoint, having the franchisee match the franchisor's dollars yields a return on ad investment of 100 percent. Although the franchisor is spending some of its money promoting franchisees' businesses, the franchisees are paying to further promote the franchisor's overall goodwill as well.

As the franchisor, as you work with your advertising agency, it is important that you never lose sight of the value of franchisee "buy-in" on your overall advertising program. You'll know you have succeeded when your franchisees start calling *your* advertising *their* advertising. Once they own it, they'll use it. Here are some factors that will help promote franchisee buy-in:

▴ *Offer proven results.* If you have a direct response ad campaign that has been tested and documented elsewhere in the system, further roll-out is usually quite easy. Use testimonials from those who have previously run the program to communicate success in a highly credible manner. This approach is usually the easiest, because what you are promoting is sharing success rather than selling the merits of advertising.

▴ *Develop award-winning creative material.* If you don't have a tried and proven success to promote, offer advertising material that is highly creative, very persuasive, truly memorable, and professionally produced. The logic here is that people would sooner invest in something they are proud of. Results aside, the better your ads look and feel, the more they'll get used.

▴ *Create overwhelming power.* In markets where you have significant outlets that can be persuaded to participate as a team, pooling the area's resources can allow individual franchisees to share in the benefits of a campaign much larger than they could afford alone. The math adds up quickly when you have ten outlets pooling $2,000 each, affording them a $20,000 blitz on radio or television when, alone, all each could afford was print.

▴ *Provide economic incentives.* Money talks. A well-placed financial incentive can provide extra mileage. In the above example, ten franchisees pooled their resources to create a $20,000 budget. If you match their expenditures with funds you had already charged against their sales, their budget quickly grows to $40,000. Your franchisee gets $40,000 worth of value for his $2,000 purchase.

Summary

I hope this chapter has helped you to understand better the value of advertising in your total marketing plan. Properly done, your advertising should be regarded as an ongoing support program for your franchises. It is tangible proof of your commitment to their success. It keeps their interest and enthusiasm high. It provides real benefit for the fees you charge. It offers promotional opportunities neither of you could afford alone. It makes you both bigger than the sum of your parts.

What Is Possible?

With advertising, almost anything is possible. Don't rule out any particular medium or creative approach because you think it might be too expensive. If you work with a good agency, you will be surprised at the number of ways to economize effectively without compromising quality. Go for the best. Your business deserves nothing less.

There is great value in keeping an open mind and in not limiting your possibilities because of preconceived notions. Retail clients are often amazed at how affordable television advertising can be. This is especially true if the target customers are women in the eighteen- to forty-five-year-old bracket. Most people think a television spot costs hundreds of thousands of dollars to buy, and some prime-time national-coverage spots do cost that much. In reality, however, an experienced television buyer can get you a daytime spot on a network-affiliated station in almost all but the top ten markets for a cost ranging from $50 to $200. Local cable television coverage and some independent stations can cost even less. And with the right agency, television producer, and professional talent, you can produce a highly effective commercial, often for less than $10,000. When you know how to stretch a budget and how to maximize return, you can afford to offer your franchises much more advertising value than you might imagine.

What Next?

When new clients ask where they should be going with their advertising, my stock answer is "Evaluate yourself." Take a long hard look at your business and your advertising. Is your advertising as good, as efficient, as revolutionary, or as practical as the rest of what your franchise offers? Is it the highlight of your offering or just something you developed as you went along? Does it stack up favorably against the competition? Does it actually help you sell franchises? Are you using it to sell more franchises? Shouldn't you be?

If the answers to any of the above questions is no, take two aspirins and call me or any good advertising agency in the morning. Better yet, call me in the afternoon; we can "do" lunch. There is this lovely restaurant in town call Tezcalipoka's. It was named after the ancient Aztec god of smoke and mirrors. This probably explains why so many of us advertising types hang out there on a regular basis.

17

Working With a Public Relations Firm

Betsy Nichol, Arthur Yann, and Kathy Moran, Nichol & Company, Ltd.

Franchise companies can use public relations to cost effectively generate leads for new franchises. Public relations can generate awareness of and interest in a franchise opportunity and can motivate potential franchisees to take the initial steps toward purchasing the rights to operate a franchise. Without this motivating process, there would be fewer franchised units, and a less successful organization would result.

The purpose of public relations is to create a favorable climate in which new franchises can be and are obtained. While there are hundreds of success stories on how public relations has contributed to the franchise expansion process, three particular campaigns that we've executed on behalf of franchise clients illustrate what we mean by "creating a favorable selling climate."

1. When *General Nutrition Centers*, the nation's largest chain of health management centers, began franchising in 1987, limited external communications meant that only thirty franchises were awarded over a two-year period. In 1990, an integrated marketing communications program including public relations and advertising began. Just twenty-one months later, more than 11,000 leads had been generated and the company boasted 127 franchises.

2. *ProForma*, a franchisor of business products distributorships, was featured in a *Fortune* magazine cover story. Two weeks later, ProForma had received more than 200 qualified leads; and this one article eventually produced enough revenue from franchise fees to pay for the entire year's public relations program.

3. *Stained Glass Overlay* had approximately seventy franchisees, primarily on the West Coast, at the time our communications program began. After we promoted the company's franchise opportunity and its decorative glass through a public relations campaign for three and one-half years in combination with the company's advertising and trade show exposure, Stained Glass Overlay had 350 franchises from coast to coast.

Now that you know what public relations can accomplish, it is important to understand fully what it is and how it works.

What Is Public Relations?

Public relations is so complex that often even the most sophisticated executives don't fully understand how it works or its importance as a marketing tool. Before explaining what public relations is, it might help to establish what it is not.

For one thing, public relations is not advertising. It isn't writing and designing paid-for ads in magazines and newspapers or creating radio and television commercials or billboards. Nor is it sales promotion, which might include a national sweepstakes to win a trip for two to Rio or mass mailings to consumers encouraging them to subscribe to a new bank card.

Like advertising and sales promotion, however, public relations *is* a powerful marketing tool that communicates persuasive messages that are important to a company's success.

One of the most widespread misconceptions about public relations is that it's strictly publicity—articles in local and national magazines and newspapers or interviews or company mentions on television and radio stations. Publicity is usually a major part of a PR program, but public relations also includes special events, press conferences, trade shows, community relations, philanthropic involvement, employee communications, and media relations and tours.

In his book, *The Marketer's Guide to Public Relations,* Thomas L. Harris offers an excellent description of how IBM applies media relations, the most basic aspect of public relations: "Media relations is one of the 'communications tools' used by the company to drive target audiences through the 'purchase path' from (1) *awareness* to (2) *interest* to (3) *desire* to (4) *action.*"[1]

Publicity about a company and its executives, products, and services carries an implied third-party endorsement by the media and is perceived as news. Because of its high credibility, media relations holds an edge over every other form of communications. For a company trying to interest investors in its franchise opportunity, a positive article about the franchise in a magazine or newspaper or an appearance by a successful franchisee on a television show has a very different impact than an ad written and paid for by the company. Similarly, a speech given by a company executive or a seminar conducted by your company on a topic of interest to prospective franchisees is less commercial than advertising and therefore tends to enhance credibility.

Both advertising and public relations play valuable roles in acquiring franchisees. Advertising is usually the hard sell, and public relations the soft sell. One study has shown that when advertising is preceded by publicity, consumers report seven times better recall of the ad. Figure 17-1 describes ways public relations can extend the impact of advertising.

Another virtue of public relations is that in tight economic times, publicity

Figure 17-1. How public relations works.

Public relations can extend the impact of advertising by:

- Telling a more detailed story and giving it credibility because its source is the news media rather than the company itself
- Positioning the company as an industry leader
- Showing top executives as experts in their field
- Making advertising seem newsworthy and complementing it by reinforcing ad messages and legitimizing claims
- Building confidence and trust in a company
- Enabling a company to reach secondary geographic or demographic markets for a relatively inexpensive price
- Reinforcing messages to weak markets
- Counteracting resistance to advertising
- Supplementing the advertising campaign by reiterating its message to the same or different markets
- Extending the reach of the company's message beyond what the advertising budget allows

can generate an enormous amount of exposure for a relatively low cost. A public relations campaign for an entire year may cost the same as a single full-page ad in a national magazine.

Public relations can also create the belief that your franchise is the "hottest" in your category. Prospective franchisees often perceive the best investments to be those that are most visible and that have been featured in the news most often, rather than those with the largest market share or that are growing the fastest.

The most important difference between advertising and public relations is that, when an advertiser places an ad, he can control the message, the particular section of a newspaper in which it will be placed, and the day on which it will appear. A publicist cannot completely control the message or when that message will be seen. But a public relations expenditure goes much farther. For the cost of a single ad, a company's public relations campaign can lead to many favorable articles in magazines and newspapers and to interviews on television and radio. And when the "big hit" occurs, such as an interview with your top franchisee on "Good Morning America" or in *The Wall Street Journal*, it will have more clout than paid advertisements in these media outlets ever could.

Getting Started

Before embarking on a public relations program, it is essential for company decision makers to agree upon corporate and communications objectives and upon what they want the agency to accomplish. Goals should be as narrowly defined as possible, and an agreement should be reached with the agency that defines the expectations for the campaign and establishes how its effectiveness will be measured.

It is also imperative for the franchise to develop a demographic, psychographic, and financial profile of its prospective franchisees. This allows the program to be targeted as narrowly as possible and maximizes the effectiveness of the budget.

After these issues have been resolved, the public relations firm should begin by analyzing your entire franchise operation, studying your company's goals and the traditional SWOT (*S*trengths, *W*eaknesses, *O*pportunities and *T*hreats) factors.

From this analysis, a number of positioning messages or ''copy points'' can be developed and used to promote your franchise. These messages should be emphasized frequently in order to elicit the desired response from prospective franchisees—that is, to have prospects call your franchise instead of another.

Copy points should describe why your franchise is an excellent investment. Factors such as a low initial investment, participation in a fast-growing industry such as health and fitness, or ability to survive recessionary economies or to generate repeat sales should be stressed frequently.

These messages should be the same throughout your advertising and public relations campaigns, as well as in all written and verbal communications (franchise literature, newsletters, brochures, press materials, and speeches). This ensures that every message sent to existing and prospective franchisees conveys your franchise's strongest assets clearly and consistently, over and over again. It's also important to convey this ''unified thinking'' to your staff, so that everyone in your organization, from the sales executives to the secretarial staff, can easily communicate your company's mission statement and strengths to others, whether inside or outside the company. A prospect judges your franchise operation by whether your organization has its act together.

If all of this sounds like an overwhelming task, a public relations agency can help you develop sales-generating copy points and then help you communicate them.

Refining the Message

You should refine the main copy points you have developed about your business to appeal to different groups of potential franchisees (for example, displaced executives, minorities, husband and wife teams). For example, displaced executives can be told that the business contacts and skills they have developed at their last job will enable them to get off to a fast start as franchisees. Minorities should be told about other minorities who have succeeded in your franchise, and a husband and wife team should be told about other couples who have successfully and happily combined their skills. These copy points can be communicated to your audience by a variety of public relations techniques.

Getting the Message Across

Some public relations techniques may meet your company's objectives better than others. Some techniques may be inappropriate. A public relations professional can determine which activities will allow your company to reach the greatest number of prospects in the quickest, most cost-effective manner.

A comprehensive public relations program designed to generate leads for new franchisees may include any of the following basic tactics.

Media relations/publicity consists of news or feature stories on your company's franchise opportunity, products, services, executives, or growth or on trend-setting developments that are placed in national and local print media or are the subject of radio and television broadcasts. Media relations includes the proactive tasks of arranging interviews and publicity as well as the reactive tasks of fielding media requests for information and arranging interviews with company spokespersons. Public relations practitioners may also supply editors and television and radio producers with background information on your company.

Special events are developed to create awareness and goodwill toward a company and its products or services. A special event can range from a seminar on car care held at local supermarkets by SpeeDee Oil Change and Tune-Up to an ongoing project such as the activities of Ronald McDonald Houses around the country.

Press conferences are held to announce timely news about your company that is of importance to a large number of media.

Franchise sales kit/literature should be developed by your public relations firm. These kits ensure that key copy points are conveyed to prospective franchisees.

Wire shorts are short articles or "fillers" that quote surveys or trends. They are written by public relations firms and placed with the Associated Press or United Press International wires. More than 1,500 newspapers across the country receive "wire short" material from the AP or UPI wires, and you can place wire shorts about your company's franchise on a regular basis.

Wire photos are visually arresting photos taken by experts. Captions are written by a public relations professional, and the photo/caption story is then transmitted over the AP or UPI wire to hundreds of newspapers. Wire photos are powerful sales tools, for they often appear in the business or main section of newspapers.

Seminars/speaking engagements provide the opportunity for company executives to position the company as an authority in a particular industry or on a particular topic and to stimulate discussions about the franchise. The media should be encouraged to cover the speech or seminar, and reprints of the resulting publicity should be made and distributed to existing and prospective franchisees.

Media tours require that a company spokesperson, usually a celebrity or a well-known person with significant media appeal, travel from city to city giving interviews about the company to local newspapers, magazines, and radio and television stations. A media tour generates significant exposure for a company and/or its products and services during a concentrated time period, thus creating a media publicity blitz. Commonly known examples of media tours are an author promoting a new book or an actor traveling to promote a new movie.

Grand openings of new franchises often include ribbon-cutting ceremonies with company executives and local dignitaries present, tours of new facilities, introductory discounts, and other hoopla. This type of support for new franchisees encourages prospects to sign on the dotted line because they feel confident that they will get customers once they open their business.

Luncheons and parties given by the company for the press serve as platforms for disseminating news about a company and for developing personal relationships with the media. It also encourages members of the media to seek quotes from company spokespersons and to use the company as a source of information at a later time when they are working on relevant stories.

Newsletters communicate company news to specific groups, such as existing and potential franchisees or customers.

Official endorsements of the franchise concept by political figures, sports stars, or heroes of industry enhance a corporation's image and stature and, of course, impress prospects.

Surveys are powerful tools that can generate publicity for your company in major publications such as *Time* and *Newsweek*. They are usually on subjects or issues that relate to your industry as a whole and have broad appeal.

Radio promotions are on-air radio contests that generate frequent on-air product/company mentions when the company's products or services are offered as prizes.

Product placement is the term used to describe the appearance of products in popular movies and TV shows where they are used as part of the story. For example, the appearance of Reese's Pieces candy in the movie *E.T.* increased the candy's sales dramatically following the release of the film.

Public service announcements, or PSAs, on radio and television feature messages offered in the public's interest. They position the company as one interested in issues of public concern and link the company to worthy social causes. For example, a home security franchise might produce a PSA on fire safety to be released during Fire Safety Week.

Video news releases (VNRs) are video productions written, directed, and produced by a public relations agency. They are produced as news segments and are sent to TV stations across the country to be used as part of the networks' news broadcasts. According to Nielsen Research, 75 percent of all local stations use VNRs regularly.

A public relations program can include many more specialized projects than those described above, such as trade show support, crisis planning and counseling, contests, and athletic sponsorships, all of which keep your franchise's name before the public.

The Importance of Keeping Franchisees Happy

When a prospect is interested in becoming a franchisee, the phone calls he makes to existing franchisees can make or break the deal. If franchisees don't have good things to say about their organization or if franchisee lawsuits are pending, closing the deal will be extremely difficult. Conversely, endorsements from existing franchisees are the best sales tools. Public relations done by the franchisor for the benefit of its franchisees can help ensure that the franchisees are successful and will provide the endorsement the franchisor needs to obtain new franchises.

One of the best ways a franchisor can support her organization is to institute a public relations program for the franchisees. New business owners are often anxious about building a customer base and usually look to the franchisor for help and reassurance. The fears faced by prospective and new franchisees will be assuaged when they know that the franchisor will be arranging articles in their local newspapers and magazines and spots on radio and television programs in their area.

The results of local publicity campaigns on behalf of individual franchisees generate business in local markets, and that in and of itself is terrific. But these media placements can also be showcased at regional and national franchisee meetings to boost the morale and egos of the franchisees and to build their confidence in you, the franchisor. Local franchisees may even be used in national publications or network television interviews, which helps promote every outlet in the organization.

Offering to support a prospect with publicity in her local market is an ideal way to convince a person that yours is the franchise in which she should invest. Often, the cost of the public relations program comes from the national advertising fund or is built into royalty payments, and instituting such a program makes good business sense.

Too often, franchisors leave franchisees to handle their own public relations, which can be a mistake. Without the proper background, franchisees don't know what is newsworthy and lack the tools and techniques to obtain publicity for themselves. Most are not media-savvy and may present a negative image of the franchise to the media without realizing it. An outside public relations agency will ensure that the agreed-upon copy phrases are included in every story and is best equipped to implement professional, objective, and effective assistance.

Measuring Results

Naturally, franchisors expect to "see" what they paid for; in other words, to evaluate their public relations investment. Public relations professionals and major corporations using public relations services have expended countless hours and dollars trying to develop effective measurement techniques. These efforts have enabled the public relations industry to validate the cost-efficiency of public relations, but only publicity, which is a small part of the total public relations program, lends itself to real measurement. The most common way to measure publicity is to total the number of readers or viewers reached by publicity during a specified time period and then to compare the cost of the publicity with the cost of advertising in print publications in the same amount of space or of broadcasts that are similar in length.

Publicity can also be analyzed on the basis of the following:

▲ *Defined target audience*. Each media placement can be measured by asking, "Are placements reaching the desired audience? Are some placements more on target than others?" A value can be assigned, for example, 3 for best audience reach, 2 for average, 1 for minimal. The circulation of each placement is then multiplied by that factor.

▲ *Appropriate message*. Some companies classify their copy points as "major" and "minor," and articles about the company are evaluated on the basis of how many copy points from each category are included in each article or broadcast.

▲ *Measured impressions, inches, airtime*. Other companies measure public relations by adding the number of impressions, column inches, and airtime accrued by the publicity. But because public relations messages offer added credibility and the ability to tell a more complete story than most ads, the total readership and broadcast audience reached is multiplied by a factor of 3.5. The higher factor is based on standard methodology established by the Public Relations Society of America.

While most PR programs fare exceptionally well under the above methodology, it is still an inadequate measurement. For example, an appearance by your company's spokesperson on CNN might not result in immediate franchise leads, but it could position your franchise as a leader in its industry. There's no way to measure the importance of being viewed as an industry leader or to gauge what it means to future prospects. Measurements deal only with what is *tangible*.

Another method of evaluating the efforts of public relations is to contrast franchisees' sales results in markets that have only advertising with other franchisees' sales results in similar demographic markets that have both advertising and public relations. Again, results derived by this method may be compromised by factors affecting one location but not another, such as tough competition or unusual economic conditions in a particular market.

Perhaps the best method of evaluating the effectiveness of the public relations expenditure is to ask a prospect who calls your office how he heard about your company. Then you can tally the replies. Tag all responses other than specific outlets (magazine ads, direct mail) under "Public Relations/General Knowledge," and compare the categories.

In theory, if a public relations campaign's sole raison d'etre is to generate franchise leads, you can evaluate the results rather easily by comparing the number of leads generated in a year without a public relations campaign to the number generated in a year with such a program (assuming that the remaining marketing elements and economic conditions remain basically unchanged).

It makes sense to have both short- and long-term goals and to make sure that short-term measurement, i.e., increased franchise leads, does not diminish your appreciation of long-term benefits such as greater industry/consumer awareness of and respect for your franchise organization, its management, and its products and services. There is no measurement for goodwill or the fine reputation your franchise enjoys. But without these, yours will be an uphill battle fraught with landmines.

When to Expect Results

"When am I going to see results?" is a question most companies ask their public relations firm after the first month of the program. Waiting to see the results of a program is often frustrating, especially for those not familiar with the public relations process.

The first month of a public relations program is usually spent preparing press materials and fine-tuning media lists. Once the materials are sent to the media, time is spent following up by placing phone calls to each editor and producer who was sent information. This may mean literally hundreds of phone calls, depending on how many publications you are trying to reach.

All magazines have "lead times," which are the number of days, weeks, or months in advance that they start working on an issue. This can vary from a few days for a weekly business magazine to six months for some women's magazines. Television shows usually have a lead time of six to eight weeks after they *accept* the idea for a segment. Your franchise might be featured in newspapers across the country in the second week of your relationship with a PR agency, but it could take at least six months or more to appear in a prestigious national magazine.

Here's an example of how long it can take to place an article. Our client, ProForma, felt that a story on the company in *The Wall Street Journal* would help generate franchisee prospects. We started working with a staff writer in April and kept in touch with him over the next several months by sending him additional information on the subject.

An article on ProForma, based on that initial contact with the *Journal* staffer, finally appeared in December—eight months later. Although it took months of follow-up and patient waiting, it paid off with dozens of names of qualified franchise candidates.

In the second week that we worked with General Nutrition Centers, we placed an article in a newspaper in New York state, where GNC was looking for an entrepreneur to open a franchise. The print article prompted local radio stations to run the story, and a prospect called that week who has since become a very successful GNC franchisee.

It often seems that feature articles and television appearances all start to happen at once, but it's not coincidence. It's the results of months of hard work that is coming to fruition.

Fee Structures

Contracts and fee structures for public relations firms vary greatly, depending on the nature of the work to be performed. Here are some basic ways that the financial aspect of the relationship may be structured:

▲ *Retainer.* In this arrangement, a set fee is paid per month for public relations services. This fee covers supervision and implementation of all day-to-day public relations activities, such as counseling and media placement. It provides for the time expended by agency management, account staff, and secretarial staff, in much the same way that lawyers and accountants are compensated for their time.

▲ *Hours.* This agreement pays an agency for the number of hours it spends providing public relations services, based on the billing rates of the individuals providing the services. A client is then charged the number of hours devoted to its account, multiplied by the billing rates of each individual working on its account. A cap is often set on time spent.

▲ *Fee plus hours.* Under this type of arrangement, an agency agrees to provide a certain number of hours of service in exchange for a retainer. Hours spent in excess of this number are billed in addition to the retainer at the individuals' billing rates.

▲ *Project.* In a relationship of this type, a client assigns an agency one specific project, such as the launch of a new product, and pays a set price for the execution of that project. Often, this is a good way for a client to determine the merits of an individual agency without entering into a long-term agreement.

Under each type of agreement, out-of-pocket expenses are billed separately in addition to the retainer fee. These expenses include telephone, photography, production, photocopying and fax, editorial entertainment, and travel expenses.

Summary

In this economy, finding qualified franchise leads is more competitive than ever. Potential franchisees are reviewing and analyzing every investment decision very carefully, and banks are more cautious about extending credit.

According to the International Franchise Association, there are over 3,000 registered franchisors in the United States either currently seeking franchisees or planning to in the near future. This means that, in the future, there will be more franchisors reaching the same pool of qualified candidates and that presenting your franchise in a positive light will be critical to your success.

NOTE

1. Thomas L. Harris, *The Marketer's Guide to Public Relations: How Today's Top Companies Are Using PR to Gain a Competitive Edge* (New York: Wiley, 1991).

18

Implementing Public Relations Strategies

Gregory Matusky, Gregory Communications

Your ads aren't working. Your direct mail flopped. Trade shows brought some sales leads, but you never closed them. There's got to be a better way to sell franchises. There is. It's called public relations.

What makes public relations so effective? First, public relations can broadcast your message to potential franchisees. An article in the *New York Times* or an appearance on "Good Morning America" can put your franchise opportunity in front of millions of Americans, many of whom would never have learned about your business otherwise.

Second, public relations adds a measure of credibility and legitimacy to your franchise. Most Americans really do believe the things they read in the newspaper. They accept as truth what they see on television and hear on the radio. Take, for instance, one example of a franchisor who appeared in an article in *Continental Profiles*, the in-flight magazine of Continental Airlines. The franchisor received more than 600 telephone inquiries from the article and wound up selling more than forty franchise territories. People actually called the franchisor from in-flight telephones to receive more information about the opportunity. An ad, with its given biases, never could have generated that much activity.

Third, public relations gives you an opportunity to describe your business in detail. Anyone who has ever written a business opportunity ad knows the difficulty in communicating all the nuances of the business in thirty or forty words. But a strategically placed article or television appearance provides a forum to tell a story in convincing and thorough terms.

All this sounds great. Every franchisor wants to generate more sales leads, especially quality leads.

But what about the price tag? Nothing comes cheap in life. Those who tell you that public relations is free advertising are telling you only half the story.

Public relations costs money. Franchise public relations firms typically charge retainers ranging from $2,000 to $8,000 a month to generate press about your business. That's a hefty amount for most small businesses, and most franchisors are small, with less than $10 million a year in home office sales.

So now the question is: Can you do your own public relations, save money, and still get results? It depends. Some of the best-publicized franchises, including AlphaGraphics and Gloria Jean's Coffee Beanery, do their public relations in-house and get marvelous results.

How? Creativity. Talented personnel. Excellent execution. Dogged follow-through. But public relations agencies provide the same skills, along with an established network of media contacts. This chapter is intended to introduce you to the fundamentals of public relations. After reading it, you'll have a pretty fair idea of whether you can do your own public relations or if the job might be better left to an outside agency.

Public Relations: The Basic Formula

Here's the formula for great PR:

$$E = MC^2$$

That's shorthand for:

$$\text{Exposure} = \text{Media} \times (\text{Creativity} \times \text{Communications})$$

Just about every franchisor wants public relations efforts to result in added exposure for her franchise opportunity. To accomplish that goal, you need to understand the media and communicate with them creatively and effectively.

Understanding the Media

We're all inundated by the media. Every day, the average American watches hours of television, listens to the radio, and reads at least one newspaper. But few of us understand how the media work and who in the media decides what will be featured and covered.

The first lesson in media relations is that media are marketers first, educators, entertainers, and informers second. This means that every medium in the United States fills a specific niche for readers, viewers, and listeners. Even seemingly similar business publications, such as *Forbes* and *Inc.* magazines, serve drastically different markets. As Paul Brown, a former writer with *Forbes* and a contributing editor at *Inc.*, explains it:

> Many stories are shot down early because they simply don't fit a publication's criteria. When I was with *Forbes*, public relations people would call me all day long and talk about small, private companies. Then when I went to *Inc.*, PR people would call with story suggestions

about Exxon and IBM. These were supposed to be professionals, yet they didn't know that Forbes typically covers large, public companies. *Inc.*, on the other hand, is for the owners and managers of emerging growth companies—firms with sales of less than $100 million.

In short, the media are in the business of satisfying the needs of their readers and audiences. Editors, writers, and program directors know precisely whom they are talking to and what they ought to say.

But few outsiders ever take the time to target their message for specific media. Few outsiders ever target the media as they would a potential customer—with a keen eye for needs and wants.

Don't get caught in that trap. Instead, learn as much as you can about the media that you want to target. Who are their readers? What topics do they cover? Who are the writers? The editors? The program directors and producers?

It's easy to gather this information. Every publication will send you free its advertising media kit. All you have to do is request it. The media kit will tell you in numbers, in graphs, and in words who reads the publication, as well as its editorial outlook and philosophy.

You can gather the same information by calling the program directors at key television and radio shows. When you get them on the line, tell them you have two quick questions. First, who is their typical viewer or listener? Second, what do their viewers and listeners get from the show?

Sounds difficult? Well, in preparing this chapter, I called Barbara Kostner, field producer for "Good Morning America," and asked her those very questions. You figure a big-time television producer doesn't have time to take telephone calls. Wrong. Barbara took the call and gladly answered the questions (she says that most PR people rarely ask; they just talk). What were her answers?

> I handle the consumer issues for the show. We always try to remember that we're talking to middle America. That's tough because we're in New York City, and our outlook might be different from the rest of the country. So we think about that busy working mother in Detroit who has a few minutes to watch "GMA" before rushing off to work. What does she need to know? We want to deliver to her news she can use— real-world information that can affect and hopefully change her world for the better. We're not looking for PR puffery. We want legitimate information about consumer trends or events that our viewers can use to protect or improve themselves.

Can you do the same investigation with publications? Absolutely. Most editors and writers love to talk about their jobs. They actually appreciate someone taking the time to learn about the publication before blindly pitching a story. And the things you can learn! Most writers and editors will tell you what they report on and how they get their story ideas. They will even tell you what not to do. For instance, Jeff Tannenbaum at *The Wall Street Journal* is quick with this advice:

> At *The Wall Street Journal* we are only interested in ideas and issues that apply to lots and lots of people. But most PR and business people start their pitch with, ''I have a really unique business that would make a great story.'' We're not looking for aberration. We report on trends and emerging issues. We look for companies that can validate those trends. The more thematically you think, the better your chances of landing your company or your client in *The Wall Street Journal*. But very few people get that point.

Sounds like common sense, doesn't it? If you want to sell something, you start by learning the needs and wants of your customer. But somehow that lesson is lost when it comes to public relations.

So start boning up on the media. Read and watch the media you want to crack and start learning what they are all about. It's called a media audit, and it's simple to do. Just order the past six copies of your target medium. You can buy them through the circulation department. Or order videos of the past six episodes of a particular program (Video Monitoring Services in New York City tapes just about every show).

Then sit down with pencil and paper, and start taking notes. Who covers what topics? Are the articles how-to or profiles? Are there monthly columns that appear in every issue? If so, who are the writers? What correspondents cover what topics? Do the television shows do regular features on food, relationships, consumer affairs?

After completing this you will have a comprehensive list of the types of topics covered by your target media.

Now you have an in. You know something about the media. You know the types of topics that are covered and the people who do the reporting. You're now ready for the next lesson in $E = MC^2$: Creativity.

The Power of Creativity

The media look for creative, fresh ideas and topics. Just imagine reporting on franchising for five or six years and hearing the same tired story lines over and over. Or as Echo Garrett, one of the nation's most respected franchise writers, tells it:

> I am always scrambling to find fresh story ideas. Most PR people don't realize that it behooves them to come up with a good story first, before contacting me. I don't think they realize how powerful that is. If, in my experience, I discover that a PR person really understands a good

story, you better believe that I will open their letters and return their calls. Conversely, if there is someone who bugs me every time a client sneezes, I don't even open their mail.

But there's a fine line between being creative and being cutesy. The media, especially the print media, hate contrived events or frilly ideas. Electronic media are much more open to highly imaginative approaches.

For instance, in print, identifying a new trend and using your business to validate that trend is a terrific way to land coverage in a major business magazine. Take, for instance, a trick used by Amy Bellinger, a free-lance publicist who once handled Signs Now, one of the many fast-sign franchises that grew quickly during the late 1980s and that sought public exposure:

> Editors were being inundated with news from these sign franchises, all saying the same thing—"Look how fast we're growing." So we focused on an indirect angle about the president, who was a franchisor and a franchisee of Burger King. How did this entrepreneur, who saw franchising from both sides, view the franchise game? The media ate it up. Signs Now made the cover of *Business Age* magazine (now defunct) and *Changing Times*. The franchise doubled its size off the public relations.

For the electronic media, you can let your imagination run a bit more free. Take a case that I worked on. The franchisor was in the automotive aftermarket— used cars, to be exact. Nothing interesting there, especially for the program directors of radio and television talk shows. They typically prefer controversial or outrageous topics. The answer? Creativity. The franchisor underwent a few hours of media training that transformed him into a veritable expert on uncovering problems with used cars. The one-page promotion that went to television and radio show producers read, "How to Defeat America's Most Hated Vermin: The Used Car Salesman." Underneath the headline, there was a photograph of a typical sleazy used car salesman. The copy went on to explain how the franchisor could teach the audience how to avoid used car rip-offs.

The one-page promotion, which was circulated to an in-house list of 2,500 program directors, resulted in forty radio interviews, a twenty-minute segment on CNN, appearances on CNBC, and one *five*-minute radio interview that generated more than one hundred telephone inquiries on its own. That's the power of public relations.

Communicating With the Media

Now that you know what the media are all about and how creativity can help you achieve exposure, it's time to tackle the second "C" in the PR formula: Communication.

Writers, editors, and program directors are communicators. They know how to use words and images to convey ideas and concepts. They expect you to communicate with them in a professional and accurate manner.

In public relations, much of the communication takes place through press releases. There are a lot of differing opinions about what makes a good press release. Just about everyone will tell you to keep a press release short—one or two pages at most. Well, you can forget that. Short press releases might be fine for reporting breaking news or for introducing new product lines to the media. But most franchisors want major feature stories about their companies. The best way to generate that type of exposure is through long, detailed releases that read more like feature articles than press releases. Take, for instance, the following release that over the course of one year triggered placements in *Time, Fortune, Entrepreneur, Success*, and scores of other media. It's long and involved, but well worth the read:

FROM:
Bassett's Original Turkey
27 W. Arlen Street
Philadelphia, PA 19106

FOR MORE INFORMATION CONTACT:
George Hendrix
(215) 647-2929

ROGER BASSETT:
PHILADELPHIA'S KING OF TURKEY AIMS FOR
LARGER MARKETS

When Roger Bassett made his father a turkey sandwich in 1983, he never expected that the seemingly inconsequential act would lead to a business that some day may topple the hamburger as the king of American fast food. But Bassett's turkey creation portended vast changes in the American diet, the life of Roger Bassett, and a business that is now franchising.

Bassett is a fifth-generation member of Philadelphia's Bassett's ice cream family—a legacy that began in 1861 when Louis Dubois Bassett plucked a tomato from the vine and concocted tomato ice cream, a nineteenth-century Philadelphia treat. Roger Bassett fully intended to spend his life serving the rich, premium flavors of his family's company. But then fate struck.

"I was working at my ice cream sundae shop at the Reading Terminal Market," begins Bassett, who now manages the company's franchise growth. "My father asked me to prepare him something special for lunch. I bought a turkey and a loaf of fresh baked bread and I borrowed a knife and oven from a neighboring merchant."

The sandwich, piled high with thickly sliced, roasted breast of turkey, attracted immediate attention from the lunch-time crowd. Roger sold his first turkey sandwich, which was later called the Original, for $1.95. The next day, he bought two turkeys and sold more sandwiches. Within a month, Bassett converted the ice cream sundae shop to Bassett's Original Turkey, and it became a big hit with noontime crowds.

"We were doing a very strong lunch trade, roasting sixteen to twenty turkeys a day and serving 250 people for lunch out of a space less than 120 square feet," says Bassett. "I knew it was a winner from the start."

Unbeknownst to Bassett, his business had struck upon the *emerging* food trend of the 1980s that promises to revolutionize the way we eat in the 1990s: healthy eating. Americans, growing weary of high-fat, cholesterol-laden red meats, wanted alternatives. Turkey breast, which has only sixty-nine milligrams of cholesterol per three-and-a-half ounce serving, was, and continues to be, high on their list of wholesome foods.

Encouraged by the success, Bassett went to work improving the business. He spent the next few years streamlining and simplifying its management, and he developed a limited menu based on customer preferences.

"The menu has sixteen items, including sandwiches and hot and cold entrees," says Bassett. "It evolved as customers asked for new twists on the old themes. When they stopped asking for variations, we stopped adding to the menu." For instance, the Original is a turkey breast sandwich served with lettuce and tomato.

By 1985, Bassett's success had attracted attention from a leasing agent with the Rouse Company who encouraged him to expand the operation and open a unit in the Cherry Hill Mall. The Rouse Company was impressed with Bassett's ability to turn big numbers in a limited space—a perfect combination for food courts.

The problem, however, was that Roger Bassett wanted to retain the same high standards as the Reading Terminal and Cherry Hill shops.

The answer to his dilemma? Franchise the concept and find motivated owner/operators who would follow the same systems and procedures that made Bassett's Original Turkey a success.

Bassett spent a year developing his franchise program, which necessitated compliance with federal law. Then he discovered a fact of franchise life: It's not easy to sell a new franchise opportunity, especially when prospective franchisees are betting an estimated $90,000 and $173,900 on a new concept.

So Bassett took a risk. Working with limited capital and without previous franchise experience, he signed leases for locations in major metropolitan and suburban malls, including Liberty Place and The Gallery Market East (two prime Philadelphia locations), as well as the Landmark Center (in Virginia) and the Columbia Mall (in Maryland).

His strategy was to secure favorable locations and use those sites to attract prospective franchisees who would pick up the cost of the lease and leasehold improvements.

If the strategy worked, he reasoned, the company would jump-start its franchise program by bringing on the first few franchisees all at once. If it failed, Bassett would run out of money before getting the franchise idea off the ground.

The risk paid off. The high-traffic locations generated the excitement Bassett needed to attract high-quality franchise prospects.

Dick Root, a veteran of the fast-food wars, was the first to open a Bassett's Original Turkey franchise. Root, who has worked for Churches Fried Chicken, Orange Julius, and Wendy's, knew immediately that Bassett's Original Turkey fit the needs of the 1990s.

"With fifteen years of food experience, I can pretty well tell whether something is going to make it. And Bassett's has all the elements of success."

Root, who lives in King of Prussia, PA, was attracted by the simplicity of the operation, the quality of the food, and [the] wholesomeness of the product.

"From a marketing standpoint, turkey has a lot of consumer appeal because it's low in cholesterol and fat. From a business point of view, the operation is exceedingly simple to manage, which keeps personnel, training, and food costs low."

Root, who opened his business in June, says the reception has been better than expected. "We have been swamped. Lunch has been very strong, and dinner has been a surprising winner."

Healthy eating is what also attracted Stephen Duffett, Medford, New Jersey, to the business. A former general manager for Domino's Pizza, Duffett believes that healthier food will offer the greatest opportunity for fast-food growth during the 1990s.

"We are not another hamburger business. We're offering customers something novel and healthy. Americans want healthier fare, but there's nowhere to get low-cholesterol food that's as convenient as fast food—nowhere except Bassett's."

Duffett, who is currently training and working in the company's Cherry Hill store, will open his Philadelphia restaurant in October at Liberty Place.

As for Roger Bassett, he is busy charting future growth for his business, which is receiving inquiries from throughout the country. "I got in the business by accident. But it's no accident that it has grown so well. We are the first and the original fast-food turkey franchise. That gives us a big jump and hopefully the momentum to grow into a national company by the end of the 1990s."

For more information about Bassett's Original Turkey, call 215-922-4614.

This release works because it tells all the details about the franchise, right down to how much the turkey sandwiches cost! Writers, editors, and program directors have held onto this release for years—literally—and pulled it from their files when they need a quick story idea. I have even seen writers bring this release to interviews, highlighted and underlined. They use it for background and insight into the company. A two-page press release never could have captured the story of this company, and it never could have generated such strong results with the press.

But press releases are only part of the communication puzzle. The query letter, a one- or two-page letter used to introduce the company to the media, can be an equally important tool in generating public relations.

Just how well do query letters work? The following query letter generated an article in *USA Today* and made a *Wall Street Journal* writer call the company president the day it hit the writer's desk! Take a look:

August 13, 19XX

Jane Van Tassel
Assistant Business Editor
Time
1271 Avenue of the Americas
New York, NY 10020

Dear Jane:

Americans are prisoners of pizza, and Kevin Abt wants to liberate them.

Abt is founder and president of Takeout Taxi, a Herndon, Virginia, restaurant food delivery business that has just announced plans to franchise across the country. The company already sponsors franchises in Virginia, Maryland, Chicago, Cincinnati, Boston, Nashville, and Huntsville, Alabama.

The concept sounds simple: Takeout Taxi picks up and delivers food (American, Mexican, Chinese, and just about anything else) from a dozen or so restaurants in its service area and then delivers it to the front door of consumers.

But in practice, delivering many different orders to many different locations is a complex, logistical challenge. In fact, Abt has tracked more than 150 attempts to copy his idea. Ninety-seven percent of them have failed.

What's the secret, then, to Takeout Taxi's success? The answer is computerization and marketing systems and procedures.

There are many angles to the Takeout Taxi story, including:

    ▴ *Imprisoned by pizza.* Forty-three cents of every American food dollar are now spent on food prepared outside the home. But if Americans want food delivered, their choices are limited to pizza and one or two Chinese restaurants. Takeout Taxi is breaking the stranglehold pizza has held over American eating by offering consumers their choice of restaurant food delivered to their homes.

    ▴ *Behind a great idea.* Ideas are cheap. It's putting those ideas into practice profitably that makes a business succeed. The Takeout Taxi concept sounds simple. In fact, many people have tried it. But most end up giving up. It took three years and the combined expertise of restaurant owners, computer programmers, and management gurus to unravel this business and make it profitable.

▴ *From parasite to partner.* Restaurants initially didn't want to work with Takeout Taxi because they had to sell their food to the company at wholesale rates. Takeout Taxi overcame the objection by using its computer technology to market on behalf of participating restaurants. The result? Takeout Taxi's direct-mail campaigns regularly record response rates as high as 60 percent. That kind of success wins over even the most conservative restaurant owners.

▴ *Big business from a small idea.* Takeout Taxi sounds like a great idea. But how much can you make delivering restaurant foods? A lot. Takeout Taxi recorded sales of $2.2 million this year. The company has already opened franchises in Virginia, Maryland, Chicago, Cincinnati, Boston, Nashville, and Huntsville, AL.

▴ *From big to small business.* Kevin Abt was the consummate corporate whiz kid—smart, articulate, and effective. In fact, US Sprint was grooming him for much bigger things before he walked away from a six-figure job to deliver food for a living. The transition wasn't easy. He made his first sales calls in a suit and tie. Restaurant owners snuck out the back door, thinking he was a tax collector.

Thanks for your interest.

Sincerely,

Again, this query letter is long and involved. But it works because it's well-crafted and makes a number of salient points about the company as well as American business. This type of written communication gets results. Just ask the companies that get the press from it!

The final form of communication is the telephone. Written communication is the icebreaker. But telephone follow-up is the key to making sure a writer, editor, or program director received and reviewed a press release or query letter. Just as in any sale, the most critical part of a sales call is the first few seconds. Publicists have used just about every trick imaginable to interest the media over the telephone. Reporters and program directors have heard just about every cliché imaginable. For instance:

▴ *The humorous line.* "Just what you wanted to hear. Some fast-talking PR pitch first thing in the morning." The media will never laugh, so don't use this line.

▴ *The apologetic line.* "I'm sorry for bothering you, but do you have two minutes for a story idea?" This might win you some sympathy, but little else.

▲ *The world's worst line.* "Do you have a minute for someone who is trying to sell you something?" The media will always say no and hang up.

▲ *The thoughtful line.* "Is this a bad time?" The typical answer is, yes, and you'll just have to call back.

▲ *The hype line.* "I have a great story I want to tell you about a dynamic company that's making fantastic advancements." Don't even try it; you won't get to the second sentence.

The only line that works. "I have been reading your column (or watching your segments) for the past few months. I particularly enjoyed the feature you did last month. I have a story idea that might interest you because it deals with the types of issues you seem to report on. May I tell you about it?"

This line works because it shows that you have done your homework. You know something about your customer. You have complimented the reporter because you have invested time to read or view her work. You have established your credibility and developed trust. It's just like sales. But few people are willing to do the up-front work necessary to get to this point. Instead, they look for the quick hit and usually come away empty-handed from a telephone call.

Playing the PR Game to Win

You have now learned the secrets to effective public relations. It's as simple as $E = MC^2$. So, now you can answer the question, can you do your own PR in-house? If you have talented people who can learn and creatively communicate with the media, chances are you won't need to pay big bucks to a franchise PR agency. But if you haven't the time or the inclination to do it yourself, then a public relations agency might be the answer to generating quality franchise sales leads.

19

Trade Shows as an Effective Means of Franchise Marketing

Nick Helyer, Blenheim Franchise Shows, Inc.

In 1991, well over one-half million Americans visited trade shows featuring companies that were there to sell franchises. Franchise trade shows are generally considered to be the best advertising method available to franchisors, including many of the high-ticket franchisors, looking for new recruitment potential.

Benefits of Trade Shows

There are a number of reasons for the spectacular success of many franchise companies at regional trade shows:

1. It is never easy to sell an expensive product, service, or business on the telephone or through the mail. Without trade shows, franchisors find it difficult to meet with many of their prospects. Without a meeting, a close is impossible, and many prospects are not willing to cross the country for such a meeting. The advantage of a face-to-face meeting at a trade show, plus the opportunity to talk again after the show, helps savvy franchisors close sales they would otherwise have no chance of even prospecting.

2. The ideal potential franchisee may not be actively looking in the trade magazines or in the appropriate newspaper classified columns at the time an advertiser places his ad. In fact, only a tiny percentage of the people that a franchisor could sell to at a certain time are even aware that such an opportunity exists. On the other hand, a well-produced franchise trade show in a metropolitan area makes a major impact upon the area's TV, radio, news, and direct-mail media. People who are simply watching TV see ads for the franchise show that the individual franchisor could not afford to purchase. The trade show combines the booth revenues of all the exhibitors and makes a major impact on the entire metro area, attracting people who are ready to buy a franchise but 85 percent of whom have not actively sought out franchise opportunity ads anywhere within the previous ninety days, according to statistics produced by the Blenheim Group, the

world's largest producer of franchise trade shows. The result in fresh, enthusiastic prospects arriving at the trade show in large numbers.

3. The choice at a metropolitan franchise trade show is not normally over-whelming. In contrast to a trade magazine, which may feature literally hundreds of ads, a franchise trade show sponsored by the International Franchise Association rarely exceeds sixty exhibitors. On the one hand, visitors to a trade show have a diverse and interesting group of businesses and investment levels to choose from. On the other hand it is practical for a visitor to examine each exhibit in detail in one day, thereby reducing the risk of becoming overwhelmed by excessive choice. The most common complaint heard from some visitors is that the specific franchise business they came to see isn't represented.

All respondents to advertising are volunteers, whether they pick up the phone, fill in and send a coupon, write a letter, or drive to a trade show. There are major differences, however, in the amounts of effort required to volunteer a response. For example, it's not much trouble to look through a magazine or newspaper, find a franchise opportunity ad, and dial the telephone number on the ad; the respondent doesn't necessarily even have to move from the spot. Mailing a letter certainly demonstrates a little more desire, since there is the inconvenience of writing and mailing.

However, neither of these responses comes close to the degree of effort required to visit a trade show. When a trade show respondent sees an ad and decides to bundle the family into the car and travel up to one hundred miles to the trade show location, her enthusiasm level is indeed high.

Another benefit of franchise trade shows is the penetration factor—that is, the number of people you can reach in your targeted market by using various advertising methods. We have already assumed that a well-produced franchise trade show, is, among other things, a comprehensively advertised one. If you, the franchisor, are targeting the metropolitan area of Dallas, which is populated by 3.6 million people, in your search for franchisees, your objective is to reach as many people as possible in that market for the dollar budget you have already allocated. If we suppose that the budget available for the Dallas metro market is $15,000, here is how it might be spent (using traditional advertising media).

You may decide to run some classified ads in the daily paid newspapers in the area; you may run a few sixty-second spots on a couple of the local news-talk radio stations; you may take a few basic TV spots (artcard only to eliminate production costs) on the local cable network; and, finally, you may have some direct mail names and addresses available to you. In this scenario, the $15,000 budget is used completely in two to three days; if you spread it any thinner, the impact will be almost undetectable.

Your alternative is to wait for a franchise trade show in the Dallas market area, which may be next week or eleven months away. (If it's the latter, there are probably other markets that need penetrating and that may be more suited to the franchise trade show schedule.) The approximate all-in cost for two salespeople to attend a franchise trade show in a single booth is $3,000, not including salaries, which may be commission, basic, or both. Tens of thousands of dollars will be spent on local advertising, and no more than seventy-five fellow exhibitors are likely to be present—enough to make a super presentation and few enough to give your franchise a great chance to create an impact.

No trade show promoter makes attendance promises, and many things influence attendances at trade shows. Nevertheless, on average, you are likely to be visited by 7,000 attendees at a well-produced Dallas-metro franchise trade show—7,000 people who have volunteered to respond, on a weekend, knowing there's an entrance fee and probably a parking fee, also. It is hardly surprising that companies that use trade shows to achieve sales allocate the lion's share of their promotional budgets to shows.

Some companies have the luxury of being able to advertise in the Dallas market area as well as participating in the trade show, but most have to make either-or decisions. One of the additional advantages of opting to be part of the trade show is demonstrated in this example.

Let's assume you had spent $15,000 (as in the previous example) on franchise recruitment advertising in the Dallas metro area. A number of people will have been exposed more than once to your mix, which is the main principle behind advertising. You are therefore justified in being confident about receiving a number of responses from potential investors. Suddenly, however, the majority of people who have seen your advertising are exposed two or more times to advertising supported by a budget of $100,000 to $150,000 put up by a trade show promoter for a franchise trade show in Dallas. The ad campaign includes heavy network and cable TV exposure, which you were unable to include in your mix. What's the potential investor likely to do? Almost certainly, she will attend the franchise trade show, even if she has responded to your individual advertising, also. The result is not necessarily a lost prospect, but the sales opportunity is certainly now in jeopardy because of the dilution influence created by other opportunities.

The International Franchise Expo

Trade shows in any industry are generally considered by the larger companies to be the most important marketing opportunity on the calendar. However, most industries in the United States have a flagship trade show—an event that is bigger, better attended, and more influential than any of the regional events. In recessionary times, many companies cut back on their magazine and other advertising and on the number of regional trade shows in which they participate. Very few cancel the flagship trade show—it's just too important.

Until 1992, the franchise industry, despite twenty-five years of prosperity, did not have a flagship trade show in the United States. In 1992, however, that changed, and the United States, as the world's largest franchisor nation, now presents the world's largest franchise expo. The IFA International Franchise Expo, or IFE, is designed to provide the franchisor with the best of everything in franchise recruitment opportunities. Despite the title, the majority of attendees (82 percent) at the April 1992 show were expected to come from the United States. Another 7 percent were expected to come from Canada and 8 percent from countries around the world. Exhibitors at the IFE benefit from an advertising and promotion campaign worth over $2 million and meet with top-quality prospects in all categories from around the world. Attendees expect to see hundreds of franchise systems under one roof and include potential franchisees ranging from couples with less than $10,000 to invest to consortiums and partnerships with more than $10 million.

Making the Most of Trade Shows

Selling at a trade show is not just a case of showing up and waiting for the visitors to do all the hard work. Many books and videos document the mistakes made by exhibit booth personnel, focusing on a few faults that are obvious to visitors but that often are not noticed by exhibitors.

Look Approachable

Sitting down, reading, eating, drinking, holding in-depth conversations with booth colleagues, folding the arms when talking with a prospect, and saying clichéd things like "Can I help you?" and "How're you today?" should all be avoided by trade shows exhibitors, but in many cases, they are not. For example, rather than saying, "How are you today?," which may prompt the reply, "Fine, thanks," followed by the prospect's just walking on, an exhibitor might say, "Good morning. Have you seen one of our [restaurants/printshops/services] in your area?" Or perhaps, "Have you seen the latest technology in [pizza production/printing/personnel placement]?" In both cases, the prospect is likely to stop rather than seem rude, allowing the salesperson to draw the prospect into the booth and expand on the reasons why the prospect should seriously consider the franchise opportunity.

Listen to Your Prospects

Another classic mistake salespeople often make is to speak for thirty minutes with a very well-dressed and sophisticated-looking couple about a $150,000 franchise, only to find they're looking for a low-cost business for their sister's son, who's moving to the area. In the meantime, 250 other prospects have walked by. Obviously, the salesperson should have clarified the prospect's needs before investing so much time fruitlessly, possibly forfeiting other opportunities in the process.

Make Your Booth Inviting

Preparation for any trade show is also key. The booth layout and content must be carefully designed, and special literature may need to be designed and printed. It's also important to ensure that the words on the booth sign are easily and quickly read; exhibitors are often so intent on covering everything that they place hundreds of words on their signs, most of which will not be read by prospects walking by. A few key phrases, on the other hand, will be read by most prospects.

Avoid putting all the furniture across the front of the booth unless you have a very good reason. How is the prospect going to be drawn into your booth if your table is blocking most of the front of the booth area? If you must have tables, place them along the sides of the booth, making it easy for prospects to enter your booth.

Know Your Clientele

Franchise trade shows have a unique feature. They are possibly the only trade shows to which the general public is invited. Public shows always emphasize entertainment and pleasure or cater to the public's curiosity; most of the visitors at boat shows don't buy boats, but they enjoy the atmosphere, looking inside all the expensive yachts. At trade shows, the visitors are there because they are in the trade represented at the expo. They can see new products, meet top executives, compare apples with oranges, and derive a definite commercial benefit from attending.

Franchise trade shows are not "fun" events and rarely attract people who expect to be entertained by them. Neither do they present industry products and services to visitors already in the industry.

Unlike the usual trade show visitor, who is already familiar with many aspects of the industry, a franchise show visitor often needs a full explanation of what she sees, even of franchising itself. Exhibitors who are sympathetic to visitors' needs for careful explanation without inferring ignorance are the companies that shout the praises of trade shows the loudest.

Follow-up is vital. Sales managers who would hound a print ad respondent into the ground frequently fail to follow up contacts made at trade shows. This a major oversight. Booth personnel must have a very deliberate system for collecting information on booth prospects and must follow them up closely without delay; after all, other exhibitors are probably following up the same people. At a typical trade show, visitors are not local; however, at all U.S. franchise trade shows except the IFE, most visitors live within one hundred miles of the show site. Probably most live within a twenty-five-mile radius of the expo location. This means that post-show local follow-up is a very practical alternative to leaving the city immediately after the show has closed.

A large majority of those franchise sales personnel who have extensive experience with trade shows attempt to prequalify booth prospects in the shortest time possible—no more than five minutes, if possible. They can then invite interested prospects to a more detailed, distraction-free seminar, either concurrent with the trade show or within one to three days following the event. Clearly anyone coming back for such a seminar has demonstrated a very high level of interest to the sale personnel. The seminar also provides an excellent opportunity for the presentation of disclosure documents, accelerating the beginning of the ten-day review period mandated by the Federal Trade Commission (see Chapter 21).

The Growth of Franchise Trade Shows

Statistics gathered by the Blenheim Group, which produces all the franchise trade shows sponsored by the International Franchise Association in the United States, Britain, France, Germany, and Holland, indicate that 85 percent of visitors to metropolitan franchise trade shows have not actively sought a franchise opportunity through other media during the ninety days prior to the franchise trade shows. This statistic suggests that visitors' knowledge horizons are limited mainly to the opportunities they see within the expo. This freshness gives a good salesperson an advantage; unless a trade show visitor knows what he wants to find at the show, the opportunity to sell him any particular franchise opportunity becomes more and more difficult the more he learns about the huge variety of opportunities available.

Franchise trade shows are becoming more commonplace in other countries, although only Canada's franchise industry is keeping up with that of the United States. In France, for example, the annual Salon International de la Franchise features up to 200 exhibitors and attracts more than 20,000 visitors. Until the advent of the IFE, the Paris show was the largest franchise trade show in the world. Several other European countries feature at least one truly national franchise event, attracting potential franchisees from all parts of the host country. The participation level at these events, as a percentage of the industry as a whole in each country, clearly indicates that most franchisors don't feel that they can afford to miss their flagship show.

Because of the high-impact nature of franchise trade show advertising, the shows never suffer from "loyalty syndrome"—the diminishing return that is often experienced by repeat advertisers in newspapers and magazines. Magazines and newspapers have regular readers, whose response generally diminishes as more and more of the readership sees the franchise opportunity ads repeatedly. If a trade magazine sells 200,000 copies twelve times a year, the majority of readers will be the same from month to month. Trade shows never suffer from this problem because they are not designed to attract repeat visitors; every show is different and is visited by different people.

With IFA and Department of Commerce figures indicating that the growth potential in American franchising is still enormous, franchise trade shows are unlikely to become outdated. It is hard to argue with proponents of franchise trade shows who assert that shows offer, dollar for dollar, more than ten times the sales potential of other recruitment methods.

Given their impact, franchise trade shows are an essential marketing tool for franchisors. The only decision still to make is "how much of the marketing mix . . . ?"

PART V

LEGAL AND REGULATORY ISSUES IN FRANCHISING

No handbook on franchising would be complete without a look at some of the legal and regulatory issues affecting the growth and development of franchise operations. Franchising is a regulated method of business growth, and the requirements surrounding the offer and award of a franchise must be carefully met during the recruitment and selection process. Once the relationship has commenced, it is critical that franchisors understand the need for ongoing compliance as well as have strategies for resolving disputes.

The first two chapters in Part V set the stage with an overview of federal and state regulations regarding franchising and the basics of the franchise agreement. In Chapter 23, we turn to building compliance systems, which are necessary to comply with regulatory issues but which also safeguard the franchisor against litigation instituted by its franchisees. Chapter 24 looks at common problems that may arise and at some cost-effective solutions for resolving them.

Chapters 25 and 26 deal with two special topics that are critical to the success of franchisors: trademark protection and strategies for evaluating and negotiating commercial leases.

20

The Regulatory Framework of Franchising

Andrew J. Sherman, Silver, Freedman & Taff

The offer and sale of a franchise is regulated at both the federal and state levels. At the federal level, the Federal Trade Commission (FTC) in 1978 adopted its trade regulation rule 436 (the FTC Rule), which specifies the minimum amount of disclosure that must be made to a prospective franchisee in any of the fifty states. In addition, over a dozen states have adopted their own rules and regulations for the offer and sale of franchises within their borders. Known as the registration states, they include most of the nation's largest commercial marketplaces, such as California, New York, and Illinois. These states generally follow a detailed disclosure format, known as the Uniform Franchise Offering Circular (UFOC), that is more stringent than the FTC format.

The UFOC was originally developed by the Midwest Securities Commissioners Association in 1975. The monitoring of and revisions to the UFOC are now under the authority of the North American Securities Administrators Association (NASAA). Each of the registration states has developed and adopted its own statutory version of the UFOC. The differences between the states should be checked carefully by both current and prospective franchisors and their counsel, as well as by individuals considering the purchase of a franchise opportunity.

A Brief History of Franchise Registration

The laws governing the offer and sale of franchises began in 1970, when California adopted its Franchise Investment Law. Shortly thereafter, the FTC commenced hearings to begin the development of a federal law governing franchising. After seven years of public comment and debate, the FTC adopted its trade regulation rule, which is formally titled "Disclosure Requirements and Prohibitions Concerning Franchising and Business Opportunity Ventures," on December 21, 1978, to be effective October 21, 1979. Many states followed California's lead, and there are now fifteen states that regulate franchise offers and sales. The states that require registration of a franchise offering prior to the offering or selling of a franchise are California, Illinois, Indiana, Maryland, Minnesota, New

York, North Dakota, Rhode Island, South Dakota, Virginia, Wisconsin, and Washington.

Other states that regulate franchise offers include Hawaii, which requires filing of an offering circular with the state authorities and delivery of an offering circular to prospective franchisees; Michigan, which requires filing of a "Notice of Intent to Offer and Sell Franchises"; and Oregon, which requires only that presale disclosure be delivered to prospective investors.

The FTC had adopted and enforced its Rule through its power to regulate unfair and deceptive trade practices. Among other things, the FTC Rule requires that every franchisor offering franchises in the United States deliver an offering circular containing certain specified disclosure items to all prospective franchisees within certain specified time requirements. It also sets forth the minimum level of protection to be afforded to prospective franchisees; to the extent that a "registration state" offers its citizens a greater level of protection, the FTC Rule does not preempt state law. There is no private right of action (right to sue) under the FTC Rule. However, the FTC itself may bring an enforcement action against a franchisor that does not meet its requirements. Penalties for noncompliance have included asset impoundments, cease-and-desist orders, injunctions, consent orders, mandated rescission or restitution for injured franchisees, and civil fines of up to $10,000 per violation.

The disclosure document required by the FTC Rule must include information on the following twenty subjects:

1. Identifying information about the franchisor
2. Business experience of the franchisor's directors and key executives
3. The franchisor's business experience
4. Litigation history of the franchisor and its directors and key executives
5. Bankruptcy history of the franchisor and its directors and key executives
6. Description of the franchise
7. Money required to be paid by the franchisee to obtain or commence the franchise operation
8. Continuing expenses to the franchisee in operating the franchise business that are payable in whole or in part to the franchisor
9. A list of persons, including the franchisor and any of its affiliates, with whom the franchisee is required or advised to do business
10. Realty and personalty, services that the franchisee is required to purchase, lease, or rent, and a list of any person(s) with whom such transactions must be made
11. Description of consideration paid (such as royalties or commissions) by third parties to the franchisor or to any of its affiliates as a result of a franchise purchase from the third parties.
12. Description of any assistance offered by the franchisor in financing the purchase of a franchise
13. Restrictions placed on a franchisee's conduct of its business

14. Required personal participation by the franchisee
15. Termination, cancellation, and renewal of the franchise
16. Statistical information about the number of franchises and their rate of termination
17. Franchisor's right to select or approve a site for the franchise
18. Training programs for the franchisee
19. Celebrity involvement with the franchise
20. Financial information about the franchisor

The information in the disclosure document must be current as of the completion of the franchisor's most recent fiscal year. In addition, a revision to the document must be promptly prepared whenever there has been a material change in the information contained in the document. The disclosure document must be given to a prospective franchisee at the earlier of either (1) the prospective franchisee's first personal meeting with the franchisor of (2) ten days prior to the execution of a contract or the payment of money relating to the franchise relationship. In addition to the disclosure document, the franchisee must receive a copy of all agreements that he will be asked to sign at least five days prior to the execution of all agreements.

The FTC Rule requires that an offering circular be provided to the prospective franchisee at the earlier of: (1) the first personal meeting; (2) ten business days before the signing of the franchise agreement or any other binding agreement by the prospective franchisee; or (3) ten business days before the acceptance of any payment from the prospective franchisee.

The FTC Rule also requires that a completed franchise agreement and related agreements be provided to the prospective franchisee five business days before the agreements are executed. A business day is any day other than Saturday, Sunday, or the following national holidays: New Year's Day, Washington's Birthday, Memorial Day, Independence Day, Labor Day, Columbus Day, Veteran's Day, Thanksgiving, and Christmas.

These timing requirements apply nationwide and preempt any lesser timing requirements contained in state laws. The ten-day and five-day disclosure periods may run concurrently, and sales contacts with the prospective franchisee may continue during those periods.

State Franchise Laws

The goal of the FTC Rule is to create a minimum federal standard of disclosure applicable to all franchisor offerings and to permit states to provide additional protection as they see fit. Thus, while the FTC Rule has the force and effect of federal law and, like other federal substantive regulations, preempts state and local laws to the extent that these laws conflict, the FTC has determined that the Rule does not preempt state or local laws and regulations that either are consistent with the Rule or, even if inconsistent, would provide protection to prospective franchisees equal to or greater than that imposed by the Rule.

Examples of state laws or regulations that are not preempted by the Rule include state provisions requiring the registration of franchisors and franchise salespersons, state requirements for escrow or bonding arrangements, and state-required disclosure obligations set forth in the Rule. Moreover, the Rule does not affect state laws or regulations that regulate the franchisor/franchisee relationship, such as termination practices, contract provisions, and financing arrangements.

Preparing the Disclosure Document: Choosing the Appropriate Format

In many ways, the choice of the appropriate format for the franchisor's franchise offering circular is difficult and complex, because the requirements of the FTC Rule, the UFOC guidelines, and any applicable state laws must all be coordinated. The format selection process determines the form in which the disclosure is to be made but not which law governs. Even if the UFOC format is selected, the federal laws governing the timing of the delivery of the disclosure document, the restrictions on the use of earnings claims, and the penalties for noncompliance still apply.

Depending on the targeted markets selected by the company, most franchisors have elected to adopt the UFOC format in the preparation of their disclosure documents. Since many registration states do not accept the FTC Rule format (even though the FTC has endorsed the UFOC format), it is simply most cost-effective to have only one primary document for use in connection with franchise offers and sales. If the franchisor is limiting its marketing activities to those states that do not have registration statutes, then the FTC Rule format may offer certain advantages. For example, the FTC Rule format generally requires less information than the UFOC format in the areas of training and personnel of the franchisor, the litigation history of the franchisor (the FTC Rule requires a seven-year history while the UFOC format requires a ten-year history), history of termination and nonrenewals (FTC, one year; UFOC, three years), bankruptcy history (FTC, seven years; UFOC, fifteen years), and sanctions under Canadian law (required by UFOC but not FTC). The FTC format also requires less stringent disclosure regarding the refundability of payments made by the franchisee.

The FTC Rule format may also be easier for the early-stage franchisor to satisfy, since it allows for a three-year phase-in period for the use of audited financials. Under the UFOC format, audited financials are required from the onset. If the financial condition of the franchisor is weak, many state administrators impose costly escrow and performance bonds. Some registration states deny a financially weak franchisor registration until its condition improves. Early-stage franchisors who are grossly undercapitalized, have a negative net worth, or have suffered significant recent operating losses should be prepared for an uphill battle with the state franchise examiners before approval is granted.

Preparing the Disclosure Document According to UFOC Guidelines

The UFOC format of franchise disclosure consists of twenty-three categories of information that must be provided by the franchisor to the prospective franchisee at least ten business days prior to the execution of the franchise agreement. Because this format has been adopted by many states as a matter of law, franchisors do not enjoy the editorial discretion to reorder the manner in which information is presented, nor may any of the disclosure items be omitted in the document. In addition, many sections of the UFOC must be a mirror image of the actual franchise agreement (and related documents) that the franchisee will be expected to sign. There should be no factual or legal inconsistencies between the UFOC and the franchise agreement.

A description of the information required by each disclosure item of the UFOC follows:

Item One: The Franchisor and Any Predecessors. This first section of the UFOC presents information on the historical background of the franchisor and any of its predecessors. The franchisor's corporate and trade name, form of doing business, principal headquarters, state and date of incorporation, prior business experience, and current business activities all must be disclosed in this section. The franchisor must also disclose the nature of the franchise being offered and its qualifications for offering this type of business, including a general description of the business operations to be conducted by the franchisee, the length of time that the franchisor has offered franchises for such businesses, and a discussion of the competition the franchisee will face.

Item Two: Identity and Business Experience of Persons Affiliated With the Franchisor; Franchise Brokers. This section requires disclosure of the identity of each director, trustee, general partner (where applicable), and officer or manager of the franchisor who will have significant responsibility in connection with the operation of the franchisor's business or in the support services to be provided to franchisees. The principal occupation of each person listed in Item Two for the past five years must be disclosed, including dates of employment, the nature of the position, and the identity of the employer. The identity and background of each franchise broker (if any) authorized to represent the franchisor must also be disclosed in this Item.

Item Three: Litigation. A full and frank discussion of any litigation, arbitration, or administrative hearings affecting the franchisor or its officers, directors, or sales representatives during the past ten years should be included in this section. The formal case name, the location of the dispute, the nature of the claim, and the current status of each action must be disclosed. Item Three does not require disclosure of *all* types of litigation but rather focuses on specific allegations and proceedings that would be of particular concern to the prospective franchisee.

Item Four: Bankruptcy. This section requires the franchisor to disclose whether the company or any of its predecessors, officers, or general partners has, during the past fifteen years, been adjudged bankrupt or reorganized due to insolvency. The court in which the bankruptcy or reorganization proceeding occurred, the formal case title, and any material facts and circumstances surrounding the proceeding must be disclosed.

Item Five: Franchisee's Initial Franchise Fee or Other Initial Payment. The initial franchise fee and related payments to the franchisor upon execution of the franchise agreement must be disclosed in this section. The manner in which the payments are made, the use of the proceeds by the franchisor, and whether the fee is refundable in whole or in part must be disclosed.

Item Six: Other Fees. Any other initial or recurring fee payable by the franchisee to the franchisor or to any affiliate must be disclosed and the nature of each fee fully discussed, including, but not limited to: royalty payments, training fees, audit fees, public offering review fees, advertising contributions, mandatory insurance requirements, transfer fees, renewal fees, lease negotiation fees, and any consulting fees charged by the franchisor or an affiliate for special services. The amount, time of the payment, and refundability of each type of payment should be disclosed.

Item Seven: Franchisee's Initial Investment. Each component of the franchisee's initial investment that the franchise is required to expend in order to open the franchised business must be estimated in this section, usually in chart form, regardless of whether such payments are made directly to the franchisor. Real estate costs, equipment and fixture costs, security deposits, inventory costs, construction costs, working capital, accounting and legal fees, license and permit fees and any other costs and expenditures should be disclosed. The disclosure should include to whom such payments are made, under what general terms and condition, and what portion, if any, is refundable. The following statement must appear at the end of Item Seven: **There are no other direct or indirect payments in conjunction with the purchase of the franchise.**

Item Eight: Obligations of the Franchisee to Purchase or Lease From Designated Sources. Any obligation of the franchisee to purchase goods, services, supplies, fixtures, equipment, or inventory related to the establishment or operation of the franchised business from a source designated by the franchisor should be disclosed. The terms of the purchase or lease, as well as any minimum volume purchasing requirements, must be disclosed. If the franchisor will or may derive direct or indirect income from these purchases from required sources, then the nature and amount of such income must be fully disclosed. *Remember that such obligations must be able to withstand the scrutiny of the antitrust laws.*

Item Nine: Obligations of the Franchisee to Purchase or Lease in Accordance With Specifications or From Approved Suppliers. All quality-control standards, equipment specifications, and approved-supplier programs that have been developed by the franchisor and that must be followed by the franchisee must be disclosed under this Item. The criteria applied by the franchisor for approving or designating a particular supplier or vendor must be included. A detailed discussion of these standards and specifications need not be set forth in the UFOC; a summary discussion of the programs with reference to exhibits or confidential operations manuals is sufficient. Finally, any income derived by the franchisor in connection with the designation of an approved supplier or as a result of an approved supplier being an affiliated corporation must be disclosed.

Item Ten: Financing Arrangements. In this section, the franchisor must disclose the terms and conditions of any financing arrangements offered to franchisees, either by the franchisor or any of its affiliates. The exact terms of any direct or indirect debt financing, equipment or real estate leasing programs, operating lines of credit, or inventory financing must be disclosed. If any of these financing programs are offered by an affiliate, then the exact relationship between the franchisor and the affiliate must be disclosed. Terms that may be detrimental to the franchisee upon default, such as a confession of judgment, waiver of defenses, or acceleration clauses, must be disclosed in this Item of the UFOC.

Item Eleven: Obligations of the Franchisor; Other Supervision, Assistance, or Services. This section is one of the most important to the prospective franchisee because it discusses the initial and ongoing support and services provided by the franchisor. Each obligation of the franchisor to provide assistance must be cross-referenced to the specific paragraph of the franchise agreement where the corresponding contractual provision may be found. Most services offered by the franchisor fall into one of two categories: *initial* or *continuing* services. Initial support includes all services offered by the franchisor prior to the opening of the franchised business, such as the provision of architectural or engineering plans, construction supervision, personnel recruitment, site selection, preopening promotion, and acquisition of initial inventory. The location, duration, content, and qualifications of the franchisor's staff responsible for conducting the training program offered by the franchisor must be discussed in some detail. Any assistance provided by the franchisor that it is not contractually bound to provide must also be disclosed in Item Eleven. Similar disclosures should be made for the continuing services to be offered by the franchisor once the business has opened, such as ongoing training, advertising and promotion, bookkeeping, inventory control, and any products to be sold by the franchisor to the franchisee.

Item Twelve: Exclusive Area or Territory. The exact territory or exclusive area, if any, to be granted by the franchisor to the franchisee should be disclosed, as well as the right to adjust the size of this territory in the event that certain contractual conditions are not met, such as the failure to achieve certain perform-ance quotas. The right of the franchisor to establish company-owned units or to grant franchises to others within the territory must be disclosed. A detailed de-scription and/or a map of the franchisee's territory should be included as an ex-hibit to the franchise agreement.

Item Thirteen: Trademarks, Service Marks, Trade Names, Logotypes, and Commercial Symbols. It has often been said that the trademark is at the heart of a franchising program. Therefore, the extent to which the franchisor's trade iden-tity (trademarks, logos, slogans) has been protected should be disclosed, includ-ing whether these marks are registered at either the federal or the state level and whether there are any limitations or infringement disputes involving the marks or related aspects of the trade identity. The rights and obligations of the franchisor and the franchisee in the event of a trademark dispute with a third party must also be disclosed.

Item Fourteen: Patents and Copyrights. Any rights in patents or copyrights that are material to the operation and management of the franchised business should be described in the same detail as required by Item Thirteen.

Item Fifteen: Obligation of the Franchisee to Participate in the Actual Oper-ation of the Franchised Business. The franchisor must disclose in this Item whether absentee ownership and management are permitted in connection with the operation of the franchised business. If direct participation is required by the franchisee, then the extent of such participation must be disclosed. If the fran-chisee may hire a manager to operate the franchised business, then the franchisor must disclose any mandatory employment terms or equity ownership require-ments.

Item Sixteen: Restrictions on Goods and Services Offered by Franchisee. In this section the franchisor must disclose any special contractual provisions or other circumstances that limit either the types of products and services the fran-chisee may offer *or* the types or location of the customers to whom the products and services may be offered.

Item Seventeen: Renewal, Termination, Repurchase, Modification, and Assignment of the Franchise Agreement and Related Information. This item is typically the longest section of the UFOC and is of great importance to the pro-spective franchisee. The term of the franchise agreement, the conditions to re-newal, the grounds upon which the franchise agreement may be terminated, the conditions under which the franchise agreement may be assigned, and the rights of the heirs of the franchisee upon the franchisee's death must all be disclosed in this section. Specific events of default, as well as any notice provisions and op-portunities to cure defaults that will be provided by the franchisor to the fran-chisee, must be defined. Obligations of the franchisee following termination, such as covenants against competition or against the use of proprietary information, must be disclosed. Finally, the conditions under which the franchise agreement may be modified, either by the franchisor or the franchisee, must be discussed.

Item Eighteen: Arrangements With Public Figures. Any compensation or benefit given to a public figure in return for an endorsement of the franchise and/or products and services offered by the franchisee must be disclosed. The extent to which the public figure owns or is involved in the management of the franchisor must also be disclosed. The right of the franchisee to use the name of the public figure in its local promotional campaign and the material terms of the agreement between the franchisor and the public figure must also be included in this term.

Item Nineteen: Actual, Average, Projected, or Forecasted Franchise Sales, Profits, or Earnings. If the franchisor is willing to provide the prospective franchisee with sample earnings claims or projections, they must be discussed in Item Nineteen.

In 1986, the North American Securities Administrators Association (NASAA) adopted new regulations for the use and content of earnings claims by franchisors. These new guidelines were adopted as the exclusive form of earnings claims permitted by the FTC as of January 1, 1989. Under the rules, which became effective in 1989, any earnings claim made in connection with the offer of a franchise must be included in the UFOC. If no earnings claim is made, then the following statement must appear:

> Franchisor does not furnish or authorize its salespersons to furnish any oral or written information concerning the actual or potential sales, costs, income, or profits of a [franchised business name]. Actual results vary from unit to unit and franchisor cannot estimate the results of any particular franchise.

If the franchisor does elect to make an earnings claim, then it must: (a) have a reasonable basis for the claim at the time at which it is made; (b) include a description of the factual basis for the claim; and (c) include an overview of the material assumptions underlying the claim.

Item Twenty: Information Regarding Franchises of the Franchisor. A full summary of the number of franchises sold, number of units operational, and number of company-owned units must be broken down in Item Twenty, usually in tabular form, including an estimate of franchise sales for the upcoming fiscal year broken down by state. The names, addresses, and telephone numbers of current franchisees should be included in this Item. In addition, the number of franchisees terminated or not renewed (voluntary and involuntary) and the cause of termination or nonrenewal must be broken down for the previous three years of operations. Many registration states require the franchisor to disclose the names and addresses of these former franchisees in the offering circular.

Item Twenty-One: Financial Statements. A full set of financial statements prepared in accordance with generally accepted accounting principles must be included in Item Twenty-One as part of the disclosure package to be provided to a franchisee. Most registration states require that the statements be audited, with limited exceptions for start-up franchisors. The balance sheet provided should have been prepared as of a date within ninety days prior to the date that the registration application is filed. Unaudited statements may be used for interim periods. Franchisors with weak financial statements may be required to make special arrangements with the franchise administrator in each state for the protection of prospective franchisees.

Item Twenty-Two: Franchise Agreement and Related Contracts. A copy of the franchise agreement, as well as any other related documents to be signed by the franchisee in connection with the ownership and operation of the franchised business, must be attached as exhibits to the UFOC.

Item Twenty-Three: Acknowledgement of Receipt by a Prospective Franchisee. The last page of the UFOC is a detachable document, executed by the prospective franchisee, acknowledging receipt of the offering circular.

Strategic Issues to Consider in Preparing the Disclosure Documents

As a franchisor prepares the required disclosure documents, she should keep in mind a number of points:

1. *The UFOC can and should be used as a marketing tool.* It is often the first, and sometimes the last, formal document that a prospective franchisee (and his advisors) ever see. Create the right first impression. Ask yourself what your UFOC says about your company. Are you flat and boring, or are you dynamic and at the cutting edge of your industry? The document need not be filled entirely with dry and boring legalese. Instead, the document should outline the franchisor's strengths, mission, business philosophy, reasons for selecting franchising as a means of growth, management team depth, initial and ongoing support and services, and operational track record. The UFOC should reflect the franchisor's philosophy, corporate culture, goals, and objectives. And there are places for each of these items within the constraints of the statutorily-prescribed format and within the bounds of the law. Stick to the facts, not opinions or puffery. For example, if the company is very committed to community service projects, then include an overview of actual involvement by the franchisor in Item I and the role of the franchisor in assisting the franchisee in those projects at a local level in Item Eleven.

2. *The UFOC should be a reflection of the thousands of management, financial, operational, and strategic decisions made by the franchisor and its team of external advisors.* It should never be a boilerplate recitation of somebody else's decisions and business plans.

3. *The UFOC is your best defense against subsequent claims by your franchisees.* When in doubt, disclose. In other words, if you have a sensitive issue

that would be material to the prospective franchisee's decision, it is better to get it out in the open and convince the franchisee to focus on the merits of your franchise program than to omit the information and run the risk of a lawsuit or investigation later.

4. *The UFOC should be user friendly.* The purpose of the UFOC is for the prospective franchisee (and her advisors) to truly read and understand the document. If it is poorly written, highly technical, disorganized, archaic, confusing, vague, and boring, then nobody will want to read it. If the document is not read and understood, then you will either lose the prospect or, even worse, sign up a new franchisee who does not truly understand her rights and obligations in the relationship. Put yourself in the shoes of the *user* of the document (prospects, spouses, friends, advisors, lenders, investors), and see if this is a document you can easily grasp. Too many franchise disclosure documents end up looking like a patchwork of drafting styles and techniques as periodic updates are made to the circular by a variety of different individuals for a variety of different reasons. As a result, the document lacks cohesiveness and creativity.

The Mechanics of the Registration Process

Each of the registration states has slightly different procedures and requirements for franchisor approval prior to its being able to authorize offers and sales. In all cases, however, the package of disclosure documents, consisting of an offering circular, franchise agreement, supplemental agreements, financial statements, franchise roster, mandated cover pages, acknowledgement of receipt, and special forms required by each state, such as corporation verification statements, salesperson disclosure forms, and consent to service of process documents, is assembled. The specific requirements of each state should be checked carefully by the franchisor and its counsel. Initial filing fees range from $250 to $500, with renewal filings usually ranging between $100 and $250.

The first step is for counsel to custom-tailor the UFOC format to meet the special requirements or additional disclosures required under the particular state's regulations. Once the documents are ready and all signatures have been obtained, the package is filed with the state franchise administrator and a specific franchise examiner (usually an attorney) is assigned to the franchisor. The level of scrutiny applied by the examiner in reviewing the offering materials varies from state to state and from franchisor to franchisor. The sales history, financial strength, litigation record, reputation of legal counsel, time pressures and workload of the examiner, geographic desirability of the state, and general reputation of the franchisor have an impact on the level of review and the timetable for approval. Franchisors should expect to see at least one ''comment letter'' from the examiner requesting certain changes or additional information as a condition to approval and registration. The procedure can require as little as six weeks or as much as six months, depending on the concerns of the examiner and the skills and experience of legal counsel.

The initial and ongoing reporting and disclosure requirements vary from state to state. For example, the filing of an amendment to the offering circular is required in the event of a "material change." However, each state has different regulations as to the definition of a "material change." A general guideline to follow is that any development in the franchisor's program, financial condition, or relationship with its current franchisees that would be relevant to the decision of a prospective franchisee should be disclosed through an amended offering and a material change filing. If in doubt, go ahead and amend the offering in order to be on the safe side.

Although *all* registration states require the annual filing of a renewal application or annual report, only Maryland and Wisconsin require that quarterly reports be filed. When advertising materials are developed for use in attracting franchisees, they must be approved in advance by all registration states except Virginia and Hawaii. All franchise registration states except Virginia require the filing of salesperson disclosure forms, with California, New York, Illinois, and Washington requiring their own special forms. It is critical that the franchisor's legal compliance officer stay abreast of all of these special filing requirements.

21

Structuring the Franchise Agreement

Andrew J. Sherman, Silver, Freedman & Taff

The principal document that sets forth the binding rights and obligations of each party to the franchise relationship is the franchise agreement. The franchise agreement contains the various provisions that will be binding on the franchisor and the franchisee for the life of their relationship and therefore must maintain a delicate balance of power. On the one hand, the franchisor must maintain enough control in the franchise agreement to enforce uniformity and consistency throughout the system, yet at the same time the document must be flexible enough to anticipate changes in the marketplace or in the franchise system and to meet any special considerations or demands caused by the franchisee's local market conditions.

The franchise agreement can and should reflect the business philosophy of the franchisor and set the tenor of the relationship. A well-drafted franchise agreement is the result of literally thousands of business decisions and hundreds of hours of market research and testing. The length, term, and complexity of the franchise agreement will (and should) vary from franchisor to franchisor and from industry to industry. Many start-up franchisors make the critical mistake of "borrowing" terms of a competitor's franchise agreement. This practice can be detrimental to both the franchisor and the franchisee, since such an agreement does not accurately reflect the actual dynamics of the relationship. To a certain extent, the franchise agreement must be an evolving document, amended and updated from time to time by the management team of the franchisor and its counsel to reflect changes and developments in the system, changes in competitive conditions, developments in the laws affecting franchising, and changes in the franchisor's management philosophies and practices.

Early-stage franchisors should resist the temptation to copy from the franchise agreement of a competitor or to accept the standard form and boilerplate from an inexperienced attorney or consultant. The relationship between the franchisor and the franchisee is far too complex to accept a compromise in the preparation of such a critical document. For example, suppose that the three principal competitors in your industry are charging a monthly royalty of 7 percent on gross sales. Not wanting to make waves, you decide to mimic this practice by also charging 7 percent. However, there may be fundamental differences between your costs and expenses and those of your competitors.

Suppose that your midwestern location affords you a lower overhead than that incurred by your New York- and California-based competitors. Perhaps you want to pass these cost savings along to your franchisees by charging only a 5 percent royalty, preserving healthy profits for yourself while likely selling more franchises than your competitors. Along the same lines, your cash flow requirements may be different than those of your competitors, suggesting that a weekly royalty payment may work better than a monthly payment. Additionally, you may wish to reward high-performing franchisees by adopting a sliding scale for royalty payments of 4 percent if a certain sales level is reached and 3 percent if an even higher sales level is reached. As you can see, a provision as simple as the royalty rate raises a wide variety of issues that must be considered by the management team of the franchisor. Merely adopting the practices and provisions of a competitor is not sufficient for building a solid foundation for franchising.

There are a wide variety of drafting styles and practices among those attorneys who regularly practice in the area of franchise law. Some franchise lawyers prefer to roll everything into a single agreement (which can develop into quite a behemoth), while others prefer to address the equipment leases, product purchasing requirements, personal guaranty, site development obligations, security interests, options for assignment of leases, and other key aspects of the relationship in supplemental agreements separate from the actual franchise agreement. The advantage to this latter approach, which I have come to appreciate over the years, is that the franchisee and its counsel are not overwhelmed (or intimidated) by the complexity and depth of a single document. This chapter examines the key elements of a basic franchise agreement and some of the various supplemental agreements that further define the long-term rights and obligations of both franchisor and franchisee.

Key Elements of the Basic Franchise Agreement

Regardless of size, stage of growth, industry dynamics, or specific trends in the marketplace, all basic franchise agreements should address the following eleven key topics:

1. *Recitals*. The recitals or preamble essentially set the stage for the discussion of the contractual relationship. This section provides the background information regarding the development and ownership of the proprietary rights of the franchisor which are being licensed to the franchisee. The preamble should always contain at least one recital specifying the obligation of the franchisee to operate the business format in strict conformity with the operations manual and the quality control standards provided by the franchisor.

2. *Grant, term, and renewal.* The typical initial section of the franchise agreement is the grant of a franchise for a specified term. The length of the term is influenced by a number of factors including market conditions, the franchisor's need to periodically change certain material terms of the agreement, the cost of the franchise and the franchisee's expectations in relation to start-up costs, the length of related agreements necessary to the franchisee's operations such as leases and bank loans, and anticipated consumer demand for the franchised goods and services. The renewal rights granted to a franchisee, if included at all, are usually conditioned upon the franchisee being in good standing (e.g., no material defaults by franchisee) under the agreement. Other issues that must be addressed in any provisions regarding renewal include renewal fees, obligations to execute the "then current" form of the franchise agreement, and any obligations of the franchisee to upgrade its facilities to the latest standards and design. The franchisor's right to relocate the franchisee, adjust the size of any exclusive territory granted, or change the fee structure should also be addressed.

3. *Territory.* The size of the geographic area granted to the franchisee by the franchisor must be specifically discussed in conjunction with a description of what, if any, exclusive rights will be granted to the franchisee with respect to this territory. These provisions address whether the size of the territory is a specific radius, city, or county and whether the franchisor will have a right to operate company-owned locations and/or grant additional franchises within the territory. Some franchisors designate a specific territory that market research indicates can support a given number of locations without market oversaturation and then sell that exact number of franchises without regard to specific location selected within the geographic area. Any rights of first refusal for additional locations, advertising restrictions, performance quotas relating to territory, and policies of the franchisor with regard to territory are addressed in this part of the franchise agreement.

4. *Site selection.* The responsibility for finding the specific site for the operation of the franchised business rests either with the franchisor or the franchisee. If the franchisee is free to choose its own site, then the franchise agreement usually provides that the decision is subject to the approval of the franchisor. Some franchisors provide significant assistance in site selection in terms of marketing and demographic studies, lease negotiations, and the procurement of local permits and licenses, especially if a turnkey franchise is offered. Site selection, however, can be the most difficult aspect of being a successful franchisee, and, as a result, most franchisors are reluctant to take on full responsibility for this task contractually. For additional protection and control, some franchisors insist on becoming the landlord to the franchisee through a mandatory sublease arrangement once an acceptable site has been selected. A somewhat less burdensome method of securing similar protection is to provide for an automatic assignment of the lease to the franchisor upon termination of the franchise.

5. *Services to be provided by the franchisor.* The franchise agreement

should clearly delineate which products and services will be provided to the franchisee by the franchisor or its affiliates, in terms of both the initial establishment of the franchised business ("preopening obligations") and any continuing assistance or support services provided throughout the term of the relationship ("postopening services"). The preopening obligations generally include a trade secret and copyright license for the use of the Confidential Operations Manual; recruitment and training of personnel; standard accounting and bookkeeping systems; inventory and equipment specifications; volume discounts; standard construction, building, and interior design plans; and grand opening promotion and advertising assistance. The quality and extent of the training program is clearly the most crucial preopening service provided by the franchisor and should include classroom as well as on-site instruction. Post-opening services provided to the franchisee on a continuing basis generally include field support and troubleshooting, research and development for new products and services, development of national advertising and promotional campaigns, and the arrangement of group purchasing programs and volume discounts.

6. *Franchise, royalty, and related fees payable to the franchisor and reporting requirements.* The franchise agreement should set forth clearly the nature and amount of fees payable to the franchisor by the franchisee, both initially and on a continuing basis. The initial franchise fee is usually a nonrefundable lump sum payment due upon execution of the franchise agreement. Essentially this fee is compensation for the grant of the franchise, the trademark and trade secret license, preopening training and assistance, and the initial opening supply of materials, if any, to be provided by the franchisor to the franchisee.

A second category of fees is the continuing fee, usually in the form of a specific royalty on gross sales. This percentage can be fixed, or it can be based on a sliding scale for different ranges of sales achieved at a given location. Often minimum royalty payments are required, regardless of the franchisee's actual performance. These fees should be payable weekly and submitted to the franchisor together with some standardized reporting form for internal control and monitoring purposes. A weekly payment schedule generally allows the franchisee to budget for this payment from a cash flow perspective and provides the franchisor with an early warning system if there is a problem, allowing the franchisor to react before the past due royalties accrue to a virtually uncollectible sum.

The third category of recurring fees is usually a contribution to a national cooperative advertising and promotion fund. The promotional fund may be managed by the franchisor, an independent advertising agency, or even a franchisee association. Either way, the franchisor must build a certain amount of control into the franchise agreement over the fund in order to protect the company's trademarks and to ensure consistency in marketing efforts.

Other categories of fees payable to the franchisor may include fees for the sale of proprietary goods and services to the franchisee, consulting fees, audit and inspection fees, lease management fees (where franchisor is to serve as sublessor), and renewal or transfer fees.

The obligations of the franchisee to provide periodic weekly, monthly, quarterly, and annual financial and sales reports to the franchisor should also be addressed in the franchise agreement.

7. *Quality control.* A well-drafted franchise agreement always includes a variety of provisions designed to ensure quality control and consistency throughout the franchise system. Such provisions often take the form of restrictions on the franchisee's sources of products, ingredients, supplies, and materials, as well as strict guidelines and specifications for operating procedures. These operating procedures usually specify standards of service, trade dress and uniform requirements, condition and appearance of the facility, hours of business, minimum insurance requirements, guidelines for trademark usage, advertising and promotional materials, and prescribed accounting systems and credit practices. Any restrictions on the ability of the franchisee to buy goods and services or requirements to purchase from a specific source should be carefully drafted within the perimeters of applicable antitrust laws. If the franchisor is to serve as the sole supplier or manufacturer of one or more products to be used by the franchisee in the day-to-day operation of the business, then such exclusivity must be justified by a product that is truly proprietary or unique.

8. *Insurance, record keeping, and other related obligations of the franchisee.* The franchise agreement should always address the minimum amounts and types of insurance that must be carried by the franchisee in connection with its operation of the franchised businesses. Typically the franchisor is named as an additional insured under these policies. Other related obligations of the franchisee that must be set forth in the franchise agreement include: the keeping of proper financial records (which must be made available for inspection by the franchisor upon request); the obligation to maintain and enforce quality control standards with its employees and vendors; the obligation to comply with all applicable employment laws, health and safety standards, and related local ordinances; the duty to upgrade and maintain the franchisee's facilities and equipment; the obligation to continue to promote the products and services of the franchisor; the obligation to reasonably process requests by patrons for franchising information; the obligation to not produce goods and services that do not meet the franchisor's quality control specifications or that may be unapproved for offer at the franchisee's premises (such as video games at a fast-food restaurant or X-rated material at a bookstore); the obligation not to solicit customers outside its designated territory; the obligation of the franchisee to participate personally in the day-to-day operation of the franchised business (required by many but not all franchisors); and the general obligation of the franchisee to refrain from any activity that may reflect adversely on the reputation of the franchise system.

9. *Protection of intellectual property and covenants against competition.* The franchise agreement should always contain a separate section on the obligations of the franchisee and its employees to protect the trademarks and trade secrets being licensed against misuse or disclosure. The franchisor should provide for a clause that clearly sets forth that the trademarks and trade names being

licensed are the exclusive property of the franchisor and that any goodwill established is to inure to the sole benefit of the franchisor. It should also be made clear that the Confidential Operations Manual is "on loan" to the franchisee under a limited use license and that the franchisee or its agents are prohibited from the unauthorized use of the trade secrets both during and after the term of the agreement. To the extent that such provisions are enforceable in local jurisdictions, the franchise agreement should contain covenants against competition by a franchisee, both during the term of the franchise agreement and following termination or cancellation.

10. *Termination of the franchise agreement.* One of the most important sections of the franchise agreement is the section discussing how a franchisee may lose its rights to operate the franchised business. The various "events of default" should be carefully defined and tailored to meet the needs of the specific type of business being franchised. Grounds for termination can range anywhere from the bankruptcy of a franchisee to failure to meet specified performance quotas or strictly to abide by quality control standards. Certain types of violations are grounds for termination, while other types of default provide the franchisee with an opportunity for cure. This section should address the procedures for notice and for opportunity to cure, as well as the alternative actions that the franchisor may pursue to enforce its rights to terminate the franchise agreement. Such clauses must be drafted in light of certain state regulations that limit franchise terminations to "good cause" and contain minimum procedural requirements that must be followed. The obligations of the franchisee upon default and notice of termination must also be clearly spelled out, such as the duty to return all copies of the operations manuals, pay all past-due royalty fees, and immediately cease the use of the franchisor's trademarks.

11. *Miscellaneous provisions.* Like any well-prepared business agreement, the franchise agreement should include a notice provision, a governing law clause, severability provisions, an integration clause, and a provision discussing the relationship of the parties. Some franchisors may want to add an arbitration clause, a "hold harmless" and indemnification provision, a reservation of the right to injunctions, and other forms of equitable relief, specific representations and warranties of the franchisee, attorney fees for the prevailing party in the event of dispute, and even a contractual provision acknowledging that the franchisee has reviewed the agreement with counsel and has conducted an independent investigation of the franchise and is not relying on any representations other than those expressly set forth in the agreement.

Sample Supplemental Agreements Commonly Used in Franchising

The franchise agreement is not the only document typically signed by the franchisee at closing upon the award of the franchise. Depending on the level of legal protection sought by the franchisor, the nature of the economic relationship between the franchisor and the franchisee, and the norms in the industry in which the franchise system operates, the following documents may also be necessary:

▲ *General release*. The general release should be executed by all franchisees at the time of renewal of their franchise agreement or at the time of a transfer of the franchise agreement or of their equity interest in the franchised business. The document serves as a release by the franchisee of the franchisor from all existing and potential claims that the franchisee may have against the franchisor. In recent years, some courts have restricted the scope of the release if it has been executed under duress or if its effect runs contrary to public policy.

▲ *Personal guaranty*. For a wide variety of tax and legal purposes, many franchisees want to execute the franchise agreement in the name of a closely held corporation formed to operate the franchised business. Although this does not present a significant problem for the franchisor, there are many advantages for ensuring that all principal shareholders of the company are personally responsible for the financial and other obligations under the franchise agreement. Under such circumstances, it is highly recommended that each key shareholder of the franchise corporation be personally responsible for the franchisee's obligation under the franchise agreement.

▲ *Sign lease agreement*. There are many reasons a franchisor might want to lease the signage bearing its trademarks to the franchisee separately. Aside from the additional rental income, the sign lease often contains cross-default provisions that allow the franchisor to remove the signs immediately upon termination of the franchisee. This can be a powerful tool in ensuring a smooth and efficient termination of the disgruntled franchisee. The sign lease agreement should set forth all specific rental terms and conditions to which the franchisee is bound.

▲ *Site selection addendum to the franchise agreement*. A site selection addendum to the franchise agreement should be executed at the time that the specific site within the geographic area designated in the franchise agreement has been selected by the franchisee. The addendum modifies the initial designation of the territory initially set forth at the time the franchise agreement was signed and is a vehicle for ensuring that the specific site meets with the franchisor's approval.

▲ *Option for assignment of lease*. The option for assignment of lease agreement provides the franchisor with the option, exercisable upon the termination of the franchisee for any reason, to be substituted as the tenant under the franchisee's lease with its landlord for the premises on which the franchisee's center is located.

▲ *Employee noncompetition and nondisclosure agreement*. This agreement, which should be executed by all employees of the franchisees, ensures that all information disclosed to these employees will be kept confidential. It also imposes noncompetition restriction on employees of the franchisees.

▲ *Special disclaimer*. This document should be initialed and signed by the franchisee at the time of closing. It serves as a written acknowledgement that no earnings claims, representations, or warranties not contained in the offering circular have been made by the franchisor or relied upon by franchisee. It also serves as an acknowledgement that the proper offering circular and related documents were provided to the franchisee on a timely basis.

▲ *Inventory purchase agreement.* The inventory purchase agreement defines the rights and obligations of both the franchisor and the franchisee when the franchise agreement or market conditions anticipate that the franchisee will be purchasing certain items of inventory, supplies, and other items from the franchisor or its affiliates. The inventory purchase agreement addresses issues such as price, shipping terms, specific product warranties, return policies, and procedures for placing orders.

22

Building Compliance Systems

Celia Garelick Spiritos, Silver, Freedman & Taff

The franchise compliance officer plays a critical role as a legal watchdog in the implementation of a franchise system, monitoring compliance with state and federal regulations that require disclosure to potential franchisees of the appropriate franchise documents, controlling timing and receipt of initial fees, monitoring advertising, and supervising the method and manner of sales.

The development of an in-house legal compliance program and the designation of a legal compliance officer is a necessity, not a luxury, for the growing franchisor operating in today's litigious society. In all likelihood, the compliance staff will periodically find itself in conflict with the sales and marketing staff as a result of the tension between the need to market aggressively and the need to market legally. A philosophy of teamwork must be fostered early on in order to avoid such tension within the company. There must be a commitment from day one to sell franchises only within the bounds of the law and to maintain complete and comprehensive compliance files. These compliance files should document, among other things, the initial meeting with the prospect, the execution of the franchise agreement, and the termination of the relationship. These record keeping requirements will often seem burdensome but will go a long way in protecting the company in the event of a subsequent dispute with the franchisee or with a federal or state regulatory body.

A compliance program means more than careful record keeping. It means a total commitment by the company to working with the compliance officer and legal counsel to guard against franchise law violations. A well-planned compliance system requires initial and ongoing training for the franchisor's sales and marketing personnel, the development of special forms and checklists, a management philosophy and compensation structure that reward compliance and discourage noncompliance, a system for monitoring all registration and renewal dates, custom-tailored verbal sales scripts and video presentations that are carefully followed and used by the sales personnel, the development of a compliance manual and periodic policy statements, a special approval and renewal process for the award of new franchises, and a periodic random and unannounced inspection of the franchise sales and compliance files in order to ensure that procedures are being followed. The success of the compliance program should not be made dependent on outside legal counsel; rather, it should be a priority for the franchisor's management team.

No compliance system is 100 percent effective in preventing franchise law violations, and most compliance problems are the consequence of innocent mistakes and statements. Human error may result in a Maryland resident being disclosed with a New York offering document because the wrong package was hastily pulled off the shelf, or the most recent financial statements may not be appended to the package due to oversight. Human nature may cause a franchise sales representative to stretch the truth a little if he has not had a sale in months and faces the loss of a job or a home. The franchisor's ability to devote sufficient resources for the compliance program, to select the right person as the compliance officer, and to foster a positive attitude toward compliance among the sales staff will directly affect the success or failure of the compliance program.

The franchise compliance officer must be selected carefully and charged with the responsibility of implementing the compliance program and enforcing its procedures. The officer serves as the in-house clearinghouse for franchise files and information, as well as the liaison with outside legal counsel. The compliance officer must gain (and maintain) the respect of the sales and marketing personnel, or the system will fail. This goal can be achieved only if a senior executive within the company assumes responsibility for disciplining those who are apathetic about compliance.

Developing Compliance Files

Organization and maintenance of compliance files by the compliance officer is critical to the operation of the management system, since the files provide immediate access to valuable information and accurate record keeping. These files are used, for example, for calculating the ten-day disclosure period and for determining prescribed dates for filing reports on material changes within a state and for timing planned advertisements.

The contents of a typical compliance file are listed below:

- Acknowledgment of receipt of offering circular
- Completed applicant questionnaire
- Executed deposit agreement (if used)
- Copy of the check for initial deposit
- Copy of executed franchise agreement
- Area development agreement (where applicable)
- Inventory purchase agreement (where applicable)
- Option for assignment of lease
- Mandatory addendum to lease
- Receipt for manuals
- Written consent of board of directors of franchisee

- Proof of insurance
- Franchisor's written approval of site
- Franchisee's certification of receipt of all licenses, permits, and bonds
- Franchisee's written notice of commencement of construction
- Franchisor's approval of the opening of the franchised business
- Copy of franchisee's lease
- Certification of completion of basic training
- All ongoing correspondence between franchisor and franchisee (post-opening)
- Inspection reports
- Notices of default

Responsibilities of the Compliance Officer

Monitoring the Activities of the Sales and Marketing Staff

- *Earnings claims.* One of the primary responsibilities of the compliance officer is to work with the sales and marketing staff in order to ensure that they are familiar with the limitations on the nature and scope of the information, including earnings claims, that may be presented to prospective franchises. Compliance officers should explain and reiterate the importance of the earnings claims regulations to all sales and marketing personnel.

An earnings claim is any information given to a prospective franchisee by, on behalf of, or at the direction of a franchisor or its agent, from which a specific level or range of actual or potential sales, costs, income, or profit from franchised or nonfranchised units may be easily ascertained. Earnings claims may include a chart, table, or mathematical calculation presented to demonstrate possible results based upon a combination of variables (such as multiples of price and quantity to reflect gross sales).

The compliance officer should work with legal counsel to ensure that any earnings claims that are provided to franchisees are prepared in accordance with applicable federal and state regulations and include a description of their factual basis and the material assumptions underlying their preparation and presentation. An earnings claim made in connection with an offer of a franchise must be included in full in the offering circular.

Note: Information limited solely to the actual operating results of a specific *existing franchise unit* being offered for sale is *not* an earnings claim if it is given only to potential purchasers of that unit and is accompanied by the name and last known address of each owner of the unit during the prior three years.

If an earnings claim is made, then the compliance officer should ensure that the Uniform Franchise Offering Circular (UFOC) Item 19 disclosure includes the following three items:

1. A concise summary of the basis for the claim, including a statement of whether the claim is based upon actual experience of franchised units and, if so, the percentage of franchised outlets in operation for the period covered by the earnings claim that have actually attained or surpassed the stated results.
2. A conspicuous admonition that a new franchisee's individual financial results are likely to differ from the results stated in the earnings claim.
3. A statement that substantiation of the data used in preparing the earnings claim will be made available to the prospective franchisee on reasonable request.

▲ *Media claims.* A media claim encompasses earnings claims contained in advertising speeches or press releases, whether contained in radio, television, newspapers, or magazines. If the media claim is to be used as a sales and marketing tool for prospective franchisees, the compliance officer must know that there is a reasonable basis to the claim and that the claim meets the following six criteria:

1. The support for the claim must be available for presentation to the FTC upon demand.
2. The underlying data on which the representation of sales, income, or profit is based shall have been prepared in accordance with generally accepted accounting principles.
3. In conjunction with the representation, the franchisor must conspicuously disclose the number and percentage of the outlets of the franchised business that the franchisor knows to have earned or made at least the same sales, income, or profits during a period of corresponding length in the immediate past as the sales, income, or profits represented, and the beginning and ending dates for the time period covered.
4. The following statements should be clearly and conspicuously disclosed:

CAUTION

These figures are only estimates; there is no assurance you'll do as well. If you rely upon our figures, you must accept the risk of not doing as well.

CAUTION

Some outlets have [sold]/[earned] this amount. There is no assurance you'll do as well. If you rely upon our figures, you must accept the risk of not doing as well.

5. If applicable, a statement that the franchisor lacks prior franchising experience or has not been in business long enough to cultivate actual business data should be included.

6. A cover sheet stating the following notice in 12-point upper and lower case boldface type should be disclosed:

INFORMATION FOR PROSPECTIVE FRANCHISEES ABOUT FRANCHISE [SALES/INCOME/PROFIT] REQUIRED BY THE FEDERAL TRADE COMMISSION

To protect you, we've required the franchisor to give you this information. We haven't checked it and don't know if it's correct. Study these facts and figures carefully. If possible, show them to someone who can advise you, like a lawyer or an accountant. If you find anything you think may be wrong or anything important that's been left out, let us know about it. It may be against the law. There may also be laws about franchising in your State. Ask your State agencies about them.

**Federal Trade Commission
Washington, D.C.**

One alternative to the presentation of the article or other medium intact is to block out the earnings claim language. This allows the prospect to see that the franchisor was named in the article or other medium in a favorable light, the rest is up to her imagination. Another option is to provide each prospect with a list of recent publications or articles in which the franchisor's name or business was mentioned. This gives the prospect the background he needs to do his own due diligence investigation.

Handling Amendments and Renewal of Offering Documents

A second key responsibility of the compliance officer is to ensure that registration documents are amended and renewed on a timely basis. For example, registration and disclosure documents must be amended whenever there is a material change affecting the franchisor, its system, or its relationship with its franchisees. They must also be amended on an annual basis to update such information as financial status and number of units sold.

The determination of what constitutes a material change can be difficult and confusing, and the compliance officer should work closely with legal counsel in order to ascertain what events fall within its scope. The term "material change" is defined by the Federal Trade Commission as "any fact, circumstance, or set of conditions which has a substantial likelihood of influencing a reasonable franchisee or a reasonable prospective franchisee in the making of a significant decision relating to a named franchise business or which has any significant financial impact on a franchise or prospective franchisee."

The following list provides examples of facts and circumstances that have been considered by federal and state franchise regulators to constitute a material change:

‣ A change in any franchise fee or other fee charged, or significantly increased costs of developing or operating a franchised outlet.

‣ The termination, closing, failure to renew, or repurchase of a significant number of franchises. Whether the number is significant depends on the number of franchises in existence and whether the area in which the actions occurred is the same area in which new franchises will be offered, except where specific states (e.g., Hawaii and New York) define what constitutes a significant number.

‣ A significant *adverse* change in any of the following eight items:

1. The obligations of the franchisee to purchase items from the franchisor or its designated sources
2. Limitations or restrictions on goods or services which the franchisee may offer to its customers
3. The obligations to be performed by the franchisor
4. The key terms of the franchise agreement
5. The franchisor's financial situation, defined as a 5 percent or greater change in net profits or losses in any six-month period
6. The services or products offered to consumers by the franchisees of the franchisor
7. The identity of persons affiliated with the franchisor and any franchise broker
8. The current status of the franchisor's trade or service marks

‣ Any change in control, corporate name, or state of incorporation, or a reorganization of the franchisor.

‣ A significant change in the status of litigation or administrative matters that have been disclosed in the UFOC. In addition, a franchisor should provide for any new claims or counterclaims that have been filed against the franchisor that may need to be disclosed.

‣ Any recent developments in the market(s) for the products or services sold by the franchisees that could increase competition or create operating problems for franchisees.

‣ A change in the accuracy of earnings claims information disclosed (if applicable).

Ensuring Compliance With Advertising Regulations

Certain states have enacted laws regulating the use of advertising by a franchisor that is directed at prospective franchisees. Many of these states require the filing and approval of such advertising and marketing materials *prior to their use*. The compliance officer should work closely with the sales and marketing staff, the outside advertising agency, and legal counsel in order to confirm the accuracy and clarity of the information presented as well as its compliance with applicable regulations.

For example, in New York, all sales literature must be submitted to the New York Department of Law at least seven days prior to its intended use. The franchisor must verify, in writing submitted with the sales literature, that it is not inconsistent with the filed prospectus. All sales literature must contain the following statement (in easily readable print) on the cover of all circulars, fliers, cards, letters, and other literature intended for use in New York:

> **This advertisement is not an offering. An offering can only be made by a prospectus filed first with the Department of Law of the State of New York. Such filing does not constitute approval by the Department of Law.**

In all classified type advertisements not more than five inches long and no more than one column of print wide and in all broadcast advertising thirty seconds or less in duration, the following statement may be used in lieu of the statement provided above: "This Offering is made by prospectus only."

The compliance officer should work with the advertising agency, media publishers, and even a clipping service to gather evidence of compliance with these regulations.

Serving as Liaison to Legal Counsel

A compliance officer may act as a link to outside counsel, with responsibilities ranging from consulting on litigation involving franchisees in which she is the chief source of data and information to reviewing all changes and issues arising out of negotiations of an agreement with a franchisee with counsel for legal and business issues and applications.

Meeting Requirements for Regulatory Filings and Licenses

In industries that are regulated on a local, state, or federal level, the compliance officer's job takes on an additional dimension—the responsibility of complying with these regulations. Examples include a franchise for an educational program that must meet state licensing requirements or a franchise in the securities industry, which is federally regulated. It is the compliance officer's duty to analyze these additional requirements and to maintain and to update all required licenses, permits, and filings.

23

Strategies for Resolving Conflict Between Franchisors and Franchisees

Andrew J. Sherman, Silver, Freedman & Taff

Conflict in a franchise system between the franchisor and franchisee is inevitable. Resolving conflicts with franchisees, however, is often an expensive and time-consuming process that can significantly impede the growth of a franchisor as well as distract the franchisor from the attainment of its business objectives. And no franchisor wants its Item Three disclosure to read like a sequel to *War and Peace*. Excessive litigation is not only costly but is also a significant detriment to franchise relations. Existing franchisees will fear that they'll be the next target, which makes them less effective operators and reduces the likelihood that they'll refer others who may be prospective franchisees. The basic rule in litigation is that there are rarely any actual winners—only successful and unsuccessful litigants.

As a result, most franchisors prefer to engage in battle in the marketplace or in the boardroom rather than in the courtroom. Nevertheless, there are instances when an amicable resolution or settlement of a conflict seems unattainable. If a dispute with a franchisee or prospective franchisee matures into a courtroom battle, franchisors must understand the fundamental rules of litigation as well as alternate means of resolving disputes.

Problems Leading to Litigation

A certain level of tension is inherent in the franchisor-franchisee relationship. The franchisor has invested a great deal of time, effort, and money in establishing a business-format franchise, including quality-control guidelines that must be followed. The franchisee, on the other hand, often desires to be his own boss and resists any such restrictions. This tension can create an exciting and dynamic atmosphere that enables both parties to achieve their goals—growth for the franchisor and independence and satisfaction for the franchisee. In many instances, however, the tension that is part and parcel of every franchise relationship leads to conflict and strife, which distract the parties from the achievement of their common objectives.

Ten Common Sources of Dispute

It is critical for franchisors to recognize and understand the problems that typically give rise to litigation and to attempt, if at all possible, to resolve these in an effort to avoid legal action. Following are ten situations that often lead to disputes and litigation between franchisor and franchisee:

1. *Franchisee recruiting*. A franchised operation is only as strong as the franchisee operating it. The franchisor must carefully evaluate and screen prospective franchisees to ensure that only qualified individuals are awarded a franchise. It is essential that all prospects be carefully scrutinized to ensure they have the financial background and experience to successfully operate a franchise. The applicant should possess the requisite financial strength to meet the demands that can reasonably be expected to arise in a franchised business, including sufficient working capital for payroll, rent, unexpected complications, product purchases, and taxes. Ideally, the candidate should have a background in a business similar to or compatible with the franchised business or other sufficient experience as a business owner or manager.

The intangible factors that contribute to a franchisee's success, such as motivation, loyalty, and commitment, are, of course, almost impossible to evaluate from a written application, and the franchisor should at a minimum speak with the applicant's references and her current employer, if any. A franchisee's level of motivation can also be evaluated by analyzing the franchisee's ownership interest or risk in the enterprise. A franchisee who is gambling with someone else's money will be far less committed to the business than the franchisee who has invested his own hard-earned dollars and personal savings. A franchisor can also learn a great deal about an individual simply through the initial screening process. An applicant who is hostile, contentious, and untruthful in the interview and negotiation process will in all likelihood be a franchisee who is hostile, contentious, and untruthful as a franchisee. It is almost inevitable that such a franchisee will cause discord and dissension, which may lead to litigation.

Many franchisors have discovered that when claims of fraud, misrepresentation, and mistake arise, they commonly grow out of misunderstandings in the recruiting and sales process. Franchise sales staff must be trained to underpromise and overdeliver. A low-key, accurate, and conservative sales presentation will go a long way in avoiding conflicts.

2. *Site selection and territorial rights*. Even the strongest franchise system in the world cannot take root and flourish in an oversaturated or underpopulated market. The franchise agreement typically imposes a duty on the franchisee to select a site for the location of the business. The franchisor often lends some

amount of assistance in the site selection process and invariably has the right to reject a site located by the franchisee. A franchisor must develop specific criteria to assist in determining whether a site selected by the franchisee is acceptable. Some of the factors considered by franchisors in such a determination include size of the site, suitability of the location and the surrounding area for the type of business being franchised, adequacy of parking, costs of development, zoning and traffic patterns, proximity and access to major thoroughfares, compatibility with other businesses in the area, and proximity to competing businesses.

Franchisors that have well-developed site selection criteria coupled with clear, fair, and flexible territorial provisions in the franchise agreement have far fewer problems with their franchisees in the enforcement of performance standards, fewer disputes pertaining to territorial encroachment, and, when necessary, fewer problems terminating problematic franchisees.

3. *Royalty payment and reporting.* The typical franchise agreement imposes various requirements on the franchisee to pay an ongoing royalty, file periodic reports, and maintain certain accounting information. Certain reports are needed to enable the franchisor to determine whether royalties are being calculated correctly, whether contributions to funds for advertising are being timely paid, and whether gross sales are accurately reported.

A clearly written franchise agreement sets forth the manner and time of such reporting, and the franchisor must act swiftly and efficiently to enforce these deadlines. As soon as a royalty or an advertising payment is overdue or an accounting report is tardy, the franchisor should notify the franchisee and demand compliance with the appropriate provision of the franchise agreement. Repeated failures by the franchisee to pay or to report may justify termination of the franchise agreement.

Franchisors should be vigilant in observing and documenting these defaults, as they may be warning signs of a failing franchisee who is in need of extra supervision and monitoring or of some other problem with either the system or the form of the reports. Failure to properly and in a timely manner notify a franchisee may result in an assertion by the franchisee that the franchisor has given up or waived its right to insist on timely compliance with payment and record keeping deadlines.

Royalties and reports become the financial and information lifeline of the franchisor. Compliance by the franchisees should be strictly enforced by the franchisor.

4. *Mismanagement of advertising funds.* Many franchisors require that all franchisees pay an advertising fee for regional and/or national promotions and advertising programs. Fees paid into the advertising fund should be kept separate from the funds used by franchisors for their operating expenses and from the funds allocated by the franchisors for advertising to attract new franchisees. Franchisors who experience temporary financial difficulties are often inclined to "borrow" from the advertising fund until their financial condition improves. Such

"borrowing" will give rise to litigation based on the failure of the franchisor to use the funds for the specified purposes.

5. *Supervision and support.* While franchisees are usually independent individuals who desire to operate a business for themselves, they are also attracted to franchising because of the guidance and support offered by a franchisor who offers an established and proven business concept. A successful franchisor not only meets the contractual commitments established by the franchise agreement but typically goes beyond the agreement to offer additional support and supervision to the franchisees. This increased support results in two bonuses to the franchisor: Such supervision alerts the franchisor to difficulties a franchisee may be having (the "monitoring" function) and demonstrates the franchisor's commitment to the system (which never hurts when prospective franchisees are talking to existing franchisees). While overzealous supervision by a franchisor is usually not needed and in fact may interfere with a franchisee's ability to run the business, maintaining routine phone contact and making occasional visits to the franchisee's place of business show a willingness to assist with problems and offer assurance that the franchisor is committed to the franchisee's goals. A lack of such support often leads to conflict in the system and ultimately to litigation.

Support by the franchisor can be made available through regular meetings and seminars, newsletters, conventions, retraining programs, and published materials related to the franchised business. Franchisors should take advantage of current communications technologies, such as modem lines, portable telephones, and facsimile machines, in building franchise support systems. Franchisors should respond promptly and in writing to specific questions and concerns of franchisees. Failure to respond to and to manage the franchisees does not make the problem go away but only compounds it by creating an adversarial relationship between the parties. In this regard, franchisors should not attempt to interfere with or impede franchisees' efforts to form a franchisee association, and, in fact, many states specifically declare any such interference to be unlawful.

Franchisors can also support franchisees by offering to provide management consulting services for special projects and general assistance at specified fees. Communication between the parties and support and assistance from the franchisor serve not only to promote harmonious relations between the franchisor and franchisee but negate any argument that the franchisor is interested only in the initial franchise fee and not in a long-term and mutually satisfactory relationship.

Meeting the service and support obligations of the agreement not only leads to happy and productive franchisees but also to a rock-solid defense in many types of subsequent litigation. The average dispute between a franchisor and franchisee almost always involves an allegation that the franchisor failed to provide critical services. Franchisors should always be fully prepared to demonstrate that this type of allegation has no merit.

6. *Quality control.* The essence of a successful franchisor is the protection of its business format, image, and trademarks, as well as the high quality and

nature of the goods and services sold and the uniformity of its business operations. The franchisor must strictly protect and defend these interests, as failure to
do so will result in a weakened system with no identifiable image. Franchisors
with a need for increased revenues are often tempted to force a franchisee to
purchase goods, services, supplies, fixtures, equipment, and inventory from the
franchisor on the basis that such items are integral to the franchisor's system and
cannot be obtained elsewhere. Because courts strictly scrutinize a franchisor's
requirements that franchisees purchase supplies only from the franchisor, many
franchisors no longer sell supplies but rather regulate the items franchisees purchase by requiring that franchisees utilize suppliers approved by the franchisor or
purchase in accordance with specifications designated by the franchisor. Many
franchisors pass through to the franchisees any discounts or rebates received by
the franchisor from its suppliers. This practice greatly allays any misgivings the
franchisee may have that the franchisor is unfairly or excessively profiting on the
sale of items that can be easily obtained from other suppliers at a lower cost.

Franchisors need to ensure that franchisees do not substitute unapproved
goods or items in place of those that meet the franchisor's quality control standards. Such action by franchisees erodes the goodwill and regional or national
recognition that make the franchised business distinctive from other business and,
if not stopped by the franchisor, signal other franchisees that the franchisor is not
interested in protecting their investment in the system. Similarly, franchisees adversely react to any attempts by the franchisor to be overly greedy in the sale of
required products or services when the franchisor or an affiliate is the sole source
of supply.

7. *Unequal treatment.* While there may be circumstances that justify a decision by a franchisor to offer to one franchisee only a benefit, such as a grace
period for the payment of royalties by a financially troubled franchisee, such
advantages should be offered sparingly and only after a thorough analysis of the
situation. Franchisees expect the system to operate uniformly, and any perceived
arbitrariness or inequality in treatment leads to resentment and hostility by other
franchisees, especially when the favorable treatment is afforded to company-
owned stores. In addition to creating an atmosphere of tension, any deviation by
the franchisor from established operating procedures also raises the issue whether
the franchisor has waived or forgone the right to demand compliance with the
franchise agreement.

Just as some franchisees should not be singled out for special treatment,
those franchisees who are difficult and demanding should not be subject to any
form of treatment that could be viewed as retaliatory or discriminatory. Any defaults or breaches of the franchise agreement by troublesome franchisees should
be carefully documented and should be handled strictly in accordance with the
franchise agreement. Franchisees who have made valid complaints against the
franchisor or the system may not be subjected to any practice that a court would
interpret as a reprisal for exercising their contractual rights. Such retaliatory treatment by franchisors leads only to litigation and further disruption of the system.

8. *The transfer and renewal process.* A franchisee who desires to sell the franchised business should be assisted by the franchisor, since an unhappy or unmotivated franchisee is an unproductive franchisee who weakens the system. The franchisor may be able to steer potential buyers to the franchisee or might even consider purchasing the location and operating it as a company-owned store until a suitable purchaser can be found. The decision to purchase a franchisee's business, however, should be carefully evaluated by the franchisor, because word of the repurchase will invariably spread to other franchisees who may believe that such a practice is the established policy of the franchisor and an absolute right of a disgruntled or noncomplying franchisee. In the event a franchisee presents a prospective purchaser to the franchisor for approval, the franchisor must ensure that the purchaser satisfies the selection criteria established by the franchisor for all applicants. Recent court decisions have held that a "reasonableness" requirement should be read into the franchise agreement and that the franchisor should not be allowed to reject a transfer arbitrarily without reference to reasonable and objective standards. If the purchaser fails to meet the objective standards and fails to qualify, written notification should be provided to the franchisee explaining the basis for the rejection.

Similarly, refusal to renew a franchise or insistance on seemingly unreasonable standards for renewal can lead to hostility if the franchisor's reasons for nonrenewal are unreasonable or self-serving (such as the desire to take back the location for itself or to transfer to a more willing buyer) or if the criteria and conditions for renewal are overly stringent. No franchisee wants to feel that after ten loyal years of operation and development of the local market, she must now "repurchase her own franchise" or jump through fifty hoops as a condition to renewal. Franchisors should strictly enforce any conditions to renewal that were set forth in the original offering circular provided to the franchisee, as well as insist on any changes that are necessary to meet current system standards. However, renewal conditions that include: (a) significant capital expenditures for refurbishment, equipment, or new signage; (b) material changes in the economic relationship between the parties; or (c) adjustments to the franchisee's territory will surely lead to conflict and dispute.

9. *Record keeping and compliance.* While the goal of every successful franchisor is to manage the business rather than to manage disputes, when disputes arise the franchisor should be well prepared to discuss and resolve the conflict. This cannot be accomplished unless the franchisor has maintained comprehensive records, including notes on all conversations, telephone message slips, memos reflecting understandings reached at meetings, correspondence between the franchisor and franchisee, copies of all documents provided to or received from the franchisee, and copies of all inspection reports and notices to the franchisee. The franchisor should develop procedures for such record keeping and file management and designate a reliable individual to assume responsibility for document control. Meetings with a troubled franchisee should be attended by at least two of

the franchisor's employees who can later verify the nature of the meeting and what was said.

10. *Rapid growth*. While the initial dream of many early-stage franchisors is to award "as many franchises as we can as fast as we can," franchising veterans will tell you that rapid growth can lead to early and certain death of a company. Franchisors who are too focused on sales rather than support, on quantity rather than on quality, and on making themselves rich instead of making their franchisees happy are destined for failure. The problems created by undercapitalization, lack of adequate field support, lack of well-defined prospective franchisee screening and selection criteria, lack of a strong management team, or lack of strategic direction or focus will spread like cancer throughout the franchise system if they are not cured immediately and detected early on.

Rapid growth *will* feed the ego of the founder, fuel headlines in the media, improve the short-term health of the financial statements, and make the sales staff fat and happy. However, without an adequate infrastructure and philosophical commitment to the long-term best interests of the franchisees through effective support and training systems, the company will not be a long-term fixture in the franchising community.

Litigation Planning and Strategy

If a franchisor determines that litigation is the most sensible and efficient way to resolve a business dispute or if a franchisee brings suit, the franchisor must develop plans and strategies, keeping in mind the following principles:

▲ The franchisor must develop goals and objectives and communicate them to legal counsel. A broad strategy such as "kick the franchisee out" is not sufficient. Rather, counsel must be made aware of any specific business objectives, budgetary limitations, or time constraints that affect the franchisor well before the litigation is initiated.

▲ The franchisor must gather all documents relevant to the dispute and organize them in advance of the time that the opponent serves the first discovery request.

▲ The franchisor should explore alternative methods of dispute resolution, clearly define parameters for settlement, and communicate them to legal counsel.

▲ The franchisor should discuss with legal counsel the risks, costs, and benefits of entering into litigation.

▲ The franchisor should review with counsel the terms of payment of legal fees (as well as those of any experts needed).

▲ The franchisor should review the terms of its insurance policies with its risk management team to determine whether there is insurance coverage for its defense costs or for meeting any judgment rendered against the franchisor.

▲ The franchisor should develop a litigation management system for monitoring and controlling costs.

▲ The franchisor should maintain clear lines of communication with legal counsel throughout all phases of the litigation and should appoint a responsible individual to serve as a liaison with counsel.

While litigation of franchise disputes does not significantly differ from litigation of other matters, the decision to resolve a dispute through litigation must be based on a genuine understanding of the legal rights, remedies, and defenses available. For example, suppose that a franchise has stopped paying royalties with the argument that payment of royalties is excused by the franchisor's failure to provide adequate field support and supervision. Before filing a complaint to terminate the franchise agreement, the franchisor should carefully review:

▲ Alternative methods for resolving the dispute
▲ The elements of proving a breach of the franchise agreement in the jurisdiction that governs the agreement
▲ The defenses that will be raised by the franchisee, such as lack of field support and supervision
▲ The perception and opinions of the other franchisees to this litigation
▲ The direct and indirect costs of litigation
▲ The damages that may be received if a breach is successfully established
▲ The probability that the location can be easily sold to a new franchisee if the franchise agreement is terminated

Only after the franchisor is satisfied that the answers to these issues indicate that litigation is a viable alternative should formal action be pursued. Similarly, if the franchisor is sued by a franchisee, it should attempt to resolve the dispute before responding with a formal answer.

Alternatives to Litigation

Franchise dispute litigation is invariably time-consuming and expensive, and a franchisor may be portrayed by adverse counsel in any of a number of unflattering ways designed to engender jury support—as a huge impersonal corporate entity with no feeling for the small and defenseless franchisee; as a greedy corporate conglomerate interested in filling its coffers at the expense of its loyal and diligent franchisees; as a vindictive and retaliatory entity motivated to get even with a franchisee who has merely exercised his contractual rights; or as a poorly managed business that has mishandled its affairs, leading to the ruin of its franchisees. Because litigation involves these drawbacks and uncertainties, many franchisors seek to resolve their disputes with franchisees through alternative methods.

The many alternatives to litigation are broadly referred to as ''alternative dispute resolution'' (ADR) methods. Each method offers certain advantages and disadvantages that may make one process far more appropriate for resolving a particular dispute than another. Legal counsel can suggest the best ADR for each particular dispute.

    ▲ *Arbitration.* Because franchise disputes often involve complex issues that are not readily disposed of and because the issues arise in a business context that lacks jury appeal, many franchisors prefer to arbitrate rather than to litigate, and their agreements contain provisions requiring the submission of disputes to arbitration. These provisions are generally enforced by courts (assuming the party who seeks to arbitrate the dispute hasn't waived this right by an express statement or conduct that implies the party intends not to enforce the right to arbitrate).

    There are many forms of arbitration. However, each is a process for parties in dispute to submit arguments and evidence in an informal and nonpublic fashion to a neutral person or persons, who will adjudicate their differences. The evidentiary and procedural rules are not nearly as formal as in litigation, and there tends to be greater flexibility in the timing of the proceedings and the selection of the actual decision makers.

    Arbitration may be a voluntary proceeding that the parties have selected prior to any dispute. To help avoid litigation, ensure that arbitration clauses appear in all agreements with franchisees, especially the franchise agreement and any guaranty executed by a franchisee. These clauses should specify:

    ▲ The place of arbitration
    ▲ The method of selecting arbitrators
    ▲ Any limitations on the award that may be rendered by the arbitrator
    ▲ Which party will be responsible for the costs of the proceedings
    ▲ That the arbitration award can be enforced in court
    ▲ Any special procedural rules that will govern the arbitration

    A key factor in arbitration is whether the arbitrator's decision will be binding. If both parties agree that the award will be binding, they must accept the results. Binding arbitration awards are usually enforceable by the local court, unless there has been a defect in the arbitration procedures. In contrast, the opinion rendered in a nonbinding arbitration is advisory only. The parties may either accept the result or reject the award and proceed with litigation. In this event, the parties have forgone any benefits of arbitration; it serves only as a dress rehearsal for a trial. Another drawback of nonbinding arbitration is that after the award is made, the losing party often threatens litigation (a trial de novo, or new trial) unless the monetary award is adjusted. Thus, the party that wins the arbitration is often coerced into paying more or accepting less than it was awarded simply to avoid a trial after arbitration.

    Unless the plaintiff, the defendant, and their legal counsel have specific rules and procedures in mind that will govern the arbitration, it is often best to follow the Commercial Arbitration Rules of the American Arbitration Association. To obtain copies of AAA rules and fees, write to the AAA at its national office, 140 West 51st Street, New York, New York 10020-1203, or call (212) 484-4000.

The services of the AAA are being utilized in disputes between franchisors and franchisees in ever-increasing numbers. In 1989 there was a 550 percent increase, representing 401 cases, over the mere seventy-three franchise disputes arbitrated during 1981. New York City had the largest number of arbitrated disputes in 1989, with ninety-eight cases, followed by Los Angeles with forty-five and its suburb Orange County, California, with thirty. The AAA expects its caseload to continue to rise with the continued growth of franchising. The franchisor-franchisee disputes arbitrated in the thirty-five AAA offices throughout the United States typically involve issues such as failure to pay fees or to make reports, termination, territorial disputes, and failure to comply with contract provisions. Franchisors who wish to arbitrate disputes with franchisees may use the following clause recommended by the AAA:

> Any controversy or claim arising out of or relating to this contract, or the breach thereof, shall be settled by arbitration in accordance with the Commercial Arbitration Rules of the American Arbitration Association, and judgment rendered upon the award rendered by the arbitrator(s) may be entered in any court having jurisdiction thereof.

When AAA services are used, the plaintiff and the defendant are presented with a list of several AAA-sponsored arbitrators. Resumes of arbitrators are provided so the parties may select an individual experienced in the area of the dispute rather than rely on jurors who may not have the requisite business background to evaluate the various documents and testimony that will be introduced. The parties then eliminate the arbitrators they prefer not to use until they select one who is mutually acceptable. A date for the arbitration is selected in a similar fashion. Arbitration under AAA rules is somewhat more formal than court-annexed arbitration but is less rigid than a trial.

Court-annexed arbitration is court-ordered, nonbinding arbitration. The plaintiff and the defendant jointly agree on and select an arbitrator from a list of arbitrators on file with the court. The parties, therefore, can select an arbitrator who is an attorney with expertise in the area of the dispute. There usually is no fee or only a moderate fee.

In a jurisdiction in which the parties and attorneys know each other, conflicts of interest can often arise, particularly when the attorney who will arbitrate has or has had a social or business relationship with one of the other attorneys. The arbitrator selected should then withdraw from hearing the matter unless both parties consent to her participation. In smaller communities, it may be extremely difficult to locate an experienced arbitrator who is unknown to both parties.

Because the arbitrator selected is usually an attorney whose expertise may be negotiating rather than adjudicating, arbitration often results in ''splitting the baby down the middle,'' not providing a clear award for one party or the other. Additionally, because no jury is involved, the likelihood of recovering punitive or exemplary damages from an attorney or an experienced arbitrator who is unlikely to be swayed by appeals to emotion rather than reason is reduced. As a result, some franchisors prefer to specify in the franchise agreement that only certain kinds of disputes will be submitted to arbitration (e.g., disputes relating to non-payment of monies due to the franchisor), while other types of disputes (those that might result in punitive or exemplary damages or those that require injunctive relief or that have jury appeal) will be litigated.

▴ *Private judging.* In many communities, retired judges are available at an hourly fee (often as high as $250) to hear and resolve disputes. Parties may agree in advance whether the decision will be legally binding.

The disadvantages of nonbinding arbitration apply to nonbinding private judging. While private judging costs are substantially higher than court-annexed arbitration costs, private judging is considerably more flexible. A private judge may be retained without court intervention and without litigation first being instituted. The parties are free to select a judge and a mutually convenient date for the hearing. The hearing itself tends to be informal, and the rules of evidence are not strictly applied. The private judge often uses a settlement conference approach, as opposed to a trial approach, to achieve a resolution of the dispute.

▴ *Moderated settlement conferences.* After litigation begins, a court may insist that parties participate in settlement discussions before a judge. If the court does not schedule a settlement conference, the parties can usually request one, often with a particular judge.

The attorneys are often required to prepare settlement briefs to inform the judge of each party's contentions, theories, and claimed damages. Parties, as well as attorneys, attend so the judge may explain his view of the case and obtain their consent to any proposed settlement. If a resolution is reached in the judge's chambers, the litigants often proceed to the courtroom so that the settlement (and the parties' consent to it) can be entered in the record to eliminate any further disputes.

Because moderated settlement conferences produce no out-of-pocket costs (other than attorneys' fees) and because information obtained or revealed is for settlement purposes only, they provide an excellent last-ditch effort for resolving a dispute prior to trial.

▴ *Mediation.* Mediation differs substantially from arbitration. An arbitrator renders a decision that is often binding; a mediator only makes suggestions or recommendations to resolve a dispute. Mediation costs are minimal and generally include only payment on an hourly basis to the mediator for his services. However, because the mediator has no authority to render a binding decision, the mediation process is effective only if both parties are committed to achieving a voluntary resolution. The participants always have the ultimate authority in the mediation process, and they are free to reject any suggestion by the mediator.

▴ *Small claims matters*. Matters that involve a small monetary amount (usually no greater than $2,500) are often best resolved in small claims court. Generally, litigants represent themselves and describe the dispute in an informal manner to a judge, who renders a decision at the time of the hearing. Court filing fees are moderate, and a trial date usually is set for within two or three months. Often a bookkeeper or credit manager may represent the franchisor as long as he is knowledgeable about the dispute and has supporting documentation.

Unfortunately, it is often difficult for a successful plaintiff to actually collect the judgment. Because of this, many courts have small claims advisers who can assist litigants in collecting the money awarded.

24

Trademark Registration and Protection

Deborah E. Bouchoux, Silver, Freedman & Taff

The foundation of every successful business is the company's intellectual property, which has been developed, improved, and expanded over the years to create a readily identifiable concept, product, or service. If proper steps are not taken by a business enterprise to protect this intellectual property, including the company's trademarks, it will be extremely difficult to achieve growth objectives, because competitors will be free to use the company's trademarks and consumers will be confused as to the source and origin of the products offered or services provided by the company.

Trademarks and Service Marks

A trademark or service mark is a word, name, symbol, or device used to indicate the origin and ownership of a product or service. A trademark is used in the advertising and marketing of a product, whereas a service mark typically identifies a service. A trademark or service mark identifies and distinguishes the products or services of one person from those of another person.

A trademark also provides a guarantee of a product's or service's quality and consistency. It assures the consumer that the products and services purchased today at one location are of the same quality as those purchased at another location. Consumer recognition of and confidence in the product or service identified by the trademark is the lifeline of a successful franchise system.

In a franchise system, the franchisor grants the franchisee a *nonexclusive* license to use the franchisor's trademarks in connection with the franchisee's sale of the products and services or with the identification of the business that constitutes the franchise system.

Types of Marks

Not all words, phrases, or symbols are entitled to protection under the trademark laws. For example, a chain of stores that sells books could not obtain a registered trademark for ''bookstore'' because the name is too generic, yet B. Dalton Bookseller is a nationally recognized mark for the same services. As a rule, the mark may not be generic in nature or merely descriptive of the type of products or services it identifies. Marks that are generally protectable are those that are coined, fanciful, arbitrary, or suggestive; in certain cases, descriptive marks may also be registered:

▴ *Arbitrary, coined, or fanciful*. This is the strongest category of mark that can be protected. The trademark is either a coined word, such as *Xerox*, or a word in common usage that has no meaning when applied to the goods and services in question, such as *Camel* for cigarettes or tobacco products. Such marks are inherently distinctive for legal and registration purposes; however, as a result of the obscurity of the mark, the burden is on the manufacturer to establish goodwill.

▴ *Suggestive*. A suggestive mark requires the consumer to use some degree of imagination in determining what product or service is identified by the mark and is the next strongest category of mark that may be protected. Owners of suggestive trademarks are usually not required to establish ''secondary meaning'' (see below). Examples of suggestive marks include *Seven-up* and *Orange Crush*, which merely suggest that they identify refreshing beverages.

▴ *Descriptive*. Trademarks that are descriptive of the goods or services they identify cannot be protected unless the manufacturer can establish distinctiveness, that is, can demonstrate that the public associates a particular mark with the goods of a specific producer (known as secondary meaning). This category includes names like *Holiday Inn* for motels, which is descriptive but nevertheless registered because it is distinctive.

There are also a host of marks that will be refused registration. They include marks that:

▴ Are immoral, deceptive, or scandalous
▴ May disparage or falsely suggest a connection with persons, institutions, beliefs, or national symbols or bring them into contempt or disrepute
▴ Consist of or simulate the flag or coat of arms or other insignia of the United States or a state or municipality or any foreign nation
▴ Consist of the name, portrait, or signature of a particular living individual unless the person has given written consent; or that feature the name, signature, or portrait of a deceased president of the United States during the life of his widow, unless she has given her consent
▴ So resemble a mark already registered in the United States Patent and Trademark Office (USPTO) that they are likely, when applied to the goods of the applicant, to cause confusion or to cause mistake or to deceive
▴ Are primarily geographically descriptive or deceptively purport to describe the goods or services of the applicant
▴ Consist primarily of a surname

A mark will not be refused registration on the grounds listed above if the applicant can show that, through use of the mark in commerce, the mark has become distinctive and that it now identifies to the public the applicant's products or services.

Protections Afforded by Registration

Trademark rights arise from either: (1) use of the mark, or (2) a bona fide intention to use the mark, along with the filing of an application to register the mark on the federal Principal Register. A federal trademark registration is not required in order for a trademark to be protected, and a mark may be used without securing registration. Although registration is not necessary, it does provide the following advantages:

- The right to use the filing date of the application as a constructive date of first use of the mark in commerce (this gives the registrant nationwide priority as of that date, unless there are certain prior users or prior applicants)
- The right to bring legal action in federal court for trademark infringement
- The possibility of recovery of profits, damages, and costs in a federal court infringement action and the possibility of triple damages and recovery of attorneys' fees
- The right to constructive notice of a claim of ownership (which eliminates a good faith defense for a party adopting the trademark subsequent to the registrant's date of registration)
- The right to deposit the registration with the United States Customs Department in order to stop the importation of goods bearing an infringing mark
- The right to use the registration as prima facie evidence of the registrant's ownership of the mark and her exclusive right to use the mark in commerce in connection with the goods or services specified in the certificate
- The possibility of incontestability, in which case the registration constitutes conclusive evidence of the registrant's exclusive right, with certain limited exceptions, to use the registered mark in commerce
- Partial protection against attacks on the registration once it is five years old
- The availability of criminal penalties and triple damages in an action for counterfeiting a registered trademark
- A basis for filing trademark applications in foreign countries

A mark that is an actual use in commerce but that does not qualify for registration on the Principal Register for one or more reasons may be registered with the USPTO on the Supplemental Register. Registration on the Supplemental Register does not provide the mark the same level of protection afforded by registration on the Principal Register but does give the registrant:

- ▲ The right to sue in federal court and to obtain statutory remedies for infringement
- ▲ In foreign countries whose laws require prior registration in the home country, a possible right to foreign registration
- ▲ Protection against federal registration by another of the same or a confusingly similar mark
- ▲ The right to use the encircled ''R'' symbol on goods

Registration on the Supplemental Register allows the owner of the mark to put the world on notice of her use of and rights to the mark. Further, registration of a descriptive mark on the Supplemental Register may confer some protection during a period of time during which the mark's use increases to the point where it becomes so substantial as to cause the mark to acquire ''secondary meaning,'' thus qualifying for registration on the Principal Register. If registration on the Principal Register is denied, it may be advantageous for a start-up franchisor to take advantage of registration on the Supplemental Register until a few franchises are sold and the mark, through increased use, gains secondary meaning. This will bolster the marketability of the franchises much more than if a franchisor were to license an unregistered trademark.

The Registration Process

Prior to the passage of the Trademark Law Revision Act of 1988, federal registration of a trademark was possible only if the mark had actually been used in interstate commerce. This requirement was different than that of most other countries, which generally allow a company to register a mark even if no actual use has been established, and generally meant that a substantial amount of time and expense might be invested in a proposed trade identity for a new product or service, with virtually no assurance that the mark could ever be properly registered and protected.

Under the new law, a franchisor may file an application to register a trademark, based on either actual use or a ''bona fide intention'' to use the mark in interstate commerce. This allows the franchisor to conduct some market research and investigation without the need to put the mark into the stream of commerce as a prerequisite to obtaining federal protection.

A franchisor should first have a trademark search conducted to ensure that no other individual or company has secured rights in the trademark or in any similar mark for the same or related products or services to be offered by the franchisor. There are several nationally known companies that perform this service for a moderate fee.

The USPTO has developed guidelines for registration under the new "intent to use" provisions. The following three procedures have been established:

1. The company files an application for registration, which is subject to all of the current tests for registrability (e.g., likelihood of confusion, descriptiveness), *except for* proof of use in interstate commerce and the requirement for actual specimens of the mark. If the mark is used in interstate commerce prior to approval of the application by the examiner, an amendment to the application should be made to allege that use of the mark in interstate commerce has occurred.

2. When the application is approved by the examiner, a Notice of Allowance is issued to the applicant.

3. If actual use does not occur until after the application is approved, the applicant has six months from the date of the Notice of Allowance to actually use the mark in interstate commerce and to file a Statement of Use, with actual specimens attached. After review of the Statement of Use and of the specimens, USPTO will register the mark. An applicant may request extensions of time for filing the Statement of Use (up to four successive six-month periods). Failure to file by this deadline results in an abandonment of the mark.

The current application filing fee is $200. A sample trademark application is shown in Figure 24-1. Applicants typically retain attorneys who are familiar with the trademark registration process to prosecute the application. (Regardless of whether the franchisor has actually used the mark in commerce or has a bona fide intention to use the mark, the application process is substantially the same.) If the mark has been used in interstate commerce, the trademark application must be accompanied by three specimens showing how the mark is actually used. These may be labels, tags, advertisements, or brochures. A trademark examiner then reviews the application to determine if it meets the statutory requirements and whether similar trademarks have already been registered in the same or similar lines of business. The examiner's concerns are usually enumerated in a formal Office Action. It is then incumbent on legal counsel to respond to all of the concerns of the examiner. This process continues until the application is either finally refused or recommended by the examiner for publication in the Official Gazette. This publication serves as notice to the general public. Individuals who believe that they would be injured by registration of the trademark may file a Notice of Opposition within thirty days of the publication date. Failure of the parties to resolve their differences results in a hearing before the Trademark Trial and Appeal Board (TTAB). The TTAB is also the appropriate body to which to appeal a final refusal by the USPTO to register the mark. If no opposition is filed or if the applicant is successful at the TTAB, the mark is then registered on the Principal Register.

Registration is a complex and often lengthy process, taking from twelve to eighteen months even if there are only minimal problems, but the commercial rewards may be substantial if the registered mark is properly used to provide the franchisor with a competitive edge. A registration is effective for ten years but may be renewed for additional ten year-terms thereafter so long as it is still in actual use in interstate commerce. The registration may, however, be cancelled after six years unless an affidavit of continued use is filed with the USPTO between years five and six demonstrating that the registrant has not abandoned the trademark.

Maintaining Rights in the Trademarks

Because a trademark provides consumers a guarantee of quality, the owner of a trademark is responsible for protecting and ensuring the quality of the products or services associated with the trademark. For a franchisor that has licensed its trademark to franchisees who may be located all over the country, maintaining a high level of quality in the products and services identified by the mark is certainly a challenge.

Along with the rights that come with owning a registered trademark come responsibilities. The licensor/franchisor must actively police the mark to ensure that an established level of quality is maintained by its licensees/franchisees. A carefully drafted license/franchise agreement should set forth, in detail, the specific obligations of the franchisee with respect to the trademarks. The license/franchise agreement must provide the franchisor with supervisory control over the product or service represented by the mark. If such controls are not retained by the franchisor, the "naked" license of the trademarks may be found to be invalid. It is, therefore, imperative that a franchisor provide its franchisees with guidelines for use of the trademarks and with guidance on maintaining quality and uniformity in products and services.

PROTECTING TRADEMARKS UNDER THE FRANCHISE AGREEMENT

Every franchise agreement should have a section devoted to the proper use and care of the franchisor's trademarks. This section should specify:

- The identity of the trademarks that the franchisor licenses its franchisees to use.
- That the franchisee shall use only the trademarks designated by the franchisor and shall use them only in the manner required or authorized and permitted by the franchisor.
- That the franchisee shall use the marks only in connection with the right and license to operate the business granted to the franchisee.
- That, during the term of the franchise agreement and any renewal thereof, the franchisee shall identify itself as a licensee and not the owner of the

(*Text continues on page 332.*)

Figure 24-1.   Sample trademark application.   [*Front*]

| TRADEMARK/SERVICE MARK APPLICATION, PRINCIPAL REGISTER, WITH DECLARATION (Corporation) | MARK (*identify the mark*) |
| | CLASS NO. (*if known*) |

TO THE COMMISSIONER OF PATENTS AND TRADEMARKS:

NAME OF CORPORATION

STATE OR COUNTRY OF INCORPORATION

BUSINESS ADDRESS OF CORPORATION

The above identified applicant has adopted and is using the trademark/service mark shown in the accompanying drawing for the following goods/services: _____

_____

and requests that said mark be registered in the United States Patent and Trademark Office on the Principal Register established by the Act of July 5, 1946.

The trademark/service mark was first used on the goods/services on _____ ;
                                                                                    (*date*)
was first used on the goods/services in _____ commerce on _____ ; and is
                                        (*type of commerce*)   (*date*)
now in use in such commerce.

The mark is used by applying it to _____

_____

and five specimens showing the mark as actually used are presented herewith.

_____
                          (*name of officer of corporation*)

being hereby warned that willful false statements and the like so made are punishable by fine or imprisonment, or both, under Section 1001 of Title 18 of the United States Code and that such willful false statements may jeopardize the validity of the application or any registration resulting therefrom, declares that he/she is

_____
                          (*official title*)

of applicant corporation and is authorized to execute this instrument on behalf of said corporation; he/she believes said corporation to be the owner of the trademark/service mark sought to be registered; to the best of his/her knowledge and belief no other person, firm, corporation, or association has the right to use said mark in commerce, either in the identical form or in such near resemblance thereto as may be likely, when applied to the goods of such other person, to cause confusion, or to cause mistake, or to deceive; the facts set forth in this application are true; and all statements made of his/her own knowledge are true and all statements made on information and belief are believed to be true.

_____
                          (*name of corporation*)
By _____
                          (*signature of officer of corporation, and official title of officer*)

_____
                          (*contact telephone number*)

_____
                          (*date*)

[Back]

DECLARATION

The undersigned being hereby warned that willful false statements and the like so made are punishable by fine or imprisonment, or both, under 18 U.S.C. 1001, and that such willful false statements may jeopardize the validity of the application or any resulting registration, declares that he/she is properly authorized to execute this application on behalf of the applicant; he/she believes the applicant to be the owner of the trademark/service mark sought to be registered, or, if the application is being filed under 15 U.S.C. 1051(b), he/she believes applicant to be entitled to use such mark in commerce; to the best of his/her knowledge and belief no other person, firm, corporation, or association has the right to use the above identified mark in commerce, either in the identical form thereof or in such near resemblance thereto as to be likely, when used on or in connection with the goods/services of such other person, to cause confusion, or to cause mistake, or to deceive; and that all statements made of his/her own knowledge are true and all statements made on information and belief are believed to be true.

_____   _____
Date   Signature

_____   _____
Telephone Number   Print or Type Name and Position

INSTRUCTIONS AND INFORMATION FOR APPLICANT

To receive a filing date, the application must be completed and signed by the applicant and submitted along with:

1. The prescribed fee for each class of goods/services listed in the application;
2. A drawing of the mark in conformance with 37 CFR 2.52;
3. If the application is based on use of the mark in commerce, three (3) specimens (evidence) of the mark as used in commerce for each class of goods/services listed in the application. All three specimens may be the same and may be in the nature of: (a) labels showing the mark which are placed on the goods; (b) a photograph of the mark as it appears on the goods, (c) brochures or advertisements showing the mark as used in connection with the services.

Verification of the application - The application must be signed in order for the application to receive a filing date. Only the following person may sign the verification (Declaration) for the application, depending on the applicant's legal entity: (1) the individual applicant; (b) an officer of the corporate applicant; (c) one general partner of a partnership applicant; (d) all joint applicants.

Additional information concerning the requirements for filing an application are available in a booklet entitled Basic Facts about Trademarks, which may be obtained by writing:

U.S. DEPARTMENT OF COMMERCE
Patent and Trademark Office
Washington, D.C. 20231

Or by calling: (703) 557-INFO

This form is estimated to take 15 minutes to complete. Time will vary depending upon the needs of the individual case. Any comments on the amount of time you require to complete this form should be sent to the Office of Management and Organization, U.S. Patent and Trademark Office, U.S. Department of Commerce, Washington, D.C., 20231, and to the Office of Information and Regulatory Affairs, Office of Management and Budget, Washington, D.C. 20503.

trademarks and shall make any necessary filings under state law to reflect its status as a licensee. In addition, the franchisee shall be required to identify itself as a licensee of the trademarks on all invoices, order forms, receipts, business stationery, and contracts, as well as display a notice at the center in a form and at a location designated in writing by the franchisor.

▲ That the franchisee's right to use the trademarks is limited to those uses authorized under the franchise agreement and that any unauthorized use shall constitute both an infringement of the franchisor's rights and grounds for termination of the franchise agreement.

▲ That the franchisee shall not use the trademarks to incur or secure any obligation or indebtedness.

▲ That the franchisee shall not use the trademarks as part of its corporate or other legal name.

▲ That the franchisee shall comply with the franchisor's instructions in filing and maintaining the requisite trade name or fictitious name registrations and shall execute any documents deemed necessary by the franchisor or its counsel to obtain protection for the trademarks or to maintain their continued validity and enforceability.

▲ That the franchisee shall promptly notify the franchisor if any litigation involving the marks is instituted or threatened against the franchisee and shall cooperate fully in defending or settling such litigation.

Additionally, the franchisee should be required to expressly acknowledge that:

▲ The franchisor is the owner of all right, title, and interest in and to the trademarks and the goodwill associated with or symbolized by them.

▲ The trademarks are valid and serve to identify the franchisor's system and those who are licensed to operate a franchise in accordance with the system.

▲ The franchisee shall not directly or indirectly contest the validity of the franchisor's ownership of the trademarks.

▲ The franchisee's use of the trademarks under the franchise agreement does not give the franchisee any ownership interest or other interest in or to the trademarks, except a nonexclusive license.

▲ Any and all goodwill arising from the franchisee's use of the trademarks in accordance with the franchisor's system shall inure solely and exclusively to the franchisor's benefit and that upon expiration or termination of the franchise agreement no monetary amount shall be assigned as attributable to any goodwill associated with the franchisee's use of the system or the trademarks.

▲ The license and rights to use the trademarks granted to the franchisee are nonexclusive and that the franchisor thus may: (a) itself use, and grant franchises and licenses to others to use, the trademarks; (b) establish, develop, and franchise other systems, different from the system licensed to the franchisee, without offering or providing the franchisee any rights in, to, or under these other systems; and (c) modify or change, in whole or in part, any aspect of the trademarks so long as the franchisee's rights are in no way materially harmed.

▲ The franchisor reserves the right to substitute different names and trademarks for use in identifying the system, the franchise, and other franchised businesses operating under the franchisor's system.

▲ The franchisor shall have no liability to the franchisee for any senior users that may claim rights to the franchisor's trademarks.

▲ The franchisee shall not register or attempt to register the trademarks in the franchisee's name or that of any other person, business, entity, or corporation.

TRADEMARK PROTECTION AND QUALITY CONTROL PROGRAM

Every franchisor should develop an active trademark compliance and protection program designed to educate the franchisor's field staff, key vendors, advisors, officers, and employees and all of its franchisees on the proper usage and protection of the trademarks. Development of a franchise agreement that imposes all of the obligations described in this chapter is a vital component of this program but alone is insufficient to prevent misuse of the trademarks and to enforce quality control standards. A trademark use compliance manual containing more detailed guidelines for proper trademark usage, grammar, and quality also plays an important role in a successful trademark protection program. Many trademarks have been converted into generic terms by the owner's failure conspicuously to identify the mark as a trade name for a product or service rather than as the generic product or service itself. Well-documented examples include *thermos, cellophane*, and *escalator*, all of which were once brand names and all of which were converted into ordinary nouns by improper generic usage. The compliance manual may reproduce a section of the franchisor's operations manual and should address the following four items:

1. Proper display of the marks (use of an encircled R, TM, or SM symbol)
2. Required state filings (fictitious name registrations) to be made by the franchisee to reflect its status as a licensee of the marks, and instructions for making these filings
3. All documents, correspondence, and other materials on which the franchisee must display the trademarks and identify itself as a licensee
4. All authorized uses and all prohibited uses of the marks

A sample compliance manual is shown in Figure 24-2.
In addition to developing a compliance manual, franchisors should create

Figure 24-2. Sample compliance manual and trademark notice.

A mark that is registered with the USPTO should always be shown in conjunction with a notice stating that fact. While a full registration notice such as "Registered in the U.S. Patent and Trademark Office" is acceptable, the short form (the letter "R" enclosed in a circle) is more often used. This simple registration symbol serves to inform the public that the mark is subject to federal registration. You must always display the mark with the symbol ® or the full registration notice.

The symbol ® should appear to the right of and slightly above the mark itself. The symbol need not be obtrusive; if you repeat the mark several times in any one brochure or advertisement, you need display it only with the first or most prominent use of the mark. Alternatively, you can display the mark with an asterisk and provide the information that the mark is a registered trademark in a note at the bottom of the page.

Style

The mark should be displayed in a manner that makes it clear that the mark is not being used in a generic fashion. Make sure that the mark is displayed in the form and style shown by the franchisor in its own brochures and promotional materials.

In the event you use the mark in other written materials, such as letters and other correspondence, and you cannot identify the mark with the ® symbol, you should always capitalize the words in the mark or put the mark in quotation marks to make it clear that you are referring to a brand name rather than a generic name.

Consistency

The mark should be displayed in a consistent manner. The addition of words or symbols to the mark dilutes the mark and leads to the conclusion that the franchisor has abandoned its original mark and is now using some other nonregistered form of the mark.

Usage

Avoid using the mark by itself. Always follow the mark with a generic noun or a description of the services the mark identifies. When other words or designs appear near the mark, leave sufficient room to allow the mark to stand out clearly.

Infringing Uses

Be aware of infringing uses of the mark by competitors and others. Under the Trademark Act of 1946, proof of infringement requires a demonstration by the owner of a registered mark that some third party is using a reproduction or imitation of the registered mark in connection with the offer or sale of goods and services in such a way to cause confusion, mistake, or deception from the perspective of the ordinary purchaser. You may observe competing uses in trade publications, the business press, and the marketing materials of competitors. Notify the franchisor of any use of any mark that you believe may cause such confusion, mistake, or deception so the franchisor can oppose those uses and thereby maintain the distinctiveness and validity of the mark.

Misuse of the Mark

Failing to display the mark properly or to notify the public that the mark is registered (either with the ® symbol or a written statement), using the mark as a generic description of the franchisor's services, varying the mark, and failing to capitalize the mark or to place it in quotes in your writings are all misuses of the mark and may result in dilution of the mark.

Carefully review all advertising copy, brochures, and any other written materials to ensure that the mark is being properly displayed by your employees, representatives, and suppliers. Do not be satisfied with materials that are substantially correct. Total compliance is required to provide protection of this valuable asset.

---

strategies to monitor franchisees, competitors, and other third parties in order to detect and to prevent improper usage or potential infringement of the mark. A staff member of the franchisor should be designated to read trade publications, business press, marketing materials produced by competitors, and in-house production, labeling, and correspondence to ensure that the mark is properly used by franchisees and not stolen by competitors. If an infringing use is discovered by a clipping service, company field representative, franchisee, trade association, or supplier, then the franchisor must be vigilant in its protection of the marks. This requires working closely with trademark counsel to ensure that all potential infringers receive letters demanding that such practices be discontinued immediately and that infringing materials be destroyed. A sample cease-and-desist letter is shown in Figure 24-3. As much evidence as possible should be gathered on each potential infringer and accurate files kept to support the franchisor's case in the event that trademark infringement litigation is necessary to settle the dispute. The registrant considering litigation should carefully weigh the costs and likely result of the suit against the potential loss of goodwill and market share. It may

Figure 24-3. Sample cease-and-desist letter.

VIA REGISTERED/CERTIFIED U.S. MAIL
RETURN RECEIPT REQUESTED

_____
_____
_____

    RE: *Infringement of Service Mark*

Dear Sir/Madam:

    We are the owners of United States Patent and Trademark Office Registration Number ____ for _____. This federal trademark was registered _____ and alleged a date of first use of _____. For almost _____ (____) years we have been a nationally known _____ and have expended a great deal of time and money in establishing consumer recognition of and confidence in the products which are distributed under the mark _____.

    It has come to our attention that your company is operating under the name _____ for the marketing of its _____. Your company is marketing, distributing and selling these products under a name which is identical to or confusingly similar to _____, which is our federally registered mark. We have been provided with a newspaper advertisement which was apparently circulated in _____ and which identifies your company as the provider of a variety of _____. Such conduct has created and will continue to create a likelihood of confusion in the marketplace concerning the source and origin of your products due to their similarity to the products and supplies distributed by us as the owner of the registered mark.

    In view of the secondary meaning and strong consumer recognition our registered mark _____ has acquired, as well as the attendant likelihood of confusion caused by your unauthorized use of an identical or substantially similar mark, the conduct of your company constitutes an infringement and violation of our proprietary rights in our registered mark in violation of the Lanham Act, 15 U.S.C. § 1125(a), prohibiting false advertising, false designation of origin and false description. Additionally, your infringement of our rights in and to our registered mark may constitute unfair competition and trademark dilution as well as a deceptive trade practice under both federal and state laws. This unlawful and unpermitted conduct has caused and will continue to cause damage and irreparable injury to us as the confusion created in the marketplace will improperly divert sales from and otherwise cause monetary damage to us and will diminish the valuable goodwill associated with our federally registered mark.

    We therefore demand that you immediately cease and desist from marketing, selling or distributing any supplies or products under the name

_____ in any locality in which you are now using or have used the name _____. Failure to comply with the terms of this letter may subject you to the payment of damages for trademark infringement (which may be trebled by the court) as well as attorneys' fees and costs incurred by us in protecting our mark and enjoining your infringement of our proprietary mark.

Please contact us within seven (7) days of the date of this letter to confirm your compliance with the terms of this letter and to advise us of the specific measures taken to remedy this unauthorized infringement. Additionally, you should provide us with all materials which bear the mark as well as examples of how the mark is used so we can ensure that any infringing materials are properly destroyed.

We strongly urge you to contact us within the time specified in this letter to confirm your cessation of the use of the mark as an alternative to the greater exposure you may face by continued unpermitted use of our federally registered mark.

Govern yourself accordingly.

Very truly yours,

_____

be wiser to allocate those funds to advertising rather than to legal fees, especially if the likelihood of winning the case is remote.

Trademark Infringement and Dilution

The principal reason for a franchisor to maintain a trademark monitoring program is to guard against trademark infringement or dilution. Under the Lanham Act (also known as the Trademark Act of 1946) an owner of a registered mark who is seeking to prove infringement must demonstrate that some third party is using a reproduction or an imitation of the registered mark in connection with the offer or sale of goods and services in a way that is likely to cause confusion, mistake, or deception from the perspective of the ordinary purchaser.

The exact definition of the ''likelihood of confusion'' standard has been the subject of much debate over the years. The focus has always been on whether the ordinary purchaser of the product in question is likely to be confused as to the source, origin, or sponsorship of the product or service. A wide variety of factors has been listed by the courts as criteria for determining whether a likelihood of confusion exists. They include:

- The degree of similarity between the infringer's marks and the registered marks in terms of visual appearance, pronunciation, and interpretation
- The strength of the registered mark in the relevant industry or territory
- The actual or constructive intent of the infringer
- The similarity of the goods or services offered by the infringer and those offered by the owner of the registered mark
- The overlap (if any) in the distribution and marketing channels of the infringer and the owner of the registered mark
- The extent to which the owner of the registered mark can demonstrate that consumers were actually confused (usually demonstrated through consumer surveys and affidavits)

Many state trademark statutes provide owners of registered marks with an antidilution remedy. This remedy is available when a third party uses a mark in a manner that has the effect of "diluting" the distinctive quality of a mark that has been registered under the state statute or used under common law. The owner of the registered mark and the diluting party need not be in actual competition, nor must a likelihood of confusion be demonstrated. However, in order to make a claim for dilution, the owner must show that the trademark has a "distinctive quality," which means that it must enjoy very strong consumer loyalty, recognition, and goodwill.

Trademark rights are often the most valuable asset of a franchisor in today's competitive marketplace. The goodwill and consumer recognition that trademarks and service marks represent have tremendous economic value and are therefore usually worth the effort and the expense to register and protect them properly. This requires a commitment by management to implement and to support a strict trademark compliance program that includes usage guidelines for all franchisees, suppliers, service providers, and distributors.

25

Strategies for Negotiating Commercial Leases

Sidney J. Silver and Steven M. Abramson, Silver, Freedman & Taff

The lease agreement is one of the most important legal documents pertaining to any franchisee business. The methodologies utilized by franchisors for selecting site locations and for entering into leases vary widely. Many franchisors administer the entire process, including site selection, construction, and leasing. Others leave this responsibility to their franchisees, reserving only the right to approve the transaction. In either case, unless certain rights are reserved in the lease, the franchise business may be jeopardized. Moreover, to the extent that franchisees enter into disadvantageous lease agreements that ultimately prevent the franchise business from being successful, the value of the franchisors' business concept is diminished. Clearly, it is harder to convince potential franchisees to invest when existing franchisees are closing their doors, even though the franchise concept might have been successful had favorable lease terms been secured.

The purpose of this chapter is to review and analyze the major issues encountered in nearly all lease negotiations and to provide a basic guide to terms and conditions that a franchise tenant should attempt to incorporate into the lease agreement. Specifically, we highlight issues concerning the entity of tenant, lease term, commencement date, use, rent and other charges, cotenancy conditions, tenant allowances, construction, maintenance and repair, restrictive covenants, assignment and subletting, and hazardous materials. We present only an abbreviated review of the subject; there are many other lease provisions not discussed here that may require close examination. Accordingly, franchising executives should bear in mind the importance of thoroughly reading any lease and of consulting an attorney experienced in lease negotiations prior to lease execution.

Economic Issues

Who Is the Tenant?

One of the most important lease decisions is the choice of the entity that will act as tenant. The choice of tenant is critical in two respects. First, it serves as a mechanism for limiting liability. Second, it affects the degree of the franchisor's control over the location.

Ideally, in order to minimize potential liability under the lease, the tenant should be a separate corporation whose assets are limited to the assets of the franchised store. To accomplish this, either the franchisor or the franchisee must incorporate a new entity for each new franchise location. With this ownership structure, even if the business were to fail in the particular location, the financial loss would be limited to the investment in the particular store, and any other franchise stores owned by the franchisor or franchisee would be unaffected.

However, most sophisticated landlords will not enter into a lease with a "shell" corporation and look for guarantees from either a financially sound corporation or the principals of the tenant (usually the individual franchisees and their spouses). In this circumstance the tenant may offer limited guarantees (i.e., a guarantee of up to one year's rent to be in force during the first two years of the lease) or other financial assurances (i.e., a letter of credit, an increased security deposit, or a larger investment in the corporation) to offer the landlord financial assurances that the tenant will have the resources to fulfill its lease obligations.

The second consideration in choosing the entity is the degree of control over the premises that the franchisor wishes to retain. In those situations where the franchisor desires to maintain maximum control over the real estate, the franchisor should execute the lease (preferably through a newly formed subsidiary corporation) as tenant and either operate the store as a company store or sublet the premises to the franchisee. In this way the franchisor, even if the store is franchised, is in the strongest position to reenter the premises and take over operations in the event of a default of either the lease, the sublease, or the franchise agreement by the franchisee, thereby preserving the real estate for the conduct of the franchise business. However, if the franchisor enters into the lease, it normally remains liable under the lease even if the space is sublet or assigned to a bona fide franchisee. In those cases where franchisors are not willing to incur the liability under the lease but still wish to maximize control, the franchisor may attempt to incorporate into the lease the right to assign the lease to a bona fide franchisee with specific provision that upon such assignment the franchisor is released of all liability under the lease. The problem with this method is that the landlord may enter into the lease on the basis of a belief about the financial strength and business experience of the franchisor and therefore condition or restrict the franchisor's ability to assign. It is also important to bear in mind that upon a sublet, and to a greater extent upon an assignment of the lease, the franchisor's control over the space is diminished even if a right of reentry is specifically stated in the sublet or assignment agreement. In many jurisdictions the franchisor, in order to exercise its right to reentry, may have to take legal action to recover its possessory interest, and landlords are unlikely to stand idly by if the payment of rent is suspended or the space is not being operated in compliance with the lease. As a practical matter, this may result in the franchisor's paying rent in order to cure a franchisee's default, even though the franchisor has not obtained possessions, in order to preserve its right of reentry under the lease.

If the franchisee enters into the lease with the landlord directly, the franchisor assumes no liability under the lease but also has no legal right of access to the leased premises absent express entry and cure provisions contained in the lease, or a collateral assignment of the lease to the franchisor. Accordingly, where there is a default under the franchise agreement resulting in the unauthorized use of the franchisor's trade name, service marks, or systems, the sole vehicle of enforcement is costly and protracted litigation seeking injunctive relief and/or a restraining order precluding the unauthorized use. It is therefore very important that the franchisor at least reserve the right to approve the lease in the franchise agreement and that the lease include a right to enter and cure a franchisee's default. However, even if this is done, the franchisor may not have access to the expedited procedures offered by landlord and tenant courts because the franchisor is not a party to the lease, again frustrating the franchisor's ability to enter and take control of the premises.

Lease Term

Once the franchisor approves the site and the franchisee decides to enter into a lease, how long should the term be? If the business format has a proven track record or is costly to develop, the tenant will want the right to transact business in the location over a long period of time. If unsuccessful, the tenant will want to be able to cut its losses and get out, particularly if the store does not require heavy capital expenditures. If a store starts out well but over time the location becomes less desirable, the tenant will want to be able to relocate. Given the uncertainty of the future, what is a tenant to do?

Generally, the longer the term, the more valuable the leasehold interest and the greater the financial exposure. Where the tenant is a shell or a newly formed corporation or where the liabilities under the lease are limited, a long-term lease is generally advantageous. For example, such a lease puts the tenant in a better position to negotiate free rent and construction buildout allowances, because the landlord will be able to amortize these expenditures against the added cash flow of additional rental over the longer period of time. For similar reasons, a longer term is desirable if the initial investment by the tenant is substantial, because the longer lease allows the tenant to recover its investment.

The key from a tenant's perspective is simply to secure the benefits of a longer term without the added risk. There are a variety ways to achieve this goal. First, the tenant can enter into a lease for a shorter initial term with several extension options. However, the procedure creates a variety of problems. The landlord may not be inclined to grant the rent concessions it would otherwise have given if the terms were fixed over the longer period. The landlord may also insist on the right to increase the rent to market and otherwise to modify the lease as a condition of extension; the tenant is generally best advised to negotiate in advance the rentals that would be payable during each option term. Moreover, the tenant will probably be required to exercise its option a specific period of time prior to the expiration of the term. In most jurisdictions, if the tenant fails to notify the landlord of its intention to extend in a timely manner, the option will be deemed to have been waived. Therefore, if a tenant elects to proceed with a shorter initial term/option structured deal, the tenant should make sure to include a provision in the lease requiring the landlord to notify the tenant of the last day that tenant may exercise its option before the option is waived.

Alternatively, the tenant can provide for a "kick-out clause" that allows the tenant to terminate the lease under certain circumstances. Typically, a kick-out clause is triggered if tenant fails to achieve a certain sales volume by a certain date, if the occupancy level of the shopping center falls below a certain percentage, or if a department store or anchor store closes. This allows tenant the flexibility of going forward with a long-term lease while at the same time providing an out if the location proves not to be successful.

Another critical issue to keep in mind is to match the terms of the lease and renewals with the term of the license granted under the franchise agreement. When negotiating lease terms, both the franchisor and the franchisee should ensure that the term of the franchise agreement is not shorter than the lease term.

Commencement Date

The tenant should negotiate for a commencement date of the lease that coincides with its opening for business. All too often, tenants enter into leases in which the commencement date is either fixed or tied to a certain number of days following the landlord's delivery of the space to the tenant (the tenant "fit-up period" or "work period"), and what ends up happening is that the commencement date is triggered long before the tenant is prepared to open. It is nearly certain that any operation that is forced to pay rent for a measurable length of time prior to opening will face a serious cash flow crisis that often prevents the business from ever getting off the ground.

As a general rule, landlords insist on some firm commencement date. In such cases the tenant needs to make sure that it reserves sufficient time to complete its construction or occupancy requirements for opening for business prior to the commencement date. Accordingly, the tenant should make sure the following contingencies are satisfied before the tenant's work period commences: (1) the landlord has approved the tenant's plans and specifications, (2) the landlord has delivered the premises to the tenant having substantially completed all required work in accordance with applicable law (including abatement of hazardous materials and/or asbestos-containing materials), and (3) all requisite building permits have been issued to the tenant. The tenant should also receive as a condition of the commencement date a certificate of occupancy or other permits necessary to transact business and should provide generally for an extension of the buildout period if events beyond the tenant's reasonable control delay construction.

Another issue to keep in mind is the importance of timing the commencement date to coincide with the tenant's selling season. In certain businesses, severe problems can arise if the commencement date falls near the end of the tenant's selling season. For example, suppose a clothing store anticipates a fall
opening, but the premises are not available until December 15. In this circumstance the tenant will probably not have sufficient time to turn over its inventory
of fall merchandise at full price and will be forced to liquidate the inventory at
reduced margins, reducing profitability. In this situation, the tenant may have
been better off deferring or postponing its opening until the beginning of the
spring season. In order to reserve the flexibility to coordinate the commencement
date with a timely seasonal opening, the tenant may wish to insert into the lease
language specifying certain periods during the year when the commencement date
cannot occur (i.e., "In no event shall the commencement date occur during the
period from December 1 through February 15 or June 1 throught August 15.").

Use/Trade Name

It is important to bear in mind that the trade name and its use are in essence
licensed by the franchisor and that the consistency of the system is vital to pres-
ervation of the franchise network. Indeed, most franchise agreements require that
the franchisee modify its operations from time to time if requested by the franchisor whenever changes in the franchise system are instituted. Accordingly, the
possibility that modifications may occur over time to both the trade name and the
use of a franchise business should be addressed by both the franchisor and the
franchisee in the lease agreement. A few examples demonstrate the importance
of this issue. Consider the franchisor whose principal business is the sale of hot
dogs. The franchisor, believing an expanded product line is necessary to generate
greater revenues, develops a new product line that includes french fries, hamburgers, and grilled chicken sandwiches. The franchise agreement requires the franchisee to modify the menu to carry these new products. What happens if the lease
use clause permits only the sale of hot dogs? Another example is a change in the
trade name of the franchisor as a result of a merger or sale to another franchisor
(i.e., the conversion of the Roy Rogers franchise operations into Hardee's operations). What happens if the lease prohibits a change in the tenant's trade name?

Narrowly drafted lease use clauses and restrictions on trade name clause are
the norm rather than the exception and can legally prevent a franchisee from
modifying or expanding its use or trade name as requested by the franchisor.
Clearly, if the rest of the franchise system is changing, a lease provision prohibiting a franchisee from adopting the changes in the system can result in disastrous
consequences. First, the failure to stay consistent with other franchise stores can
create the impression with the public of a dated store. Moreover, in the case of a
change in franchise trade name and system, if the franchisor ceases to market and
to support the old franchise trade name and system, the franchisee will lose the
market value and goodwill of the franchise business purchased as the trade name

disappears over time. To complicate matters further, there will likely be a conflict between the franchise agreement and the lease agreement.

For these reasons, every effort should be made to try to keep the use clause as broad as possible and to eliminate trade name restrictions from the lease. This is especially important if the franchisor's trademarks have not yet been registered by the United States Patent and Trademark Office (USPTO) or have not yet become "incontestable" (see Chapter 25 on trademark registration) because the franchisor may need to reserve the right to change or modify its trade identity if its chosen name or mark conflicts with an existing registered trade name or mark. In those instances where the landlord's consent is required to change the tenant's use and/or trade name, the lease should state that such consent will not be unreasonably withheld, conditioned, or delayed. The tenant should also make it clear in the lease that in connection with a change in its trade name or in the franchise system, the tenant will have the right to change its signage to reflect the new trade name or new logo, service marks, or designs adopted by the franchise system. Similarly, if franchise stores are changing their color schemes or cosmetic appearance, the tenant should also reserve in the lease the right to make alterations in the space consistent with the franchisor's new designs.

The tenant should also be careful to provide in the lease that the tenant's intended use is permitted under applicable laws and that the landlord has the right to enter into the lease. Under the law of many jurisdictions, it is the tenant's responsibility to make sure that its intended use is permitted under applicable law. Accordingly, if a tenant enters into the lease, only later to discover that its use is prohibited, it may still be liable for rent and other lease obligations even though it cannot use the leased premises as intended. Moreover, a landlord may have entered into an agreement with another tenant that prohibits or restricts the use afforded the tenant under the lease. If this happens, the tenant may find itself in the middle of a lawsuit challenging its ability to use the leased premises as intended. It is therefore strongly recommended that the tenant incorporate the following clause into all leases:

> **Landlord represents, covenants, and warrants that tenant's use is permissible under all applicable laws and that landlord is not a party to any agreement or restrictive covenant granted any other tenant which would prohibit or give rise to any claim by third parties that tenant is not free to use the premises as permitted under this lease.**

In a related issue, what happens if, as a result of a change in an applicable law, the tenant is either precluded from engaging in its permitted use under the lease or the cost necessary to allow such use to be in compliance with applicable law is excessive under the circumstances? Again, this is a very real and contested issue. A prime example of the importance of this issue is the passage and enforcement of the Americans with Disabilities Act of 1990, which requires businesses to make their stores and landlords to make their shopping malls accessible to the handicapped. It appears that the burden of compliance with the Act will be determined by the lease. Accordingly, the tenant should attempt to shift the cost of compliance to the landlord. If such language cannot be attained, the tenant should reserve in the lease the right to terminate the lease. A sample clause addressing this issue is as follows:

> **Anything contained herein to the contrary notwithstanding, in no event shall Tenant be required to comply with any such laws, rules or regulations after the date hereof which would require Tenant to make structural or material alterations, modifications or repairs (material alterations, modifications or repairs, meaning those costing in excess of $2,500 in any lease year) necessary to comply with future laws, rules or regulations including environmental laws, rules or regulations and including laws, and rules or regulations adopted pursuant to the Americans with Disabilities Act of 1990 for which the cost of compliance shall be Landlord's sole responsibility.**

Both franchisors and franchisees must recognize that, as a practical matter, landlords, in their effort to build up the goodwill of their shopping center, attempt to attract a balanced mix of different tenants with well-established trade names, often including well-established national and regional franchisors. Good landlords also attempt to narrow use clauses to protect all tenants from excessive competition within the shopping center (that is, if a landlord has a pizza operation in a food court, it is unlikely to give another tenant the right to sell pizza, even if the tenant is in the food service business). It is also common for landlords to grant significant rent concessions (such as free rent and construction allowances) in order to secure proven, recognized businesses.

Depending on the nature of a franchise business and on competitive synergy, it may be appropriate to insert into the lease an "exclusive use" clause. Generally, an exclusive use clause provides that the tenant will be the only operator in the shopping center offering the type of products or services permitted under the lease. For example, a frozen yogurt store may request a provision in its lease that no other tenant in the shopping center will be allowed to offer for sale frozen yogurt or any frozen dessert product. A quick-service oil-change franchise operator may simlarly request a provision stipulating that no other tenant in the shopping center will be allowed to offer oil changes. Most well-advised landlords will not agree to such absolute restrictions because it limits their flexibility in marketing and their control over their real estate, but they will agree to grant tenants some reasonable protection.

Rent and Proportionate Share Charges

What is the rent? While this seems like an easy question, it often proves to be a major area of disagreement between franchisors, franchisees, and landlords. Consider the following example: A landlord advises a tenant that the rent is $25 a square foot. The tenant understands this to mean that its rental obligations under the lease for a 2,000-square-foot space will be $50,000 a year and bases its decisions to enter into the lease on this conclusion. The landlord's understanding is that the ''minimum annual rent'' is $50,000 and that the tenant will also pay its proportionate share of real estate taxes, common area maintenance expenses, insurance, advertising and promotional fund costs, utilities, and, in some cases, percentage rent. So, what is the rent? Probably more along the lines of $40 per square foot, or $80,000 a year, according to the landlord's point of view.

The point is that the tenants should focus on what the total occupancy costs are, occupancy costs being defined as rent and any other charges payable by tenant to landlord, including utilities, under the lease. Each business should have a general idea as to what percentage of its sales can be allocated to cover occupancy costs and still allow for profitable operations.

MINIMUM ANNUAL RENT

As minimum annual rents are generally a function of the bargaining position of landlord and tenant, the existing market conditions, and the term of the lease, they are not discussed at length in this chapter. In general, the obvious is true — the lower the rent, the better the deal. The phrase ''in general'' is emphasized because in leasing, as in anything else, a tenant often gets what it pays for. If the rent is extremely low or if the landlord is giving extraordinary incentives, it may be because the location and/or the center is poor.

Tenants may want to keep in mind the following ideas in order to help keep the rent in line with cash flow projections. First, tenants can average the minimum rent over the term. For example, if the minimum rental is $10 per square foot on a three-year lease, the tenant may wish to set the minimum rent at $9 per square foot in year 1, $10 per square foot in year 2, and $11 per square foot in year 3. Not only will this structure help cash flow in the first year, it may result in below-market rents in year 3. A second point the tenant should keep in mind when negotiating minimum rents is that if a reduced rent or free rent is offered initially and the deal is a percentage rent deal, the percentage rent breakpoint should be based on the full negotiated rent. Otherwise, the benefits of the minimum rent or free rent may be lost. For example, assume the tenant's minimum rent is $50,000 per year and the percentage rate breakpoint is 5 percent over the natural break of $1,000,000. Suppose the tenant receives as an allowance half-rent during the first lease year. Absent provision to the contrary, the natural breakpoint will be $500,000 during the first year, which means that for every dollar of sales between $500,000 and $1,000,000, the tenant's rent concession is proportionately reduced.

PERCENTAGE RENT

In many cases landlords insist on percentage rent in addition to minimum annual rent and other charges. Percentage rent deals are most common in regional shopping centers but can also be found in strip centers and even freestanding store deals. As a general rule, most tenants are better off avoiding percentage rent transactions, particularly if the tenant believes it is likely to attain substantial sales volumes per square foot. However, in some cases, a percentage rent deal may be advantageous because it can allow the tenant to reduce its overhead. For example, instead of paying $25 per square foot, a tenant may be able to negotiate a $15 per square foot minimum rent if it agrees to pay percentage rent of 5 percent. Under this example, if the leased premises consist of 2,000 square feet, a tenant will need to generate $1.25 million in sales volume to pay an aggregate rental equal to the $25 per square foot deal. Clearly, if the tenant realistically projects sales of less than $1.2 million, it is better off entering into a percentage rent deal.

The actual percentage paid by the tenant is normally determined by the nature of the tenant's business and the type of shopping center. Some landlords even have charts that fix percentages for specific industries. The actual percentage is, of course, subject to negotiation, but landlords generally attempt to secure higher percentages in businesses that have higher margins (i.e., jewelry stores, food court operators) or that are located in high-end shopping centers. Similarly, landlords often agree to lower percentages from tenants that have lower profit margins (i.e., discount stores) or that are located in shopping centers that feature moderately priced operators or in strip centers or freestanding buildings.

In percentage rent lease deals, tenants should make sure that the definition of gross sales is not overly expansive. Specifically, the tenant should make sure that the lease excludes those charges that the tenant does not include in its own accounting of gross sales. For example, typical exclusions from gross sales include:

Any exchange of merchandise between stores of the tenant if such an exchange is made solely for the convenient operation of the tenant's business; returns to shippers or manufacturers; cash or credit refunds to customers; sales of trade fixtures, machinery, and equipment used in connection with the tenant's business; delivery charges; amounts collected and paid by the tenant to any government for any sales, use, or excise tax; discount sales to the tenant's employees; charges made in connection with alteration of merchandise; sums received in settlement of claims for loss or damage to merchandise; interest charges earned in connection with the tenant's own credit sales; uncollectible or bad debts (generally with a percentage limitation); service charges assessed against the tenant by national credit card companies; and bulk sales of inventory outside the ordinary course of the tenant's business.

In a franchise business, it is also important to try to exclude gross royalty fees paid to the tenant's franchisor. If the landlord will not agree to exclude the royalty fee, the tenant must recognize in its projected cash flow analysis that it may be paying percentage rent on the royalties it pays to the franchisor.

Finally, tenants should also make sure to delete lease language that allows the landlord to increase the tenant's minimum annual rent if the tenant's gross sales are not in excess of the percentage rent breakpoint.

PROPORTIONATE SHARE CHARGES

Many tenants find that if proportionate share charges are passed on to the tenant, there may be no way of controlling the occupancy costs for which the tenant is liable under the lease. It is becoming more and more common to hear tenants complain that what may have appeared to have been an advantageous lease on the date of execution has proven to be cost-prohibitive in later years. Accordingly, tenants must understand proportionate charges and what measures can be undertaken to control them.

The pass-through charges of the lease are a repeated source of confrontation between landlords and tenants. More and more landlords are expanding the scope of expenditures to be included in common area charges, while at the same time tinkering with the calculation of tenant's proportionate share. Moreover, in large regional shopping centers, it is becoming more and more apparent that landlords' lease administrators do not review each lease for negotiated exclusions and that the only way to protect a particular tenant's negotiated rights is an audit or a cap on the aggregate amount for which the tenant will be liable. As discussed in more detail below, tenants should try to secure limitations or a cap on all proportionate share pass-through charges. However, in practice, landlords will probably not even consider caps on utilities, taxes, and insurance charges. Tenants should also make sure that their proportionate share is calculated on the basis of the gross leasable floor area of the shopping center, as opposed to the leased and occupied floor area. If not, a tenant's share of operating expenses will increase as the shopping center vacancies increase. If the landlord refuses to use gross leasable floor area as a baseline, the tenant should at least insist on a floor amount, such as 85 percent of the gross leasable floor area, as a basis for the proportionate share calculation.

▲ *Common area charges.* There are several ways a tenant can control its proportionate share of common area charges (CAM). The best way to control CAM charges and to reduce future disputes with the landlord is to agree upon a cap formula. However, as a practical matter, unless the tenant is in an extremely strong bargaining position, it is unlikely that a landlord will agree to a cap, and even if a cap is agreed to, the landlord is likely to set it at a number that is unlikely to be reached. Assuming for the moment that a cap can be successfully attained, tenant and landlord can arrive at a cap formulation in a variety of ways. The parties can agree to an overall occupancy cost cap equal to a percentage of the tenant's gross sales (i.e., 8 to 10 percent of gross sales). Alternatively, the parties can tie the cap to the percentage increase in the Consumer Price Index or can limit increases to a fixed percentage (i.e., no increases greater than 5 percent in any one year). Regardless of the calculation method, the tenant should bear in mind that any cap is better than no cap and should address the issue up front during negotiations as a material economic term.

The tenant should also try to limit the types of costs that may be passed through. However, without an audit right and a penalty provision for improper pass-throughs, the tenant's exclusions lose practical significance.

▲ *Taxes.* Tenants can do little to alleviate their proportionate share charges for taxes, and few landlords will grant a cap on tenant's proportionate share charge for taxes regardless of the tenant's bargaining strength. However, before signing the lease, tenants should make sure that the definition of taxes does not include personal property taxes assessed against the landlord's personal property not located upon and used exclusively in connection with the maintenance of the shopping center or the landlord's corporate, franchise, inheritance, or income taxes. Moreover, tenants should make sure that in mixed-use complexes (i.e., those combining retail, hotel, and office space), the allocation of taxes is fair and not arbitrarily skewed to require that the retail portion pay the greater share. Finally, in those cases where the landlord estimates the tenant's proportionate share of taxes, the landlord's estimate of taxes should not exceed the actual taxes for the prior year, adjusted by the then applicable CPI, and the landlord should be required to furnish the tenant with actual copies of the tax bills each year. Tenants should also be careful to make sure the landlord is not adding an administrative fee to the tax bill.

▲ *Promotional/merchants association.* Many landlords establish mandatory advertising programs and promotional funds to market the shopping center for the collective benefit of all tenants. While in concept this may be appealing, as a practical matter it often increases a tenant's financial obligations under the lease without providing much benefit. Most advertising brochures or programs assembled by the shopping center amount to a poor use of the tenant's advertising budget. Indeed, in many franchise relationships, the franchisee's local advertising budgets are already fully committed due to its obligations to make contributions to a cooperative fund under the franchise agreement. Accordingly, whenever possible, the franchisee should try to eliminate required advertising and promotional fund charges from the lease. If such costs cannot be eliminated, the tenant should specifically limit the number of advertisements it is required to participate in and the aggregate cost of its participation in the promotional/merchant's association.

Moreover, the tenant should make sure that landlords cannot arbitrarily force an increase in the promotional dues. Recently, a major shopping center, faced with new competition from a recently remodeled and expanded nearby center, doubled its promotional charges. The landlord justified the increase by pointing to a lease provision that stated that if the landlord and a majority of a tenants' committee, to be comprised of four tenants, voted to increase the promotional dues, the tenants had to pay the increase as additional rent. The lease provision did not specify how the tenants' committee was to be selected, and it appeared that the landlord had picked the tenants to serve on the committee. Several tenants are investigating the matter for foul play, but the cost of litigating will probably exceed the increase itself.

Finally, tenants should attempt to secure a representation from the landlord that it will expend all monies collected currently for the promotion of the shopping center. Tenants should also ask for a provision relieving them of their obligation to participate if all tenants do not participate in the promotional/merchants association.

▲ *Utilities/trash removal*. Tenants, when negotiating utility and trash removal provisions, should make sure that the lease provides that tenants pay only for the services they use. This can most easily be accomplished by installing separate meters and paying the utility company for services directly and by separately contracting for trash removal. However, in a number of shopping centers this is not possible because the landlord contracts for such services for all tenants. If the landlord purchases utilities and trash removal services, it is important that the tenant read the common-area provisions and the utility and trash removal provisions of the lease carefully to make sure charges are not duplicated. Moreover, the tenant should insert in the lease a requirement that utility charges, when service is furnished by landlord, will not exceed those charges that the tenant would be required to pay to the public utility company had such service been purchased directly from the public utility company. Provisions should also be inserted requiring that the landlord contract for utility and trash removal services at competitive rates and that any cost savings obtained by the landlord be passed on to the tenant, it being the stated intention of the parties that the landlord not profit by providing such services.

Tenants should also consider the nature of the tenant's use when reviewing this matter. For example, a restaurant tenant has special utility and trash removal requirements and in fact may be able to procure such service more cheaply on his own. In such cases, tenants may wish to reserve in the lease the right to contract separately for such services and to receive a credit against pass-through charges equal to the tenant's proportionate share of such charges.

TENANT ALLOWANCES

It is no secret that financing for franchise businesses has always been difficult to obtain. Accordingly, a great deal of time is spent in negotiating tenant allowances from landlords to help finance new stores. Allowances can take many forms, including free rent, reduced rent, or construction assistance in which the landlord actually performs fit-up work for the tenant's benefit or pays cash construction allowances to reimburse all or some of the tenant's construction cost. While issues can arise in nearly all allowance situations, it is the actual payment of cash allowances that proves to be the most problematic. In practice, most landlords attempt to have the tenant fund the build-out, deliver appropriate lien waivers, and complete any and all punch-list items prior to payment of the allowance. This can create severe cash flow problems for franchisees, inhibiting their ability to perform other obligations under the franchise agreement. Tenants are not banks and generally lack the resources of the landlord. Accordingly, where cash construction allowances are negotiated, franchisors and franchisees should attempt to negotiate payment draws of the allowance that coincide with their contractor's draw requests. Tenants should also minimize the documentation required for each draw request. Generally, a statement from the tenant or from the tenant's architect certifying the progress on the construction work, together with the contractor's application for payment, should be sufficient to release partial payments of the tenant's allowance. The backup documentation required by the landlord, such as final lien waivers and paid invoices, can be furnished in connection with a final application for payment of the allowance.

Alternatively, some landlords agree to set up procedures by which the tenant's contractor can submit its draw request directly to an escrow account created by both landlord and tenant. This system can work wonderfully if the escrow is funded properly and if documentation is kept to a minimum. Moreover, with the financial condition of many landlords being more and more suspect, this method may provide the tenant with the best assurance that promised allowances will be readily available. However, many landlords require that the tenant contribute to the escrow account the difference between the contract price of the work and the landlord's contribution. Under these circumstances, the goal of preserving the tenant's cash reserves is somewhat frustrated. However, the security of the known availability of the landlord's funds may be worth funding the difference in advance.

Despite the virtue of progress payments, it is a fact that, as a practical matter, tenants seldom get paid allowances in a timely fashion. It is helpful to insert interest and penalty clauses into the lease in the event the landlord fails to pay allowance requests promptly. The tenant should also attempt to negotiate a right of offset (the right to withhold payments against overdue allowances) should the landlord fail to pay tenant's allowances on time. Landlords are not known to willingly grant tenant any offset rights, and if a tenant does hold back payment without a stated offset right, it will probably receive notice of default shortly thereafter. Moreover, in instances where the tenant has also negotiated a certain free-rent period, there may be little to offset against. Although it seems unfair, there is very little a tenant can do with a delinquent landlord other than to bring a separate action to recover allowances. This reality makes the creation of an escrow account for the allowance money all the more attractive.

Construction Issues

The initial construction of a store nearly always brings with it issues not initially considered by the franchisor and the franchisee. In fact, there are more than a few cynical operators who claim that the best way to estimate the cost and time of construction is to figure out the most the job will cost and add 15 percent, then figure out the longest it will take to build and add thirty days. The bottom line is that in nearly all cases, certain complications will be encountered during the construction period. What follows is a summary of frequently encountered problems and practical considerations that relate to construction.

Plan Approval

The plan approval process is critical if the parties hope to achieve a timely opening without unforeseen costs. This is especially critical if the franchise agreement or the lease agreement sets a fixed date by which time the franchisee has to open its business to the general public. (See previous discussion under "Commencement Date.") In order to assure the parties that the transaction will proceed as intended, certain prerequisite materials must be delivered to the tenant, the franchisor (if the franchisor is not the tenant), and their architects and contractors *prior to* the execution of the lease. Examples of such materials include "as built" drawings, the landlord's building outline criteria, and notices of special zoning or code requirements (or a representation from the landlord that the construction and the use of the space as contemplated are consistent with applicable zoning requirements). If these materials are delivered and reviewed prior to the lease execution, many disputes as to design, cost, and "above building standard work" may be avoided.

It is also important, particularly with seasonal retailing, that the stores open when scheduled. In order to keep to the schedule, both landlord and tenant must cooperate to deliver plans and approvals in a timely manner. But timely plan submittal and approval are only the beginning of the process. Once the plans are approved by the landlord, the tenant must still obtain governmental approval and building permits before commencing work. Unfortunately, it is not uncommon for the approval process to drag on well beyond the period contemplated in the lease. When the approval process is delayed, the following disputes almost always arise between landlord and tenant: (a) What is the proper rent commencement date?, (b) Is tenant's work period extended?, and (c) Is the "force majeure" clause (see section on "Delays") applicable?

If the rent commencement date is defined in the lease as the first day following the tenant's buildout period and if the lease states further that the buildout period does not commence until the landlord has approved the tenant's plans and until permits for the tenant's work have been issued, the tenant will not suffer because of delays in plan approval. Similarly, the tenant may also wish to make it clear that the landlord cannot be said to have delivered the premises to tenant until the landlord has completed the landlord's work in accordance with all applicable laws and has approved the tenant's plans. Without such provisions, the tenant may find itself with a rent commencement date well in advance of its opening date.

Field Conditions/Delays

Directly related to plan approval and to the timely completion of both landlord's and tenant's construction work is the condition of the premises at the time of delivery. Again, a great deal of time, money, and trouble will be saved if, prior to executing the lease, the tenant inspects the premises to verify the square footage and to make sure that the field conditions conform to the "as built" drawings. Unfortunately, this is not always possible. Consider the situation where the tenant must demolish an existing space before commencing construction work. A visual inspection prior to demolition will not necessarily confirm the "as built" drawing. Indeed, once demolition begins, it is not uncommon to find conduits and feeds behind party walls that are not reflected on the landlord's plans, structural discrepancies, asbestos-containing materials, code violations, and similar problems.

Under the customary "as is" deal, these problems can not only frustrate the tenant's construction schedule but can in fact make the entire transaction economically disadvantageous. Accordingly, when negotiating the lease, tenants should be careful to exclude from the "as is" conveyance latent defects and discrepancies from "as built" drawings furnished by the landlord. The tenant should also make the landlord agree to bear the cost of redesign necessitated by nonconforming field conditions and make the landlord responsible for the removal of asbestos and related hazardous materials. Again, be sure to clarify that any delays attributable to any of these conditions will extend the tenant's construction period and postpone the rent and term commencement date. Moreover, seasonal tenants should provide in the lease that if opening is delayed for any of these reasons and if such delays force the tenant to miss the season, then the tenant may either terminate the lease or postpone its opening to the next season.

Not to be overlooked is whether the building outline criteria as specified by the landlord will accommodate the tenant's contemplated use. Again, the parties are advised to discuss, prior to execution of the lease, any special needs required over and above base building standard. A leather or fur store may require special HVAC (heating, ventilation, air conditioning) capacities. A restaurant may require special gas, exhaust, sprinkler, or plumbing lines. The type of special requirements and the cost allocation should be negotiated as part of the overall economic deal. If they are not, the tenant, in all likelihood, will be required to bear the additional costs associated with such requirements.

Charge-Backs

A tenant charge-back is an amount that the landlord will bill the tenant for certain work performed by the landlord that benefits the premises. The construction exhibits and building outline criteria usually state in detail the charge-backs the landlord expects to recover from the tenant. Often the materials are never seen by counsel or by the principals of the tenant, because they are incorporated by reference and sent directly to the tenant's construction personnel. *Do not let this happen!* Charge-backs can aggregate anywhere from $10 to $25 per square foot per store and should be negotiated as a basic economic term of the lease. It is important to note that certain charge-backs, such as trash removal and temporary utility service for the tenant's work, are reasonable and customary. However, tenants should attempt to negotiate landlords' waiver of other charge-backs for temporary barricades, studs and demising walls, floor slab, piping, delivery of utility lines to the premises, and similar charges.

Delays

In recent years, landlords have come to look upon clauses that excuse performance for events beyond the tenant's control (so-called force majeure clauses) unfavorably. The reason for their objection is that excused delays have been successfully used by tenants to postpone the day rent commences. Nowhere is this trend more apparent than in the drafting of the excused delay/force majeure provision. Consider the following recent example. A tenant's opening was delayed because government authorities refused to promptly inspect the stages of the tenant's work and to issue a certificate of occupancy. The tenant claimed that the commencement date was postponed as a result of such delays. The landlord insisted that the commencement date not be delayed and further argued that the tenant was in default because it failed to open and to pay rent on time. In support of its position, the landlord argued: "The force majeure provision in the lease specifically states that the payment of rent is not excused by force majeure."

In this particular instance the force majeure provision did exclude from its scope the obligation to pay rent. However, the lease did not state that the rent and term commencement date could not be postponed by reason of force majeure; indeed, nearly all of the items listed as being subject to force majeure related to the original construction of the store. In order to avoid disputes of this nature, tenants should modify the force majeure provisions specifically to postpone both the rent and the term commencement dates.

Continuing the example, the landlord also argued: "The force majeure clause only applies to delays caused by landlord."

Most force majeure clauses simply do not state this, and, in this case, the landlord asserted this position without legal foundation. However, the invalid argument put forth by this landlord is perhaps the strongest evidence of landlords' resolve to fight tenants on delay claims. It is therefore critical that, at the first sign of delay, tenants keep accurate chronological records of all events causing delays, including the length of each delay, and consistently notify landlords in writing of each event causing delays and the length of the delay.

Of course, not all delayed openings are attributable to force majeure events. There are also times when a tenant may wish to delay opening for business reasons. Examples include a restaurant delaying its opening until it receives a liquor license or a seasonal store delaying opening until the beginning of its season.

Generally, the failure of the tenant to open under these circumstances will not be excused, and the tenant's term and rent commencement date, plus penalties for late opening (if any), begin to accrue on the commencement date stated in the lease. Moreover, the failure to open on time may also result in a breach of the franchise agreement. In order to avoid a default, the tenant should specify during lease and franchise agreement negotiations any other business prerequisites to opening and arrange to have the term and commencement dates of both the lease and the franchise agreement postponed until these prerequisites are satisfied.

Another problem that surfaces repeatedly is an attempt by the landlord to prevent a tenant from opening, even though the tenant's work is completed. In some cases, the delay is requested by the landlord to effectuate a grand opening. In other cases, the delay results from the landlord's failure to inspect and to approve a tenant's work promptly. To avoid these problems, a tenant should make sure that the lease requires that the landlord inspect the premises within twenty-four hours after receipt of tenant's certification that the premises are substantially complete, stocked, fixtured, and ready to open. The lease should further state that the landlord's failure to inspect promptly will constitute a waiver of the right of inspection and that minor punch-list items shall not be a basis for preventing the tenant from opening. With respect to effectuating a grand opening, if the delay is minimal, it is usually in the tenant's best interest to go along. However, if the delay materially cuts into the tenant's selling season, the tenant should either be allowed to open or be entitled to reimbursement for lost sales and extra inventory carrying costs.

Mechanics' Liens

Nearly all leases require that the tenant keep the premises free of mechanics' liens and deliver to landlord lien waivers within a certain number of days following completion of the tenant's work. Unfortunately, as a practical matter, this covenant may be out of the tenant's control. If the tenant's contractor and subcontractors are involved in a dispute and cannot resolve their differences, the tenant is generally not obligated to pay the general contractor until it receives final lien waivers from all subcontractors. Accordingly, the subcontractor files a lien, and the tenant, the landlord, and the landlord's lenders have to deal with it.

What do you do when faced with a situation where liens are threatened or no lien waivers are received? First, deal with reputable contractors who have histories of working repeatedly with the same subcontractors. Many established national and regional franchisors have already assembled a list of contractors with whom they have had positive experiences, and franchisees are well advised to solicit bids from these contractors. Second, reserve the right to deduct the amount of subcontractors' claims from payments due the general contractor. Third, reserve the right to cut two-party checks in exchange for lien waivers. Finally, incorporate into the lease the requirement that final payment of the allowance be made upon the landlord's receipt of written notice that the applicable statutory period for filing liens has expired.

Maintenance/Repair

Normally, repairs inside the premises that affect only the premises are the tenant's responsibility; maintenance and repair items that affect the structural portion of the shopping center or that benefit all tenants generally are the landlord's responsibility. In cases where the tenant leases the entire building, structural repairs are generally the landlord's responsibility, with the tenant bearing the responsibility for all other repairs. However, even though the obligations of maintenance and repair are normally spelled out clearly in the lease, practical problems do arise.

Access to Premises

Most leases allow landlords access to the premises for necessary maintenance and repairs. However, what does a tenant do when the landlord arrives unexpectedly at his store with the work crew? To avoid this problem, tenants should be careful to include in the lease restrictions on the landlord's access. Typical requirements include (1) access only after written notice, (2) access only during nonbusiness hours, (3) access only when accompanied by the tenant's security personnel, and (4) a general covenant to perform maintenance and repair in a manner so as to minimize interference with the tenant's business. The tenant should be aware that the landlord needs to reserve to itself the right to enter without notice in case of emergency, but the tenant may want to either define the circumstances that constitute an emergency or have the landlord indemnify and hold the tenant harmless against any damages or liability resulting from emergency repairs.

Nature of Maintenance/Repair

As we have indicated, the assignment of responsibility for maintenance and repair is normally a function of the type of maintenance or repair being conducted and of who benefits directly from the maintenance or repair. If the maintenance or repair item falls within the premises and benefits the tenant, the tenant is normally responsible. If the maintenance or repair item is for the benefit of other tenants or of the shopping center, whether it is done within the premises or outside the premises, generally it is the landlord's responsibility. But what does the tenant do when the maintenance/repair is in the premises and solely benefits the tenant but is necessitated by the negligent acts or deferred maintenance of the landlord or of another tenant? The law generally places the financial burden for the maintenance or repair on the party at fault. However, most leases provide that the responsibility of repair/maintenance in such instances is the tenant's alone and that the tenant is to look to its insurance company for reimbursement. In cases where the damage is caused by other tenants, the tenant is normally able to make a claim against the tenant causing the damage. However, some landlords are now incorporating waiver of subrogation provisions between tenants of the shopping center into new leases that, if effective, may preclude the tenant's remedies against the responsible party.

An even bigger problem is what happens when the landlord refuses to perform its repair obligations. Self-help is not practical if the landlord's maintenance and repair obligations are capital in nature, affecting structural or common elements of the shopping center (for example, when the shopping center needs a new roof). A tenant can try to withhold rent, but here again, the landlord will probably prevail in an action for default absent specific offset rights. Moreover, the cost of the repair item may be so great as to make the offset right inconsequential. Ordinarily, the tenant's sole remedy in such cases is litigation seeking to force the landlord to live up to its obligation. However, the tenant may strengthen its ability to force the landlord to perform by including in the lease the right to terminate the lease and to recover the unamortized cost of the tenant's improvements and inventory should the landlord fail to repair the shopping center within the applicable notice and cure period.

Still other problems arise when a landlord undertakes a major remodeling of the shopping center. Though the remodeling normally is beneficial when completed, the disruption to the tenant's business during the remodeling can be devastating. Tenants may attempt to alleviate some of the burdens of the remodeling period by providing for a rent abatement in the lease during remodeling periods or during any time that maintenance/repair efforts by the landlord force the tenant to close.

Unfortunately, recent leases specifically provide that the tenant must continue to pay rent and other charges due under the lease, regardless of the cause of the interruption. The landlord's reasoning is that the tenant can recover this money by carrying business interruption and/or rent insurance. The reader should note that under these same new leases, the landlord generally also carries rent insurance and passes through the cost as part of the common-area charges. Such provisions are grossly unfair and should be corrected prior to executing the lease. Specifically, the lease should be redrafted to provide that if the interruption lasts for a period longer than forty-eight hours, the tenant's rent and additional rent (i.e., occupancy costs) should abate in proportion to the part of the leased premises rendered unusable until the tenant's full use and enjoyment of the property are restored. If the disruption lasts for a period of thirty days or longer, tenant should also reserve the right to terminate the lease and recover from the landlord its unamortized cost of improvements and inventory.

Tenants may also negotiate into the lease a provision stating that the remodeling will not take place during peak business seasons and that the landlord will notify tenants at least nine months in advance so that they can properly adjust their inventory commitments. Tenants should also guard against modifications to the shopping center or leased premises that will alter or adversely affect their ability to conduct business. For example, tenants should insert lease provisions that prevent the landlord from being able to erect or locate kiosks or other structures in front of the leased premises; that prohibit the landlord from erecting new conduits or feeds through the leased premises; and that restrict the landlord's ability to materially reduce or relocate parking areas.

Restrictive Covenants

Thou shall not . . . ! The landlord's commandment list continues to grow with each redraft of its standard lease. It is difficult from a tenant's point of view to appreciate that some of the restrictive covenants contained in the lease do protect the continued viability and image of the shopping center, which in turn benefits the tenant. As alluded to earlier, these covenants and restrictions should be checked carefully against the key terms of the franchise agreement, and especially the operations manuals, to ensure consistency. There are commonly areas that may conflict, such as provisions governing signage, hours of operation, and use, and trade name restrictions that may impose varying requirements.

Use

As discussed under ''Use/Trade Name,'' landlords often attempt to narrow the scope of the tenant's permissible uses. (A more detailed discussion of how best to modify use clauses is provided in that section.) We reiterate that the tenant should be sure to draft a use clause that provides for flexibility to allow for merchandising changes over the term of the lease.

Continuous Occupancy

When a tenant plans to open a new store, it expects that the store will be profitable and that the shopping center presented by landlord's leasing agent will prove to be everything promised. Landlords know this is not always going to happen. Therefore, they include in their leases disclaimers that state that any and all claims of the leasing agent are of no legal effect and that the tenant came to the decision to enter into this lease based on its own careful study of demographics and other relevant factors. The lease further states that the tenant must continuously operate during all days and hours required in the lease.

There are a number of ways a tenant can address the going-dark provisions that prohibit or that limit the acceptable conditions for closing the store. First, as discussed in the section on ''Lease Term,'' the tenant can negotiate a kick-out clause into the lease. Second, the tenant can use its corporate structure to get around the continuous occupancy restrictions by having a separate corporation enter into each lease. Finally, the tenant can cap its occupancy costs so that the store continues to be viable even if the shopping center is not.

Tenants should also bear in mind that, as a practical matter, the landlord's remedies to prevent a tenant from closing up shop depend on the importance of the tenant to the shopping center. Recent decisions have allowed the landlord the remedy of specific performance (i.e., a court order demanding specific action) against a major tenant going dark. However, it is more than likely that a nonanchor tenant will not be subject to the specific performance remedy, regardless of the lease language, because it is unlikely that the landlord can prove irreparable harm in such circumstances. Moreover, if the tenant inserts in the lease an obligation on the part of landlord to mitigate damages by reletting the premises, the tenant may be better off simply going dark despite the lease language, because the losses from continuing operations may exceed the maximum amount the landlord can recover in damages.

Radius Restrictions

Many landlords, particularly when the lease includes provision for percentage rent, impose restrictions preventing the tenant from opening a competitive business within a certain geographic area surrounding the shopping center. Tenants should attempt to negotiate radius restrictions out of the lease and should bear in mind that, once given, a radius restriction becomes harder and harder to get deleted in future deals. In negotiating its radius restrictions with the landlord, a tenant should also consider the nature of its business, as in many cases the goal of the radius restriction—preventing a decline of gross sales from the leased premises—is not achieved even if the radius restriction is inserted. For example, if the tenant's business is a low-cost, impulse item, like bulk candy, having a store in Mall A and a store in Mall B across the street will not adversely affect the sales of either store. In fact, quite the opposite is likely to occur as name recognition and customer loyalty develop in both locations.

If a tenant does have a radius restriction in the lease, there are certain limitations it should insist upon. First, it should make sure that the radius restriction applies only to stores operating under the identical trade name and carrying identical merchandise. Second, it should make sure the radius restriction is consistent with the underlying franchise agreement. This is especially important when an area development agreement requiring the franchisee to deploy a minimum number of sites within a specific territory over the course of a development schedule is signed. Moreover, tenants should limit the distance and the duration of the radius restriction to no more than is absolutely necessary under the circumstances and should exclude from the restricted area any existing stores or contemplated stores.

Relocation Clauses

Many modern leases reserve to landlords the right to place the tenant in another location within the shopping center in the event the landlord remodels, expands, or alters the shopping center. Tenants should try as hard as possible to delete from the lease the landlord's relocation rights. If this proves impossible and the deal is still desirable, then a fallback position is to identify on the shopping center plans, and agree upon, other locations that would be acceptable should relocation be necessary. If the landlord can relocate the tenant to one of the preapproved other locations, make sure the lease requires that the landlord not only pay the tenant the unamortized cost of the tenant's improvements but finance the construction and fixturing costs of the new space as well. Also, make sure that the relocation occurs during a soft selling season and that the tenant is not required to move until the new space is ready for occupancy. If the landlord cannot relocate the tenant to one of the other preapproved locations, the tenant should make sure that the lease provides that the right to relocate is waived, *not* that the parties may terminate the lease. Of course, the franchisor should carefully examine any relocation clause to make sure alternate locations are acceptable and should approve any relocation, which may have a significant impact on the performance of the franchisee.

Other Restrictions

Some other restrictions landlords incorporate into leases include covenants not to operate as a discount store, conduct going-out-of-business sales, or sell out-of-season merchandise. These covenants should also be checked carefully against the terms of the underlying franchise agreement, the key portions of the operating manual, and the tenant's own business practices. The covenant against discount operations may be construed as price fixing and is rapidly disappearing from more sophisticated landlords' leases. The covenant against going-out-of-business sales can be and usually is enforced by landlords. However, by the time the landlord gives notice and the stated cure period expires, the sale may be over. Moreover, if the tenant files for bankruptcy, the restrictions against a going-out-of-business sale will probably not be enforced. The covenant against selling out-of-season merchandise, though a default, can probably be corrected within applicable notice and cure periods and, in any event, is a factual issue that may be difficult to prove if seasonal merchandise and out-of-season merchandise are sold at the same time.

Assignment and Subletting

Because most courts favor a tenant's right to assignment or sublet, landlords have gone to great lengths to make sure that their leases expressly prohibit assignment and subletting. If the tenant has not previously negotiated exceptions or at least a reasonableness standard for the landlord's consent, there is little the tenant can do short of bankruptcy to force an assignment or subletting. Moreover, as a general rule, even if an assignment is either approved by the landlord or permitted by the terms of the lease, the original tenant will not be released from liability.

Tenants must also consider the implications of an assignment or a sublet on use restrictions, trade name restrictions, reporting of percentage rent, reporting of consideration for assignment, and franchise fees. These issues and others are discussed in more detail below.

Sale of Business

Whether large or small, a tenant must negotiate into its lease the right to sell its business. Ordinarily, the sale of the business constitutes an assignment or subletting requiring the landlord's consent. However, in many instances, tenants are able to negotiate the right to sell the business so long as the landlord receives some protection and assurances that the assignment will not materially alter the operations in the leased premises. In general, typical landlord requirements of any prospective purchaser/assignee include: (1) a comparable net worth, (2) comparable retail experience, (3) same use, (4) same trade name, and (5) that the assignment be in connection with the sale of all of the tenant's stores. Where the business is franchised, most landlords will consent to an assignment, and some will even allow such an assignment without their consent, if the sale is to the franchisor or to a bona fide franchisee having a net worth comparable to that of the tenant, provided the assignee agrees to continue to operate the business as a franchise under the same trade name, use, and system. Landlords will also normally except from assignment restrictions the sale of stock of publicly traded companies and tenant reorganizations where the resulting entity has a comparable net worth and continues the same use and trade name as the tenant.

As discussed in the section on defining who is the tenant, the issue of assignment of a franchised business is further complicated by the fact that nearly all franchise agreements reserve to the franchisor the right to reenter the premises and to take over operations should the franchise fail to follow operating rules of the franchisor, breach the lease, or breach its franchise agreement. However, absent express language in the lease to the contrary, entry by the franchisor would probably be construed as a prohibited assignment of the lease.

Financing

Many lenders, including the United States Small Business Administration, are now requiring that leases be assigned as collateral for the loan. Nearly all landlords will object to this provision and will fight vigorously to prohibit an assignment of the lease as collateral. However, if the only way to finance the store is to obtain a collateral assignment of the lease, many landlords will acquiesce if given assurances that the store will continue to operate under the trade name and use even if the bank forecloses. It is therefore important to address the financing issue and its implications for assignment restrictions in the lease prior to lease execution.

Relationship With Other Clauses

We have already discussed how an assignment or sublet can be affected by the use clause and trade name requirements. However, of equal significance are certain claims that a landlord may make for the consideration received by a tenant for the assignment. Most leases specifically state that the landlord is entitled to any consideration over and above the rent for the premises. Moreover, in the case of a percentage rent deal, the landlord's definition of gross sales may include all consideration received from the transaction of business from the premises. Accordingly, the landlord may argue that sums received in consideration of the sale of the business are either the landlord's property or, at the very least, are to be included in determining the tenant's percentage rent.

It is best that the lease specifically state that consideration received in connection with the sale of the tenant's business will not be included in gross sales and is the tenant's property. However, even if this distinction is not in the lease, the tenant may sell the trade name, goodwill, and inventory by separate agreement and argue persuasively that the landlord has no right to consideration received for the trade name, goodwill, and inventory of the tenant (this position also applies to franchise fees). However, where the assignment is to an entity with a wholly different use or trade name, the facts favor the landlord's argument that the assignment is in essence a sale of the landlord's real estate and that the proceeds belong to the landlord. Tenants should review each lease very carefully to make sure that the landlord will not have the right to claim any proceeds received by the tenant as a result of an assignment or sublet.

Finally, tenants should bear in mind that the assignment clause can also affect the amount of damages the landlord may receive if the tenant is in default. Specifically, the furnishing of a proposed assignee or subtenant to the landlord may serve as evidence against the landlord's damages claims when the landlord is under an obligation to mitigate damages.

Cotenancy Clauses

As important as any other lease issue is the ability of a tenant to assure itself that the shopping center it believes it is entering will not wither away. In today's economy, when major department stores such as Bloomingdales, Macy's, Ames, and Garfinkel's have sought the protection of bankruptcy laws and scores of smaller retailers are closing their doors, it is a realistic fear of any tenant that the shopping center it bargained for will cease to exist. Absent provision in the lease to the contrary, the fact that one or more anchor stores and scores of smaller mall tenants are no longer transacting business will not relieve a tenant of its obligations under the lease, including the obligation to pay rent and to remain open. The problem is compounded if the tenant is located in a wing of a shopping center with high vacancies or with a closed anchor store. One way of addressing these concerns is through the cotenancy clause.

Simply stated, a cotenancy clause conditions the tenant's obligation to open on other tenants in the shopping center being open. Often landlords modify the cotenancy provisions by tying the tenant's obligation to a provision calling for a certain number of other tenants "being required to be open." Since nearly all leases now have continuous occupancy requirements and set mall hours, the cotenancy clause is of little benefit to the tenant if the phrase *required to be open* is inserted in place of *open*.

There are generally three occasions when the cotenancy clause comes into play: (1) when determining the tenant's hours of operation, (2) when determining the commencement date, and (3) if after the tenant's opening a certain number of stores or one or more department stores close their doors. In each instance, the tenant should subject its obligations under the lease to: (1) all department stores (specifying the names of each department store) being open, and (2) a significant percentage of leasable floor area being leased, occupied, and open for business. Tenants should also insert provisions allowing for rent abatement or adjustment if the cotenancy conditions are not satisfied and for a right to terminate if the cotenancy conditions remain unsatisfied for a certain period of time. Moreover, tenants should include, in connection with any termination right, the right to recover from the landlord the unamortized cost of the tenant's improvements.

Dispute Resolution

Except in rare instances, the express language of the lease governs disputes between the parties. Landlord/tenant disputes can be very expensive, and the landlord is usually in a better financial position to litigate the dispute. While arbitration is available, we have found it to be just as costly as litigation, with far more suspect results.

The remedies available to tenants for landlord violations, such as self-help and set-off, are either not practical or else subject tenants to suit for default. Even if the tenant prevails, a tenant's recovery for a loss is often limited to the landlord's equity in the shopping center, which, given the popularity of leveraging in recent years, may be nonexistent.

There are times when a landlord and tenant have a bona fide dispute. In these circumstances, many landlords choose to protect their rights and serve the tenant with notice of default. Tenants (and, where applicable, tenants' franchisors) should make sure that the lease provides them with a guaranty of written notice and a reasonable opportunity to cure (usually thirty days for nonmonetary defaults, ten days for monetary defaults). If the notice of default is without foundation or is based on an error, the tenant should notify the landlord immediately that it is not in default. If the tenant is in default and it knows it cannot or will not cure, then the options of bankruptcy and assignment rights need to be explored, as should the landlord's mitigation obligations. Tenants should keep in mind that most state courts have landlord and tenant divisions that provide for expedited hearings in cases involving a tenant's default. Sometimes these expedited proceedings can be frustrated and postponed by tenant demands for a jury trial or by assertions of meritorious counterclaims. They may also be delayed by requesting discovery as to the basis of the tenant's default. Such a delay may benefit the tenant in a variety of ways. First, it may help attain a settlement with the landlord, as few landlords can afford a nonpaying tenant controlling their space. Second, it may allow the tenant the time to conclude its affairs in the store, including inventory liquidation sales.

In the final analysis, the ability to resolve lease disputes between landlord and tenant is a function of the past relationship between the parties and whether the parties wish to make deals again in the future. With national tenants and landlords, each party depends on the other for future growth opportunities. Accordingly, most disputes tend to be resolved without litigation in a fair and equitable manner. However, if the relationship between the parties is volatile and if neither cares about jeopardizing future deals, litigation and additional expense prove the rule, rather then the exception.

While kicking a tenant when he's down may give some landlords pleasure, at some point down the road the tenant may be critical to a new shopping center. By the same token, suing landlords, particularly those with other prime space, may frustrate tenants' ability to reach attractive markets. In short, regardless of the nature of the dispute, it is better, to the extent possible, to walk away at the end of the day on good terms.

Other Lease Concerns

Although not spoken of frequently, there are a variety of other lease concerns that tenants should address during their negotiations. A summary of these are discussed below.

Asbestos/Hazardous Materials

Nearly all leases provide that the tenant accept the leased premises "as is" and that tenant comply with all applicable laws. While these provisions may on the surface appear to be reasonable, they can shift to the tenant the financial responsibility for abating friable asbestos (asbestos that is exposed and that presents a hazardous condition requiring removal) and hazardous materials, even if the materials were not brought upon the leased premises by tenant. Accordingly, tenants should take extra care to make sure the leased premises are free of friable asbestos and hazardous materials on the commencement date and to shift to the landlord the responsibility for abatement or compliance with applicable environmental laws if hazardous materials are subsequently discovered and not brought on the leased premises by the tenant.

Tenants should realize that many landlords will insist on similar restrictions prohibiting tenants from bringing hazardous materials onto the leased premises. Although in most retail franchise businesses this is not an issue, certain businesses will by necessity have to use substances defined by law as hazardous materials. For example, a film development business, an auto service station, or a print shop all may use hazardous substances every day. Accordingly, tenants should be careful to carve out exceptions in the lease that allow for the use of hazardous materials if they are necessary for the tenant's business, so long as they are properly stored and disposed of. Finally, tenants should make sure that costs incurred by the landlord to comply with environmental laws are not included in common area costs.

Bankruptcy

In recent times, a struggling tenant's ultimate weapon against an uncooperative the landlord has been to petition the United States Bankruptcy Court for relief. However, in order to avail itself of bankruptcy protection, the entity owning the store must be insolvent (i.e., not paying its obligations as they come due). Therefore a strong tenant cannot file bankruptcy for one bad location (which again favors the concept of making each store a separate legal entity).

By filing bankruptcy before termination of the lease a tenant can in effect circumvent the assignment restrictions of the lease. First, a bankruptcy filing effectively allows the tenant to control the leasehold. This can be very significant in situations where the lease itself is valuable. The bankruptcy court will generally approve an assignment so long as the tenant assigns the space to a tenant who can provide adequate financial assurances and can demonstrate the same or similar use. Second, the filing of bankruptcy, where the lease is of little or no value, effectively forces the landlord to take back the space and to discharge the tenant from its future rent obligations. Finally, because of the severe consequences a bankruptcy filing may have on the landlord's ability to control its space, the threat of bankruptcy tends to enhance negotiations with landlords.

Nondisturbance Agreements

Most leases contain provisions that require tenants to subordinate its leasehold interest to any existing or future lenders of the landlord and to accept new owners of the leased property. In essence, this means that the tenant agrees to allow the landlord's lenders or successors in interest to treat the tenant's leasehold interest as secondary to the interest of the landlord's lenders or successors in interest, even if the lease was in force before the date of the loan. The problem with granting unconditional subordination and attornment rights is that if the landlord defaults on its loan, the lender or successor in interest can proceed as if the tenant's lease did not exist on the date of the loan, effectively giving the lender or the lender's successor in interest the ability to terminate the tenant's leasehold interest. In order to avoid this situation, the tenant should attempt to secure a nondisturbance agreement from existing and future lenders of the landlord who have liens against the shopping center. The nondisturbance agreement constitutes the existing party's assurance that so long as the tenant is not in default it will continue to enjoy those rights afforded under the lease.

As a practical matter, landlords will generally attempt to avoid any provision that conditions the tenant's obligation to subordinate or to attorn its interest to the tenant's receipt of a nondisturbance agreement, particularly concerning any existing lender. If such is the case, the tenant may consider recording the lease in the land records office as one alternative. If the lease is properly recorded, any future lien holder or successor in interest (including purchasers) will have to take the property subject to the lease. However, the problem with recording is that in many jurisdictions it is very costly. In any event, tenants should keep in mind that even if landlords are unwilling to secure nondisturbance agreements, it is unlikely that a lender or a party seeking subordination or attornment will not honor the tenancy because, in most cases, the decision to finance or to acquire the property is based on the rent generated by the property. Accordingly, lenders and purchasers generally will not take any action to diminish or to jeopardize the rental income stream, and tenants' use and enjoyment will generally be unaffected.

This chapter is meant to provide the reader with a general understanding of the important decisions and issues to be addressed prior to entering into a lease. The reader should always keep in mind that each business and each lease is different and that other issues not discussed in this chapter are bound to arise. It is therefore our recommendation that the reader use this chapter only as a guide for evaluating its lease decisions and consult experienced counsel prior to executing any lease. After all, the lease is arguably one of the most important legal documents the franchisee will sign.

PART VI

FINANCIAL MANAGEMENT ISSUES IN FRANCHISING

One of the most critical, yet often overlooked, aspects of building a franchising company is the financial aspect, including tax management and capital formation.

Early-stage franchisors are notoriously guilty of conducting financial analysis in a vacuum (if at all), being undercapitalized (which has both regulatory and franchise relations implications), largely ignoring key accounting and tax issues (until they reach crisis levels), and failing to develop strategic relationships with third-party lenders and leasing companies to facilitate opening for business quickly and cost-efficiently.

The chapters in Part VI address the critical tax, accounting, and financial issues that are at the heart of building a franchising company.

26

Raising Growth Capital for the Emerging Franchisor

Andrew J. Sherman, Silver, Freedman & Taff

Owners and managers of growing franchisors have come to understand that meaningful and effective business planning is critical to the long-term success and viability of any business and to its ability to raise capital. Only recently have the investment banking and the commercial lending communities given franchising the attention it deserves. There are finally enough franchisors whose balance sheets have become more respectable, who have participated in successful public offerings, who have played (and won) in the merger-and-acquisition game, and who have demonstrated consistent financial appreciation and profitability. These developments have played a role in providing young franchisors access to affordable capital in recent years. Nevertheless, a growing franchisor must be prepared to *educate the source of capital* about the unique aspects of financing a franchise company compared to financing a conventional business. And there *are* differences. Franchisors have different balance sheets (heavily laden with intangible assets), different allocations of capital (directed as expenditures for "soft costs"), different management teams, different sources of revenues, and different strategies for growth.

The Business Plan

Before you consider the various methods of financing available to the growing franchisor, *it is critical that you understand the key elements of a business plan.* A well-prepared business plan demonstrates management's ability to focus on long-term achievable goals, provides a guide for effectively implementing the articulated goals once the capital has been committed, and constitutes a yardstick by which actual performance can be evaluated. Regardless of the method chosen for raising capital or the type of capital to be raised, virtually any lender, underwriter, venture capitalist, or private investor will expect to be presented with a meaningful business plan. The following is a broad outline of the fundamental topics to be included in a typical growing franchisor's Business Plan.

A. Executive Summary.

This introductory section of the plan should explain the nature of the business and highlight the important features and opportunities offered by an investment in the company. The Executive Summary should be no longer than one to three pages and should include: (1) the company's origins and performance; (2) distinguishing and unique features of the products and services offered to *both* consumers and franchisees; (3) an overview of the market; (4) an overview of its franchise sales track record and its relationship with its franchisees; and (5) the amount of money sought and for what specific purposes.

B. History and Operations of the Franchisor.

This first full section of the Business Plan should discuss the history of the franchisor in greater detail; its management team (with resumes included as an exhibit); the specific program, opportunity, or project being funded by the proceeds; a discussion of the prototype; an overview of the franchisor's industry (with a specific emphasis on recent trends affecting the market demand for the franchises); and the products and services offered by the franchisee.

This first section should also address the following questions:

- When and how was the prototype facility first developed?
- Why has the company decided to expand its market share through franchising?
- What are the company's greatest strengths and proprietary advantages with respect to its franchisees? Consumers? Employees? Shareholders? Competitors?
- What are the nature, current status, and future prospects in the franchisor's industry?
- What is the franchisor's track record for sales and growth?
- How effective are current franchisee relations and communications programs?

Many of these issues will be discussed in greater detail in later sections of the Plan. Therefore, each topic should be covered summarily in two or three paragraphs.

C. Marketing Research and Analysis.

This section must present to the reader all relevant and current information regarding the size of the market for both franchisees and consumers, trends in the industry, marketing and sales strategies and techniques, assessments of the competition (direct and indirect), estimates of market share and projected sales, pricing policies, advertising and public relations, strategies, and a description of sales personnel.

The following questions should also be addressed:

- ▲ Describe the typical consumer. How and why is the consumer attracted to patronize the franchisee's facility? What relevant market trends affect the consumer's decision to purchase products and services from the franchisee's facility?
- ▲ Describe the typical franchisee. How and why is the prospective franchisee attracted to the franchisee's business format? What factors have influenced the prospect's decision to purchase the franchise?
- ▲ What is the approximate size of the total market for the services offered by the franchisee? The approximate market for franchisees?
- ▲ What marketing strategies and techniques have been adopted to attract franchisees and consumers? Where do referrals for prospective franchisees come from? Do existing franchisees make referrals? Why or why not? (Include sample promotional materials as an exhibit.)
- ▲ Describe the performance of the typical franchisee. Are the stores profitable? Why or why not?

D. Rationale for Franchising.

This section should explain the underlying rationale for selecting franchising instead of one of the other growth and distribution strategies that may be available. Discuss the ratios between company-owned units and franchise units and the relationship underlying this ratio. Under what circumstances will additional company-owned units be established? Explain to the reader which method(s) of franchising will be selected—single units only? Sales Representatives? Area Developers? Subfranchisors? Special risks and legal issues triggered by the decision to franchise should also be discussed.

E. The Franchising Program.

This section should provide an overview of the franchising program. It should discuss key aspects of the franchise agreement and include a description of the typical site, the proprietary business format and trade identity, the training program, the operations manual, support services offered to franchisees, targeted markets and registration strategies, the offering of regional and area development agreements, and arrangements with vendors. A detailed analysis of sales and earnings estimates and the personnel needed for a typical facility should be included. Discuss marketing strategies relevant to franchising, such as trade shows, industry publications, and sales techniques. Explain the typical length of time from the first meeting with a prospect to grand opening. What are the various steps and the costs incurred during this time period (from the perspective of both the franchisor and the franchisee)? Discuss strategies for the growth and development of the franchising program over the next five to ten years.

F. Corporate and Financial Matters.

This section should briefly describe the current officers, directors, and shareholders of the corporation. An overview of the capital contributed to the company thus far should be provided, along with an explanation of how these funds have been allocated. Discuss the anticipated monthly operating costs to be incurred by the corporation, both current and projected, not only for operating and managing the prototype facility but also for the administrative expenses incurred in setting up a franchise sales and services office. Discuss the pricing of the franchise fee, royalties, and promotional fund contributions. Discuss the payment histories of the franchisees thus far. Are they complying with their obligations under the franchise agreement? Why or why not?

What portion of these fees collected from the franchisee will be net profit? Discuss the amount of capital that will be required for the corporation to meet its short-term goals and objectives. How much, if any, additional capital will be required to meet long-term objectives? What alternative structures and methods are available for raising these funds? How will these funds be allocated? Provide a breakdown of expenses for: personnel, advertising and marketing, acquisition of equipment or real estate, administration, professional fees, and travel. To what extent are these expenses fixed, and to what extent will they vary depending on the actual growth of the company?

G. Operations and Management.

Provide the current and the projected organizational and management structure. Identify each position by title, with a description of duties, responsibilities, and compensation. Describe the current management team and anticipated hiring requirements over the next three to five years. What strategies will be adopted to attract and retain qualified franchise professionals? Provide a description of the company's external management team, such as attorney and accountant.

H. Exhibits.

Include in the presentation copies of the franchisor's trademarks, marketing brochures, and press coverage, as well as sample franchise agreements and area development agreements.

Legal and Strategic Issues in Private Placements

Franchisors are increasingly turning to private placements of their securities as a viable method of raising equity capital. In general terms, a private placement may be used as a vehicle for capital formation any time a particular security or transaction is exempt from federal registration requirements under the Securities Act of 1933, which regulates the offer and sale of securities. In order to determine whether a private placement is a sensible strategy for raising capital, it is imperative that franchisors: (1) have a fundamental understanding of the federal and state securities laws affecting private placements; (2) be familiar with the basic procedural steps that must be taken before such an alternative is pursued; and (3) have a team of qualified legal and accounting professionals who are familiar with the securities laws to assist in the offering.

Private placement generally offers reduced transactional and ongoing costs because it is exempt from many of the extensive registration and reporting requirements imposed by federal and state securities laws. Franchisor generally enjoy even greater cost saving because much of the disclosure information required for a private placement memorandum (PPM) has already been assembled and disclosed in a franchise offering circular (FOC). Since the franchising business is inherently disclosure-driven, the management teams of franchisors generally have an easier time with the process of preparing the PPM than their nonfranchisor counterparts.

The private placement usually also offers the ability to structure a more complex and confidential transaction, since the offeree is typically a small number of sophisticated investors. In addition, a private placement permits a more rapid penetration of the capital markets than does a public offering of securities requiring registration with the Securities and Exchange Commission (SEC).

An Overview of Regulation D

The most common exemptions from registration that are relied upon by franchisors in connection with a private placement are contained in the SEC's Regulation D. The SEC promulgated Regulation D in 1982 in order to facilitate capital formation by smaller companies. Since its inception, Regulation D has been an extremely successful vehicle for raising capital, with billions of dollars being raised each year by small and growing businesses. Regulation D offers a menu of three transaction exemptions:

1. *Rule 504.* The first exemption created by Regulation D is a Rule 504 offering, which permits offers and sales of not more than $1 million in securities (provided that no more than $500,000 is offered and sold without registration under state securities laws) during any twelve-month period by any issuer that is not subject to the reporting requirements of the Securities Exchange Act of 1934 and that is not an investment company. Rule 504 places virtually no limit on the number or the type of investors that participate in the offering. Even though no formal disclosure document needs to be registered and delivered to the offeree under Rule 504, there are many procedures that still must be understood and

followed. In particular, since most states do not include an exemption similar to 504, it is necessary to prepare a formal private placement memorandum.

2. *Rule 505.* This second exemption under Regulation D allows for the sale of the franchisor's securities to an unlimited number of "accredited investors" and up to thirty-five nonaccredited investors regardless of their net worth, income, or sophistication, in an amount not to exceed $5 million in a twelve-month period. Many franchisors select Rule 505 over Rule 504 because its requirements are consistent with many state securities laws. An accredited investor is any person who falls within one or more of the eight categories set out in Rule 501(a) of Regulation D. Included in these categories are officers and directors of the entity who have "policymaking" functions, as well as outside investors who earned $200,000 per year for the last two years (or $300,000 for each of the last two years in conjunction with a spouse) or whose net worth exceeds $1 million. The issuer should keep in mind, however, that if one or more of the purchasers is not an accredited investor, then a full private placement memorandum must be prepared and delivered to all purchasers. There is an absolute prohibition on advertising and general solicitation for offerings that fall within Rule 505 or 506.

3. *Rule 506.* This exemption is most attractive to growing franchisors requiring large amounts of capital because it has no maximum dollar limitation. As under Rule 505, the issuer may sell its securities to an unlimited number of accredited investors and up to thirty-five nonaccredited investors. The primary difference is that, under Rule 506, any nonaccredited investor must be a "sophisticated" investor. In this context, a sophisticated investor is one who does not fall within any of the eight categories specified by Rule 501(a) but is believed by the issuer to ". . . have knowledge and experience in financial and business matters that render him capable of evaluating the merits and understanding the risks posed by the transaction, either acting alone or in conjunction with his purchaser representative." Rule 506 does eliminate the need to prepare and deliver disclosure documents in any specified format if only accredited investors participate in the transaction. The same absolute prohibition on advertising and general solicitation imposed by Rule 505 applies to Rule 506 offerings.

The Relationship Between Regulation D and State Securities Laws

Full compliance with the federal securities laws is only one level of regulation that must be taken into account when a franchisor is developing plans and strategies to raise capital through an offering of securities. Whether or not the offering is exempt under federal laws, registration under applicable "blue sky" laws may still be required in the states where the securities are to be sold. This often creates expensive and timely compliance burdens for growing franchisors and their counsel, who must contend with this bifurcated scheme of regulation. Generally speaking, there are a wide variety of standards of review among the states, ranging from very tough "merit" reviews (designed to ensure that all offerings of securities are fair and equitable) to very lenient "notice only" filings (designed primarily to promote full disclosure). The securities laws of each state where an offer or a sale will be made should be checked very carefully prior to the distribution of the offering documents.

Venture Capital as a Source of Growth Financing

A rapidly growing franchisor should strongly consider venture capital as a source of equity financing when it needs additional capital to bring its business plans to fruition but lacks the collateral or the ability to meet the debt-service payments that are typically required to qualify for traditional debt financing from a commercial bank. This is especially true for franchisors, who often need capital to finance "soft costs," such as personnel and marketing, for which debt financing may be very difficult to obtain. As franchising as a method of expanding a business matures, a growing number of private investors and venture capitalists have been willing to consider a commitment of capital to emerging franchisors.

Some recent trends within the venture capital industry may increase the chances for early-stage franchisors to obtain venture capital. For example, many venture capital firms have recently expressed an interest in making smaller transactions in more traditional industries that offer lower risk and more moderate (but stable) returns. Many franchisors that operate in basic industries (e.g., food, hospitality, entertainment, personal services) can meet these investment criteria. There has been a definite shift away from high-tech deals, which are largely dependent on a single patent or on the completion of successful research and development, and toward investments in more traditional industries even if they result in less dynamic returns.

Negotiating and Structuring the Venture Capital Investment

Assuming that the franchisor's business plan is favorably received by the venture capitalist, the franchisor must then assemble a management team capable of negotiating the transaction. The negotiation and structuring of most venture capital transactions revolves around the need to strike a balance between the concerns of the founders of the company, such as dilution of ownership and loss of control, and the concerns of the venture capitalist, such as return on investment and reduced risk of business failure. The typical end result of these discussions is a Term Sheet setting forth the key financial and legal terms of the transaction, which then serve as a basis for the negotiation and preparation of the definitive legal documentation. Franchisors should ensure that legal counsel is familiar with the many traps and restrictions that are typically found in venture capital financing documents. The Term Sheet may also contain certain rights and obligations of the parties. These may include an obligation to maintain an agreed valuation of the company, an obligation to be responsible for certain costs and expenses in the event the proposed transaction does not take place, or an obligation to secure commitments for financing from additional sources prior to closing. Often these obligations are also included as part of the "conditions precedent" section of the formal Investment Agreement.

Negotiations regarding the structure of the transaction between the franchisor and the venture capitalist usually center upon the types of securities to be used and the principal terms, conditions, and benefits offered by the securities. The type of securities ultimately selected and the structure of the transaction usually fall within one of the following four categories:

1. *Preferred stock.* This is the most typical form of security issued in connection with a venture capital financing to an emerging growth company. This is so because of the many advantages that preferred stock can offer to an investor, such as convertibility into common stock, dividend and liquidation preferences over the common stock, antidilution protection, mandatory or optional redemption schedules, and special voting rights and preferences.

2. *Convertible debentures.* This type of security is basically a debt instrument (secured or unsecured) that may be converted into equity securities upon specified terms and conditions. Until converted, it offers the venture capitalist a fixed rate of return and offers tax advantages (e.g., deductibility of interest payments) to the franchisor. A venture capitalist often prefers a convertible debenture in connection with higher-risk transactions because the venture capitalist is able to enjoy the elevated position of a creditor until the risk of the company's failure has been mitigated. Sometimes these instruments are used in connection with bridge financing; the venture capitalist expects to convert the debt to equity when the subsequent rounds of capital are raised. Finally, if the debentures are subordinated, commercial lenders often treat them as the equivalent of an equity security for balance sheet purposes, helping the franchisor to obtain institutional debt financing.

3. *Debt securities with warrants.* A venture capitalist often prefers debentures or notes in connection with warrants for the same reasons that apply to convertible debt, namely the ability to protect downside by enjoying the elevated position of a creditor and the ability to protect upside by including warrants to purchase common stock at favorable prices and terms. The use of a warrant enables the investor to buy common stock without sacrificing the position as a creditor, as would be the case if only convertible debt were used in the financing.

4. *Common stock.* Venture capitalists rarely prefer to purchase common stock from the franchisor, especially at early stages of development. This is because "straight" common stock offers the investor no special rights or preferences, no fixed return on investment, no special ability to exercise control over management, and no liquidity to protect against downside risks. Common stock might be selected if the franchisor wishes to preserve its Subchapter S status under

the Internal Revenue Code, which would be jeopardized if a class of preferred stock were to be authorized.

The Use of Initial Public Offerings by Growing Franchisors

An initial public offering (IPO) is the process by which a growing enterprise registers its securities with the SEC for sale to the general investing public for the first time. Many growing franchisors view the process of "going public" as the epitome of financial success and reward. And many national franchisors have successfully completed public offerings in recent years, including Shoney's (family restaurants), Wendy's International (fast food), TCBY Enterprises (frozen yogurt), Snelling & Snelling (personnel placement), McDonald's Corporation (fast food), Medicine Shoppes International (pharmacy stores), Ponderosa (steak houses), and Postal Instant Press (printing centers).

However, the decision to go public requires considerable strategic planning and analysis from both a legal and a business perspective. The planning and analysis process involves: (a) a weighing of the costs and benefits of being a public company, (b) an understanding of the process and costs of becoming a public company, (c) an understanding of the obligations of the company, its advisors, and its shareholders once the franchisor has successfully completed its public offering, and, most important, (d) choosing the timing of the offering carefully.

Costs and Benefits of the IPO

For the rapidly expanding privately held franchisor, the process of going public presents a number of benefits, including: (1) significantly greater access to capital; (2) increased liquidity for the franchisor's shares; (3) greater prestige in the financial markets; (4) enhancement of the franchisor's public image (which may have the effect of increasing franchise sales); (5) opportunities for employee ownership and participation; (6) broader growth opportunities, including the potential for merger, acquisition, and further rounds of financing; and (7) an immediate increase in the wealth of the company's founders.

However, the many benefits of being a public company are not without their corresponding costs, and the latter must be seriously considered in the strategic planning process. Among these costs are: (1) the dilution in the founders' control of the entity; (2) the pressure to meet market and shareholder expectations regarding growth and dividends; (3) changes in management styles and employee expectations; (4) the need for compliance with complex regulations imposed by federal and state securities laws; (5) stock resale restrictions for company insiders; (6) vulnerability to shifts in the stock market; and (7) the sharing of the franchisor's financial success with hundreds, even thousands, of other shareholders.

Note that many franchisors have not been intimidated by the disadvantages of being publicly held, primarily because they: (1) are already operating in a disclosure-oriented business; (2) are already compelled to provide audited financial statements; and (3) feel that being publicly held will increase credibility, which generally increases franchise sales.

Preparing the Registration Statement

If, after weighing the costs and benefits of an IPO, this financing route is selected, then the franchisor should locate experienced securities counsel (that is also sensitive to the special issues raised by franchising) to assist in the preparation and filing of the Registration Statement. The Registration Statement, which must be filed with the SEC by the franchisor's counsel, consists of two distinct parts. The first part is the offering prospectus, which is the document that is widely distributed to underwriters and prospective investors to assist them in analyzing the franchisor and the securities being offered. The second part includes the exhibits and additional information that are provided directly to the SEC as part of the disclosure and registration regulations. The SEC has also established special provisions for small offerings by companies that are not already subject to the reporting requirements of the 1934 Securities Exchange Act. This is Form S-18, which is available for offerings which will not exceed $7.5 million over a twelve-month period. Form S-18 is somewhat less detailed than a disclosure and requires less detailed financial statements.

An Overview of the Registration Process

Once the registration statement has been prepared and is finally ready for filing with the SEC, franchisor's counsel has two choices: either to file the document with the transmittal letter and required fees *or* to schedule a prefiling conference with an SEC staff member to discuss any anticipated questions or problems regarding the registration. Once the registration statement is officially received by the SEC, it is then assigned to an examining group, composed usually of attorneys, accountants, and financial analysts, within a specific industry department of the Division of Corporate Finance. The length of time and the depth of the review afforded by the examining group to any given registration statement depend on the history of the franchisor and the nature of the securities offered.

In addition to individual state and SEC regulations, a franchisor offering its securities to the public must also meet the requirements of the National Association of Securities Dealers (NASD) and of state securities laws. The NASD analyzes all elements of the proposed compensation package for the underwriter in order to determine reasonableness.

Once the final underwriting agreement is signed and the final pricing amendment is filed with the SEC, the registration statement will be declared effective, and the selling process may begin. To facilitate the mechanics of the offering process, it is recommended that a franchisor retain the services of a registrar and transfer agent, who will be responsible for issuing stock certificates upon closing, maintaining stockholder ownership records, and processing the transfer of shares from one investor to another.

The issuer is usually required to file Form SR, which is a report on the franchisor's use of the proceeds raised from the sale of the securities. An initial Form SR must be filed within ninety days after the registration statement becomes effective and once every six months thereafter until the completion of the offering and the application of the proceeds toward their intended use.

Ongoing Reporting and Disclosure Requirements of Publicly Held Companies

Section 13 of the Securities Exchange Act of 1934 grants broad powers to the SEC to develop documents and reports that must be filed by companies that register their securities for sale to the general public. The three primary reports required by Section 15(d) of the Exchange Act are Form 10-K, Form 10-Q, and Form 8-K.

1. *Form 10-K.* This is the annual report, which must be filed ninety days after the close of the fiscal year covered by the report. Form 10-K must include a report of all significant activities of the franchisor during its fourth quarter, an analysis and discussion of financial condition, a description of current officers and directors, and a schedule of certain exhibits.

2. *Form 10-Q.* This is the quarterly report, which must be filed no later than forty-five days after the end of each of the first three fiscal quarters of each fiscal year. This quarterly filing includes copies of the financial statements for the quarter (accompanied by a discussion and an analysis of the franchisor's financial condition by its management), as well as a report of any pending litigation.

3. *Form 8-K.* This is a periodic report that is designed to ensure that *all material information* pertaining to significant events that affect the franchisor are disclosed to the investing public as soon as they are available but not later than fifteen days after the occurrence of the particular event that triggers the need to file the Form 8-K. The duty to disclose "material information" to the general public, whether as part of a form 8-K filing or otherwise, is an ongoing obligation that continues for as long as the franchisor's securities are publicly traded.

Debt Financing Alternatives for the Growing Franchisor

Early-stage franchisors have not had much luck with commercial banks over the past two decades. This is because most lenders prefer to see "hard collateral" on the balance sheet of a borrower, which is often lacking with start-up franchisors who have only their intellectual property, a projected royalty stream, and a business plan to pledge. A second problem is that most lenders prefer to see a use of proceeds that is allocated primarily to the purchase of "hard assets" (to further serve as collateral), which is the opposite of what many franchisors want to do with their capital. Most early-stage franchisors need capital for "soft costs," such as the development of manuals, advertising materials, and recruitment fees. Certainly these intangible assets can be pledged; however, they are likely to be given far less weight than equipment, inventory, and real estate. By the time that the franchise system has matured to the point that a lender is willing to extend capital based upon the franchisor's balance sheet, royalty stream, and track record, no capital is likely to be required.

Despite these problems, it is likely that the optimal capital structure of a growing franchisor will include a certain amount of debt on the balance sheet. The use of debt in the capital structure, commonly known as "leverage," affects both the valuation of the company and its overall cost of capital. The maximum debt capacity that a growing franchisor will ultimately be able to handle usually involves a balancing of the costs and the risks of a default of a debt obligation against the desire of the owners and the managers to maintain control of the enterprise by protecting against the dilution that an equity offering would cause. Many franchisors prefer to maintain control over the affairs of their company in exchange for the higher level of risk that is inherent in taking on additional debt obligations. The ability to meet debt-service payments must be carefully considered in the company's financial projections.

If a pro forma analysis reveals that meeting debt-service obligations will put a strain on the franchisor's cash flow or that insufficient collateral is available (as is often the case for early-stage franchisors who lack significant tangible assets), then equity alternatives should be explored. It is simply not worth driving the company into voluntary or involuntary bankruptcy solely to maintain a maximum level of control. Overleveraged franchisors typically spend so much of their cash servicing the debt that capital is unavailable to develop new programs and to provide support to the franchisees, which triggers the decline and the deterioration of the franchise system. In addition, the level of debt financing selected by the franchisor should be compared against key business ratios for its particular industry, such as those published by Robert Morris Associates or Dun & Bradstreet.

27

Raising Capital for the Prospective or Expanding Franchisee

Howard A. Davis, Franchise Capital Advisors, Inc.

In the past, the typical growing business's single source of external capital was a commercial bank. However, for some reason, banks have paid scant attention to franchising and the specific needs of franchisors and franchisees.

Since the mid-1980s, the former Finance, Accounting, and Tax Committee of the International Franchise Association has attempted to educate bankers across the country on what franchising is and on the opportunities available to them. Franchise companies have been forced to seek alternative sources of financing for both the franchisor and the franchisee.

According to a study recently conducted by Francorp, the average-sized franchisor has approximately sixty-five outlets, hardly comparable to McDonalds, which is the kind of franchise most lending institutions are familiar with. Regardless of size, franchisors are always seeking new and additional sources of capital. A policy decision by a bank to stop funding franchise companies or specific industries can have tremendous impact.

This chapter deals with financing in general and specifically addresses techniques for financing franchisees and the various alternatives a franchisor can take in assisting its franchisees in obtaining capital.

The Role of the Franchisor

In most cases the prospective franchisee perceives the franchisor as an expert in all phases of its franchise business and assumes that the franchisor has established relationships with various types of lenders. To what extent the franchisor takes an active role in helping its franchisees obtain funding depends on the specific system and on what involvement the franchisor chooses to take on. Most franchise agreements contain provisions protecting the franchisor if it chooses to assist the prospective franchisee in obtaining financing. The reality is that the franchisor knows the real value in providing assistance, which allows it to open new units and generate franchise fees, ongoing royalty fees, and other sources of revenue. (Typical franchisee financing needs are listed in Figure 27-1.)

There are numerous ways a franchisor can assist a franchisee in obtaining financing, including:

- Creating a source book identifying the various types and sources of financing
- Establishing a relationship with various lenders
- Providing its own financing
- Assisting in the presentation of a loan package
- Establishing vendor programs
- Providing internal leasing programs
- Guaranteeing loans
- Providing remarketing agreements
- Teaching the prospective franchisee to package and present a loan
- Developing creative approaches to obtaining financing

The key issue is, *at what point does the franchisor accept a deposit from a prospective franchisee and execute a franchise agreement—before or after financing has been committed or put in place?*

When money changes hands, the franchisor is motivated to complete the transaction and usually is not happy to refund any monies. Therefore, the franchisor has a definite incentive to get the financing in place as quickly as possible.

In most cases the applicant will have a financing situation that requires special attention for one reason or another. Keep in focus that we are dealing strictly with financing issues, not operational issues. It is quite possible that even with financing in place, the prospective franchisee will fail training or prove unable to obtain a site.

The Financing Approach

Once the franchisor has made the decision to assist the prospective franchisee in some fashion, it becomes its responsibility to understand the financing market

Figure 27-1. Franchisee financing needs.

Land and building	Signage
Equipment	Marketing
Leasehold improvements	Expansion
Working capital	Consolidation
Renovation	Inventory
Conversion	

and the requirements of the specific lenders. Its reception by the lenders will depend on what stage the franchise company is in (start-up, growth, emerging, or maturity), each of which has a different impact on different lenders. Remember, just as in law and medicine, there are specialists in lending, too. The commercial banker or real estate lender probably knows very little about factoring or equipment leasing, whereas an equipment lessor knows enough to be wary about term loans or real estate loans.

In all cases, lenders are going to be concerned about (1) the borrower, (2) the amount of financing, (3) the primary source of repayment, (4) a secondary source of repayment, and (5) collateral issues.

Markets and conditions change, and it is crucial to maintain a list of all available alternatives and to be prepared for a sudden change. Banks used to be a primary source of capital for small businesses. The current environment for lending to any company below the stature of a Fortune 500 company is very difficult, but not necessarily impossible. Many lenders and institutions have changed their views, and it is not inconceivable for even a seasoned franchisor to lose sources of financing as a result of a policy change or a change in financial condition at its traditional lender.

Internal Analyses

The franchisor must first understand and identify each and every cost associated with setting up its franchise operation. In addition to the actual hard costs, such as equipment and signage, soft costs, such as working capital, special permits, and licenses, must be identified. It is imperative to identify as many hidden costs as possible. Even the seasoned franchisor should keep information updated on an ongoing basis. This information is also required in the Uniform Franchise Offering Circular, which in most cases does not include a sufficiently detailed breakdown.

A franchisor may set *absolute* net worth requirements in selecting franchisees or may allow for more flexibility, establishing particular financing arrangements with certain lenders and allowing potential franchisors a free hand in seeking financing. My experience suggests that the average franchisor has to allow itself flexibility. It may be in the franchisor's best interest to work harder with an experienced candidate who could be an excellent franchisee for the particular system but who needs creative financing methods or with an employee of a franchisee or the franchisor.

Unit Cash Flow Analyses

Obviously, it is important to understand the range of potential cash flows that can be generated from a franchised unit. Historical information is the best. If a franchisor has not exercised good internal control procedures, information can be obtained by requesting current financial data or by reviewing the tax returns of franchisees. If the franchise is new, the financial data available may be limited to company operations. The franchisor should have this information to determine the health of its system. Keep in mind that the more information the lender has, the easier it will be to obtain financing. The unavailability of information or the existence of a poor track record may necessitate an alternate means of financing.

The key information being sought is the available cash flow after taking into consideration a provision for the franchisee's own personal cash requirements, which are often overlooked.

The Matching Principle

Each asset (tangible or intangible) identified in Step I needs to be evaluated on an item-by-item basis and viewed as an appropriate source of funds. Each asset should be matched to an appropriate *type* of financing (there may be more than one appropriate type).

Organizing the Search

Since we are dealing with an environment where there are thousands of lending sources, it is important to organize your data bank. A financial source book should be set up using colored tabs separators for each type of *source* you are planning to contact or already conduct business with. For example, tabs might name commercial banks, leasing companies, venture capitalists, government programs, and commercial finance companies. Behind each separator place a data sheet with the name, address, telephone number, and contact person at the institution you have contacted or will be contacting. As new sources are developed, it is easy to update your source book. Understanding each lender's criteria is an important element of your data sheet, and each type of lender should have its own data information. (Forms of financing are listed in Figure 27-2, and potential sources are listed in Figure 27-3.)

Beginning the Search

Now you are organized and ready to begin the search for financing. Again, a lot depends on the specific growth plans of the individual franchisor, who may decide to assist in providing sources for particular geographic areas and in tailoring presentations for specific lenders. On the other hand, the franchisor may have a new area targeted for development, in which case a "fishing expedition" may take place to attract new franchisees.

Current or past contacts are a good starting point; remember, lender decisions change regularly. The initial mission is to begin assembling your source book. Referrals are the next best source; trade associations, vendors, and other franchisors are other ways to find sources.

Completing the Search

Updating the source book and searching for new sources of financing is an on-going task. The purpose of the initial search is to establish a base and to match financing and lending requirements to individual franchisor requirements and historical information. For example, it may be determined that certain commercial banks provide term loans for only three years or that they are interested only in providing Small Business Administration (SBA) loans or loans backed by real estate. Some may not be interested at all. Similarly, certain equipment leasing companies lease equipment such as cash registers or computers, in which case several lessors may be required to accomplish the financing objective. Finally, certain financing sources may restrict themselves to certain geographic areas.

Now that a data bank has been established, the franchisor must decide which, if any, sources it wishes to establish a relationship with.

* * *

Up to this point, we have identified the specific financing needs, unit cash flows, and various lending sources. Much valuable information can be obtained from this: (1) Maybe the franchisor has to set different qualification standards for prospective franchisees; (2) new sources of financing may be available that could reduce the franchisees' capital requirements; (3) there may be ways to combine the sources and to create a customized financing package; (4) the franchisor may have revealed new ways to obtain financing; or (5) the franchisor may have the ability to establish an internal financing program and have an outlet to support a certain number of franchises or to sell the paper on a nonrecourse basis to an unaffiliated third party.

Establishing a Relationship With Lenders

The franchisor is in business to expand via franchising new units. In most cases, a prospective franchisee is going to need external capital to be able to proceed in purchasing a franchise and will turn to the franchisor for assistance and potential sources. Experience says that the more sources of financing a franchisor has and the better the understanding of each lender's requirements, the greater the competitive advantage that company has over the others.

A major problem that most franchisors face is how to approach a lender. Assuming the franchisor has taken the time to create a source book, it is important to understand what information various lenders require. More important, it is the role of the franchisor to educate the lender about franchising prior to submitting a loan request, because most lenders do not understand the subject. *Establishing a relationship is a two-way street—the franchisor wants to learn about the lender and the lender wants to learn about the franchisor.*

The relationship that begins today may not provide immediate results, but it

Figure 27-2. Types of financing.

Financing comes in two forms: debt or equity.
The following is a list of types of financing available:

Debt Instruments

Trade Credit

- Open account trade credit
- Notes payable trade credit
- Consignment trade credit
- Trade acceptances

Bankers acceptances

Letters of credit

- Export letters of credit
- Import letters of credit
- Standby letters of credit
- Revolving letters of credit
- Irrevocable letters of credit
- Transferable letters of credit

Transaction loans

Floor planning

Commercial paper

Revolving credit

Term loans

Banks

- Debentures
- Subordinated debentures
- Insurance bonds
- Mortgage bonds
- Zero coupon bonds

Mortgages

Equity Financing

Common stock

Preferred stock

- ▴ Cumulative/noncumulative
- ▴ Callable

Asset-based financing

Accounts receivable financing

Accounts receivable factoring

Inventory financing

Other Financing Alternatives

Warrants

Convertible bonds

Leasing

Sale leaseback

Employee Stock Ownership Plans (ESOPs)

could save you a tremendous amount of time in the future. As business goes up and down, different sources of capital will be used to finance franchisees. Lenders will come and go. Even large companies need to cultivate new lenders, because existing ones at some point may have too much concentration in one industry or company. The object of the financing game is to demonstrate the ability to get lending sources under all circumstances.

Generally, lenders are concerned about risk, because they have to report to their shareholders and/or governmental agencies. Different lenders will assume different risks. Currently, an abundance of money is being loaned by nonbank lenders, which are not subject to the same regulatory constraints as traditional banking institutions.

The franchisor's goal in establishing a relationship with the lender is to make sure the lender understands the franchisor's business and to prove to the lender that (1) there is evidence of customer acceptance of the product or service; (2) the company is focused and committed to supporting the franchise system and not moving in too many directions at once; (3) the proprietary position in the market has value and that a franchisee joining the system should not be viewed as another start-up business; (4) a strong management team is in place, even if it means identifying outside consultants or companies that provide services to the franchisor; and (5) the operations will generate an acceptable return on investment (ROI)

Figure 27-3.   Sources of financing.

Barter financing	Mortgage bankers
Broker's commission	Option financing
Commercial banks	Other people's credit
Commercial finance companies	Partnership with seller
Commercial paper brokers	Pension funds
Consumer finance companies	Prepaid subscriptions
Credit unions	Preselling
Customers	Private underwriting
Deposits	Real Estate Investment Trusts
Employees	(REITs)
Equipment manufacturers	Savings and loans
Equity sharing	Seller financing-earnout
Existing business versus new	State sources
business	Suppliers
Factoring companies	Third-party guaranty
Financial brokers	U.S. Government Sources
Future commitments	• Small Business
Investment bankers	Administration (SBA)
Investment companies	• Small Business Investment
Landlord improvements	Companies (SBIC)
Leasing companies	• Minority Enterprise Small
Leveraged buyouts	Business Investment
Life insurance companies	Companies (MESBIC)
Limited partnerships	Venture capital

and will provide enough cash flow to repay the lender, provide a good income to the franchisee, and build the franchisee's retained earnings.

Additionally, the franchisor is interested in (1) establishing a contact at the lending institution; (2) defining who the decision makers are; (3) determining what the lending approval process is and the specific lending authority of the contact; (4) understanding what lending criteria the lender uses; (5) identifying what issues the lenders are sensitive to; (6) pinpointing what information they require in a loan package; and (7) estimating the time needed for the approval process.

This information will help the franchisor in reviewing a particular franchise candidate and in determining if a specific lender might be interested in financing a particular operation. Additionally, by establishing different relationships, the franchisor will be able to continually monitor its own requirements in selecting franchisees.

The benefits of establishing and maintaining good relationships with lenders are numerous and include having a direct contact that understands your system to discuss a particular need, reducing turnaround time in getting a decision, knowing that a loan package will get immediate attention, and obtaining a more favorable rate than a traditional start-up venture. Additionally, the franchisor knows how to send the franchisee into the lender and can assist in the preparation of the loan package.

The first meeting should take place at the franchisor's office. Lenders like to see the environment in which the company operates. At this time the lender should receive a tour of the franchisor's facility and meet the key management players. A presentation of marketing materials and marketing research is also a good idea, and the franchisor should provide the lender with a current Uniform Franchise Offering Circular (UFOC) and supporting documents for review.

If possible a tour of the company and the franchise operations should take place to help the lender get a feel for the whole operation.

The franchisor should also request several documents from the lender, including (1) a current financial statement; (2) a copy of the spreadsheet on which it conducts its loan analyses; (3) a loan offering form or write-up guidelines; and (4) a list of documents required in a loan presentation.

The Loan Package

Preparing the loan package is the first step in actually obtaining the financing. The franchisor should have a good understanding of the information the specific lender requires in making its decision. There are a few basic understandings that should be mentioned. First, assume that the person receiving the package is not going to make the decision. Second, the more complete the package, the quicker the response and funding. Finally, the information should be precise, to the point, and supportable.

The lender is going to judge the applicant on a number of factors, including the character of management; the balance sheet and the net worth of the applicant; the applicant's capacity to earn money; cash flow; conditions in the economy, industry, and region; collateral; and current information provided by the franchisor. The lender also understands that there are four ways a loan can be paid back: (1) refinancing elsewhere, (2) obtaining an investor, (3) selling an asset, or (4) from earnings and cash flow (the preferable way).

The following items should be contained in the loan package:

Section 1: Executive Summary. The executive summary should contain a brief description of how much is being requested, how long it is being requested for, the purpose of the loan, how the loan is to be repaid, and alternative sources of repayment.

Section 2: Source and Use Summary. This section should contain a detailed list of the source of funds (equity contribution by the franchisee and proceeds from the lender) and a detailed description of where the funds are going. In developing the source book, the "use" elements should have been identified. Material items should be discussed in footnotes to the statement.

Section 3: Location Information. If a particular site has been selected or a lease prepared, a description of the lease terms and supporting demographic information should be included.

Section 4: Statement of Projected Earnings and Cash Flow. This is a key section of the loan package, since it must demonstrate to the lender the primary source of repayment and indicate any cash flow deficits that may occur in the beginning months of the business. Included in this section should be the franchisee's personal requirements. Detailed footnotes should accompany this statement with full support of the assumptions. The more detailed, the better the chance of getting the deal done. If the site is a new one or if the franchisor is expanding into a new area, information on competitors should be obtained to provide additional support of the assumptions. *The franchisor should provide the guidelines in preparing this information and should require the franchisee to prepare the information. This will force the franchisee to take an active role and obtain a better understanding of the business.*

Section 5: Personal Financial Statement and Cash Flow. This should be completed on the lender's application form, if available. Any supporting documents, such as current bank statements, brokerage accounts, and loan information, should be included. Remember, the support you provide will prove your knowledge, minimize the time the lender has to take in obtaining information, and expedite the approval process.

Section 6: Tax Returns. Most lenders require a minimum of two years' tax returns, which should be included in their entirety, including K-1's from partnerships the applicant is a participant in.

Section 7: Personal Biographies. The lender will be interested in your past, in your plans for operating the franchise business, and in who you intend to hire as additional management if required, and how. If an absentee owner owns the franchise, a contingency management plan will be important.

Section 8: Industry Information. Current financial statistics and articles pertaining to the industry and the franchisor should be included. You are not submitting a marketing plan but rather enough information for a third person to review the package and understand the business.

Section 9: Franchise Agreement and UFOC. The proposed Franchise Agreement and supporting documents should be included.

28

Developing Franchisee Equipment Leasing Programs

Richard M. Contino, FirstStreet Credit Corporation and
Executive Online! Company

A franchisee's ability to lease needed equipment can increase a franchisor's profits. The high cost of franchise startup and operations can limit available operating cash, cash often critical to a franchisee's initial survival and future success. Leasing, because it is 100 percent financing, conserves working capital. Additional working capital creates more operating time, and that, in turn, increases a franchisee's chances of success. More successful franchisees mean greater franchisor profits.

The Need for a Financing Strategy

In today's competitive market, an equipment leasing program must be an integral part of a franchisor's marketing effort. Franchisors with effective financing programs have a competitive edge over those that lack one. Having ready financing for necessary equipment reduces a franchisee's required capital outlay and increases the attractiveness of a franchise offering. Very simply, the easier it is for a franchisee to get financing, the greater the chance of a franchise sale.

For the uneducated franchisor, the leasing market can have some unhappy surprises. Leasing companies are sometimes not what they seem; financing programs change without notice; available funds unexpectedly dry up; worse yet, enthusiastic lessor marketing is all too often misleading.

To further complicate matters, there is no general financing program approach that works for every franchisor. Packages offered, customer credit profiles, equipment involved, and franchisors' abilities vary widely. As a result, the franchisor's approach must be tailored to fit its potential customers' needs and capabilities, all within the context of its financial and management strengths. In other words, in order to have a successful equipment financing program, a franchisor must develop its own financing strategy. Attempting to assist franchisees on a deal-by-deal basis does not work.

The typical franchisee seeking financing faces unique financial hurdles. If they are not properly taken into account early in the financing process, problems will occur. For example, franchises by their nature are start-up operations. Start-ups present increased credit risks to a lessor and, since leasing is a credit business, may be cause for an automatic turndown. Specific management experience, something often lacking, is also an important consideration.

Common lease misconceptions also get in the way. Some franchisors, for example, believe leasing companies will finance anyone on the basis of having the equipment as collateral security, regardless of credit standing. They reason that a lessor has little financial risk in a lease default because it can repossess and sell the leased equipment to recover any remaining invested cost. Unfortunately, this is not generally true. Used equipment sale proceeds rarely cover a lessor's remaining lease balance, particularly if a lessee defaults in the early years. The fact that equipment is involved is a secondary consideration; high potential resale equipment makes a deal sweeter but does not provide the basis for a financing approval. For example, machine tools traditionally have high end-of-lease resale values, something that increases lessor deal profit and, therefore, increases the lessor's interest in a transaction.

The franchisor that anticipates difficulties and creatively handles them before they become problems is in the best position. Those that attempt to find leasing companies to approve customer financing outside normal guidelines are in for disappointment.

Relying on the Franchise Risks Sales

Relying on a prospective franchisee to find necessary equipment financing is risky; many have limited financing experience. In all fairness, even people with solid business backgrounds typically don't approach the leasing market effectively. As we have already suggested, a franchise situation can present difficult financing roadblocks. Putting together a salable franchise financing package takes experience. Knowing how to overcome approval objections is often an art. Relying on the leasing salesperson for suggestions can be a mistake. Most work on a commission basis and quickly move to the next deal when problems are encountered.

Developing a Financing Strategy

Developing an effective, reliable, and attractive customer equipment financing program can be done, but it takes careful preparation. The franchisor has to understand the realities of the leasing market—the benefits, the risks, and the players. In some situations, for example, lessors require substantial financial guarantees or cash collateral, such as certificates of deposit, that prospective franchisees cannot, or will not, provide. In others, an equity interest in the franchisee's, or the franchisor's, business may be requested. In many cases a lessor will attempt to tie up as security all of a franchisee's personal and business assets, something that may be unacceptable.

The best way for a franchisor to ensure the availability of franchisee financing is to establish its own financing company. That, however, takes money, expertise, and management time and can create undue financial risks for the franchisor.

The next best alternative is to establish a solid primary relationship with a compatible, well-established lessor and secondary relationships with at least two other funding sources. With each, the franchisor should develop a financing plan that spells out approval criteria, documentation requirements, and necessary customer credit support. If the franchisor fails to do this well in advance of franchise marketing, effective and timely customer equipment financing is problematic at best. Time and money are easily thrown away pursuing financing structures that have little chance of acceptance.

An effective financing program must provide the franchisor with, for example, the ability to obtain financing for the weaker, in addition to the strong, credit franchisee. Unless pinned down in writing, most lessors avoid approving all but the top credits. If the issue is put on the table in advance, it can be solved. Offering, for example, to provide the leasing company with a right of first refusal on all business may convince it to provide financing in the less desirable situations. Without planning, the franchisor may be forced to provide unreasonably restrictive or open-ended financial or other guarantees to get a franchisee financed.

A word of caution: Franchisors should not rely on a lease salesperson's verbal assurances that a lease will be approved. Most work on a commission basis and have little to lose by throwing another deal in front of the credit committee to see if it will pass.

An Overview of the Leasing Business

The concept of the lease as a property right, and the rights and duties of lessors and lessees, has been part of our legal tradition for centuries, particularly with respect to real estate. During the 1950s, leasing began to emerge as a viable alternative for acquiring equipment. Today, the equipment leasing industry plays a major role in the financial community: A user can lease virtually any type of equipment on a variety of terms. There is however, a drawback; the legal requirements and financial considerations are, at times, extremely complex. In fact, many transactions involve concepts so sophisticated that even the most experienced people sometimes make mistakes that could cost them or their customers thousands of dollars.

To get the best deal, a franchisor has to understand the leasing basics. It cannot randomly approach the leasing market and hope that someone will figure out and offer an enticing customer financing program. The franchisor must know where to start, what to ask for, and how to assist in effectively supporting a franchise credit without giving away more than necessary. Never forget: A leasing company's objective is to make its lease investment as secure as possible—and then some.

The increased interest in leasing as an alternative means of acquiring equipment has made it necessary for franchisors to be able to assist in arranging it. To do so, the franchisor must know, for example, the common lease structures, who the potential lessors are, how different lessors work, and what risks are involved. Understanding the lease pros and cons is also essential. There are many pitfalls for the inexperienced. Leasing companies know every marketing trick in the book and use them to cut their investment risk to a minimum. For example, some notoriously offer extremely low financing rates and later, when competition has been eliminated, find a way to justify an increase. If you don't know the rules, you will make mistakes that can hurt business. Always keep in mind that a leasing company is out to make as much money as possible as quickly and as safely as possible.

The tax aspects of a lease transaction can be another important consideration. The rules are extremely complex. For certain types of lease transactions, the rapidly changing tax laws have created problems and uncertainties. Major changes, for example, enacted by the 1986 Tax Reform Act (1986 TRA) took away the investment tax credit (ITC) and expanded the alternative minimum tax (AMT). Additional tax law changes intended to stimulate business could have a significant impact on leasing. A knowledge of the key aspects is essential in structuring the most effective customer financing program.

Because of the many variables that can be involved in establishing an effective customer leasing program, this chapter cannot answer all the questions involved for a particular franchisor. The approach used by one company may be totally inappropriate for another company. This chapter does, however, introduce the reader to the essential issues that must be taken into account in developing a solid financing approach.

Tax Reasons for Leasing

The General Tax Picture

Although any type of equipment can be leased, the critical question for the prospective lessee is, at what cost? While the answer is complex, as a threshold matter leasing often is not an economical way to acquire equipment unless the lessor can take advantage of certain tax benefits and indirectly pass them on, at least in part, in the form of relatively lower lease rents.

Example: The Tax Advantage. Company Able wants to acquire the use of a $20,000 computer. It can borrow funds from its bank for five years at the prime rate, assumed for this example to be 10 percent a year. If Able were able to borrow 100 percent of the funds required, its cost to finance the computer would be the cost of the $20,000 loan.

As an alternative, Able could lease the computer from Company Baker. Assume Baker also borrowed "at prime" from the same bank and that it would fund the computer purchase entirely from its bank borrowing. If there were no computer ownership tax advantages, the only way it could make a profit would be to charge a lease rate greater than its cost of funds. Thus, Able would have to pay something over prime rate to Baker, not a very attractive arrangement.

Although this example is admittedly oversimplified and not completely realistic, it makes the point—leasing may not make any economic sense for a lessee unless the lessor is able to use available ownership tax benefits.

The Lessor's Tax Benefit

What tax benefits are available to the lessor? For equipment placed in service before 1986, the lessor can obtain both an investment tax credit (ITC) and depreciation deductions as an equipment owner. With limited exceptions, the 1986 Tax Reform Act (TRA) did away with the ITC for equipment placed in service after 1985. Thus, the tax benefits for the lessor today are the depreciation deductions available under the Modified Accelerated Cost Recovery System (MACRS), introduced by the 1986 TRA.

Under MACRS, a lessor generally can write off his equipment's costs over a period significantly shorter than its useful life and at an accelerated rate. For example, a lessor can deduct the cost of the leased computer equipment over a six-year period, with the percentages for each year 20 percent, 32 percent, 19.2 percent, 11.52 percent, 11.52 percent and 5.76 percent. In a typical lease, the lessor's deductions in the early years exceed the rental income, permitting the lessor to offset other income with those excess deductions.

A word of warning: A franchisor intending to establish its own leasing company must consider the effect of the revised corporate alternative minimum tax (AMT) rules; depreciation deductions will be deferred significantly. This in turn could have a major impact on what rents should be charged.

The Lessee's Tax Consequences

Basically, an equipment user decreases its tax benefits by becoming a lessee rather than an owner. As lessee, the user can deduct rental payments, but those will be less than the depreciation she could have deducted in earlier years. Then why should leasing be considered? As explained later in this chapter, there are numerous financial and business reasons for a prospective lessee to lease rather than to buy. Also, leasing is particularly attractive to equipment users who cannot take timely advantage of the depreciation deductions. Two types of users basically fall into this category. First are those who have negative taxable income or carryover losses so that they have no taxable income to offset; second, to a lesser extent, are those subject to the AMT, because the AMT reduces the value of an equipment owner's tax benefits but does not in most cases affect deductions for rent. For those users, the rental payments charged by a lessor who is taking ownership tax benefits into account in setting his lease rate can be worth more than the ownership tax benefits.

The Importance of Lease Structuring

When the lessor anticipates tax benefits, he will suffer an economic loss if those benefits are unavailable. Those benefits will be available only if the lessor remains the equipment owner for tax purposes. The lessor will be treated as the tax owner only if the lease is a true lease. To qualify as a true lease for tax purposes, certain tax guidelines must be met. A discussion of these guidelines is beyond the scope of this chapter, and the reader is referred to the many excellent technical books on leasing available today.

Poor lease structuring can lead to disaster. If the transaction does not qualify as a true lease, the lessee will not be able to deduct the rental payments and the lessor will not be able to use the ownership tax benefits. For example, if the lease was classified as a loan, the lessee would be deemed the equipment owner and the lessor deemed the lender. If the lessee cannot use any tax benefits and the lessor must have them for the transaction to make economic sense, everyone loses.

Observation: While all leases must be true leases for the lessor to obtain tax benefits, for leases where the lease term is significantly shorter than the equipment's useful life, there will be little risk that the lease will not be treated as a true lease, because the lessor's ownership status will be clear. Generally, the closer the lease term comes to matching the equipment's useful life, the more attention must be paid to the true lease rules.

Potential Lessors

In order to begin to develop a financing strategy, a franchisor must know the types of individuals and companies that provide lease financing and how they operate. Each has unique characteristics, with accompanying benefits and risks that must be taken into account.

For discussion purposes, it is useful to separate the potential lessors into five categories: individuals, independent leasing companies, lease brokers, captive leasing companies, and banks. The categories can be helpful in narrowing the field of potential lessors. For the franchisor considering setting up its own leasing company, the categories are helpful in determining an approach to take.

Individuals

Prior to the 1986 TRA, the role of the individual as lessor was limited because of the rules restricting an individual from claiming ITCs on leased property. Now that ITC is no longer available to lessors, wealthy individuals can be rate-competitive. This, coupled with the fact that they often take greater business risks than traditional leasing companies do, can make them a good choice in difficult financing situations. A few innovative equipment leasing companies and investment bankers have begun to develop interesting investment programs for individuals that will make them an increasing part of the equipment financing business. For example, some railcar lessors have set up individual investor programs that provide individuals with opportunities to invest in short-term railcar leases.

An individual considering becoming an equipment lessor must, however, now contend with the passive loss rules. An explanation of those rules is outside the scope of this chapter. The franchisor or prospective lessee receiving a lease proposal from an individual lessor, however, need not be concerned with the passive loss rules, except to be sure that any indemnities do not require the lessee or the franchisor to reimburse the lessor for deductions lost under those rules.

A word of caution: A prospective lessee considering leasing from an individual must look at more than the rent advantage. For example, because individuals often take aggressive tax positions, they may run afoul of the IRS. The IRS may then put a lien on all the individual's property, including the leased equipment. Also, individuals can be somewhat more arbitrary to deal with when variances from the lease terms are required.

Independent Leasing Companies

Independent leasing companies provide a major source of equipment lease financing. Because leasing is their principal source of revenue, they have to be extremely aggressive and, in some cases, are willing to bend the rules for the lessee's benefit to win a transaction. For example, some will give a lessee the right to buy the equipment at a low predetermined fixed price when the lease ends—a practice that can run the risk of adverse tax consequences.

There are two types of independent leasing companies: those that merely buy and lease equipment to the user (finance companies) and those that also offer other services, such as maintenance and repair of the equipment (service leasing companies).

FINANCE LEASING COMPANIES

Finance leasing companies—lessors of millions of dollars' worth of equipment each year—operate in much the same manner as banks or other financing companies. They do not maintain an equipment inventory but rather, after agreeing on a lease with a lessee, buy the specific equipment needed for the lease. The lessee orders and receives the equipment from the vendor. When it arrives, the finance leasing company pays for it, takes title, and leases it to the equipment user.

Finance leasing companies typically write leases, referred to as finance leases, that run from 70 to 80 percent of the equipment's useful life. The total amounts received under these leases, including the rents payable and the equipment residual value proceeds, are usually sufficient to provide the lessor with a full return of his equipment investment and a profit. If the equipment purchase is leveraged with third-party debt, the rents will also usually be enough to cover the full repayment of the debt. This type of long-term lease is net to the lessee; that is, the lessee must assume substantially all the equipment ownership responsibilities, such as maintenance, taxes, and insurance.

SERVICE LEASING COMPANIES

Service or specialized leasing companies provide nonfinancial services to lessees in addition to the equipment financing. Services may include equipment maintenance and repair or advice on the equipment's operation and design.

Service lessors typically limit their activity to a single type of equipment, such as computers, or to a single type of industry, such as the mining industry. The in-depth experience gained through the specialization enables them to reduce many leasing risks. For example, because they frequently handle used equipment, they know how to deal efficiently with equipment when it comes off lease, which, in turn, reduces their re-leasing or sale risk. Furthermore, because of that reduced risk, they can offer attractive lease termination or equipment exchange privileges.

Observation: Many industry participants believe that product specialization is less risky for a lessor than industry specialization. They reason that an industry-specialized lessor would likely suffer more if his industry were to hit hard times than an equipment-specialized lessor would if one of the industries in which his equipment was used were to experience a downturn.

Service lessors typically write leases with much shorter lease terms than finance leases. Nonpayout in nature, those leases do not permit the lessor to recoup her entire equipment investment during the first lease term. Thus, to recover her investment and make a profit, the service lessor must continue to re-lease the equipment. If the equipment becomes obsolete sooner than expected, the lessor may incur a loss. To be compensated for taking that high risk and for providing other services, service lessors generally charge higher rents than finance lessors.

When should a franchisor consider using a service leasing company? Basically, when the lessee needs the specialized services offered by the service lessor or wants a shorter lease term or early termination rights. A user may want the shorter term when, for example, there is a high risk of equipment obsolescence.

Lease Brokers

Also referred to as lease underwriters or syndicators, lease brokers package lease transactions for the account of third parties. Put simply, they match up prospective lessees with prospective lessor-investors. They charge a fee for their service, usually ranging from 0.75 to 8 percent of the leased equipment's cost, which is typically paid for by the lessor-investors.

To put the lease broker's role into perspective, it is helpful to understand how a broker normally operates. Generally, a lease broker begins by contacting all types of equipment users and vendors to determine whether they have any leasing needs. In the case of a prospective lessee, he defines the rough parameters through discussions with the prospective lessee. At this juncture, the broker may perform a credit check on the prospective lessee to make sure the credit is marketable. If there are not any problems, he formulates a concise lease structure, including rental rate, and offers it to the equipment user, generally through a formal proposal letter.

If the user finds the proposed arrangement acceptable, the broker then proceeds to find prospective lessor-investors, commonly referred to as equity participants, or, in the case of smaller transactions, a leasing company. If the transaction is to be leveraged with third-party debt, a leverage lease, he may also put out feelers for prospective lenders, commonly referred to as debt participants, although usually the debt side is handled by an investment banker. Having located the equity and the debt participants, the broker proceeds to shepherd the transaction through documentation to completion.

Although generally acting exclusively as a broker, a lease underwriter may, on occasion, invest some of his own funds in the equipment along with other third-party lessor-investors and, thereby, become a part owner. By doing so, the lease underwriter can add credibility to the investment and thus be able to sell the lease transaction to potential investors more readily.

One of a lease broker's major assets is his knowledge of the leasing industry. Because he is continually in the market, he knows where to find competitive, cooperative, and realistic equity participants. And he knows how to get those equity participants to agree to what meets the lessee's needs, including, for example, lease rates, overall transaction structure, and documentation.

There is a risk in dealing with brokers. If they cannot find the funding participants, you must start over looking for financing. So long as you understand this risk and put some realistic performance time limits on the broker arranging the funding, you can plan for any nonperformance possibilities. The problem is, particularly in the small-ticket lease marketplace where transactions range from $1,500 to $100,000, the broker may not state that she is a broker for fear of losing your business. Some companies simply won't deal with intermediaries but insist on negotiating with the actual money source. So, if you are led to believe that you have a firm deal when the lease proposal is signed and you rely on that belief, you may find yourself in difficulty if the leasing company is acting as a broker and cannot perform and no contingency plans have been made.

Captive Leasing Companies

In increasing numbers, equipment vendors are setting up their own leasing companies, generally referred to as captive leasing companies, to service their customers. Although the purpose is usually to offer lease financing on equipment sold by an affiliated company, some captive leasing companies also may be willing to buy and lease equipment sold by a nonaffiliated company.

A captive leasing company marketing its affiliated company's equipment can often offer attractive rates, because, when it markets its affiliated company's equipment, that company makes a sale profit, allowing the captive lessor to work with a lower financing profit. Coupled with its knowledge of the equipment's potential residual value, this can result in attractive rents for a lessee.

Recommendation: When considering a certain vendor's equipment, always find out whether the vendor has a captive leasing company. If so, it should be seriously considered in developing your financing strategy.

Observation: Although captive leasing companies have a theoretical advantage over other types of lessors because of their connection with the vendor, in practice they often do not know how to take advantage of that position effectively. Perhaps this is because the equipment vendors do not have extensive experience in using leasing as a marketing tool and may not support the leasing operation as fully as they should.

Banks

Many banks, particularly national banks, are actively involved in equipment leasing. They usually are lessors in net finance leases because of regulatory requirements and because those leases provide the least risk and most similarity to their lending activity. (Finance leases are explained later in this chapter.)

Banks are not generally inclined to take aggressive equipment residual value positions and may therefore demand higher market lease rates. Their cost of funds, however, in many cases is lower than that of nonbank lessors, often offsetting their conservative residual value positions.

The terms and rates offered by bank lessors often vary significantly from one transaction to the next. Internal bank policies may contribute to that variation. Banks are not as dependent as most nonbank lessors on their leasing activities for revenues and so can afford to miss out on many deals. Periodically, however, they can go on major drives for lease business and, at those times, can be extremely rate-aggressive.

There is a hidden risk in dealing with banks. Since leasing is not considered their main line of business, if they experience general financial difficulties, as they have in the late 1980s and early 1990s, their leasing department is usually one of the first to go. Management's rationale is that the bank must go back to basics to get its financial house in order. Chase Manhattan Bank's sale of its profitable leasing subsidiaries in 1991 is a good example of what can happen when a bank experiences general financial problems.

Recommendation: Given the unpredictability of bank lessors' responses to potential lease transactions and of their commitment to the business, a franchisor is well advised to avoid relying exclusively on one to service all its financing needs.

Many bank lessors typically operate with a limited lease marketing staff. As a result, the transactions they see are fundamentally limited to those coming in through existing customer or lease brokers. Today, however, an increasing number of bank lessors are establishing strong marketing organizations; as a group, they will undoubtedly become more of a factor in the marketplace.

It is worth mentioning that banks directly participate in the leasing market in a another major way: They frequently act as lenders in leveraged lease transactions.

Types of Leases Used

Significant differences exist among the various types of leases. Unfortunately, the industry jargon used to label the different types is sometimes less than precise. Further compounding the problem is the fact that many hybrid arrangements have surfaced that cross over the lines of the standard descriptive terminology. Once the fundamental characteristics of different leases are identified and understood, however, the confusion can be eliminated.

For explanation purposes, it is helpful to separate all equipment leases into two main categories: financial leases and operating leases. The financial, or finance, lease typically represents a long-term lease commitment in which the sum of the rents due approximates the equipment's purchase cost. Decisions to enter into a financial lease should be part of a company's financial, as opposed to operating, policy considerations. All equipment leases not fitting within the financial lease category can be put into the operating lease category. Because operating leases involve shorter-term financial commitments, decisions as to their use typically come within the scope of a company's operating policy.

Within those two broad categories, there are a number of basic variations: leveraged leases, nonleveraged leases, and service leases. These variations are sometimes incorrectly considered to be separate types of leases rather than what they are, descriptive forms of the basic types. For example, finance leases can be leveraged leases or nonleveraged leases, and service leases can be financial or operating in nature. They will, however, be explained individually to give the reader a working perspective.

Figure 28-1 sets out a general overview of some fundamental lease characteristics.

Figure 28-1.　Lease characteristics.

Type of Lease	Lease Term	Typical Type of Transaction	Comments
Finance Lease	Substantial portion of asset's economic life	Underwritten and direct lessor	Payout-type lease
Net Finance Lease	Substantial portion of asset's economic life	Underwritten and direct lessor	Payout-type lease. Lessee has basically all ownership responsibilities.
Leveraged Lease	Usually, substantial portion of asset's economic life	Underwritten	Usually net finance lease
Nonleveraged Lease	Hours to substantial portion of asset's economic life	Direct lessor	Any lease where no third-party debt involved
Operating Lease	Hours to years	Direct lessor	Usually nonpayout

The Finance Lease

A common type of equipment lease, finance leases are considered long-term leases because the primary lease terms usually run for most of the equipment's useful life. Typically, the total cash flow over the term—from rents, tax savings, and equipment residual value—is sufficient to pay back the lessor's investment, take care of administrative expenses, pay off any equipment-related debt obligations and commissions, and provide a profit. Because they are entered into by lessors as long-term financial commitments, finance lessors usually impose a substantial repayment penalty for a lessee's early lease termination in an amount that ensures a return of the lessor's investment and a profit, at least up to the date of termination.

Consistent with its financial nature, a finance lease is usually a net lease. A net lease is one in which the fundamental ownership responsibilities, such as maintaining and repairing the equipment, paying for the necessary insurance, and taking care of property, use, and sales taxes, are placed on the lessee. A net finance lease can be compared to an equipment loan in that the lessor, like a lender, is involved only in asset funding. The lessor's only basic responsibilities are to pay for the equipment, lease it to the lessee for the agreed-on term, and not interfere with its use.

Because a finance lease's term runs for most of the equipment's useful life, the lessee bears most of the risk of the equipment's becoming obsolete. The degree of obsolescence risk that the finance lessor assumes depends on the equipment's anticipated residual value. If, for example, a lessor computes the rent on the basis of a zero equipment residual value at the lease term's end, the lessor has no residual value risk and, thus, no obsolescence risk. This, of course, presumes there is not risk of premature equipment return as a result, for instance, of a lessee default. As a practical matter, however, a lessor must generally use a residual value greater than zero to be price-competitive. The risk of obsolescence is then on the lessor to the extent of the value estimated. If her profit is in part dependent on the anticipated residual value, the greater the risk of obsolescence, and the greater the chance the transaction will not turn out to be as profitable as anticipated.

One of the financial lessor's principal concerns is the protection of her investment in the event of a lease default or an equipment casualty. Toward this end, finance leases usually include provisions to make the lessor whole if any of these events occur. From a casualty loss standpoint, the lease may include stipulated loss value provisions. Those provisions set out the amount the lessee must pay the lessor if an equipment casualty occurs, depending on when it occurs. The amount of the stipulated loss value is intended to guarantee the lessor a return of her investment, reimburse her for any tax benefit losses, and assure her of at least some profit. These stipulated loss values are also sometimes used as a measure of lease default damages, although there are other methods.

Finance leases frequently contain a ''hell-or-high-water'' rent commitment. Under this type of obligation, a lessee must pay the full rent when due unconditionally and cannot reduce the amount paid even though he has a legitimate claim against the lessor for money owed. This is not as bad as it sounds for a lessee, because he can still bring a lawsuit against the lessor for any claims.

Finance lessors seek hell-or-high-water rent provisions most often in leveraged lease transactions involving nonrecourse loans. The reason for this is that, in a nonrecourse loan, the lender agrees to look only to the lessee's rent payments and the equipment for a return of his investment. With a hell-or-high-water provision, the lender need not be concerned that a dispute between the lessor and the lessee will result in the lessee's withholding rent and therefore may well be willing to offer an attractive loan arrangement.

The Operating Lease

If a lease's primary term is significantly shorter than the equipment's useful life, the lease is referred to as an operating lease. Operating leases typically run anywhere from a few months to a few years, although some are as short as a few hours.

Because the lease terms are relatively short, an operating lessor usually cannot earn back much of his equipment investment through the rents from one lease transaction. Thus, he must either sell or re-lease the equipment on attractive terms to come out ahead. The danger to an operating lessor, of course, is that the equipment's market value will be inadequate to allow him to sell or re-lease it on economically favorable terms. In other words, he has the risk of equipment obsolescence. As a result, such a lessor attempts to earn back his money faster to lessen his investment exposure by charging higher rent than a finance lessor.

Their short lease terms and easy cancellation provisions make operating leases attractive to users in several situations—if the user anticipates using the equipment for only a short time or if the user wants to be able to change equipment if something better comes out. Users often lease computer equipment under operating leases in view of the constant technological improvements of that equipment.

The Leveraged Lease

In a leveraged lease, a percentage of the funds to buy the equipment, usually 60 to 80 percent, is loaned by a bank or other lender. Because the lessor has put up only a small percentage of the equipment's cost, her investment is said to be leveraged, because her return is based on 100 percent of the cost. Leveraging generally enables a lessor to provide a lessee with relatively lower rents while at the same time maintaining her return. Frequently, net finance leases are structured as leveraged leases.

The debt used to leverage a lease transaction is usually nonrecourse debt. With nonrecourse debt, the lender has no recourse against the lessor for nonpayment of the loan but he can look only to the rental stream, the lessee, and the value of the equipment for its repayment. In such an arrangement, the lessor must assign to the lender its rights under the lease, including the right to the rental payments.

Observation: While a lessor has no repayment obligations to a nonrecourse lender if the lessee defaults, he does bear some risk because his rights against the lessee and the equipment are subordinated to the lender's repayment rights.

The Nonleveraged Lease

Also referred to as an unleveraged or a straight lease, a nonleveraged lease is one in which the lessor pays for the equipment from his own funds. Leasing companies often enter into nonleveraged leases.

A distinct advantage in using a nonleveraged lease structure is that there are usually only two principals involved, the lessee and the lessor. Because of the limited number of parties, the mechanics of putting together a transaction are simpler, saving time and documentation costs, such as legal fees. One disadvantage for a lessee, however, is that the rent is usually higher than it would be if the lease were leveraged.

The Service Lease

Leases in which the lessor assumes equipment ownership responsibilities, such as maintenance, repair, insurance, record keeping, or payment of property taxes, in addition to providing the asset financing, are usually called service leases. Service leases generally have relatively short lease terms.

The Pros and Cons of Leasing

Leasing is not always the best way for every user to acquire equipment. In some circumstances, it is advisable; in others, buying equipment is the right decision. In each situation, a user must weigh all the advantages and disadvantages. In order to establish the most effective financing program, the franchisor must understand the issues that could affect a franchisee's decision to lease or to buy. This section provides the reader with the basic considerations essential to a comprehensive evaluation.

Observation: Putting together lease financing can require less red tape and less time than a loan transaction. There are situations in which the shorter documentation time and expense saved can make up for a higher interest cost. This is particularly true when the cost of the equipment involved in relatively small.

The Advantages of Leasing

▲ *Reducing obsolescence concerns*. When a user is concerned that equipment may become obsolete before the end of its useful life, leasing can reduce that concern, provided part of the lessor's investment return is based upon a sale or re-lease of the equipment when the term ends. High-tech equipment, such as computer equipment, often gives rise to that concern because new, more efficient models that quickly make their predecessors obsolete are continually being developed.

As a practical matter, as long as the equipment does its job, does it really matter whether there is better equipment available? In some situations it does. For example, a more efficient item of manufacturing equipment can lower production costs by a sufficient amount that the user has to acquire a new model before the old model has been written off to ensure the user's price-competitive position in the market. If the user has bought rather than leased the equipment, the overall cost of replacing it would be expensive. And if the old equipment's market value is significantly less than its book value at the time of replacement, the user may be confronted with a potentially undesirable book loss in addition to the replace-ment cash outlay.

Observation: A lessor also runs the risk of financial loss through equipment obsolescence. Thus, to protect himself he will undoubtedly build a premium into his rate to compensate for the risk. A prospective lessee may be willing to pay the premium as a form of insurance against a loss through obsolescence. Of course, if the equipment does not become obsolete the increased rental rate will have reduced the profits he could have made had he owned the equipment.

▴ *Meeting limited use needs.* If equipment is needed for a limited period of time, leasing can be an effective way of acquiring its use. It eliminates the remar-keting risks an owner would have at the end of a short use period, and it also permits a more defined estimate of the effective cost of using the equipment. For example, public utilities building their own plant often must acquire certain spe-cialized construction equipment to do the job. Once the plant is finished, the equipment may be of no further use to the utility, but it may still have many years of useful life left. If it cannot be sold for a reasonable price, the overall cost of its use can be high. Leasing removes the resale risk and allows the utility to determine in advance the total effective usage cost.

▴ *Preserving capital.* An advantage of leasing to some users is that it helps preserve their existing funds or bank lines for other uses. The absence of a down payment—in effect 100 percent financing—can assist high-growth-rate compa-nies in maximizing their use of funds. That can be particularly attractive in peri-ods of tight money.

Observation: When evaluating whether to lease or to buy equipment, a user must carefully consider the real cost of borrowed funds. For example, a high compensating balance requirement can easily increase the effective cost of a bank loan. As this type of collateral loan cost increases, the attractiveness of leasing usually increases.

▴ *Obtaining technical or administrative services.* Users lacking the staff or the expertise to attend to specialized equipment needs can lease equipment as a way to acquire those necessary technical or administrative services. Through ser-vice leases, users can avoid tying up time and manpower in activities that are outside their normal operations. There is, of course, generally a charge, built into the rent, for the nonfinancial services supplied. Typically, lessors of office equip-ment, trucks, automobiles, and railcars offer some form of nonfinancial services as a supplement to their financing. For example, railcar lessors frequently offer maintenance services.

▴ *Overcoming borrowing problems.* Users with credit or borrowing prob-lems may have an easier time getting leasing companies to fund their equipment needs, as leasing companies often impose less stringent financial requirements than traditional lenders. They are willing to take greater risks because (1) they actually own the equipment and (2) they can more readily handle used equipment than can traditional lenders if they must take possession from a defaulting lessee.

This is not to say that leasing companies will provide equipment financing to a user regardless of its financial condition. There still must be a reasonable assurance that the user will be able to meet the lease payments.

▴ *Benefiting from inability to use tax benefits*. It is common for a user to be in a situation in which it cannot use the tax benefits—currently depreciation deductions—that result from equipment ownership. It may, for example, have an excess of accumulated tax benefits or insufficient earnings, because of either poor performance or major acquisitions, that have used up its tax bill, or the user may be subject to the minimum tax and find the tax benefits deferred. Such a company can indirectly take advantage of most of the ownership tax benefits through leasing from a tax-sensitive lessor. Because such a lessor takes these tax benefits into account when calculating the transaction's economic return, he, in effect, passes these benefits through in the form of a relatively lower rent.

Observation: A lessor will not pass on 100 percent of the equipment ownership tax benefits to a lessee through a reduced rental charge. He will make a profit on those benefits by adjusting the rent to reflect only a partial recognition. The rent adjustments vary with each lessor and each situation.

▴ *Avoiding capital budget restrictions*. Decisions to lease equipment are sometimes made to avoid a user's internal capital budget restrictions. For capital equipment purchases above a certain amount, a manager may be required to obtain prior approval, and that approval may be difficult or impossible to obtain. If the equipment is leased, she may be able to account for the rental payments as an operating expense—even though the lease represents a long-term financing similar to a capital expenditure—to get around the approval problem. In this way, she may also be able to maximize her capital budget.

Observation: Top management in an increasing number of companies has prescribed rules in this area to avoid budget end-running, particularly with finance leases. For example, since long-term equipment leases can have a significant negative future impact on a company's earnings, particularly when cutbacks are necessary, very often these transactions require senior management or board of directors approval.

▴ *Deriving off–balance sheet benefits*. In the early days of leasing, many users leased equipment, instead of taking out long-term loans to buy equipment, to avoid burdening their balance sheet with long-term debt liabilities. The lease, regardless of its duration, was basically treated as an operating expense. As a result, a company's profit-to-fixed-asset ratios were improved, in turn generally permitting a greater bank borrowing capability. Today, the circumstances have changed. Regardless of whether significant leases obligations have to be recorded on the balance sheet, sophisticated lenders factor them into their evaluation of a company's financial condition. Also, and certainly most important, the accounting rules now effectively eliminate the traditional ''off–balance sheet'' benefit in most situations.

The Disadvantages of Leasing

▴ *Loss of residual upside*. When a user leases equipment, he forgos the possibility of realizing a gain if the equipment appreciates in value during the lease term. Any such gain instead goes to the lessor. This is a common occurrence. For example, through inflation or buyer demand, a ten-year old river barge may be worth more than it originally cost.

Many leases give lessees the option to buy the leased equipment at the lease term's end for its fair market value at that time. If the fair market value turns out to be high, the purchase price, coupled with the rent paid, can result in a very expensive transaction. In such a situation, the lessee would undoubtedly have been better off if he had originally bought the equipment. The problem is that there is no way of telling what the future value is going to be.

There is, however, one way for a prospective lessee to limit his cost exposure if he believes it is likely he will want to buy the equipment at the end of the term and also share in any residual upside—a fixed price purchase option. Under this option, a lessee has the right to buy the equipment at the end of a lease at a fixed price, say 25 percent of original cost, that is agreed on at the time the parties enter into the lease. If the equipment's market value at the lease terms end is high, say 75 percent of cost, the lessee has the option of taking advantage of the favorable market by buying it for 25 percent of cost and selling it for 75 percent of cost. There are, however, two problems with fixed price purchase options. First, not all lessors are willing to grant them and give up their residual upside. Second, fixed price purchase options can jeopardize a lease's true lease status for tax purposes.

Frequently, a prospective lessee's concern over the loss of residual value upside is more emotional than practical. The potential loss must always be kept in the proper economic perspective. This can be done by attempting to put a realistic value on it by, for example, bringing in a qualified appraiser to give an opinion as to what the equipment is likely to be worth in the future and discounting the value to its present worth.

Example: A Residual Perspective. Company Able is considering whether to lease or buy a heavy-duty crane. Able's financial vice-president recommends that it be leased; however, the operational vice-president believes that it should be bought because of its favorable market value at the end of the period of use. The facts are as follows:

Crane cost	$3 million
Lease term	20 years
Depreciated book value at end of twenty years	$300,000

If the market value of the crane is estimated to be $500,000 at the end of the lease term, Company Able will lose the chance at a $200,000 upside gain ($500,000 − $300,000) if it leases the equipment.

What if, however, the potential loss is considered in terms of current dollars? The present value of such a loss twenty years out, computed using an annual discount rate of 10 percent, is approximately $30,000. Compared to the original cost of $3 million and considering the fact that the upside gain may not materialize, the residual concern may be overstated, particularly if any down payment that would have been required in a purchase is put to productive use.

▴ *Limiting of equipment control.* When a lease ends, so does a lessee's right to use the equipment. This can create a problems for an equipment user if suitable replacement equipment is not readily available and if the lessor refuses to re-lease or sell it to the lessee. While purchase or renewal options theoretically eliminate this risk, from a practical standpoint, when a third party owns the equipment, there is no guarantee she will abide by the terms of the options voluntarily. Also, there is always the possibility, although remote, that a lessor will interfere with the lessee's right to use the equipment during the lease term, even though she may have no legal right to do so. Having the legal right of continued use may be of little consequence to a lessee when equipment essential to its continued operations becomes unavailable.

Key Franchisee Credit Considerations

A franchisee's creditworthiness is the most important consideration in the lessor's decision to provide financing. If the franchisee's credit is weak, financial support from the franchisor or other third party must be supplied.

Although specific credit criteria can vary from lessor to lessor, certain basic areas are always of review interest in the lessor's approval process. For example, the types of criteria found on a typical lessor's credit information sheet for lease transactions ranging from $5,000 to $250,000 might be as follows:

▴ *Minimum time in business.* The applicant must have a minimum verifiable time in business of two years. Three years is required in the case of applications over $25,000, and four years in the case of applications over $100,000.

▴ *Existing banking relationship.* The applicant must have a business bank relationship of at least two years, and the bank account must show a minimum low-four-figure average balance. In the case of transactions exceeding $25,000, the minimum average account balance must be in the low five figures. There cannot be any overdrafts or check returns for insufficient funds.

▴ *Trade references.* The applicant must provide three significant trade references, each of whose relationship goes back at least six months. COD trade references are not acceptable.

▴ *Good personal credit.* Personal credit reports must contain no derogatory information.

▴ *Financial statements*. Financial statements must be supplied for transactions exceeding $25,000. Current assets must exceed current liabilities and, for transactions in excess of $50,000, a minimum equity of $75,000 must be present.

The franchisor that conducts it own preliminary "lease acceptability review" before submitting a transaction to a prospective leasing company can head off problems. Very often, issues that might result in a turndown can be addressed to facilitate an approval before the application is submitted. Once a franchisee is turned down by one leasing company, it is more difficult to get a funding approval. The reason may not be logical, but it is a fact of business life—credit managers at times turn down business they might otherwise have accepted merely because they're afraid another credit manager spotted a problem they couldn't find.

Financing Program Suggestions and Tips

Equipment financing programs must be tailored to fit a franchisor's customer profile while taking into account its management and financial capabilities. In doing so, there are some general tips and suggestions that can help in the development process.

One critical point should always be kept in mind: If the success of your sales effort depends heavily on third-party franchisee funding, do not rely on one funding relationship. Historically, bank-affiliated and nonbank leasing companies have closed their funding doors without warning and, at times, with indifference to customer commitments. One day management decides leasing is bad and fires its employees. The next day it decides leasing has possibilities, hires new employees, reenters the market and tells prospects it is NOW in it for the long haul. Same story, different year.

A legal word of caution: The fact that a franchisor or a prospective lessee has a contractual right to funding is often of little practical value in today's sluggish and uncertain court environment. Worse yet, on careful reading a franchisor will find most funding commitments are heavily qualified, providing lessors with many ways to walk away. A franchisor that plans accordingly will stay on top.

Some of the following tips and suggestions may seem obvious, yet time and time again they are forgotten in the rush to put business on the books. For example, everyone agrees that maintaining good customer relations is essential, yet many overlook the fact that once a third-party leasing company is involved it may be out of their control. One major bank lease marketing group was known for aggressively and effectively establishing relationships with equipment vendors and franchisors. And their customer service/administration group became equally well known for damaging customer relationships through inattention and indifference.

To begin with, a franchisor must ensure that its overall customer equipment financing program does the following:

▲ Preserves good customer relations at all times.
▲ Allows it to control its customer relationships.
▲ Avoids the whims of individual financing sources.
▲ Gives the impression of financing continuity.
▲ Is reliable under all circumstances.

In order to achieve these objectives a franchisor should:

▲ *Consider establishing its own financing company.* Although setting up a financing subsidiary may be difficult, doing this properly can go a long way to controlling a franchisor's marketing destiny. Of course, setting one up may not be within a franchisor's financial or management capabilities, but, if it is, a franchisor will have a significant marketing edge.

Very often those with the capability to set up a financing company do not because of the difficulties of starting and running a business they know little about. There are alternatives that can be explored, such as setting up a financing joint venture with an experienced lessor.

▲ *Establish multiple funding relationships.* If establishing its own financing company is not feasible or desirable, a franchisor must establish a committed working relationship with at least three lease financing companies. Their financial backgrounds, years in business, and track records must be investigated thoroughly. Not doing this puts a franchisor unnecessarily at risk. For example, many leasing companies simply don't have the funds available to service a vendor's repeated financing needs properly. An investigation can prevent unfortunate surprises.

▲ *Control document flow.* A franchisor should control the lease application and documentation process. This ensures that problems will be properly addressed in a timely manner. For example, a franchisor's salesperson should prepare the lease application and documents, submit them to the leasing company, and monitor the transaction weekly.

▲ *Develop uniform lease documentation.* Developing one set of lease documents generally acceptable to all funding sources is an important marketing step. If a deal is turned down by one lessor, documents don't have to be resigned to use another source, saving time and possible embarrassment.

▲ *Avoid lease brokers in small transactions.* Lease brokers have no control over whether a deal will be approved or funded. They often send financing packages out to multiple sources, hoping someone will approve it. In small transactions some brokers spend more time sending financing offerings to sources than preparing a good financing package. Improper packaging alone can result in turndown, something that increases the difficulty of finding future funding.

In addition, lease brokers often charge a high fee for their services. In large transactions they are worth the fee; in small transactions they are not. Their answer is that the lessor pays the fee so a lessee should not be concerned. The fact is a lessor needs a minimum deal profit and the fee is based upon the rent level. And brokers establish a rent level that permits the largest possible fee.

▴ *Avoid lease investment funds.* Lease investment funds promoted by investment bankers and lessors surface from time to time. They are public or private limited investment partnerships that raise money to invest in equipment leases. Historically, many have had problems from poor management or improper structuring. The result: When problems arise, funding is cut off. Franchisors working with an investment fund must not rely on it exclusively.

▴ *Consider guarantees carefully.* Franchisors should not readily give financial guarantees. They can adversely affect its ability to finance growth. Worse yet, many lease guarantees permit collection from the guarantor without having exhausted all remedies against the lessee.

▴ *Be realistic about what will entice a lessor.* Very often franchisors have financial misconceptions that lead them down blind financial alleys, such as trying to find a lessor that will finance credits others won't. And any funding source that offers to provide what others will not is rarely reliable.

In summary, there is a customer financing program structure that can work for every franchisor, but care must be taken to guarantee the best possible program. A franchisor that works within the financial market realities has the greatest chance of arranging an attractive and reliable financing program.

Good luck!

29

Financial and Tax Reporting Issues for the Growing Franchisor

John L. Allbery, Deloitte & Touche

Careful strategic business and tax planning are vital to the successful operation of a franchise organization. The Internal Revenue Code is littered with pitfalls for franchisors and franchisees. So are many state and local tax statutes—and these laws are being enforced more vigorously in response to cutbacks in federal assistance.

The application of federal, state, and local tax laws to the franchise industry requires franchising executives and their advisors to anticipate and to address the tax implications of most transactions. A thorough understanding of the statutory and regulatory provisions affecting the taxation of franchising organizations is the necessary first step toward developing a sound tax strategy.

IRC Section 1253: The Statutory Basis for Taxing Franchise Transfers

Prior to the Tax Reform Act of 1969, the Internal Revenue Code did not specifically address the tax treatment of payments for franchising operations. Parties to a franchise agreement were left to characterize each transaction for tax purposes as they saw fit. This lack of legal guidance led to instances in which franchisors and franchisees took inconsistent positions on the same transaction. Conflicting court decisions on similar franchising arrangements added to the confusion. To help clarify these issues, Congress in 1969 added Section 1253, "Transfers of Franchise, Trademarks, and Trade Names," to the Code. In passing this legislation, Congress sought to address completely the tax treatment of franchise payments, as well as payments received for trademarks and trade names.

The major issue addressed by Section 1253 is whether payments received by the franchisor from the franchisee should be considered capital gain or ordinary income. Section 1253 provides that if the franchisor retains any significant power, right, or continuing interest with respect to the franchise, these payments to the franchisor do not constitute the sale or exchange of a capital asset and are there-fore considered ordinary income.[1] The franchisor's power, right, or continuing interest is deemed to exist if the franchise contains any of the following provi-sions:

- A right to disapprove any assignment of such interest, or any part thereof
- A right to terminate at will
- A right to prescribe the standards of quality of products used or sold or of services furnished and of the equipment and facilities used to promote such products or services
- A right to require that the transferee sell or advertise only products or services of the transferor
- A right to require that the transferee purchase substantially all of his sup-plies and equipment from the transferor
- A right to payments contingent on the productivity, use, or disposition of the subject matter transferred, if such payments constitute a substantial element under the transfer agreement[2]

Since giving up all significant control of the franchise would defeat the purpose of the typical franchise relationship, most transfer payments fall within this defi-nition and must be recognized as ordinary income.

The IRS has a long-standing policy of taxing prepaid income in the year of receipt, whether the income is derived under contracts to furnish services or con-sists of prepaid rent, royalties, or bonuses. Thus, for tax purposes, the franchise fee generally is income to the franchisor upon receipt.

With proper planning and documentation, initial franchise fees sometimes can be deferred into the following tax year. If the initial franchise fees are re-ceived "substantially for services," if the services are not performed by the end of the tax year, and if the services are required to be performed by the end of the succeeding tax year, then that portion of the initial franchise fee associated with the services not yet performed can be deferred to the following tax year.[3]

The tax problems that confront franchisees often center on the question of whether or when payments made to the franchisor become deductible. Tax treat-ment of these payments depends on the nature of the payments to the franchisor.

Amounts paid to franchisors that are contingent on the productivity, use, or disposition of the franchise are deductible as ordinary and necessary business expenses when paid or accrued, regardless of whether the transaction is treated as a sale or exchange of a capital asset or as a mere licensing arrangement.[4] These contingent payments, often referred to as royalties, license fees, or service fees, usually are assessed on an ongoing basis to compensate the franchisor for the intangible rights transferred. Often these payments are based on some perform-ance measurement, such as a percentage of the franchisee's receipts.

Noncontingent payments to franchisors generally are made for initial fran-chise transfers. The tax treatment of these payments is more difficult to determine. If the franchise transfer is treated as a sale or exchange, noncontingent payments must be capitalized whether they are down payments or installment payments made to discharge any portion of the initial franchise fee assessed to the franchisee.[5] If the franchise has a limited useful life that can be estimated with reasonable accuracy, the capitalized amounts of the initial transfer fees can be depreciated.[6] However, the burden of proof of a determinable life of a franchise is upon the franchisee. If the franchise can be renewed at the franchisee's sole option or if it is renewable indefinitely, then depreciation is not allowed.[7]

If noncontingent payments for a franchise transfer are treated as other than a sale or exchange of a capital asset, determine whether the payments are lump-sum payments or periodic payments. Lump-sum payments are deducted ratably over the lesser of: 1. the period of the franchise agreement or 2. ten years.[8] Equal payments made periodically over either the period of the franchise agreement or a period of more than ten years are deductible in the year paid.[9] Of course, many other possible payment arrangements exist that fall within the parameters of Section 1253.

Congress later added a provision to Section 1253 that places a $100,000 limitation on the deductibility of principal amounts subject to the ten-year amortization treatment. This limitation applies to all payments that are part of the same transaction or of a series of related transactions.[10] Furthermore, the taxpayer can elect to capitalize amounts exceeding the $100,000 limitation and recover the amounts over a twenty-five-year period beginning with the taxable year in which the transfer occurs.[11]

Sometimes the initial franchise fee can be allocated to specific services to be provided. These services may include site selection, lease negotiations, equipment and other fixed-asset planning, and the development of marketing plans and advertising campaigns. An allocation of the initial fee can benefit the franchisee, because payments for many services may be deductible currently or may be depreciable over a shorter period than that authorized by Section 1253 and the accompanying proposed regulations.

Multiple Unit Transactions

Franchisees are not always mom-and-pop buyers; often they own many outlets. Large franchisees commonly enter into a variety of multiunit relationships, of which four are most common:

1. *Subfranchising*. This is a two-tiered relationship in which the franchisor enters into a franchise agreement with a subfranchisor, who in turn enters into a separate agreement with the subfranchisees who actually operate the sites.

2. *Area development agreements*. This is an agreement between a franchisor and a franchisee who is buying a large territory that will support a number of outlets. As part of the agreement, the franchisee, or area developer, is obligated to open a certain number of sites within a specific time period.

3. *Area representative agreements*. This is an arrangement between a franchisor and an area representative who markets the franchises within a specific area and performs supervisory functions for the franchisor. The agreement usually includes a timetable requiring the area representative to sign up a certain number of prospective franchisees within a given time period.

4. *Brokers*. Franchise brokers are similar to stockbrokers in that they are salespeople who work on commission.

From a tax accounting standpoint, each of the above franchise relationships is governed by Section 1253. In a subfranchising arrangement, Section 1253 provisions apply to both franchisor-subfranchisor and subfranchisor-subfranchisee relationships. In an area development agreement, the area developer is considered the franchisee for purposes of applying Section 1253. It is still unclear whether the $100,000 limitation on amortization of the franchise fee discussed earlier in this chapter applies to each site or to the entire development area. In an area representative agreement, both the franchisor and the area representative recognize ordinary income to the extent of their respective shares of the franchise fee and the royalty income.

Financial accounting for each of these arrangements generally is governed by "Statement of Financial Accounting Standards No. 45—Accounting for Franchise Fee Revenue." This Financial Accounting Standards Board (FASB) pronouncement states that revenue from franchise fees should be recognized "when all material services or conditions relating to the sale(s) have been substantially performed or satisfied by the franchisor."

Pooled Advertising Funds

A uniform advertising program lies at the heart of most successful franchise operations. Typically, the franchisor requires franchisees to contribute a certain percentage of sales to a pooled advertising fund. These monies are used to create marketing and advertising campaigns designed to build sales and promote the chain's identity.

The Internal Revenue Service has been trying for many years to tax pooled advertising receipts. But time and time again, in such landmark cases as *The Seven-Up Company*[12], *Broadcast Measurement Bureau, Inc.*[13], and *Insty-Prints*[14], the Tax Court has rejected the IRS's position. Thus, for now at least, these payments, if structured properly, generally are not considered taxable income upon receipt by the fund, and the subsequent disbursements from the fund for advertising are not deductible by the fund.

To the franchisee, pooled advertising payments might at first appear to be deductible as ordinary and necessary business expenses. However, proposed regulations released by the IRS indicate that in many cases such payments are not deductible until expended by the fund.[15] For this reason, franchisors may wish to issue correspondence at least annually informing franchisees that only a specified percentage of contributions to the fund are deductible in the current year.

Since the IRS has yet to acquiesce to the Tax Court decisions on the taxability of pooled advertising payments, prudent taxpayers should assume that an attack by the IRS is possible and should plan accordingly. One excellent planning strategy is the creation of a separate entity, such as a trust or a corporation, to administer and disburse the funds. This approach has several advantages: (1) It substantially reduces the likelihood of the sponsor being deemed taxable; (2) any earned interest that is deemed taxable will be taxable to the separate entity rather than to the franchisor, presumably at a lower rate; and (3) the documents executed in formation of the separate entity can be used to memorialize the tax filing positions for the fund.

Case precedent suggests that the franchisor should consider the following points when completing the franchise advertising fund documents:

▴ The governing instrument for the advertising fund should expressly restrict the use of the funds, and the income thereon, solely to advertising purposes.

▴ The documents should state clearly that the franchisor shall realize no profit, gain, or other benefit from the entity.

▴ Contributions to the fund should be segregated from the franchisor's corporate assets and treated separately for accounting purposes.

▴ Governing instruments should require that no contributions to the fund, or income thereon, can revert back to the franchisees or the franchisor prior to termination of the fund.

▴ The documents should allow occasional contributions by the franchisor as long as they are subject to the same restrictions on use as franchisee contributions.

▴ Franchisees should be given some role in the administration of the fund through reporting of fund activity by the franchisor or by the fund itself.

There are also some operational strategies that can help minimize tax risks. If the IRS were to be successful in arguing that the fund income is taxable, for instance, the IRS would be forced to allow ordinary and necessary business expenses to be deductible against that income. Therefore, the entity should try, as much as possible, to expend or to specifically commit its funds in the fiscal period in which the funds are received.

Passive Royalty Income: Personal Holding Company and S Corporation Considerations

If a successful corporate franchisor is a closely held regular corporation of if the franchisor has made or will make an S corporation election, the receipt of payments deemed to be royalties can result in unpleasant tax consequences. To a regular corporation, such payments can constitute personal holding company income and thereby subject the corporation to a penalty tax on its undistributed earnings—the personal holding company (PHC) tax. To an S corporation, the payments can be characterized as passive investment income, subjecting the corporation to a penalty tax and/or the termination of its S election.

The PHC tax was enacted in 1934 in an effort to discourage individual taxpayers from incorporating their investment assets to take advantage of lower corporate tax rates. Although corporate tax rates today actually are higher than individual rates, the PHC tax lingers as a trap for the unwary.

The PHC tax, as defined by the Internal Revenue Code, currently equals 28 percent of the undistributed personal holding company income of a personal holding company.[16] The Code defines a personal holding company as a corporation of which: (1) at least 60 percent of the adjusted ordinary gross income in the taxable year is personal holding company income, and (2) greater than 50 percent of the stock was owned by five or fewer individuals during the last half of the taxable year.[17] Personal holding company income can come from a variety of sources, including franchise royalties.[18]

A review of legislative history leads one to believe that Congress did not intend to subject active franchisors to the personal holding company tax on franchise-related revenues, even though such revenues are considered royalties. However, under the IRS's mechanical approach, the risk of inclusion is real, and the stakes are substantial.

As protection against the characterization of franchise fee receipts as royalties for PHC tax purposes, the franchisor should pay close attention to the language of the franchise agreement. If possible, the agreement should specifically allocate a portion of the fees as compensation for services, because this compensation clearly qualifies as active income. If it is not possible to avoid PHC tax status by reclassifying income as compensation for services, the franchisor should consider generating or purchasing another source of high gross income that is not from any of the PHC sources listed in the Code. Another possible remedy is to elect S status, since S corporations are exempt from the PHC tax. Alternatively, a franchisor with a good set of facts and a strong constitution might request an IRS private letter ruling stating specifically that the royalties received by the franchisor are not PHC income.

Although S corporations are not subject to the PHC tax, a small business corporation may run into trouble if a large portion of its receipts are passive investment income. Royalties specifically are included in the Code's definition of passive investment income.[19] A corporate-level tax is triggered if a corporation having Subchapter C earnings and profits (i.e., from a time before the S election) derives over 25 percent of its gross receipts from passive investment sources.[20] If the corporation's passive investment income exceeds 25 percent of gross receipts for three consecutive taxable years, the corporation will lose its S status.[21]

One method of avoiding this tax is to eliminate the corporation's earnings and profits by making a dividend distribution to shareholders. In such a situation, the corporation should make a valid election on a timely-filed return under Section 1368(e)(3). This election ensures that, contrary to normal tax rules, the distribution will be considered first a C corporation dividend, with the balance a distribution of S corporation previously taxed or current taxable income.

State and Local Income Tax Nexus

There is a flip side to the "active" versus "passive" distinction—that is, there are potential negative results of having too much "active" income. For example, a foreign corporation earning active income within a particular state may unwittingly establish a nexus, or connection, with the state sufficient to subject the corporation to the state's tax laws. As used here, the term *foreign corporation* refers to a U.S. corporation organized and existing under the laws of a state other than the taxing jurisdiction.

With the explosive growth of franchising in recent years, several states have stepped up their efforts to tax foreign corporate franchisors. These states generally seek to tax foreign corporations that do business, employ capital, own or lease property, incur payroll costs, or maintain an office within the state.[22]

The definition of tax nexus varies greatly from state to state. The New York State franchise (income) tax, for example, is imposed on every foreign corporation that is, among other things, "doing business" or "employing capital" in New York. Since the statute implies, but does not state specifically, that some activities within the state do not rise to the level of "doing business," many questions remain unanswered about the taxability of foreign franchisors in New York State. In contrast, New Mexico's definition of tax nexus is highly specific. Statutes and court decisions clearly establish that a franchisor receiving license fees or royalties from a franchisee operating within New Mexico is subject to the New Mexico gross receipts tax.

Other states impose substantially different tests, which must be reviewed carefully on the basis of the facts and circumstances of each situation. In any event, continued cutbacks in the distribution of federal funds to the states likely will force more states to interpret their nexus rules more liberally in an effort to raise additional revenues.

State Sales and Use Tax Nexus

All states except Alaska, Delaware, Montana, New Hampshire, and Oregon assess a sales tax on sales within their taxing jurisdictions for franchise companies having sales and use tax nexus. Each state levying a sales tax also has a parallel use tax that must be assessed by the taxpayer for items consumed internally by the franchise company.

The definition of nexus for sales and use tax purposes is basically the same as for income tax purposes, referring to a taxpayer's connections to or activity within a state. However, the criteria for determining sales and use tax nexus are different from those used for determining nexus for income tax purposes.

The requirements that must be met to establish nexus differ from state to state. However, these requirements fall into three main categories:

1. Establishment of a physical presence within the state
2. Solicitation of sales through employees or agents working within the state
3. Establishment of an ''economic presence'' within the state[23]

Until recently, the first two categories were the standard for determining sales and use tax nexus. However, as we have discussed, federal subsidies to the states have declined since the Reagan Administration, and many states have now recognized the need to raise additional revenues. Some states, most notably California, Connecticut, Minnesota, North Dakota, and Tennessee, have responded in part by expanding the definition of nexus from a physical to an economic presence. These states have also become more aggressive in auditing and assessing sales and use taxes due by companies that meet the newly expanded definition of nexus.

As a result, franchisors, which previously were not responsible for registering, collecting, and remitting sales or use tax on transactions spanning state lines, may find states knocking at their doors requesting payment. Franchisors must be aware of these changes and be prepared to challenge the states' positions where necessary. In addition, franchisors should be ready to register, collect, and remit sales and use taxes when required in order to limit their exposure to taxes, penalties, and interest.

International Franchising Tax Considerations

Many U.S. franchisors are now franchising abroad. According to the International Franchise Association, 374 American business format franchisors were operating more than 35,000 outlets outside the United States in 1988, with many others considering foreign operations.[24] Although international franchising has expanded significantly, entering foreign markets can be difficult. The success of these ventures depends on several factors, including the franchisor's domestic market position and its ability to adapt its system to accommodate differences in language and culture.

The main objective of tax planning for an international franchising entity is to structure the franchise relationships in a way that minimizes overall effective tax, both domestic and foreign, on the franchisor. Because of the complex interaction of the Internal Revenue Code and the tax laws of the various foreign countries and possessions, transactions that appear to be similar in nature can result in remarkably different tax effects. In fact, if not properly structured for tax purposes, a transaction that appears to make business sense to the franchisor may not be advisable after consideration of the adverse tax consequences. Therefore, we caution that this area of tax law is extremely complex, and the franchisor should investigate possible ramifications thoroughly before proceeding with such arrangements.

When structuring the international franchise relationship, the franchisor has three basic options:

1. Directly licensing franchises to unrelated foreign franchisees
2. Licensing (or selling) franchises to foreign subsidiaries or other related parties, who then sublicense (or license) the franchises to unrelated foreign franchisees
3. Licensing (or selling) franchises through territorial master licensees who then sublicense (or license) the franchise to foreign franchisees unrelated to the franchisor or the master licensee

An examination of the relative merits of these structuring options is beyond the scope of this chapter. Which arrangement is most favorable depends on whether franchise fees earned are subject to tax (and the level of tax) in the franchisee's country, whether any tax treaties are available to eliminate or reduce the foreign tax, and whether related party on-licensing can reduce the overall effective domestic and foreign taxes. Because of the complexity of these arrangements and the multitude of structuring options available in international franchising, the construction of a flow chart or other model is advisable in order to make the decision tree easier to comprehend.

Other Services to Franchisees and Tax Planning Considerations for the Franchisor

There are many other tax planning opportunities that, while not unique to franchising, should be considered by the franchisor. Many of these concepts can be packaged and offered to franchisees as value-added services:

▴ *Targeted jobs tax credit*. Many franchisor or franchisee operations hire significant numbers of members of designated socioeconomic groups targeted by the federal government. These employees may qualify the employer for an income tax credit equal to 40 percent of the first $6,000 paid to the qualifying employees during their first twelve months of employment.[25]

▴ *Ad valorem tax studies*. Franchisors may realize substantial property tax savings by reviewing and, whenever appropriate, protesting real and/or personal property tax valuations for retail and warehousing locations. In addition, the franchisors may wish to keep warehoused property in states offering a property tax exemption for such property.

▲ *Franchisor-sponsored retirement programs for franchise owners.* A good way to improve franchisee relations without spending a great deal of money is for the franchisor to sponsor a "private label" retirement plan. "Private label" means that all plan documents and correspondence refer to the plan as the franchisor's specific plan and that the plan is customized to suit the desires and needs of the franchisees. By pooling contributions, franchisees gain investment opportunities that otherwise would be unavailable to them.

▲ *"ZEESOP" or "ZSOP" plans.* As a tool for retaining franchisees, some franchisors have established nonqualified deferred compensation plans, sometimes referred to as "ZEESOP" or "ZSOP" plans. Under such a plan, the franchisor contributes on behalf of the franchisee a certain percentage of royalties, sales, or purchases over a prescribed amount. These funds are placed into a trust and are nontaxable to the franchisee during the lifetime of the trust. A well-structured ZEESOP or ZSOP plan can help attract and retain good franchisees, as well as encourage franchisees to increase sales and productivity.

▲ *Passive losses from royalty arrangements.* As discussed earlier, income derived from franchise royalties may be considered "passive" for personal holding company and S corporation purposes. Using the same logic, losses incurred from these activities also can be considered passive and may be subject to significant passive loss limitations.[26] Regular corporations that are not closely held generally are not subject to these loss limitations.

▲ *Affiliated company considerations and elections.* Many franchising concerns, particularly those involved in separate businesses, try to limit their legal liability by setting up a separate corporation for each business. For instance, a franchisor may have separate legal entities involved with such activities as equipment leasing, sale of supplies or certain proprietary products, finance, and real estate. In these situations, many affiliated company considerations must be addressed, depending on whether the entities are subsidiaries of the common parent corporation or brother/sister affiliated companies. Among these considerations are apportionment of surtax exemptions, tax preferences, investment tax credit property limitations, and Section 179 expense limitations.

▲ *Succession planning.* Because of the variety of restrictions customarily found in a franchise agreement, creating a sensible estate plan for the franchise owner is far more difficult than for the owner of a sole proprietorship or closely held business. For instance, franchise agreements typically prohibit the franchisee from transferring or assigning the franchise without the franchisor's consent, making it difficult for the franchisee to pass along the franchise freely to a spouse or children. To reduce the possibility of future legal complications, the franchisee should enlist the cooperation of the franchisor throughout the estate planning process.

As franchising has become a more powerful force in the world economy, the accounting and tax issues faced by franchisors and franchisees have grown more complex. This chapter has highlighted some of the more significant statutory and regulatory pitfalls franchising executives and their advisors should anticipate when planning franchise transactions. The preceding discussion is hardly exhaustive; each situation presents a unique set of facts and issues, making careful business and tax planning all the more important. Franchisors and franchisees who make the effort to anticipate the tax consequences of their actions will be rewarded with more successful and profitable operations.

NOTES

1. IRC §1253(a).
2. IRC §1253(b)(2).
3. Rev. Proc. 71-21, 1971-2 CB 549.
4. IRC §1253(d)(1).
5. Prop. Reg. §1.1253-1(c)(2).
6. IRC §1253(d)(2).
7. *Victor E. Stromstred*, 53 TC 330 (1900).
8. IRC §1253(d)(2)(A).
9. Prop. Reg. §1.1253-1(c)(3)(ii).
10. IRC §1253(d)(2)(B).
11. IRC §1253(d)(3)(B).
12. *The Seven-Up Company*, 14 TC 965 (1950).
13. *Broadcast Measurement Bureau, Inc.*, 16 TC 988 (1951).
14. Frank and Freida Schochet, Trustees of Insty-Prints, Inc., *National Advertising Fund Trust* TC Memo 1982–416.
15. Proposed Income Tax Regulation §1.461-4.
16. IRC §541.
17. IRC §542(a).
18. Income Tax Regulation §1.543-1(b)(3).
19. IRC §§1362(d)(3) and 1375(b)(3).
20. IRC §1375(a).
21. IRC §1362(d)(3).
22. See, e.g., New York Tax Law, §209.1; 20 MYCRR 1-3.2.
23. Judith A. Shanley, *1990 Multistate Corporate Tax Guide* (New York: Panel), pp. 70–72.
24. *Franchising in the Economy, 1988–1990* (Washington, D.C.: U.S. Department of Commerce, 1988).
25. IRC §51(a).
26. IRC §469.

30

Developing the Franchise Fee Structure

Michael Howard Seid, Strategic Advisory Group

In December 1988, *Venture Magazine* published its annual Franchise 100 ranking, listing the one hundred fastest-growing franchise companies for the prior twelve months. What struck me at the time was not the rate of growth of these systems (first-ranked Subway sold 617 franchises, and last-ranked Jr. Food Mart sold twenty-seven,) but that a significant number of these franchisors had either lost money or were still significantly dependent on franchise fees to remain profitable. When, in 1990, *Success Magazine* published its first Gold 100 using a more sophisticated approach to franchise ranking, a significant number of these ranked franchisors still had lost money or continued to rely on franchise fees to remain profitable. Interestingly enough, earnings were not included in the 1991 Gold 100 rankings.

Success in franchising has historically been measured in number of units sold, and logical readers might surmise that a system that is in rapid expansion, or a system that is high in one of the publisher's rankings, is a financially healthy company worthy of consideration for their franchise investment. Often this is not the case.

Although every company, whether franchised or vertically integrated, has periods of time in which the company survives on stockholder's investments or, in the case of franchises, on franchise fee income, there needs to be a time early in a company's existence when ongoing revenue from continuing operations exceeds ongoing expenses. Unless the company's revenue stream is structured to accomplish this goal, the company, for all its publicity and quick sales, is at financial risk. In the case of vertically integrated companies, the risk is primarily borne, except for debt, by the stockholders or the owners. In franchising, the risk is also shared by the franchisees.

Over the years, as I have worked on the restructuring and repositioning of established franchise systems, I have been struck by the method franchisors have used to establish their fee structure. To probe the thought processes used, I often pose a seemingly simple question that I have called the Big Bang Theory: "How did you develop your fee structure?" By listening to management's response, I can begin to understand the methodology, the care, the understanding the systems creators put into the structural design of the system.

Properly developed, a franchisor's income stream is carefully planned after all the strategic and other operational components of the system have been determined and their revenue and cost effects have been determined. If the franchisor's response centers heavily on the competitive environment in the franchise industry or on its feeling that the level of franchise fees has created a salable package, I begin to understand that a true strategic process never occurred.

One of the most significant criticisms of certain franchise packagers and of the franchise media is that they see franchising as a sales-driven event. Unlike company-owned systems that can adjust revenue by increasing their products' selling price or their product mix, franchising is highly inelastic. Once franchise fees, royalty payments, and other continuing income are established, except as they may be affected by future franchisees or renewal franchisees, the franchisor's unit revenue is substantially locked. The old adage "I will make up for the loss on the sale of each unit by selling more units" may be a business staple, but for a franchisor who has not properly developed its system's revenue stream, it represents a tragic reality.

Fees need to be kept at competitive rates, but pity the poor franchisor who is so similar to its competition that its only distinguishing feature is lower fees. While it can be argued that excessively high fees are a barrier to the sale of franchises, the reality is that if the fees are too low the franchise system won't be able to provide the support and guidance its franchisees need, and the system won't survive.

Two areas where "market-driven" fees have most frequently played havoc with franchise systems are in the initial franchise training and in ongoing support programs promised to franchisees. Every franchisor I have ever met desired, when the system was established, to provide its franchisees with the finest training programs and ongoing field support in the industry. Unfortunately, these desirable services were translated into statements in franchise sales literature and into guarantees in franchise legal documents without having been costed out ahead of time.

Recently, in providing "franchise therapy" for a franchisor who had been "packaged" several years before, this problem became critical. The franchisor, when describing its initial training program in Item 11 of its offering document (Obligation of the Franchisor), had provided for six weeks of training, three of which were to take place at the franchisee's location. While the franchisor was new, with only a handful of store openings a year, this was not a problem, and the training department could service this requirement. The first time that two or more franchises were scheduled to open during the same time period, the problem became immediately apparent. Without hiring additional field trainers or reassigning other personnel, causing other systemwide problems, the franchisor was unable to provide the required level of support. Had the system been properly developed through strategic planning, either the cost of the field training in dollars and in additional staffing would have been determined and included in franchise fees or a training curriculum would have been developed that better suited the systems capacity.

The problem was twofold: The franchise fee was market-driven and did not support the cost of the program, and without proper strategic planning, the entrepreneurs' vision of the perfect training program was incorporated into the franchise documents even though the franchisor did not have the capability to perform according to its agreement. Resolving this situation required redeveloping the training program to include more training at the franchisor's training center and rewriting and reprinting the franchise sales literature and franchise legal documents to change the promised location and the duration of the training. This was costly and disruptive for the franchisor. Because the franchisor wished to have the franchisees attend advanced training to increase quality and efficiency throughout the system, a continuing certification program that required the franchisee and certain staff to attend advanced training programs periodically was adopted, along with a fee to cover the cost of these programs.

Similarly, when franchisors incorporate into their literature promises of a minimum level of field support, problems can occur. Field support requirements can be an ongoing financial drain. Two factors in packaged franchise systems frequently drive this problem. One is a written promise in the legal agreements of a set level of field visits, and the other is the high cost of these visits, which often exceeds royalty income derived from the franchisee. Many new franchisors who lack the number of units necessary to establish critical mass in a marketplace find that the cost of servicing these units is more than the franchise fees earned. While this is a common problem in new systems and in new markets, those franchisors who have not established clear and defined target markets and critical mass requirements institutionalize this occurrence. Any philosophy of franchise sales that ignores critical mass issues creates problems that are avoided by strategically developed systems. The cost of field service, together with the distance and duration of field visits, is one of the integral components analyzed in strategic planning.

A separate but equally important reason to avoid defining the level of field support is a recognition that franchisees differ in the level of support they require. A system that has contractually defined the level and frequency of field support may not be in a position, because of a lack of qualified personnel, to provide those franchisees who need additional assistance with the support they require to regain or to maintain profitability. Simply put, the franchisor, by trying to promise a high level of support in its legal documents, actually lessens its ability to improve the performance of its system. Franchise system expansion and the costs of providing adequate support are issues to be determined before the company signs its first franchise agreement.

In franchising there is a symbiotic relationship between the health of the franchisor and the health of the franchisee. This makes the strategic development process critical. Most continuing franchisor earnings are based on a percentage of gross sales; the franchisor's income is not directly connected to the profitability of its franchisees. The structuring of the fees, therefore, can be determined only after every other integral component of the franchise system, at both levels, is determined and their cost and relationship to profit are known.

The financial structuring of the franchise system must examine the culture, position, quality, value, consistency, organization, operations, expansion, marketing, advertising, customer profile, critical mass, distribution, training, legal requirements, field services, home office support, and unit profitability of the franchise system relative to cost, profit, and, ultimately, return on investment. Franchisor's fees are therefore one of the last things determined in the strategic process.

Franchising has historically been used by smaller companies as a method for growth. In the future, I believe, large established vertically integrated companies will turn to franchising as a method to distribute some of their products and services or will use franchising as a method of reorganization and restructuring, a method I call "Retrofranchising."

In order to understand the strategic process, an understanding of the advantages and disadvantages of franchising is important. Since the Retrofranchising strategy was created as a restructuring tool, a logical place to begin the examination of the strategic process is with its effect on traditional businesses.

Retrofranchising

Even a cursory glance at the business section of any newspaper reveals that many businesses are reeling from the sins of corporate overexpansion and the by-products of their leveraged buyouts during the 1970s and 1980s, including high debt-to-equity ratios and excessive real estate and other lease obligations. In addition, many of these companies are facing the pressure of a soft labor market, with high labor turnover and a shortage of quality management.

Traditional reorganization strategies revolve around contraction of the company, and many businesses today are making strident reorganization decisions that include protection under the bankruptcy laws. It was because of this modern retailing phenomenon that the Strategic Advisory Group, along with our strategic allies at Price Waterhouse, developed the reorganization technique of "Retrofranchising."

Retrofranchising is an attractive alternative distribution system for classic vertically integrated organizations that fall into one of two broad categories:

1. Companies with a product or service for which their traditional distribution system or corporate structure is inadequate for maximum profitability

2. Companies with profitable individual units burdened by excessive debt acquired during expansion in the 1970s and 1980s; management and labor concerns; and lease- or real estate-related obligations

Retrofranchising offers several significant advantages for a company, and the use of retrofranchising as a restructuring and reorganization technique is very exciting and very timely.

The issues facing many distressed companies fall into two broad categories, economic issues and organizational issues.

Economic Issues

Traditional reorganization strategies provide for systemwide contraction to reduce ongoing operating costs, coupled with the closing of locations to provide relief from real estate obligations. The company traditionally liquidates excess inventory, furniture, fixtures, and equipment, providing some modest inflow of required capital to reduce debt. Retrofranchising is not a contraction strategy but in essence looks to the sale of available assets while preserving and often enhancing existing revenue streams without disruption to established distribution systems. It is essentially a reverse LBO, with the selling company retaining control over what it has sold. The following financial issues flow from the Retrofranchising strategy.

▲ *Capital infusion.* Franchisors charge an initial fee (franchise fee) to franchisees upon their entrance into the system. The franchise fees range, on average, from $500 to $100,000, with average fees ranging from $10,000 to $30,000. In addition to the standard franchise fee, under Retrofranchising, the retailer has the additional economic incentive of selling ongoing local operations at a fair market value based on sales multiples or other predetermined formulas. An additional incentive is the elimination of dilution issues that management may wish to avoid.

▲ *Cost of modernization.* Within reason, the Retrofranchisor can require costs of modernization of local operations to be borne by the franchisee at either the inception of the relationship or over the term of the franchise agreement. Should the rate of return allow for additional capital contribution by the franchisee, the passing on of modernization costs will allow for capital improvements that may have been delayed when the company was experiencing financial problems.

▲ *Ongoing revenue.* With knowledge of the profit potential for its local units, the company is in a position to determine a proper royalty that allows the franchisee an adequate return on its investment. Traditionally, royalties are based upon gross sales; while the franchisor does not share in bottom-line profits, it also does not share in unit shortfalls. A passive royalty income stream is typical in franchising.

In 1989, a small sample study conducted by DePaul University and Francorp examined, among other issues, the sales per unit in company-owned locations and franchised locations. The study confirms what most industry experts have recognized for a long time: Franchised units tend to have higher sales than comparable company-owned units. "Franchisors who favor franchisees as managers say the difference in sales can be as much as 100 percent, but the mean is 44.4 percent and the median 20 percent.''

It is also a recognized reality that the cost of sales and other operating costs in franchised units tend to be lower than those in company-owned locations. These two factors—higher sales and lower operating costs—can make marginal corporate locations extremely viable when converted to franchises.

▴ *Marketing and creative costs*. Franchisees contribute to a fund for the creation and placement of advertising and for other local marketing and point-of-purchase costs. In addition to these contributions, local franchisees often are either obligated or voluntarily agree to expend additional sums for local marketing.

Shifting the expense for advertising to the local operator has a dual effect. It removes from the franchisor the expense of local unit advertising. Also, local management can also exploit opportunities that corporate managers would not be able to react to, expanding the effectiveness of the advertising budget.

▴ *Distribution and sales to franchisees*. In closing local retail operations, manufacturer/retailers often incur serious disruptions to their established distribution networks. With Retrofranchising, the distribution network is not disrupted. By selling products to franchisees at wholesale prices, the company will continue to profit from these sales as well as continue manufacturing levels at prereorganization levels.

In some situations the distribution system may be the franchisable portion of the business. Franchises, because of their individual ownership, are difficult to unionize, although union-related concerns must be addressed in the conversion should the company have union contracts in place. The capital cost of distribution equipment, maintenance facilities, insurance, and operating costs can be passed on to the franchisee, and some cost centers, such as maintenance facilities, can be converted from a cost to a profit center.

I recently studied the conversion of the route distribution system of a major bakery to a franchised distribution system. In addition to removing the cost of the employee salaries and benefits, truck maintenance, and other related expenses, the maintenance facility, which had been a significant cost center, was converted to a fee-generating maintenance facility that will be utilized by route franchisees. An additional benefit will be increased sales for the bakery.

Because the route franchisee's income is determined by the sales in its territory, franchisees have a new and added incentive for expansion of their customer base that was missing from their prior status as employees. Thus, the route franchisees become a significant sales force for the company's products.

There is other income potential, as well. Typically, large retailers have established preferred pricing on equipment, cabinetry, and other items used by local operators. Franchisors may establish buying groups or develop third-party leasing arrangements by which a portion of the cost paid by the franchisee is earned by the buying group, which is owned either by the franchisor in total or in partnership with the franchisees. Franchisees benefit from lower costs by buying through the franchisor's buying group, and the franchisor earns additional income through its traditional buying power.

Organizational Issues

Franchising offers some unique advantages at the corporate, field, and local levels. Although the franchisor has an obligation to ensure that his franchisees are equipped to operate their business (not dissimilar to the training provided to local unit management), they are not burdened by direct supervision of local operations.

CORPORATE ORGANIZATION

Franchisors typically are able to operate with a smaller corporate and field organization than are classic retailers. As the burden of supervising local operations is eliminated, the franchisor's field organization takes on the responsibility of ensuring franchisee compliance and assistance. Often, field organizations that previously assigned one field supervisor or general manager to five or eight locations can now reduce this level of organization by four- or fivefold. Field operations personnel may be able to work with twenty-five or more franchise locations, because they are no longer burdened with day-to-day responsibilities and can focus on quality and consistency issues. In addition, depending on the size and structure of the prefranchised corporation, significant savings in financial and administrative areas can be made as payroll and other administrative functions are transferred to the franchisees.

LOCAL MANAGEMENT

After the conversion to franchisee ownership, it is the franchisee's responsibility to staff its locations and to supervise its employees. The motivational difference between salaried management and franchisee ownership can be startling, as the DePaul study found.

The motivation of direct ownership enables the franchisee to monitor the salary structure, staffing levels, and other cost areas better than a salaried manager would. Because the franchisee is motivated by both profit and the pride of ownership, she is in a better position to react to local opportunities. This can both increase local profitability as well as customer satisfaction and quality control.

An often cited reason for not franchising is the loss of control the franchisor has over the quality of the product and service delivered by the franchisee to the customer. In any organization there are good and bad franchisees, as well as salaried management, which can affect quality. However, the franchisees, with their investment on the line, tend to provide a higher quality of service and product delivery to their customers. Quality level is not only a nonissue but may actually prove to be one of the reasons companies decide to franchise.

Who Can Retrofranchise

Not every established retailer is in a position to Retrofranchise. Some of the components required for successful retrofranchising are:

▲ *Name recognition and public perception.* Although the company is under increasing economic or organizational pressure, the public awareness of the company's name and its perception of the company's product or service quality needs to be positive in order for franchising to be successful.

Recently I met with representatives of a major retailer of electronics to discuss converting its out-of-state locations into franchised locations. During the initial phase of our discussions, the company announced in the press that it was under severe economic pressures and had closed a significant number of its locations (which Retrofranchising could have avoided). Had our discussions commenced before financial conditions became so dire, successful Retrofranchising could have not only averted the contraction of the company but provided the opportunity for continual growth.

▲ *Local operations.* Often the difficulty facing distressed corporations is not in the core businesses but the lack of income required to service accumulated debt. In these circumstances, where the local units, taken as individual operations and combined into regional organizations, are profitable, the investment is reasonable, and the return on investment for the franchisee and the franchisor is likely to be adequate, successful retrofranchising is possible.

▲ *Market trends.* If the products or services have a high degree of acceptance by customers and this trend is likely to continue into the foreseeable future, Retrofranchising is possible.

The need for long-term product and service acceptance is universal. There is a heightened responsibility in franchising in providing your franchisees with the expectations of long-term profit and stability. To the extent that the core business has a stable and growing customer base, long-term successful expansion is possible.

There are some significant obstacles that may make Retrofranchising impossible. One in particular is the management of the corporation.

▲ *Independence.* Franchisees are not employees, and the management skills needed to run a chain of stores are markedly different from those necessary for operating and growing a franchise system. A significant amount of independence will be lost as local franchisees examine and comment on all management decisions, whether it affects them or not. While there is a franchise agreement that binds the relationship, good franchise management is based on moral persuasion. Franchisees, as independent business people, cannot be fired or reprimanded as can a local employee.

Often, when the corporate culture is so rigid that it makes direct franchising impossible, the establishment of a separate organization, in terms of both management and franchising, may need to be established to create the right atmosphere.

A psychological evaluation of the management team should be conducted prior to the transfer of established management to the franchise environment. Given the radically different management skills required in the franchise culture, existing executives may not be suited to the franchise process.

▴ *Marketing and repositioning.* A great degree of flexibility is lost because of the involvement of franchisees. Not insignificant is the loss of ability to control pricing and promotional campaigns, as well as image. Often the other franchisees in a franchisee's market are your best allies and can bring moral pressure to bear when the franchisor cannot.

Although not every company can or should choose Retrofranchising as a strategy for reorganization, it highlights many of the advantages and disadvantages all franchisors must address in the development of their strategic plan.

The Traditional Start-Up Franchisor

The starting point in the development of any franchise system, whether it be reorganization through Retrofranchising or traditional start-up, is the positioning of the local unit. An understanding of where you are currently in the consumer's mind and how that position is likely to change in the future is key to determining the changes that may be required for success. An error many franchisors make is the assumption that change is only positive. The reality is that market conditions are likely to change and customer satisfaction requirements are likely to change.

Management Horizons, the retail consulting division of Price Waterhouse, upon whose wisdom I and many major retailers and service companies rely, speaks of the "Field of Dreams" mentality and the changing retail paradigms of the 1990s.

The Field of Dreams Mentality

The Field of Dreams mentality assumes: "If I build it they will come." Unfortunately, in the 1990s they may not. (The "they" refers to the consumer of your franchisee's products and services and also to the prospective franchisees.)

Many of the franchisors I work with have developed very strong concepts and have created superb organizations. Unfortunately, belief in the Field of Dreams philosophy, relying on both media-induced perceptions and the sales strategies of franchise packaging companies that suggest that a franchisors's growth can be extremely rapid, can cause significant cash flow and financial problems when the true realities of franchise expansion set in.

In 1988 I wrote "Growth Decisions Study on Franchise Expansion," which analyzed the growth of the franchise industry from 1978 to 1987 by examining 2,141 franchisors. The key results of the study are quite interesting for new franchisors estimating their future growth:

1. Franchisors that had begun the sale of franchises after 1977 represented 69.6 percent of the total population studied, although they represented only 29 percent of the franchises sold during the ten-year period. The majority of franchise sales were made by established companies established prior to 1977.

2. For franchisors established since 1977, the average number of franchises sold annually in years one through three was between 2.4 and 5.9.

3. During the ten-year period following their establishment, franchisors sold an average of 9.6 franchises a year.

4. The average size of all franchisors, regardless of when they were established, was 106.9 franchisees. The industry median was only 13.

The essential lesson to be learned is that growth rate, while higher for franchisors than for company-owned operations, is still measured in realistic rates.

Reliance on media perception or on entrepreneurial enthusiasm in forecasting sales can leave a company with significant financial problems. Improper franchise fee structure and poorly planned critical mass and marketing strategies for their franchisees are among the concerns. The same results that traditional retailers faced after absorbing high debt in the 1970s and 1980s are faced by franchisors whose growth is driven by a Field of Dreams philosophy. Unrealistic growth projections, whether measured in square foot sales or franchise unit sales, can be disastrous.

The Retail Paradigm for the 1990s

The changing retail paradigm of the 1990s is that customer loyalty and quality perception will be the key to consumers' purchasing decisions. Past performance is no longer the clear indicator it once was. Quality has been a management buzz word and the root of business writer Tom Peters's management philosophy for the past decade. However, its role as a driving force in purchasing decisions and in the creation of customer loyalty will become paramount in the decades to come.

In "Retailing 2000," Management Horizons discusses the future of retailing. Regarding customers in the future, it suggests:

> While shopping frequency will decline among a large segment of the population, customer loyalty will increase as older (35+), time-pressed consumers become almost exclusively destination-store-oriented in their shopping behavior. Most older consumers do not view shopping as a social experience or leisure-time activity. They do not

enjoy walking the mall from one end to the other to shop a variety of stores. Small, mall-based specialty stores that depend on impulse purchasing from passersby will suffer as the percentage of older buyers increases.

Specialty stores will be "reinvented" to encompass an expanded mix of merchandising in larger stores that will make a more powerful marketing statement to targeted customers. These specialists' strategies will depend on getting a larger portion of the shopping budget of a smaller but more loyal customer base.[1]

The change in the method by which customers make their purchasing decisions will have a significant impact on the future growth of franchisees and on the franchise systems they are part of. In developing their strategic plans, franchisors need to recognize that positioning and long-range acceptance are the keys in planning system expansion. For this reason, the theory of low fees for marketability has little merit.

Given the basic philosophy that successful systems must be based at every level on consistency, quality, and value and that customer loyalty will be the driving force in the future, the determination of financial structure can result only from a clear understanding of the system, its goals, and its future customers.

The Franchise Operation

The ultimate goal of every franchise is to have each unit operate as a mirror image of the franchisor's program. This requires two basic assessments:

1. The realities of the existing operations and how the franchisor wants the franchisees to operate
2. The types of support programs and corporate organizations the franchisor must develop to enable the first assessment to happen

The operations section of the strategic plan focuses on all levels of the franchisor's organization. While typically this plan refers only to the franchisor and the franchisee levels, depending on other expansion methods utilized (master franchising, area development, and international expansion), each level has its own unique requirements for which the system must provide.

Operating systems and support, in addition to needing to be established at each level, must also be established for each period in the franchise relationship: start-up, early development, and continuing operations. In addition to the obvious creation of standards and procedure manuals for franchisee operations, the franchisor must define the services it will provide to the franchisees and must establish procedures to provide these services, together with training programs, at all levels. These services include both home office and field support as well as support services that address the differing needs of the franchisees as they mature in the system. The realization that franchisees require a differing level of service depending on their time and performance in the system is one of the keys for franchise success.

Modern franchising is a complex business. Franchisees require access to information on a real-time basis, and the franchisor needs to create mechanisms to collect this information, analyze the results, and communicate it effectively. The use of point-of-sales and management information services are no longer uncommon in franchising. Innovative systems of communications include monthly newsletters, trained field personnel able to assist franchisees on the basis of systemwide and local information created on a timely basis, and even voice mail systems that enable the franchisor to communicate with its franchisees daily. Each of these programs of franchisee support is identified in the strategic process, and the costs and benefits of each are calculated.

Once these critical operations questions are answered, the development of the proper organizational structure to implement the franchisor's strategy can then be created. If every franchise organization were identical, this process would be simple.

Although titles may be similar across organizations, their functions may vary. Therefore, the franchisor should draw up an organizational chart detailing function and reporting responsibilities. As the system requires, individuals are then recruited to fill responsibilities, not just titles. The careful matching of individual skills and temperaments to responsibilities is essential in the creation of the organization. While not common in franchising, there is movement toward the use of corporate psychologists who can profile the personality types of management individuals. The cost and timing of organizational staffing is not a function exclusively based on time. In a properly designed system, staff is added as the system can both utilize the skills and afford their addition.

Training Requirements

The goal of the training section of the strategic plan is to determine the level and types of training required to operate the system effectively at all levels. Areas to be considered include: requirements needed to develop a standardized training program; the location of the training program; who should teach each component of the program; who should attend; length of training program; and content of the training programs. In addition to evaluating training requirements, the strategic plan looks again at the costs associated with the training process.

The training program provides the basis for consistent and quality service to the organization and its customers by providing franchisees and corporate staff with the tools to operate their businesses as they were designed to be operated.

Should the expansion plans for the system include multiunit ownership and master franchise programs, a recognition that these operators need additional skills must be built into the system. An often-cited criticism of multiunit ownership is their poor performance and their lower operating standards. Many times I have found that the multiunit operator was not trained by the franchisor to have the organizational skills required to operate at this level of management. Additionally, while master franchisees are often responsible for the training and continual support of their subfranchisees, the training programs offered to them differ little from the training provided to individual franchisees, except for franchise sales. Thus master franchisees are not able to implement system changes, further damaging the program.

Training, support, and communications systems and the cost associated with them are realities that need to be addressed in the strategic plan.

Marketing Strategies

The franchise marketing strategy is essentially an analysis of the company's concepts relative to the franchising arena. The objectives of this analysis are: the determination of the most effective means of market entry; markets to be penetrated and their critical mass and distribution requirements; the definition of the franchisee's profile; the creation of the franchise marketing package and marketing methodologies, including not only advertising but public relations and the proper use of franchise trade shows; and the mechanisms to search, screen, approve, select, and close the franchise sale.

A qualitative analysis of each of the alternative expansion methods (company-owned, individual, master, area development, international) is followed by a quantitative analysis of the most attractive prospect for the company.

Without detailing all the risks and rewards of each method of expansion, it is important to note that the method chosen needs to make long-term sense, both financially and organizationally. Because it is touted as a rapid method of expansion and I believe that rapid expansion for its own sake is not a respectable goal, except in special situations and for uniquely capable individuals or organizations, I am not a great proponent of classic master franchising. I am convinced that the exchange of initial fees for reduced royalties can mortgage a systems future; in addition, the inherent problems with quality and consistency that come with allowing a separate organization to select, train, and communicate system culture and changes to franchisees are unnecessary risks I feel franchisors should avoid. For master franchising to be successful, the franchisor must establish performance standards for the master franchisee and must preserve and execute its right to recapture markets should performance standards, in expansion as well as unit quality and performance, not be met. Even should the master franchisee meet its expansion schedule and the franchisor continue to support the ultimate franchisees, there may be inadequate revenue to provide quality support for the master franchisee's system if royalties and other continuing fees are shared. If the franchisor requires a royalty of 5 percent to provide proper service, its ability to support its franchisees profitably may be problematic if that royalty is shared with the master franchisee.

Once the decisions have been made on the type or types of franchising methods to be used, the geographic strategy, critical mass requirements, distribution requirements, and territorial rights that may be granted to the franchisee need to be determined.

Franchising is a critical-mass business. Critical mass allows franchisees to achieve market dominance over the local independents while allowing the franchisor to have the revenue required to provide a heightened level of service at an affordable cost. When a market is critical-mass-planned, franchise systems benefit in a variety of ways, including their ability to secure better locations at better base rents with better landlord assistance. Landlords and developers recognize the stability of franchise systems and prefer franchisees over independents if for no other reason than franchisees advertise more than the local independent, resulting in more overall traffic to the center.

The establishment of critical-mass requirements allows the franchisor to evaluate those factors important for its locations and to determine how many locations it should establish in the market. Assessments should include a determination of the customer profile (demographic, socioeconomic, market characteristics), site criteria profile (size, viability, traffic, parking, signage), and market or trading areas, taking into account natural trade barriers, such as roads, bridges, rivers, and highways.

While the calculation of mileage radius to determine protected territories is easy, it is inherently unscientific. In developing a market overlay analysis for a franchisor on the East coast, I determined that fifty separate trading areas were available to support individual locations. Utilizing the standard protected market area measured in miles, the franchisor had planned for a maximum of twenty locations. Had the franchisor limited himself to a radius definition of protected territories, large sections of the market would have been left undeveloped and the future growth of the system would have been unnecessarily contracted. It would also have provided fertile ground for competitors to penetrate a market in which they had already identified and developed a product and service demand.

Just as every franchise is different, every potential franchise candidate is also different, economically, demographically, and philosophically. One of the largest expenses incurred by franchisors is marketing their franchise opportunity, and it is important that their efforts be targeted to the proper candidates. Unfortunately, many new franchisors rely upon the "typical" franchisee profile (married, thirty to fifty years of age, and so on) in developing their marketing material. Marketing efforts (brochures, advertising, media buys, public relations, and trade shows) need to address themselves to the profile of potential franchisee developed in the marketing section of the strategic plan. Multitudes of leads provide a sense of accomplishment to the franchisor's marketing professionals, but it is the selection and closure of the proper candidate that makes the system healthy. Lead generation and follow-up are expensive, and franchise candidates who do not meet the franchise profile only increase this expense. Franchisors need to target their marketing to an identifiable franchisee profile. If this specific franchisee profile is not developed and communicated through the marketing effort, all the franchisor does is create activity.

An identified franchisee profile allows the franchisor to customize the message, allows potential franchisees to self-screen, and enables the franchisor to target the publications and vehicles that these potential candidates read. It is the most cost-effective approach to recruitment.

On the basis of its analysis, coupled with the realities of franchise sales and unit performance, a company can begin to project its future revenue streams. A simple but common mistake in the area of income projection is entrepreneurial optimism. Not only must the franchisor realistically estimate the number of franchises sold, but the timing of these sales, taking into account seasonality if appropriate, will have an impact on the cash flow requirements of the franchise system. Additionally, franchisors must realistically assess the timing from franchise sale to opening and the monthly sales each franchisee will earn, which will translate into royalty income and available advertising dollars.

With quality real estate becoming harder to locate and zoning restrictions affecting site selection more and more, the average time to unit openings often is longer than the franchisor would desire. If overly optimistic, franchise system revenue projections, and the projected timing of these cash inflows, may be unattainable, resulting in severe system disruption and possible failure.

Corporate overhead requirements are tightly projected against system size and revenue availability. Without realistic income projection, the size of the organization, in both staff and overhead, may outstrip corporate resources.

Legal Issues

The franchise system and the franchisor/franchisee relationship are shaped by strategic planning, policies, procedures, ongoing administrative monitoring, and support services spelled out in the strategic plan. The legal agreement between the franchisor and franchisee details the relationship and system the franchisor intended.

The role of the legal section of the strategic plan is to direct the franchisor and its counsel to potential areas of conflict and to provide business advice on which policies should be implemented to protect the system and to ensure that the legal documents are complete, accurate, and marketable and include all aspects determined in the strategic plan.

Working with competent legal counsel, the strategic plan should clearly determine, among other things: franchise terms, renewal policies, and fees; territorial exclusivities; lease/sublease policies; the franchisee's reporting and audit responsibilities; and states into which the system will begin to expand.

Once all of the requirements of the system are determined and all basic system assumptions are made, financial projections for each level of the organization can be created. Financial performance and realistic start-up expenses are analyzed to determine rates of return for franchisees and to help in the determination of fees. With the goal that franchisees at all levels remain profitable and their rate of return on their investment be conducive to the purchase of additional units, the franchisor can begin to determine the system's fee structure. Those fees include the initial franchise fee, continuing royalty fees, and advertising contribution and training fees, among others. Coupled with the realistic franchise sales projections and the known timing of unit openings, the projected monthly sales volume for each franchise location and the income stream for the franchisor can be determined.

Each segment of the strategic plan identifies areas of responsibility and cost for the franchisor. With the identification of the systems costs, both start-up and ongoing and with the revenue stream projections developed, the franchisor can also calculate its cash requirements and rate of return. This process of modeling fees for the franchisees and projecting the resulting income stream for the franchisor, while time-consuming and tedious, provides the franchisor with a realistic assessment of the financial needs and resources of the system.

Without a careful organizational analysis and realistic financial projection created through the strategic process, the franchise system is no more than a shelf package. The determination of fee structure without a complete understanding of the system will place fees either too high or too low. Neither alternative is acceptable.

A quality franchise system for either a traditional start-up franchisor or a Retrofranchised company needs to be developed with care. Planners should understand that franchising is only one method of distribution and that an analysis of other methods should be made in tandem with the franchising analysis.

NOTE

1. Management Horizons (the retail consulting division of Price Waterhouse), "Retailing 2000" (Columbus, Ohio: 1991).

PART VII

CURRENT TRENDS AND TOPICS IN FRANCHISING

A wide variety of topics and issues directly and indirectly affect the growth and development of a franchising program. These are also the same topics and issues that are regularly discussed by the franchising community and the business media.

In Part VII, we have assembled some of the leaders in their respective fields to discuss issues such as the growing role of women and minorities in franchising, the costs and benefits of launching an international franchising program, the insider's view on multiunit franchising, and the lack of formal educational programs on franchising at the university level.

31

Women and Minorities in Franchising

Susan P. Kezios, Women in Franchising, Inc.

Today, more than ever before, women and minorities are investigating franchise business ownership. Why? Because during the 1990s, for the first time, women and minorities will come to constitute a majority of the work force. By the year 2000, white women will become the single largest group of American workers, making up almost 40 percent of workers. And nonwhite men and women will total close to 23 percent of the American work force.[1]

However, moving into the work force in larger numbers does not necessarily mean moving into the upper echelons of that work force. Most women and minorities plateau at middle-level management positions in major corporations.[2] And like many traditional entrepreneurs before them, women and minorities opt for business ownership as a career move that will rid them of current job frustrations.

White women call these frustrations the glass ceiling, while minorities call it the invisible white wall. Whatever it is called, the result is the same—women and minorities often encounter a ceiling that limits their upward mobility in larger organizations. Couple this ceiling with the downsizing of major corporations, and you have an exodus of talented, enterprising individuals who happen to be women and minorities, many in their peak income-earning years.

Self-employment is one way women and minorities can control their own destinies. For those individuals who do not have a burning desire to start a particular business from scratch and for those who do not have a strong entrepreneurial heritage, buying a franchise is a chance to be a provider of products and services instead of forever being a consumer.

Terminology

Why do we use the phrase "women and minorities"? White women are not considered a minority under federal law but are, rather, a separate protected group. Minorities include minority men and women and persons who describe themselves as being one of the following four ethnic or racial minorities:

1. *Black*. Black, Jamaican, Puerto Rican, West Indian, Haitian, Nigerian
2. *Hispanic*. Cuban, Mexican, Puerto Rican, Latin American, Hispano, Latino, European Spanish
3. *Asian/Pacific Islanders*. Asian Indian, Chinese, Japanese, Korean, Vietnamese, Guamiam, Cambodian, Laotion, Pakistani/Filipino, Hawaiian, Samoan, Fijian
4. *American Indian/Alaskan natives*. Aleut and Indian, Eskimo, Canadian Indian, French-American Indian, Spanish-American Indian

The physically challenged, or "differently abled" as many prefer to be identified, consider themselves the largest minority in the country. The U.S. Small Business Administration (SBA) Office of Advocacy sponsored research into business ownership opportunities for the physically challenged and found that there are few if any types of business that cannot be owned and operated by the physically challenged.[3] One study in the SBA report talked of a woman with multiple sclerosis who owns a Mail Boxes, Etc., franchise. Another described amputees who own one or more McDonald's restaurants. A man who lost his leg in an accident joked that "When I had two legs, I didn't even have one McDonald's. Now I have one leg and two McDonald's."[4]

Finally, majority or minority men and women can be considered "socially or economically disadvantaged citizens," that is, unable to obtain adequate financing on reasonable terms for one of the following reasons:

- The applicant belongs to a historically deprived group because of race, creed, sex, religion, or national origin
- He or she has a physical handicap
- He or she possesses other social or economic impediments (e.g., lack of formal education)

Terminology becomes important to the prospective franchisee searching for financing because it can affect the franchisee's ability to gain access to special management or business consulting services earmarked for women or minorities. Terminology also becomes important to the franchisor in the never-ending quest to expand the franchise owner network. A franchisor beginning to expand into urban locations may well find that a person's ethnicity can be an important factor in running a successful, long-term franchise in certain communities.

Current Status of Women and Minorities in Franchising

Despite the recent proliferation of newspaper and magazine articles about the large numbers of women and minority franchisees, as late as 1985, *Megatrends* author John Naisbitt reported that women and minorities were just beginning to discover the opportunities available to them as franchise entrepreneurs.[5]

Statistics seem to support Naisbitt's observation. For seventeen years the U.S. Department of Commerce's Industry and Trade Administration published an annual survey, "Franchising in the Economy," which included a report on the number of minority franchisees. However, the final edition of "Franchising in the Economy," published in 1986, indicates that minorities owned 8,116, or 1.7 percent, of the approximately 478,000 franchised outlets nationwide (see Figure 31-1). Since that time there has been no accurate compilation of figures regarding minority franchise ownership.

An analysis of Department of Commerce statistics shows that minority franchise participation fell from almost 30 percent between 1983 and 1986 to an estimated 25 percent in 1989. Simply stated, black, Hispanic, and Native American ownership of franchises has actually dwindled since 1983. The only racial minority to increase its ownership of franchises over that same period has been Asians.

In its seventeen years of tracking franchise statistics, the Department of Commerce never tracked women's ownership of franchised businesses. In 1987, Women in Franchising, Inc., conducted the first nationwide survey of women's ownership of franchises (see Figure 31-2). It found that 10.9 percent of all franchised outlets were owned solely by women. Another 20 percent were owned by women-men partnerships. A 1990 follow-up survey showed that women continue to own just 11.1 percent of all franchised outlets, while the number of woman-man partnerships increased to 23.9 percent. While there has been no drop in the number of franchises owned by women, neither has there been any real growth. Women have merely maintained their position as franchise entrepreneurs.

Rates of Business Ownership by Minorities and Women

Generally speaking, the number of women- and minority-owned businesses still lags behind the number owned by majority entrepreneurs. The state of minority and women's entrepreneurial inequality is illustrated in Figure 31-3. White men

Figure 31-1. Minority franchise ownership.

	Black	Hispanic	American Indian	Asian	Total (numerical)
1983	38%	31%	2%	29%	7,360
1986	36%	28%	1%	36%	10,142
Net Gain or Loss	−2%	−3%	−1%	+7%	+2,782

Source: U.S. Department of Commerce, *Franchising in the Economy,* 1983, 1986.

Figure 31-2.   Franchise ownership by women.

1987 Survey of 137 Franchising Companies			
	Women	*Women-Men*	*Men*
Percentage of Outlets	10.9	20.0	60.6
No. of Outlets	2,041	3,717	1,339
1990 Survey of 260 Franchising Companies			
	Women	*Women-Men*	*Men*
Percentage of Outlets	11.12	23.95	60.21
No. of Outlets	3,826	8,242	20,715

Source: 1987, 1990 surveys conducted by Women in Franchising, Inc.

own the largest number of businesses, at 6,856,665. White men own more than 2.5 times the number of businesses that white women own. White men's gross receipts are also the highest, at $599,841,888. Gross receipts of businesses owned by white men are five times greater than those of women-owned businesses.

Even though black-owned businesses outnumber those that are Hispanic-owned, black companies' gross receipts lag behind those of Hispanic businesses. The "Other Minorities" category, which includes Asians, has only slightly more establishments than the Hispanics category, yet gross receipts are higher than at either black- or Hispanic-owned companies.

Figure 31-3 clearly illustrates that women- and minority-owned firms are smaller and less profitable and grow more slowly than those owned by majority men. The businesses owned by women and minorities resemble separate under-developed nations within a nation.

Looking at the United States as a nation of immigrants offers some interest-ing food for thought when it comes to ancestry and the likelihood of women and minorities owning their own business. Figure 31-4 illustrates business ownership rates for different ancestry groups, calculated by dividing the number of persons in a particular ancestry group who identified themselves in the 1980 U.S. census as self-employed by the total number of persons in that ancestry group. The rate of business ownership varies widely by ancestry group.

Russians (likely a proxy for Eastern European Jews) rank at the top, and Lebanese are ranked second (this group has also historically engaged in mercan-tile activities).

Puerto Ricans, considered to be one of the most disadvantaged of the His-panic groups, rank at the bottom. Just above them are sub-Saharan Africans. This

Figure 31-3. Business ownership and gross sales by ethnic group.

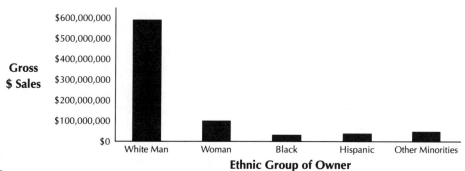

Key:
■ = Total No. of Companies

Key:
■ = Gross Receipts of Companies

Source: U.S. Department of Commerce, Bureau of the Census, 1982, Characteristics of Business Owners.

group includes native American blacks, although not all native American blacks consider themselves sub-Saharan. Also ranking in the bottom five are the Vietnamese, most of whom emigrated to the United States in the early 1980s.

Of the intermediate-ranked groups, Koreans have the highest participation in business ownership among Asians, and Cubans have the highest rate of business ownership among Hispanics. So, for some women and minorities, history itself is against their chances of becoming self-employed.

Despite the obstacles they face, women are turning to business ownership in increasing numbers. The U.S. House of Representatives Committee on Small Business issued a June 28, 1988, report entitled, ''New Economic Realities: The Rise of Women Entrepreneurs.'' At the time of the report,

▲ Women were starting businesses at a national average twice that of men.
▲ The federal government estimated that, given recent trends, the percentage

Figure 31-4. The ancestry factor.

Rank	Business Ownership Rate
1. Russian	11.7%
2. Lebanese	10.7%
3. Romanian	10.4%
4. Swiss	10.4%
5. Greek	9.5%
18. Korean	6.9%
23. Japanese	6.5%
24. Chinese	6.0%
30. Polish	5.2%
32. Irish	5.0%
34. Cuban	4.8%
Five Lowest	
46. Vietnamese	1.7%
47. Haitian	1.6%
48. Dominican	1.5%
49. Sub-Saharan African	1.4%
50. Puerto Rican	1.1%

Source: 1980 census calculated from Fratoe, 1986.

of women starting businesses could reach 50 percent of total new businesses by the year 2000.

▲ The vast majority of women-owned businesses were emerging in the service sector.

The service sector is the fastest-growing sector of the U.S. economy. It is also the sector that requires the least financial resources and tends to rely on human resources or human capital.[6]

The significance for both women and minorities, and for franchisors, lies in the fact that new service areas are where the most explosive growth is expected in franchising over the next ten years. New service franchises include those that provide a variety of business and personal services, all of which are finding that some of their best operators are women and minority owners.

Traditional Obstacles to Business Ownership

The major obstacle facing women and minorities contemplating small-business ownership is their inability to obtain capital. Money is a problem partly because the average woman typically earns seventy cents for every dollar a man earns. All men earn close to twice what all women earn. Black and Hispanic men earn close to twice what all black and Hispanic women earn, and white males earn the highest wages and therefore have more capital to form businesses.

A lack of entrepreneurial skills and restricted access to quality technical and managerial training is a major reason for the lower gross sales of women- and minority-owned businesses. The House of Representatives report on women entrepreneurs cites continuing technical and managerial training as necessary to break down barriers that hinder the growth of women-owned businesses. Without a strong entrepreneurial heritage it is difficult for anyone, not only women or minorities, to consider business ownership as a viable option.

Franchising offers a way to overcome both of these obstacles. First, the franchisor's expertise typically includes information on sources of financing. Franchisors know who has experience in and who wants to finance restaurant, hair care, or print shop franchises. If the franchisor does not directly offer financing, it is often able to direct the woman or minority candidate to those who can help.

Second, the essence of all successful franchise systems is ongoing technical and managerial assistance. Business training must be long term. There is no way to learn how to run a business day to day other than by doing it. And there is no better place for women and minorities to learn entrepreneurship than from an entrepreneur, specifically a franchisor, who has already developed a business plan that can be successfully replicated by others.

Access to Information

If women and minorities can overcome traditional obstacles of business ownership by purchasing franchises, why aren't more of them doing so? Why isn't the franchise industry embracing this heretofore untapped pool of franchisees?

Although the process of investigating a franchise is basically the same for both men and women, gaining access to the necessary information does not occur naturally for women and minorities in the United States. To begin with, women and minorities often don't know where to go to ask about owning a franchise. Women especially may feel they're supposed to give help, not receive it.

Women and minorities need mentors, especially in the field of business ownership. Franchising provides them with one of the oldest mentoring systems in the United States. The franchisor must begin to close the information gap, however, to tap into the obvious resource that women and minority franchise candidates represent.

Target Marketing

While everyone else in franchising is trying to figure out why their available pool of candidates is diminishing, franchisors can tap a wellspring of talent by beginning a dialogue with enterprising women and minorities. To begin that dialogue, however, franchisors have to know where to hold the conversation.

Women and minorities tend to gather information more from formal than from informal sources: government agencies, small or minority business development centers, network-oriented clubs, and publications targeted to their special interest group.

As a franchisor, your first step to increasing your visibility to potential women and minority franchisees is to find your target group and provide it with information. But where do you find women looking to go into business for themselves? How can you target black or Hispanic franchisees?

Special-interest print media are a good place to start. Monthly magazines like *Black Enterprise, Hispanic Business,* and *Minority Business Entrepreneur* all run regular articles and special feature sections on franchising. If franchise editorial is not part of the magazine's regular fare, wait for franchise editorial to appear so your advertisement will have more impact on the reader.

A caveat about advertising in women's magazines: Do not get sold on women readers who may not fall within your target profile. Some publication may have a large number of readers who are at a "consuming" point in their lives and who are not at a "looking to get out of their jobs" point.

Never use a special-interest advertising medium unless you can be dominant, and never add a second medium until you are dominant in the first. With a limited advertising budget, be sure you have strong frequency against your target and then begin to spread your reach. If one of your major marketing strategies is to increase market share, you will probably have to back it up with a substantial communications budget for advertising and sales promotion. If funds are not available to handle special-interest advertising, then you have to change your strategy.

COMMUNITY-BASED ORGANIZATIONS

An important part of the more formal network women and minorities use to gather information are the many community-based business and professional organizations. These groups may have either an ethnic or an economic development focus. Developing relationships with these groups is the first of many grass-roots steps to promoting new franchise concepts to special-interest groups.

Utilize community-based organizations to recruit women and minorities by (1) looking for those groups with the largest number of your target; (2) identifying the programs they have available; and (3) understanding the relationship you are building with these groups.

Community-based organizations can help you acquire credibility by allowing you to cohost or to sponsor an event, underwrite the cost of a newsletter, or participate as a panelist on an economic development program. You will be building a relationship with one or a handful of several key people within the organization. Value and nurture these relationships. These key people will "secure" your franchise as reputable and worthy of consideration in the minds of their membership. A single violation of that relationship not only will tarnish your future efforts but will damage franchising's credibility within that particular community as well.

An example of a community-based organization is the Asian American Small Business Association (AASBA) of Chicago. Founded a little more than a decade ago, the AASBA supports legislation for small businesses and establishes good governmental relationships with the city and the state. Its projects focus largely on economic development efforts within the Asian American community of Chicago.

A second example is the United States Hispanic Chamber of Commerce, an alliance of over 200 Hispanic chambers and business associations nationwide, collectively representing 400,000 Hispanic business enterprises. The U.S. Hispanic Chamber of Commerce was begun in 1979 and has grown to be the most influential Hispanic trade association in the United States. Based in Washington, D.C., its primary goal is to promote the economic growth and development of Hispanic business.

Obtaining Financing for a Franchise

As stated earlier, the major obstacle to women and minorities seeking to own a franchised business is lack of access to capital. This is also one of the reasons franchisors haven't been successful in recruiting more women and minority franchisees. Many franchisors complain that it is difficult to find potential women and minority applicants with the economic resources needed to start a franchise. Very often talented individuals are not given the opportunity to explore an identified franchise if the franchisor has determined that they do not have the equity needed to cover costs associated with the start-up of a franchise.

If a woman or a minority candidate has the qualifications you're looking for in a franchisee, then take the lead to help put the deal together. If you don't, you'll find yourself saying, "That person was perfect, but we just couldn't get the money together."

Franchisors can utilize a cookie-cutter approach to franchise financing that leaves no stone unturned and works in any part of the country. This involves tapping the new "old boy" network of people at the state, county, and city levels who are committed to furthering economic development in their areas. This network also includes a number of "helper agencies" that offer business planning assistance and financing help to your prospective franchisee.

First, review private-sector financing sources. There are two places to go for private-sector money: banks and nonbanking financial institutions. Traditionally, banks have been unwilling to finance new businesses, franchises included. Recently, however, the attitude of some lending institutions has begun to change. The Community Reinvestment Act (CRA), a federal law revised in the mid-1980's, has fueled some of this new interest. A low CRA rating has forced some bankers to take a look at how many of the transactions they have completed have put depositor dollars back into the community. A bank with a small business division is likely to be more attuned to satisfying its CRA requirements, and you will have a better chance of financing your woman or minority candidate by working with this type of institution.

Second, the franchisor can utilize creative equity financing strategies, provided the prospect has access to the majority of the equity required. Some creative equity financing strategies include:

- Deferring the franchise fee
- Providing a portion of up-front equity to be factored back through royalty payments
- Exploring public financing programs that permit lower equity participation to finance the fixed asset portion of the project

Taking on debt as part of the franchise financing package is a necessary evil. The word "evil" is used because attempting to service a costly debt structure will doom a franchise from the start.

Equity and debt have an inverse relationship—the less the equity, the more the debt. Therefore, the cost of the debt and how it is structured become critical components of the financial package. The challenge is to identify and then to secure the least expensive debt for your prospect. Some creative debt strategies include:

- Structuring the term for a longer amortization
- Structuring an interest-only six- to twelve-month plan
- Deferring principal and interest payments
- Seeking a debt source that can be more patient about repayment, such as a friend, a relative, or an investor, or using self-financing.

In both items 2 and 3, the deferred debt balloons at the end of the amortization period.

A third possibility is public-sector financing programs. These programs vary from state to state and from city to city. However, the most important factor to remember is to know what exists and what is available in your target area and how these programs can be utilized in structuring a proposal and making the deal happen.

Most public-sector programs have three major objectives:

1. *Offering opportunity*. These programs provide the borrower with the means to get the deal done. The loan is guaranteed by another agency that gives the lender a comfort zone within which to operate. There is no interest rate reduction in this type of program.

   Example: SBA 504 Program and the SBA 74 Loan Guarantee.

2. *Providing incentives*. These programs offer a reduced interest rate to the borrower. They do not, however, reduce lender exposure.

   Example: Linked Deposit Program.

3. *Combining opportunity and incentive*. These programs have characteristics of both opportunity and incentive programs. They reduce both the interest rate and lender exposure.

   Example: Ohio Mini-Loan Program (low-interest-rate direct loan plus a loan guarantee).

In addition, your target state, county, or city may have financing programs tied into the number of jobs created. These programs are typically available to both men and women, regardless of ethnicity. For every job created by opening a business, you are able to borrow a certain dollar amount per person at a very reasonable interest rate, sometimes as low as 3 or 4 percent.

For example, one successful program that has financed franchises is the Build Illinois Minority and Women Business Loan Program. Loans offered under this program range from $5,000 to $50,000. A minimum of one job must be created or retained for every $6,000 borrowed from the state. The interest rate is currently set at around 4 percent.

Some states, counties, and cities have special franchise financing programs for persons who want to open franchised businesses. One of the oldest such programs is administered by the state of Maryland. The Equity Participation Investment Program (EPIP) provides loans to "socially or economically disadvantaged" individuals, i.e., women and minorities, who will locate their franchises within the state of Maryland. The state actually invests up to 45 percent of the total cost of the franchise and becomes an equity partner with the franchisee.

Finally, many women and minorities limit their search for a franchise to one that offers help with financing. Franchisors that do not offer direct financing can successfully compete by knowing how to utilize resources such as those I have discussed to mix and match sources of money for their candidates.

Helper Agencies

In certain locations your woman or minority franchise candidate may have been referred to you by either a Small Business Development Center (SBDC) or a Minority Business Development Center (MBDC). Small Business Development Centers are partially funded by the U.S. Small Business Administration (SBA).

Minority Business Development Centers are funded by the U.S. Department of Commerce Minority Business Development Agency (MBDA).

These centers provide services that result in an increase in the number of local small and minority-owned businesses. Candidates go to a local SBDC or MBDC for counseling and assistance in writing a business plan, sourcing financing, and marketing and to learn about their business ownership options.

From time to time these agencies have special trade fairs, seminars, or workshops on franchising in which your company may want to participate. On a larger scale, franchising was recently chosen by the MBDA as a major avenue for increasing the number of minority businesses. Through its National Franchise Initiative, MBDA intends to develop a climate and a support system for accelerating the growth of minority franchise businesses.

MBDA has worked closely with more than one hundred MBDCs throughout the United States and has developed materials and programs to support the National Franchise Initiative. MBDA has provided MBDCs with written materials and a computerized listing of franchisors interested in recruiting minority franchisees and has run a series of in-depth franchise training seminars for interested minority candidates.

Franchisors interested in beginning the process of networking within a target community should contact the local Small or Minority Business Development Center. Schedule a meeting with the counselors, introduce them to your concept, and offer to participate in any economic development programs they may have. While you help the SBDC or MBDC counselors to understand franchising, they can help you by screening and referring qualified candidates.

Increasing Your Company's Appeal to Women and Minorities

The first place to start increasing your company's appeal to women and minorities is at the top. If the chairman or president isn't behind the marketing department's objective to recruit more women and minority applicants, your special-interest marketing plan will be that much harder to implement. Often the old boys at the top of the franchise pyramid need new outlooks.

Part of the problem is that some of the old boys are out of touch with what is really going on in the marketplace. Diversity training for all levels of upper management will bring viewpoints regarding women and minority franchisees out on the table. This kind of training will also help identify elements in your corporate culture that prevent you from retaining good women and minority owners.

To get a reality check on how women and minorities perceive your franchise, schedule one or more focus groups, groups put together to find out what women or minorities think about such things as your advertisements and the atmosphere at your home office.

If the idea of hiring a consultant to hold one or more focus groups does not appeal to you, then at least get upper management to talk with your current women and minority franchisees, executives, and prospects. Find out what they think about your organization and your advertisements. If you want women and minorities as franchise owners, you must involve them in your sales process.

Your franchise sales department has probably been accustomed to a mass marketing approach. Targeting special-interest groups involves utilizing rifle-shot techniques—profiling your target, identifying the geographic area in which your target lives and works, and developing relationships with people and organizations within the community who can communicate your message.

Above all, do not sabotoge your preplanning when your franchise sales team comes to town. If the franchise sales process is controlled totally by white men, then have them talk regularly to women and minorities. This may sound elementary, but franchise salespeople often forget to listen to and act upon what (in this case women and minority) prospects are saying.

Sensitize your salespeople's eyes to issues that normally go unnoticed. Develop sales talent in women and minorities in your company so that they can screen your message before it gets out the door and communicates ignorance to those you are trying hardest to reach. Not only do you need the right attitude at the home office to attract women and minorities, you must communicate that attitude to attract the right candidates.

One promotional technique guaranteed to backfire is to announce to the world that 75 percent of your franchisees are (female, black, etc.). This kind of tactic kills more ad campaigns than it helps. A better place to start is by using black or women role model testimonials in your ads.

Marketing to Women and Minorities

Women and minorities sometimes come to business ownership with less confidence than white men bring. Women especially act more tentatively as they go through parts of the franchise-buying process. As you would with any franchise candidate, you as a franchisor should talk about the goals of safety and security and emphasize that risk taking is part of the franchise-buying process.

Franchisors sometimes talk about how much hand-holding they must do after the sale with some of their women and minority franchisees. If this becomes a recurrent theme in your company, an examination of your training program may show you don't need to provide more training for women and minorities, just different training. Issues that franchisees may be dealing with, such as sexism and racism, now become the franchisor's issues.

Some franchisors state that, if they openly recruit women and minorities, they will deter some of their more traditional candidates from purchasing the franchise. Most franchisors, however, discover the opposite effect. They find they are opening franchises in more diverse marketplaces than ever before.

Another myth is that it takes more time to educate women and minorities about franchising. There is also a perception that putting together franchising for women or minorities takes more time. This is often a function of the franchisor's knowing which resources to tap into and how to utilize them efficiently to the benefit of the franchisee. Ninety-day closes are not the norm for women and minorities. Special-interest marketing is a long-term strategy—a six- to twelve-month close. Women and minority candidates are known to gather more information before they make their decision, hence the longer lead time.

Marketing to women and minorities also has its advantages. With many suburbs already saturated with franchises, urban areas are one of the last frontiers in which franchisors can increase market share. The centralized nature of the black, Hispanic, and Asian communities, all primarily urban populations, makes marketing to these groups a natural rifle-shot approach. Rifle-shot your target market by locating the major community organizations, identifying the leaders in economic development within those communities, and purchasing advertisements in special-interest publications.

In an effort to accelerate women and minority business development, innovative financing programs specifically designed to open franchises within certain cities and states are available. Find your qualified woman or minority candidate, and take him or her to the program that will help get the prospect into your business.

The result of many of these targeted financing programs is more money to the franchisor's bottom line, both before and after the sale. Utilizing a combination of public- and private-sector financing programs for women and minorities often brings all-cash deals to the franchisor. A Kentucky Fried Chicken spokesperson claimed that franchises owned by minorities rack up as much as $100,000 more in sales per year than nonminority operations. A McDonald's spokesperson stated it simply: "It makes sense to be represented in every community by the people who live there."[7]

The Future of Women- and Minority-Owned Franchising

Advocacy groups, the franchise industry, and women's and minority organizations have recently started to provide information to prospective women and minority entrepreneurs about franchising. However, it will be another decade before we can truly measure the results of today's efforts.

To ensure a level playing field between franchisor and franchisees, the U.S. House of Representatives Committee on Small Business held a series of hearings on the subject of franchising in the early 1990s. One of those hearings touched upon the experience of women and minorities as purchasers of franchises. Another hearing focused exclusively on the experience of minorities in franchising.

Issues discussed ranged from women's and minorities' lack of access to capital to the poor choice of locations offered minority applicants. The committee is determining how best to protect the interests of all franchisees, majority or minority, men or women.

Most franchisors recognize that a healthy reciprocity exists between the strategic needs of their marketing efforts and the human needs of the women and minorities they recruit. Franchisors can certainly accomplish their business objectives of increased market share without compromising the interests of the women and minorities they solicit.

Without the leadership of franchisors, female and minority business ownership through franchising will not happen within an acceptable time frame. Continuous business development is critical to the expansion of every franchisor's network. Women and minorities are an integral part of that development.

NOTES

1. Howard N. Fullerton, "Projections 2000: Labor force projections 1986 to 2000," *Monthly Labor Review*, September 1987.
2. *Dataline: The Glass Ceiling*, August 1991 (subscription newsletter).
3. Associated Enterprise Development, Inc., *Businesses That Can Be Owned and Operated by Handicapped Veterans* (Annapolis, Md.: 1984).
4. Ibid.
5. The Naisbitt Group. *The Future of Franchising: Looking 25 Years Ahead to the Year 2010* (Washington, D.C.: International Franchise Association, 1985).
6. U.S. House of Representatives Committee on Small Business. *New Economic Realities: The Rise of Women Entrepreneurs* (Washington, D.C.: GPO, June 28, 1988).
7. Erika Kotite, "Opening Doors for Minorities," *Franchise and Business Opportunities* (The Entrepreneur Group, 1990).

32

Trends and Developments in International Franchising

James H. Amos, Jr., "I Can't Believe It's Yogurt"

Macroeconomically, roughly one-third of U.S. corporate profits are generated by international business. In fact, American competitiveness abroad has had a direct effect on domestic employment levels as well as on the economic health of the nation. For every billion dollars of export, 25,000 new jobs are created at a time when it appears that the growth potential of the U.S. domestic market is leveling off. Five million new jobs created in manufacturing in the United States in the last five years were export-related. The Office of Technology Assessment of the U.S. Department of Commerce reports that "where a global market exists, firms operating on a worldwide basis may have advantages over those that restrict themselves to a domestic market."

The global marketplace has become highly competitive. The United States is losing not only to Japan but to South Korea, Taiwan, Brazil, Mexico, and other nations. In 1990 our share of the world's exports declined from 15.4 percent to below 12 percent in one year. Eighty percent of our industry now faces international competition. We simply do not have the best goods at the best prices, nor are we anymore the only game in town. U.S. foreign trade is producing record deficits, and our dominance in world agriculture is decreasing. We are facing competition in service industries and losing shipping to companies such as Taiwan's Evergreen Marine Corporation.

In addition, *international* no longer means outside this country. There is already a plethora of foreign corporations operating in the United States today. Not a single black-and-white television set sold in the United States is American-made, and foreigners own companies like Baskin Robbins, Saks Fifth Avenue, Alka-Seltzer, Bantam Books, Paul Masson, and Nestle's.[1]

In 1992, the European Community (EC) brought its 321 million consumers to a collective trading table. The rules for international trade are clearly changing. Since change is inevitable, using it to your corporate advantage is only prudent. Centuries of institutionalized trade barriers are being swept away under the guidance of twelve member states that encompass nine languages. The EC market is more than one-third bigger than the United States market and yet maintains different cultures and tastes. The EC is changing commercial, financial, legal, tax, and other business areas so much that U.S. companies cannot sit idly by and ignore them. New structures will be necessary to take advantage of these opportunities.

Within the EC, technical standards will be based on minimum European requirements. Physical barriers at internal frontiers will be removed, and fiscal systems will be harmonized. Capital movements will be completely liberalized, with a single market established for delivery of goods. In today's environment, both large and small companies should recognize that the process of integrating European communities into a truly single market is a significant step toward creating a global economy and, thus, global markets.

Competition will not ease under the new system. In fact, it will become more difficult. As trade barriers fall, additional regulations will emerge in their place that could undermine the potential for growth within the EC. The creation of "Fortress Europe" is a distinct possibility. In addition, European companies will be in direct competition with one another. Already cross-border acquisitions and mergers have increased. What is even more interesting is why there have not been more acquisitions and mergers. Instead, what we are seeing are strategic alliances and minority investments that will probably end up being poor substitutes for complete mergers. However, this may well indicate an even riper market for international business format franchising. The successful franchising company that is considering entering these markets is well advised to have an international business development system that follows a clearly defined critical path.

What questions should a senior level franchising executive ask prior to globalization? Some of the questions my company asked itself prior to entering the international arena were:

- ▲ How has our market changed, or is it likely to change?
- ▲ Should we look at Europe as one market, rather than as individual countries?
- ▲ Do we need to reorganize our business to take advantage of economies of scale?
- ▲ Should we form joint ventures and strategic alliances, merge with or acquire new businesses to strengthen our market presence?
- ▲ Are our management and structure appropriate to exploit new opportunities or to defend our position?
- ▲ Who in our company will be responsible for deciding how to make the most of the single market?
- ▲ How should our information flows be managed?
- ▲ Should we reconsider how we manage our financial resources?
- ▲ Will we need to modify our products based on new EC regulations or technical standards?
- ▲ Should we establish closer links with the European Commission in Brussels?

The fact remains that, whether it is the EC, the Pacific Rim, or any other world market, moving your product into the marketplace effectively and efficiently may be the most critical task you face as an executive, even as other executives formulate their own strategic directions and operating plans for the rest of the 1990s. The value chain concept, as an example, reexamines where products are manufactured, how they are manufactured, and how they get into the market. More than ever, an approach is needed to integrate the product development, production, marketing, finance, and distribution objectives of the business.

Clearly the 1990s will bring a revolution in business realignments. Many U.S. companies will experience great difficulty in adjusting their global strategies. Exporters will have to tighten up partnerships or be squeezed out by competitors seeking to take away their market share. Continued success in overseas markets will require new alliances with new strategies. Multinational concerns are emerging in the form of strategic alliances, joint ventures, mergers, and acquisitions. Eventually, these new entities will set their sights on U.S. markets. It is therefore imperative to fight the competitive battle overseas, formulate a strategy, and weigh the risks and rewards of strategic alternatives such as licensing, joint ventures, branches, subsidiaries, and company-owned, master, or direct franchising.

One of the reasons business format franchising is so attractive is that historically U.S. companies and corporate leaders have looked toward more complex and financially expensive options such as acquisitions or mergers. However, these are very risky, requiring a great deal of time, often maturing too late to take advantage of a rapidly emerging market. What we have is an international environment where the rules are being rewritten. A highly competitive global market has promulgated a rash of international business collaborations.

Primary Methods Utilized for International Expansion

Among the main methods of international expansion are company-owned-*only* operations, direct franchising, branch operations, subsidiaries, joint venture, and master franchise rights.

Company-Owned-Only Operations

You decide not to franchise in the target country but to establish your own operations. This obviously requires financial resources and manpower. It, of course, can also provide the basis for future franchise development.

Direct Franchising

You, as the franchisor, enter into a franchise agreement with each individual franchisee. This is limited in scope because of the distance from the target country.

However, direct franchising combined with the establishment of a branch or subsidiary can provide tax advantages.

Branch

This method is used in two circumstances:

1. A branch is set up to service country franchisees.
2. A branch is established as a regional base. This action is usually driven by fiscal and legal considerations, not business reasons.

Subsidiary

A subsidiary may fulfill any of four functions:

1. The subsidiary may service franchisees that are directly franchised into the target territory.
2. The franchisor may grant the franchisee the right to the subsidiary.
3. The subsidiary may joint venture.
4. The subsidiary may be used as a regional base to support franchisees or master franchisees in the region.

Joint Venture

In this scenario, along with selecting the right person, you face the added problem of determining what share you wish to take and how you want to finance your contribution. The joint venture vehicle becomes the master franchisee. Sometimes the franchisee's contribution to the JV takes the place of the front-end fee, and sometimes that fee is returned by the franchisor as its contribution. There is also an operational loss risk and a broader scope for disagreement on operational matters. It should be noted that it is infinitely more difficult to divest oneself of an unsatisfactory JV partner than to terminate a master franchisee.

Master Franchise Rights

A master franchisee or master developer is entitled to open its own outlets or to subfranchise, or both. If you are considering this option, take these four factors into account:

1. Selection of the right master franchisee is difficult.
2. There is a need for a strong home base to meet demands.
3. The set-up will divert both staff and financial resources from domestic operations—more than you think.
4. The start-up will always take longer than you think.

The master franchise or master development agreement may be the most appropriate method of penetration for the following three reasons:

1. It establishes a global network and family of franchisees.
2. It requires the master franchisee to provide the financial resources to establish and exploit the business development system. Whatever these resources are, they must be found by the master franchisee.
3. It requires the master franchisee to recruit staff for the pilot as well as for his own business organization. This blends your business development system into local conditions through the master franchisee's local knowledge.

The three essentials for penetrating international markets are:

1. Correct choice of partner
2. Correct choice of arrangement format
3. Legal documentation

Some of the factors necessary to establish and operate international franchises are:

- Supporting franchises outside the United States
- Recruiting enough qualified franchisees
- Training franchisees for units outside the United States
- Controlling franchisees outside the United States
- Maintaining adequate quality controls
- Dealing with trademark and copyright regulations
- Committing sufficient managerial resources from headquarters to international expansion
- Satisfying governmental and legal restrictions
- Analyzing potential of different markets
- Arranging sufficient local financing
- Making the product acceptable to foreign consumers
- Repatriating royalties
- Overcoming language and cultural barriers
- Arranging supply channels for inventory and other material
- Dealing with tax structures and import duties in host countries
- Obtaining enough suitable locations
- Adapting promotional approaches to host countries
- Coping with foreign currency uncertainties
- Redesigning franchise package to make it marketable outside the United States
- Beating competitors in host countries

"I Can't Believe It's Yogurt": A Case Study

It was my belief that either the joint venture or the master franchise agreement was the most appropriate method of international expansion for "I Can't Believe It's Yogurt," a division of Brice Foods in Dallas, Texas. Franchising is a particularly attractive vehicle for international expansion because it requires substantially less capital than ownership or the other forms of expansion, including joint ventures. In addition, few companies can afford the capital investment required to do the due diligence necessary to assess every foreign market. Therefore, local expertise is paramount in the master franchise relationship. There are really two factors that determine the method a company might choose to expand into international markets. One is the franchisor's willingness and ability to devote the financial and human resources necessary to provide direct support to its international franchisee. The second is the availability of suitable potential partners in the host country. In the March/April 1990 edition of *Export Today*, Peter Holt, the manager of international development for "I Can't Believe It's Yogurt," wrote:

> There's plenty of money abroad for the right deals coming out of the United States. Thanks to franchising's outstanding record of success in this country—which now accounts for more than one-third of retail sales—franchised companies are enjoying an advantage in the foreign marketplace. Consequently, more and more franchisers, even some who have barely cracked the domestic market, are looking to expand abroad.
>
> Nearly 400 American franchisors have expanded into overseas markets in the past twenty years, opening more than 31,000 outlets, according to the U.S. Commerce Department. In 1988, 228 franchisors—mostly small and mid-sized—told the Commerce Department they were considering foreign expansion by 1990. Of that number, there were fifty franchisors of business products and services; thirty-eight restaurant chains; thirty-seven retailers of nonfood products; and thirty-four retailers of food products and services.
>
> In order to successfully franchise overseas, the franchisor must have a sound and successful home base that is sufficiently profitable. The financial position of the franchisor must be secure and he must have resources which are surplus to—or can be exclusively diverted from—his domestic requirements. He must also have the personnel available to devote solely to international operations, and above all he must be patient. On the whole, the development of international markets will always take longer and make greater demands on the resources of the franchiser than first anticipated.[2]

The facts are that control issues, difficulties in offering adequate support, increased costs, cultural and language differences, difficulties in assessing local markets, governmental regulations, repatriation of dollars, and timing as an issue unto itself all carry great demands. However, increased growth, increased revenue, larger market share, and the benefits of increased brand recognition are strong motivators. Given the changes in the global community, the timing issue becomes a question of whether to seize an opportunity when it is offered.

Once a method of international expansion has been chosen, the next crucial step is to determine which domestic strategies can be transferred directly to foreign markets and which strategies should be modified or not used at all. As an example, as with all negotiations, you must know what cannot be compromised when sitting down to the table. At "I Can't Believe It's Yogurt," that meant trademark, logos, service mark, quality of product, and presentation. Beyond this, some degree of flexibility would be necessary. Minor changes in the menu to meet cultural differences might be appropriate. International markets are littered with the residue of companies that failed to be flexible enough to allow some differences in domestic models. Overall, international business development systems should mirror domestic models but allow for a critical path that reflects local markets and cultural differences. Finally, if franchising is the chosen vehicle, the most crucial element in international expansion becomes the selection of the master partner. We decided that we needed to create a profile of a potential master partner. That profile would drive our international development worldwide. What we wanted was a partner that had the vision and the desire to seek disproportionate market share within its country; it would not only have to want market dominance but would have to have the financial capability to educate the consumer and to advertise in its market. Further, in choosing a partner, special consideration had to be given to the political connections, human resources, and business resources that the potential master would bring to the partnership. The importance of these considerations cannot be overestimated in both the developmental and the ongoing operational phases of the master partnership. With these factors satisfied, we would want to grant exclusive rights to the master partner to penetrate its market with all phases of product development.

Relationship development then became the driving force behind the selection of a master franchise partner. It became obvious that there were numerous candidates in most countries with the wherewithal to penetrate their markets financially. However, we soon learned that, regardless of the structure of the agreement or indeed the legal documents supporting that agreement, it was the relationship that would drive the documents, not vice versa. I think this concept is often overlooked in domestic business format franchising, and, if the careful selection of the franchisee is important in domestic growth, it is absolutely imperative in international growth. We at "I Can't Believe It's Yogurt" were patient until we had the profile of the candidate that was a strategic fit for us. We have walked away from agreements because we believe that in some instances no agreement is better than one based on the wrong relationship.

Mutual advantage is the key to selecting the proper partner. The right partner will have integrity, and the company or group represented will display a cooperative culture. A proper matching of strengths, weaknesses, and motivation is necessary; your strength should be the weakness of the partner. In general, this means labor, raw materials, and an expanding market merge with technology, know-how, and marketing and management expertise to maximize business opportunity. I suppose "chemistry" is the glue that keeps things working, but it is an intangible, often defined as trust, that binds the relationship. The result is an implicit understanding that both partners will live up to the unwritten terms of the agreement.

At any rate, companies that are new to European business after 1992 or that hope to take advantage of the move toward globalization in other world markets will need to examine each of the three principal areas of their company to determine a strategy for entering the single European markets. These areas are:

1. *Marketing*—customers, distribution and pricing
2. *Production*—supplies, product range, and processing technology costs
3. *Infrastructure*—organization for human resources, financial resources, and information technologies

In Europe, as artificial competitive advantages disappear, national champion companies will no longer be granted state aid. Monopoly power will disappear, and major joint ventures between European partners will increase. The new harmonious standards will encourage multinational companies and will make it more difficult for small to medium-sized business to survive market forces such as pricing policy. As Europe regulates itself into an integrated economy and new harmonious standards apply, it could become increasingly more difficult for American companies to do business in the EC.

The real question today is not whether you should go global, but when, where, and how. As Napoleon once mused, "Ground I can recover, time I can never retrieve."

NOTES

1. Lennie Copeland and Lewis Griggs, *Going International* (New York: Random House, 1985).
2. Peter D. Holt, "Franchising: The Overseas Advantage," *Export Today* (March/April 1990).

33

Multiarea Development and Expansion Strategies

Milli Stecker, SPAR (Special Projects As Required)

The era in which we are living is marked by the ever accelerating pace at which things change. In order for new businesses to grow, they must grow fast, and the definition of just how fast is extremely difficult to standardize. A strategic concern for any new business concept is its "window of opportunity," the time that an organization's competitive advantage can be exploited in the marketplace before external pressures slow the business's rapid growth. Issues surrounding multiarea development are key because they are primarily concerned with growth—maximizing and sustaining the business's unique competitive advantage in the marketplace. Franchising is a strategic alliance formed to share risks, and the multiarea development agreement strengthens that alliance by linking territorial expansion, revenue growth, and market share of the franchisor and the franchisee to an even greater degree.

Types of Growth Strategies

The person or organization that develops a business concept chooses to franchise in order to maximize growth and to minimize cost. The advantage of growing a company-owned operation is that the owner has total control over standards and procedures. Branch operations accelerate expansion across regions. However, the resources needed to acquire the capital for multiarea expansion are usually beyond those available to an emerging organization. Franchising offers the owner a way to grow the chain without incurring large capital costs. The simplest form of business format franchising is direct franchising of individual units across multiple regions, requiring a sales, training, and system support staff. Direct franchising offers faster expansion with no capital outlay for the franchisor. Conversion franchising, the development of a franchise system primarily through the conversion of independent going concerns, is similar to direct franchising. It usually is more time-consuming to negotiate with and then mesh an independent company with the existing franchise system, and it may not be possible in some markets because there are no independents to convert.

To utilize the sales and support staffs more effectively, franchisors can offer a multiarea development agreement, requiring the franchisee to open a number of stores in a specific territory in a set amount of time. The advantage to the franchisee is that he knows has secured selected territory in advance of being operationally or financially able to develop it. A second possibility, known as master licensing or subfranchising, is an arrangement that grants a license to a company or a person for a territory; the company or person then operates the company and units under the license or grant sublicenses within the territory to the operational franchisees. The advantage of multiarea and master franchising arrangements is that they allow large territories to be defined and exploited at relatively little per-unit-sales or maintenance expense. The disadvantage to the franchisor is the loss of direct control over standards and procedures; the arrangement may become similar to product trade name franchising.

Master licensing is common in international franchising arrangements. Other common international expansion strategies are the establishment of a subsidiary to sell franchises in a given country and the creation of piggyback franchises that physically place the franchise unit in existing department stores.

Multiarea development agreements are probably considered the most attractive way for the franchisor to maximize domestic growth, particularly for concepts that are capital-intensive and that have high start-up costs, such as hotels and restaurants. The multiarea development scheme offers the lowest cost to the franchisor compared to other franchise growth strategies, such as direct franchising of individual units and master franchise agreements. Individual franchise agreements are more expensive because the franchisor has to duplicate his sales, development, training, and maintenance expense for every unit sold; no economies of scale or learning curve benefits are derived from the franchisee pool. Master franchise agreements are more expensive because they require more start-up effort securing a suitable franchise. It is often necessary to hire brokers to help the franchisor find appropriate franchises, and a longer time is usually needed to establish the organization and the target territory. Finally, master franchisors may be the target of lawsuits and other entanglements because the increased number of relationships formed may generate an increased number of problems and disputes.

In the multiarea franchise sales effort, the franchisor seeks to recruit financially capable investors who are ready and eager to develop the business concept in as wide an area as the franchisee can afford and as quickly as possible. Other arrangements are made to ensure the successful operation of the franchise by the investor franchisee group. The franchisee is promised exclusive rights to develop within a specified radius, with the guarantee that the franchisor will not franchise another unit in this protected area.

The franchisor thus secures a cost-effective means of executing its regional or national development plan in a time span that is much smaller than the franchisor could have achieved selling individual franchises. The disadvantage of multiarea (and master) franchises is that they give the franchisee greater bargaining power with the franchisor and enable the franchisee to resist strategic changes dictated by the franchisor. Franchisors may have no alternative than to buy out some franchisees in order to maintain consistency in policies and standards within their system. Young franchise organizations typically seek a formula for the optimal size of the exclusive territories they grant. As a franchise system begins to grow, there is an urgency to develop units as fast as possible. The initial challenge to any new franchisor is to have a system that can support the cost of continuing services, as well as make a reasonable profit, from the revenue derived from ongoing operations of the franchise system, either from royalties or from the sale of other goods and services.

Determining the Size of the Territory

Knowing that it is essential to reach the point where the franchise system is large enough to support the cost of continuing services, and also knowing that external pressures can substantially delay that time, the tendency for the young franchisor is to grant exclusive territories that are too large. Several problems can arise with large exclusive territories. Often the franchisee gets wrapped up in the operations of the newly developed units and has little incentive to develop as rapidly as the franchisor expected. Another problem that may slow development, especially in today's economic climate, is that the franchisee's lender may want to see the establishment of a track record before the lender commits additional funding to further development. Sometimes, franchisees' financial status changes and consequently their interest in developing their territory wanes. This may happen even when the franchise is doing well, if other investments have distracted the franchise owner. When these things occur, the franchisor has to negotiate to buy back the territorial rights. The negotiation process and the resale of the territory further delay growth in the territory.

   Paradoxically, the same pressures on the franchisor can result in the opposite mistake—granting exclusive territories that are too small, especially in rapidly developing regions. Probably the most basic conflict between franchisee and franchisor centers on how many outlets should be in a particular market. In the long run the franchisor cuts its own throat if it overpopulates a market with outlets. Nevertheless, it may be difficult for the franchisor to resist the additional revenue derived from selling franchises and from expanding the flow of royalty income. The pressure to sell franchises while the window of opportunity is still open may obscure the potential diminution that excessive growth in a particular market may cause in the average outlet's revenues.

   Obviously, it is not in the best interest of the franchisor or its franchisees to place outlets too close to each other. Failed franchisees damage the expansion of a franchise system. Nevertheless, even with the best intentions, it is extremely difficult to define a territory optimally, especially for the young franchise organization expanding into new territories. Controlling the zeal, on the one hand, to oversaturate a "hot" market with outlets or, on the other hand, to grant territories that are too large for any single operator group to build and operate within its window of opportunity is a practical problem for the rapidly expanding franchise system.

The size of each multidevelopment agreement should be evaluated on a case-by-case basis, granting territories after taking into account the nature of the franchise concept, the territory in question, the financial strength of the franchisee, the prevailing economic climate, and the competitive environment in the particular market. For instance, it may be reasonable for a franchisor of retail frozen dessert shops to grant territorial exclusivity rights to an individual for the state of Montana, yet be unwilling to grant exclusivity rights for the city of Boston. The lack of development in the latter case would leave too great a gap in the marketplace and would invite competition. The penalty for delayed expansion in the former case would be much less severe.

Industry trends suggest that the nature of franchising itself is changing. The demand for large territorial exclusivity rights will slacken in the future as the characteristics of franchisees change. In the past, the franchisor sought investors with "deep pockets," those who could financially afford rapid expansion of relatively capital-intensive concepts. However, the growth of franchising is expected to continue into the next century, with early retirees and female entrepreneurs leading the growth. Nearly one-third of all franchised operations in the nation are currently owned, wholly or in part, by women. The International Franchise Association reported in 1989 that more than half of new franchisees used the equity in their homes as collateral on loans to buy franchises. These are not the kinds of franchisees that will seek large territorial exclusivity rights. Obtaining financing for first and second units will be the primary challenge faced by the entry-level entrepreneur, and franchise organizations that want to attract this new breed of franchise owner will have to offer new and creative ways to help their franchisees find sources of capital. This scenario may suggest a return to single-unit franchising, more participation by the franchisor in multiarea unit financing, lower cost outlets such as piggybacking, or other creative approaches that will make growth feasible for the "typical" franchise buyer.

Alternatives to Area Development

Since rapid expansion of large territories is probably not feasible for the fastest-growing franchise owner group, franchise organizations will have to find other ways to expand. Conversion of existing outlets is probably the next best alternative for the franchisor, since costs of conversion are low and the revenue flow is almost immediate. However, the recruiting effort can be very time-consuming, the number of suitable targets may be small, and the breach of existing agreements may entangle the franchisor in potential legal disputes. A less time-consuming approach may be the acquisition of small regional chains that will be flipped to franchise owners once the sale is finalized. This approach suggests that the franchisor has achieved a certain level of maturity and can afford an acquisition and the associated activity it entails. We will probably see a greater willingness among established franchise organizations to expend the resources necessary to seek conversions as development costs become prohibitive for the entry-level franchisee. One other means for multiarea expansion is to develop a variety of outlet mechanisms that can be exploited within a trade area. It may be the case that a trade area is suitable for only one freestanding retail outlet, but the market for one product or service can be expanded through alternative distribution systems, which adds incremental revenue for the franchisee or franchisor. The "I Can't Believe It's Yogurt" organization was able to negotiate with a large regional grocery chain to install minishops called kiosks in the chain's stores. By addressing prevailing market segmentation, the franchisor was able to penetrate the market deeper than it could have had it been limited by its traditional retail configuration. Issues concerning encroachment are not too difficult to dismiss when countered by the economic reality of increased brand awareness, volume efficiencies, and increased co-op marketing fund contributions.

Summary

Business owners seek to franchise their business format primarily for the sake of the format's rapid market penetration. Franchising allows for fast expansion with less exposure to franchisors than they would face by attempting growth internally. Franchising allows the franchisee to enter the market place with minimized risk as well. The franchisee purchases a tested business format and a level of corporate knowledge that would be unattainable for the independent owner without years of experience and presumably costly errors, if the business survived at all. The rapid expansion of the franchise format is to the franchisee's benefit because the franchisor's strength allows him to face the competition in a stronger position thanks to marketing and product development, and the franchisor can offer the franchise system high levels of operational support.

In spite of these advantages, the pace at which new franchise systems expand has come under scrutiny from industry analysts in recent years. Many articles have been written warning prospective franchisees to beware of franchisors who boast of the dozens or even hundreds of franchises that will be added to their franchise systems annually. The analysts state that franchisors who make such claims usually are more interested in selling franchises than in providing adequate support to existing franchisees. The young organization considering expanding through franchising needs a steady and well-planned growth strategy to balance the demands of growth with the needs of the existing system. Areas targeted for expansion need to be extensively analyzed for long-term growth and profit potential before any franchise offering is made. Only then can the franchisor determine the optimal vehicles for growth.

The multiarea development agreement is not the only way for a franchisor to expand the franchise system regionally, nationally, or even internationally. Acquisition of competitors and company store development are two schemes for rapid growth at a much higher level of cost for the franchise owner. However, all of the alternatives to multiarea development require a larger investment of capital and management resources from the franchise owner. For the early stages of franchise system growth, the multiarea development agreement will probably continue to be the most economically viable expansion strategy.

34

Trends and Developments in Franchising Education

William J. Keating, Dickinson School of Law

It would be logical to assume that the dynamic growth of domestic and international franchising over the past thirty years has captured the attention of our nation's business universities and law schools. It would also be safe to assume that the growth of franchising has spurred the development of hundreds of courses and programs designed to educate the future executives and managers of these franchised businesses.

Unfortunately, American education has yet to realize that the franchising phenomenon sweeping our nation will, according to U.S. Department of Commerce studies, account for about one-half of all retail sales in this country by the year 2000. Despite the growth of franchising, only a handful of universities offer any formal courses on the topic. The core courses in business management, marketing, and commercial law do not go far enough in discussing the special relationship between franchisor and franchisee, the strategic issues in building a franchised business, or the regulation of franchising at the federal and state level.

This chapter surveys what is being done, both publicly and privately, to educate students in the United States about franchising. I hope it will stimulate greater interest by the franchising community in getting courses adopted at the grass-roots level.

To be successful, franchisors and franchisees must understand the franchise systems in terms of operational requirements, legal regulations, and successful marketing strategies. Counseling and support services to potential franchisees and franchisors by trained counselors, comprising a cadre of well-trained, experienced advisers in franchise marketing and management, is also necessary. Yet, except for a few special programs in a limited number of schools, today's educational environment does not seem to be responding to the need for training potential franchisors and franchisees, as well as counselors and consultants having a basic understanding of the dynamics of franchise systems.

University and Law School Programs on Franchising

University Programs

Several universities in the United States offer programs on franchising. Four are discussed in this section.

1. *University of Nebraska-Lincoln.* The University of Nebraska-Lincoln (UNL) has established the International Center for Franchise Studies (ICFS), which is currently directed by Professor Vance Mehrens, who also teaches an undergraduate course on franchising at UNL. The ICFS is a unit of the Nebraska Center for Entrepreneurship, established in 1987, as an affiliate of the management department of UNL's College of Business Administration. The ICFS also generally facilitates the annual and periodic meetings of the Society of Franchising; this society consists of faculty members from around the world who teach courses in or who have an interest in franchising. The Society's annual meeting is usually held in February in conjunction with the annual meeting of the International Franchise Association. The published proceedings of the annual meeting are available from ICFS and make for valuable reading for interested franchising executives.

The objectives of the Center for Entrepreneurship are to provide students with the skills and knowledge necessary to create and operate new businesses successfully, as well as to assist businesses in improving their profitability and performance levels. The program also benefits the state of Nebraska by promoting employment and industry, increasing tax revenue, and generally promoting economic growth.

2. *Louisiana State University.* Louisiana State University (LSU) has founded an International Franchise program under the direction of Dr. Robert Justis, formerly assistant director of the University of Nebraska-Lincoln International Center for Franchise Study. Dr. Justis also teaches a regularly offered undergraduate course on franchising at LSU and is considered one of the pioneers in the areas of franchise education.

The objective of the LSU Franchising Center is to provide a full-service educational program covering all levels of franchise operations. The Center offers college-level courses on various aspects of domestic and international franchising, including marketing, financing, and regulatory and operational considerations.

Dr. Justis, and coauthor Dr. Judd, have published a text, titled *Franchising*, which was published by the Southwestern Publishing Company in 1989. The book is divided into six parts, with twenty-two chapters and an appendix, and covers all phases of franchising. It has been adopted as a textbook by several universities.

3. *University of St. Thomas.* The University of St. Thomas (UST), located in St. Paul, Minnesota, has established a Franchising Institute, including eight

courses (twenty-two credits) in franchising that are offered at the MBA level. The director of the Institute is Professor Cheryl Babcock. Professor Babcock was formerly director of the University of Nebraska-Lincoln International Center for Franchise Studies. UST now offers the only MBA program in the country where a student can earn a certificate in franchising management. The graduate courses include:

- ▲ New Venture Statistics
- ▲ New Venture Finance
- ▲ Franchising Statistics
- ▲ New Venture Marketing
- ▲ Venture Policy
- ▲ Financial Accounting for Managers
- ▲ Persuasion
- ▲ Franchising Management

Undergraduate students are permitted to attend.

The university also has a program for people who already have an MBA and who wish to update it with courses in franchising. It also offers a continuing education program consisting of a ten-week (three hours per week) miniseries for persons involved in the franchise field.

4. *University of Maryland.* The University of Maryland recently offered a course exclusively on franchising and licensing, taught at the MBA level, thus becoming one of the first universities in the United States to offer a course exclusively on franchising at that level. The three-credit course met once a week and was taught by franchising lawyer Andrew J. Sherman. Students were required to take a midterm examination and to prepare a term paper on special topics in franchising. The paper topic list and syllabus are presented in Figures 34-1 and 34-2.

While I am not aware of every franchising program offered by colleges and universities, there appears to be a dearth of such courses. An informal survey that I conducted in 1991 leads to the conclusion that few schools offer courses dedicated to franchise operations. Several schools indicated that they had previously offered such courses but had discontinued them. Other schools responded that they had considered such courses but did not adopt them. Some of the schools stated that a few classes in franchising were included in general business courses. Many schools claimed that they did not identify a strong or profitable market in this area.

Law School Courses

The focus of undergraduate school programs in franchising seems to be on the operational aspects of franchising. Law schools, as might be expected, tend to

Figure 34-1. List of proposed paper topics.

1. Trends and Developments in International Franchising: A Focus on Strategic Issues
2. Strategies for Dealing with Nonperforming Franchisees
3. Advantages and Disadvantages of Multiunit Expansion Strategies in Franchising
4. Methods for Site Selection and Determination of Franchise Territories: A Comparison of Current Approaches and Demographic Analysis in Franchising
5. The Role, Structure, and Importance of Franchise Advisory Councils
6. Strategic and Financial Planning for the Growing Franchisor: A Discussion of Key Issues
7. Managing Quality Control in a Franchise System: Legal and Strategic Issues
8. Anatomy of a Franchisor's Bankruptcy and Reorganization
9. The Role and Importance of Field Support in a Franchising System
10. Marketing Strategies for Recruiting and Selecting Qualified Franchisees
11. Franchise Fees and Royalty Structures: Financial Analysis and Comparison
12. The Use of Computer Systems and Software to Improve the Performance of the Growing Franchisor
13. Business Plan, Pro Forma and Development Strategy for a Hypothetical Franchisor
14. The Impact of Franchising on a Selected Industry
15. Initial and Ongoing Training Systems in Franchising
16. Development of Operations Manuals and Key Operational Issues in Building a Franchise System
17. Alternatives to Franchising: Advantages and Disadvantages
18. Key Accounting, Tax, and Financial Issues in the Development of a Franchise System

Source: Andrew J. Sherman, adjunct professor, University of Maryland.

emphasize franchising offering circulars, the Federal Trade Commission (FTC) Rule, franchise agreements, trademarks, trade secrets, antitrust statutes, and other areas of the law as it pertains to franchise marketing. While the division of emphasis is a natural one, a certain amount of crossover exists. The undergraduate schools generally include a reference to the legal rights and duties of the parties, as well as a discussion of general regulatory controls. A course in law school dedicated to the legal aspects of franchising would be incomplete without an explanation of how franchise systems are structured, as well as how they operate.

The course in the law of franchising that I teach at the Dickinson School of Law grew out of a trademarks course, particularly the section on trademark licensing. Franchising systems were used as an illustration of trademark licensing,

(*Text continues on page 478.*)

Figure 34-2.   Syllabus for a business school course on franchising and licensing.

(a) Required Reading:	1. *Franchising,* by R. Justis and R. Judd (Southwestern, 1989)
	2. *Franchising and Licensing: Two Ways to Build Your Business,* by Andrew J. Sherman (AMACOM, 1991)
(b) Grading:	1. Sixty percent of the final grade will be based on the preparation of a twenty- to thirty-page paper, with 45 percent being allocated to the written paper and 15 percent to a fifteen-minute oral presentation of the paper by each class member during the last two weeks of the semester. Paper topics will be discussed in greater detail on February 11, 19xx, the fourth week of the semester.
	2. Thirty percent of the grade will be based upon a midterm examination on March 3, 19xx.
	3. The remaining 10 percent will be based on class participation. All students are encouraged to actively participate in class discussion.
(c) Course Objectives:	1. To gain insight into the important role of franchising in the domestic economy and international marketplace
	2. To understand franchising and licensing as strategies for business growth, as compared to alternative strategies for growth
	3. To understand the key operational, management, training, and financial issues in building a franchised system
	4. To learn the legal and regulatory issues involved in the recruitment and selection of franchisees, as well as in the ongoing relationship between franchisor and franchisee
	5. To learn about the importance of intellectual property and quality control as an integral part of a growth strategy

Source: Andrew J. Sherman, adjunct professor, University of Maryland.

(continues)

Date	Topic	Reading Assignment
1/21/xx	(a) Introduction to Franchising (b) Strategies for Business Growth (c) The Foundation for Franchising	
1/28/xx	(a) Impact of Franchising in the Domestic and International Economies (b) Regulatory Aspects of Franchising	Justis & Judd, pp. 3–60; Sherman, pp. 81–100
2/4/xx	(a) General Management and Administration of the Franchise System (b) Product Distribution, Quality Control, and Antitrust Issues in Franchising	Justis & Judd, pp. 139–156, 238–262, and 338–370; Sherman, pp. 58–77 and 15–42; *Siegel* v. *Chicken Delight* and *Krehl* v. *Baskin Robbins*
2/11/xx	(a) Overview of the Franchise Agreement (b) Multiunit Expansion Strategies (Area Development Agreements and Subfranchising) (c) Discussion of Paper Topics	Justis & Judd, pp. 97–118; Sherman, pp. 120–157
2/18/xx	(a) Business and Strategic Planning in Franchising (b) Financial Management Issues and Analysis in Franchising	Justis & Judd, pp. 61–94 and 271–316; Sherman, pp. 259–283
2/25/xx	(a) Franchise Recruitment and Selection Strategies (b) Operations, Training, and Field Support in Franchising	Justis & Judd, pp. 159–199, 319–336, and 372–399; Sherman, pp. 213–236 and 43–47
3/3/xx	MIDTERM EXAMINATION	
3/10/xx	SPRING BREAK	
3/17/xx	(a) Strategies for Protecting Intellectual Property in a Franchise System (b) Unfair Competition, Implied Duties of Good Faith and Fair Dealing, Common Law Business Torts	Justis & Judd, pp. 119–138; Sherman, pp. 158–185; Handouts

(continues)

Figure 34-2. (cont'd.)

Date	Topic	Reading Assignment
	(c) Review and Discussion of Midterm Examination	
3/24/xx	(a) The Franchisee's Perspective: Analysis and Red Flags in Evaluating a Franchisor (b) Progress Reports and Discussion of Papers	Justis & Judd, pp. 403–430 and 475–493; Sherman, Handout—*Inc.* Magazine (January 1992)
3/31/xx	(a) Management of the Franchisor-Franchisee Relationship (b) Franchisor-Franchisee Communications and Advisory Councils	Justis & Judd, pp. 263–266 and 497–531; Handouts
4/7/xx	(a) Sources of Conflict, Dispute Management, and Compliance Issues in Franchising (b) Dealing With the Breakaway Franchisee and Noncompliance Issues (c) Managing the Transfer, Renewal, and Termination Process	Justis & Judd, pp. 517–548; Sherman, pp. 101–119 and 186–209
4/14/xx	(a) International Franchising (b) Territorial and Real Estate Issues in Franchising	Justis & Judd, pp. 549–567 and 201–237; Sherman, pp. 237–255; Handouts
4/21/xx	(a) Alternatives to Franchising (b) Licensing as a Growth Strategy	Sherman, pp. 301–332
4/28/xx	PAPER PRESENTATIONS (All papers due 4/24/xx)	
5/5/xx	PAPER PRESENTATIONS	

and it soon became apparent that there was a need for a law school course dedicated to franchising.

The course in trademarks must be taken as a prerequisite to, or concurrently with, the course in the law of franchising. The course includes sixteen students who have indicated a strong interest in franchising. The students are organized into four groups. Each group is assigned a franchise system for purposes of role-playing. Two students in each group are selected to represent the franchisor, and two students represent the franchisee. Over the semester the students are required to meet with their respective groups to negotiate and draft a franchise agreement. A copy of a typical syllabus is shown in Figure 34-3.

During the course of the semester, regular class meetings are held and the students are instructed in the background of franchising—history, structure, relationship of trademarks and trade secrets to franchising, and Uniform Franchise

Figure 34-3. Syllabus of franchising course at the Dickinson School of Law.

Schedule

Aug. 30	Introduction
Sept. 6	Trademark/Trade Secret License
Sept. 13	Development of Franchise System
Sept. 20	State and Federal Regulation of Franchise
Sept. 27	Structure of Negotiated Franchise Agreement
Oct. 4	First Franchise Team Meeting—Each Law Firm to Meet Separately
Oct. 11	Pairs of Franchise Teams Meet Separately
Oct. 18	Antitrust and Franchise Litigation
Oct. 25	Speaker: Andrew J. Sherman Silver, Freedman & Taff Washington, D.C.
Nov. 1	Pairs of Franchise Teams to Meet Separately With Professor in His Office 12:30–1:55 P.M. McDonald's Group 1:55–2:20 P.M. Holiday Inn Group 2:30–2:55 P.M. Arthur Murray Group 2:55–3:20 P.M. Midas Muffler Group
Nov. 8	Antitrust and Franchise Litigation
Nov. 15	Final Team Meetings
Nov. 22	Students Discuss Antitrust Cases: *Siegel* v. *Chicken Delight* } Arthur Murray Group *Kentucky Fried Chicken* v. *Diversified Packaging* } McDonald's Group *Principe* v. *McDonald's* } Holiday Inn Group *Susser* v. *Carvel* *Krehl* v. *Baskin Robbins* } Midas Muffler Group
Nov. 28	All Agreements Due

Offering Circulars. The presentation includes lectures, role-playing and model-building and requires reading assignments. Antitrust cases are assigned to be presented by the students; each franchise group must present a section of antitrust analysis for class discussion.

The role-playing exercise culminates in the presentation of a franchise agreement negotiated, drafted, and executed by each group. During the final classes in the semester, each group must present its franchise agreement to the class, along with a discussion of why the agreement was structured in a particular way. The professor critiques the presentations and encourages discussion.

Three other law schools in the United States also offer courses in franchise law. These include: Creighton University Law School (Professor Gary Batenhorst, general counsel for "Godfather Pizza"); Fordham University Law School (Professor Byron Fox); and University of Florida College of Law (Professor Sheldon Cohn). These courses are excellent and are conducted by skilled professionals. However, four law schools offering courses in franchise law, out of the approximately 175 major law schools in the United States, seems woefully inadequate to me. It may be that some schools include lectures on franchise law as part of another course, such as courses on corporations or trademarks. It seems that the range of legal topics affecting franchise operations would justify offering a discrete course. It also seems that the volume of marketing accomplished through franchising justifies having more law schools offer such courses.

Trade Associations Programs

The two major trade associations that have taken a leadership role in educating the various players in franchising are the IFA and the Forum on Franchising section of the American Bar Association. Both groups are extremely active in conducting continuing education programs in all phases of franchise operations and management.

IFA

The IFA was created in response to a situation that developed in the early days of franchise development after World War II. The success stories of McDonald's, Holiday Inn, and other well-managed franchises created a myth that all franchise operations guaranteed success. Unfortunately, a number of investors were victims of misleading franchise offerings that tended to give the entire industry a bad reputation. State and federal agencies threatened to impose regulations that would have chilled the growth of legitimate franchises.

The IFA was formed by responsible franchisors to impose a code of ethics that would permit the orderly growth of franchising while encouraging fair dealing with franchisees. As part of its mission of improving the quality of the franchise industry, the Association has developed a series of educational programs covering every aspect of franchising. The Association comprises primarily representatives of franchisors, and it strives to impress upon its members the ethic that fair dealing benefits the system as a whole.

The IFA also publishes a wealth of information on franchise management and conducts seminars throughout the country on all aspects of franchise operations. The programs include an annual two-day seminar in Washington, D.C., dedicated to discussing current legal issues affecting franchise law. The program focuses on pending legislation, as well as on analysis of legal trends developing in franchise marketing and on the impact of these trends on lawyers who counsel clients in this area.

The IFA also publishes the Franchise Legal Digest, which reports on all areas of franchise operations having regulatory implications. The Digest is published semimonthly and contains an abstract of the articles in the issue.

While the programs of the IFA and the Forum on Franchising have some overlap, they tend more often to complement each other. Most of the IFA seminars are dedicated to general topics of franchise management and are not limited to legal aspects. Areas such as financing, quality control, site location, operations manual preparation, accounting, personnel management, advertising, and franchise relations are presented. The thrust of the presentation is to assist franchisors in establishing and operating successful franchises. While the programs are directed to franchisors, they recognize the necessity of treating franchisees fairly to achieve a quality franchise system.

Executive Certification Program

The IFA has recently instituted a comprehensive educational program titled, "The IFA Executive Education and Certification Program." As the title suggests, the program is dedicated to improving the expertise of franchise executives.

The course is developed into eight modules:

1. Franchise Marketing
2. Strategic Business Management
3. Economic and Demographic Forces Shaping the Future of Franchising in the 1990s
4. Human Resource Management
5. Finance and Accounting
6. Real Estate in Franchising
7. Legal and Ethical Considerations in Franchising
8. Franchising Operational Systems

Each course module is scheduled for a one-week presentation. Modules 1 and 2 have been presented at Louisiana State University by IFA staff and LSU faculty. Modules 3 and 4 were offered in fall 1992, and Modules 5 through 8 are yet to be scheduled.

Participants in the program earn credits toward a Certified Franchise Executive (CFE) certificate, issued by the Institute of Certified Franchise Executives, which is sponsored by the IFA. Completion of the eight-module course, along with meeting certain formal requirements, entitles the candidate to use the designation "CFE" (Certified Franchise Executive), indicating the achievement of a high level of proficiency in the franchising field.

The program has received praise from a number of executives associated with successful franchises. The courses are valuable in improving the skills of franchising executives, as well as in assisting them in recognizing and dealing with continuing changes in the franchising field. However, the program is not a substitute for a basic education in franchise marketing and operation at the college level. Nonetheless, I find it commendable that franchise executives wish to hone their skills through continuing education courses. It is equally desirable that students intending to pursue a career in franchising have the opportunity to understand the dynamics of the industry through courses offered at the college level before they enter the field.

IFA Educational Foundation, Inc.

The IFA has also developed a support program, the IFA Educational Foundation, to finance educational programs in the franchise field. The Foundation has an immediate goal to create an endowment of $3 million to support franchise education programs at all levels. In addition to supporting courses in franchising at the university level, the foundation intends to support "practically oriented educational (programs) below the four-year college level." The program is intended not only to support college-level courses but also to provide training in the fundamentals of business to financially and educationally disadvantaged people who are unlikely to go to college.

Forum on Franchising

What the IFA does for franchisors, the Forum on Franchising of the American Bar Association does for lawyers who specialize in representing members of the franchising community. The Forum focuses on the legal aspects of franchise regulations, such as taxation, agreements, antitrust regulations, real estate, trademarks, and litigation. The section includes approximately 1,500 members who have an interest in franchise law.

The Forum Committee of the American Bar Association presents a number of continuing education programs, including a two-day seminar every fall. The programs are excellent and are presented by leaders of the franchise bar. Topics are presented in five or six general sessions, supplemented by about fifteen workshops. Attendance usually includes between 300 and 400 lawyers.

The plenary sessions cover current developments in general areas of the law, such as antitrust law, franchise registrations, and international franchising. The subject matter is presented in lecture form by a practitioner who specializes in the particular area. The lectures are excellent and are quite helpful in keeping lawyers abreast of current developments.

The workshops are small-group discussions of specific areas of law affecting franchises, such as tax law, bankruptcy, and litigation. Each is limited to thirty attendees. The discussion is led by a panel of experts, and audience participation is encouraged. The format is relaxed and offers an opportunity for the attendees to exchange views and share experiences. Each session lasts about an hour and a half.

The Forum also publishes *The Franchise Law Journal*, a quarterly that includes a wide variety of articles on all phases of franchise law. The articles are of excellent quality and are contributed by lawyers specializing in franchise law.

Goals for Franchising Education

Given the paucity of courses in franchising, the question arises as to whether additional courses are desirable or necessary. The answer is a resounding ''Yes.''

I am concerned about the lack of schools offering courses in the franchising field. While accurate current information is difficult to collect, a significant number of major colleges and universities apparently do not offer courses in franchising. An even greater need for such courses appears to exist in law schools if they are to train business lawyers to work in an area that currently accounts for 35 percent of all retail sales in the United States, is predicted to expand to 50 percent of all retail sales by the year 2000, and is experiencing phenomenal growth in international markets.

A few law schools that do offer courses in franchising limit the classes to continuing education seminars that run over several days. What is needed is a broad curriculum that exposes students to an overview of franchising early in their college and law school careers. This kind of program would go a long way toward providing an understanding of the dynamics of franchising, as well as promoting an awareness of the opportunities for careers in franchising. Advanced courses in specific areas of franchise operations, marketing, finance, and support would give the students opportunities to develop expertise in these areas. A separate course in law school devoted to franchise law would be beneficial in training franchise lawyers.

While some of the operations of a franchise system are common to all commercial systems, the special relationship between franchisor and franchisee, which affects the ability of each party to achieve success, is unique. A business or law school graduate who goes into franchising will eventually become familiar with this relationship. Having an understanding of the dynamics of franchising will be a substantial advantage as the student prepares for a career in this field.

Problems Facing the Franchising Industry

There seems to be a perception that franchisees are not being treated fairly by franchisors and that franchisors are imposing harsh conditions on franchisees. Several states have enacted statutes imposing a ''good faith'' requirement on franchisors in dealing with franchisees. Others have found a common-law requirement. The definition of ''good faith'' is somewhat ambiguous, leaving both parties to wonder that their rights and duties are. Abroad, France has enacted laws requiring registration by franchisors, and other countries are considering similar legislation.

The U.S. House of Representatives Small Business Committee has held hearings on problems in the franchise industry. Congressman John La Falce, chairman of the committee, has indicated that he sees a need for legislation increasing the federal role in franchise regulation. One problem that concerned the committee members is the failure of some franchisors to provide sufficient training, support, and continued assistance to their franchisees. The committee found that some franchisees are being used merely as a means of creating revenue and are not receiving any meaningful assistance from the franchisor in establishing and operating the franchise.

The other problem that concerned the committee was the lack of any viable legal recourse for franchisees in the event of a dispute between the franchisor and the franchisee. The superior bargaining position of the franchisor permits it to insist that the franchisee waive rights and remedies, particularly with respect to choice of forum, choice of law, and similar provisions.

I believe that the franchise industry does not need more regulation. If anything, it needs less regulation. More important is the need for improved understanding of the dynamics of the entire system by the people who are responsible for establishing and operating the franchise systems. It needs franchisees who understand the franchisor's justification for adopting and exercising tight controls. It needs franchisors who understand the franchisee's need for training, support, encouragement, and incentive to operate the franchise unit successfully.

Continuing education programs are excellent. However, they are no substitute for a fundamental understanding of the franchise industry, developed through college and law school courses during an academic career.

I believe that there is a substantial need for students to be trained in the special needs of the franchise industry. Students who appreciate the dynamics of the industry, the objectives of the parties (sometimes complementary, sometimes adversarial), the components of a franchise, the flow of money, and the need for fairness on both sides to achieve success are well positioned to enter the franchise field as franchisees, franchisors, and professional advisers.

35

The Americans with Disabilities Act (ADA)

Andrew J. Sherman, Silver, Freedman & Taff

Beyond the franchising laws discussed in Chapters 20 and 22, there are also a wide variety of nonfranchising laws and statutes that directly affect the day-to-day operations of both franchisors and their franchisees. One of these is the Americans with Disabilities Act (ADA or the Act), which protects individuals with disabilities in the workplace. So whether you are recruiting for a new executive at corporate headquarters or one of your franchisee's sales clerks is wheelchair-bound, the ADA is going to impact every aspect of your organization. In fact, it is critical that these guidelines are incorporated into your personnel policies and operations manuals.

The guidelines affecting the recruitment and retention of persons with disabilities are one of the most rapidly changing and complex areas of employment law. The problem lies in balancing the important social and economic objective of creating meaningful employment opportunities for all persons in our society who want to work against the degree to which companies can afford to make accommodations for those individuals who require special assistance.

For example, polls taken in 1986 during the consideration of the ADA indicated that two-thirds of all disabled Americans between the ages of 16 and 64 were unemployed, despite their desire for work. In absolute terms, this means that approximately 8.2 million people with disabilities want to work, but cannot find a job. Compare that 67 percent unemployment rate in the disabled community to the current national unemployment rate of 7.8 percent, which most Americans find unacceptable, and the necessity to hire the disabled appears clear. Forty-seven percent of the poll participants who were not employed, or not employed full-time, attributed their employment status to discrimination.

What the Americans with Disabilities Act
Means for Franchises

The ADA is designed to help alleviate employment discrimination against the disabled. A disabled person has been defined to include anyone who has a physical or mental impairment that substantially limits a major life activity, or one who has a record of such an impairment, or one who is regarded as having such an impairment. Thus, people who have continuing medical problems will be considered disabled, including those who have been hospitalized in the past for their medical condition. Furthermore, persons with an infectious disease, including those with AIDS or the HIV virus, are considered legally disabled and are entitled to protection under the Act.

Franchisors should also keep in mind that in addition to federal law, more than forty states have enacted legislation that prohibits discrimination against persons with disabilities. Since each state defines the scope of a disability differently and sets out a wide-ranging list of "prohibited practices," your franchisees should carefully check their own state laws to ensure that they are in compliance. For instance, in some states, the definition of a "handicap" is limited to physical disabilities, whereas under federal law, the term has been interpreted to include mental or psychological disorders (such as mental retardation, emotional or mental illness, or specific learning disabilities), cosmetic disfigurement, and certain types of contagious diseases. In the event that the state law differs from the federal law, you must comply with both.

Among other purposes, the ADA is designed to help alleviate employment discrimination against the disabled or, as more recently referred to, "the differently abled." The ADA also expands the scope and clarifies certain issues under the Rehabilitation Act of 1973, which had previously applied only to federal agencies and departments, employers receiving federal financial assistance, and federal or government contractors.

To receive protection, disabled persons must be qualified handicapped employees able to perform the essential functions of the job, with franchisors or franchisees making a "reasonable accommodation" at their place of business for any disability that such an individual may have. The ADA lists examples of reasonable accommodations, such as wheelchair ramps, braille keyboards, job restructuring, part-time work, modified work schedules, reassignments to vacant job positions, acquisition or modification of equipment, adjustments of qualifying exams, modification of testing procedures or training programs, and the provision of qualified readers for blind employees.

The accommodations, however, may be viewed as unreasonable if they create an "undue hardship" to the franchisor or individual franchisee. An undue hardship is determined by examining the overall size of the business, the size of its budget, the nature of its operation, the number of its employees, the composition and structure of its work force, and the nature and cost of the accommodation. Thus, a larger employer might be required to spend more money or to undertake a greater effort than would a smaller company to accommodate an individual's disability.

Prohibited Employment Practices

Employers cannot conduct medical examinations of job applicants nor can they inquire whether a job applicant has a disability. Even where the disability is obvious, the ADA prohibits asking about the nature or severity of the disability. However, franchisors and franchisees may ask if job applicant to voluntarily disclose any personal disability so that the employer can consider reasonable accommodations. Steps should be taken to make the applicant aware that the disclosure is voluntary and will be kept confidential.

With respect to medical examinations, the *pre-offer* use of pre-employment medical examinations is prohibited in all circumstances. However, employers may require a physical examination or make medical inquiries of an applicant *after* an offer for a job has been made if the five following conditions have all been fulfilled:

1. All entering employees are tested or interviewed about relevant health problems, regardless of whether they appear to have a disability.
2. The results of the tests and questions are kept in a file that is separate from the employee's personnel file and are treated as confidential information.
3. Examination results are not used for any purpose prohibited by the ADA.
4. Access to an applicant's medical files may be given only to supervisors and managers who need to make accommodations, personnel responsible for first aid and safety, and government officials investigating compliance with the ADA.
5. All tests and inquiries are job-related and consistent with business necessity.

Franchisors and franchisees cannot ask questions that relate directly to the disability. Questions to be *avoided* include: ''Will your disability impair your job performance?'' or ''Have you filed any workers compensation claims?'' However, employers *may* ask general questions about an applicant's ability to do the work involved such as, ''Are you fully qualified to perform the job?'' or ''Is there anything that might prevent you from completing the job requirement?'' Questions must stay focused on the tasks required by the position that is being filled, emphasizing the candidates' *abilities*, not their *disabilities*.

Franchisors and individual franchisees should always follow general employment law guidelines in the interviewing and hiring process. Therefore, questions that are also prohibited in the vast majority of recruitment situations include inquiries concerning the applicant's race, color, religion, sex, or national origin, questions regarding pregnancy, and inquiries regarding arrest records or military status. Certain types of queries pertaining to an applicant's birthplace, maiden name, sexual preference, or marital status may also be prohibited.

Steps Toward Compliance

The following steps may be taken to avoid violations under the ADA:

- Issue a company policy of nondiscrimination setting forth company goals in affirmatively hiring differently abled persons.

▲ Create the position of an ADA officer who educates all managers responsible for hiring about the specifics of the Act.

▲ Review the hiring process, job descriptions, personnel records, and promotion requirements to determine if any discriminatory procedures are taking place or could take place. (Good faith is *not* a defense to an ADA violation.)

Deadlines

Franchisors and franchisees with twenty-five or more employees must have complied with all applicable sections of the ADA by July 26, 1992. Franchisors and franchisees with fifteen to twenty-four companies must comply no later than July 26, 1994. The Act is not directly applicable to those employers with less than fifteen employees.

36

Franchising for the Growing Company

Craig S. Slavin, Certified Management Consultant and founder of The Franchise Architects

One of the most critical aspects influencing the ultimate success of franchising is often overlooked: *the corporate evolutionary and growth process*. What the growing company must understand is how the franchise efforts impact the "core" business and how the "core" company accommodates the many changes that occur as a result of franchising and rapid growth.

Companies are like people. They follow a predictable course of evolution with distinct stages of growth. When franchising is used to grow a company, these changes tend to occur faster and with greater velocity—that is, the faster a company adds franchises, the faster the evolution occurs. I have established five distinct growth stages through which a franchise company will evolve. They chart a company's evolution from dependence on a single source (the founder/entrepreneur) to the development of more complex structures. The changes that occur during these transition periods are significant and result in a series of "crises." How well a company manages these growth stages and crises will significantly affect its franchising success.

Stage One: Entrepreneurial

Of course, the first stage of any business is highly entrepreneurial. Typically the founder/entrepreneur is at the helm of this new business. The company's growth is predicated on the ability of the founder to make decisions; in fact, the founder makes all the decisions relating to the operation of the company. Therefore, the company is only as effective as the entrepreneur can make it. This is a very difficult and risky stage of growth for any company.

Franchising, in its purest sense, is a "transference" process, meaning the parent company (the franchisor) transfers to the participant (the franchisee) the methodologies and prescribed specifications of operating the business. A Stage One company has very little ability to perform these functions. The Stage One crisis is the inability of the founder/entrepreneur to make effective decisions and delegate responsibilities as needed in both the original "core" business and the franchise program. Until the founder can delve into the details of the business sufficiently enough to define, refine, discipline, document, and, if possible, computerize the business, effective transference is very unlikely. This is why a Stage One company is not yet ready to franchise.

Stage Two: Management Discipline

It is at this stage that the founder makes one of the most important decisions he or she will ever make: to turn ideas and concepts into a more structured and disciplined business environment. Systems building can be achieved two ways. One involves hiring an outside, impartial management consultant or consulting firm. Or the founder can hire, as staff, a business manager. Either way, the intent of this stage is to develop a more prescribed and orderly direction for both the prototype location and the growth program.

This often means that the organization becomes vertical in nature from the standpoint of rank and horizontal from the standpoint of specialization. A centralized core of objectives, with standards and controls, communicated through a directive management approach begins to surface. At this stage of growth, franchising may still be premature because of its accompanying crisis: instability, caused by the clash between the company's need to complete the building of systems and programs and the founder/entrepreneur's level of willingness to let go and allow the business manager to develop the business.

Stage Three: Delegation Specialization

In the third stage of growth, franchising should begin for the emerging company. It is without question the hardest stage to reach, but the one that possesses the greatest rewards because the company's organizational structure becomes even more horizontal by incorporating a collaborative and decentralized management style.

Middle-level managers are recruited to head newly created departments and to establish effective internal and external communications. Senior management adopts a "Management by Exception" style that allows each middle-level manager to do his or her job, while senior management focuses on long-term strategic issues such as new products, services, acquisitions, and franchising.

In Stage Three, the business manager, with the assistance of the middle-level managers, can further define the specifications of the business that will be franchised and establish the managerial controls necessary to enforce these guidelines. The long-term focus of the Stage Three company also includes developing people, both internal employees as well as external franchisees and business affiliates. The company now has two sets of customers: (1) the end-user (consumer) and (2) the franchisee, each with its own demands and needs for customer satisfaction. The Stage Three company requires two management structures in place to manage the company-owned unit and the franchise unit.

The crisis that occurs within a Stage Three company is one of transition. The entire composition of the company has changed—and is still changing. In addition, the day-to-day decision making process is now made collectively by the middle-level managers.

What has happened to the founder/entrepreneur of the business? Well, if that individual is not on a boat in the Caribbean, he or she is working with senior management on long-term strategic planning.

Stage Four: Bureaucracy

The type of bureaucracy most common in Stage Four is that of a slow-moving and very passive type of organization. This is the result of the buildup of layers within divisions, separating the line personnel from management. The Stage Four company can take the meaning of control to its extreme and create a more rigid and less flexible system. Therefore, it is in a franchisor's best interests to avoid Stage Four altogether. If a Stage Four company wants to initiate a franchise program, then it must either rid itself of lethargy or establish a separate entity that has the structure and culture of the third stage.

The Stage Four crisis is that this type of organization is impersonal by its very nature. Because of the bureaucracy, the company will encounter great difficulties being responsive to the needs of its franchisees, impacting on its ability to grow.

Stage Five: "Intrapreneurial"

Greater spontaneity in management action through teams and the skillful melding and collaboration of diverse personalities is the definition of Stage Five. The company that understands how to integrate the myriad of disciplines, personalities, and complex issues of business management—including franchising principles and environmental and political issues—into a well-run and cohesive organization has evolved into Stage Five.

Also indicative of a Stage Five company is the introduction of "matrix" teams, which are assembled to resolve problems or discuss issues. In addition to employees, franchisees are often asked to participate in these teams, creating a unity between the company and the franchisees, which is not possible in any other stage of growth.

Unlike the earlier growth stages where employees are either compensated for hard work or obedience, Stage Five employees are typically compensated on the basis of the overall productivity and profitability of the entire company. In the

Stage Five company, entrepreneurialism has been internalized within the corporate entity and so "intrapreneurialism" prevails. The Stage Five crisis involves a further shift in philosophy and management style. Employees who have been with the company for some time may have difficulties embracing this new style of management and communication.

The Stage Five organization encompasses all the elements for successful franchising because it is able to generate a level of enthusiasm and collaboration between corporate employees and self-employed franchisees, whose individual goals then become one and the same.

*   *   *

The main goal for any company desiring expansion through franchising is not to become a franchise company, per se, but to focus on the necessary steps to becoming a Stage Five organization. Stages One and Two are where the greatest amount of risk is associated with any business. Most business failures occur in these stages because the business is not yet defined, refined, and professionally managed.

The operational refinements that occur in Stage Three significantly increase a growth company's ability to succeed, because they enable a Stage Three company's franchisees to bypass the first two growth stages, where trial and error exist and the risk of mortality is the greatest. This factor alone is the reason why the franchising success rate is so high and why franchising in general will continue to be such a widely used method of expansion.

Index

[Page numbers followed by the letter *n* refer to footnotes.]

About the Editor

A recognized national authority on the legal and strategic issues affecting small and growing companies, **Andrew J. Sherman**, J.D., is Of Counsel with Silver, Freedman & Taff, a Washington, D.C.-based law firm.

Mr. Sherman serves as legal counsel to a diverse range of more than 125 growing businesses. He represents both international and domestic franchising and corporate clients and practices primarily in the areas of franchising, licensing, and distribution; corporate finance, private placements, and venture capital; intellectual property law; and business planning and general corporate law.

Prior to practicing law, Mr. Sherman worked for The White House Conference on Small Business, the Department of Commerce, and as a management consultant to the Navy. He also served as a vice-president and cofounder to a Maryland-based franchisor from 1978 to 1982.

Mr. Sherman has published more than 175 articles on legal and management topics affecting business growth in such well-known and worldwide publications as *Inc. Magazine, Dun & Bradstreet Reports, Nation's Business,* and *Small Business Reports*. He is the author of four special reports published by the International Franchise Association and the Michael C. Dingman Center for Entrepreneurship at the University of Maryland. In addition, he has been interviewed on television, radio, and in the press in such publications as *The Wall Street Journal* and *U.S.A. Today* on strategic issues influencing franchising and business growth.

A frequent national lecturer, Mr. Sherman has been a featured speaker at various national and regional meetings of the International Franchise Association. He is the developer and lecturer for the American Management Association (AMA) course on "Strategies for Protecting Trademarks, Copyrights, and Trade Secrets" and for the AMA's Council on Growing Companies courses on "Growth-Oriented Distribution Strategies" and "How to Grow Your Company in Cash-Tight Times."

Mr. Sherman is an adjunct professor in the M.B.A. program at the University of Maryland, where he teaches a course on franchising, licensing, and business growth.

He is an active member of several professional associations, including the American Bar Association's Forum Committee on Franchising, the Society of Franchising, the American Bar Association's section on Business Law, the District of Columbia Bar section on Corporations and Business Law, and the International Association's Council of Franchise Suppliers.

Mr. Sherman is deeply committed to the education and development of children. He serves on the board of directors of the Maryland Chapter of Special Olympics, the board of directors of The National Foundation for Teaching Entrepreneurship to Disadvantaged and Handicapped Youths and is a speaker and author for Junior Achievement International. He has served as legal counsel to the Young Entrepreneur's Organization and to the Association of Collegiate Entrepreneurs since 1988.

He received his undergraduate degree in political science from the University of Maryland and his law degree from American University.

About the Contributors

Steven M. Abramson, J.D., joined Silver, Freedman & Taff in 1986. His primary areas of expertise are in retail, restaurant, office, commercial, and industrial leasing for small and mid-sized franchisors and retail businesses. Mr. Abramson works very closely with clients on all lease negotiations including workouts when lease obligations can no longer be timely satisfied. He also has extensive experience in the acquisition and sale of small and mid-sized companies.

John L. Allbery is the office managing partner for the Des Moines office of Deloitte & Touche. He is also the director of the franchise industry for the firm nationwide. He has been a speaker on franchising at numerous functions for clients, professional accounting organizations, and franchise trade-industry groups. Mr. Allbery serves on the International Franchise Association's Finance, Accounting and Tax Committee and Legal/Legislative Committee, and on the Executive Advisory Board of the International Center for Franchise Studies at the University of Nebraska.

James H. Amos, Jr., is senior vice-president international of "I Can't Believe It's Yogurt." An accomplished public speaker and author, his most recent work, *The Memorial*, was chosen by the American Library Association as one of the best books of 1990. Mr. Amos has successfully negotiated master franchise agreements in twenty-five countries and has participated in all phases of international development from recruitment to marketing.

Neal Anstadt is president of Parcom Technologies, Inc., a business system developer and integrator. Mr. Anstadt has codesigned and developed some of the first air express parcel computer systems, which have been placed in mail and shipping rooms throughout the United States, Canada, and parts of Europe. He has also codeveloped several franchise/franchisor computer systems for utilization in shipping, inventory control, billing, and order entry.

Gary Blake is the founder and CEO of The Blake Group, Inc., a "micromarket" information consultancy. He actively works with clients, including several franchises, to solve strategic planning problems through utilization of information, database, and mapping technologies. Mr. Blake also manages a development group that is designing new techniques and technologies to help franchise systems expand with micromarket strategies.

Deborah E. Bouchoux, J.D., joined Silver, Freedman & Taff as Of Counsel in 1990. She practices principally in the areas of franchising, intellectual property, and trade regulation. Ms. Bouchoux has both provided advice to and represented numerous corporations in connection with a variety of general corporate issues. She is currently teaching courses on the topics of legal research and writing, business associations, and advanced writing at Georgetown University.

John A. Campbell is the founder, CEO, and chairman of the board of Franchise Masters, a company that, through his leadership, has served more than 250 clients nationwide. Having seventeen years' experience in franchising, Mr. Campbell is an expert in the area of franchise development and marketing. He is a member of the board of directors of several professional organizations, including the International Franchise Association, the Council of Franchise Suppliers, and the Advertising and Promotion Committee of the IFA.

Richard M. Contino is a businessman, consultant, and attorney, actively involved in the development and implementation of equipment leasing and financing programs for business. He is chairman of the board and cofounder of FirstStreet Credit Corporation, a national equipment leasing company, as well as managing director and founder of Executive Online! Company, a national electronic information provider. Mr. Contino is the author of the *Handbook of Equipment Leasing: A Deal Maker's Guide* (AMACOM Books) and *Legal and Financial Aspects of Equipment Leasing Transactions* (Prentice-Hall).

Mark E. Czejak serves as director of sales and marketing, national accounts, for Safeguard Business Systems Inc. Safeguard, a member of the International Franchise Association, manufactures and markets business and financial management systems and services to the franchise community in the United States as well as in several other countries. An accomplished speaker/trainer, Mr. Czekaj has written and produced corporate sales motivation programs, and has conducted skill development workshops for corporate sales organizations and professional associations across the United States.

Jerry R. Darnell is executive vice-president of Sterling Vision Inc. In the past he directed all phases of franchising for a franchised financial services company. His franchise management system has enhanced franchise development staffs across the nation, both in private consulting practice and from corporate executive positions. As a consultant, he assisted start-up and established franchisors with the design and redesign of their development programs. Mr. Darnell's commitment to franchising keeps him active in International Franchise Association symposiums and issues.

Howard A. Davis is director and president of Franchise Capital Advisors, Inc. Mr. Davis specializes in financing and franchise-related matters. He currently serves as CEO of several companies in the field of corporate finance, venture capital, and franchising. One of these companies, The Stanton Group, Inc., is a syndicator and investment banking firm that deals primarily with financing privately held companies and growing franchisors. This company also assists small businesses in developing and implementing financing strategies. He was formerly president of a regional pizza franchisor.

Margaret Dower joined the management consulting firm of Management 2000 as an editor and technical writer. Management 2000, with offices in Houston, Texas, and Edmonton, Alberta, has developed a specialized practice in helping companies use franchising as a strategy to grow. At the firm, which has worked with more than 400 franchisors in many areas, among them manual writing, Ms. Dower has created manuals for client recruiting and field and international operations as well as used operations manuals to strengthen franchise management.

Robert Gappa is president of Management 2000. He has served as a strategic consultant to hundreds of franchise systems. In his twenty-four years of experience as a consultant, he has become a recognized leader in the field of franchise consulting. In addition to franchise development, his areas of expertise include strategic planning, marketing strategies, operations, compensation planning, and human resources management. He is a frequent seminar leader for International Franchise Association programs.

R. M. Gordon is senior vice-president and chief operating officer of The Original Great American Chocolate Chip Cookie Company, Inc. A certified franchise executive, Mr. Gordon is a member of the board of directors of the International Franchise Association and chair of the IFA education committee. He also holds membership in the American Management Association, the American Marketing Association, and the Financial Management Association.

Ron Guberman is president and CEO of Media Reactions, Inc., a company that introduced a remarkable tracking system that demonstrates to clients exactly what part of their advertising produces the best results. Mr. Guberman has been involved in advertising for more than twenty-five years, and he possesses a wealth of experience and knowledge in working with franchises to advertise and expand. He is a guest speaker and lecturer at a variety of functions, including the International Franchise Association's winter marketing workshop.

JoAnn T. Hackos, Ph.D., is president of Comtech Services, Inc., an information design firm, which she founded in 1978. She is also president of JoAnn Hackos & Associates, Inc., a strategic planning and management consulting firm, which she began in 1991. Over the past ten years, she has advised franchise organizations in the design of information, the development of training programs, and the development of strategic plans for marketing, franchise management development, and staff training and productivity issues.

Nick Helyer is president of the U.S. division of the Blenheim Group Plc., the world's largest independent trade show producer. Mr. Helyer's division produces the World of Franchising Expos, sponsored by the International Franchise Association, as well as the International Franchise Expo, the world's largest franchise event. Prior to Blenheim's entry into the United States, Mr. Helyer produced franchise expos in the United Kingdom.

Sid Henkin is a senior consultant for Prism·CLS. His expertise is in quality training, and his experience includes, but is not limited to, consulting for franchising organizations. He has a far-reaching knowledge of human behavior and systems that is of great benefit to his clients in all realms of business. Before joining Prism·CLS, Mr. Henkin was director of marketing and development for Contemporary Learning Systems. He is a frequent writer and speaker for International Franchise Association programs and publications.

William J. Keating, J.D., is professor of law at Dickinson School of Law in Carlisle, Pennsylvania. He teaches in the areas of patent law, trademark law, copyright law, franchising law, food and drug law, and transnational business organizations. He was formerly a patent attorney and general patent counsel for AMP, Inc. He is the author of *Franchising Advisor* and various law review articles.

Susan P. Kezios is president and founder of Women in Franchising, Inc., the only industry association devoted to the professional interests and advancement of women in franchising. The organization, which started in 1987, is now recognized as the leading advocate for both women and minorities in franchising. It is noted for its series of conferences on Franchising for Women and Minorities, which is broadcast via satellite to simultaneously reach large numbers of potential franchisees. Ms. Kezios is a member of the International Franchise Association's Minorities and Women in Franchising Committee.

Jan Kirkham is executive vice-president of Management 2000. A recognized expert in the field of franchise operations and franchisee training, Ms. Kirkham has trained field consultants and other franchise personnel for hundreds of companies. She has fourteen years of consulting and training experience in operations, management development, communications, and development of trainers.

Gregory Matusky is founder and president of Gregory Communications, Inc., a franchise communications, marketing, and public relations firm based in Ardmore, Pennsylvania. Mr. Matusky is one of the nation's foremost writers on franchising. He is the author of two books on the subject—*Blueprint for Franchising a Business* and *The 100 Best Home-Based Franchises*. He also serves as a contributing editor to several national publications.

Timothy McGowan is a vice-president of Management 2000. Mr. McGowan has fourteen years of marketing, franchise development, and financial management experience. He has designed and improved franchise and marketing systems and has helped direct the growth of franchise marketing activities for several national companies.

Kenneth J. McGuire is cofounder and CEO of Performance Group, Ltd., a franchise consulting, development, and marketing firm with offices in Tallahassee and Chicago. He is a long-standing and active member of the International Franchise Association and the International Council of Shopping Centers. A frequent contributor to articles on franchising, Mr. McGuire also speaks regularly at seminars and other events devoted to franchising issues.

Kathy Moran is an account supervisor at the public relations firm of Nichol & Company, Ltd., and serves on the agency's executive committee. Ms. Moran's experience with the firm includes work on many accounts, ranging from Fortune 500 companies to franchise companies.

Betsy Nichol is president of Nichol & Company, Ltd., a public relations firm that serves a diversity of prestigious accounts. She was formerly an account supervisor for two of the country's largest public relations agencies. Ms. Nichol is active in the Counselors Academy of the Public Relations Society of America, and serves as vice-president of publicity for the International Furnishings and Design Association.

Robert L. Perry operates The Hunter Group, an Annapolis, Maryland, consultancy specializing in franchises. Regarded as one of the nation's foremost independent franchise consultants, Mr. Perry has studied hundreds of franchises in the area of franchisor-franchisee communications and has provided marketing assistance to more than thirty leading franchisors. Having fourteen years' experience in franchising, he has conducted seminars on how to buy franchises. He also serves as a contributing editor to *Income Opportunities* magazine and writes articles for many national business and consumer publications.

Michael Howard Seid is managing director of Strategic Advisory Group, an integrated provider of franchise advisory services and corporate and investment banking. The Strategic Advisory Group has its headquarters in West Hartford, Connecticut. Mr. Seid advises companies on whether franchising is appropriate for them as well as works with established franchises to improve their financial effectiveness. He has been a senior operations executive or consultant for companies within the franchise, retail, restaurant, and service industries and has conducted seminars on franchising for major accounting firms, chambers of commerce, trade associations, and major corporations.

Sidney J. Silver, J.D., is a senior partner in the firm of Silver, Freedman & Taff, where he regularly represents a variety of both mature and growing companies in the retail, wholesale, service, and manufacturing businesses. He has been a panelist and lecturer at the Georgetown University annual commercial lease negotiation seminar. He is a member of the Murray H. Goodman Center for Real Estate Studies Roundtable of Advisors at Lehigh University and is a regular panelist and lecturer at the U.S. Real Estate Today conferences held annually at Lehigh. Mr. Silver has represented an extensive number of clients, both as tenant and landlord, in commercial lease negotiations, including dealing with most of the major mall developers in the United States. Mr. Silver has negotiated a wide variety of merger, acquisition, joint venture, and license agreements in Europe, North and South America, and Asia during his many years of practice.

Robin Ballard Simeonsson is currently a graduate student in the MBA program at the University of Maryland—College Park. Prior to attending graduate school, she worked in the telecommunications industry for IBM and BellSouth Corporation. While at BellSouth, she served as telecommunications systems designer for Coca-Cola Enterprises and the southeast region of the Digital Equipment Corporation.

Craig S. Slavin is a certified management consultant with more than twenty years of solid experience in franchising. He has helped many franchise companies improve their competitive positioning. In all, he has directed expansion programs for hundreds of companies in more than forty industries on four continents. Founder of The Franchise Architects and former managing director of the franchise division at Arthur Andersen & Co., Mr. Slavin has conducted seminars in franchising for prestigious institutions of many different types. In addition, he has been featured in numerous television and radio broadcasts and in articles in major publications on franchising issues.

Celia Garelick Spiritos, J.D., joined Silver, Freedman & Taff in early 1991. Her primary areas of practice include securities, acquisitions, and various general corporate matters. Ms. Spiritos is a member of the New York State Bar, the District of Columbia Bar, the New York State Bar Association, the District of Columbia Bar Association, and the District of Columbia Women's Bar Association. Prior to joining Silver, Freedman & Taff, she was an attorney-advisor at the Securities and Exchange Commission in the Division of Corporation Finance from 1987 to 1990.

Milli Stecker is president and founder of SPAR (Special Projects As Required), a contracting firm specializing in business analysis and planning. Ms. Stecker was the manager of financial planning and analysis for Brice Foods, Inc./I Can't Believe It's Yogurt. She was responsible for the initial design of the corporate financial reporting systems. While she fulfilled her position at Brice, the franchise system grew from fewer than 50 to more than 400 units.

Robert F. Turner is a self-employed business consultant specializing in small businesses, strategic planning, and franchise operations. He is the former chief operating officer of General Business Services, Inc., the nation's leading franchisor of financial management services for small businesses. Having more than twenty-five years' experience in virtually every aspect of franchising, Mr. Turner has consulted with more than two hundred small businesses, and has often been a speaker, panelist, and lecturer on the subject of franchising.

Arthur Yann is vice-president of Nichol & Company, Ltd. He is responsible for the management of Nichol & Company's largest and most prestigious accounts. In addition, he maintains an active management role in the supervision of all agency accounts and serves on the agency's executive, planning, and new business committees.